HAZEL PETRIE HAS AN MA IN HISTORY AND PHD IN MĀORI STUDIES from the University of Auckland. She has contributed chapters to numerous books on history, ecology, and religion, both in New Zealand and overseas, and has also written or delivered academic papers on related topics. Hazel is also the author of *Chiefs of Industry: Māori Tribal Enterprise in Early Colonial New Zealand*, which was shortlisted for the Montana New Zealand Book Awards in 2007. She won a CLNZ Writers' Award in 2012 for her work towards this book.

OUTCASTS OF THE GODS?
THE STRUGGLE OVER SLAVERY IN MĀORI NEW ZEALAND

HAZEL PETRIE

AUCKLAND
UNIVERSITY
PRESS

First published 2015

Auckland University Press
University of Auckland
Private Bag 92019
Auckland 1142
New Zealand
www.press.auckland.ac.nz

© Hazel Petrie, 2015

ISBN 978 1 86940 830 5

Support for this book is provided by

A catalogue record for this book is available from
the National Library of New Zealand

This book is copyright. Apart from fair dealing for the purpose of private study,
research, criticism or review, as permitted under the Copyright Act, no part
may be reproduced by any process without prior permission of the publisher.
The moral rights of the author have been asserted.

Cover painting: Augustus Earle, 'Slaves preparing food', from
PUBL-0015-03, Alexander Turnbull Library, Wellington
Cover design: Spencer Levine

Printed by Printlink Ltd, Wellington

CONTENTS

Acknowledgements	ix
Introduction	1
A note on usage and orthography	16

Chapter 1: By black and red together, the work is done — 17
Race and skin colour	19
Cosmology	21
Red feathers and chiefly garments	22
Māori traditions relating to skin and hair colour	24
Rangatira disguising themselves as slaves	26
Skin colour as an indicator of status	29
Western attitudes towards Australian Aborigines	33
Māori attitudes towards Moriori and Aborigines	35

Chapter 2: Tapu and mana: losing and regaining — 39
Deeper connotations?	42
Could 'slaves' have had no mana or tapu?	46
Vulnerability of 'slaves' to tapu	48
Could captives return home?	50
Did attitudes change over time?	52
Retrieving the lost	54
The significance of eating one's enemy	58
Rangatira captives	62
Ransom	64
Deferential treatment and peaceful intervention	67
Rangatira who returned home to become leaders of mana	71
Gaining mana within their captors' communities	72

Chapter 3: The roles, status, and rights of Māori war captives — 76
Slave or servant? — 78
Degrees of usefulness — 79
'Stray slaves' — 82
Daily life on the edge of society — 84
Relationships between slaves and masters — 89
Marriage between slaves and free people — 93
The crime of adultery — 95
Changing hands — 98
Runaway slaves — 99
Punishing delinquents — 100
Tikanga and the treatment of slaves — 109
Rights to land and cultivations — 114
Refugees and vassalage — 118
The final insult — 120

Chapter 4: The value of captives and the impact of muskets — 123
Utu — 124
Captive taking before muskets — 126
Captive taking becomes more efficient — 127
Captives as trade items — 133
Ritual sacrifice — 138
Maintaining chiefly mana — 139
Released captives become independent entrepreneurs — 140
'Slaves' as workers for hire — 143
'Slaves' as guides for Pākehā travellers — 144
Captives introduce new skills — 145
Toi moko or moko mōkai — 147

Chapter 5: Dark Helens and aboriginal Messelinas — 155
The eighteenth century — 156
Sexual hospitality — 161
The development of a sex trade — 164
Sex and muskets — 166
Māori attitudes — 167
Enthusiastic participants? — 170

Western attitudes	172
Kororāreka: the hell-hole of the Pacific?	174
Missionary attitudes	175
'Slave labour' in the sex trade	176
The problem of illegitimacy	183
The involvement of very young girls	186
Chapter 6: Taking British liberty and freedom to Māori	188
Motivations behind abolitionism	194
The 'saints' come marching in	195
Protecting the aborigines	197
Inquiring minds	200
Questions and answers	201
British government in New Zealand	207
Māori responses to British government	211
Chapter 7: Plucking brands from the burning	215
Early missionary attitudes toward slavery	217
More gently does it	221
From slaves to servants	223
Working conditions at the mission	224
The Bible and slavery	227
Missionary understandings of slave redemption	229
Spiritual redemption	235
Plucking brands from the burning	237
Chapter 8: Breaking the spiritual bonds	242
Why were captives released?	243
Released captives as converts, teachers, and catechists	247
Rangatira conversions	249
Missionaries as peacemakers	253
Slaves who did not want to go free	254
The demands of conversion	256
Christianity's war on mana and tapu	257

**Chapter 9: 'Offensive to the English in the next
degree to man eating'?** 261
The Busby era 261
Following the Treaty 265
Protecting New Zealand's aborigines 270
Slaves or prisoners of war? 273

Chapter 10: Enslaved by the British? 283
Pākehā as slaves of the Māori 285
'Enslavement' through land loss 287
The denial of chiefly mana 294
Arresting rangatira 298
The economy of chiefly mana 302
Fishing up the island: hardening attitudes and the Kīngitanga 306
Bound for Canaan 317

Chapter 11: The language of slavery 324
The changing vocabulary of 'slavery' 327
In the beginning was the word 330
Political correctness 334
Summing up 336

Appendix 342
Notes 348
Bibliography 383
Index 398

ACKNOWLEDGEMENTS

There is a saying, 'Mā te huruhuru te manu ka rere', or, 'It is the feathers that enable the bird to fly'. In this case, the feathers, or funds, enabling the research to take place were provided by the Royal Society of New Zealand's Marsden Fund. Financial support during the final writing stage of the work was subsequently provided by Copyright Licensing Limited. To both institutions I am extremely grateful.

I am also grateful to many individuals who have generously contributed in a wide variety of ways. My family, especially my husband Tony and father-in-law Ian Petrie, have offered consistent personal support. And special thanks go to Mrs Hohipere Tarau, who not only translated a great deal of Māori-language material but was also a very empathetic sounding board for my ideas in the early years of the project. So, too, were the staff of the Māori Studies Department at the University of Auckland. Philip Abela and the staff of the Auckland University Library, as well as those at the Alexander Turnbull, Auckland City, and Hocken libraries have been sources of information and great courtesy over the project's several years of incubation. Patu Hohepa, Hone Sadler, Jane McRae, Chris Tremewan, Patricia Te Arapo Wallace, Maureen Lander, Tanengapuia Te Rangiawhina Mokena, Angela Wanhalla, Anne Salmond, Sally Nicholas, Vavao Fetui, Ross Clark, Michael Belgrave, Hirini Kaa, Angela Middleton, and Ian Smith are just a few of the many individuals who have been kind enough to give of their time and expertise as and when I sought it. I have also benefited from the comments and suggestions of two anonymous referees. Finally, I am very grateful for the expertise and boundless patience of editor Mike Wagg, proofreader Ginny Sullivan, and the staff of Auckland University Press. But, in the end and despite all their help and advice, the responsibility for errors or omissions remains mine alone.

INTRODUCTION

JAKE 'THE MUSS' (OR MUSCLES) HEKE, LEAD CHARACTER IN THE novel and movie *Once Were Warriors*, has acquired almost iconic status in popular New Zealand culture. He represents the stereotypical hard-drinking, wife-beating, irresponsible, disenfranchised Māori male of modern times. Apparently by way of justifying his bad behaviour, Jake tells his family that his violent nature is a consequence of his slave ancestry and the family's 500 years of humiliation. Māori used to fight each other, he explains, and, because his line was defeated, they were taken as slaves. For his wife Beth, that revelation conjures up images linking Māori slavery with that suffered by Africans in America, so she tells their children:

> Us Maoris used to practise slavery just like them poor Negroes had to endure in America.... Yet to read the newspapers, on the TV every damn day, you'd think we're descended from a packa angels, and it's the Pakeha [New Zealander of European descent] who's the devil. Clicking her tongue: Just shows, we're all good, and we're all bad.[1]

Despite the wide variety of forms of slavery or bondage throughout world history, familiarity with African-American history, acquired through books, films, and television documentaries, has led many Westerners, including New Zealanders, to comprehend 'slavery' in a particular way — as black people, bought and sold, labouring on plantations, beaten, abused, and dehumanised. Strands of New Zealand popular culture emerged crediting the arrival of British colonists with putting an end to slavery — as well as intertribal warfare and cannibalism — among Māori.[2] Some have made the additional claim that Māori sought a treaty with Britain 'as a means of protection' from those customs.[3] One research scientist (in mathematics and physics) went so far as to claim that 'Maori culture was not just dysfunctional but mad, criminally insane', and, presumably, hell-bent on self-destruction.[4] But because the history of Māori 'slavery' and the place of war captives in Māori society has been largely unexplored thus far, popular assumptions relating to Māori so-called slavery, its function, and British impacts on it have not been subject to scrutiny and may have been too readily accepted.

The trans-Atlantic trade in Africans and debate over the possibility of abolishing it were at the forefront of Western, especially British, minds as the colonisation of New Zealand was being contemplated. Consequently, that system became the key point of reference for understanding the place of those people already referred to as slaves by missionaries and others who reported on New Zealand affairs. That loose labelling of war captives in Māori society as 'slaves' has had the effect of conflating two, quite different, institutions and led to these captives being perceived in much the same way as African slaves in the Americas rather than as the prisoners taken in intertribal warfare that they almost always were.

Misapprehensions began early. Even contemporary observers could not agree on the general tenor of what was referred to as Māori 'slavery'. Some said it was benign but others referred to cruelty, the degraded status of 'slaves', and the tenuousness of their hold on life. In later times, the victory achieved by Christianity and English law in securing their freedom through the introduction of new moral and legal codes appears to have been an assumption made without supporting evidence.[5]

Nevertheless, it is the shock-horror descriptions of the 'slave' experience recorded by some outsiders that continue to resonate especially loudly today.[6] Their inability to return home, abandonment by their kin, and the misery of precarious lives that could be snuffed out at any moment because their master or mistress was having a bad day are recurring themes. Yet while the despair, the drudgery, and the fragility of life that are said to have been the captive's lot have frequently been stressed, oral traditions tell of slaves as faithful companions, who risked life and limb to save their masters and mistresses or facilitate the path of true love. Such stories contain their own biases, of course, but nineteenth-century accounts confirm the great variety of experience. There is also evidence that those who abused war captives could be subjected to severe censure or even banishment from their community, implying that such behaviour, without just cause, breached accepted codes. As will be seen, captives elicited different responses and lived in varying degrees of comfort or discomfort. Cruel, inhuman treatment was not a universal standard.

Even when free to go home, some captives chose to stay where they had settled. Their individual responses almost certainly related to their personal situations. Remarkable differences in their lives after capture related to a number of variables, including the circumstances of their acquisition, their pre-captive rank, and their capacity to improve their position through their abilities or attitudes.[7] Status could be enhanced by marrying members of their 'host' tribe, especially members of rangatira (chiefly) families, but highly respected skills such as those of the carver, the tattooist, or even the military strategist could have the same result. In a variety of times and places, some slaves have been treated harshly, while others have enjoyed better lifestyles than the free – and such was the case in Māori society.[8]

Glimpses of what life was really like for war captives in Māori society appear in a variety of sources and provide a foundation for considering whether 'slavery' is an appropriate term for each situation and whether it should be universally applied. 'Slavery' is an all-purpose word, rarely to be trusted. So the key to much misunderstanding appears to lie in how it is defined and how systems of slavery are perceived. Possibly 'the most misused word in the English language', slavery 'has become a metaphor for extreme inequality, for subordination, deprivation and discrimination'.[9] The fact that it continues to be used rhetorically to argue against various institutions or circumstances considered to be major moral evils has been credited to the ongoing power of abolitionist language.[10]

Despite the multitude of applications of the word 'slavery', it has all too often been assumed that those many institutions (if that is what they were historically) can be discussed and theorised cross-culturally.

Yet different environments produce entirely different products, which are liable to alter as the environment changes. Therefore, understandings need to take account of time, place, cultural values, kinship and economic structures, social stratification, and spiritual implications.[11] The last, which is rarely discussed and which may often be immaterial, is particularly relevant with regard to Māori — as it was in other Pacific societies.[12] That was recognised by early ethnographers who described Māori 'slaves' as '[o]utcasts of the gods' or said that they had ceased to count 'in things spiritual'.[13]

Given that slavery, being a nebulous concept, is a difficult word to define, it should not be surprising that translations of Māori text have served to confuse the historical record even further. Political and ideological impulses may also be responsible for distortion in translation, but cultural differences go some way towards explaining why English words such as slave and slavery have been applied to a variety of situations and circumstances that are not necessarily analogous to English meanings. When a word from one language is translated into another, its original connotation may not be conveyed with the translation. Instead it may conjure up quite different meanings that are not appropriate or relevant.

A wide vocabulary of words referring to people of low status, including war captives, has been used by Māori historically, many of them being translated, apparently randomly, into English as 'slave' (see Chapter 11 and Appendix). More significantly, the use of those words has altered over time. Changes in usage appear to reflect the adoption of new moral values, especially those associated with Christianity. While that has had the effect of distorting some of the written history pertaining to Māori war captives, it also indicates the extent to which those new values became embedded in the Māori psyche. However, that is only one factor that needs to be kept in mind when drawing on written records for clues to lived experiences.

The wide variety of impressions in the contemporary record not only highlights the different qualities of life experienced by Māori captives but also reminds us of the need to read the observations of early explorers, missionaries, and other Westerners with an appreciation of their likely preconceptions. Besides their religious, social, and political agendas, time and place — where they were and when — surely influenced their observations. Attitudes were not fixed — either among Māori or those who commented on or sought to alter customary practices.

The writings of eighteenth-century explorers provide some clues to the extent and nature of captive taking prior to Western contact, but the most substantial body of eyewitness accounts relating to war captives or 'slaves' comes from the missionaries, sailors, and others who lived in or visited New Zealand from the late 1810s and into the 1830s. The fact that the first missionaries arrived in late 1814 means we have access to many of their letters and journals from that time on; but because their presence encouraged more Western shipping to visit New Zealand ports, we can also draw on the writings of a variety of British and French ship's officers during that period as well. Other works written by Westerners who either lived in or visited New Zealand in the nineteenth century, but especially those who arrived before 1840, provide valuable information along with insight into the ideologies and beliefs they carried with them. Artists like Augustus Earle, who visited in the 1820s, and George French Angas, in the 1840s, as well as adventure-seeking travellers like John Nicholas and Edward Markham with the privileges of spare time and money, have left their impressions, which are pious or ribald, supporting or at odds with those of the missions.

While we can access many of these accounts and glean much about the ways in which war captives were employed and treated as well as the personal reactions of the writers, we must also remember that the very presence of these observers — missionaries, mariners, and others — set a period of very rapid economic and spiritual change in motion. Nor were their writings entirely spontaneous. They were reporting their observations and work among Māori communities for the mission societies or naval authorities at 'home' or recording impressions for books they intended to publish for audiences hungry to hear about exotic peoples in far-flung corners of the world.

Yet another factor skewing the evidence is that prior to the mid-1830s, mission stations were limited to the northern part of the North Island, the region most visited by overseas shipping. The upshot is that most of the observations left to us as 'evidence' of Māori practices come from that region, and other areas, including the lower North Island and entire South Island, are less well endowed with written records. The extent to which that imbalance affects the overall picture is unclear. According to Atholl Anderson, there is little evidence of slavery in southern New Zealand. He suggested that because there was little horticulture in the south, there would have been no continuing demand for large labour forces, or the means to feed one. Moreover, enslaving one's own kin was usually carefully avoided, and given the smaller population, there would have been fewer opportunities to capture genealogically distinct people within the South Island.[14]

The fact that a disproportionately large body of writing about Māori warfare and captive taking comes not only from a fairly limited geographic area but also an abnormal period in New Zealand history surely added to the false impressions and distorted understandings of earlier practices. To counter those problems somewhat, a parallel history approach, placing Māori records and perceptions beside Pākehā or European ones, is used in the chapters to come. There is a significant body of Māori writing from the 1840s onward, but examples from earlier times, when captive taking was more common, are thin on the ground. Some Māori letters mentioning slaves or captives are available from the 1830s; and oral traditions recorded in the Māori language during the early years of settlement offer some correctives to the written record and glimpses of what might loosely be referred to as 'customary' practices and attitudes towards 'slaves'. Māori proverbs or sayings, oral traditions, waiata (songs), karakia (incantations), and extracts from Native Land Court minute books indicate changes to the ways in which those people fitted into the social framework. They also offer further clues to the spiritual and psychological impact of captivity, as do associations revealed figuratively through metaphors, language, and the symbolism of colour.

As others have noted, historiography — especially that which was produced prior to the second half of the twentieth century — tended to overemphasise the virtues and successes of missionary and colonial endeavours. In the later twentieth century, however, the pendulum swung the other way and their role was placed under a far more critical light.[15] Heightened tensions between Māori and settler as the latter swamped the former by sheer force of numbers, and the hostilities that broke out in 1860 were neither the only nor the first factors that impacted viewpoints in the written record.[16] An example of that process is offered by Alexander Maxwell and Evan Roberts's analysis of multiple accounts of a single event that occurred in 1824 but which were published over the following half-century. That study revealed how those many reworkings reflect changes in Western perceptions of Māori as well as the writers' standpoints at the time of reworking.

The incident forming the basis of their analysis took place while a ship named the *Endeavour* was visiting Whangaroa Harbour and trading with the local Ngāti Pou people. Cultural misunderstanding appears to have instigated an altercation in which the crew and three missionaries were held hostage for some two hours. The standoff ended peacefully thanks to intervention by neighbouring chief Te Ara of Ngāti Uru, but some 30 subsequent accounts of the events reveal a pattern of shifting portrayals of the various actors and the parts they played in those proceedings.[17] Whereas the earliest published narratives stressed Māori savagery, setting that characteristic beside the writers' confidence in their innate potential for civilisation, conversion, and redemption, those published during the 1830s no longer needed to persuade their readers of that potential. As many had now been converted, accounts shifted to depicting 'the pre-Christian Māori in the darkest possible terms so as to draw a dramatic contrast with the happy Christian present'.[18] Versions published from the 1850s, however, 'exaggerated the importance and accomplishments of European missionaries', overshadowing the part played by Te Ara in achieving a peaceful resolution. As Maxwell and Roberts explained, 'various incarnations of the story', told from different perspectives, at different times, with different purposes in view, enabled the authors 'to draw diverse moral lessons' and provide a window into the variety of Western attitudes towards Māori as well as more general shifts over time. Much the same process — of shifting attitudes and shifting heroes — appears to explain why conclusions relating to Māori 'slavery' drawn from post-1850 accounts are often at odds with what was said by those who were present during the earlier events these accounts purport to describe.

Quite apart from misapprehension and bias in the records is the fact that a very large proportion of the evidence for the situations that war captives found themselves in comes from a period of unprecedented captive taking. Because the so-called 'musket wars' were a very atypical period of New Zealand history, they have played a significant part in misunderstandings of Māori 'slavery' to date. During this time, from around 1820, the balance between economic and spiritual imperatives for Māori shifted dramatically. The advent of foreign trade, the arrival of British missionaries, and the new cultural and religious ideas that came with them had set off a chain of adaptations to Māori society — economically, spiritually, socially, and politically — as Māori attempted to take maximum advantage of exciting new opportunities.

My previous research into the ways in which Māori engaged with the new commercial opportunities arising from European contact indicated that one consequence of the process was the ability of one-time war captives or 'ex-slaves' to become independent entrepreneurs while hereditary chiefs struggled to sustain their role as effective providers for their people.[19] That circumstance aroused my curiosity and highlighted the dearth of existing studies relating to the lowest section of Māori society.

The only specific study of New Zealand practices, 'Maori Prisoners and Slaves in the Nineteenth Century' by Andrew P. Vayda, was published more than 50 years ago. Associated with a broader examination of Māori warfare,[20] his pioneering paper noted the significant discrepancy between reports from eighteenth-century visitors to New Zealand that Māori took few captives in warfare and those from the early nineteenth century who observed the taking of large numbers. He suggested that two factors might account for this apparently dramatic change: the introduction of muskets and the newly acquired value of war captives in producing goods for overseas trade.[21]

In his subsequent 1970 article, 'Maoris and Muskets in New Zealand: Disruption of a War System', Vayda put forward the argument that aggressive expansion for fertile land, which encouraged the dispersal of the population over underexploited territory, had been the key driving force behind Māori warfare before European contact.[22] His ideas were challenged by Angela Ballara's 2003 book *Taua: 'Musket Wars', 'Land Wars' or Tikanga?*, which investigated the subject in much greater depth and offered a different perspective on the causes of warfare among Māori. Ballara argued that the term 'musket wars' should not be applied to the series of wars from the late 1810s to the 1830s because their fundamental nature was not altered by the introduction of new weaponry.[23] She also disagreed with Vayda's fundamental premise concerning war captives, suggesting that the 'capture of prisoners later used as slaves was as common before the introduction of muskets as after'. Ballara nonetheless accepted that whereas women and children were most often taken prior to that time, the number of adult men being captured increased as their labour could bolster agricultural expansion or other aspects of what was now vital foreign trade.[24]

The concentration of external trade being initially confined to a few key regions, especially Northland's Bay of Islands, certainly meant that its benefits could be enhanced by the larger involuntary workforces more readily acquired as a people once equipped only with hand-to-hand weapons gained access to firearms that enabled them to muster those workforces more efficiently. However, the unprecedented level of warfare which began in the late 1810s, and which was accompanied by an equally exceptional degree of captive taking, was a relatively short-lived phenomenon. The 1830s saw a reversal of the situation as intertribal warfare subsided and victorious tribes began to release their captives. Some have claimed that this emancipation was due to the influence of missionary teachings. Others have given the credit to the imposition of British law (a problematic conclusion given that it did not commence until 1840). However, historians have more recently begun to suggest economic reasons for that phenomenon. There is much to support the argument that the impetus was a more pragmatic response to changed circumstances — that they were divesting themselves of excess labourers or that Māori society was simply returning to equilibrium, to a more normal situation: similar to that prior to the 1820s.

As for the first and probably most widespread understanding, it is true that Christian influence had begun to take hold during this period and that that influence would eventually be significant, but it was still very limited in the 1830s. Chiefs and fighting men of rank were slower to accept the new religion than captives or women and young people, yet many began releasing their captives before conversion. Such anomalies mean that it is hard to distinguish between cause and effect. Reports of customary practices being hidden from missionary neighbours, at least in the North Island where they were initially confined, confirm that Māori were anxious to avoid offending the sensibilities of valuable sources of trade goods, foreign intelligence, literacy, and other new technologies. So were they indicating an acceptance of Christian ideas relating to the humane treatment of prisoners in order to curry favour or would these people have been released regardless of non-Māori influence? That is one of the questions that will be examined in the following chapters.

By the 1830s, when large numbers of captives were being released, the campaign to abolish slavery throughout the British Empire had reached a fever pitch. The slave *trade* had been abolished in 1807 but the subsequent Slavery Abolition Act, passed in 1833, outlawed slavery itself. Union Jacks were to serve as fluttering symbols of freedom that would shame the United States and other allegedly less noble nations. But abolition was neither a simple nor straightforward process. Consequently, in 1838, when the pros and cons of colonising New Zealand and how it might be best achieved were very much on Britain's political mind, so, too, were issues relating to how the new slave-free regime might best be managed.

The leading British abolitionist Sir Thomas Fowell Buxton published a book that year entitled *The Slave Trade*. He followed that very soon after with a lengthy supplement, *The Remedy*. Having concluded that previous anti-slavery policies, which emphasised forceful suppression, were not working, Buxton shifted the emphasis to mobilising Africa's own resources against the trade. Africa's wealth, he argued, could be better tapped by co-operating with indigenous leaders in mutually beneficial commerce. But while it might be thought that this argument would have had its strongest appeal among those who favoured establishing colonies to supply both raw materials and markets for British manufactures, others, who connected the suppression of the slave trade with their own moral redemption, also supported Buxton's proposals. The idea of atonement for national or personal sin may have provided as powerful a motivation for some as the expected economic advantages did for others.[25] The motives and rationales behind the abolition movement remain the subject of debate, but the clamour to outlaw slavery meant that the indigenous institution in New Zealand would come under close scrutiny from the British Colonial Office.

Slavery had become anathema to British identity and was not to be tolerated within any of her colonies. With that in mind, the lobbying of abolitionist campaigners, especially during that decade, provided one of many 'good' reasons for the British to colonise New Zealand.[26] British government, arm in arm with Christianity, would prohibit slavery in New Zealand as it had, allegedly, throughout the Empire.[27] William Hobson probably did not need reminding of the maxim that 'the British flag never flew over a nation of slaves' when he offered Māori a treaty with Britain in 1840[28] — although prior to the establishment of formal government, and to some extent after it, British attitudes towards Māori 'slavery' remained far less consistent than such slogans imply. Some Māori customs, including warfare and cannibalism, considered to be inconsistent with principles of humanity, were suppressed immediately following the Treaty of Waitangi, but 'slavery' was initially tolerated because of its role in Māori social organisation and sometimes, perhaps, for settler convenience. Some of those involved in colonisation recognised the devastating effect that giving war captives equality with hereditary leaders would have on Māori society. But others did not — or chose not to.

The beliefs and ideologies of missionaries, early government officials, and settlers, all of whom had their own ideas about what slavery was or is, not only fostered varied and sometimes contradictory impressions but would also impact Māori society and its leadership profoundly. For that reason, the examination of freedom and unfreedom in the Māori world that follows not only considers how and why customary practices came to an end but also the implications of the process.[29]

In many respects, slavery ran counter to the needs of the colonisers who hoped to encourage individual self-reliance and self-discipline among Māori. 'Communism', a label often applied to the communally organised Māori society, was almost as unloved by church and state in nineteenth-century New Zealand as it was during the United States' McCarthy era of the mid-twentieth century. The needs of the Industrial Revolution in Britain had led authority figures to focus strongly on individual self-reliance. Samuel Smiles's 30-page book called *Self Help*, first published in 1859, became an international best-seller, but the American Ralph Waldo Emerson had pitched the same ideas much earlier, in 1841.[30]

He even used Māori as an example of a problem society. What a contrast, he wrote:

> between the well-clad, reading, writing, thinking American, with a watch, a pencil, and a bill of exchange in his pocket, and the naked New Zealander, whose property is a club, a spear, a mat, and an undivided twentieth of a shed to sleep under.[31]

The undivided share of a shed is, of course, a message about the need for individual ownership, especially of land. The need to encourage self-reliance as well as responsiveness to the market as consumers of British manufactures were key concerns for everyone involved in colonisation. Moreover, contemporary ideas pertaining to freedom, morality, and incentives to industry combined to produce an expectation that the existence of slavery would inhibit attempts to civilise Māori even if, within these ideological frameworks, slavery was deemed to be 'sentenced to extinction by the laws of human progress'.[32]

So it was during the 1830s, when the eyes of Britain's Colonial Office were scanning a very distant horizon — not for evidence of slavery in New Zealand (which was taken as a given), but to understand its nature — that the need to formulate means of abolishing it was a taken-for-granted necessity. Consequently, despite differing points of view in the historical record, the legacy has been a narrative of dishonoured Māori captives and their triumphal release as a result of Christian teachings or British intervention.

The notion that Māori warfare was especially cruel has supported those ideas. Thomas Lambert, for example, whose book *The Story of Old Wairoa* was first published in 1925, wrote that the people of Waikaremoana knew nothing of clemency: 'When they went to war they went to kill, not to take prisoners. . . . [I]t was the recognised custom to kill them, not solely for the sake of the larder (though it was often borne in mind) [but because] the value of the victory was measured by the total number slain.'[33] Lambert's intimation of anthropophagy, or cannibalism, here is far from unique. That practice, which excited particular attention among Europeans from early modern times, has lost little of its emotive strength. But although most twenty-first-century historians tend to take a more cautious view, similar perspectives have been argued recently, including the assertion that 'hundreds of prisoners' were seized 'to serve as supplies of meat for whole communities'.[34] Different understandings of and attitudes towards the consumption of human flesh tend to be disregarded. In response to the allegation that Westerners 'did not understand the history of cannibalism', John Robinson argued that 'either there was cannibalism and infanticide or there was not. Understanding of history is not ethnically determined.'[35] One of the aims of the present study is to show that while the understanding of history is not so much ethnically (whatever that means) as culturally determined, understanding the context of practices and their rationale is vital.

Cannibalism now features less often in scholarly literature, but the characterisation of Māori as natural-born fighters has continued for more than two centuries. In 2006, scientific evidence appeared to bear out the notion of a people genetically predisposed to violence. In that year Rod Lea was reported as telling an Australian genetics conference that a high proportion of Māori carried a 'warrior gene' (monoamine oxidase A or MAO-A), which may have helped them to survive intertribal warfare and long-distance migration but may also have been responsible for higher rates of addiction and criminality. Media hype ensured widespread outrage that modern science could seemingly accuse an entire racial group of an inherited tendency to criminal behaviour. Lea and his colleague Geoffrey Chambers subsequently sought to clarify the intention behind their research as being aimed at seeking ways to best deal with addictive behaviours. But the violent-Māori genie was out of the bottle once more.[36]

As historians have shown, the 'martial race myth', or the idea that Māori are 'culturally staunch', has been used in a variety of contexts and often by Māori themselves. Given that the British had been at war almost continually for most of the century prior to their first contact with Māori, Christina Thompson argued that the characterisation 'can be read both as a description of something empirically encountered [in the sense of resistance to invasion] and as a displacement of a European ethos of war onto the Maori people'.[37] Similar use of the Māori warrior icon is evident in realms beyond military endeavours as well — in the sporting arena, for example. However, the regular re-emergence of the idea that Māori are predisposed to war has ensured a continuous supply of oxygen to associated ideas that the race is innately violent and cruel — towards war captives and others.

Limited research relating to Māori and other Pacific prisoners of war (whether referred to as slaves or not) probably explains why, despite a very substantial body of literature concerning forms of unfreedom around the world from ancient times to the present, global studies have tended to restrict their scope to Europe, Asia, Africa, and the Americas.[38] Blackbirding, or the Pacific labour trade carried out by Westerners, has received considerable attention, but indigenous Oceanian systems have, by contrast, been largely overlooked, as the editors of one substantial collection of slavery studies admit.[39] Some articles relating to the Solomon Islands have appeared in scholarly journals, but even that attention was slow in coming.[40] It has been suggested that because head-hunting and cannibalism captured the imagination of generations of Europeans, captivity has been treated as a mere afterthought less worthy of investigation.[41] Perhaps it is cannibalism, which often served as a means of measuring civility or barbarity among indigenous peoples, that accounts for the lack of attention to war captives or slavery in other parts of the Pacific.[42] Yet it was there, where the concepts of mana and tapu (kapu or tabu in some areas) were effectively universal, that the logic behind Māori practices must lie.[43]

Mana for the New Zealand Māori has been described as the 'enduring, indestructible power of the gods ... the sacred fire that is without beginning and without end'. Derived from the ancestor gods, it is often referred to as the power of the gods, the power of the ancestors, the power of the land or of the individual.[44] Supported by mana, tapu is a complex concept with many meanings and conditions that defy simple explanation. It is often glossed as 'spiritual restriction' and sometimes applied in ways similar to the English word 'sacred'.[45] Both concepts, mana and tapu, will be discussed more fully in Chapter 2, but suffice to say here that they were powerful forces which, together with utu (satisfaction or redress), provided the framework of social control in Māori society. Captives not only did the unpleasant dirty work essential for the smooth running of any community, but also allowed those of high rank to protect their tapu and maintain or even elevate their mana by avoiding tasks that would damage those conditions.

The logic of slavery is very often said to be economic — a means of increasing productivity and profit — but, as David Brion Davis and others have stressed, such motives may often fuse with issues of identity, ideology, and power.[46] That was certainly the case in New Zealand where, prior to Western contact, captives served economic needs but the spiritual aspects were fundamental. In many times and places, too, the social positions of outsiders including war captives and chattel slaves have encompassed a variety of relationships.[47] Adoption into the conqueror's community was a strategy practised in a number of societies, including Māori, especially when the captives were women or children.[48] Oral traditions show that North America's Cherokee related slavery to failure in warfare, but saw it as a temporary status pending adoption or release.[49] In the Solomon Islands, Cameroon, and elsewhere, 'slaves' might be war captives but could also be those who had offended social norms or infringed the ethics of their society — in other words, criminals.[50] Such people lost kinship rights in the society of their birth and lived on the margin of another. There was a similar mutability in Māori society. They were outsiders.

Internationally, slaves are commonly said to be the 'Other', a term that typically means people of different ethnicity or religion, but the New Zealand situation was somewhat different. Despite belonging to different tribal groups, they were not ethnically or linguistically distinct from their captors or, in the case of social outcasts, their hosts. Religious beliefs were much the same, too, but being captured or outlawed altered their spiritual status. That was the primary distinction. During the second quarter of the nineteenth century, however, Māori spirituality was being reshaped. Old values were being replaced by new — but gradually and not totally. So although the ways in which war captives or 'slaves' were treated and perceived evolved from within Māori spiritual and cultural parameters, the spiritual and cultural contexts were themselves evolving in tandem with the arrival of outside influences, especially the advent of international trade and adoption of Christian principles. That meant that their situations were changing, too, but in ways that were not necessarily consistent or clear cut.

It seems that perceptions and representations have had longer-lasting legacies than lived experiences and that misapprehensions may, in part, be due to omission. Of all the paintings and drawings from the early years of European–Māori contact, only a few depict those from the bottom of the social heap. The clothing, tattoos, and other adornments of their social betters have had far more appeal for artists — at least until the early twentieth century when, as fictional characters, captives might appear as players in a romanticised or even erotic past.

Discrepancies in the treatment of slaves and prisoners of war have been observed and recorded across societies since the third and second millennia BC, so it should not be surprising that the same anomalies appear in Māori society. The chapters that follow are intended to show how and why some of those discrepancies might be explained and to shine some light into several dimly lit corners of New Zealand history.

A note on usage and orthography

Although changes over time are very important to our understanding of how the people deemed to be slaves fitted into Māori society, a thematic rather than a strictly chronological approach has been applied here in order to suggest how and why, as well as when, those changes to their position and circumstances occurred. And, because not all Māori war captives were treated like slaves and not all 'slaves' were captives, the word 'slave' will be used to denote people treated or referred to as such by contemporary observers while 'captive' will be used elsewhere. That admittedly fuzzy distinction is not intended to suggest that the difference is unimportant, only that the records are not always clear with regard to the specific status of individuals. Finally, it should be noted that long vowels in Māori words and proper names have been indicated by macrons where the correct form could be ascertained. Where that was not possible, they have been left unmarked.

CHAPTER ONE

By black and red together, the work is done

MA PANGO, MA WHERO, KA OTI, WHICH LITERALLY TRANSLATES as 'With black and with red it will be done or the work completed', is probably the best-known Māori whakataukī, or saying, relating to people from the bottom of the social heap. Perhaps the earliest published explanation, from missionary Richard Taylor's 1855 book *Te Ika a Maui*, refers to the combined efforts of 'gentlemen' (rangatira, chiefs, or people of high rank), represented by the colour red, and slaves, represented by black. Taylor wrote that it referred 'to the custom of chief's [sic] painting themselves with red ochre and slaves with charcoal, before they went to war'.[1] William Colenso also used the word 'slave' to explain the whakataukī's reference to black, but modified the terminology and the reason for the metaphor of colour somewhat by saying that '[t]he slaves and plebeians, naked and unwashed, were black enough'.[2] Those differences aside, it is generally agreed that the essential message is that all members of a community must contribute to communal wellbeing. However, although the distinction between red and black is (or was) clearly meaningful and suggests one potential pathway into past understandings, disentangling its multi-levelled metaphorical, spiritual, and physical associations is not an easy task.

Nevertheless, an attempt at disentanglement may reveal glimpses of how pre-Christian Māori conceived their social hierarchy.

The key to understanding slavery in any past society is to get inside the heads of the people who lived in that society. But if it is a past society, its people are no longer around to interview. Even their descendants, let alone historians from other societies, have lived their lives in other times and cultures and with more recent value systems. We might, therefore, look to oral traditions to suggest some clues as to how those long gone perceived their world and the varieties of people who shared it with them. Often, it is the everyday, common-sense perceptions that the historian will miss because they were unspoken in the record. But attitudes once taken for granted may be discernible if we look for subtle undercurrents.

Along with many other insights, oral traditions may allow us to probe beneath the superficial level of outsider accounts and better understand how war captives were perceived prior to European contact. 'Slaves' feature in many of those old stories, and certain themes occur in different stories and in different versions of them. So those recurring themes are likely to tell us something about pre-European contact perceptions, especially when the narratives were recorded in the Māori language at an early stage in Māori written history. The association of slaves with the colour black is one strong and recurring theme.

The colours red and black (as well as white), commonly used in Māori art and iconography, carry cosmological significance. Consequently, their use tells us much about the relative positions of war captives and rangatira in terms of mana (authority, power, prestige), tapu (spiritual restriction), and social status, as well as how each was perceived. It must be borne in mind, though, that although a number of different Māori words have been translated into English as 'slave', a word that can be used to cover a wide variety of situations in that language, Māori-language texts are equally imprecise. As will be seen, the same individual may be described by more than one term within the same text, which means that their more specific position in society is very cloudy indeed. Nevertheless, the association of the colour red with mana, tapu, and high rank is consistent, as is the association of black with its opposite counterparts.

Race and skin colour

The notion of race from which modern popular understandings have evolved derives from a period of colonial expansion when scientific developments in Europe provided a means of classifying the earth's many peoples into different social and cultural groups. Skin colour, a key marker, proved a useful way of identifying them as belonging to particular races and ranking them as either superior or inferior. Conveniently for those doing the classifying, that process implied their innate suitability for positions of either servitude or domination. Consequently, a set of purportedly Negro characteristics, which became the negative standard for describing and comparing human beings, was encouraged by the consolidation of the Atlantic slave trade in the sixteenth century.[3] Those ideas not only assisted the ideological justification of colonial exploitation but also served to justify slavery, especially in the United States, as well as colonisation more generally. As Morgan Godwyn explained in a 1680 publication, the words:

> *Negro* and *Slave*, being by Custom grown Homogenous and Convertible; even as *Negro* and *Christian*, *Englishman* and *Heathen*, are by the like corrupt Custom and Partiality made *Opposites*; thereby as it were implying, that the one could not be *Christians*, nor the other *Infidels*.[4]

So Negroes were not Christian but natural slaves and Englishmen could not be heathen or, presumably, slaves. Such theories likely lie behind the perception of some early European observers that Māori slaves belonged to a different and inferior race from their masters.

These connotations of skin colour within the Western world are assumed to have evolved from earlier ones that associated positive characteristics such as purity and goodness with white, and death and evil with black. The use of black and white as metaphors for dark and light in the English language is often said to have derived from the Bible. Yet, as the Bengali theologian Mukti Barton pointed out, the origins of the Bible lie in the East, not Europe, and he has argued that such metaphors are not evident before the Bible was translated into English. Barton explained that in his Bengali language, darkness and blackness are not the same thing. *Andhokar*, the Bengali word for darkness, refers to blindness or something that impedes vision; it is not a colour as *kalo* (black) is. He therefore reread the Bible to consider whether the association of darkness with blackness originated there or was a purely European concept. Having done so, he concluded that European interpreters have sometimes read black and white into the texts when they were not present previously and, on other occasions, have interpreted less specific terms through the lenses of their own prejudices. That tendency, he suggested, began with Greco-Roman culture which associated black with death and the devil and is evidenced by representations of Africans and Blacks as demons or the devil throughout Christian writings from the first century CE. In other words, white is normative in European ways of thinking and to describe people as coloured carries negative connotations.[5] However, such associations have not been limited to the Christian world. The colour black has evoked highly negative symbolism from ancient times, not only in Western culture generally, but also among various Asian, Native American, and even sub-Saharan African peoples.[6] So we need to consider whether Barton's thesis concerning the connotations of black holds with regard to Māori understandings and symbolisms and whether those pertaining to red altered over time.

As the proverb 'Ma pango, ma whero, ka oti' indicates, the lowest members of Māori society were signified by the colour black and people of rank by red. Explanations of the saying often refer to the chiefly practice of smearing the body with a mixture of kōkōwai (red ochre) and oil. Although it is sometimes said to have been only those of rank and, therefore, with a considerable degree of tapu whose bodies were besmeared with kōkōwai, there is evidence to suggest that it was sometimes more widely available. Archdeacon Walsh, for example, suggested that it was used by minor rangatira on festive and ceremonial occasions.[7] More interestingly, though, George French Angas described a young slave woman he encountered gathering flax, saying: 'Her only garment was a coarse brown mat, extending from her waist to her knees, and her limbs were anointed with kokowai, or red ochre, to keep off the attacks of the sand-flies.'[8] René Primevère Lesson, a doctor and naturalist aboard the French ship *Coquille*, also mentioned young slave girls rubbing their bodies with fish oil to make red ochre dust adhere.[9]

So, on the surface, such instances would appear not to conform to the colour coding of social rank indicated by the proverb, but the difference may have lain with the type of oil the kōkōwai was mixed with. Fish oil was effective but smelly. Vegetable oils were far more desirable but rarer, so more expensive and prestigious. Tītoki trees, for example, which were one important source of oil, do not produce fruit every year, hence its rarity. When they did fruit, the oil was stored in gourds and scented by adding aromatic leaves to produce a far superior and more pleasantly perfumed product. Another saying: 'Ko nga rangatira a te tau tītoki' ('They are only chiefs of the season in which the tītoki tree bears it berries') is a reference to the years of tītoki fruiting when it was said that anyone could procure it and look like a chief, whether or not they were. It was applied to a person who suddenly turned out in fine dress.[10] Or, as a nineteenth-century Englishman might have said, was getting ideas above their station.

But if red was generally associated with chiefly folk, by contrast, ashes, soot, and charcoal were most often associated with slaves or war captives, perhaps because of their role as fire makers and cooks. Because cooked food represented a serious danger to the chiefly classes whose tapu was vulnerable to contamination or neutralisation by such contact, food preparation was very much the work of lowly folk. That is why kāuta, or cookhouses, were built away from the sleeping quarters and other buildings, allowing rangatira to keep a safe distance from them. The humble folk, obliged to spend their days tending fires, were more likely to have skin discoloured by smoke, soot, and ashes.

Cosmology

Another explanation for the metaphorical association of war captives with black and people of rank with red lies in the realms of cosmology. Some traditions tell that kōkōwai is the blood of the sky parent Ranginui that soaked into the body of the earth mother Papatūānuku when the primordial couple were being separated by their children in order to bring light into the world. In that version of the creation story, Ranginui clung so fast to his wife that they had to cut off his arms causing his blood to flow, which is one explanation for its use as body paint signifying high social status.[11]

Whatever the origin of the symbolism, red is the colour of the gods in much of Polynesia and, to a lesser extent, other parts of the Pacific. In Māori society, mana is the fundamental basis of chiefly leadership, and since the rangatira represented the most direct lines of descent from the gods, it follows that red would also be considered a chiefly colour. But whereas, in cosmological terms, red signifies tapu or spiritual restriction, power, rank, and the gods, black is the opposite. As in Greco-Roman culture, black represents the world of death, 'a dark, defeated underworld of the ill, the dead and the beaten'.[12] 'Whiti te ra, ka whakatika; to te ra, ka kino', or 'When the sun rises things are all right but when the sun sets the situation is bad', is another 'message about good and bad, expressed clearly by the contrast between light and dark, daytime and night'.[13] Such sayings have particular relevance for a discussion of captivity in Māori society which was very much about its spiritual and psychological elements.[14]

Red feathers and chiefly garments

Although other forms of red dress or adornment have served similar purposes, red feathers indicated chiefly status in a number of Pacific societies. The *Bounty* mutineers, surprised that they were able to purchase a bull and a cow for just a few red feathers when they visited Tahiti in 1789, had assumed the islanders considered the cattle of little value, not realising that the feathers were such highly desirable treasures.[15]

Memories of the significance of red feathers appear in Māori traditions such as one recorded by George Grey concerning the migration of the *Arawa* canoe to New Zealand. As the travellers neared land, they saw a mass of pōhutukawa trees in bloom and one of the rangatira is said to have called out:

> "See there, red ornaments for the head are much more plentiful in this country than in Hawaiki, so I'll throw my red head-ornaments into the water;" and, so saying, he threw them into the sea. The name of that man

was Tauninihi; the name of the red head-ornament he threw into the sea was Taiwhakaea. The moment they got on shore they ran to gather the pohutukawa flowers, but no sooner did they touch them than the flowers fell to pieces; then they found out that these red head-ornaments were nothing but flowers.[16]

So the new arrivals quickly discovered their mistake. The blossoms of the pōhutukawa do not last and New Zealand was sadly lacking in red-feathered birds.

They were not entirely unfamiliar, though. According to Walter Buller, the amokura, or red-tailed tropic bird (fig. 7), was well known to Northland's Ngāpuhi people. Almost every year, following easterly gales, a few would be washed ashore (generally dead) at North Cape or Spirits Bay and the local people would set out to look for them systematically. Because the bird was so rare, its long red tail-feathers could fetch a high price when exchanged with southern tribes. Buller claimed that a Hawke's Bay chief gave a valuable slab of pounamu (greenstone or nephrite jade) in exchange for just three of those feathers.[17]

In other parts of the Pacific, where nature also failed to provide adequate supplies of red feathers, other symbols and colours have been employed to indicate chiefly status. Whether due to the lack of indigenous sources of red feathers or the new land's distance from other trade sources, kōkōwai provided a substitute and cloaks replaced headdresses as signifiers of rank in New Zealand.

William Brougham Monkhouse, the surgeon aboard James Cook's ship the *Endeavour* on its first voyage to New Zealand, described a variety of types of cloak. Some had geometric patterns on the borders, woven into the garment in shades of cinnamon red, cream, and black. Also reported, though less often, were fine cloaks ornamented with red breast feathers from a native parrot (presumably the kākā) or strips of white-haired dog skin. As well as noting that the people's faces and limbs were dressed with kōkōwai mixed with oil, the ship's company also reported that carvings on canoe prows and sterns were coated with a similar paint and that fine cloaks were reddened by being rubbed with dry ochre. Even the hafts of some weapons were bound with flax from which red feathers or white dog's hair was suspended.[18]

Some fine cloaks made for persons of high birth were made from fibres that had been coloured with kōkōwai before being woven, as opposed to colouration after the weaving was completed. James Barry's famous painting of the great Ngāpuhi leader Hongi Hika (fig. 5) during his visit to London in 1820 with Waikato and Thomas Kendall shows him wearing a red cloak, which may have been treated that way, but red kākā feathers can also be seen at the base of the gannet feathers in his coronet.[19] He clearly chose to be immortalised in his finest ensemble. An oral tradition concerning Tamainupō tells how the loss of such a garment could cause a devastating loss of standing: the hero, who was the son of a rape victim and her attacker, took revenge on his father by stripping him of the red cloak that symbolised his chiefly status.[20]

Once Western travellers began arriving on New Zealand shores, Māori were keen to acquire other items of red clothing and adornment. Moehanga, from Northland, was very keen indeed. Believed to have been the first Māori to reach England, in 1806 aboard a British whale ship, he asked Captain Peter Dillon to take him to Calcutta twenty years later. That was apparently where he thought he might get himself a red soldier's jacket to complement his old cap.[21] Edward Markham, an English adventurer who spent a few days at Waitangi in 1834 while the British naval ship HMS *Alligator* was in port, noted the significance of red clothing and the power it implied. Māori had 'much greater fear of the Red [soldiers] than the Blue Jackets [sailors]', he reported.[22]

Māori traditions relating to skin and hair colour

Attitudes towards physical attributes including skin and hair colour also come through in oral traditions and imply that certain looks were favoured. A number of stories refer to a 'race' that inhabited New Zealand prior to the arrival of the Māori, variously known as patupaiarehe, urukēhu, or tūrehu. Indeed, one of the patupaiarehe tribes was called Pakepakeha which, according to some, was the origin of the modern term Pākehā for a person of European descent. It is quite probable that their skin colour gave early explorers and traders an advantage when they first arrived in New Zealand. Māori memories of their first meetings with Europeans suggest that their unusual appearance, if nothing else, suggested a supernatural origin. Patuone used the term 'tupua' (goblin, demon) to describe his father's first impression of Europeans,[23] but a Ngāti Porou account recorded by Mohi Tūrei was even more explicit. He wrote that:

> They were turehu [fair people], punehunehu [misty-looking], ma [fair], ma korako [pale, like albinos], whero takou [red, like red ochre] . . .[24]

However, Ngāti Hotu, the tribe remembered as already living in the Taupō area when Ngātoroirangi and Tia from the *Arawa* canoe arrived, were similarly described as urukēhu, or fairy people, because of their unusual red hair and fair skin. A Ngāti Ira saying also links fair colouring with descent from an ancestor of high rank. When asked about the colour of a child's hair, the response might be:

> Kapatau he uru korito, he koraki, he uru ariki no Pipi.
> If it is flaxen hair, a chiefly blond, then it is the noble hair of Pipi.[25]

Traditions relating to the patupaiarehe vary but generally suggest that cooked food (which has the power to whakanoa, or neutralise, tapu) was offensive to them. Others state that albino birds and eels as well as red flax and red eels were considered the property of the patupaiarehe and that trouble would befall any Māori who took them.[26] Curiously, one term applied to slaves in the Taranaki region is 'ngoringori' which is also the name given to a small variety of black eel. Another black eel called tuna-tuhoro was considered an ill omen in the nearby Whanganui area and consequently never eaten. Similar dark-coloured eels were also avoided in parts of Northland and Southland, so perhaps it was the black or dark colour and its negative associations that lay behind the dual meanings of ngoringori.[27]

Other writings from the early twentieth century imply or refer directly to fair skins as signs of chiefly status. For example, in 1905, Paora Haenga described the people who came on the waka (migration canoes) *Tainui*, *Te Arawa*, *Takitimu*, *Matatua* [sic], *Kurahaupo*, *Tokomaru*, *Aotea*, and *Nukutere* as being:

> he Tohunga katoa, he tapu, he urukehu katoa.
> all experts, tapu and all fair (or reddish) haired.[28]

That appears to contradict the tradition that it was the predecessors of Te Arawa in the Taupō region who were fair and may have been influenced by the contemporary political climate, an assertion of comparative rank. But associations between fair skin and chiefliness turn up over and over again. An article published in the Māori-language newspaper *Te Toa Takatini* in 1926 is one that makes the association explicit. In that, Reweti T. Kōhere described Te Kani-ā-Takirau as being:

> he tangata tu rangatira, he roa, he kiritea, he ataahua. He urukehu ona makawe, he mingimingi. Kaore he tohu o te rangatira i ngaro atu i a ia. I te mea he tangata tino rangatira ia ko tona ahua ki tona iwi he tangata tapu.[29]

> a man of high rank, tall, fair-skinned, handsome. His hair was fair (or reddish) and curly. He lacked no chiefly attributes. Because he was of very high rank, he was considered by his people as a tapu person.[30]

So was it the fairness of his skin and hair or the intimation that he was descended from urukēhu that represented his chiefly attributes — or were they one and the same?

Rangatira disguising themselves as slaves

The contrasts between the physical appearances of rangatira and taurekareka (captive, slave, or despised wretch) come through clearly in a number of oral traditions. A frequent motif in oral traditions, including the stories of Tāwhaki, Whakatau, Paowa, Tama, and Tinirau, is that of demigods and rangatira disguising themselves as slaves in order to infiltrate another community. They typically messed up their hair and wore old, shabby clothing, as well as smearing their faces and bodies with charcoal, ashes, or soot. So ridiculous was the idea that these tales were considered to be very humorous. The comic aspect is made specifically in one version of the story of Whakatau, son of Tūwhakararo and Apakura, who attempted to avenge his father's death. In that account, Whakatau had his hair cut short before rubbing his face all over with charcoal in order to conceal his moko (facial tattoo), or chiefly identity, and mingle unobtrusively among the workers in his enemies' village. The effect was so amusing that they said: 'What a black-looking fellow he is! and his quarry, Poporokewa, burst out laughing at his appearance.'[31]

The account of Tama's attempts to find his wife, who had left him for a better-looking man, refers to a similar disguise. In German missionary Johann Wohlers's version, having gone through the painful process of acquiring a moko to make himself more handsome, he then disguised his newly acquired beauty with dirt and ashes and made himself look like a mean man.[32] In that case, when he finally revealed his true self, Tama washed off the dirt, dressed his hair into a topknot, and clothed himself in his treasures.[33] Similarly, when Tinirau's son Tūhuruhuru wanted to find his mother, he was advised to disguise himself by rolling around on the ground where some fern had been burnt off in order to gain entry into her village as a stray slave.[34] One story, belonging to the Moriori people of Rēkohu, or the Chatham Islands, has a woman unknowingly take her two brothers as slaves. In this tradition, she immediately blackened their faces with charcoal, which suggests that it was a way of marking or identifying them as such rather than a natural process related to their work.[35]

In Ngāti Wai's account of the adultery of Manaia's wife, as told by Taipari Munro, the identity of his wife's lover was exposed by the ashes transferred from his body to hers. Her infidelity was discovered when Manaia returned home from a fishing trip and called to his wife to help him haul his canoe to shore. Because the water was deep, she hitched up her clothing to swim out towards him but, when she did so, her husband saw that her body was covered in ashes. That was Manaia's proof that she had lain with his slave because he knew that the man kept himself warm on cold nights by sleeping in the embers of the fire.[36]

It seems from the way that dirt, soot, ashes, and charcoal were used as a means of disguise that it was not the natural skin colour that equated with status but the fact that slaves and those of the lowest orders were the ones obliged to light and maintain fires and take care of cooking, which blackened their skin. John Turnbull Thomson, who came across a female slave in the early years of European settlement, described her just as we might expect, having: 'dark brown skin . . . blackened with smoke', and eyes 'red with the fumes of the manuka and black pine'.[37] The nature of their work and less spare time for personal grooming would hardly have improved the dirty and unkempt look of slaves.

Some early Pākehā writers, including Richard Taylor, referred to Māori warriors smearing themselves with charcoal when going into battle, as indicated by his explanation of the saying about red and black working together. Missionary William Yate found the habit very annoying when he and two of his brethren felt obliged to break up a fight between some of the Ngāpuhi chief Moka's slaves. Having entered the fray with a clean white jacket and nankeen trousers, Yate was not happy to come out of it covered from head to foot with charcoal and hair oil.[38] The practice of smearing with charcoal was not restricted to war captives, though, as it served as camouflage and assisted the body to retain warmth.[39] John Wilson, another Church Missionary Society (CMS) missionary, referred to the Ngāti Hauā rangatira Te Waharoa blackening his face before battle, too, so this use of charcoal was clearly for practical purposes and unrelated to rank.[40] John (Jacky) Marmon, a Sydney-born son of convict parents and a very early European arrival in the Hokianga area, loved to recount colourful and often highly suspect stories of his life 'as a Māori'. But his description of Ngāpuhi warriors returning from an assault on Ngāti Pāoa with faces streaked with charcoal and heads and bodies smeared with red ochre indicates how both colours might be used.[41]

Cosmetics aside, the evidence suggests that, prior to European contact and, perhaps, for some time after, Māori associated fair skin with high rank, regardless of whether the link between dark skin and low status was related more directly to the nature of the work typically done by slaves. In post-contact times, however, Māori appear to have absorbed something of the Western attitude which associated black-skinned people with slavery and, in some instances, as people less worthy of humane treatment than may have previously been the case. With that in mind, some inkling as to how Māori attitudes towards skin colour altered following European contact can be gleaned from the impressions of eighteenth- and nineteenth-century outsiders.

Skin colour as an indicator of status

Early European explorers and travellers paid a lot of attention to skin colour. George Robertson, who visited Tahiti in 1767 as master of HMS *Dolphin*, found 'three distink [sic] colours of people' there, 'the red or Indian Colour'; 'the Whitest sort'; and the 'Mustees'. The last he said was a colour that sat between the whitest and the red.[42] His remarks that the 'Servents' who paddled the great canoes were of a 'coper [sic] colour' and that 'the whole of the fair people sit under the Canopys' imply that he considered fairer skin to be the result of status and less exposure to the sun.[43] Victor Charles Lottin, who visited New Zealand in 1824, also thought that the married women were fairer than their slaves because they were 'more sedentary'.[44] In other words, menial labour out of doors darkened the skin.

Much later, in 1868, William Colenso, who had spent over 30 years in New Zealand by then, reported that Māori varied more in colour than any other Polynesians:

> Various hues of olive, of yellow-brown, and of an approach to the copper-colour were common. A few were of fair complexion; while others were very dusky, particularly of the more Northern tribes. Such colours, however, were not invariably perpetuated by descent; seeming rather to follow the abnormal law of all domesticated animals.[45]

Richard Taylor agreed that complexions and hair colour varied. For him, Māori were a decidedly mixed race, some of whom had woolly hair, others brown or flaxen, with skin colours equally varied. 'So dark are some of these natives', he added:

> that they are joked by others as being *Pokerekahu*, which is a name for a very black kind of kumara; in fact, they have many terms of reproach amongst themselves for these dark persons, such as *kiwakiwa, pangopango*, signifying black.[46]

Taylor's use of the word 'reproach' implies that he considered darker skin to be less esteemed than fair. It is possible that he was conditioned to interpret remarks which, in reality, were neutral, as being negative or insulting when they were not, but a pepeha, or saying, relating to Punga, a son of Tangaroa, tends to support his perception:

> Kātahi ka auraki mai ki te whānau a te mangumangu kikini, i te aitanga a Punga i a aue e!

> Now you come back here to the family of the ill-favoured dark one, a descendant of Punga such as I.

This was the sarcastic response uttered by a man whose lover returned after deserting him. Punga was said to be the progenitor of repulsive lizards, so ugly people were referred to as his offspring. The saying is a reminder that appearance is not the only basis for judging people, but, again, the suggestion is that dark people were ill-favoured.

Colenso and Taylor's impressions that there was significant variation in Māori skin tones are supported by the fact that Māori had a number of terms for describing people on the basis of complexion. In 1893, Ngāti Porou's Tuta Tāmati explained that dark-skinned people were referred to as kiri-parauri, light-coloured people as kiri-tea, and those considered to be red-skinned as kiri-waitutu, or the colour of tutu berry juice.[47] However, although there are suggestions that whiteness or fair skin was especially admired in Māori society, those connotations could have related to the greater cleanliness of the rangatira class and/or suggestion of descent from the earliest races of people to have settled the land. The latter may have conferred greater status or rights as tangata whenua (original inhabitants or people of the land). But, as they began interacting more frequently with Europeans and travelling overseas themselves, Māori cannot have been oblivious to Western ideas of racial superiority based on skin colour.

During the nineteenth century and earlier, Western ideas of race were typically conflated with class. The same was true in many other societies and cultures that historically associated skin colour with social rank. Often, this has related to the idea that the lower classes, being the workers, spend more time in the sun and are consequently darker-skinned than their more leisured compatriots. Paler skin is thus a sign of wealth and status. David Brion Davis's claim that '[i]t would be hard to overemphasize the importance of this linkage between low social class and the physical markers of menial labor' was certainly borne out in the observations of early European visitors to the Pacific.[48] The idea was not only evident when George Robertson visited Tahiti in 1767 but also in Edward Tregear's *Maori-Polynesian Comparative Dictionary*, published in 1891. With regard to the word 'whero' meaning red or reddish brown, Tregear noted that the Hawai'ian proverb *'He weo ke kanaka, he pano ke alii'*, or 'Red is the common man, black is the chief', was in direct contrast to the Māori conception of colour and rank. He sought to account for this by suggesting that:

> The Hawaiian proverb, speaking of black as a chief's hue, probably refers to the heavy tattooing of a noble.... The Polynesian chiefs of ancient descent were often very fair, probably owing to long lines of ancestry descending through ladies kept in close seclusion, and protected from the heat of the sun, in which the common people worked almost naked.[49]

That idea, perhaps combined with contemporary associations of race with class, may have supported the belief of some European observers that Māori slaves were an inferior race to free Māori.

However, another reason for these perceptions is the idea promoted by Richard Taylor and other early European ethnologists that the Māori had conquered and dispossessed a Melanesian people who had settled New Zealand before them. That alleged earlier race was often associated with or said to be the Moriori people of Rēkohu, the Chatham Islands. According to Taylor, Māori enslaved New Zealand's 'first sable colonists', just as the descendants of Shem (ancestor of the Jews) and Japheth (ancestor of Europeans) had enslaved the children of Ham (Africans). Elsdon Best was not a fan of biblical analogies, but was influential in promoting much the same understanding: that Māori had enslaved the Moriori and other early settlers of Melanesian origin.[50] They were ideas that gained considerable traction by way of justifying the Pākehā treatment of Māori as a conquered people. By waging war and confiscating Māori land, the settlers claimed to be acting just as the Māori had before them. It is an idea that continues to crop up today in online blogs, talkback radio shows, and the like. In his 2003 book *Quest for Origins*, Kerry Howe noted that there were by then websites offering elaborate details of claimed early arrivals in New Zealand. One with a sequence of Phoenicians 1666 years ago, others with Mauryans (an ancient Indian empire) 2240 years ago, Greeks 2180 years ago, Celts 300 AD, Arabs 790 AD, Tamils 1170, Portuguese in 1522, and Spanish in 1576.[51] There is no sustainable evidence for any of these assertions but, if any of these ideas were true, Māori claims of injustice could be very conveniently dismissed with the suggestion that they were merely having done to them what they had done to others.

The assumption that lighter-skinned people were superior to darker was shared by the German Ferdinand von Hochstetter, geologist aboard the *Novara* for an Austrian scientific expedition which visited New Zealand in the late 1850s. For him, Māori skin colouring was evidence of other attributes and higher rank on the scale of human civilisation:

> Two human races differing widely in physical and mental qualities, in language, manners and customs, inhabit the islands scattered over the Pacific Ocean. One race of very dark complexion, almost black, of ungainly make, of an extremely low grade of mental faculties, savage and for the most part incapable of civilization, occupies the southwestern part.... They are generally designated as Melanesians or Papuas....
>
> The second race, of a lighter complexion, in all the various shades of brown, of an admirably regular make, ranks much higher.[52]

With regard to the second group, von Hochstetter continued:

> To these Polynesians proper the natives of New Zealand belong; they are moreover the most important family of the Polynesian race both as to number, and mental and physical faculties.[53]

But, in the eyes of some, not all Māori were superior: only certain ones. Robert Carey was a military man involved in the Taranaki war that began in 1860 when Wiremu Kīngi Te Rangitāke refused to sanction the government's purchase of his land at the Waitara. So his poor opinion of Kīngi's people, as well as those of Ngāti Ruanui and Taranaki people more generally, was typical of those who adopted the common practice of dehumanising the enemy, representing them as barbarians or lesser human beings in one way or another. Carey's 1863 book *Narrative of the Late War in New Zealand* described the Taranaki people as 'men whom the Waikato looked down on as slaves, and whom our own people acknowledged as an inferior race, in customs, independence, build, and courage'.[54]

Although Reverend Abraham, Bishop of Wellington, did not face either of them in battle, he nonetheless made a similar comparison between Waikato Māori and the conquered Moriori in 1869:

> I have had the teaching of some of the Ma-ori-oris, and found them duller of intellect and heavier in body and mind than any other Polynesians I have ever seen — in fact, more like some of the Australian Papuens whom I have had to teach, and whom I observe Mr. Wallace connects with Polynesians. But as with the Maoris, so with the Australians, I have seen and taught two perfectly distinct types of mental and bodily structures in both races. One Australian was as heavy, thick-lipped, broad-featured, and *amiable* as a Ma-ori-ori; the other was as keen, sharp-featured, and self-willed as the highest type of Maori; I say the highest type, because the chiefs generally, and some of the finest tribes, such as the Waitakos [sic], have the high forehead, the straight nose, long hair, and intellectual haughty expression of what is, or used to be, called the Caucasian race; while the great mass of the people have the crisp woolly hair, the thick lips, the broad face, and the good-humoured look of the negro, though highly improved and developed.[55]

The implication, perhaps, is that being of an 'inferior' type explains their defeat. They were assumed to be too physically and mentally feeble to survive.

Western attitudes towards Australian Aborigines

The 1860s were a time of particular tension between Māori and Pākehā, but the ranking of racial types, evident in the Bishop's comparison, had a long history. Western visitors to the Pacific in the late eighteenth and nineteenth centuries often compared Melanesians and Australian Aborigines most unfavourably with Polynesians, including Māori. Their responses, partly based on skin colour and partly on cultural and environmental factors, were passed on to Māori very candidly. The *Maori Messenger: Ko Te Karere Maori*, a bilingual newspaper published by the government, followed that tradition, assuring Māori that they were a superior race of men, whilst the Australians, unhappily, were an inferior one. In an 1849 editorial, readers were told that:

> [Australians] are a most savage race of people. They go entirely naked (unless in towns, where the whites have taught them decency), and paint their bodies with various colours, and ornament themselves with beads and shells.... They are too ignorant and too indolent to dig the ground.

The item went on to explain more fully why the Aboriginal Australians were both pitied and held in contempt for the various attributes it ascribed to them. It also sought to flatter its Māori readers by explaining that Australians belonged to a lower order of people. Seeking to allay fears about the rapid alienation of their land and suggestions that they would be reduced to a position like the one indigenous Australians found themselves in, the paper told Māori readers that those on the other side of the Tasman Sea did not meet the prerequisites of land ownership:

> Bad and designing men may tell you, and we believe have told you, that Englishmen are anxious to strip you of your lands. They may, to induce you to believe them, point to Australia where the natives occupy no land. It is true they do not — but why? Because they are savages with no brains — no industry — no intellect and, like brutes, they but roam the surface of the earth, instead of (as you do) rendering it the means of supplying them with food and habitations.[56]

Those ideas would not have been new to Māori, though. Sealers and whalers, who had previously spent time in Australia, were visiting New Zealand from the 1790s and in greater numbers from around 1803. Having established themselves in a number of coastal areas, they often shared their less than flattering impressions of the indigenous inhabitants of that country with their hosts. But Māori were travelling themselves, too. According to Governor King, both Tuki Tahua, who called at Sydney on his way to Norfolk Island in 1793, and Te Pahi, who visited during 1805 and 1806, had poor impressions of the Australian Aboriginals, remarking similarly on their lack of clothing and agriculture as well as their disinclination to kill enemies worsted in battle.[57] How common these reactions were is hard to know. Te Pahi was also very critical of many European customs and habits, in Sydney and elsewhere, and many other Māori visitors expressed concern at the poor treatment the indigenous Australians had received.[58] European opinions of the Aborigines, though, whether in Australia or New Zealand, must have been hard to miss.

Māori attitudes towards Moriori and Aborigines

So it should not be surprising if Māori absorbed something of the Western attitude which associated black-skinned people with slavery and regarded them as lesser human beings. A case in point is the way that the Moriori were treated by the Māori tribes Ngāti Tama and Ngāti Mutunga who invaded their homeland in 1835. Although indigenous to Rēkohu, the Moriori are understood to share the same Polynesian ancestry as Māori and to have left the mainland around 1500. Yet the invaders appear to have acted with unusual brutality — probably much more so than was the case in other times and places. Significantly, the conquered Moriori were not referred to by any pre-existing words in the Māori language but by the newly coined 'paraiwhara', a transliteration of the English term 'black fella'.[59] The epithet is said to have been adopted because the conquerors had heard it used by sealers and traders to refer to Aboriginal Australians, and that they treated the Moriori in the harsh ways they understood Europeans to have treated those people. Because the word was used regularly with evident contempt, and from the impressions gained during their own visits to Australia, Māori understood their Australian counterparts to have been enslaved by the British. Within this mindset, Māori might have considered that their status was so degraded it would have been unthinkable to intermarry with them — for the British and, therefore, for Māori too. All the same, there were cases of intermarriage between Māori and half-caste Australian Aboriginals in South Island whaling communities but possibly not with full-blooded Aboriginals.[60] Indeed, the author of one article about the half-caste whaler Tommy Chaseland, who married a Māori woman, was asked by an informant not to publish her name as 'members of her family were not "terribly impressed" that they had Aboriginal ancestors'.[61]

Such responses may also explain why the Māori conquerors forbade intermarriage with Moriori, contrary to customary practice. Moriori were not only debarred from marrying Māori but also prohibited from marrying within their own community. The existence of some half-castes confirms that not everyone obeyed the rule, but their Moriori mothers may have been considered concubines rather than wives.[62] Another aspect of the Rēkohu situation that differed from norms on the mainland was the fact that the Moriori were not taken back to the lands of their masters or conquerors but enslaved on their own lands. It would seem then, that in this context, the term 'black fella' and its equivalents implied status rather than skin colour.

However, while the origin of the word 'paraiwhara' as applied to the Moriori has been acknowledged, another name, recorded by Elsdon Best, may have similar roots. In a version of 'The Legend of Rata', concerning migration from Eastern Polynesia to New Zealand, he recounted that:

> Manu-korihi was a chief of the clans Pakau-moana and Te Ahi-utu-rangi, who led a party of his people from Whiti-anaunau to a strange land in the south-west, where two chiefs named Matuku-tangotango and Pou-hao-kai lived at a place called Pariroa. Hine-komahi, daughter of Turongo-nui, Te Rara-a-takapu, Whakaaupara, and Mohokura were other important persons of Pari-roa. The folk who lived at that place were *pakiwhara* — that is, a shiftless people who lived in poor huts not good houses, and scattered about. They subsisted on fish, shellfish, birds, and vegetable products, but did not cultivate food. They often moved their place of abode, hence they did not construct good houses.[63]

This description of a nomadic, non-agricultural people is in line with nineteenth-century European ideas relating to race which typically categorised such societies as savage.⁶⁴ Therefore, it might be wondered whether the term 'pakiwhara' was another transliteration for black fella. Best's informant appears to have been describing a people he expected the ethnologist to recognise as inferior to Māori. A similar process of thought exchange might account for the tradition of the Hāwea, associated with the Waitaha people of the South Island. They are said to have been very dark-skinned with thick curly hair, thick lips, and flashing white teeth, apparently similar to the Zulus of South Africa. 'They did not come from Hawaiki, the fatherland of the Māori.'⁶⁵ Elsewhere, Best suggested that some Melanesian people arrived in New Zealand aboard the migration canoe *Horouta* as slaves of the Polynesian navigators who went on to become ancestors of the Māori.⁶⁶ So, once again, the idea was that darker-skinned people were inferior to lighter and probably more suited to slavery or liable to be enslaved.

Preconceptions work both ways, however, because George French Angas reported in 1844 that an Australian Aboriginal, known, ironically, as Black Charley, had heard much of the cannibal propensities of the New Zealanders. Charley worked on a schooner and was, according to Angas, afraid to go ashore for fear of being devoured.

> [H]e always exhibited the most violent signs of fear whenever any of the natives came on board the schooner, fully expecting they would purchase him for a cooky, or slave, to be killed and eaten. The young New Zealanders, on the other hand, were greatly amused at the dark colour of his skin, and laughed at him for being so ugly; calling him Mango, Mango [sic] or black fellow.⁶⁷

The idea that Māori treated the Moriori as they understood the British to treat indigenous Australians is also supported by the fears articulated by Māori rangatira when they were being asked to sign the Treaty of Waitangi in 1840. At the Hokianga gathering arranged to obtain further signatures, Taonui, who had previously visited Sydney, pointedly asked:

> How do the Pakehas behave to the black fellows of Port Jackson [Sydney]? They treat them like dogs! See! A Pakeha kills a pig; the black fellow comes to the door, and eats the refuse.⁶⁸

It is in the nature of sayings and metaphors that they are typically multi-levelled in their meaning, and the fundamental message of 'Ma pango, ma whero, ka oti' has been applied to many new circumstances over the generations. But, as proverbial sayings evolve to serve new purposes, so, too, are oral traditions reshaped to meet contemporary needs. As Ranginui Walker put it:

> The moral truths which are the myth-messages are relatively stable but points of detail may be altered to suit local circumstance.[69]

Local, in this case, may also mean contemporary. So should these matters confuse us or do those shifts offer insight into changing societal modes and perceptions? To quote Walker again:

> In some cases the myth-messages are so close to the existing reality of human behaviour that it is difficult to resolve whether myth is the prototype or the mirror image of reality.[70]

There can be little doubt that cosmology, a lack of mana and tapu, and the common physical condition of taurekareka, or captives, were all embodied in explicit perceptions of them as black. So, conceptually, they must have been connected. However, although semiotic connotations are ever shifting, it does seem that in many, if not most, contexts black has been a colour with negative connotations for Māori. Connections between black and darkness on the one hand and white and lightness on the other are very apparent in the Māori worldview and suggest that to be 'enslaved' was to enter a dark and gloomy world indeed. What is not so clear, though, is whether all captives were subsumed into a deep or permanent state of darkness as 'outcasts of the gods'.

CHAPTER TWO

Tapu and mana: losing and regaining

As BLACK IS THE COLOUR OF DEATH AND DESPAIR, RED IS THE colour of tapu and, therefore, of mana and rangatiratanga, or chiefliness. Tapu has many meanings and applications, including legal ones, and important spiritual implications. Although close to the Judaeo-Christian idea of sacred or holy, it lacks the New Testament connotations of 'moral righteousness'. A person or thing placed under tapu is removed from the sphere of the profane and placed within that of the sacred; untouchable and no longer to be put to common use.[1] Tapu induced awe and fear as well as respect. Together with its counterpart mana, tapu regulated human behaviour and social order. Mana has been defined as 'lawful permission delegated by the gods to their human agent to act on their behalf and in accordance with their revealed will'. It is a spiritual gift, delegated by the gods. As mere agents or channels of that authority, humans must be careful not to abuse the endowment. The late Reverend Maori Marsden stressed the distinction between authority and power, adding that to exercise the gift of spiritual power outside its delegated limits would result either in its withdrawal or in 'that power running rampant and causing harm to the agent and others'. This was a threat that supported another fundamental principle: that of maintaining balance. To explain the difference between authority and power in modern terms, Reverend Marsden offered the analogy of a person approaching traffic lights:

> The lights turn green but his car stalls at that moment. He has permission to cross, but no power. His car starts and the lights remain green. He has both authority and power to proceed.[2]

Since mana was vital to chiefly authority and the wellbeing of the tribal group, it was absolutely essential that it be maintained or, better still, enhanced. So attacks on the mana of an individual or the community had to be dealt with and dealt with effectively. Insults, often considered trivial by non-Māori, could represent a serious attack on the mana of the victim or the group. So warfare, which offered an opportunity to restore mana and ensure spiritual and material wellbeing, played an important role in inter-group relations. Wars were fought to avenge personal insults or killings, to settle disputes, or to achieve political dominance. But while success in battle restored or enhanced the mana of the victor, captivity and enslavement represented a significant loss of tapu and mana for the defeated. The people referred to as slaves in the English language were generally war captives forced to perform not only the unpleasant work despised by people of higher status, but also that which was most damaging to tapu and mana — such as making fires and cooking food. A large number of 'slaves' symbolised the high status of successful tribal leaders and the degraded state of the vanquished. To lose one's mana was social and spiritual death, to become a non-person — a lost soul.[3]

As mentioned in the Introduction, the concepts of mana and tapu were widespread throughout the Pacific region, as were the associated symbolisms of colour. So language may offer other insights into ancient understandings of what it meant to be a war captive or to be 'enslaved'. As many aspects of Māori society and spiritual belief were carried across the Pacific with the first migrants to New Zealand, some terms or concepts pertaining to captives or slaves would have made that same journey from the Polynesian homelands and offer clues to their original connotations. However, despite the fact that similar institutions were present in other parts of Polynesia, Māori have inherited few words that originally designated the status of slave.[4] Nevertheless, there are some likely linguistic remnants. For example, in Rarotongan or Cook Islands Māori, the word '*unga*' means little people or insignificant crumbs. According to the Reverend W. Wyatt Gill, the people of Rarotonga drew on the root system of the indigenous arrowroot plant to refer to their social hierarchy. The plant has one or two large tuberous roots which are surrounded by many smaller ones as well as a large number of even smaller tubers which Gill claimed were called *unga*. He explained that large roots metaphorically represent the chiefly people, the smaller ones the 'landed proprietors' who owe allegiance to the chiefs or who are their relatives, while the many tiny *unga* represent the serfs or *tangata rikiriki* (little people) who were of no account in Rarotongan society.[5] No further references to this specific usage have been located, but a near equivalent in New Zealand Māori, 'hunga', can mean 'people', or a group or crowd of people, 'the masses', and has also been translated to mean a slave or refugee. Another related term, 'kahunga', also has 'slave' as its primary meaning, so this similarity suggests a shared metaphorical development that was carried to New Zealand regardless of whether it originated with the arrowroot plant or merely something small and insignificant.[6]

Perhaps the best-known Māori word for a slave is 'taurekareka' and it is generally assumed that it refers to a war captive, although it was and still is used pejoratively as a very severe insult applied to someone the speaker despises. It suggests that the person is a worthless wretch. This is more curious as the equivalent word had positive connotations elsewhere in the Pacific. *Taulekaleka* means 'youth', 'young man', or 'handsome' in Proto-Polynesian.[7] However, a clue may lie in the Samoan *taule'ale'a*, which could be applied not only to a young man, who would, of course, be subservient to others, but also to a person without a *matai* (chiefly) title.[8]

But while taurekareka is always used in a thoroughly debasing way in New Zealand Māori, there are other words such as 'mōkai' and 'pononga' that may be used less harshly. As the *Tai Tokerau Dictionary* explained:

> Many of these terms can also be used to denote relationships other than those marked by the complete subjugation of one party by another; thus for example mōkai can refer to a pet or the youngest member of a family.[9]

Pononga is often translated as servant. In today's world, it might refer to an office assistant or volunteer worker. It could be that, in some historical instances, they were favoured war captives, selected as attendants to people of rank, but in others, they may have been free-born members of the same tribal group who performed a similar role for someone of higher rank than themselves. Some people today use pononga to mean a faithful follower — a disciple, perhaps — of a political or spiritual leader.[10]

Deeper connotations?

As Richard Taylor said, Māori used 'many terms of reproach' among themselves which related to skin colour,[11] and a variety of words relating to slavery or low status appear to have been employed in much the same way. Several terms have been used metaphorically or with a political purpose — to insult or put down an enemy or rival. In 1860, the newly established Māori King, Pōtatau Te Wherowhero, took that approach when pronouncing his high regard for the Governor and European people generally, but referred (in English translation) to Tāpihana and Te Whaitere at Kāwhia and Waipā as 'troublesome characters' . . . 'descendants of fern diggers, or slaves'.[12]

Apart from the most common terms — taurekareka, mōkai, and pononga — several others may offer clues to deeper spiritual or metaphorical connotations. Two less well-known words that referred to both captives and fish — 'ngoringori' and 'parakau' — may be cases in point. A story published in the Māori-language newspaper *Te Korimako* in 1884 used ngoringori to describe the sons of Canute, King of England, and parts of Scandinavia. The article, entitled 'Ingarangi i mua ai', or 'England in past times', was likely to have been written or translated by Charles Oliver Bond Davis.[13] But whoever the writer was, he clearly did not hold Canute's sons in high regard.[14] Interestingly, though, ngoringori does not seem to have been used in the northern part of New Zealand where most of *Te Korimako*'s readers lived (unless, perhaps, to mean an eel). *Te Aka*, an online Māori Dictionary, says it is an adjective denoting lowly status.[15] H. W. Williams's *A Dictionary of the Maori Language* says that 'ngori' means weak or listless, which might be another clue to its origin, and that it means a slave in the Taranaki dialect.[16] Taranaki was the origin of a story collected by Elsdon Best, which applauds the praiseworthy attributes of a woman named Raumāhora:

> Ki te kite ia i etahi tangata o etahi iwi ke, o etahi hapu ke, ka karangatia e ia kia peka ki te kainga, ahakoa ope tino tangata, ope ngoringori noa iho ranei ka karangatia e ia ki te kainga, ka manaakitia e ia.
>
> Should she espy persons of other tribes or clans, she would call to them to stop at the village; whether a party of influential folk or one of low caste persons, they would be invited by her to the village and hospitably entertained.[17]

So ngoringori here relates to people of 'low caste' or little account.

Parakau is also a species of fish, possibly a young flounder. Many rituals pertained to fishing, and it was customary to return the first fish caught, te ika whakataki, to the sea, to Tangaroa god of the sea, as an offering or sacrifice. So it is unlikely to be mere coincidence that people caught in battle, those killed, and even human sacrifices could be referred to as 'ika', or fish. New Zealand Māori and other Pacific peoples have traditions that refer to catching enemies as being akin to catching fish. In Tahiti, human sacrifice was called *'i'a avae roroa'* — 'the long-legged fish'.[18] In the Solomon Islands' New Georgia, captives from other islands were referred to either as pigs that were hunted or fish that were caught.[19] Since there were no pigs in New Zealand until they were introduced by Europeans in the late eighteenth century, it was the concept of captives as fish that Māori carried with them when they migrated. Thomas McDonnell, who lived in the Hokianga from the early 1830s, was given a nineteenth-century explanation for eating the enemy which referred to them as fish:

> If [a man] won't kill his enemy when he catches him, what is the use of going to fight? A man goes to fish for whapuku. Well, he catches a fish. What does he do with it? Does he let it go again? That would be a foolish thing! No, for if he did, he would be laughed at, and people would say he was mad. So he eats it. What else did he catch it for? And so with fighting.[20]

A number of Māori phrases referring to victims of warfare or sacrifice include one or other of the words 'ika' or 'ngohi', both of which can mean fish:

> ika koangaumu: human sacrifice or sacrificial fish (see Chapter 4)
> ika paremo: human victim slain to propitiate Tangaroa, god of the sea
> ika takoto a Tiki: human corpse
> ika hui rua: the slaying of two men together, at one and the same place
> ika purapura: human victim buried during erection of a house
> te ika a Tiki, matāika or mātāngohi: the first man killed or captured in a fight
> he maroro kokoti ihu waka: 'a flying fish cut off by the bow of the canoe': the first person encountered on the way to battle
> ngohi: victim (or troop, company of fighting men)
> whakatakoto ngohi: to lay an ambush

Williams's *Dictionary* includes the word 'pārau' as meaning a slave or a captive, or, as a verb, to lay hold of. Williams also notes the word's relationship to the verb 'rau', 'to catch as in a net'. Perhaps more curiously, Richard Taylor explained that 'tipai', which means a mollusc or scallop, can also refer to an untattooed face: 'a sign the man would be made a slave of'.[21]

Besides fishy words and phrases being applied to captives (an association surely enhanced by the fishy smell they would often give off), there was logic behind terms related to food, cooking, and eating being applied to them and others of low status. That is why the term 'kuki' or 'cookee', which was not derived from any pre-contact Māori word but rather from the English 'cook', often appears in nineteenth-century writings. It refers to the role that captives were typically obliged to perform. 'Tūmou' and its variant tūmau, for example, can also refer simultaneously to both 'slave' and 'cook'. 'Kaitoa', which signifies that the toa (courage or strength) of the conquered has been consumed,[22] may refer to a brave man or a warrior, but can also mean 'satisfaction', so 'kaitoa koe' means 'serves you right'. 'Toenga kai' or 'toenga-kaitia' (left-over food) were other terms used contemptuously of captives, implying that the rest of their people were eaten.[23]

One Ngāi Tahu woman was so furious with her husband after an argument that she decided to rub salt into his wounds by applying connotations of food to belittle his ancestry through another tribal group. She used the names of some of his ancestors in such a way, saying:

> He taurekareka koe, no roto i te kakakaiamio; i puta mai koe i roto i te pohatu paremoremo, i te aruhe taratara.

The sentence cannot be simply translated because, as Jim Williams explained, although Pōhatu Pāremoremo and Aruhe Taratara, mentioned in that sentence, are names of her husband's Waitaha ancestors, they can also refer to food, so she was implying that he was of little mana:

> Kaiāmio is the practice of seasonal wanderings in family groups to gather food, but by replication of the initial sound she makes a pun, implying a kākā scratching around for food. Pōhatu pāremoremo are umu stones, slippery with the juices of cooking, and aruhe taratara is fern root — a very low class of food.

Although his hapū, Kahea, is still acknowledged as having been the most prestigious line of Ngāti Māmoe and 'a feature of their morganatic marriage', she created an overall image of his descent from demeaning lines of ancestry.[24]

Like many others, Raymond Firth was inclined to treat the New Zealand institution from a European perspective and, therefore, in relation to concepts such as 'the division of labour'. Yet despite his reference to Nieboer's 1910 *Slavery as an Industrial System*, Firth correctly took issue with several aspects of Nieboer's analysis. He pointed out that the background of the New Zealand institution should be sought 'not merely in general economic conditions alone, but also in the whole scheme of magico-religious ideas centring around food and its preparation, as well as in the complex set of customs and emotional attitudes relating to war'.[25] Firth had grasped that significance almost a hundred years ago, yet it is still overlooked today by those who suggest that the '[u]nderstanding of history is not ethnically determined'.[26]

Could 'slaves' have had no mana or tapu?

In Māori society, being captured in war and enslaved was extremely humiliating and is frequently said to have resulted in the total loss of an individual's tapu and mana. However, the evidence frequently confounds that idea, which appears to have been overstated. Was it possible for human beings to have no tapu? Tapu and mana are so closely related that, as Father Michael Shirres put it: 'explicit references to mana are implicit references to tapu'. There could not be one without the other.[27]

For Edward Tregear, '[a] slave was nobody spiritually; his gods had forsaken and forgotten him; therefore he was essentially non-existent'.[28] Firth also seems to have understood captivity in terms of spiritual death, saying that 'his capture removed from [the captive] the mana of the gods and in things spiritual he ceased to count'.[29] In Hawai'i, people referred to as *kauwā*, believed to have been the descendants of captives but isolated far more severely from Hawai'ian society than Māori were from theirs, were referred to as corpses.[30]

Nevertheless, the idea of humans living without tapu troubled Elsdon Best who remarked:

> It is interesting to note that slaves were held to be free from *tapu*, and yet no explanation is given as to their condition of welfare and their survival, why they did not perish in such a defenceless condition.... If it is necessary to a freeman, in order that he may retain life, how is it that the slave exists without it?[31]

Oral traditions, too, often credit 'slaves' with having tapu and, by implication, mana. In one version of the story of Tamaāhua, which explains the origins of pounamu in the South Island, the protagonist's 'slave' Tumu-aki burnt his fingers while cooking birds for their evening meal. But his unthinking reaction to suck his fingers cost him dearly. In so doing, he destroyed his tapu and was punished by being turned into a mountain.[32]

On the basis that they had no mana or rights, it has been suggested that the killing of slaves was not a crime.[33] Yet, again, that cannot have been strictly true because a number of instances of masters or mistresses being rebuked for mistreating captives or executing them without just cause have been recorded, which suggests that there was tikanga, or a customary code of conduct, relating to their treatment. And, if captives had no tapu or mana, why were they not all treated alike? Rangatira or captives of high rank were treated differently from commoners, as women were treated differently from men. Captive men did beat aruhe or fern root, a basic everyday carbohydrate staple, but food preparation and cooking seem to have been performed by women more often than by men, albeit not exclusively. Obliging men to cook may also have been a means of putting male captives more firmly in their place. But work appears to have been gendered in other ways, too, which also puts into question the widely held view that slaves were completely devoid of tapu.[34] It seems more appropriate to talk in terms of degrees of tapu and mana.

Because the logic behind the Māori concept of tapu has proved difficult for present-day scholars to comprehend, Shirres drew on early Māori texts to derive a better understanding. His analysis concluded that the term tapu is neither univocal nor equivocal but analogous. By that, he meant it has meanings which 'though different when applied to different things are nevertheless related in some way'.[35] He went on to explain that there are many different tapu:

> Individuals and groups of people are *tapu*; children, parents, war parties, sick and so on. Some of the *tapu* mark off places; houses, gardens and special ritual areas. Others mark off special times, so we have *tapu* days. There are *tapu* which need to be protected, strengthened and confirmed, for instance the *tapu* of the child. There are *tapu* which give protection, for instance the *tapu* of the *iraamutu*, the chief's sister's daughter.[36]

A Ngāti Pāoa source, almost certainly Wiremu Hoete, explained that: 'the *mana*, and therefore *tapu*, of man is seen as beginning with . . . "the very coming of the child into his mother"', but comes from his ancestors. Shirres's nineteenth-century informants agreed that a person's tapu and mana is not lost until the time of death when it passes to his or her descendants as long as the family continues to exist.[37] So, for those scholars, both attributes last a lifetime.

Although Shirres did not refer specifically to captives, he did note the difference between the tapu of a rangatira and that of an ordinary person and variations in the degree of mana pertaining to individuals. Key points clarified by his analysis are that the tapu of one person or thing may be in conflict with that of another as well as with 'intrinsic' tapu relating to people or things that are tapu in themselves. Based on the different levels or strengths of tapu and the fact that the tapu of individuals may be in conflict with each other, it is possible to grasp why war captives could both threaten and be threatened by the tapu of the rangatira.

Vulnerability of 'slaves' to tapu

Joel Polack, a Jewish merchant from London who arrived in New Zealand in 1831, explained that people assigned to perform certain types of work, such as preparing the bones of the dead for interment, cutting hair, or undergoing the process of tā moko (tattooing), were forbidden to touch food. They were 'fed like babies from the hands of another party' and '[i]f a slave is thus tapued, he has to swallow his allotted food as best he can, as it lies on the ground, taking especial care his fingers do not touch a morsel'.[38] He recounted one particular incident when several Māori he had employed were carrying bags of flour and biscuit from a boat into his store on their backs:

> [A] corner of one of the bags came unsewed and the biscuit fell out — this bag was carried by an inferior chief; a slave man standing by, picked the bread up, for which I offered him some; the chief carrier stopped me, "Give him something else for his trouble," said he, "but a slave must not eat of that which has been carried on my back; he would die."[39]

This 'inferior chief' appears to have been concerned for the other man's welfare and the impact of the extension of his own tapu onto the captive via the biscuit. It could have been the kiss of death.

Missionary John Morgan and merchant-politician William Brown recalled similar incidents. Morgan wrote that when he was near

Matamata in 1834, some of the young rangatira who accompanied his party 'were very particular as to what burden they carried. One of them said: "If I was to carry a bag of flour, and a slave should afterward eat of it, I should die in consequence of his having partaken of it."'[40] Brown recalled that a friend of his once gave some tobacco to a slave 'who, after having used it, was informed that it had been on the roof of the chief's house'. 'The poor fellow, in the greatest consternation, went immediately to the chief telling him what had happened, and beseeching him to take off the tapu from the tobacco to prevent the evil consequences.'[41]

As Edward Tregear pointed out, captives had to be very careful indeed not to violate the tapu of rangatira because, although the consequent harm would fall on the rangatira, the penalty for causing that harm would be harsh:

> [W]hat he had to dread was the vengeance of the offended person, not the wrath of deities. The celestial penalty of the breach would fall upon the chief whose *tapu* had been broken, not on the slave, who was below divine notice. Such pleasant absolution from individual holiness allowed the slave to execute many tasks which it was impossible for more exalted persons to perform, such as cooking food, carrying burdens and other menial duties which it was to the advantage of the community should be executed, and which he was therefore valued for being able to do. The warrior whose person was so holy that it would be contaminated by going near a cooking-oven and whose back was too sacred to bear a burden had a good friend in "the outcast of the gods."[42]

Although rangatira joined their people to work at various projects, they could not carry food or firewood, or involve themselves in cooking or food preparation, amongst other things.[43] So, as Shirres put it: 'all *tapu* can be seen as needing to be treated with respect, and sometimes fear, but this depends on which side you are on, on the relationship of your *tapu* to the other *tapu*'.[44] War captives were not immune to the forces of tapu, although they were in some ways freer than their captors in that regard.[45]

Could captives return home?

Regardless of however free or otherwise they might have been, it has been asked why, given the large influx of captives into many communities, especially during the 1820s, running away was not more common. It has often been said that, because their shame and ill fortune fell on their wider tribal group, their kin would not have wanted them back and they could not go home. In the same vein, the captives themselves are assumed to have felt so dishonoured that they would not have considered it anyway.[46] Edward Tregear, who had arrived in New Zealand as a seventeen-year-old in 1863, was one who believed that escape would serve little purpose:[47]

> It was useless for [a slave] to try to escape to his own people, for they would not have received him; he was an unlucky man whose gods had forsaken him, the proof being that they had allowed him to be captured. He was to his own tribe as one dead, or worse, his presence would be a living insult to them. They wanted neither him nor his bad luck again in their fort or war-party; it was misfortune enough that one of their number should be "a morsel spared from the oven" but the offence could not be wiped out by the return of the captive; only the blood of his captors could avenge the degradation.[48]

Augustus Earle, who visited New Zealand in 1827 when captive taking was the preferred method of recruiting compliant workers, was somewhat less dogmatic. But he still felt that going home would offer little improvement to a captive's status:

> If the slave effect his escape to his own part of the country, he is there treated with contempt; and when he dies (if a natural death), his body is dragged to the outside of the village, there to be made sport of by the children, or to furnish food for the dogs![49]

In other words, they would be treated as slaves among their own.

For Polack, on the other hand, the reason slaves rarely escaped was the Māori's innate inability to keep a secret. He claimed that, once a friend was told of the plan, word would almost always reach the master or mistress via a series of people passing 'the secret' along (supposedly in confidence).[50] His was surely a jaundiced and racialised view but supports the idea that captives would have liked to get away from their situation. It might also help to explain why they rarely combined in their escape attempts. Once at their conquerors' home places, they were not confined or restrained as was sometimes the case in other societies, but were, in the practical sense, free to roam.[51] However, because they came from many different tribal areas, there were formidable obstacles to their organising a united escape.[52] Could they really trust fellow captives from other tribal groups?

From the 1820s, missionaries and others often reported that slaves who failed in their attempts to run away were killed or otherwise punished.[53] But where were they planning to go? Some may have run to the missions, but certainly not all. And even if they did, the missionaries were usually obliged to hand them over. Christianity had taken little hold by that time, even in the Bay of Islands area where the first missions were located, and much less so in the more distant places from where they had been seized.[54] So who would have taken in fugitives if not their own kin? Were they all planning a new career as itinerant outlaws? A career as a 'highway robber' was unlikely to appeal to runaway women or girls who must have expected to be welcome if they made it home. But even when their kin received them warmly after a successful return, that welcome could put them all in danger. One of John White's informants told how Ngāti Kōpirimau of Hauraki suffered massive losses when Ngāti Raukawa paid them a visit looking for a woman who had fled from them at Te Aroha. The encounter that followed cost them dearly with many of their men killed and their women captured.[55]

For a lucky few escapees, there may have been opportunities to negotiate an arrangement with another tribe. That appears to have been how Waikato of Te Hikutū in Hokianga became aware of the chance to obtain utu or redress for a previous insult by Te Tātua, a rangatira of Ngāti Wai and Ngāti Toki. It was 1820 and an escaped slave is said to have let him know that Te Tātua's home on Tawhitinui (the Poor Knights Islands) had been left largely undefended while he was away fighting with one of Hongi Hika's war parties. That intelligence allowed Waikato to seize the moment and lay waste to Tawhitinui along with the people who had stayed behind. The escapee surely expected to enjoy a more comfortable lifestyle with Te Hikutū after giving them that helping hand.[56]

Despite claims to the contrary, happy reunions do not seem to have been untypical when captured people made it home. Indeed, family members often encouraged them to flee. And more regular opportunities came with the arrival of overseas ships. Two of Te Rauparaha's captives, known aboard ship as Diky and Tomy, seized the chance when they were offered 'on trust' as crewmen to the Danish voyager Captain Thomas Sødring who visited Cloudy Bay. He was obviously embarrassed as well as annoyed when they fled:

> Their escape had been planned with much cunning. Two days before having had a visit from some of their relations, who possibly had talked them into escaping, they had acquired complete new clothes which they then took with them.[57]

So their relatives appear to have been keen to welcome those now smartly dressed family members home — but that was in 1840.

Did attitudes change over time?

Like Diky and Tomy, captives certainly did return home after European contact and were often warmly welcomed by their kin. But it has been suggested that such readiness to take back captives was an innovation; that in non-Christian times, most would have been too shamed by their loss of tapu to want to return to their own people.[58] Yet such a change would not only have been quite dramatic but also appears to have come about very quickly. Not only that, but captives returned to places said to be untouched by missionary influence, so, presumably, unaffected by new worldviews.

Large numbers of captives had been taken north from the late 1810s, where they often came under missionary influence. However, as discussed more fully in Chapter 8, there was a reversal in the trend from the late 1820s and many northern leaders began releasing their captives. Many of those allowed to go home were responsible for introducing

Christianity into their home communities and their names are still remembered. Logically, that means that they must have been welcomed back before they had time to share those new ideas. Which begs the question of why it would have been so different in earlier times — or even whether it was.

Significant conquests had damaged the viability of tribal groups at various times in history, prompting survivors to adapt to new situations. The extraordinary loss of people and, therefore, of their labour force and source of future children during the so-called 'musket wars' may have been so great for some communities that their survival depended on a more receptive attitude towards returning captives. Besides, warfare tends to result in losses on both sides, so the impact went both ways. As the losers might welcome back successful escapees, the victors could take captive women as wives or adopt others as a way of bolstering their numbers. The latter was a natural and logical response which occurred in pre-colonial Nigeria, Native America, the Solomon Islands, and elsewhere, where captives were adopted into the ranks of their hosts to avoid their own extinction or strengthen their gene pool.[59]

But as an entry in John White's *Ancient History of the Maori* acknowledges, there were contradictions in responses towards the return of family members who had been captured:

> A chief who lived in the south near Wellington whose son had been taken slave by one of the northern tribes would not own his son who had returned from his captivity. The chief said he had been so degraded by being taken alive in war, that he would not own such a child, yet in July 24th, 1849 a young man came from the East Cape to Hokianga and bought his brother with mats and greenstone who had been a slave to Wharepapa.[60]

White does not say when the chief from near Wellington refused to acknowledge his son. It may have been at an earlier date, or, perhaps, that father was more 'old school' than the young man from the East Cape. Alternatively, it may have been that the son failed to live up to his people's expectations in battle and let the side down. Regardless of specific circumstances, attitudes were altering as Christianity offered new ways of coping with what was, by now, a very abnormal situation, but not in a consistent way. The numbers of people captured and the proportion of the population who had been captives at some point in their lives must have exceeded previous experience enormously. Yet deaths in battle still fell well below deaths from introduced diseases, childbirth, and other causes.[61] Lack of immunity to diseases common in the Western world meant that Māori death rates rose significantly from the time of European contact. Although the most rapid population decrease occurred subsequently, between 1840 and 1860,[62] those tribal groups that had suffered outside assault during the 1820s and 1830s would have felt their losses most keenly in that period. Apart from deaths in combat and starvation from lengthy sieges, large numbers of captives were taken from single battles or expeditions. According to Samuel Marsden, on one early 1818 expedition, Hongi burned 500 settlements between the River Thames and the East Cape, captured 2000 prisoners, and brought back about 70 heads in a single canoe.[63] Barnet Burns claimed that about 400 were taken when Te Aitanga a Māhaki attacked Whakatōhea around 1831, with some 60 of them being killed.[64] Even a prearranged limit could imply that a high number of casualties was expected. Before a battle for a pā (fortified settlement) between Wairoa and Gisborne commenced it was agreed by the rangatira that only half the pā would be destroyed and the number of people killed would be restricted to half the inhabitants.[65] Those realities may well have contributed to warmer welcomes for captive kin who managed to escape or gain their freedom through other means.[66] But it does not appear to be the whole story. As early as 1819, a young man told Marsden that a woman taken as 'part of his spoil' on an expedition to the East Cape would be allowed to join the mission ship *Active* when it visited her home so she could 'see the place' but that he would need to accompany her and ensure she did not land 'as she would run away'.[67] So even at this early stage in the 'musket wars', her captor assumed she would have been welcomed home.

Retrieving the lost

In the early 1840s, Edward Shortland recorded a karakia, or incantation, together with its associated ritual, which was used to cleanse people

FIGURE 1. The frontispiece of Alexander Strachan's *The Life of the Rev. Samuel Leigh* (1870) is an example of how Māori 'slavery' has been conflated with the slave trade in Africans. It includes an image at the bottom right said to show 'Mr. L. defending a slave', but the drawing on the top left, purported to depict Leigh being 'attacked by New Zealanders', has them carrying shields unknown to Māori and living in huts very reminiscent of South African rondawels. It is apparently an African rather than a New Zealand scene. Leigh did not visit Africa but made frequent visits to a slave market in Pernambuco, Brazil, on his return voyage to England from New Zealand. *Image courtesy of Special Collections, University of Auckland Libraries and Learning Services*

FIGURE 2. This image of a supplicant male slave in chains appeared on several medallions made for the Society for the Abolition of Slavery by Josiah Wedgwood from 1787. However, it was not ultimately restricted to medallions but also appeared on various china and ceramic items, jewellery, blocks for wax seals, and even on patch boxes (used to hold black silk patches for women's faces). A ubiquitous icon, it would have been the image that many people internalised and recalled whenever the word 'slavery' was used.

FIGURE 3. A piece of kōkōwai, or red ochre (haematite). *ME017175, Museum of New Zealand Te Papa Tongarewa, Wellington*

FIGURE 4. The centre kōwhaiwhai (rafter pattern) in this grouping is named Mōkai. Many recorded patterns feature a red, black, and white colour combination and this is certainly not the only pattern without any red, but the absence of the colour denoting mana and tapu accords with the name of the pattern (mōkai: slave, captive, subject, pet) and a lack of rangatiratanga. *Drawings of Maori rafter patterns, 145 [1942], Albert Percy Godber: E-302-q-5-144/146, Alexander Turnbull Library, Wellington*

FIGURE 5. This painting of Hongi Hika (centre) with Waikato and the Reverend Thomas Kendall was commissioned by the Church Missionary Society and made during his visit to England. Hongi's kiwi-feather cloak has been coloured with red ochre and the gannet feathers in his coronet have red kākā feathers at their base. *James Barry, 'The Rev. Thomas Kendall and the Maori chiefs Hongi and Waikato', 1820: G-618, Alexander Turnbull Library, Wellington*

FIGURE 6. Rawiri, a chief from Taranaki, wearing a red blanket. Red blankets were far more highly regarded than grey ones. In 1845, the Kaitaia-based trader Gilbert Mair found that he could get twice as much kauri gum (resin) for red blankets as for grey ones. *William Strutt, 'Rawiri, a fully tattooed chief, a rare specimen of new specimens, New Plymouth, Taranaki', 1856: E-452-f-006-3, Alexander Turnbull Library, Wellington*

FIGURE 7. An amokura, or red-tailed tropic bird (*Phaeton phoenicurus*), from John Gould, *Birds of Australia* (1840–48). *Plate 73 in vol. 7, courtesy of Alexander Turnbull Library, Wellington*

FIGURE 8. Pōhutukawa tree.

FIGURE 9. Portrait of Rev. William Yate by C. John M. Whichelo, c. 1840. *NK9642, Rex Nan Kivell Collection, National Library of Australia, Canberra*

FIGURE 10. Portrait of Te Rangihaeata, c. 1850, holding the mere pounamu named Te Tuhiwai, given to him by Te Rauparaha who had received it as a gift exchange sealing peace between himself and Ngāi Tahu chief Te Mātenga Taiaroa. *Richard Aldworth Oliver, A Series of Lithographic Drawings from Sketches in New Zealand, London, 1852: PUBL-0032-1, Alexander Turnbull Library, Wellington*

FIGURE 11. A group of Moriori survivors on the Chatham Islands photographed in 1877 by Alfred Martin. *19XX.2.481, Canterbury Museum, Christchurch*

FIGURE 12. Toki poutangata — an adze of authority — held by a chief. It has been suggested that toki poutangata were originally used for the ceremonial execution of captives (Skinner, *Comparatively Speaking*, p. 149). *OL000491, Museum of New Zealand Te Papa Tongarewa, Wellington*

FIGURE 13. Photograph of Hākopa Te Ata-o-Tū, c. 1860s, by Daniel Louis Mundy. *PA1-Q-232-08-3, Alexander Turnbull Library, Wellington*

FIGURE 14. South Island Māori converts to Christianity, with Eliza Stack, wife of the Rev. James Stack, outside St Stephen's Church, Tuahiwi. The bearded man third from left is believed to be Hākopa Te Ata-o-Tū. *Photographed by Alfred Charles Barker, 1867: PA7-01-23, Alexander Turnbull Library, Wellington*

FIGURE 15. 'Aranghie, the tattooer of New Zealand'. *Augustus Earle, A Narrative of a Nine Months' Residence in New Zealand in 1827, London, 1832*: PUBL-0022, Alexander Turnbull Library, Wellington

FIGURE 16. Presentation of a carved pare, or lintel, said to represent 'the emancipation of a slave who rose to the position of a chief because of his fighting prowess' to David Graham, the Auckland War Memorial Museum's research officer (far right), in 1929. 1/4-018223-G, Alexander Turnbull Library, Wellington

who had been held captive by other tribes and assimilate them back into their home communities.⁶⁸ The existence of this karakia implies that Māori were able to respond to captivity or enslavement within their own spiritual framework and did not need Christian teachings to facilitate the reintegration of those people.

There is other, earlier, evidence of this, too. For example, a South Island tradition tells how someone whose tapu had been despoiled by other means could also be reintegrated into their society. That example related to the grave predicament Ngāi Tahu faced when they lost their wisest tohunga (expert in spiritual matters) Tūhiku during hostilities with Ngāti Māmoe. Left with few options when it came to finding someone else to read the omens, forewarn them of danger, and identify the most propitious time for attack, Ngāi Tahu leaders approached Tūhiku's daughter for advice. She recommended that they look to her brother Pōhatu. Pōhatu had never stood out as a boy, consorting with slaves rather than people of his own rank, so the idea of his taking over the role was soundly ridiculed. 'Can such a one as Pōhatu enlighten and direct us?' they asked. 'His place is in the kitchen beside the cooking fire; what can the defiled know about sacred things!' But his sister was unmoved so the people eventually gave in, stripped him of his clothes, and took him to water where they cleansed him and performed incantations to make him tapu.⁶⁹ Having completed the ceremonies, they asked the meaning of Tūhiku's last message, which he had conveyed by his holding up two fingers as he was taken away, bound, in a Ngāti Māmoe canoe. Pōhatu explained that they must wait two years before attempting to gain utu for his death because that was the length of time required for grass to grow over the place where his body was cooked.⁷⁰ So, through the administration of appropriate ritual, Pōhatu was able to fill the important position previously occupied by his father. Although he had not been a captive, the example offers some clues as to how others who were might be able to regain positions of power or influence.

Under the impression that capture by another tribe removed from a chief 'the *mana* of the gods', Raymond Firth considered that 'cooked food and all its adjuncts' would consequently have 'no destructive effect upon him'.⁷¹ But there were ways of protecting the mana and tapu of people once they had been captured. For example, an unnamed Tainui source explained that a 'karakia whakanoa', or incantation to remove tapu, had the purpose of protecting rangatira captives who might be obliged to cook food for their masters:

> Tu-kai-kera kera is the god who takes the tapu from a chief who is made a slave so that if he has to cook food for his master he will not die.[72]

In this case, John White explained that the karakia was to ensure that the captive's mana mākutu (power to bewitch) remained with him.

Because there is limited specific evidence for times before European contact, it may be impossible to make a sound judgement as to whether tribal groups were always reluctant to be rejoined by kin previously captured in battle. Nor is it clear whether captives were too humiliated to return or whether their kinfolk would not have welcomed them if they had. Men were the warriors and, therefore, more directly implicated in military defeat, so women and young children may have suffered less shame and loss of mana from being captured. As Chapter 7 will show, parents made desperate attempts to retrieve captured children during the 1820s, but examples from earlier times indicate that such responses were far from new. Around the sixteenth century, the son of Tāraia of Ngāti Tamaterā was captured by the people of Waitahora pā when he was among a party encroaching on their forest resources at Te Pakiaka. Tāraia responded by following his captors' trail until he was able to rescue his presumably adult son and take him back home.[73] The circumstances of a person's capture are almost certainly relevant, as, perhaps, might be the length of time they remained in captivity. Those recently taken, like Tāraia's son, may have been more easily welcomed home than those long gone and perhaps more thoroughly degraded by the tapu-destroying activities they may have been obliged to perform. But there may always have been a variety of responses to captured kin.

An incident that occurred in 1833 has two puzzling aspects. The first concerns the circumstances surrounding how some Ngāti Porou people from Waiapu came to be landed at the Bay of Islands and handed over to the local Ngāpuhi people as captives or slaves by the English whaler *Elizabeth*. The Waiapu people had recently been at war with those from the Bay of Islands but peace had been made. According to William

Williams, they were visiting the whaler in one of their harbours when a gale sprang up leaving the captain with no option but to head out to sea and continue his voyage with his 'guests' still on board. William Yate, however, who was at the Bay of Islands when they arrived there, and Barnet Burns, a more colourful reporter,[74] suggested that the captain had deliberately enticed them on board and landed them at the Bay as a way of ingratiating himself with the northerners.[75] Whichever was the case — kidnapping or misadventure caused by weather — the circumstances of their detention should surely have affected their reception in the north. Given either scenario, retaining them as 'slaves' would not seem to have been tika, or lawful, under customary systems. It was said that local Ngāpuhi were about to share the dozen or so Māori 'passengers' aboard the *Elizabeth* amongst themselves but that missionary persuasion ensured that they would be returned home safely. However, as many other captives, taken earlier, were being released by this time it is hard to avoid the suspicion that the northerners neither wanted to add to their labour force nor intended to keep them as 'slaves'. Now that muskets were much more widespread with retribution a real possibility, returning captives made more sense as pre-emptive peacemaking initiatives. That may have been the case in this instance, but their 'humane' response would also have scored them some pats on the back from their missionary neighbours, not to mention some nice new blankets in return for their visitors' 'redemption'.[76]

The second curious aspect of this incident relates to the party's journey home from Northland aboard the CMS vessel. On arrival at Pūriri in the Hauraki region, en route to the East Coast, they were surprised to find that the local Ngāti Maru people joined them in their hymn singing. Another captive, previously redeemed by the missionaries, had taught them.[77] So he must have been accepted and reintegrated into their community even though they apparently had had no exposure to Christian teachings or hymn singing until he brought them. Two weeks later, having reached Hicks Bay with the Waiapu people on board, their kinfolk, too, were astonished but delighted to have their relations home. They had assumed them to have been murdered. 'The scene when the parties met was most affecting and all the routine and ceremony of a native meeting as practised after a long absence took place', wrote Yate. 'Nothing could possibly have exceeded their gratitude.' Yet, as he also noted, '[n]o missionary [had] ever set his foot upon this part of the island' before.[78] Among the arrivals was a man called Piripi Taumata-ā-Kura who would be very successful indeed in introducing and converting Ngāti Porou to Christianity, but the changes he wrought were yet to come.

Some three years later, in 1836, Te Mutu and other leading rangatira from Maungatapu near Tauranga approached missionaries John Wilson and William Wade for help in redeeming Te Mutu's wife and children, taken by Te Arawa when Te Tūmū pā fell. Wilson's description of their homecoming captures the emotion of the occasion vividly:

> On landing a short pause was made, and then the redeemed captives, with their band of friends who had brought them, slowly advanced from their canoes. They moved on in order till they came within twelve yards of the tribe, which stood in a solid irregular form — men, women, and children — ready to receive them. Both parties then extended their arms towards the other, not moving from the spot on which they stood, and then commenced their lamentation for the dead, fallen in battle, or for those afterwards killed, all of whom had been eaten. Their movements of the body and tone of voice, though exciting, were easy — even graceful. The women, naked to the waist, with dishevelled hair and bathed plentifully with tears, sometimes bent forward to the ground till their heads touched it, as though incapable of supporting so much sorrow at this greeting recording the past. There were many stout hearts and fierce men who wept as children, and it was with no little difficulty that I restrained the power of sympathy and did not equally weep with them.[79]

The significance of eating one's enemy

As Wilson intimated, being killed and consumed was at the other end of the range of captive experience. Missionary writings were at their most colourfully vitriolic when reporting the practice of eating enemies, but they either failed or chose not to comprehend its full significance. That significance, as a means of destroying the tapu of the consumed, is evident in traditions relating to Ranginui and Papatūānuku and the creation of the earth. They differ in many aspects but frequently recount that, because of the primeval couple's close embrace, their many children enclosed between them were forced to live in darkness. In order to free themselves and let in the light, most of them agreed that their parents should be separated. Tāne (god of the forest) plays a leading part in several versions, as the one who forced them apart. In some traditions, he achieved that by lying on his shoulders and pushing them apart with his legs. But Tāwhirimātea (god of the winds) opposed the separation, so after the painful deed was done, he devastated the forests of Tāne and the waters of Tangaroa (god of the sea). Rongomātāne (god of agriculture) and Haumia (god of fern root and wild plants), who avoided their brother's retribution by being hidden in the bosom of their mother Papatūānuku, thus remained passive gods. However, the one sibling Tāwhirimātea could not subdue was Tūmatauenga (god of war), who finally conquered Tāne and Tangaroa. Tūmatauenga consummated his conquest by eating the children of the others: the birds of the forest, fish of the sea, kūmara (sweet potato), and fern root. It was that total destruction and consumption that destroyed their tapu. The enormity of such an act is embedded in well-known curses. One of the most contemptuous of Māori insults was to call someone a 'remnant of the feast' (toenga kāinga), meaning 'you are not even worth cooking', which implies a person of little mana.[80] Another extreme invective is to say 'upoko kōhua', or your head (the most tapu part of the body) will be boiled.

    In his account of the 1836 taking of the pā at Maketū in the Bay of Plenty, John Wilson described his journey towards Ngāti Hauā's encampment. At one point, his party noticed a head that had been literally boiled and placed on a post with a raw kūmara in its mouth.[81] The cooking of the victim's head was a very potent attack on his mana and tapu, but the placement of the kūmara suggests additional ritual significance.[82]

    Te Rangi Hīroa, who wrote that the gaining and losing of mana related to success in battle and was not connected with its digestion, nonetheless described the creative strategy employed by one warrior to ensure that his body would not suffer that fate. Having been wounded in battle, Ngātokorua knew he was likely to be killed. So he broke off the point of his weapon and concealed it in his clenched right hand as he was overpowered. Although bound behind his back, he managed to free his hands but kept them behind him so the loosened ties would not be noticed. He then called to the leader of the opposing force, indicating that he wished to hongi him, or press noses, in a gesture of farewell. As that rangatira bent down, Ngātokorua seized him by the hair and pulled him towards him, stabbing him several times in the neck so that the blood gushed onto him. By ensuring that the blood of the opposing rangatira was daubed over his face and body, he rendered it tapu to his enemies so they could not eat him. In so doing, said Te Rangi Hīroa, he did not preserve his mana but saved his descendants from 'the food stigma'.[83]

More recent scholars, however, have offered other opinions. Maori Marsden wrote that when a warrior of rank, of great mana and ihi (essential force), fell in battle, his conquerors would cook his body and eat those portions that they believed held his mana:

> By eating his flesh they consumed his mana and ihi, and thereby replenished their own. Eating the enemy's mana not only depleted the mana of the opposing tribe, it also brought the gods of those tribes under the subjection of the conquering tribe.[84]

Patu Hohepa explained that although capture and enslavement would cause a rangatira woman to lose her mana, loss that could be made permanent by her captor's killing and eating her, it could still be retrieved if her family successfully avenged her capture or death: that is, by achieving satisfactory utu.[85]

According to Elsdon Best, it was common for war parties fighting at a distance from their homes to cremate those who fell in battle in order to prevent their bodies falling into the hands of the enemy. When a rangatira fell in such circumstances, his head would be removed to be taken home and preserved, then the body would be cremated. This might occasionally be done in times of peace to ensure the deceased could not be eaten nor their bones be made into fish-hooks, tools, or other profane items.[86] So, when Ngāti Manu's Whareumu was killed at Waimā in 1828, Te Wharerahi (also known as Wharenui), a recognised peacemaker, attempted to retrieve his body and prevent the situation being further inflamed by its being eaten.[87]

About that same time, on a visit to Kaiapoi in the South Island, Te Pēhi Kupe and several other Ngāti Toa warriors were killed while they slept, apparently following an argument over a block of pounamu. In this case, Te Pēhi's body was cooked and eaten and his bones were indeed made into fish-hooks.[88] Te Rauparaha, warrior chief of Ngāti Toa, sought to avenge this terrible insult by hiring a vessel called the *Elizabeth*, captained by William Stewart, to transport his warriors to Akaroa on what was purported to be a trading visit. All went according to plan. The inhabitants were caught off guard and the high-ranking Ngāi Tahu rangatira Tama-i-haranui (Te Maiharanui) was captured. The bitterness of Te Pēhi's son Te Hiko spilled out as he drew back the prisoner's upper lip, saying: 'those are the teeth that ate my father'. In absolutely no doubt that Te Hiko was there to obtain utu for his father, Tama-i-haranui sent for his wife and daughter, and one of the parents strangled their daughter aboard ship. According to several published accounts of this incident, that was done so she might not be enslaved. Best was one who gave that explanation. He likened it to another occasion when a man killed his own son who had 'returned from a state of slavery, in order that the evil name should not go down to his descendants'.[89] But Te Hiko's phrase 'the teeth that ate [his] father' implies another reason for Tama-i-haranui killing his daughter. The Reverend James Watkin wrote that the Ngāi Tahu rangatira was himself cooked and eaten.[90] So he may not have killed his daughter to save her from slavery but more specifically from the threat of being eaten and having her inherited mana destroyed forever. That would have been assured by her body being disposed of at sea, possibly through a porthole on the ship.[91]

As for Tama-i-haranui, he was flogged while aboard the *Elizabeth*, either by or on the orders of Stewart. Whether this was a response to his defiant demeanour or punishment for killing his daughter depends on who is telling the tale. Nevertheless, despite his ultimate end, Tama-i-haranui's Ngāti Toa captors are said to have reacted badly to the flogging, saying that 'he was still a Chief, and not to be treated as a slave'.[92] Te Rauparaha's capture of Tama-i-haranui was entirely just, the two having equal status from the Māori point of view, but 'for any common person to lay violent hands on the sacred person of a chief, even one destined for the oven, was highly offensive to Māori susceptibilities'.[93]

His execution some two weeks later at the hands of Te Pēhi's widow was also tika, or correct, in terms of utu because he had been responsible for her husband's death. But the flogging he received by or at the command of Captain Stewart was not.[94]

Rangatira captives

It is often said that rangatira were more likely to be killed in the field and that it was the lesser mortals who were taken captive and enslaved. John Butler implied as much in February 1822 when he reported the departure of a large war party heading towards Hauraki and Waikato: 'They have already destroyed almost the whole Mogoia [Mokoia/Panmure] Tribe, brought away most of the heads of the chiefs, and many slaves', he wrote.[95] Not all rangatira were killed, but evidence regarding their capture and treatment is often contradictory. It makes sense that male rangatira, typically the military leaders, would be particular targets on the battlefield and less likely to be taken alive. But reports concerning differences in the way those captured were handled are more puzzling.

Augustus Earle, who visited New Zealand in the 1820s, was one who said that chiefs were never made prisoners: 'they either fight to the last, or are killed on the spot, and their heads are preserved . . . as trophies'.[96] Joel Polack agreed that chiefs were seldom taken alive, but that this was because they were usually surrounded and protected 'by a staff of relations and friends'.[97] However, Jules Dumont d'Urville, who was in New Zealand a little earlier than Earle or Polack, wrote of a Hauraki rangatira he came across in the Bay of Islands:

> One day a chief . . . showed me one of his slaves crouching at his feet waiting in silence for his orders, and . . . told me proudly that his slave had once been one of the most famous warriors of the Shouraki [Hauraki] region. In fact, this unfortunate man bore on his face all the marks which belong exclusively to those of high rank, and I could not help pitying him for not being eaten on the battlefield like his fellows, rather than being reduced to the shame of serving his triumphant enemy.[98]

The missionary Richard Davis wrote similarly of a rangatira family from Taranaki who were captured by enemies from Waikato and subsequently 'sold' to Ngāpuhi in exchange for muskets and powder. Davis felt that being saved from the general fate of prisoners of war — 'being cooked and eaten' — was not a merciful act on the part of the 'bloody victors' and added that other captives had advised them to run away while they were being marched towards Hokianga on the opposite coast.[99]

Chronology does not seem to account for the differences in treatment as these apparently opposing impressions come from similar periods in time: Dumont d'Urville and Earle in the 1820s, Polack and Davis in the 1830s. One possible explanation might be that, despite their alleged rangatira status, they were not of significantly high rank to begin with or had somehow lost mana or status prior to being captured. Whatever the case, a very different fate befell Ngeungeu, the beautiful daughter of the high-ranking Ngāi Tai rangatira Ōtara Te Irirangi. Captured by Ngāpuhi on one of their raids to Tāmaki in the 1820s, Ngeungeu was considered so tapu that Patuone, a prominent rangatira in the Hokianga region, sent a message to her father assuring him that she would be treated with respect and kept safe. Had he not done so, the wrath of Ngāi Tai might have been more than Ngāpuhi had bargained for. But Patuone was a businessman and directly responsible for establishing a shipbuilding industry in his district.[100] Somewhat paradoxically, he was also involved in the start of shipbuilding at Waiheke Island in the Hauraki Gulf near Auckland. That came about with the arrival of a Scottish boat builder named Thomas Maxwell soon after Ngeungeu was taken to the Bay of Islands. The newcomer took a great shine to Ngeungeu who was equally taken with the Scot. Cupid won out, Patuone consented to their marriage and arranged safe passage for them to Tāmaki, much to her father's great delight. With his father-in-law's support, Maxwell established a successful business at Waiheke. So everyone seems to have lived happily ever after, but the fact that Ngeungeu was a highborn captive was crucial to things working out so well. Her status secured favoured treatment and, in this case, everyone was able to benefit from the situation.[101]

Preserving the mana and dignity of rangatira was vitally important. So a war party that had suffered losses during an 1835 battle in the Waikato was not cheered up by assurances from a group of women that the warriors who had opposed them were 'only slaves'. Missionary Henry Williams blamed their gender for a lack of diplomatic nous. Rather than mollifying them, the idea that chiefs should have been shot by slaves had only served to rile them even more.[102]

Ransom

The importance of rangatira and the protection of their mana was such that they might be returned to their people by ransom. Alexander McCrae, who visited New Zealand on the British Navy store ship HMS *Dromedary* in 1820, noted that prisoners 'of distinction' could be ransomed for articles of value, such as pounamu or muskets.[103] Just three years later, while Hongi Hika's military might was striking terror into hearts throughout the country, Samuel Leigh reported that a party from the Hauraki region had travelled north with desperate hopes of arranging peace on any terms but was especially anxious to redeem one of their women who had been captured. They managed to secure her freedom in exchange for four of their own captives, the two parties separating 'in great friendship' and 'in hopes that the good understanding which prevailed on both sides would secure a permanent peace'.[104] According to Polack, prisoners were often captured alive with a view to their being exchanged for canoes or slaves.[105]

During the 1824 battle of Waiorua, when Ngāti Toa's Te Rauparaha and some of his allies attacked Kāpiti Island, a young rangatira of Ngāti Toa and Ngāti Koata named Tawhi was captured. He, too, was located and reclaimed by his family in exchange for the release of Tūtepourangi, paramount chief of Ngāti Kuia, who had been captured by Ngāti Koata. While this may have been a simple exchange, it has been suggested that it began a process in which land was gifted and intermarriage took place to finally settle the peace between the parties.[106]

A number of people who went on to become well known in the annals of New Zealand history were rescued through ransom. Wiremu Maihi Te Rangikāheke, the Ngāti Rangiwewehi leader and scholar who became a close associate of Governor George Grey, was reclaimed by that means when he was a child. Having been taken captive by Ngāpuhi at the siege of Mokoia Island in 1823, his father secured his release, together with that of his mother and siblings.[107]

Prisoners treated as hostages were 'preserved' or set aside and presumably able to avoid tapu-damaging work such as cooking. So when Ngāti Toa's Te Rauparaha took a close relative of Ngāti Rārua's Te Pukekōhatu captive in the late 1820s following a dispute over the settlement of the Nelson district, he kept him as his personal attendant. He did so to protect him against further hostilities. Nevertheless, because Te Pukekōhatu was anxious to bring his relative home safely, he sought his tohunga's advice as to how that might be achieved. The tohunga responded by taking a prestigious hei tiki (pendant made from pounamu) named Te Maungarongo from Te Pukekōhatu's neck. He then instructed Te Pukekōhatu to firstly secure this precious pendant, which had originally belonged to a tohunga from the Wairau Valley, to the neck of his wife's female attendant before presenting them both to Te Rauparaha. Te Rauparaha was so moved by the gesture that the captive was returned immediately.[108] The hei tiki was one of a number of valuable items Te Rauparaha received as components in peacemaking processes. But gifts of such importance required another gift in response. So when Te Rauparaha was given a mere pounamu, or jade weapon, named Te Tuhiwai by the Ngāi Tahu chief Te Mātenga Taiaroa in 1843 (see fig. 10), he presented them with a war canoe called Waikahua. The binding contract these exchanges of valuable gifts represented was known as a tatau pounamu, or greenstone door.[109]

But ransom was not necessarily immediate. Rāpata Wahawaha, who was also captured as a child, is thought to have remained a captive of Rongowhakaata's Rāpata Whakapuhia for at least a year before his freedom was purchased by Tama-i-whakanehua-i-te-rangi. Wahawaha, who went on to prove himself a very able soldier, became a leader among his own Ngāti Porou people. In later years, however, he not only took utu against Rongowhakaata, but also changed the pronunciation of his name to Rōpata to lessen the stigma of his connection with Whakapuhia.[110]

Because the exchange of hostages, especially captives of rank, was potentially key to securing peace through diplomacy after hostilities, it was important to keep their mana intact.[111] So, ensuring the possibility of subsequent peacemaking may have been the reason for treating a captive like Rēnata Kawepō of Ngāi Te Ūpokoiri and Ngāti Kahungunu especially well. While he was a young man, in the early 1820s, his Ngāi Te Ūpokoiri people took refuge at Taupō after their defeat at the battle of Te Whiti-o-Tū. However, when his cousin Tiakitai, the rangatira of Waimarama, invited them to return to their home area, Kawepō and his sister opted to do so, settling close to Te Roto-a-Tara, a lake near Te Aute in Hawke's Bay. But this was a time of turmoil, and Ngāi Te Ūpokoiri and their allies were again defeated a short time afterwards. Things heated up considerably this time when Kawepō was taken and put over a fire but Tiakitai's brother intervened in the nick of time and had him turned over to their Ngāpuhi allies as a captive. Initially taken to Nukutaurua, Kawepō was subsequently taken to Waimate North in the Bay of Islands about 1837 where he was converted to Christianity and took the baptismal name Rēnata, or Leonard. During the more than ten years he lived among Ngāpuhi, he was always treated with deference to his rank and even tattooed as a rangatira before he was eventually released and returned to his own people. Back home, he worked as a teacher for over four years, eventually becoming a senior leader of Hawke's Bay Māori. Changing attitudes may have helped him in the long run, but the evidence indicates that his status as a man of rank, especially through his mother's family, had been recognised and upheld.[112] Many rangatira are said to have found it difficult to reconcile their hereditary rank and status with newly acquired Christian beliefs and values, but some, like Kawepō, gained mana on their return home.[113] Although the 'taint' of captivity might still be invoked by those who sought to minimise an individual's status, Christianity offered a new form of mana for leaders like Kawepō.[114]

So it was with Te Ua Haumēne. He, too, was captured with his mother while a very young boy. Taken north from Taranaki to Kāwhia, where he spent most of his childhood, his Waikato captors taught him to read and write in Māori. Under the guidance of Reverend John Whiteley, he began to study the Bible and Christian philosophy and was eventually baptised.[115] Te Ua went on to found the Hauhau religion (which will be discussed in Chapter 10) with its guiding principle of pai mārire, or goodness and peace. So, for him, too, a period of captivity laid the groundwork for a different type of leadership.

As with the man that Te Rauparaha took as his personal attendant, those who served people of high rank were typically of relatively high birth too, much as is the case with ladies-in-waiting and other staff who act as attendants to members of European royal families. It might then be asked, at what point did a captive became a 'slave' or lose tapu? It seems likely that their status changed meaningfully once they had been obliged to perform tasks such as fire making or cooking that damaged their tapu rather than merely being captured. The evidence suggests that rangatira captives were typically treated with respect and often returned to their own people without significant loss of mana. As we know, such returns could be arranged by ransom or through subsequent peacemaking arrangements, and it appears to have been with the latter in mind that they were allowed to avoid tapu-damaging tasks. Nevertheless, they would have had to 'pay their way' in the host community, so looking after people of high rank among their captors, providing specialist skills, or acting as advisors in some capacity would have been appropriate ways of contributing to their hosts' community. Usefulness seems to have been another key to preserving one's dignity and quality of life after capture.

Deferential treatment and peaceful intervention

One of the Ngāi Tahu warriors captured by Ngāti Toa at Kaiapoi in 1831 was the rangatira Te Ata-o-Tū. Together with his wife Te Ao Paki, he was taken north of Wellington. According to some accounts, they became 'slaves' to Te Rauparaha, but Hākopa, as he was later known, was liberated when his captors embraced Christianity.[116] James Cowan, however, tells a more detailed and exciting story. He wrote that Te Rauparaha admired Te Ata-o-Tū's abilities as a warrior which were demonstrated at Kaiapoi. Armed only with a long-handled tomahawk (toki kakauroa?), he had managed to dodge two musket balls from Ngāti Toa's Te Pehi Tahau before killing him. Not being one to 'waste' such an exceptional warrior, Te Rauparaha spared his life to serve in the ranks of Ngāti Toa in their future battles. With no battles to fight at that time, though, the couple were evidently reduced to the sort of work normally done by captives. Te Ata-o-Tū was sent to work for a Ngāti Koata chief at Kukutauaki on the mainland opposite Kāpiti Island while his wife went to work for a family in an adjacent village. Being separated was heart-wrenching but, because they were not too far away from each other, they managed to arrange the occasional secret meeting. However, when Te Ao Paki overheard that her husband was to be gifted to some Ngāti Raukawa visitors from Taupō, who would take him home with them — hundreds of kilometres to the north — they decided to make a run for it. But it was not an unplanned escape. They went to Waikanae, then a large Ngāti Toa and Ngāti Awa settlement, and approached Te Pēhi Kupe's son Te Hiko, one of Te Rauparaha's lieutenants. Te Ata-o-Tū's reputation as a warrior ensured that they were received warmly and taken under Te Hiko's protection. The women from Taupō were initially upset at losing the gift they had expected but some fine cloaks and pounamu put things right. As for Te Ata-o-Tū, Cowan's anonymous Ngāi Tahu informant said he was treated as an adopted relative and entrusted with a number of important missions. In particular, he was charged with protecting Ngāti Toa's wāhi tapu, or sacred places. Given the unpolished manners of the typical whaler who frequented the area, it was not a cushy job.[117] But Hākopa Te Ata-o-Tū did eventually return home to Kaiapoi where he settled down to become a renowned carver of pounamu (see figs 13 and 14).[118]

These examples suggest that people of rangatira birth or evident skills were treated with respect before the establishment of English law. And following the battle of Moutoa Island in the Whanganui River in 1864 it was evident that the same sensitivities remained despite it. That battle was fought between upriver supporters of the Pai Mārire movement, fearful of rampant land loss and settler encroachment on their territories, and others from downriver who feared the implications of that movement for their independence and the economic benefits of Pākehā settlement. Their close genealogical connections were bound to cause difficulties, which were apparent when the Superintendent of Wellington ordered those who had fought in support of the government to hand over their captives to the Crown. Hōri Kīngi Te Ānaua made their reluctance to surrender them very clear:

> We have fought for the Queen and for the protection of the Pakehas. We have killed . . . many of our nearest relations and friends. We have taken others of them prisoners. Have we not done enough . . . ?

Special concern was expressed for the Pai Mārire chief Raimona who, as they said, was 'nearly related to every Chief of this river', and they repeatedly asked for his release. The importance of maintaining his chiefly dignity was evident when Mete Kīngi Te Rangi Paetahi explained:

> If we lay hands on him he will be degraded, and looked upon as a slave for ever. We are, therefore, trying to persuade him to walk down to the canoe without our touching him. Give us time.

They were eager to find a solution that would not involve the humiliation of physical contact.[119]

Tribal groups were split internally as well as externally on the basis of supporting or fighting against the settler government when this battle took place, but it was not a new phenomenon for Māori combatants to find themselves set against kinfolk on the battlefield. The reaction to the taking of Raimona highlighted the need for delicate handling of rangatira captives but there were other processes aimed at deferential treatment.

Since polygamy was the norm for men of rank, diplomatic marriages with a rangatira woman from the contending party was one means of sealing the peace when hostilities ceased. Captive women of any rank might be taken as secondary wives by the victors but were not necessarily deemed 'slave' wives and might be accorded chiefly status.[120] The same could apply, albeit less often, to men taken as husbands by a woman on the winning side.

Because people of rank were tapu in their physical person, items in contact with their body were imbued with that tapu. So, placing a garment, usually their cloak, over someone about to be slain was another way of signifying that the individual was now under their mana and protection.[121] Elsdon Best referred to a number of instances of the practice. For example, when Tūhoe were on their way to attack Ngāti Manawa at Te Tāpiri, they took one of their rangatira, Harehare Aterea, captive along the way. He was about to be killed when the Tūhoe rangatira Kererū intervened by throwing his cloak over him. Ngāti Awa's Awatope did the same when his father's murderer was defeated in battle.[122]

In 1818, Te Rātūtonu was among the Ngā Māhanga rangatira who had unsuccessfully defended the Tāpuinīkau pā in Taranaki against a Ngāti Toa attack. He was a handsome man who had proved himself a brave and skilled warrior, features that had not gone unnoticed by Te Rangihaeata's sister Te Rangi Topeora. Te Rātūtonu had been her lover when he had visited Kāwhia previously and, much taken by him, she persuaded her uncle Te Rauparaha to have him 'called' once the hostilities at Tāpuinīkau had ceased. The ceremony involved someone approaching the beleaguered pā under guarantee of safety to invite the warrior into the besiegers' camp. Te Rātūtonu chose to accept the invitation and went down to meet Te Rangi Topeora. Nekepapa of Te Āti Awa was also keen to secure Te Rātūtonu as her husband but Te Rangi Topeora won the 'race' by throwing her dogskin cloak over him and claiming him for herself. Following a number of speeches, 'rich in eulogy of their new-found kinsman, and full of admiration for the virtues of his bride', the couple were duly married.[123] In this case, the call was instigated by the love-struck woman but, in others, the ritual may have been a means of avoiding the humiliation of rangatira kinsmen as Edward Tregear suggested:

> In taking war-prisoners a curious custom was sometimes observed in cases where a chief was nearly related to both sides and when if likely to be taken he would assuredly become a slave. To obviate this, when a battle had taken place and one of the contending armies was evidently about to give way and be routed, it was permitted to the chief of the winning party to call out the name or names of certain warriors among the enemy. If one of those named immediately accepted the invitation and joined the number of his foemen he was then treated as a visitor and not as a prisoner, indeed being often kept as a highly-honoured guest.[124]

There were a number of other ways in which enemies, chiefly or not, might be spared even though defeated. According to Thomas Downes's account of the taking of Maungaraki pā in the Wairarapa district, the conquering rangatira spread his cloak on the ground and invited the defeated leader Haupapa-o-te-rangi, who had been captured, to sit on it. By agreeing to do so, Haupapa-o-te-rangi not only saved his own life but also those of his people who would likely become a vassal tribe.[125] Similar policies allowed members of a war party with relatives among the people about to be attacked to go ahead and warn them of the approaching danger.¹²⁶ Much the same applied when the first war party was approaching the settlement from which they sought utu. They would not attack until they had been seen by their intended victims.¹²⁷ An expectation of military fairness surely lay behind the response of the leading chief at the battle of Rangiriri in 1863, who initially declined the opposing British general's call for surrender, saying: 'Ho mai he paura' ('Give us some gunpowder') as they had run out but hoped to continue the fight.¹²⁸ Unfortunately for him, the British fought according to different rules.

Fleeing the battlefield, on the other hand, would incur a very serious loss of mana, as John White explained:

> [I]t is a sign that those who flee are the degenerate offspring of those of low birth, and is an indication that their tribe will become less and less in power and numbers, and is also a sign that the homes of their tribe will be taken by other people, and the honour and the name of the tribe be blotted out by the power of the weapons and bravery of their enemy.¹²⁹

Rangatira who returned home to become leaders of mana

Kinship links could be very helpful to those who could demonstrate them, as was the case for Ngāti Hauā's Te Waharoa. While he was a child, he and his mother were captured by Te Arawa. But because his mother was able to explain her genealogical connection to their captors, they were neither killed nor treated as slaves. Nevertheless, being raised away from his own people, Te Waharoa was denied the preparation for leadership that would otherwise have been his birthright. Fortunately, however, he displayed such great skill as a warrior that he went on to become principal leader of Ngāti Hauā regardless of his unfortunate start in life.

Like Te Waharoa, Te Ua Haumēne, Rāpata Wahawaha, Rēnata Kawepō, and Wiremu Maihi Te Rangikāheke, many others went on to become leaders of high rank among their own people despite periods of captivity. Tāmati Hone Ōraukawa, who had been captured as a boy by the future Māori King Te Wherowhero, went on to be a leader of his own

Ngāti Ruanui people and, perhaps more ironically given his history with Te Wherowhero, was one of those whose names were put forward in 1856 as a candidate for the Māori kingship.[130]

Gaining mana within their captors' communities

Describing one of Te Rauparaha's raids down the west coast as far as Wellington and the Wairarapa in 1819–20, one man told Elsdon Best, 'we enslaved those that took our fancy and killed the others'.[131] On what basis certain people took their fancy can only be surmised, but it might be guessed that they included attractive young women or people thought to have useful skills or abilities. Ngāti Toa's Te Waari Carkeek said that captives had an obligation 'to serve and maintain the honour of the Rangatira who spared their life'. Perhaps more significantly, he also said that people were not considered 'lesser mortals just because they were captured in battle' and that captives were often given a great amount of responsibility.[132] Hongi Hika and Te Morenga are said to have deliberately brought skilled craftsmen from the East Coast back to the Bay of Islands with them when they undertook the first documented raids with muskets.[133]

Desirable skills were not limited to the material arts, though. According to a tradition retold by Kepa Ehau of Ngāti Tarāwhai and Ngāti Whakaue, Hongi ordered two of his chiefs to capture a Ngāti Tarāwhai tohunga renowned for his spiritual powers as their party was heading towards Mokoia Island in Lake Rotorua in 1823. That tohunga, Tumakoha Te Whanapipi, drew on those powers to call up the winds and turn the lake dark and rough as the Ngāpuhi invaders approached him at Okataina. In this version of events, the strategy worked and Hongi's warriors paid with their lives for their failure to capture their quarry. The expertise they hoped to acquire had ensured that he slipped through their fingers.[134] Other versions, however, say that the combined powers of Tumakoha and other tohunga had no effect and that Ngāpuhi 'sailed serenely on'.[135]

Another man, referred to as Aranghie but whose correct name was probably Rangi, was a celebrated tohunga tā moko, or tattooist, whom

Augustus Earle met when he visited Kororāreka in 1827 (see fig. 15). According to Earle, 'men of the highest rank and importance were in the habit of travelling long journeys in order to put their skins under his skilful hands'. He was gratified 'to behold the respect these savages pay to the fine arts'. This 'professor', said Earle, 'was merely a kooky or slave, but by skill and industry [had] raised himself to an equality with the greatest men of his country; and as every chief who employed him always made him some handsome present, he soon became a man of wealth'. Rangi's clients included well-known leaders of rank such as Pangopango, Rukiruki, Kiwikiwi, Rangituke, and others. And while some captives are said to have survived on a meagre diet of scraps, Rangi evidently dined well. Earle reported that 'Shulitea' (King George or Te Whareumu) 'sent him every day the choicest things from his own table'.[136] Yet, despite the claim that he was 'merely a kooky or slave', this man had received training in a highly esteemed art before being taken prisoner so was unlikely to have been of lowly birth.

The introduction of Christianity was probably incidental to the gaining or regaining of mana within a captor's community; not only because these examples pre-date the conversion of rangatira, but also because there are oral traditions from before European contact times that attest to the same process — sometimes to the great displeasure of the masters.[137] One rather gruesome example concerned Ariki or Arikinui, who accompanied the great rangatira Tōhē as he famously explored the north en route to visit his daughter at Kaipara. It seems that although a pononga (slave or servant?), Arikinui (meaning of very high rank) was not only ironically named but also very strong. In Nicky Conrad's version of the story, Arikinui is portrayed as getting too big for his metaphorical boots. So much so, that Tōhē feared people might think Arikinui was the chief and he the slave. The threat worried him so much that Tōhē used his spiritual powers to cause the 'pononga' to sleep, and while he slept, he was castrated. After that rather drastic comeuppance, Arikinui was treated as a captive all the way to their destination.[138]

But Māori captives did not always seek to return home anyway. According to Cowan, Wi Te Parihi, also known as Pirihongo or Pirihonga, was a Te Arawa captive from the Bay of Plenty taken north long before the

Northern War of 1845–46, when he chose to fight for Hone Heke against the British and was considered one of his two greatest warriors.[139] White, on the other hand, says he had travelled north to visit relatives who had been taken captive earlier and subsequently chose to settle there. Either way, he joined his people's one-time enemy.

As the then former missionary William Colenso indicated, this was not an uncommon situation:

> Slaves have been known to rise to very important positions among their new masters; and, even when having opportunities to escape, or set at liberty, to choose to remain and live and die with them. The writer has known several instances, especially among the Ngapuhi (Bay of Islands) tribes, in which the slave, although without original rank, has become the principal man, or leader, in the sub-tribe in which he was a slave.[140]

That was the case with Hākopa Te Ata-o-Tū, as we know, but something similar might occur in the case of refugees or others living away from their home areas. For example, in the 1830s, Te Mau-Paraoa, who Angela Ballara says was a captive from Ngāti Kahungunu of Mōhaka, was living with other members of Ngāti Kahungunu under Pōmare II's protection at Ōtūihu. He became a leading warrior who fought with Pōmare at Waikato in 1826 and at Ōtūihu when it was assaulted by Tītore in 1837.[141] When Pōmare died in 1850, Te Mau-Paraoa became a leading rangatira of Pōmare's people.[142] According to Dan Munn, Te Mau-Paraoa was allied to both Pōmare and Te Whareumu and, 'through them with Kawiti, of Ngāti Hine, and, again through the latter's tribe to Te Urikapana and the rangatira Te Haupokia'.[143] So he certainly found a powerful niche for himself in the north.

On a visit to Northland in 1929, David Graham, the Auckland War Memorial Museum's research officer, was presented with a carved pare, or lintel, said to represent 'the emancipation of a slave who rose to the position of a chief because of his fighting prowess' (see fig. 16).[144] The museum's records show that the Reverend Riri Kawiti, a grandson of the famous Ngāti Hine leader Te Ruki Kawiti, presented the lintel to the museum and that it had once adorned a wharenui, or meeting house, at Waiōmio,[145] which was opened in 1863 or 1864. The carver is named as

'Kapetoru' of Te Arawa, a lieutenant to Kawiti, so he may have been the captive who rose to a position of mana among Ngāti Hine.[146]

Captivity had important spiritual ramifications but they were not necessarily permanent ones. Before the practice of captive taking ended altogether, it is clear that there was no one way in which captives were treated and that the lives they led and the status they occupied while in captivity were closely related to their rank prior to capture and their usefulness as members of their conquerors' tribal group afterwards. They were expected to help rather than hinder. Christianity made inroads into customary belief systems, often led by released captives, but other Westerners affected the social order too. Christianity and British legal systems eventually provided some with new forms of leadership, but potential reasons and motives for change were plentiful. Warfare had served as the ultimate means of dispute resolution when peaceful methods failed, but with the level of warfare intensifying and expanding, deaths and dislocation reached new heights and communities were driven away from their established territories in a domino-like process.[147] 'Outside' forces in the form of new economic opportunities played their part in initiating change from within.

CHAPTER THREE

The roles, status, and rights of Māori war captives

BEING CAPTURED BY THE ENEMY DID NOT NECESSARILY MEAN instant 'slavery'. In the worst-case scenario, captives taken back to the conquerors' home could be killed immediately by grieving widows. But, as Angela Ballara pointed out, to refer to those people as slaves, as missionaries often did, obscures the purpose of their death. They were killed by the bereaved as utu for the fallen.[1] By contrast, though, people with desirable skills might be taken selectively so their captors could take advantage of their talents. Men like Rangi, the expert tattooist, might be valued and respected, just as young beautiful women could gain status as beloved junior wives. And captives of either sex could become close friends and confidants of their masters and mistresses, especially if they were of chiefly birth. Others sat anywhere between the two extremes.

A number of early residents and visitors to New Zealand offered their assessments of the institution they referred to as 'slavery'. In 1824, Dumont d'Urville thought that captives were 'treated fairly kindly'. James Busby, who arrived in New Zealand as the official British Resident nine years later, reported that chiefs treated all their people with civility, saying: 'even the Slaves are never ordered by their Masters. But always spoken to in some such manner as the following "Will you do this my good fellow".'[2] William Colenso, who had lived in New Zealand since 1834, had a similar view:

> All things considered, ordinary slavery among the New Zealanders was not so bad as the word imports, and as some Europeans, from want of due knowledge, have made it to appear.[3]

Thomas Buddle, a Methodist missionary who arrived in 1840, agreed that the condition of war captives:

> bore no resemblance to the slavery of what are called civilized nations. It was not reduced to system. No grinding labour was exacted. They were not treated with cruelty. But any misdemeanour, any insult offered by a slave to his chief, would be visited with instant death . . .[4]

Thomas McDonnell, Britain's one-time Additional Resident, told an 1844 Select Committee on New Zealand that slaves sometimes received more for their labour than chiefs. Slavery was 'so mixed up with the system', he said, 'they become parts of the family'.[5] Reverend Frederick Wilkinson, who visited Northland with Samuel Marsden in 1837, had told the previous 1838 House of Lords Select Committee on the state of New Zealand that he had seen many slaves 'a great deal better off than their Masters'.[6] Other witnesses to that inquiry said they were treated harshly and frequently killed.[7] Those witnesses included Joseph Barrow Montefiore and Robert FitzRoy, who had made only brief visits to New Zealand, and Samuel Hinds who had not visited at all. As will be discussed in Chapter 6, contemporary politics would have skewed their evidence, but it is equally certain that there was no one reality. Most captives appear to have been accorded some degree of respect, but not all.

In addition to the plethora of comments that Māori 'slavery' was a relatively benign institution, overseas visitors to New Zealand in the early part of the nineteenth century often remarked on the autonomy of individuals and kin groups.[8] John Liddiard Nicholas, an author who accompanied Marsden from Sydney to the Bay of Islands in 1814, thought that the stubborn independence of the people of Te Puna was unknown or only partially experienced in other districts. His remark that 'the immunities they enjoy have a visible effect on their manners, which assume in consequence rather an unaccommodating tone' paints a picture of individual haughtiness.[9] But other accounts suggest that personal independence was far from unique to Te Puna. Marsden, who had enjoyed far more interaction with Māori, wrote that chiefs 'cannot command the people as a body to labour on their ground, etc'. They 'have their domestics [presumably captives] to dress their provisions, attend them in their canoes, cultivate their land, or do any other menial services; and these only are wholly under their authority'.[10] As New Zealand's first historian, Arthur Thomson, would put it, their language was not 'that of lacqueys'.[11] Lieutenant-Colonel Thomas Gudgeon contrasted the aristocratic character of Māori with their fellow Polynesians, suggesting that chiefs in the Pacific islands were 'treated with a slavish deference that is unknown among the New Zealanders'. He considered the Māori system healthier because there were only 'two classes, the gentleman and the slave'. He quoted the Poverty Bay proverb: 'Turanga tangata rite — In Turanga all men are equal' as a principle that governed the Māori character, adding that the 'all men' of this saying referred to 'free-born warriors descended from the common ancestor' and did not include slaves or the descendants of slaves.[12] That saying may also allude to the desirability of collective action — in other words, that all of Tūranga should act together in times of crisis. But his use of the quotation underscores his understanding that there was a significant degree of personal autonomy.

Slave or servant?

'Jake the Muss' claimed that his family had suffered generations of humiliation because a long-distant ancestor had been captured in war. But the scenario is unlikely given that Māori almost always have options when it comes to tracing their line of descent. As one nineteenth-century storyteller explained:

> Ko ngā tūpuna o te tāngata ehara i te wāhi kotahi; no tērā wāhi, no tērā wāhi.

> People don't trace their descent from a single place, they trace it from many different places.[13]

That is because Māori ancestry can be traced through the father's or mother's line and most people (in most societies?) tend to opt for the one of greatest nobility. Just how long the taint of slavery might persist remains an open question, but Gudgeon's impressions oversimplified reality. There were gradations of rank between rangatira, and not all of their attendants were 'slaves' or captives. For example, it is said that because several very important descent lines converged in the person of Te Kani-ā-Takirau, prominent leader of Ngāti Porou in the early to mid-nineteenth century, his servants were restricted to only a few people of high rank themselves. To preserve his particularly great mana and tapu, Te Kani-ā-Takirau never grew his own food and was accompanied by a guard of honour when he travelled. He was unable to gain a reputation as a military leader because if he was ever in danger of being captured a bodyguard of warriors would find a way to whisk him off to safety.[14]

Degrees of usefulness

While it is generally said that 'slave' status was not hereditary, the children of captives did sit lower in social ranking. The children of male or female captives married to rangatira men or women were certainly not slaves, but those born to two slave parents were considered to be still slaves themselves. According to Earle, male slaves were not permitted to marry or to have any sexual relations with women, but exceptions could be made.[15] The individual's usefulness or value were ultimately the key factors when it came to how well he or she fitted into the community.

Commenting on the propensity of slaves not only to steal from each other but also to maul and kick each other over the spoils, Polack claimed that 'to the southward', where they had less value, it was wiser for them to keep quiet about their thefts, especially at times when provisions were in short supply.[16] At such times, he explained, the chiefs 'are strictly severe in putting the laws in execution, and, fearful amid contrary evidence that the guilty should escape, orders are issued to have them both killed instanter, often before the merits of the case are heard'.[17] Placing food supplies, especially the favoured kūmara, under tapu was a means by which the rangatira could protect vital resources and his people's wellbeing. To ignore the force of his mana was to dice with death.

In a communal society, everyone was expected to contribute to the common pool. Communities could ill afford to carry people who were unable to pull their weight, especially in difficult times, so orphaned infants and elderly or chronically sick captives lived on a razor's edge. This may have been especially so in the 1820s when food supplies that might be traded for muskets and ammunition were being carefully rationed.[18] Children left fatherless seem to have been particularly vulnerable to infanticide. Missionary John King reported that a woman from the Bay of Islands was so distraught by the news that her husband had been killed in battle, she prepared to hang herself. But, realising that would leave her baby with no one to nurse it, she decided to kill the child, too. Fortunately for the baby, some slaves heard it groan, rushed in and saved its life by cutting it down from where the mother had hanged it.[19]

Incapacitated adults often fared badly, too. Missionary Francis Hall wrote of a woman among a group of captives taken to Waimate North in 1821 who was killed and eaten because, being tired and lame, she was unable to keep up with the rest.[20] Much the same could happen to someone who became ill or disabled after settling at the victors' village. In 1823, John Hobbs reported that an elderly captive was killed because he 'had become troublesome through old age and infirmity'.[21] Three years later, William Williams recorded that an elderly female captive from a village near Rangihoua had been despatched with a bullet in the back because, as her master told him, she had been sick for a long time and was unable to help herself.[22] Times were tough in the 1820s, when it seems that the expense of maintaining these people was not matched by their usefulness, especially during a period when potatoes and other foods were being carefully rationed so that surplus supplies could be traded for all-important muskets. There could be little room for sentiment when the very survival of the group was tenuous.

A letter accompanying the photograph of 'Old Mihaka' (see fig. 21), which was probably taken during the first decade of the twentieth century, says that he was 'a slave whom Te Rauparaha left behind on the coast when retreating from Kawhia'. The writer explained that Mihaka:

> lived on Hari Hare[?] run & Mr Turnbull used to feed him. The heap of wood in the photo is the whare he live [sic] in being a slave he had no standing with the local natives & when he got old they had no use for him. Rauparaha left him behind because he had a sore foot & could not walk at the time he was not 20 years of age he must have been 90 when I took his photo.

Since Te Rauparaha left Kāwhia around 1820, Old Mihaka may have been much younger than twenty, possibly a small child who had little value regardless of his sore foot. Whether a child or a young man, his life story appears to reflect his original status as a captive combined with a physical disability. Te Rauparaha was moving on when Mihaka had difficulty walking, so there was no need to kill him. He was simply left behind.[23]

Given those harsh realities and, perhaps, for similar reasons, it appears that members of the same tribal group who were physically or mentally impaired might be treated as downtrodden workhorses or 'slaves' among their own. An example from the South Island suggests that that may have been the case. When New Zealand's first Surveyor-General John Turnbull Thomson visited Tūtūrau in Southland in 1856, he described the subject of his painting (see fig. 22), 'Reko's slave', as a fifteen-year-old girl. If that age were correct, she would have been born about 1841, some four years after the last-known battle in the area.[24] Thomson described her gait as not that

> of a human, for she crouched about so bent as to be almost on all fours. . . . Her back at that tender age was bent quite double with humility, oppression, and degradation. How brute like is insensibility — how inhuman like is the callous indifference that would perpetuate such misery on a fellow being!

Yet the artist's biographer pointed out, in 'fairness to Reko', that 'Thomson's painting reveals a classical case of Ankylosing spondylitis or fusion of the spinal column' and that the disease is not caused by ill-treatment.[25] It seems probable that her status was reduced by her medical condition.

In 1846, Charles Heaphy, also an artist and surveyor, had joined another fellow surveyor, Thomas Brunner, to explore a coastal route from Golden Bay to the South Island's West Coast. On reaching Pākawau pā in western Golden Bay, they hired an extra bearer to help carry their loads. This man was a 'slave' called Tau, who Heaphy described as:

> sulky, indolent, and self-willed, with one of the ugliest untattooed faces conceivable. His intellect was not of the highest order, and he wanted an eye; he, however, possessed two excellent qualities for bush work — he could carry a tremendous load, and was an unfailing snarer of woodhens.[26]

Tau, who belonged to Ngāi Tahu, is thought to have been captured in the late 1820s during an invasion by Niho, one of Te Rauparaha's lieutenants from Taranaki.[27] However, Heaphy's description of him seems to support the idea that the status of a 'slave' was, at least in part, dependent on talent, personality, and usefulness. In this case, he was not very smart and his lack of physical attractiveness did little to boost his appeal.

'Stray slaves'

Atholl Anderson's suggestion that slavery may have been relatively uncommon in southern New Zealand may well be correct, although oral traditions, including those recorded at Ruapuke, one of the southernmost islands of New Zealand, do refer to them in the more distant past.[28] In the tradition of Whakatau, recorded at Ruapuke, the hero sought to avenge the murder of his father by infiltrating his killer's village in disguise. He stooped and 'disfigured his body with ashes and charcoal, so that he had the appearance of an old mean man' or 'an old stray slave'.[29] In the north, William Yate was somewhat unconvinced by the suggestion that 'stray slaves' may have roamed the countryside as outlaws. Nevertheless, he was obliged to acknowledge that Māori were reluctant to go out alone, especially at night, or beyond the confines of their village for fear of such people:

They are possessed with a kind of indefinite fear, and indescribable dread, which, with all their efforts, they are unable, or profess themselves to be unable, to shake off: at times, they say it is the fear of meeting the Paraus, or slaves, who have run away, and are living by murder and robbery in the bush; though no one was ever known to have been either robbed or murdered by them, nor does any person ever recollect to have seen one of these poor runaways.[30]

'Stray slaves' may have included unwanted criminals or troublemakers who had been banished or absconded from their communities for wrongdoing and found themselves roaming from place to place with no one keen to take them in. Writing long after the events he described, John White recounted a tale of a 'robber chieftain' which might have convinced Yate to sympathise with his Māori neighbours who feared robbers and murderers hiding in the bushes. That story concerned a man named Moko who had a stronghold at Waipara, North Canterbury, near a cave close to a main trade route. He and his band of thieves were evidently in the habit of robbing and murdering small parties of carriers who came their way. The carriers were mostly slaves, who carried goods such as preserved mutton-birds, dried fish, and kauru (the edible stem of the tī tree, or cordyline) northward to be exchanged for preserved forest-birds, woven items, and other products from the north. The thefts must have been very annoying but, because most of the carriers were slaves, there was little enthusiasm for obtaining utu for their deaths. Things changed, however, when Moko killed a close relation of Tūtewaimate, an important rangatira. That murder pushed Tūtewaimate and his people over the edge. The party sent to seek him out found him sleeping alone in his cave and should have killed him easily but, due to his treachery, it was Moko who killed Tūtewaimate. Moko's lack of chivalry suggests a man of little mana, so the robber 'chieftain' may have been a criminal or runaway captive who had gathered others around him and managed their activities.[31]

But some captives, even when not enslaved, were destined to attract bad luck. Two such people were Ngāti Ira's Te Kēkerengū and his mother Tamairangi who were captured by Ngāti Mutunga in the 1820s. Believing she was about to die, Tamairangi asked to formally farewell her people and her land with a waiata (song) that she composed. But the song was of such beauty and pathos that Te Rangihaeata, then visiting Ngāti Mutunga, offered his protection to her and her family. So it was that they went to live on Kāpiti Island. However, Te Kēkerengū was a very handsome man and was suspected, possibly unfairly, of seducing one of Te Rangihaeata's wives. Feeling that they were in danger, mother and son hurriedly took their leave. Accompanied by some of their people, they continued southward.³² What happened next is not entirely clear, but things turned out badly in the long run. According to one account, they found refuge at Ōmihi near Kaikōura, where Te Kēkerengū's protector, a man named Rerewaka, foolishly taunted Te Rangihaeata's Ngāti Toa people that if Te Rauparaha headed to Kaikōura he would rip his belly open with a niho mangā, or shark's-tooth knife. That curse provided Te Rauparaha with the perfect invitation to attack Rerewaka's people and begin his incursions into the South Island.³³ Like Hongi Hika in the north, Te Rauparaha was a warrior chief and businessman who acquired an impressive arsenal of guns. He used them to begin a campaign of conquest over the areas of southern New Zealand where the valuable pounamu could be found. As for Tamairangi and Te Kēkerengū, whatever the precise details of their story, it was clearly one of twists and turns in which they were eventually killed with (or at the hands of) their erstwhile protectors in the south.

Daily life on the edge of society

The wide variety of situations that war captives, criminals, and refugees experienced highlights the problems of definition. We might pause to wonder whether all of them or, indeed, any of them were 'slaves', but such finer points were not the concern of politicians. Before the colonisation of New Zealand began, the British government was keen to determine what proportion of the New Zealand population were slaves. William Yate had told an 1836 Select Committee concerning aborigines in British settlements that about half the northern population was slaves but that the figure was probably less than 10 per cent in the south.³⁴ Despite never having visited the country, Samuel Hinds told the 1838 Select Committee that 90 per cent of the New Zealand population was slaves. The CMS missionaries, who had lived beside the Māori community for almost a quarter-century by then (and still were), responded that a third would be closer to the truth: a figure that likely related to the North Island.[35] They also confirmed that although chiefs did not carry food or firewood, or engage in the preparation or cooking of food, they did work at various projects together with their people.[36] Rangatira worked alongside commoners and captives in many activities, but as there was demarcation with regard to the types of work they could undertake, so did their tapu require separation of their living quarters.

Although forms of accommodation varied from region to region, precisely how and in which part of the kāinga, or village, people lived related to their status and role in the community. George Sisson Cooper, used to the ostentation typical of Europe's rich and powerful, was surprised to find that the residence of the great Tūwharetoa ariki, or paramount chief, Iwikau Te Heuheu Tūkino III at Pūkawa, on the shores of Lake Taupō, was not carved or elaborately ornamented as he thought befitting a leader of such high rank. However, his description of the settlement offers some clues as to how other communities may have been laid out in the early nineteenth century in relation to the rank of the residents. Cooper noted that houses of equal size to Te Heuheu's sat on either side of the marae (courtyard or village common) where members of his family and other rangatira lived. But on the other side of the central space were the more roughly built homes of the 'inferior' inhabitants. He explained that they lived in 'small wretched huts' adjoining the cookhouses placed at the opposite end of the enclosures where their bosses lived. So there was clear segregation between those of little and those of great tapu when it came to the distance between them and the cooking area. The spiritual threat posed by exposure to cooked food was an important factor in the arrangement of the buildings. A few, apparently luckier, 'slaves' (perhaps attendants would have been a more appropriate word in this case) — those who served the rangatira families — were housed closer to their masters and mistresses.[37]

Differences in climate influenced the type of housing, too. Victor Charles Lottin, who visited the warmer Bay of Islands in 1824, described all the houses he saw there as 'huts' that were fully exposed to winds from the north, northwest, and northeast. Tuai, the local rangatira, told him that they were built close to the ground to protect them from storms which would otherwise blow them over. Scattered around those houses were simple reed hedges providing shelter from the wind and the sun and it was in that area that the slaves were usually to be found.[38] Slaves here, both male and female, either slept in the open or sheltered under lean-tos.[39] The way in which war captives were typically perceived by their captors was evident from the living conditions that Western visitors described as well as the daily round of chores that typically fell to them. Gutting fish for drying was one of the duties usually assigned to young girls.[40] Lottin noted that fish, gutted and headless, were hung from poles to dry in the sun and smoke — presumably near the reed hedges where they sheltered.[41]

Among the key jobs given to war captives were lighting and managing fires and preparing and cooking food. As explained earlier, this related to the power of cooked food to destroy tapu. It was thus a vital role, not only to cater for the home people, but also to enhance their ability to provide hospitality to guests. That practice continued after the establishment of British government. So when Governor George Grey and his party visited Te Heuheu's people at Pūkawa in 1850, some of the slave girls were sent to dig up and prepare potatoes before talks began.[42]

Those chores having been done, Grey's party was treated to a great feast. Kits of pork, kūmara, potatoes, and taro, calabashes of preserved pigeons, kākā, and tūī, as well as piles of dried fish were ceremonially divided out before 'dessert' was prepared. That part of the meal consisted of fern root roasted and beaten by a group of female slaves who sat near the fires where it was roasting. Each of the women had a large smooth stone on the ground in front of her and held a wooden mallet in her hand. The guests sat in a semicircle in front of them ready to eat their portion as soon as it was prepared.[43] Aruhe, or the root of the bracken fern, was not as palatable as kūmara or the introduced white potato but a more readily available, everyday carbohydrate staple. After drying and soaking, the roots were cooked and then pounded into a paste, which could be made into cakes — but the pounding was a very laborious process.

Raymond Firth considered that beating fern root was women's work, but, as Figures 25 and 26 show, it was a job that might be performed by men or women.[44] Dressing and weaving flax (harakeke, or *Phormium tenax*), on the other hand, was more specifically women's work. During the 1820s and 1830s, large numbers of female captives were employed to prepare flax that could be traded for muskets. It was big business, carried out on an unprecedented scale. New Zealand flax prepared by Māori women was highly regarded at this time and much in demand for ropes and cordage in this age of sail, but it was another slow and laborious process. Te Rauparaha put his Ngāti Toa people and their allies, but especially their huge corps of captives, to work dressing flax. He established an important trading centre at Kāpiti Island where ships increasingly called, keen to supply arms and ammunition in exchange for this local product.[45] That trade was vital to Te Rauparaha's building a well-armed force of fighting men ahead of his rivals.

Flax was also used for fine weaving, including the making of high-quality garments, but that was usually the work of rangatira women. Their superior skills and artistry were demonstrated in the fine cloaks and other prestigious items they produced, which might be presented to honoured guests or as payment to other skilled craftspeople. Everyday utilitarian items, including baskets for serving food or storing potatoes, were more likely made by female captives or slave women.

Edward Shortland noticed some women engaged in that sort of work when, unconvinced of Māori abilities to call up the spirits, he was taken to visit an elderly woman living near Matamata, renowned for her supernatural powers. When he and his companions found her, she was in her cultivation grounds, sitting beside a fire and wrapped in a blanket. Opposite her were two female slaves chatting while they worked at weaving potato baskets — presumably for storing her crop.[46]

Concern for personal tapu ensured that there was a never-ending demand for disposable plates. As Major Richard Cruise pointed out after attending a hākari, or feast, with Hongi Hika's people:

> It is customary, when the natives of this country sit down to their meals, for the slaves to put the portion of each individual before him, in a new basket, made of a kind of flag; nor are those baskets, under any circumstances, used twice; and at the termination of the repast every person carries away the remnant of the food originally set before him.[47]

The importance of not sharing containers for food or drink was made very clear to Marianne Williams when the local rangatira Te Koki visited the Paihia mission in 1824. Having drunk 'a large basin of tea', he warned her not to allow 'his kuki', a servant to another missionary wife, to drink from the same vessel. If he were to become ill and discovered that she had done so, the girl would have been killed.[48]

Suggestions that captives were too ashamed to go home may have been correct, at least for those who experienced the worst situations. But their shame may have related more closely to the degrading ways in which they were treated and the demeaning work they were obliged to perform rather than simply having been captured. Elsdon Best narrated the story of Te Papa, a young Ngāti Raka rangatira, who fled from the battle of Te Pou-o-Urutake where his father had just been slain, grabbing a hīnaki, or eel pot, as he ran. He was sure the enemy would assume that anyone carrying such a thing would be a slave or at least a man of small consequence and pay little heed — as with the heroes of oral tradition who disguised themselves with charcoal or ashes. The ploy paid off. His pursuer did mistake him for a commoner or slave and 'pressed on in pursuit of higher game'.[49] So, despite his people's defeat, Te Papa lived to see another day.

Jobs typically assigned to captives included carrying loads, especially on the back. The back was a highly tapu part of the rangatira's body, as was clear from the rangatira's reaction when Joel Polack offered a piece of dropped biscuit to a slave. So warriors generally took captives from previous battles on subsequent military expeditions, to carry supplies and ammunition as well as to prepare their food along the way. They also reloaded guns and were sometimes given their own weapons to support their conquerors in battle.[50]

As captives or 'slaves' served to carry loads and avoid the tapu of the rangatira's back, so were their services necessary to feed rangatira and tohunga who were unable to touch any food or drink while under particular types of tapu. That might apply to those who prepared the bones of the dead, cut the hair of rangatira, or were undergoing tā moko (the process of tattooing).

In a version of the story of Pare and Hutu, it was explained that Pare was a puhi (ritually set aside virgin) of such high rank and, therefore, great tapu that when food was taken to her it was first given to one of her slaves, who passed it to a second, then to a third, before it could be given to Pare.[51] Best described a similar process involving three intermediaries, explaining that one attendant would prepare the food for people under the strictest tapu, then another would take it to a particular point, from where the last would pick it up and feed it to them (see figs 30 and 31).[52]

Relationships between slaves and masters

When the *Coquille* called at the Bay of Islands in 1824, Tuai pointed out one of his slaves to Dumont d'Urville, saying that he had brought him back from Whitianga but had not killed him as the Northland rangatira claimed was 'the usual custom'. Instead, he had been set free and given a wife. Dumont d'Urville took this to be an example of compassion on Tuai's part but he also added that the 'man was a chief in his homeland' so might have expected to be treated with far greater deference than the hoi polloi. He also noted that this man was 'sincerely attached' to Tuai, acting as his agent in all his trading negotiations with Europeans as well as accompanying him to war. According to Tuai, the man would no longer have any great standing among his own people and that was why he had chosen to act in support of Tuai's interests.[53] However the man from Whitianga felt about his situation, he was making the most of his circumstances, and the remark that he was 'sincerely attached' to Tuai implies a measure of mutual respect.

Like so many others, Charles Darwin asserted that 'among savages the chief has absolute power of life and death over his slave', but added that there was nonetheless 'an entire absence of ceremony' between master and slave. Also like others, he was surprised by the degree of personal autonomy retained by individuals regardless of their social rank. He noticed that a slave would 'press noses with any one he met, indifferently either before or after his master the chief'. Darwin went on to claim that societies needed to have arrived at a 'certain point' in civilisation before complex formalities were 'instituted between the different grades of society'.[54] His stay in New Zealand was a brief one (nine days) and he was evidently oblivious to the significance of tapu.

Tregear thought that strong bonds of friendship or even of family loyalty were common between master and slave and used the traditional story of Pāoa to illustrate his point. Pāoa was a very great rangatira, the founding ancestor of the Ngāti Pāoa, who was smitten by a beautiful slave girl while living apart from his rangatira wife who had left him after a quarrel. So love-struck was he that he abandoned his wife of rank permanently in order to live with his new love. One of Pāoa's male slaves, however, resented his betrayal and returned to serve the first wife. He and his mistress worked their kūmara gardens together, while 'Paoa and his slave-wife worked theirs'.[55]

Dumont d'Urville, one of many observers who felt that Māori prisoners were treated kindly, had added that they were 'sometimes sincerely devoted to those whom they are forced to serve'.[56] John Butler saw it differently, saying that Māori looked on their 'cookies' (captives) as mere dogs but with less than half their value.[57] Other missionaries were sometimes inclined to agree with Butler's opinion. Reverend Alfred Brown, for example, in his November 1832 report to the CMS, wrote with dramatic flourish:

> O cursed Slavery whether practised by gentlemen in the West Indies, or by Barbarians in New Zealand! In the former country there is a semblance of Justice (bitter mockery though it be) the Master being allowed to tell his own tale, while the Slave is compelled to be silent — but here the savage Master has uncontrolled power over his Slaves whom he may murder at his lawless will.[58]

His remarks reflect a notion dating back to the early 1700s that Africans were better off in the West Indies than their homelands. The rationale was that being sold into slavery and taken to Christian lands would actually rescue Africans from the likelihood of being killed, starved, or cannibalised in 'primitive Africa'.[59] Brown surely shared the common view among evangelical missionaries that replacing the prevailing Māori social systems and spiritual beliefs with Christian ones would have similar effect. But the perspective was not only a Christian one. Nineteenth-century Māori often expressed the view that enslavement was kinder than slaughter.[60] Nevertheless, the idea that they could be 'murdered at will' is questionable.

As the section 'Tikanga and the treatment of slaves' later in the chapter will show, Māori society was not 'lawless' and neither was it acceptable to kill 'slaves' without just cause. However, Butler and Brown were not disinterested observers but among those who strove to bring the 'light of civilisation' to a supposedly dark world of barbarism. There can be little doubt that their evangelical outlooks closely associated civilisation with Christian principle and that they expected adoption of the faith to have moral, social, and practical outcomes.[61] However, given that others described friendly relations between masters and slaves, overstating their benighted state may, on occasion, have served to boost support for their mission. By contrast, though, William Brown, a member of the Legislative Council of New Zealand who sought to encourage further British immigration, was keen to counter readers' fears of Māori cannibalism and warlike propensities by characterising them as 'hopeful subject[s] of civilization and refinement'.[62] In his book, first published in 1845, he wrote that although 'a slave must not eat of the same food — not even cook at the same fire, lest the chief's attua [sic: god] should kill them', after eating it was a different situation: 'the slaves will squat down by the side of their chief, and talk and joke with a familiarity which would not, of course, be permitted, were their masters naturally of a haughty disposition'. William Brown also mentioned a chief who was 'constantly making presents to other members of his tribe, and even to his slaves'.[63] William Yate agreed that some masters were 'peculiarly kind to their captives', and allowed them to chat freely with their chief.[64] Not only were there as many perspectives as there were observers, but also many agendas that Māori practices or alleged practices were enlisted to support.

Relationships between slaves and their masters or mistresses could certainly be warm. And despite the suggestion that some refused opportunities to be manumitted and returned to their families through shame,[65] others remained because of the close bonds they had formed. Such bonds were evident in 1831 when Richard Davis wrote of a young slave lad who had converted to Christianity, saying that he had 'a very kind master, and his anxiety for the conversion of his master is very great'.[66] Another man belonging to a rangatira named Ripi from Mawhe, who had taken the baptismal name William, was overjoyed to learn that Ripi 'was likely to receive the truth' and rejoiced 'to hear of the salvation of [his] master's soul'.[67]

Stories of slave companions accompanying their masters on journeys of exploration or supporting their mistresses in romantic exploits abound in oral traditions. These frequently identify the two people as having close, friendly relationships. But even though they may be referred to as 'slaves' in those stories, it is usually unclear whether they were war captives or simply people of a somewhat lower rank who served as attendants. Nor can we be certain that such intimate relationships were typical between captor and captive. It is also virtually certain that traditions handed down orally over the generations altered somewhat as their retellers adopted Christian values. Slavery, if that is what it was, did not magically end with the signing of the Treaty of Waitangi in 1840, but attitudes had begun to change by then. Indeed, the church and British legal systems offered those from the lower social ranks alternative forms of protection against injustice or ill-treatment. And those 'slaves' who were not fully integrated into their captors' kin groups had elements of freedom denied to those who were. Since Māori society was communally based and all were expected to contribute to the communal pool of resources or lose mana for failing to do so, some one-time captives may have seized opportunities to become independent entrepreneurs. As John Johnson, New Zealand's first Colonial Surgeon, explained: 'The taurekareka or slaves do not consider it necessary to maintain a reputation for munificence, consequently many of them are possessed of property.' His remarks were intended to applaud the 'taurekareka' for acquiring 'property' and condemn rangatira for distributing their wealth as gifts. But he followed them with the more telling comment that if Europeans like himself were to make Māori industrious, they would first have to make them avaricious.[68] As for those ex-captives who became businessmen, some specific examples discussed in Chapter 4 indicate that they may not have operated as independently as Johnson seems to have believed.

By the time Johnson wrote his 'notes', some former captives had already left their conquerors' communities, but others appeared content with their lot and remained. Angas, the travelling artist, came upon a slave girl at Tūhua near Lake Taupō in 1844 gathering flax with her pet dog. She was delighted to take a European visitor to her village, 'laughing and chattering in high spirits' as she went to light a fire and cook a meal for him.⁶⁹ She was fulfilling a traditional role, but was her cheerfulness the result of new attitudes on the part of her master or mistress? There are many reports of cheerful slave girls two or three decades earlier, so probably not. Johnson had a similar impression two years later in Auckland, then the seat of government. He said that it was often difficult to 'distinguish the rangatira from the taurekareka' in that town, although he did come across an exception in the case of the handsome fifteen-year-old son of Te Pakaru from Kāwhia and his 'poor diminutive attendant'. The young rangatira had been to Auckland to buy some Western clothes and a pair of shoes which he intended to wear when he rode one of his father's horses in an upcoming race. Johnson was scathing of the 'young *gentleman* [who] seemed fully aware of his own importance, and strutted on' (emphasis in source), comparing his demeanour to the 'subdued look and meagre frame' of the attendant, who 'was the very personification of slavery'. '[T]ottering under a pack', he sat silently during meals behind everyone else, 'receiving thankfully the coarsest part of the fare thrown to him'. Johnson said that he only smiled once and that was when he gave him a portion of his breakfast. He emphasised the slave's downtrodden status by saying that he seemed almost afraid to accept the offering until 'the proud young stripling his master' unwillingly granted him permission to take it.⁷⁰ Perhaps the arrogance of youth gave this 'gentleman' a self-importance not shared by his elders? Or, the differences implied by a few random examples may simply reflect the universal variety of relationships between individuals.

Marriage between slaves and free people

Although circumstances and attitudes varied greatly, marriages between captives and free people appear in oral traditions and the historical record. It is true that they were particularly common when the captive was an attractive young woman, but while some were viewed as mere concubines, others were highly favoured and treated with great respect. Regardless of their status, most of those women appear to have been reasonably well treated as were their children.[71] Although it was not common, some did marry other captives, and their offspring were considered to have the same status as their parents.[72]

Diplomatic marriages between men and women of rank were a time-honoured means of securing the peace after prolonged or particularly bitter fighting between tribal groups. The defeated party might give one or more of their rangatira women to the victorious chiefs as a means of initiating peace negotiations and cementing alliances. Whether the victorious rangatira was already married was irrelevant. Puhi or other women of high rank were ideally offered in these circumstances because they would greatly enhance the conquerors' mana. Moreover, children born from such unions, having inherited rank from both tribal groups, would make the peace even more secure. But, while it was more unusual, the gifting of a married woman might not be out of the question if the situation demanded more desperate measures.[73] An example of that occurred following the battle of Te Whetū-Matarau when Ngāti Porou's Rangi-whakatatae gave his wife Te Hiku-poto to Taotao-riri of Ngāpuhi.[74]

It was suggested by a witness to the 1838 Select Committee that slaves became free when their master or mistress died, but the CMS missionaries denied the truth of that statement, saying that they would be claimed by relatives of the deceased or one of the rangatira.[75] They also attested that women and men had equal rights over both slaves and land.[76] And women were not without rights when it came to their partners. Rangatira women might be allowed to live with a captive for a time without the relationship being formalised. The woman would not be considered tied to the man any longer than she chose or until others felt it appropriate for her to be married to a man of more suitable rank. Ngāti Tūwharetoa's Te Heuheu, for example, was happy for his young daughter to live with a Pākehā of little consequence so that he could say that he had a European living under his mana. Such arrangements were likely to come to an end, however, when the rangatira decided to give her as a wife to a man of rank. According to Richard Taylor, when unapproved liaisons produced a child, the grandfather was likely to kill it. Taylor told of an occasion when a rangatira from Rotoaira killed his daughter's illegitimate baby by tying it up in a basket and attaching it to one of the rafters of his house to perish, much as the widow mentioned by John King had done. Taylor felt that the woman from Rotoaira 'did not seem to grieve for her infant's death'.[77]

The crime of adultery

The rationale behind these actions related to inheritance, especially mana whenua, or land rights. For the same reasons, adultery was a very serious crime in Māori society: all the more so if the husband of an adulterous woman was of high rank. Many oral traditions relate to such goings-on. But it was not only the cuckolded husband who would be affected by the birth of a child of an uncertain father. John King told of an incident in 1824 when a young chief shot one of his dead brother's wives and her lover for adultery after having a bad dream about the brother. The doomed couple were both slaves.[78]

During the 1830s when the timber trade was in full swing around the Hokianga Harbour, a chief, appropriately named Rangatira, who was working as a sawyer with a Scots timber merchant,[79] was roused by a message brought by a slave messenger. In the words of Edward Markham, the slave 'whispered some News not pleasant to a married ear'. Rangatira immediately asked his employer if he might borrow his double-barrelled gun as there were two kūkupa (pigeons) about. Oblivious to what he was about to do or who the 'pigeons' were, his workmates watched him head off with the gun, powder flask, and ammunition. When he reached home, the furious husband found that his wife, who had been unfaithful with not just one but two of his slaves, was out. One of her lovers, unlucky enough to be in, was despatched on the spot. The sound of the shot brought most of the village — including his wife — out to see what had happened. Seeing her shot, the second slave took to his heels. It took two days for Rangatira to track him down, but track him down he did, and the third member of this illicit *ménage* met his demise.[80]

A particularly heart-wrenching case of family involvement in the discovery of an adulterous liaison occurred in 1841, after the Treaty of Waitangi, when William Symonds, an Auckland magistrate, visited the Waikato's Waipā district. Te Waru, an elderly rangatira, accompanied Symonds to his village where he announced that, from that time on, his people would live according to English law. This was a deeply painful decision because, shortly afterwards, he solemnly handed his only daughter over to Symonds, accusing her of murder (see fig. 33). Because her brother had committed suicide when his adulterous relationship with a female slave was exposed, she had killed his erstwhile lover.[81] Happily for the girl, she was not tried for murder as the incident had occurred before Te Waru announced his decision to follow English law. However, it is a poignant example of the emotional torment that could accompany the acceptance of new laws and new value systems.

Not all rangatira were so prepared to submit to English law. Early in 1847, the Auckland merchant John Logan Campbell called attention to a recent series of 'murders' which had been committed in the Hokianga district. Aware of the different concepts of justice, Governor Grey responded by sending Captain Nugent and Lieutenant Symonds on a mission of inquiry with strict instructions to avoid giving offence. The Herekino chief Pukeroa had killed one of his wives for an infidelity that had led to her pregnancy. Others, including Pukeroa's neighbour Mangumangu, and another man named Whau, had taken the same action about the same time: late 1846.[82] Whether the 'wives' concerned were captives or of rangatira rank is not recorded, but the circumstances all having been proven, Grey turned to his trusted advisor the Hokianga rangatira Tāmati Wāka Nene. Nene confirmed the victims' guilt under Māori law but explained that English law was not suited to dealing with their crimes. And, if any attempt were made to apprehend the husbands, Māori would certainly take offence and protect them, he warned. In other words, their reaction to the arrest or imprisonment of a rangatira would be much the same as when they were captured in battle. Manhandling or detaining a person of such tapu would be greatly resented and a very dangerous move on the part of government. On this occasion, Grey appears to have taken Nene's advice.

Women of rank would not suffer damage to their mana lightly either. When Te Rangi Topeora's husband Hauturu had an affair with a slave on Kāpiti Island in 1840, his furious wife saw to it that the adulterous woman was killed and eaten.[83] It was not always the guilty parties who suffered, though. Compensation might also be achieved through the death of an innocent person. The wife of one Bay of Islands rangatira killed 'a large fine woman slave because her husband had cast her off for a season to live with another of his wives'. John King explained that this was how she took revenge despite the slave woman being quite uninvolved in the husband's choices. King was told that the wife had been pregnant twice prior to this incident but aborted the baby each time out of anger with her husband for taking so many wives. Hell's fury had a fair bit of competition with this only partly scorned woman.[84]

Although there were certainly exceptions, Angela Ballara noted that the deaths of slaves in connection with dispute resolution would not normally require utu.[85] So, when a man was accused by members of another tribe of having relations with a woman of bad repute, he was so enraged by the slur on his reputation that he shot a slave who belonged to his accusers. Locally based missionary Samuel Leigh must have been under the impression that such an act did require utu because he anticipated that a war would result, but Ballara found no evidence to suggest that it had.[86]

In early 1841, after English law had officially been established, a man named Tipako ignored a rāhui (spiritual restriction or ban) near North Cape and killed a shark. Perhaps not surprisingly, he was killed for his transgression. But according to missionary John Hobbs, because Tipako was closely related to the rangatira who had set up the rāhui, some of his nearer relatives responded by killing four of the rangatira's people and taking two of their slaves as compensation. As was often the case with Europeans, Hobbs did not think the crime a serious one but feared, nonetheless, that the hostilities were about to ratchet up.[87] He advised Māori who consulted him that all of the deaths were improper, but we can assume that their response was in line with those of earlier times, including the 'payment' of slaves as compensation.

Still later, in 1860, when war was under way in Taranaki and Pākehā began to leave his area of Kāwhia, Kikikoi emphasised his family's commitment to protecting them. He recounted the painful tale of his father's response when his people plundered a ship that had arrived from Sydney under the captaincy of a Mr Brown. Pikia, Kikikoi's father, was not present but was furious when he heard of it. He insisted that the plundered goods should be paid for, which they were obliged to do. After the payment of over 2000 baskets of potatoes and 200 pigs had been loaded aboard the vessel, Pikia gave another of his sons as a slave (taurekareka) to the Europeans. Precisely what this son's position was intended to be is not clear, but Pikia surely took the action to provoke his people because they had disregarded his professions of friendship towards Western visitors. Much like the scorned wives who killed their infants when angered by their husbands, the loss was to the community. Pikia was taking utu against his hapū but also sending a strong message to potential business partners that he would protect them.[88]

Changing hands

Less painfully than being killed or shipped overseas, captives might be gifted as utu for crimes committed by others or for loss of face. One man's serial gifting began when Patuone from the Hokianga was living among Ngāti Pāoa in the Hauraki area and a Ngāti Maniapoto party came to visit them at Wharekawa. At their hosts' request, the guests dressed themselves in their finest clothes and feathers and began to dance. One of the best dancers found such favour with Patuone's young and attractive wife that she quietly arranged to elope with him. However, the plot was discovered by the Ngāti Pāoa chiefs who demanded compensation for this assault on their mana. Having acknowledged the disgrace brought on them by the seductive dancer, the Ngāti Maniapoto rangatira put things right by handing over one of their captives, a Ngāti Kahungunu man named Hami Hone Ropiha (or John Hobbs). As fate would have it, Hobbs went on to become a great ally of the government and served as George Grey's orderly during the Northern War of 1845–46.[89] He had apparently been gifted to the British troops by Patuone's brother Wāka Nene[90] and was ultimately rewarded for his services with a grant of land in Auckland's highly desirable Official Bay. His portrait, commissioned by Grey, hung in the drawing room of his Mansion House on Kawau Island.[91]

Runaway slaves

Not all captives attained such heights, of course, and some opted to run away from their captors. The oral traditions that mention people laying claim to stray slaves support Samuel Marsden's statement that runaways became the property of anyone who caught them.[92] Some unlucky ones who failed in their attempts to escape received the death penalty, but others did make it home.

Instances of captives escaping immediately after capture might be discounted on the basis that they had not actually been 'enslaved' or submitted to any form of bondage. One Ngāpuhi veteran, who told of being away from home for twelve months during one of their 'musket war' campaigns, said that captives 'escaped here and there on our journey as we went from place to place'.[93] However, there are also accounts of people making their escape after being held captive for a period of time, which would seem to be a different matter. Although death was the penalty for unsuccessful attempts, some took their chances anyway. Augustus Earle 'felt sick almost to fainting' when a handsome young man of 'mild and genteel' demeanour told how he had tied a pretty young girl to a post and killed her for trying to run back to her own people. Having told her that he only intended to give her a flogging, he shot her instead.[94] Earle felt that the man had 'cheated' the girl with his lie, but Māori under penalty of death were often despatched without warning on the basis that it was less cruel to die quickly and unexpectedly than to live with the torment of a looming death sentence.

Missionary writings imply that escape attempts were not uncommon. James Kemp reported in 1824 that two servant girls ran away from James Shepherd's home, taking 'many things' with them. They were planning a return to their home but their Māori masters followed them and ordered them back. Kemp feared they would be 'very ill treated' by their masters but offered no hint that they might be killed.[95] Edward Tregear recounted the story of a rangatira, who having been away on a long journey, returned to find his sister cooking food — definitely not appropriate work for a woman of rank. When she told him that her 'maids' had deserted, the indignant man went straight to the runaways' homes and killed them both.[96]

Enslavement was a dark and painful experience for many reasons, not the least being the splitting up of families. John Hamlin reported how a captive from Taranaki, taken to Waikato, came across his wife who had also been taken north to serve another master. Romantic notions led them to take to the bush in hopes of escaping together, but their dreams of living happily ever after were shattered when someone recognised them as runaways and shot the man dead. The woman was then obliged to become the wife of her first husband's executioner.[97]

Others had better luck, though, and successful escapes could become the stuff of legend. When artist and explorer Charles Heaphy was planning an expedition over the mountains between the Rīwaka Valley at Motueka and Tākaka at Golden Bay in December 1843, a report that a female runaway had made her escape by travelling from valley to valley over the mountains convinced him that a route could be found.[98]

Punishing delinquents

Escape attempts aside, some captives failed miserably when it came to obedience and seem to have deliberately courted danger. That could mean that their life was well short of total terror or that it was so miserable they cared not what their fate might be if caught. In the case of young children, it might simply have been that they had not yet learned the rules or potential consequences of their wrongdoing.

It is to be expected that missionaries would be horrified when small children, who had been living among their Māori neighbours as slaves or captives, were killed for stealing kūmara. It was often mentioned that they were tapu kūmara, or taken from a tapu store. Kūmara were vital to the Māori economy, among the most prestigious foods, and consequently subject to a considerable degree of ritual and spiritual restriction.[99] So for both economic and spiritual reasons, the theft of stored kūmara was a very serious crime indeed and subject to the death penalty. Small children were particularly vulnerable to capital punishment, not only because of the severity of the crime but also because their value to their conquerors' community was negligible.

One young man, who John King referred to as 'Toodieka', killed a young boy he had brought north as a captive because he had stolen kūmara from a chief's house that was under tapu.[100] Three years later, in 1822, King reported that an old woman tied a young captive girl's hands together before tying her up more completely in a large potato basket and throwing her down the steep hill running from the top of Rangihoua (see fig. 34). In this case, the girl was not too badly hurt, managed to bite through her ties, and escaped to Te Puna, but was killed a few months later apparently by an eight-year-old 'chief's son'.[101] The same old woman was reported as using the same method on another slave a short while later.[102]

There were many such instances, but late 1823 to 1824 was a particularly bad period for light-fingered captives. King reported six executions between 19 November and 7 December alone, but he and his Wesleyan counterparts recorded several others over the next few months. An entry in Hobbs's journal for February 1824 recorded that 'about a half dozen Boys and Girls had been killed . . . for stealing potatoes this Season'.[103] Hunger was surely getting the better of them, but the penalties for getting caught were very high indeed. Quite apart from customary tapu conditions, these deaths occurred in the early years of the 'musket wars' when access to muskets was literally vital to survival. That likely explains why another captive, who failed to prevent a chief's pigs from getting into his potato gardens, was killed for his negligence.[104] Potatoes were one of the principal currencies used to purchase arms.

Saleable foodstuffs like potatoes were being carefully stockpiled as trade items and kūmara were very important for offering hospitality to guests. But if missionary journals are anything to go by, the theft of food was not an uncommon crime among captives, who may have suffered from greater hunger at a time when supplies, which might otherwise be traded for the all-important guns, were often strictly rationed. For the missionaries, these thefts were trivial crimes and the punishments excessive, but given the significance of tapu and the vital importance of food supplies, captives whose lives had already been spared once and whose contribution to their captors' community was likely a small one, should, perhaps, have known that they were skating on very thin ice and could expect harsh penalties. A warning sign displayed by the Kawakawa River might have made some think twice. Exploring the area in 1820, Richard

Cruise spotted a head stuck on a pole which he and his companions were told was that of a slave thief put on display to remind others of the fate they could expect if similarly tempted.[105]

Descendants of convicts sent to the Australian colonies in the late eighteenth century often refer to what now seem the minor crimes that caused some of them to be sent packing to the other side of the world. 'He only stole a loaf of bread' is a common cliché. But desperate times call for desperate measures, so, in October 1788 when food supplies were critically short in the newly founded colony of New South Wales, Governor Arthur Phillip introduced strict rationing there. Despite his usual aversion to the death penalty, during those precarious times, anyone who stole food was liable to be punished by hanging. So Phillip's response was virtually identical to that of Māori, the only difference being the method of execution.[106]

Unlike Augustus Earle, who thought the runaway captive had been 'cheated' by being shot without warning, Cruise thought the Māori form of execution was 'one of the most humane customs of the country'. He felt that to be struck on the head with a mere or patu without prior warning was kinder than leaving the condemned on death row while they awaited the inevitable.[107]

Just how afraid captives were of their masters or mistresses would reflect what they knew of the latter's attitude and degree of compassion. That was predictably variable but, from the time of their arrival, missionaries might sometimes negotiate leniency. For example, in 1827, James Kemp reported that Rewa pursued a number of his slaves who had escaped. He managed to seize them at Waimate, where others were planning to join them. According to Kemp, Rewa would have put them to death except for the missionaries' intervention because '[a]ccording to the New Zealand laws, it is death if a slave run away and is caught'. On this occasion, however, he promised the brethren that they would not be harmed if they returned.[108] In this instance, we must rely on Kemp's version of events and that does not explain why Rewa agreed to the missionaries' proposal. He may have been anxious to maintain good relations with them or he may have needed an excuse to retain valuable workers.

Compassion was not something introduced along with Christian teachings but neither could it be relied upon. A few years earlier, in February 1824, Kemp had recorded that a slave of the great and much-feared warrior Hongi Hika robbed him not only of some muskets but also of the helmet and coat of armour given to him by King George IV. The muskets may have been to assist the thief's escape, but to have stolen such significant symbols of Hongi's mana as the helmet and armour would surely have been pushing his luck rather far and intensified the owner's determination to apprehend him.[109] Kemp made no mention of Hongi's likely or actual response but Rusden wrote that John Rutherford, a shipwrecked seaman and convicted thief, witnessed the killing of a slave who had attempted to steal Hongi's armour in 1825 or 1826. He 'smote him dead and devoured his heart upon the spot', Rutherford reported gleefully. Unfortunately, as Rutherford and Rusden are vague about the date, we cannot be certain whether this was a reference to the same incident or whether attempts to steal these particular items had become fashionable.[110]

Dealing with one's own captives was one thing, but since their status was similar to that of other belongings, it was not lawful to punish, let alone kill, someone else's. That was evident when Motoki, a rangatira from Taiāmai, did just that. The man was discovered to have been stealing but, because that was not sufficient cause to kill a 'slave' who was not one's own, Motoki's enemies responded by killing one of his.[111] About a year later, in 1825, serious hostilities broke out in the South Island following an incident that occurred when the high-ranking Ngāi Tahu rangatira Tama-i-haranui went to Kaiapoi to fetch a canoe. He had left Pōtahi and his wife Murihaka to look after his house at Waikākahi, but during his absence and for reasons now unknown, Murihaka put on a tōpuni (a fine dogskin cloak) which was tapu to Tama-i-haranui.[112] Having witnessed her act of sacrilege, his relations killed a slave who belonged to one of her relatives. Although his owners were enraged by the death, they were not prepared to attack Tama-i-haranui's relatives and so killed a member of Murihaka's people, Ngāti Koreha, who lived at Tai Tapu on Banks Peninsula, as retribution. After that, events began to spiral out of control instigating far more widespread warfare. These were times of great tension between related tribal groups, the implications of which were so unusual and tragic that the events became known as the Kaihuanga (or 'eat relations') feud.[113]

Yet while the killing of someone else's captive or slave was unlawful, responsibility for their behaviour would seem to have fallen on their master or mistress. So, in that same year, 1825, a northern rangatira named Moka was grossly offended when one of his slaves was accused of stealing a pig belonging to another rangatira from the Hokianga. Having first threatened to shoot the accuser, the outraged Moka was subsequently appeased by a gift of two pigs.[114] Three years later, some of the crew of the mission vessel the *Herald*, who had been living on a small island in the Bay of Islands, were plundered while attending evening service. It was soon discovered that three slaves, including one belonging to the local tohunga Tohitapu, were responsible. The rangatira, who was very friendly with the mission folk, turned up soon after 'in a great bustle' insisting that he be tied up as the thief had been. He repeated that request several times, saying that he was so ashamed of his slave's conduct he had not eaten since learning of it.[115]

As with Rewa's act of compassion in promising not to harm his runaway slaves, how much of Tohitapu's anger was due to his wanting to avoid upsetting the missionaries is hard to know. Most rangatira were doing their best to stay in their good books since maintaining friendly relations with them was very closely linked to their trading opportunities. That concern was apparent when one of Hongi's slaves, working as a servant to James Kemp, reported that his sister and another captive had been shot as a 'satisfaction' for the adultery of Hongi's wife with his son-in-law: an action taken without the offended husband's knowledge or sanction. Conscious of the need to protect not only the missionaries' bodies and possessions, but also their sensibilities, Hongi had asked that none of his slaves be killed for her crime.[116]

Although 'slave owners' were responsible for the doings of their underlings they also had reciprocal obligations, rather like the European concept of *noblesse oblige*. As Te Ao-o-te-Rangi angrily proclaimed following the trial of a man called Huntly for murdering a Māori in 1855:

> Ka haere pai te Pakeha, e ahatia hoki. Tena ka pa kau ki taku wahine, i patu ra nei i taku tamaiti i taku tema, ki taku pononga ra nei, ko reira, ka maru ia i au, ekore ia e tohungia.

If the European goes on his way quietly, he will not be interfered with; but if he touches my women, or strikes my child, or my brother, or even my slave, then, I will pounce upon him without mercy.[117]

Some offences, like theft, adultery, and unjustified violence, were understood cross-culturally, but others were viewed in very different lights. Among these were cursing and verbal insults. The CMS missionaries had been horrified when a female slave, who they believed to have been ill-treated by her master at Te Puna, was summarily executed on the beach for having cursed him.[118] That was in 1820 when the reaction might have been expected, but the seriousness of the offence did not diminish over the following decades. Christian teachings and English law sometimes softened responses — but certainly not in all cases. It has been suggested that a one-time captive uttering a particularly dreadful insult towards her master, coupled with the culprit's Pākehā husband refusing to pay a much lighter penalty, was one of the sparks that ignited the Northern War in the 1840s.

That reckless woman was Kōtiro Hinerangi of Ngāti Umutahi and Ngāti Tū, who had been captured by Ngāpuhi around 1829 and given to Hone Heke as a 'slave'. She eventually married a Scot named Alexander Grey, but when he died soon after, she went on to marry William Lord, a butcher and storekeeper at Kororāreka. Heke, the first Māori to sign the Treaty of Waitangi, had quickly become disillusioned with its effects and, according to Hugh Carleton, decided to provoke a reaction from the European settlers at Kororāreka in 1844 by reasserting his rights over Kōtiro under Māori law. However, when she received word that Heke was coming to take her away, she went into high dudgeon and pointed to one of the pigs hanging in her husband's butchery, referring to it as Heke.[119] Another version claims that she made a similar comment during an argument with other women.[120] But whichever is correct, likening a man of mana to a pig was quite outrageous, especially for someone who had been his captive. Accounts of what happened next vary somewhat. One has it that Lord's shop was ransacked by a taua muru (retributive plundering party), which removed his goods and his wife for the insult, while another says that the looting was because Lord failed to redeem his wife with an agreed payment of a cask of tobacco. He may have cheated the defamed rangatira by giving him only half a cask of tobacco instead of the whole one demanded and agreed. Regardless of the details, Kōtiro's insult seems to have set things in motion.[121]

Other forms of name-calling or character assassination were also liable to arouse passions. Missionaries, who generally lacked enthusiasm for getting involved in such cases, nevertheless understood their mission to include introducing British systems of dispute resolution along with Christianity. So, in 1835, when Pūmuka was the victim of a false accusation made by someone else's slave, Henry Williams held 'a court' to discuss the matter. Having been found guilty, Pūmuka took the culprit in charge as his slave until his master made a satisfactory compensation for the attack on his mana.[122]

British teachings about 'civilised' ways of dealing with dispute resolution or matters of law could be a cause of confusion, however. For example, when a rangatira at Waiōmio in the Bay of Islands area hanged one of his wives for having relations with a slave, he did not expect to be rebuked by a missionary for doing so. Taken by surprise when he was, he said 'he thought he was exactly following the English method'. Hongi Hika had been in England during the trial of George IV's wife Queen Caroline for just such a crime and had 'expressed great disapprobation at the whole proceeding'. Having five wives himself, Hongi, who had perhaps heard of Henry VIII as well, thought that the trial process was an unnecessarily protracted procedure, saying that 'he would rather cut off all their heads than be so much troubled about one'.[123] It seems that Hongi had shared his impressions with his compatriots.

In many instances, while the crime may have remained the same, attempts were made to modernise approaches to obtaining utu. Henry Williams's 'court' approach was more formalised by George Grey on his return to New Zealand in 1861 for a second governorship. Based on a customary model, rūnanga, or tribal assemblies, were redeployed as a vehicle for the introduction of indirect rule through a form of local government. The scheme was intended to provide new and more efficient forms of governance for and over Māori communities.[124] Salaried Māori magistrates would deal with local issues under the leadership of European commissioners. However, when Henry Hanson Turton was sent to report on the workings of this initiative in 1862, the people of Kauaeranga in the Thames area were divided as to whether they should be following British or Māori law. Ngāti Whanaunga were happy to follow English law but Ngāti Maru, under a rangatira named Rīwai, were emphatic about their preference for returning to customary systems, not only in law but 'language, trade, religious instruction, and local habitation'. They did not support the Queen but neither did they support the Māori King. They were adamant that they would 'rule themselves by their own laws'. After three hours of argument, proceedings commenced anyway with Rīwai acting as judge. The first case concerned a claim for £50 in damages by the mother of a girl, aged about ten, who had been called a taurekareka. When the woman's demands were met with laughter, the girl's father stood to say that although her mother was a slave, he was a man of great standing, a view that was supported by copious aunts and uncles who had gathered in support. After much commotion, during which the Māori lawyers hired to take the case came close to blows, the defendant 'assailed the plaintiff', abused the witnesses, poured scorn on others, and insisted on repeating her slander, matters were in chaos. Rīwai, whose inclination had been for a customary proceeding in the first place and who was now in a 'nervous sweat', asked Turton to take the matter in hand. Turton awarded the plaintiffs ten shillings' compensation. Although content with the judgment, the defendant exclaimed that she did not have such a large sum and never would have. Not to worry, a collection was immediately taken up, which saw an assortment of clothing and coins to the value of 25 shillings handed over to the defamed mother.[125] So Turton was still thwarted in his attempt to introduce British forms of justice as he intended.

Elsewhere, in Ōpōtiki, a man who let loose with that same affront in the same year earned himself a substantial fine of £5 from the local rūnanga. And here, too, the penalty was not to official liking. When the region's Resident Magistrate Charles Hunter Brown heard of the £5 fine and other 'severe' penalties for 'trifling offence' he lambasted the rūnanga as a 'purely Native Runanga . . . in its most rampant state'. He firmly believed that it was 'worse for the Maoris than the old "taua" (plundering party)'.[126] Insults and derogatory words still had powerful force in the Māori world, but that reality had gone right over the head of Charles Hunter Brown, Esq.

As studies by Vincent O'Malley have shown, Māori communities responded to Grey's rūnanga initiative in various ways. Supporters of the Māori King tended to see the salaries and appointments offered to Māori officers as 'a thinly disguised attempt to deceive the Māori people and reduce them to subservience'.[127] Others used the system as far as they chose to and in their own ways, as the people of Kauaeranga did, but nowhere was it embraced as Grey had hoped. Charles Hunter Brown reported considerable distrust in the remote Urewera region, for example, where people feared for their land and their nationality 'lest they should be made slaves to the Queen'.[128] Māori failure to simply roll over or let government agents control proceedings saw the government system finally dismantled at the end of 1865.[129] But matters of Māori law continued to be debated in more traditional rūnanga.

Mākutu, or bewitching, was an especially serious crime, whoever the perpetrator. In 1869, however, it was an elderly 'slave' woman called Atereta whose death featured in Auckland's *Daily Southern Cross* newspaper. Atereta's powers of mākutu were said to have been responsible for over 50 previous victims, including ten relatives of another slave named Pera. When Pera became ill, a rūnanga of tohunga met to determine the cause and eventually cast suspicion on Atereta. As Pera's condition deteriorated, he added fuel to the smouldering fire by claiming that his spirit had seen an apparition of Atereta that confirmed her guilt. He repeated this 'verdict' three times to the tohunga, according to custom law. Atereta was called to appear before another rūnanga of the people when Pera had passed away. But Pera's brother Ruka took matters into his own hands. He intercepted her on the way and struck her dead with his tomahawk. That rather dramatic ending to the case meant that her sentence was never decided. Ruka's action may have been customary in some sense but was not 'tika', or correct, under custom law. The paper reported that 'the whole of the people should have consented to her death'. So it seems doubtful that she would have been condemned to die. That was implied by the crying of the people as she was buried and by Ruka taking to his heels.[130] Aside from attitudes towards mākutu, this case confirms not only that people in the community were still being spoken of as slaves almost 30 years after British government began in New Zealand but also that they were not utterly despised and their lives could be valued.

Tikanga and the treatment of slaves

That case touches on another theme in contemporary accounts that has recurred in more recent literature: that, prior to the adoption of Western legal systems, captives could be beaten or even killed at their master's or mistress's whim.[131] Arthur Thomson wrote that 'the word of their masters was law, and a refusal to obey death' and that '[t]he people never defended the cause of slaves'. Yet, he came close to contradicting that statement when he added that 'slaves were not ill-treated as long as they did what was required of them' and that cruelty towards them was the exception rather than the rule.[132] The evidence points strongly towards 'tikanga' or rules concerning the correct ways of treating slaves and that abuse was not condoned.

In his *Ancient History of the Maori*, John White recorded one example of seemingly mindless murder, apparently from Māori informants during the late nineteenth century. In that account, a group of children who deliberately killed a slave during a game of mock warfare were praised by their parents who proclaimed that 'they all would be brave in battle when they became men and women'.[133] However, another example, which White called 'Murder love and suicide [sic]', is more ambiguous. In that story, a man called Paopao, who was rejected by the woman he desired, vented his anger by killing one of his slaves and attempting to kill another. But, having done so, he disappeared into the forest and committed suicide. His bones were not discovered until four years later.[134] The treatment of captives clearly had to be tika, or just, according to Māori law and this man's rash act must have preyed heavily on his mind. As Edward Tregear put it: 'it was considered "bad form" to abuse an inferior'.[135] It could also lead to warfare.

During his stay in the Bay of Islands in 1824, Dumont d'Urville asked Tuai of Kahuwera 'what would be done to a chief who killed a slave without any reason'. Tuai responded 'that nothing would be done; but ... it would be a wrong act and that this in itself would prevent it from being committed'.[136] Like greed, neglecting to entertain visitors hospitably, or a lack of knowledge regarding oral traditions and tribal history, being too hard on captives could see rangatira lose mana or personal power.[137] These were obligations that must be met, much as Europeans would understand the moral obligation of the highborn or powerful to act with honour and generosity towards those lower down their social scale. The principle was also much the same as that of tuakana–teina, or senior–junior, relationships in other Māori contexts. Wrong-acting in respect of a teina or junior relative would result in loss of mana and a possible shift in leadership from the one to the other.[138]

Public rebuke for the ill-treatment or unjust killing of slaves is evident in oral traditions as well as written history. For example, Terehunga from Poverty Bay was banished from Te Aitanga a Māhaki for killing a slave — and whakapapa (genealogical) charts indicate that this event must have occurred pre-1700 — well before European influence.[139] The story of Tamaāhua, in which he travelled from the North to the South Island in search of his wife, also refers to his killing his slave or attendant named Tūhua. There are several different versions of this story which seems to blur the lines between a genuine oral tradition and myth, but at least two recount that Tamaāhua was condemned for his action. One version states that his three wives were turned to stone as his punishment. Another says that Tūhua was killed because Tamaāhua suspected that his wife was attracted to Tūhua, but that the act was nonetheless 'condemned by his companions'.[140]

Nor did excessive punishments pass unnoticed. So when Te Puhi of Whangaroa struck one of his slaves on the head for setting fire to the fern on an old cultivation, some of his relatives, including his uncle, an old man called Mahue, felt that that response was overly harsh. The man had tried to make his job of collecting food roots easier by clearing the fern but his attempt at efficiency had not gone down well. Mahue told his nephew off, saying that such treatment was 'kino rawa', or very wicked. Highly offended by his remarks, the tetchy Te Puhi loaded his musket and shot Mahue dead. This was one of several instances in which the mistreatment of a slave led to wider hostilities. In this case, Te Puhi's nephew and namesake was so angry that he had to be restrained from killing his uncle for having killed the old man. Worse was to come for the slave, though, as Te Puhi, getting grumpier and grumpier, went on to order him killed and baked. But that still did not end the matter. Three days later, a taua muru of between 200 and 300 warriors arrived from a nearby settlement to punish Te Puhi for killing Mahue. The killing of the slave may have been tika, or just, as the rebuke for his punishment had been the cause of Te Puhi's ungovernable rage, but utu was nonetheless due for the killing of Mahue. Two other slaves were taken away alive in this raid and one more was killed.[141]

Sometimes, though, obtaining justice for an abused captive required a degree of subterfuge. That was the case when a young man named Te Ratu was captured by Hunaara from Kōkai on the East Coast. Hunaara is said to have made Te Ratu's life one of abject misery. One particularly terrifying experience involved having a large crayfish placed on his bare back, which tore into his flesh and cut it to ribbons. Offended by his mistreatment, a benevolent old chief named Te Whi-o-te-Rangi took pity on him and put forward a plan. He suggested that when Hunaara sent Te Ratu for water, he should contrive to break the calabash, so that his master would beat him. Having done as suggested, Te Whi-o-te-Rangi not only protected Te Ratu, but also made sure that he was returned to his own people.[142] The rationale for Te Whi-o-te-Rangi arranging for Te Ratu to be beaten is likely to have been to ensure that the abuse occurred publicly so he would be justified in stepping in to protect him, but it is also possible that Te Ratu was a rangatira by birth.

In one version of the story of Manaia and his family, their slave, a man named Paeko, interceded when Manaia beat his wife Maungakiekie during a family argument.[143] But since another account has him as her lover, the story may be more complicated.[144] Nevertheless, there are enough examples to confirm that, as well as being entitled to just treatment, captives were not necessarily obsequious.

One of many differences between the Māori practice and chattel slavery was the response that European buyers were likely to receive if they abused someone they 'purchased'. When the 1838 House of Lords Select Committee on New Zealand asked Dr John Watkins whether slaves who found themselves in European hands were content with their lot, he said they would be if well treated but, if not, they would run away. As to whether Europeans who had purchased those slaves would try to get them back, he replied that it would require intervention from his 'first owner'. If that first owner thought the slave had been ill-used, they would not only help him but also seek retribution for the ill-treatment.[145] In other words, European buyers were still subject to Māori custom law.

An item written by someone 'recently returned from New Zealand' appeared in an Australian weekly in July 1840. It implies that British systems had affected Māori approaches to the punishment of offences by that time, but customary sensitivities are also evident:

> A slave of one of the chiefs having committed a misdemeanor, the chief went to ascertain from the whitemen what would be the English mode of punishment for him. They immediately replied — Oh! give him a dozen lashes. They all, therefore, assembled together, the injured chief being perched on the top of a house crying. The boy was tied, but before they would allow him to be touched the chiefs ordered their different tribes to go away, for that it was not right to see one of their men hurt; he, however, got his twelve lashes, and the feeling manner in which some of those present appeared to be affected, induced me to entertain a favourable opinion of them.[146]

As with so much of the evidence offered by Western observers, there are no clues in the 'recently returned' person's letter as to how serious the misdemeanour was, nor what the rank of the culprit had been prior to becoming a 'slave'. Perhaps he was a rangatira by birth and the 'different tribes' were his own people told to disappear so that his mana was not severely damaged in their eyes? That is pure conjecture, but the sending away of the people was not likely to have related to the contemporary 'English mode of punishment', which was more typically a public event.

It is hard to know what was meant when Richard Davis referred to 'a kind of gentleman slave' who belonged to Kaitara (apparently also known as Hara), but perhaps he, too, was of rangatira birth. Davis wrote that this man, whoever he was, had committed adultery 'with one of his master's many wives', and that Kaitara and his brother spoke to him about the matter, 'in a quiet way'. Not quietly enough, apparently, because the accusation 'roused the slave's anger and indignation to a great pitch'. So much so, that he fastened his cartridge box about him and stomped off down the road with his gun, determined to kill the first animals he came across as utu. Having failed to kill those first animals — some pigs which ran away while he was loading the gun — he shot a missionary's cow instead. On his return to Taiāmai, he announced that he had killed the cow in order to bring the white people's wrath on his master and that, having done so, he was heading off to Mangakāhia to revenge himself more thoroughly at the expense of the rangatira's pigs. Having been told of all this by a messenger, Kaitara was finally wound up enough to track down and kill the recidivist troublemaker. From Davis's point of view, Kaitara and his people had 'hardened their hearts against the Gospel and [were] no doubt becoming more & more wicked'.[147] Yet this 'gentleman slave' not only possessed his own gun and ammunition but had also been effectively getting away with sleeping with the chief's wife, which suggests that some captives could get away with quite a lot of misbehaviour. However, while it may have been that the naughty captive was a man of high rank among his own people and Kaitara may have been slower to rein him in than someone of lesser social standing, it may also be pertinent that this occurred in 1836, after northern leaders had begun setting their captives free. At this stage, Kaitara may not have felt that it was worth spending much time on 'taming' him. As William Yate had said a little earlier, 'some slaves of a bold and daring spirit' had 'thrown off the yoke' and 'assumed an authority which their possessors dared not to repel'.[148] Yate, who wrote that the burden of slavery was a heavy one, does not imply that that boldness and daring was a new thing, merely that some had it hard while others were well treated. Whether those different attitudes were the result of Christian teaching or a more relaxed attitude to captives now that many tribal groups had more than they could profitably use is open to conjecture. However, oral traditions and evidence from earlier times suggest that different attitudes were more likely due to the vagaries of human nature.

As Kaitara's rebellious 'slave' sought to cause trouble for his master, others might seek revenge on a tyrannical or cruel master by taking advantage of their tapu state and their need to have food and water administered by a servant. John White gave as an example the fact that the former could not speak while a servant was pouring water for them to drink and that they would have to indicate when to stop by raising their eyebrows. An annoyed servant might therefore choose to deliberately look away when he thought that the master might wish to indicate a stop to the flow. Spillage was to be avoided due to the tapu state of the water that had come into contact with the rangatira or tohunga's person, so such an 'innocent diversion' could be very inconvenient for the drinker who had to keep drinking![149]

Rights to land and cultivations

So, captives who held a grudge evidently found ways of getting back at their masters or mistresses, but they also had rights under custom law. Raymond Firth was adamant that '[a] Maori slave, not being a member of the tribe, could never possess land, and it is to be doubted if, except in rare instances, he could cultivate for himself a piece of ground allotted to him by his owner'. He denied the claims of William Brown and John Nicholas, who said that 'many of the cookees have ground which they hold by an independent tenure', arguing that the people they were referring to were clearly not slaves.[150] However, Te Whaiti, who gave evidence to the 1838 parliamentary inquiry in Britain under the name Nayti, indicated much as Nicholas did. Moreover, those who found their way back home retained land rights there, too.

Hōri Rōpiha, a Ngāti Kahungunu rangatira from Pōrangahau who visited England in 1884 with King Tāwhiao, was struck by the extraordinary riches of the English lords and the 'awful squalor and poverty of the Taurekarekas, landless men or slaves'. He was reported to have said that the condition of the latter was due to land monopoly.[151] But much earlier, in 1845, Samuel Martin supported the argument of released captives who returned to their original homelands, that their 'loss of liberty did not entail the loss of property'. This sometime newspaper editor, president of the New Zealand Aborigines' Protection Association, magistrate, and fierce opponent of the government, agreed that custom law allowed them to reclaim their rights to tribal lands.[152]

John White also agreed that people of rangatira rank who had been captured might still retain their birthrights to land. He cited the example of a South Island woman who was taken north and became the wife of a Ngāpuhi rangatira. In that case, the people living on her people's land wanted to sell it to a European settler, but the transaction could not take place without the agreement of her son who had been born to a Ngāpuhi chief. The circumstance suggests that the woman had already died when the sale was proposed but a portion of the sale price was duly sent north.

In another example, the capture of a Bay of Plenty rangatira and his subsequent marriage to a northern woman created difficulties for his relatives when they sought to assert their rights to land. They were compelled to offer gifts to his captors' people to procure the return of the man and his son. But while their return confirmed his rights in the Bay of Plenty, his wife and daughters were obliged to remain with the Ngāpuhi people. If they had accompanied the men southward, they would apparently have lost their rights to land in the north, although it is not clear why. White recounted other examples of captives who, having married into their conquerors' tribal groups, retained their birthrights to land. He noted specifically that 'the great-grandchild in the female line has a claim to land'. Māori custom law allowed people who had left their ancestral land to reclaim their rights to it on the basis of 'ahi kaa', or lighted fires, as long as they returned within three generations, so those great-grandchildren would have needed to return within that time. White reported several other cases in which the children of captives, who married into the tribes of their conquerors, acquired land rights as a consequence, although he implies that this may only have been the case when the captives were themselves of rangatira rank.[153] Nevertheless, there is considerable additional evidence to support the view that war captives could be granted the right to cultivate or build homes on particular areas of land. Chief Judge Seth-Smith and Judge Jackson Palmer of the Native Appellate Court accepted that circumstance as a principle of custom law when a case relating to a slave marrying into his owner's tribe came before them in 1905.[154]

The Waitangi Tribunal, a permanent commission of inquiry established to research and report on claims brought by Māori concerning breaches of the Treaty of Waitangi, has considered such matters in more recent times. It found, for example, that those Ngāi Tahu people who had been captured by Ngāti Toa but released during the late 1830s and early 1840s were able to rekindle the fires on their own land because they had returned within a generation. As the Tribunal's report noted, those rights were also supported by the fact that:

they could not be classified as still subject to their former masters because of the Christian ethos as well [as] the assumption of British sovereignty over New Zealand and the fact that all Maori post treaty held British Citizenship.[155]

While the introduction of English law may have complicated things somewhat, in this case, rights were retained under either system of law.

In Māori law, rights of 'ownership', or mana whenua, over land was one thing, but being given the right to use it for a specific purpose was another, and what rights were granted to captives was usually dependent on the interests of the person to whom they owed homage. Pressure from government officials following the Treaty of Waitangi in 1840 appears to have granted some additional rights to slaves under English law, too — at least officially. And there may have been pragmatic reasons for that concession. John White wrote to Native Minister Donald McLean in 1871 recommending that any subsequent legislation include provision for slaves to be granted rights to a portion of their captors' lands for their lifetime. Failure to do so would, he felt, result in a 'lot of poor fellows like Dick Turpin of old living on what they can take from others'.[156] In other words, a return to the days of stray slaves and roaming bandits.

Regardless of what rights captives or slaves may have had to land, it appears that they could assist their masters or mistresses to retain theirs. Evidence given in the Native Land Court implies that people with mana whenua over land they did not occupy could maintain those rights by directing their slaves to cultivate that land thereby satisfying the demands of ahi kaa roa; that is, keeping their rights alive through 'long-burning fires' or continuous occupation. Heremaia Kauere of Ngāti Tū claimed rights on the basis that, after establishing a cultivation on the Waimamaku Block in the Hokianga area, his uncle Te Whata left two slaves to maintain it. Although Te Whata did not return to that land, his slaves 'remained behind and died there', he attested.[157] Ruatara Taurapoko claimed that Pōmare did likewise at Hariru in the Bay of Islands.[158] It is tempting to see those people as having something of a sinecure — a fairly free hand without anyone constantly hovering about but making themselves useful by keeping their masters' rights alive.

One case that came before the Native Land Court in the 1890s concerned a man called Rāpata Te Rou, a captive from Taranaki, whose master granted him land rights on Waiheke Island in the Hauraki Gulf. The question of succession came up at that time because Te Rou had recently died and left no issue. Some contradictory evidence was given as to whose 'slave' he was and who was entitled to succeed to his land rights, but certain points were agreed by the contending claimants. These included the fact that he was taken captive as a child by Waikato but later taken to Waiheke Island by his mistress, and that much later, as an adult, he and other captives from Taranaki had been allowed to return home. Te Rou, and apparently others of that group, had subsequently chosen to leave Taranaki again and return to their erstwhile masters on Waiheke who granted them rights to land in the form of Crown grants.[159] Some ten years later at Paeroa, another court was told that it was contrary to Māori custom law for those who granted land to people without an ancestral right to it to try and take it back. The court appears to have taken the view that if a one-time captive left direct descendants, they would be entitled to succeed unless they had 'permanently severed themselves from the tribe, by taking up their residence in other districts'. Should they have done so, it was decided, they would have forfeited any claim.[160]

However, when success in battle had been followed by occupation of the conquered lands and marriage to women of mana from those lands, the rights of descendants could become more complicated, especially in the era of the Native Land Court. For example, at hearings held between 1898 and 1901 concerning land at Rāwhiti in Northland, Ngāpuhi claimants argued their right to the land on the basis of conquest during the early 1800s. However, two of the Ngāpuhi rangatira, Te Kēmara and Wharerahi, had taken wives from among Ngare Raumati, the group conquered on that occasion. The Ngāpuhi claimants argued that Ngare Raumati had been completely subjugated and, consequently, lost their mana and tapu as leaders as well as any previous administrative role concerning the land. Ngare Raumati, however, claimed that the marriages of Te Kēmara and Wharerahi to the Ngare Raumati women and their living on Ngare Raumati land meant that their fire had not been extinguished. In other words, their rights were still intact.[161]

Refugees and vassalage

Raymond Firth discerned differences of circumstance and status with regard to the relationship between tribal groups, which he described in terms of either vassalage or slavery. He considered that '[t]he institution of vassalage' was of 'no great importance in the economic life of the Maori, save for the tribute which it afforded to the chiefs of the superior tribe'.[162] But it is difficult to understand how this tribute could not have been of very real economic importance.

People defeated in battle were sometimes allowed to remain on their lands as subject tribes. They had been conquered but not enslaved. As Tregear explained it, 'the condition of servitude was more that of a tributary [sic] than of personal service'.[163] The majority of the defeated would be spared, whether men or women, although a few of the more desirable women might be taken as wives by the conquerors. Their kinfolk might be left on their own land but obliged to offer tribute in the form of food, labour, or other produce as a reminder of their subjugation and to give the victors an economic boost. Vassal tribes also had obligations to support their conquerors in battle if and when called on to do so. Failure to oblige was likely to worsen their position.

That there were distinctions between different states of vassalage is indicated by a variety of different terms. For example, one of Elsdon Best's informants told him that the term 'awhenga' 'was applied to people saved from an enemy out of a kind of pitying contempt':

> Should the Pu-taewa of Te Whaiti be defeated in war, and the survivors fly to us for refuge, and we give them shelter — that would be an *awhenga* because they are not our friends, although we have saved them. There is a certain amount of degradation in the term. If we assisted friends in that manner, it would be termed *awhina*, not *awhenga*. Awhina means "to befriend," whereas awe [sic: awhe?] signifies "to gather in a heap."[164]

'Pori' also refers to a subservient tribe, people, or dependants, as does 'rahi'.[165] Ngāti Hauā's Wiremu Tāmihana Tarapīpipi said that rahi was 'applied to a tribe reduced to a dependant condition by a conquering tribe'. He went on to say that their lands were held by right of conquest, 'that

FIGURE 17. An 1844 portrait of Toea, daughter of Te Awaitaia, by George French Angas, who explained that 'the boy is an attendant, the son of an individual of inferior rank' and that both Toea and the young boy were members of Ngāti Mahanga, which implies that he was not a captive but born into the tribe. *George French Angas,* The New Zealanders Illustrated, *London, 1847: PUBL-0014-54, Alexander Turnbull Library, Wellington*

FIGURE 18. Portrait of Nga Waka Te Karaka and 'attendant', by George French Angas, c. 1852. Again the status of the attendant is ambiguous. The boy, who appears to be wearing a high-quality cloak, may well have been a free-born member of Nga Waka Te Karaka's tribal group. Alternatively, he might have been designated 'attendant' because Nga Waka Te Karaka was Christian and assumed not to have any slaves. *C-114-005, Alexander Turnbull Library, Wellington*

FIGURE 19. Whatever their original status, the dress and demeanour of the two 'attendants' on the previous page are much brighter than the subject of this 'Portrait of an aged slave woman, at Pouketouto, in the interior, beyond Mokau [Waitomo]', which is also by Angas. Taken together, they suggest very different circumstances and positions in society. *'Implements and domestic economy', George French Angas,* The New Zealanders Illustrated, *London, 1847: PUBL-0014-55, Alexander Turnbull Library, Wellington*

FIGURE 20. Portrait of three young Māori women, c. 1827–28. 'The older two were about 25 years of age; the third, Hepee, was a 13-year-old girl, one of Amoko's slaves. Amoko was the daughter of one of the chiefs living on the Mongo-Mongo River.' *Augustus Earle, Sketches Illustrative of the Native Inhabitants and Islands of New Zealand, London, 1838: PUBL-0015-010-a, Alexander Turnbull Library, Wellington*

FIGURE 21. 'Old Mihaka', the slave Te Rauparaha left behind when retreating from Kāwhia. *V. S. Jackson letter to Miss Wilton: [c. 1919?], MS Papers-1052, Alexander Turnbull Library, Wellington*

FIGURE 22. 'Reko's Slave girl, Tuturau', by John Turnbull Thomson, 1856. *Hocken Pictorial Collection, Hocken Library, Dunedin*

FIGURE 23. Heaphy, Brunner and Fox held Hone Mokehakeha (also known as Hone Mokekehu or Kehu) in much higher regard than their other bearer, the ugly and dull-witted Tau. William Fox painted Kehu snaring a weka (woodhen) in 1846. *'In the Aglionby or Matukituki Valley, looking into the Otapawa. 20th Feb. [1846]': B-113-008, Alexander Turnbull Library, Wellington*

FIGURE 24. Richard Taylor drew this sketch at Taiāmai, inland from the Bay of Islands, showing how a chiefly dwelling with a pitched roof was fenced off from the cooking shed on the right. *'Titari's house and cooking place at Taiamai, August 20 1841', Sketchbook, 1835–1860: E-296-q-025-3, Alexander Turnbull Library, Wellington*

FIGURE 25. A scene at Kororāreka, 1827–28, showing four slaves pounding fern root. One appears to be a woman but three are men. *'Slaves preparing food', from Augustus Earle, Sketches Illustrative of the Native Inhabitants and Islands of New Zealand, London, 1838: PUBL-0015-03, Alexander Turnbull Library, Wellington*

FIGURE 26. This scene of a courtyard in Pipitea pā in 1842 also shows a man pounding fern root. *William Mein Smith, from illustrations to Edward Jerningham Wakefield,* Adventure in New Zealand, from 1839 to 1844, *London, 1845: PUBL-0011-04-1, Alexander Turnbull Library, Wellington*

FIGURES 27 AND 28. This 'aged woman of Te Mutu making a basket of the leaves of the tawara', whom Angas described as 'reduced almost to a skeleton', may or may not have been a captive. Everyday items such as these could be made in the open, but it was important that fine weaving was done under shelter. The women working beneath the shelter of the porch (below right) were likely to have been free women of status. *'Interior of a house at Rangihaeata's pa at Porirua, with women engaged in manufacturing flax garments', 'Domestic sketches', from George French Angas,* The New Zealanders Illustrated, *London, 1847: PUBL-0014-59, Alexander Turnbull Library, Wellington*

FIGURE 29. Portrait of Tuai, painted during his visit to England. *James Barry, 'Tooi, a New Zealand chief', October 1818: G-608, Alexander Turnbull Library, Wellington*

FIGURE 30. A man and a woman under tapu being fed by others. *Louis Auguste de Sainson, 'Personnages taboues', twelve engravings from Dumont d'Urville,* Voyage pittoresque autour du monde, *Paris, 1839: A-433-017, Alexander Turnbull Library, Wellington*

FIGURE 31. This tohunga is being fed by a child because his tapu was such that he could not touch food himself. *Gottfried Lindauer, 'Tohunga Under Tapu', c. 1902: Accession No: 1915/2/50, Auckland Art Gallery Toi o Tāmaki*

is lands fallen to the brave (*kua riro i te toa*)'. However, Tāmihana also indicated that the reduction in their status would not occur until they had been defeated more than once, perhaps three times:

> till at last the tribe becomes small, and is reduced to a mean condition. It is then made to do the work of dependants — to cultivate the land for food, to catch eels, and to carry wood. In short, its men are treated as slaves.

In such cases, he said, 'their land passes into the possession of the tribe whose valour conquered them' and they would not consider 'striving against their masters; because their power to fight has gone from them':

> They were not brave enough to hold possession of their land, and although they may grow numerous afterwards, they will not seek for a payment for their former losses; for they are fearful, and say among themselves, "Don't let us strive with this tribe, lest we perish altogether, for it is a brave tribe."

However, as Edward Shortland pointed out:

> Thompson [Tāmihana] belonged to a victorious tribe; his sentiments therefore have a natural bias in favour of the sole right to the lands of the conquered tribe being with their conquerors. If, however, a member of the conquered tribe were to be consulted on this point, we should learn that he had not abandoned all idea of a right in the lands he had been allowed to retain, and was then occupying.[166]

Those remarks highlight the problem of evidence given to Europeans looking for customary rights and procedures with a view to how Crown grants under the British system should be allocated.

The condition of vassalage, in any form, was not tolerated happily and was one that the conquered would try to cast off at the earliest opportunity. Thomas Gudgeon referred to the reaction of the Ngāti Ruanuku and Wāhineiti people who, having been defeated by Tūwhakairiora, were required to give him presents of food, such as birds and rats.[167] Although unable to avoid those obligations, they were not carried out meekly. According to Gudgeon, they remained defiant, carrying the food 'on the points of their spears and in this fashion laid the birds, &c.' before Tūwhakairiora who eventually 'took the hint and released them from their state of vassalage'. Ngāti Ira were said to have been similarly defiant when living under the mana of Toko-rākau.[168] Rather than sit submissively under the domination of others, defeated groups could, over time, regain enough strength and confidence to recover the mana over their lands. That was why, in the era of Westerners buying land for cash or goods, 'vassal' tribes frequently resisted the right of the conquerors to sell what they considered to be still their rights over it.[169]

As with land, so, too, could the conquest of one tribe over another result in a transfer of mana over the losing tribe's vassals from their first conqueror to the next. For example, in the wake of the wars of the 1820s, people from Ngāti Tūmatakōkiri and Ngāti Wairangi, previously captured by Ngāti Apa, Ngāti Kuia, and Rangitāne in the Nelson-Marlborough region and by Ngāi Tahu in other areas of the South Island, found themselves under the mana of chiefs from Kāwhia and Taranaki when their conquerors were themselves worsted. So it was that Eruera Te Wata Pakoko, also known as Eruera Puhiohio, was first captured by Ngāti Apa when they conquered his Ngāti Tūmatakōkiri people, but subsequently became the personal attendant of Hōhepa Tāmaihengia of Ngāti Toa. Kehu, who acted as guide, bearer, and weka-catcher for Charles Heaphy and other explorers (fig. 23), was passed around in much the same way. He had been captured around 1810 by Ngāi Tahu when he was about twelve years old but was later transferred to Motueka by Ngāti Rārua.[170]

Those unable to remain on their own land, through defeat or their inability to defend themselves, might take shelter in the domains of others. The mana of their rangatira might remain intact and they might retain their position as leaders of their people, but their status as refugees would render them subservient to those who gave them shelter. Under such circumstances, the situation would be expected to benefit both parties.

The final insult

In 1839, when the New Zealand Company vessel the *Tory* arrived at Wellington to buy land (the background to which will be discussed more fully in Chapter 6), agreement appeared to have been reached with Te Wharepōuri and his cousin Te Puni-kōkopu regarding the purchase of six areas or settlements in the district. Te Wharepōuri had favoured the sale of land, assuming that it would bring settlers, economic opportunities, and advantages in terms of defence to the region. He told the Company's agent Edward Jenningham Wakefield that Te Aro was a 'slave settlement' and the people a 'tributary tribe':

> *Warepori* himself took charge of the portion assigned to his immediate followers at *Nga hauranga*, and dispatched a share which had been made purposely smaller to the pa *Te Aro*, the most southerly of the settlements, where a tributary tribe, called the *Taranaki*, had their habitation.[171]

However, they did not have the right to sell the land at Te Aro, and Te Wharepōuri was obliged to explain to the inhabitants why they had received a disproportionately smaller portion of the purchase goods. It was because 'the free settlements had required a large proportion', he told them. Then, in order to try and 'sell' the sale to the people of Te Aro:

> He dwelt on the promotion in caste which they would by this means obtain, as "each man that fell would now be buried with his musket and cartouch-box, and be mourned over as a warrior that died with his arms in his hands".[172]

Not surprisingly, the people of Te Aro were less than satisfied by the posthumous elevation of status he proposed.

What this alludes to, however, is the difference in burial arrangements according to the rank of the deceased. As in Britain, where the rich and powerful might have grand memorials while others suffered a pauper's grave, so did Māori funerary arrangements relate to rank. In the case of individual war captives, the disposal of their body was usually the final insult to their mana, differing greatly from that of the rangatira. The bodies of people of rank were treated with very great respect and care. Customs varied from place to place and from tribal group to tribal group, but a common practice was described by Elsdon Best. He explained that the knees would be drawn up until they touched the body, then held in that position by a cord passed around both. The deceased were then covered with superior garments; their hair combed, oiled, and arranged, and probably adorned with feathers. The face might be smeared with kōkōwai and jewellery placed around the neck or in the ears in preparation for lying in state. Weapons, carved items of pounamu, or other treasures might also be laid with them at this time and when taken to their final resting place.[173] Far less consideration was given to captives and others from the bottom of the social heap. Polack confirmed, perhaps not surprisingly, that: 'Slaves who die by disease are seldom devoured, but hastily flung either into the sea or a hole, where the dogs often feed upon the remains.'[174] Richard Taylor recorded a very similar attitude, saying:

> [A]s for poor slaves, little thought was bestowed upon them; they were buried or not, according to circumstances. If the corpse laid in a spot where it was not offensive to the living, there it was left; if otherwise, a hole was dug, and it was thrown into it.[175]

Curiously, though, the Wesleyan missionary Nathaniel Turner understood that 'slaves' retained a presence even in death. Māori believed that when someone died, their left eye became a star, and it seems such immortality was not denied to anyone. The brightest stars may have been those of the great, but war captives still shone in the sky, albeit more dimly.[176]

Samuel Martin probably summed up the New Zealand situation when he wrote that:

> With the exception of the insecurity of life, the slaves in New Zealand have been, and are now, at least better treated than in any other part of the world — enjoying both a larger amount of freedom, as well as the right of property. It is true that they work for their master, but they are at the same time permitted to cultivate provisions for themselves, which they may either use or sell, at their own discretion.

Records left to us imply that it was the old, the ill, and the weak or otherwise problematic for the community who tended to lead the unhappiest lives and suffer the most miserable deaths.[177]

CHAPTER FOUR

The value of captives and the impact of muskets

I T IS LOGICAL TO ASSUME THAT WAR CAPTIVES WITH THE MOST value to their captors would enjoy the best quality of life. So, at this point, we should perhaps look back to much earlier times, when captive taking was less prevalent than during the 1820s. It is probable that warfare had occurred from the time that the ancestors of the Māori first arrived in New Zealand and it has been suggested that, in that early or Archaic Period, it was more likely motivated by the possibility of gaining mana.[1] But, from around 1500 AD when the supply of indigenous animal food had diminished, warfare is more evident.[2] Overhunting saw the moa (a giant flightless bird) head for extinction and seal numbers seriously depleted. With the decline of those food resources, fishing and the gathering of other marine and riverine resources increased in importance, as did horticulture. Those factors, along with some dramatic climate changes, are thought to have resulted in significant population movements and competition for good horticultural land. And with human survival at stake, competition could turn hostile. So this was the era of pā building (the establishment of fortified settlements), the clearer marking out of territory, and identification of mana over resources. Those circumstances gave rise to new motivations for warfare with strong leadership all the more vital.

As the power to defend and manage crucial resources came from and was dependent on mana, so was mana supported by tapu. So, as it became increasingly important to protect the tapu of tribal leaders, it would follow that the need for war captives to undertake duties destructive of tapu would increase at the same time. And more prevalent warfare would also have provided more opportunities for taking captives to boost the labour force.

Building pā and their associated earthworks required an enormous effort in terms of manual labour. But other major engineering exercises were also undertaken to increase productivity and expand resources as populations grew. For example, in Northland, Marlborough, and probably elsewhere, significant networks of channels, variously referred to as canals or drains, are believed to have facilitated the harvest of riverine and marine life, including fish, eels, and waterfowl, as well as draining land for further cultivation. Digging those channels with kō, or wooden spades, was an enormous expenditure of labour, but then the spoil had to be removed as well. As in most societies around the world, that sort of heavy labour seems to have fallen primarily on the lowliest members of the community.[3] So the economic and social pressures to improve productivity appear to have very conveniently facilitated the emergence of leaders with the mana and labour forces necessary for these and other large-scale projects, such as preparing deforested lands for cultivation.[4]

Utu

The demand for labour that could be met by acquiring captives would have ebbed and flowed in different times and different places, and the spiritual value of captives may have been more important when times were most dire. Rangatira of mana wielded powerful spiritual as well as physical forces that not only controlled but also protected those under their leadership. However, because threats to their mana could come from many sources, utu was an essential means of protecting and maintaining it.[5]

Tensions raised by the pressure of population on previously abundant resources may have created a climate in which warfare flourished, but custom law still required assaults to have just cause. Utu, often translated as revenge, provided that cause, but because its key purpose was to restore balance, it was important not to go too far in taking revenge or seeking compensation for wrongs. The level of compensation was typically measured against the seriousness of the offence. It was not tika, or correct, to take too heavy a retribution. When positive utu was required to restore balance (following receipt of a gift, for example), it was equally important not to be so generous that the receiver of largesse would be unable to respond sufficiently. If a chief or his tribe wanted to damage the mana of another, it could be done just as effectively by overwhelming them with gifts or hospitality they could not reciprocate.

So responses were usually made with caution, and non-violent means of resolving conflicts were preferred. Muru, a form of ritual plunder or process of restorative justice, was one method of obtaining utu and tended to be the preferred option when close relations were involved. But when such systems failed to satisfy, human sacrifice or warfare might be unavoidable. Even in those situations, however, pre-emptive peacemaking could take the heat out of a hostile situation. Rangatira captives might be escorted home ceremonially with gifts as part of such initiatives. Land Court minutes record that they were sometimes 'whakarangatira'd', meaning that they had their former rank and status formally reinstated. This may have been a long-established process, but was probably occurring on an unprecedented scale by 1845.[6]

Utu is different from Western legal systems, and some customary responses to misfortune can seem unjust to non-Māori. For example, when a Te Whānau-ā-Apanui rangatira who had joined his tribe's Whakatōhea allies was killed fighting the people of Whakatāne, his people sought utu, not from Whakatāne but Whakatōhea, because it was their appeal for support that led to his death.[7] Similarly, when a chiefly woman was killed by a fall from a horse, it was the horse that paid the ultimate price.[8] Other responses strike Westerners, who privilege individual responsibility, as abhorrent. But in communal societies, responsibility is communal, the blame and penalty falling to all members of the culprit's group as the loss of mana impacts on all members of the victim's. The greater the mana of the victim, the greater the loss to the group. Māori law did not distinguish between injury and mere harm either. Whether the hurt was deliberate or inadvertent, utu was required. As one man explained with regard to pre-Christian times, it was customary 'to kill someone in revenge for the death of a relative, and provided that someone was killed it did not matter whether the person who committed the crime or others suffered for it'.[9] Because the culprit's people would want to avoid sacrificing one of their own, they might prefer to substitute a surrogate, and a captive from another tribe could fit the bill. But a life for a life was not necessarily sufficient either. Several captive deaths might be necessary to restore balance following the loss of a person of rank.

Captive taking before muskets

Oral traditions refer to rangatira men and women having slaves or attendants, but although the circumstances of pā building and warfare over the most desirable land suggest that reasonable numbers of captives might have been an advantage, the numbers taken were probably not great in those times. Until the late 1810s, vanquished enemies appear to have been more often killed than taken away as captives. Comments left by members of early expeditions led by Captains James Cook and Marion du Fresne between 1769 and 1772 tend to support that view. Joseph Banks, for example, thought that Māori rarely took prisoners, saying:

> The dispositions of Both Sexes seems mild, gentle, and very affectionate to each other but implacable towards their enemies, who after having killd they eat, probably out of a princ[i]ple of revenge, and I beleive never give quarter or take prisoners [sic].[10]

First Lieutenant Le Dez of du Fresne's ship *Marquis de Castries* reported from the Bay of Islands that he thought Māori warfare must be cruel, because he and his fellow crewmen had seen 'neither slaves nor any signs of slavery'.[11] In other words, he assumed that enemies were slaughtered. So if slavery existed in the various Māori communities they visited, it cannot have been highly visible. Ensign Lottin, who visited in 1824 — after the musket had made an impact on warfare — had a very jaundiced view of Māori. He called them ferocious cannibals prone to total destruction, but mentioned that only women and children were taken into slavery. '[M]en are devoured', he said.[12] Ngāpuhi's Rewa told John Butler that little boys might be spared, and brought up 'as slaves' so 'as they grew they would have neither knowledge of their father or mother, or any enmity against them'.[13]

It seems safe to assume that prior to the 1810s, only a modest number of captives were taken and that these were most often women and children rather than men.[14] A preference for women and children could pose something of a puzzle if performing heavy labour was a key role, but major engineering projects were not a constant and women typically carried out much of the agricultural and load-bearing work anyway. Besides, as Firth pointed out, captives were not forced to perform excessive labour. They may have performed 'the heavy *tapu*-less tasks' but were 'saved from participation in other work, such as canoe-making, because of its *tapu*'.[15] However, if captives once constituted a smaller proportion of Māori communities, a new phase was looming.

Captive taking becomes more efficient

Changing economic conditions and the advent of the musket appear to have been responsible for a dramatic growth, not only in the extent of intertribal warfare, but also in the numbers of captives taken. Western ships were visiting New Zealand and purchasing cargoes of pigs and potatoes from 1803, if not earlier, and Māori leaders were keen to take full advantage of these new trading opportunities.[16] And those opportunities received a massive boost with the arrival of the first missionaries in the Bay of Islands in 1814.

Since 1805, the mission's first patron, Ruatara, had made some determined but frustrated attempts to reach England and meet King George III. He finally reached the River Thames in 1809 but his hope of meeting the King was thwarted when he was not allowed to leave the ship. Ruatara had been subjected to fraud, abandonment, and beatings during his five years at sea and was ill, vomiting blood from beatings, as he began his journey back to Australia that year aboard the convict ship *Ann*. Fortunately for him, Samuel Marsden, Chaplain of New South Wales, was also on board and ensured that he was looked after for the rest of the journey. Ruatara subsequently lived with Marsden at his seminary in Parramatta near Sydney. During his stay he studied agriculture and learned about Christianity, eventually inviting Marsden to establish the Church Missionary Society in his territory in the Bay of Islands. Having made preparations for their arrival, Ruatara accompanied Marsden to New Zealand, together with Hongi Hika, Korokoro, and other Bay of Islands leaders. Their party arrived on 23 December 1814 aboard the *Active* with the first missionaries, Thomas Kendall, William Hall, and John King, their wives and children, and three tradesmen. They anchored near Rangihoua, on the northern side of the Bay, where the first mission would be established.[17]

When Ruatara died shortly after their arrival, Hongi took over the role of the mission's patron. Knowing that a reputation for peace and security would encourage traders, he continued to defend the missionaries as well as Western traders and seamen, but determinedly contained their activities within his territory. Hongi and many other tribal leaders had expected the mission's presence would bring more shipping and more trade to areas under their mana or control — and they were right. Trading ships felt safer coming to a place with a Christian presence and English-speaking residents who could advise them on local customs and conditions. They could also tell them who to approach with regard to products they wanted to purchase. That might be spars, timber, or flax to take to other markets, or food and water to restock their vessels. The location of the first mission at Rangihoua was not well suited to missionary needs, though, so others were soon established at Kerikeri in 1819, Paihia in 1823, and gradually further afield.[18]

As patrons of the first missions, the Bay of Islands people gained an early monopoly on foreign trade and grew wealthy in terms of access to processed foods and manufactured items from Europe and elsewhere. It was that trade advantage that allowed Hongi's people to acquire muskets ahead of those in other areas. A visit to England in 1820 saw him return home with an even more substantially increased armoury and strengthened his political position still further. That massive military advantage meant Hongi was well ahead of the pack as the arms race began in earnest during an unprecedented period of warfare lasting over ten years. Initially motivated by the need to secure utu for the defeat of his Ngāpuhi people by Ngāti Whātua at the battle of Moremonui, Maunganui Bluff, in the first decade of the nineteenth century, his military predominance and effective control of the musket trade enabled him to take utu for a number of other unavenged injuries and acquire enormous numbers of captives in the process. In what became a vicious circle for his enemies, those captives were taken to his domains and put to work producing goods that enabled him to buy yet more muskets and further increase his power.

Acquiring a supply of muskets required access to foreign traders on one hand but a large supply of goods they were keen to buy on the other. One in-demand product was the white potato. They were particularly sought after by visiting ships for their good keeping qualities and the scurvy-fighting attributes of their vitamin C content. Consequently, tribes in the northern areas, where foreign ships most often called, expanded their potato gardens exponentially. Marsden estimated that the area of land under cultivation had increased tenfold in the Bay of Islands district between the time of the missionaries' arrival in December 1814 and September 1819.[19] Captive labour went a long way towards achieving this massive and ongoing expansion.

Naturally, those areas with good supplies of muskets were able to increase the number of captives brought to their region significantly. There are also suggestions that some military assaults, or taua muru, were undertaken primarily for the purpose of acquiring captives.[20] At a time when the demand for muskets was at its peak, the productive capacity of captive labour put those tribes able to take large numbers of prisoners in the strongest position. It was very much a case of the rich getting richer as Hongi expanded his potato production in order to buy more muskets, tools, and other manufactured items. His wealth and his arsenal (not to mention the suit of armour given to him in England by King George IV) gave him an aura of invincibility and struck fear into the hearts of tribes throughout the country.

Further south, at Kāpiti Island, Ngāti Toa's Te Rauparaha is reported as having some 2000 captives. According to his son Tāmihana, members of their immediate family had between 30 and 200 slaves each.[21] Muskets were the key to his success, too. As one Taranaki man put it, his people were 'opehia taewatia', or gathered up like crops of potatoes.[22] Gathered up like potatoes to grow more potatoes, but especially to dress flax for sale as the raw material for cordage. Ropes and rigging were very much in demand by Western sailing ships, so this production provided Te Rauparaha with the wherewithal to obtain muskets and powder, or tobacco and rum, as the mood took him. As was the case with Hongi, captives not only augmented his labour force to an unprecedented extent but also freed up their own able-bodied men for other activities including more warfare.

The contribution of individual warriors was taken into account when new captives were allocated following a successful military expedition. That was evident in 1823, when John King recorded that a man from Rangiu (Rangihoua?), who had not engaged in military action since the mission was established some eight years earlier, was about to depart with a war party. Feeling that he was no longer in a fit state to fight, King asked why he was going. The man replied that he preferred not to 'but his neighbours told him if he went not — when they came back — they would take his mats — break his canoes & set on fire his Huts'. They argued that since the man had previously enjoyed the benefit of captive labour on his cultivations, he should continue contributing to the acquisition of this involuntary labour force or do without such assistance in the future. King added that this man 'had no slaves but what he bought & paid for'.[23] That may have been the interpretation of a European with an individualistic mindset, because it was the leader of a war expedition who had the right to distribute the captives taken. And he did so with regard to the strength of the force they brought to the field and the degree of their tribal group's involvement with the 'take', or cause, of the fight. Any 'buying' or 'selling' of captives would have occurred subsequent to that initial distribution. Nevertheless, the practice reinforces the idea that captives were not merely an economic asset but also a reward for helping to acquire them and why a large number of captives enhanced an individual's mana.[24]

Hongi's military expeditions did not expand his territories. He took captives north to his domains but did not occupy the lands of the defeated. Te Rauparaha's approach was somewhat different. The Ngāti Toa leader often left people on their own land as vassals. So when Rangitāne were heavily defeated in 1828, the year that the flax trade really took off,[25] (their rangatira Te Ruaoneone had foolishly threatened to pulp Te Rauparaha's head with a fern-root pounder), he left them on their lands to provide food and dressed flax he could trade for more muskets.[26] However, the Ngāti Toa leader took other captives back to Kāpiti to prepare flax on the spot for sale to ships. To use the words of one of John White's informants (in translation): 'Rau-paraha came back to Kapiti with his slaves, so that he might tame them here at his own place.'[27]

Muskets not only allowed the victors to round up large numbers of captives but also to take them back home more easily: whether on foot overland or by water in canoes. But even with the benefit of guns, simpler, probably customary, systems were still employed. Sometimes, prisoners had their hands tied behind their backs and ropes placed around their necks so they could be led like horses.[28] Others might be fenced in with stakes (as dogs once were, apparently). Following a joint Ngāpuhi/Ngāti Toa raid into the Wairarapa during 1819–20, the male prisoners, who had been corralled that way, managed to escape by digging a hole under the fence.[29] Women were obliged to scrape flax and make it into ropes that were plaited into their hair to tether them together while they were marched off to their new home with one of their captors holding the rope. Those ropes would be tied to their captors' arms while they slept, intended to ensure that the prisoners could not escape unnoticed.[30] On this occasion, though, the women also managed to escape by cutting through the cords with shells. Elsdon Best related a story from Māori mythology about a taniwha (supernatural creature) who kidnapped a woman and forced her to live with him as his wife. Fearing that she would run away, he plaited a long rope into her hair, keeping hold of the other end whenever he went to bathe, or she left their home. This reluctant 'wife' also managed to make her escape by cutting the rope with a shell one day when she was meant to be fetching water.[31] Perhaps the Wairarapa women remembered that story?

Trading ships visiting Northland as well as other coastal ports were keen buyers of Māori dressed flax, especially during the 1830s, but for Hongi and others the white potato was a very important trade good. They were being sold by the ton by 1803.[32] The interconnection between potatoes and muskets led James Belich to suggest that the popular term 'Musket Wars' might be more accurately termed 'Potato Wars'. He was referring to the fact that, as well as providing a more reliable food supply and trade good, white potatoes were hardier than kūmara, the previous staple carbohydrate, and had a better ratio of output to labour which freed up warriors for more and longer campaigns.[33] However, the introduction of this new crop also affected Māori patterns of production and brought about significant changes in the roles assigned to various sections of society. Spiritual restrictions relating to the cultivation of the kūmara excluded captives and women from planting and harvesting. But, as a newly introduced crop, white potatoes were subject to a much lesser degree of tapu, which meant that more of the work could be carried out by anyone.[34]

When Marsden attempted to impart Christian and other Western values to a group of Kawakawa rangatira, one agreed that it was better to have just one wife, 'for, where there were many, the women always quarrelled'. However, others remarked that their wives made the best overseers, ensuring the efficient cultivation of their lands, so having several wives made better business sense (see fig. 42).[35] According to Marsden, the considerable increase in Northland's productive capacity was 'wholly owing to the tools of agriculture which [had] been sent out from time to time by the Church Missionary Society'.[36] But the availability of captive labour, which could be overseen by local women, was surely a significant factor in that increase, too. It was Marsden who reported that Hongi had acquired 2000 captives in the course of just one expedition the previous year. Moreover, the increasing numbers of ship visits to the Bay of Islands — which rose from two in 1813 to eleven in 1819 and 25 in 1820[37] — increased access to agricultural and other metal tools from other sources as well.[38] The availability of war captives as a labour force not only freed tribal leaders to stay away from their communities for longer periods and to undertake longer, more distant military expeditions, but also to devote more time to trading activities when they were home.

Their negotiating skills were essential to the success they enjoyed marketing products such as pigs, potatoes, dressed flax, and timber to foreign buyers. Timber was one of the trades managed by chiefly entrepreneurs, but captive labour was useful in that industry, too, especially for heavy work like dragging spars to waiting vessels.[39]

Tribal groups without either muskets or a large body of captive labourers, but anxious, especially for the former, needed to find other ways of protecting themselves as well as increasing production. Agreeing terms with neighbours, even erstwhile enemies, could prove mutually beneficial. Ngāi Te Rangi, who had seized the flax-rich area of Maketū in the Bay of Plenty from Te Arawa about a century earlier, took that approach in 1830. They had acquired a much sought-after trader but lacked sufficient people to dress the large quantities they now had the opportunity to sell. An invitation to the Arawa people at Rotorua to return to Maketū and share in the proceeds of their sales resolved the problem.[40] It was a win-win situation for both parties.

In accordance with the laws of supply and demand (or demand and supply) there can be little doubt that captive taking increased dramatically from the late 1810s when their usefulness was at a peak. Warfare and captive taking on the scale attributed to Hongi and Te Rauparaha, for example, could not have been feasible in earlier, musket-less times. All of which means that the evidence of people whose experience was of those years of unprecedented warfare cannot be taken as typical of earlier times.

Increased opportunities for trade increased the economic value of captives and, possibly, engendered a greater respect for them as individuals. Punishments, which may have been particularly severe in the 1820s, appear to have declined in the 1830s, as did the chance of being killed for ritual purposes.

Captives as trade items

It is often said that Māori did not buy or sell slaves, but while there was no slave market as such, there were circumstances, even in earlier times, when they might be gifted or exchanged by way of trade, ransom, or compensation. Oral tradition refers to the practice of gifting. An example occurs in one version of the story of the ancestor god Tāwhaki who went in search of his daughter. She had been taken up to the heavens by her mother who hailed from the celestial realms, but on his journey to find them he came across a blind old lady, his grandmother Matakerepō. It was she who showed him the pathway to his daughter, so he gave her his attendant as a token of his gratitude.[41] But the practice was not restricted to mythology. William Yate, who worked in New Zealand from 1826 to 1834, wrote that:

> Transferring the services from one master to another, is a matter of frequent occurrence amongst the natives; for which an equivalent is given and received, and the bondsman's former master has no more claim upon him.[42]

Yate's view that such exchanges were considered permanent appears to have applied when both parties were Māori but, as examples in Chapter 6 will note, different rules may have been applied to Pākehā 'buyers'.

Still later in the nineteenth century, historian John White agreed that captives could be exchanged or bartered in 'older times' when the price of one might have been a mako, or shark.[43] His view is supported by remarks from one of the first Europeans to touch on New Zealand shores. At Doubtless Bay in December 1769, one of the first points of contact between Māori and European, the Frenchman Guillaume Labé aboard the *St Jean Baptiste* reported that: 'They know what slaves are because they offered to sell some to the captain and even to the soldiers in exchange for pieces of cotton cloth.' The offer may not have been understood by the French as the Māori intended, but the remark does suggest that captives were thought of in terms of commodities and potentially available to be traded. In this case, the French opted not to make a purchase 'for fear of desertions'. The extent to which more regular European and American contact or conditions resulting from the 'musket wars' may have seen captives being offered for sale to foreigners more frequently is difficult to assess but visiting ships were approached. Victor Charles Lottin reported a man attempting to sell a young boy for a double-barrelled musket when Dumont d'Urville's corvette *Coquille* visited the Bay of Islands in 1824.[44] Missionaries and others also referred to tribes from further south taking captives north to trade them for the muskets and ammunition that Ngāpuhi in particular had in greater abundance.⁴⁵ There can be little doubt that captives were a saleable commodity during the 'musket wars' arms race.

Like other commodities, the price of captives rose and fell with demand. Polack claimed that while a small hatchet would have purchased three or four in 1814, one was worth 30 times that amount in the Bay of Islands twenty years later.⁴⁶ His suggestion of peak prices in the mid-1830s may be doubtful as this was when many were being released, probably surplus to requirements at that time. However, as warfare reached unprecedented levels through the 1820s, the survival of tribal groups was dependent on access to muskets, and trading captives along with other goods was one way that communities living away from the coastal areas favoured by Western ships could access manufactured goods, including muskets. Teretere, or trading parties, with supplies of captives or specialty products such as woven cloaks called at the Bay of Islands or places in the far south where sealers were known to have congregated. However, because only the local people, or tangata whenua, had the rights to control activities in their anchorages, all trade had to be conducted through them rather than directly with the shipping.⁴⁷

When Elsdon Best reported that Ngāi Tūhoe had bartered captives for muskets, he implied that it was not typical of earlier practice. The suggestion seems to be that they were driven to it by the need to defend themselves at a time when those tribes armed with muskets had a frightening advantage. Fortunately for Tūhoe, who lived well away from harbours visited by overseas shipping, they had connections with Ngāti Maru who, thanks to the many European traders who visited their area in the Hauraki Gulf, were well stocked with arms and ammunition. A problem remained, though: Tūhoe lacked suitable trade goods to exchange for weapons. They 'had practically no flax-growing country' and very few pigs, the most in-demand trade items. However, they did have a good supply of captives, with the added advantage that they could be walked to Hauraki much more readily than other goods. Those luckless people had been unfortunate enough to have been captured during fighting with Ngāti Kōtore and Ngāti Kahungunu as well as at Hauturu pā, Poverty Bay. Best understood that ten of them were paid for the first musket they acquired. That musket was named Te Riaki, which indicates its importance and would have given it the potential attributes of mana.[48] However, the price of muskets in Northland subsequently fell in terms of pigs and flax, dropping first to five captives, then to one. Overall, though, Tūhoe's expedition was successful. Through their Ngāti Maru friends, they gained twenty muskets, six kegs of powder, and a supply of lead for making bullets.[49]

By the time London-born merchant John Israel Montefiore claimed to 'have seen a full-grown woman bought for a shark's tooth!' in the 1830s (which is at odds with Polack's claim about high prices that decade), muskets were well and truly distributed around the country, so whether this was a simple economic transaction could be doubtful.[50] Since captives were already being released by this time, the shark's tooth may have been a mere token to conclude an exchange that was convenient for all the parties.

However, barter was not the only way by which commodities might be exchanged. Taua muru was another. Often referred to as 'plundering raids', they were one means of obtaining utu, or compensation, for wrongs without resorting to warfare. Hostile expeditions would remove or destroy property (the consequence John King's reluctant warrior from Rangihoua had been threatened with), thereby wiping out the offence and restoring the balance of mana. Although taua muru were generally designed to avoid bloodshed, 'slaves' did not enjoy the same protection as free people and might be removed by the plundering party along with crops, canoes, and other goods. If caught, they could be 'destroyed in the same spirit that houses were burnt'. Therefore, the deliberate killing of slaves by anyone other than their own masters or mistresses might warrant retaliation, but in much the same way as damage to other possessions or livestock as opposed to the murder of kin.[51]

So it was when one of Tītore's slaves was found dead on the Kerikeri road in 1836. One of the two men accused of the murder was a member of Richard Davis's congregation. The missionary rose to their defence, claiming that there was no clear evidence against them, and urged their accusers to 'act with caution and deliberation'. Perhaps anxious to protect a convert, Davis suggested that the victim may have died as a result of inclement weather. But the locals did not buy that idea, so, with the offended party 'in an uproar', Tītore sent another slave with a very inflammatory message on the subject.[52] Unfortunately, Davis neglected to record the final outcome or fate of the accused.

In some cases, captives redeemed by missionaries were returned to their kinfolk, but more often, perhaps, they were employed as servants on the mission stations — which naturally involved ongoing costs. Squirming under significant pressure and threats from Hongi Hika in 1824, Davis lamented that he was unable to purchase a slave from their patron because the mission's food supplies could not bear the strain of another mouth to feed.[53] This was when food supplies were being strictly rationed, so even the gun- and captive-wealthy like Hongi were offering to sell their excess stock for other goods at this time.

Yet while the exchange of captives between Māori groups or individuals was likely a permanent arrangement, the situation was somewhat different when they were 'purchased' by non-Māori. Missionaries and merchants like Joel Polack often complained that their former 'owners' would expect to take them back, albeit on a temporary basis, when extra hands were needed — such as at planting or harvest time. The frequency of such demands indicates that their redemptions or purchases were considered neither absolute nor permanent. Pākehā 'buyers' may have acquired use rights rather than ownership of captives.[54] The nature of their rights to those people may have been misunderstood by dissatisfied purchasers, but it might also have related to their relationship with the 'seller'. Missionaries kept themselves apart from Māori communities and, like Polack, did not marry into the local Māori community. The trader Phillip Tapsell (fig. 43) did, however. He married two Māori women and successfully ransomed a number of war captives.[55] An Englishman and two Americans, suffering a 'very miserable' situation among Ngāpuhi in the Bay of Islands, had pleaded with him to ransom them. They were among a variety of captives, including English men, women and children, black and white Americans, Māori, and an East Indian, whom he rescued by that means. The list Tapsell kept of people whose freedom he purchased noted that he generally paid the equivalent of £20 value. Cash was rare in those times, so the currency was likely to have been a musket, which was then worth around that amount. He spent around £450 ransoming a total of 23 people, most of whom he had no prior connection with, and does not appear to have received any recompense for rescuing them. James Cowan thought that the Māori recipients of Tapsell's largesse may have been more grateful than the whites.[56]

Missionaries often reported saving slaves from imminent death with urgent, on the spot, redemptions. But they were not the only ones to do so. John Hughes, who had a whaling station at Moeraki in North Otago, protested in the strongest terms when he realised that a slave was about to be killed. Those protests proving fruitless, he bought the man for a few second-hand clothes. Yet neither the man himself nor his former captors regarded him as free. He was now Hughes's slave and remained with him until he died. Much as an Englishman might have referred to his valet, Hughes and his friends called the man 'Rogers', which suggests that he was probably treated like an English servant.[57] Whether a transfer of ownership was a good or a bad thing for the individual concerned was a matter of serendipity, but destiny could offer much worse alternatives.

Ritual sacrifice

When a member of the rangatira's family died, it was generally felt necessary to sacrifice one or more people, and non-kin such as war captives were typically the preferred choice — though not always. Oppenheim referred to this custom as an 'act of mourning', but the underlying principle behind the practice is not entirely clear. It was often said that the purpose was to provide a companion or servant for the deceased in the afterlife, although Elsdon Best claimed that that was not the case for Tūhoe. He suggested that it was done to add prestige, or mana, to the occasion and associated the custom with the term 'ika koangaumu'. Ika koangaumu, which loosely translates as sacrificial fish, refers in other contexts to a fish speared and eaten as an element of the ceremony in which the tapu was lifted from an important new waka, or canoe.[58] In the case of human sacrifice, however, the person was not eaten.[59]

It may have been possible to avoid such a fate, however. A woman was pointed out to Richard Cruise and other members of the *Dromedary*'s crew as having been twice selected for the purpose. Apparently not without friends among her captors, she was tipped off in advance on both occasions. So, by making herself scarce and hiding in the bush until the funeral ceremonies were over, she lived to serve another day.[60] However, another young girl on Waiheke Island who found herself in a similar situation was more fatalistic. She had been the favourite slave of an old woman who died and the bereaved family felt their loved one would be 'uncomfortable in the other world without her attendant'. Despite being forewarned that she would meet her doom in three days' time and being offered help from Europeans in making her escape, she resigned herself to her fate. She reasoned that she would eventually be killed to accompany someone else into the afterlife anyway and preferred the lesser misfortune of sharing eternity with her earthly mistress.[61]

If the purpose was important enough or the emergency extreme, it might be considered necessary to sacrifice a loved one.[62] According to Best, slaves might be killed to provide food for a funeral feast, but a person of rank, possibly even a relative of the deceased, could be sacrificed 'as in exaltation of, and a token of respect to, the dead'. In this case, it was referred to as 'putu kai'.[63] The initiation of significant projects like the building of a pā, the launch of a large war canoe, or, in later times, the opening of an important house, might also require a major sacrifice.[64] Rāniera (Sonny) Tau of Ngāpuhi recounted the tradition handed down from his ancestors concerning a very highborn woman of long ago who insisted on the sacrifice of a chiefly woman to satisfy her pregnancy cravings. The mother-to-be was Kareroariki, an ariki in the distant homeland of Hawaiki who expressed a particular appetite for human heart. Being of such high rank, she could demand that her wish be granted, and so it was that a young maiden of a similar rank to Kareroariki lost her life to satisfy that desire.[65]

Maintaining chiefly mana

Maintaining chiefly dignity, or mana, was more often at the expense of war captives. So if a person of rank was suspected of theft, a 'slave' was likely to take the blame. Joel Polack recalled an incident during the 1830s when a 'respectable chief' was seen concealing a pair of his pantaloons under his blanket at the end of a visit. When tapped on the shoulder, 'he turned round with great sang froid and an expressive wink, pointing to his slaves, that his consequence might not be lowered in their estimation'. This chief presented Polack with a pounamu ornament and large pig 'as an acknowledgment for his appropriation'.[66] These were significant gifts, especially the ornament, and acknowledged the importance of maintaining his mana.

And woe betide a slave who witnessed their master or mistress committing a misdemeanour and blabbed about it, for they, too, were likely to face punishment for the damage done to the miscreant's mana. In 1824, a young girl, foolish enough to publicise her master's adultery, was rewarded with a severe wounding.[67] But when three slaves belonging to a rangatira named Putu (perhaps Paora Te Putu) were killed at Hauraki in 1837, things initially looked more dire. These unfortunate people had witnessed three men stealing potatoes from Putu and were killed to ensure they did not spill the beans as to who the culprits were. Putu obviously found out anyway because he killed one of the thieves, a man named Ngoi. When Ngoi's Ngāti Maru people assembled to seek utu for the death of their kinsman, they were instead presented with a gift of sixteen baskets of potatoes. Regarded as sufficient utu in the circumstances, peace was made. However, John Morgan, who reported these events, made it clear that had war resulted, it would have been in response to the killing of Ngoi and not the slaves.[68]

Released captives become independent entrepreneurs

Edward Tregear thought that a lack of tapu was a boon to war captives, but he was writing in the early twentieth century, long after attitudes towards them had altered their position and opened up new opportunities to them:

> Slaves had one great consolation for the misfortune that had taken away their rank or position as freemen; it had delivered them from the discomforts of the *tapu*. A slave was nobody spiritually; his gods had forsaken and forgotten him; therefore he was essentially non-existent.[69]

However, as captives began to be released, their having little tapu or mana to maintain may have meant they were freer to act independently. Assured of protection from the new institutions of the church and English law, those who went on to become independent entrepreneurs might have felt less need to be members of a collective. But that is by no means clear.

When Richard Davis mentioned in 1836 that mission horses were being used to plough some land for two of his 'married natives' who had recently purchased it, he not only implied that they had the means to buy land but also, in his mind, were in a position to do so. What rights they actually acquired from the point of view of the 'sellers' may no longer be discoverable. Both of these men were 'slaves', and only one was 'redeemed', so it is difficult now to understand how a slave, let alone an unredeemed one, was able to purchase land from his conquerors and equally difficult to imagine the sellers were anyone else. Given the date, by which time many captives had been released, it may simply have been that neither was still considered a slave by their previous master or mistress and had been effectively set free, but Davis's comment that '[t]hey will soon outstrip their masters' was prophetic.[70]

Rāpata Te Rou, who appeared in the previous chapter, went on to become a successful businessman within the territory of his captors. Taken from Taranaki as a child, his name was one of five that appeared on the title when a reserve was created over an 850-hectare area of land at Mātiatia on Waiheke Island in 1869. Evidence was given to the Native Land Court that the land had been gifted to the Taranaki captives by Wiremu Hoete through the process of tuku whenua — the gifting of land from one group to another. Prior to 1840, tuku whenua had been used when groups with mana whenua over land had been reduced in their numbers and sought to strengthen their position by incorporating others who wished to settle among them. The rights granted were those of use only. Once the outsiders ceased to occupy the land, mana whenua would return to those who made the gift. Rāpata, however, was a very enterprising fellow. He is said to have owned and operated several sailing ships at different points in time, and to have run firewood and horticultural businesses, as well as managing a farm with 1100 sheep. During the 1890s, he also received royalty payments for sand that was sent to Auckland by the scow-load, which indicates that his rights were unexpectedly extensive for a one-time captive.[71] However, those rights are likely to have acknowledged the benefits he was bringing to the community that adopted him. Being well respected in both Māori and Pākehā societies, Rāpata's house was an official polling place for elections in the 1880s, and his funeral was attended by a big crowd when he died suddenly from measles in 1894.[72] His grave, near the foreshore at Mātiatia, is still carefully looked after.

Reihana Te Kamo was another captive turned entrepreneur. A Te Āti Awa man, he had been taken north where he became a Christian teacher and took the baptismal name of Richard Davis. In 1839, Henry Williams took him from the Bay of Islands back to Port Nicholson (Wellington) where he regained some land rights.[73] Colonel William Wakefield, Chief Agent for the New Zealand Company, wrote of Davis's opposition to the Company buying any land in the region and of his reluctance to sell his own. The Company appears to have responded to that opposition by disputing his claim to the land on the basis that 'he was only a slave' and thus had no right to it. Williams took up Davis's cause, however, and arranged for an acre to be set aside for him.[74] Regardless of his land rights, Davis went on to become a wealthy entrepreneur with a timber house at Pipitea pā said to be well above the general standard of Māori homes at the time.[75] He sent agents, including other one-time captives, to settlements outside Wellington with little or no access to European goods to trade with them for their pigs. Within five years, he owned a horse and a schooner and had £300 in the bank. He planned to take the ship to coastal areas where potatoes and grain could be bought cheaply and resell them in Wellington for a healthy profit.[76] There are likely to have been other such entrepreneurs for whom living an individualist lifestyle had advantages. But while they may have conducted their business interests on a personal basis, we also know that both of these men, Rāpata Te Rou and Reihana Te Kamo, worked with and for the wider communities they lived among. Like Rangi, the expert tattooist who became wealthy within his captors' community in the 1820s, Rāpata and Reihana had not been cowed by their period of captivity but assumed leadership roles through their business acumen: one in a new community, the other among his own.

In the mid-1840s, John Johnson the Colonial Surgeon suggested that because slaves did not need a 'reputation for munificence', many of them acquired considerable personal wealth.[77] Having less mana to begin with, the lowlier members of Māori society had less obligation to distribute material goods among their community, so were, in theory, freer to pursue individual wealth accumulation. Apparently individualist approaches were applauded by church and government authorities but, as the examples of Rāpata Te Rou and Reihana Te Kamo suggest, those who expressed their approval may have overlooked the contribution those businesspeople were actually making to either their own or their captors' communities. Nevertheless, other released captives, with or without good business skills, may have chosen independent enterprise over continuing to contribute to communal resources. Rangatira had no such option. Bound to distribute their wealth and take care of their people in order to preserve their mana, many struggled to do so, especially when the once booming economy of North Island Māori slumped dramatically in the late 1850s. Now that church and government offered different forms of support, those from the bottom of the social ladder could drift away in search of new freedoms.

'Slaves' as workers for hire

But the luxury of personal choice was still in the future when early Pākehā arrivals claimed to have purchased slaves outright. Surgeon John Watkins's statement to the 1838 parliamentary inquiry that Englishmen generally paid slaves no wages contradicted other evidence that they were paid. Indeed, the CMS missionaries responded to Watkins's testimony by saying that 'slaves hired by Europeans [were] regularly paid their wages, but their native masters share[d] the payments with them'.[78] Ngāti Toa's Te Hiko was said to be paying his slaves in 1839.[79] When questioned by an 1844 Select Committee in Britain — in other words, after the establishment of British government in New Zealand — Thomas McDonnell explained that he offered labour contracts to groups of perhaps eight or ten people headed by a chief. The 'heads of the tribes work, as well as the merest slave', he said, but he did not enquire as to how the payment was distributed among them.[80] But the expectation of payment may not have been a new thing. According to Charles Baker, when he and James Kemp purchased some food at Pukenui in 1829, the slaves, ordered to carry it to their settlement at Kerikeri, refused to move without payment.[81]

Tregear claimed that slaves allowed to work for someone other than their own masters would be paid for their labour in the form of goods. He added that a portion of these would usually be offered to their master or mistress but that it was seldom demanded as a right.[82] In a communal society, extra compensation was generally given to those who did most of the work, but free people employed by outsiders would typically give a portion of their earnings to their rangatira, too.

Not all Pākehā were grateful for the services slaves or captives provided, though. Polack, who had little sympathy for the poor benighted slave, said they were 'the most annoying of the several classes in the country; having no character to gain or lose, they subject the commercial trader to much inconvenience'.[83] In many instances, however, they were essential.

'Slaves' as guides for Pākehā travellers

Having traditionally carried burdens, 'slaves' were often hired as bearers and guides by Pākehā travellers. Surveyors found them invaluable in the South Island where the terrain and the climate made haphazard wandering potentially lethal. Hone Mokehakeha, known as Kehu, was a Ngāti Tūmatakōkiri captive held by Ngāti Rārua chiefs at Motueka, who accompanied Thomas Brunner on his survey of the region and its hinterlands in 1842. He did the same again when Brunner was joined by Charles Heaphy and William Fox to explore the North Island's lake districts in early 1846. Heaphy's description of Kehu's fishing methods reveals how Christian teachings were still far from displacing Māori customs but were being combined with other European influences as well. His Pākehā travelling companions having given up their attempts at eeling, Kehu went back across a river near their campsite and:

commenced chanting his Wesleyan missionary service, mixing with the translated version of the ritual special incantations to the taipo [taipō: spirit] of the lake and the river for propitious weather and easy fords, together with request to the eels to bite quickly, and not keep him longer in the cold. Then, as he caught one which would not die quick enough to please him, would he introduce some decidedly uncomplimentary language which he had learnt at a whaling station, and again subside into the recitation of his Wesleyan catechism and hymnbook . . .

His calling on a variety of spiritual and profane forces appeared to have worked well because the travellers found 'four fine eels' already roasting for breakfast when they awoke next morning, not to mention another four hanging from an adjacent tree.[84] Equally skilled at birding, Kehu was 'worth his weight in tobacco!' wrote Heaphy.[85] But he was remembered especially fondly by Brunner for having saved his life on a later expedition. Another Ngāti Tūmatakōkiri captive, Pikiwati, had been with Brunner and Kehu on that journey, which began in late 1846. Inconveniently for Brunner, because the wives who accompanied the two guides had absconded from their rangatira and feared being recognised, he could not explore some of the routes he had intended. The expedition turned out to be an eighteen-month struggle against the elements during which Brunner suffered paralysis. Pikiwati and his wife eventually deserted Brunner during his illness but Kehu and his wife remained and looked after him.[86]

Captives introduce new skills

Pākehā like Heaphy and Brunner must have picked up some useful skills from guides like Kehu but, in earlier times, captives from other areas may have been the source of new ideas, techniques, and even artistic styles for their captors' community, too. Rangi, the war captive who achieved fame in the Bay of Islands as a tohunga tā moko, or specialist in tattooing, likely brought his techniques and designs with him from wherever he originally hailed.

The same must have occurred with other skilled artists, including women with expertise in weaving. Weaving skills were passed down through the generations, typically within families. Certain areas were famed for their expertise, and the women with those skills were highly regarded within their own hapū.[87] Women from Taranaki, for example, were renowned for their weaving, so it is highly likely that they passed on patterns, techniques for preparing or dying fibres, and information about the suitability of different fibres for particular uses to the communities among whom they were obliged to settle. Oral traditions tell that women learned of new varieties of flax with ideal qualities for making particular types of garment or other items from visitors. They would sometimes make long journeys to acquire plants to take home and cultivate locally. While no specific examples of such information being transferred by war captives are known to have been recorded, logic suggests that they would have been potential sources of new knowledge.

For reasons lost to time, carving seems to have died out in North Auckland during the eighteenth century. Dependent on skilled craftsmen from other areas, the Bay of Islanders commissioned tohunga whakairo (expert carvers) from Tauranga or the East Coast to undertake projects for them.[88] Acquiring them as captives would have been far more convenient and cost effective, of course. So the practice of deliberately identifying and bringing back skilled craftspeople from the East Coast to do their captors' bidding appears to have begun when Ngāpuhi undertook their first documented raids with muskets in 1818.[89]

Ensign McCrae recorded that a man, probably captured from the East Cape, had carved a 'whare tapu' (pātaka, or storehouse?), which he described in 1820 as: 'a complete piece of carved work consisting of representations of human and other figures, a work of much labour and time, and by no means defective in execution'.[90] Richard Cruise, in Northland at the same time, stressed the labour and ingenuity of Māori carving but also noted that skilled artists were rare.[91] He explained that Wētere of Ngāi Tāwake had brought the carver then decorating his storehouse some 200 miles (322 km) from the Hauraki region.[92] Much later, a witness to the Native Land Court said that when Tarawheti of Whirinaki was building a carved house at Tiakiruahine, Te Whareumu from Kororāreka sent his slave, a skilful carver, to help.[93] Since Te Whareumu died in 1828, he must have done so before that date.

Tene Waitere was one celebrated carver from later years whose career may have been influenced by the circumstances of his birth at Mangamuka in Northland. His mother Ani Pape had been captured during a Ngāpuhi attack on Rotorua in 1823 and was taken as a wife by Waitere, against her will. However, while Tene was still an infant, an uncle arrived on the scene and somehow arranged to take Ani and her children back to Rotorua. Having settled at Ruatō, on Lake Rotoiti, he was trained in the arts of carving by Wero Tāroi, a master carver of the celebrated Ngāti Tarāwhai school. Over time, Tene Waitere built his reputation by working with other renowned carvers on a number of new meeting houses around Rotorua and Taupō. But from 1892, when he was employed by Charles E. Nelson, manager of the Geyser Hotel at Whakarewarewa, commercial carving became a primary source of income for him. From the hotel, he carved large pieces to decorate the building and the thermal areas, as well as tobacco pipes, walking sticks, and replicas of traditional artefacts for sale to tourists or for presentation to distinguished visitors. However, he is particularly remembered for his work on Rauru, a fully carved meeting house intended to illustrate the local legends that guides would tell to tourists. Waitere stopped carving for Europeans about 1912, when his work became more stylised and strictly orthodox. Although he preserved the traditions and integrity of his art while creating work for Westerners, he was one of the first carvers to lift some of the tapu from Māori woodcarving. His birth, in effective captivity, coupled with his having worked so closely with Europeans, may account for his not playing any major roles in Ngāti Tarāwhai leadership. But that background may also have given him the freedom to be innovative with his carving and to become Rotorua's most prominent carver of the time.[94]

Toi moko or mokomōkai

While the possession of muskets allowed northern tribes to acquire skilled artists as well as general labourers, Ensign McCrae noted other recent effects when he visited the Bay of Islands in 1820. The heads of those slain in battle, which in earlier times might have also been available for ransom by their own people, had by now become trade items because of the demand for them among Europeans.[95] Like some other skills and customary practices, the art of preserving heads was corrupted in the face of market forces. Those changes were encouraged by the Western fascination with Māori facial adornment. Moko, or tattoos, not only indicated mana but also contained mana itself. They were very important aspects of identity and, for that reason alone, they would be restricted to people of rank.[96] But the level of expertise and length of time necessary for their execution and the many restrictions placed on those involved also made the process expensive. It was a procedure which was unavoidably bloody, too, so that a collective ritual was held at the completion of the moko as utu, or recompense, for the chiefly bloodletting. Part of that ritual might be the sacrifice of a slave or war captive.[97]

Because the head is the most tapu part of the body, those of deceased rangatira, including women, were frequently preserved by an elaborate curing process and were highly valued by their people. The practice offered a means of keeping those dear to them close at hand, even in death. But following a battle, the heads of slain enemy chiefs were kept as trophies of war.[98] While these might be derided and treated with great disrespect, they were also important components in the rituals of peacemaking. Because the exchange of chiefly heads could settle the peace between contending parties, they were unlikely to be traded unless the conqueror was determined on never making peace.[99] Not until the arrival of Europeans, anyway. Visitors with deep pockets and an irresistible array of exciting new goods had the power to change things. What would seem to be an early example of shifting attitudes occurred when Samuel Marsden visited the Hokianga in 1819. As he wrote: 'Nothing is held in so much veneration by the natives as the head of their chief.' Yet, an elderly rangatira 'with a very long beard and his face tattooed all over' was so keen to secure an axe, he offered his most valuable possession to get one. But he did hope that Marsden might allow him a little time to die naturally. Having no axes left at this point on his journey anyway, Marsden asked who it should be given to once he had acquired the head and was told to give it to the man's son. But when Marsden explained that he had more axes back at Rangihoua, the old man gave him two mats to secure the deal and arranged for a man to be sent to collect the precious tool from the mission.[100] Marsden made no further comment about his intentions to collect the old man's head at any future date.

The purchase of Māori preserved heads (mokomōkai, mokamōkai, toi moko, or ūpoko tuhi) by Europeans had begun much earlier with James Cook's ship *Endeavour* in 1770. Joseph Banks, a scientist and Fellow of the Royal Society, was evidently keen to purchase one, for he wrote that an old man, who he supposed to be the local chief, brought six or seven to the ship at the explorers' request. This man was not as eager a seller as Banks a buyer, for the Englishman described him as 'very jealous of shewing them' and said that his purchase was 'much against the inclinations of its owner'. Although the elderly man liked what Banks had to offer in exchange, he was reluctant to part with a head until threatened with Banks's musket, at which point he grudgingly conceded. All he got for it 'was a pair of old Drawers of very white linnen'.[101] What he planned to do with those second-hand undies we do not know, but had he retained the head, it may have proved more valuable for making peace with its original owner's people. That might explain his reluctance to trade it for the underpants. However, there would be many more eager buyers, and the temptations to trade preserved heads for desirable new goods would become harder and harder to resist.

This was an age of scientific curiosity when macabre exotica were fashionable and Europeans with the means were eager to study pieces of non-white bodies. So much so, that the early nineteenth century saw the popularisation of what have been referred to as human zoos. These were exhibitions that took supposedly scientific ideas about race into the popular arena and made notions of racial difference seem common sense. Suggestions that race was biologically or genetically based and that skin colour or other biological markers reflected levels of intelligence, psychology, sporting ability, or even humanity are now referred to as 'scientific racism'. They were ideas that took deep and long-lasting root. One early example of prurient interest was the exhibition of Saartjie Baartman, a Khoisan slave, promoted as the 'Hottentot Venus'. Saartjie was abducted from South Africa and taken to London in 1810 where she was exhibited naked in a cage and made to show off her protruding buttocks and large genitals, physical features that were not so unusual among her own people.

Scientific interest was the reason Samuel Marsden gave to Pōmare for wanting him to supply a preserved head. They were 'much in demand among scientists in England', he told the Bay of Islands rangatira.[102] That interest was really ideologically based, emanating from the society the scientists lived in, and has long been discredited. But the opportunities offered for scientific racism were apparent when M. J. Fontenelle presented a Māori head to the Royal Institute of France in 1827. The sutures of the skull, the occipital region, frontal cavity, and a vertical bony septum having been closely examined by members of the academy, Monsieur Fontenelle concluded 'that this race may be considered as a sort of link between man and the ourang outang'.[103]

Sydney was the centre of the trade in preserved Māori heads. As a newspaper correspondent calling himself Verax (Truthful) recalled, he had seen two tattooed human heads in a private house in Sydney around 1812. They were then valued at 20 guineas each. Seven or eight years later, in January 1820, he was astonished and horrified to spot a man casually walking along George Street in that town with a head wrapped in a handkerchief under his arm. He was particularly outraged to learn that the price had now dropped to two guineas, which he attributed to the fact that 'dealers in that traffic are not only supplied in proportion to the increased demand, but even on terms much lower than formerly'. He suggested that they might eventually be bought for 'a dollar each'.[104]

Advertisements for preserved Māori heads began to appear in London newspapers from 1820.[105] According to one auction house, the finely tattooed head of a New Zealand chief was among some fine specimens of 'exotic conchology' and other items that belonged to a gentleman about to leave London for the country.[106] Mr Alexander Hume presented the head of a young chief, 'beautifully tattooed, and embalmed in a manner unknown to the civilised nations of modern times', to the Museum of the Royal College of Surgeons in 1822. He promised to supplement his gift by giving the museum an account of the Māori process of preservation. Mr Hume was a surgeon in the Royal Navy which might explain how he came by the head.[107] As an advertisement, from January 1827, addressed to 'MEDICAL GENTLEMEN and

Others' implies, the items were expected to appeal to the scientifically minded.[108]

Medical men were eager buyers of preserved heads as curiosities. When a Mr Way — a surgeon and apothecary living in Southwark, London — took his neighbour to court for allowing 'quantities of filth' to collect in the yard of her livery stables, *The Times* described the prosecutor more fully than the defendant. He was said to be a 'man of considerable practice' whose windows in Park Street exhibited 'besides medicine, several preparations, and amongst them the heads of two New Zealanders "grinning with a ghastly smile" at the passers-by in the street'.[109] When a policeman was called to testify to the 'most nauseous' smell coming from the livery stables, he noted that he had first thought it came from the prosecutor's shop. To which the defendant's counsel asked: 'Did it smell like a New Zealander preserved?' — a question which 'excited great laughter'.[110] Perhaps this indignity was little different to what they may have been subjected to had they remained on stakes within the pā of their enemies where the conquering party would likely have 'danced naked before the heads, uttering all manner of abuse to them in terms of bravado and insult, as though they were still alive'.[111] The description of the Southwark heads as 'grinning with a ghastly smile' indicates that the lips of these men were drawn back to expose their teeth. It was those of the enemy that would be pulled back that way in the process of preservation. The heads of one's own people were cured with their lips brought together.[112]

Marsden withdrew his request to buy a head when Pōmare offered to shoot some people who had killed his son. For some gunpowder and an axe, he offered to bring their heads back to the Bay and show Marsden how to preserve them.[113] But once the market was better established, other sellers offered stocks of merchandise ready to take away. Lottin recounted a visit by a party of people from the Hauraki area to the Bay of Islands while the *Coquille* was there in 1824, saying that they had 'brought tattooed, preserved heads to sell'. He had assumed that the trade was carried on in secret, but 'in this case they had stuck them on sticks and were playing with them as with the most indifferent of objects'.[114] His shipmate René Primevère Lesson reported similarly. Two large canoes had pulled up beside the French vessel eager to trade but, at first, they offered only 'a few trifling curiosities' for sale. More valuable items followed, including fish- (shark's-?) teeth ear ornaments as well as axes and jewellery made from pounamu. But then, as the trading started to slow down, one man pulled out a preserved head 'gaily, waving it above his head'. Still more were produced, including one from under a woman's loincloth, a situation that was surely the ultimate insult to the deceased. She, too, is said to have played with the head with indifference. Lesson purchased one 'as an anatomical curiosity' in exchange for a pound of powder — which may have been used to replenish their stocks.[115]

It may only have been while they were in New Zealand that overseas buyers contemplated the potential for the trade to spur victorious tribes to kill their captives as items of merchandise. Although Lesson thought that the traffic in heads was 'strictly forbidden by the administration in Sydney', it was actually another seven years before Governor Darling of New South Wales issued a proclamation banning their sale.[116] However, by 1835, there was evidence that Darling's proclamation had the effect of reducing the value of heads even more greatly than Verax had predicted. The remains of a human head, supposed to be that of a New Zealander, was discovered in the neighbourhood of Bligh Street, Sydney, having been thrown away and burned or buried in an ash heap.[117]

However, despite advising others that it was not 'safe or prudent' to purchase heads, it appears highly likely that Marsden did arrange for William Hall to purchase one for a 'gentleman' at Oxford University who had specifically asked for a specimen 'without hair'.[118] Why he wanted a bald head is unclear, but perhaps it was thought more suitable for scientific examination. Elsewhere, however, in 1885, a local historian recalled visiting the 'sombre apartment beneath the Music Hall' of the Sheffield Literary and Philosophical Society as a child where he had seen 'the head of a New Zealander, with long black hair, behind the Presidents chair'.[119]

To be fair to those involved, this was probably before most buyers appreciated that such purchases were creating a market and encouraging those with a supply of captives to kill and cure on demand. Nevertheless, Reverend John Graham, rector of two York churches, who, like Marsden, received his appointment through the good offices of the famous abolitionist William Wilberforce, donated 'the head of a New Zealand Chief, recently slain in battle' to the Yorkshire Philosophical Society towards the end of 1828.[120] How Graham, who was also vice-president of the Church Missionary Association in York, secretary of the Bible Society, and president of the Religious Tract Society, came by the head remains a mystery.[121]

But Darling's decree clearly failed to end the trade. J. Pitts Johnson, who visited Kāpiti Island in 1837, was keen to buy a head that was taken aboard his ship the *Persian*.[122] He was outbid by the ship's doctor, who secured the purchase for a very small blanket and an old dirty shirt, but the sellers were still keen to trade. Through Samuel Cherry, master of a whaling ship, who translated for him, they told Johnson that they had now run out of stock of the heads of slain enemies. Not to worry, though — Te Hiko lined up seventeen live slaves along the side of the ship, saying that he could take his pick. If there was one whose tattooing particularly took his fancy, his head could be served up in three days' time. The price would be a cask of gunpowder. The head of a previously slain enemy was apparently quite a legitimate purchase for Johnson, but the thought of a man being killed to order horrified him. Having been told that this was now common practice when it came to trading with foreigners, the would-be buyer turned to urging great punishment 'on those inhuman and brutal whites, who thus encourage the crime of murder among an ignorant race of beings'.[123]

Lieutenant Charles Wilkes, commander of the United States Exploring Expedition which toured the Pacific between 1838 and 1842, was another keen buyer. Among those on board the vessels comprising the expedition were naturalists, botanists, taxidermists, a mineralogist, and a philologist. With regard to their visit to New Zealand in 1840, Wilkes remarked that the trade in 'native curiosities', particularly in tattooed heads, was not as great as it had been, presumably due to the legal restriction. It was still going on, but with 'great precaution', as he discovered when some of his men wanted to buy some. Wilkes was surprised to find that the willing though discreet seller was the steward on the missionary vessel anchored in the Bay of Islands. He wrote that when they had finished buying other goods, the steward:

> invited our officers to step down to his little store-room, under the forecastle, where he had a curiosity which could not be brought out. After this

mysterious enunciation, they followed him to the bottom of the ladder; he then told them he was about to put his fate into their hands, believing that they were too much men of honour to betray him. He then proceeded to inform them that he had two preserved heads of New Zealand chiefs, which he would sell for ten pounds. He could not venture, he said, to produce them on board the brig, but if they would appoint a place, he would bring them. The penalty for selling them was fifty guineas, and he conjured them to the most perfect secrecy. These proved to be beautiful specimens, and now form a part of our collections.[124]

So, representatives of an official United States government expedition were among those keeping the market going.[125]

The tables were turned for one dealer, though. A whaler from Kāpiti Island named Joe Rowe, who was dealing in preserved Māori heads, was mortally embarrassed the day he came across a party of Ngāti Tūwharetoa at the mouth of the Whanganui River. That first recorded meeting between Māori and Pākehā in the area ended badly for Rowe when the Tūwharetoa people noted that his stock consisted of members of their tribe. Rowe and two other men in his party were killed, but he received more poetic justice by having his head severed, dried, and preserved. Presumably with his mouth open and teeth exposed.[126]

What should be remembered before moving on is that the 'musket wars', which began in the late 1810s and continued to the early 1830s, were an aberration in Māori warfare: in captive taking, numbers killed and eaten after capture, and in many other ways, too. It is important to keep that in mind because the end of the wars saw the release of many captives and, to a large extent, the end of captive taking by Māori. Yet, despite it being a brief interlude in Māori history and a very atypical one, most of our historical accounts concerning Māori 'slavery' are based on primary source material from that period. Many of those accounts came from missionaries whose Christian sensitivities were shocked by different attitudes and different spiritual practices. Other early visitors from Europe were also horrified by practices they considered uncivilised. The sale of toi moko, or mokomōkai as they were commonly known, was a case in point, even though it was Westerners, including clerics and surgeons, who wanted to purchase them and thus created the market.

CHAPTER FIVE

Dark Helens and aboriginal Messelinas

DEAD ENEMIES COULD HAVE ECONOMIC VALUE, BUT THAT OF living war captives was more lasting and flexible. Besides growing potatoes, dressing flax, cooking, paddling, carrying, and even helping in the field of battle, young women and girls proved lucrative in a somewhat more passive field of enterprise. The sex trade was not a degrading or tapu-destroying activity but, because it was also a form of employment that received particular attention in the writings of both missionaries and visitors to New Zealand, we know rather more about that than their other commercially driven activities.

For many Westerners, the thought of women being directed to offer such services for pay represented the proverbial 'fate worse than death'. But that perception does not correctly reflect reality in all times and all places and should not be taken for granted. Prostitution, which the *Oxford English Dictionary* defines as 'the practice or occupation of engaging in sexual activity with someone for payment', did not exist in all societies — despite the common claim that it is the world's oldest profession. It certainly did not exist in Māori society.

Unfortunately, there are few contemporary Māori sources from which indigenous attitudes might be gleaned. Evidence for the late eighteenth and early nineteenth century comes predominantly from the writings of outsiders — many of whom had little understanding of Māori society or social mores. Although they had much to say about the sex industry in that period, especially in Kororāreka and other northern ports, there are many contradictions in their remarks and opinions which are puzzling. Much of the confusion may be due to their not always making it clear whether those participating in the trade were war captives or free women. But apart from the ideologies and social conditioning of the writers, the date and place from which their remarks were made may also have influenced their observations. So, a sketched history of Western comments on and attitudes towards sexual interactions between Māori women and non-Māori men, taking those factors into consideration, may offer some clues as to what was really going on.

The eighteenth century

The sex trade began with the first visit of James Cook's *Endeavour* in 1769 but it is not entirely clear whether or not the women involved were primarily war captives. Te Weherua, a young man thought to have been about sixteen or seventeen years old when Cook visited Tōtara-nui, or Queen Charlotte's Sound, in 1777, said that the 'especially selected' girls who went out to the vessel were 'the mere refuse & outcasts among them'. Te Weherua had a good long chat with the surgeon's mate, David Samwell, presumably with the help of Cook's Tahitian interpreter Mai, and told him that 'none of the fine Girls were suffered to come near us but were kept with great Care' at their homes. It is probably safe to assume that those of the highest social standing were not offered to the sailors, but Samwell's comment that the women who did visit were daubed with red ochre is more curious. Although not always the case, as previously mentioned, kōkōwai, or red ochre, is generally believed to have indicated chiefly rank. Yet Cook himself reported that few of the sailors were keen to sleep with these women who had too strong an odour for their taste and did not did measure up to the other 'cleanly & handsome' women they had also spotted.[1] This suggests that the red ochre they wore was mixed with shark oil, producing the smell that Westerners frequently turned up, or perhaps held, their noses at. The 'cleanly & handsome' women were perhaps of higher rank and able to wear ochre, or kōkōwai, mixed with sweeter-smelling vegetable oils.² Apart from that, the fishy odour of captive women may have been enhanced by one of the occupations typically assigned to them: that of gutting fish in preparation for drying. It was work that caused them to be 'covered with a thick layer of scum', which gave off a penetrating odour.³ Some 'greasy brown nymphs' did appeal nonetheless.⁴

Te Weherua's insistence that only women of low rank were offered to Cook's crew appears to be supported by reports that they were less than 'cleanly'. But, on his second visit to New Zealand, Cook himself not only remarked on the relative chastity of Māori women but also compared the attitudes of their menfolk concerning sexual relations with his crew to the experience of his previous expedition:

> [W]hatever favours a few of them might have granted to the crew of the *Endeavour* [in 1769] it was generally done in a private manner and without the men seeming to intrest [sic] themselves in it, but now we find the men are the chief promoters of this Vice.⁵

That might imply that the 'promoters' were enlisting women slightly higher up the social scale.

In 1772, First Lieutenant Le Dez of the *Marquis de Castries* was obviously bothered by the fact that gifts his fellow sailors had given to the local people at the Bay of Islands were passed on to the chief. He assumed that 'the women even gave them the fruit of their gallantry' because they feared and hated the chiefs.⁶ However, it was more likely they considered it appropriate to give precious manufactured items to their rangatira for him to distribute as he thought fit. Keeping personal gifts for one's self was a Western expectation which was not necessarily shared in a communal society. William Brown complained similarly almost 70 years later with regard to quite different circumstances:

> The slaves who become servants to the white people generally save the greater part of the clothes which they may procure, in order to present to their chief. A boy lived with me for upwards of a twelvemonth, and I was

greatly annoyed to find that all the clothes which had been given to him were regularly presented to his chief whenever he paid a visit.

Brown nonetheless recognised that this practice was 'in obedience to custom'. If the boy had not conformed to this usual practice, 'he would have been looked upon as wanting in attention to his chief'. Yet Brown also knew that the boy was handing the goods over on a purely voluntary basis because, as he said, the chief would have had no way of knowing what property his slave possessed unless he told him.[7]

As for which women would be offered to visiting seamen, a greater recognition of opportunities for trade had possibly made the difference by 1773 when Cook reported from his second voyage that: 'for a spike nail or any other they value [they] will oblige their Wives and Daughters to prostitute themselves whether they will or no and that not with the privicy [sic] decency seems to require'. George Forster, the naturalist on that voyage, wrote that when the *Resolution* entered Queen Charlotte's Sound in May, local men boarded the ship and walked through it, offering their 'sisters' and 'daughters' to the crew — despite some tears and protests.[8] While it is not possible to know how many were unhappy about the duties expected of them, Cook's remarks are somewhat puzzling as they imply quite a different attitude with regard to 'wives' than was more frequently reported. Other European visitors, including Forster, stressed that married women were strictly out of bounds, and the penalties that continued to be imposed in cases of adultery well into the second half of the nineteenth century indicate that the marital fidelity of women was a very important matter.[9] However, Joseph Dubouzet, who visited Otago in 1840, believed that the availability or even promotion of their wives' involvement in the sex trade was a change that had come with time. 'The chief concern of the natives [consisted] in handing over their wives to the foreigners', he wrote. '[F]ormerly none but the chiefs had this privilege and they only gave their slaves as prostitutes.'[10] It is possible that both Cook and Dubouzet misunderstood the situation, and that the women were not formally recognised 'wives', but war captives whose status related more closely to that of a concubine. However, like Dubouzet, René Primevère Lesson also felt that the availability of married women in

Northland was an innovation, and his comments based on an 1824 visit appear on the surface to be the most revealing:

> The navigators who have written that the Zealanders [sic] prostituted their wives have been in error up until now. Married women, especially the wives of chiefs, are punished by death if they are caught committing adultery. However, one can sometimes buy the complaisance of the husband and close his eyes with some present or other, and Tuhi [Tuai] himself, chief of the eastern part of the bay, did not seem far off handing over his wife, requiring only the greatest secrecy.

Yet this implies that Tuai did not actually 'hand over his wife', and Lesson continued by adding that:

> Several natives brought their wives on board with them, and when we sought their favours, the wives showed a sort of disgust, and replied hotly that they were taboo, and that it was forbidden to touch them. The girls enjoy a greater liberty . . .[11]

Regardless of their social status, though, most visitors recognised clear distinctions between single and married women. As Forster explained following his 1773 visit: 'Their ideas of female chastity are, in this respect so different from ours, that a girl may favour a number of lovers without any detriment to her character; but if she marries, conjugal fidelity is exacted from her with the greatest rigour.'[12] Julien Crozet, second in command to Marion du Fresne, whose expedition had visited New Zealand the previous year, was also in no doubt about the need to approach only single women:

> The married women were distinguished by a sort of straw plait which confined their hair on the top of the head; the girls had no such distinctive mark, their hair hanging naturally over their neck without anything to bind it.
>
> It was the savages themselves who pointed out these distinctions and who gave us to understand by signs that we must not touch the married women, but that we might with perfect freedom make advances to the girls.

The latter, he sounded pleased to add, could not have been more approachable.[13]

Samuel Marsden found them to be more than just 'approachable'. During his first visit to New Zealand in 1814 aboard the mission vessel *Active*, he felt himself obliged to prohibit a woman who had become known as Mary while dispensing her 'unlimited favours' among the crew from having any connection with the vessel. Mary was outraged by what she considered to be his unwarranted restriction and regarded the missionary wives with 'green-eyed' jealousy, believing them responsible for the boycotting of her visits. Climbing onto her high horse, she informed Marsden that 'New Zealand women were quite as handsome as those of *Europee*, and ought to be suffered as well as them to remain on board'.[14] The sex trade certainly did not end with Marsden's visit, but his ban, coming as it did with the establishment of a mission in the Bay of Islands, heralded more regular chastisement of it.

The lack of premarital chastity among unmarried Māori women was often remarked upon by outside observers because their own backgrounds had programmed them to find it surprising. However, with the exception of a few women of very high rank who were ritually set aside as virgin brides for strategic marriage alliances (puhi), Māori society placed no special value on virginity.[15] But the reaction of Tohitapu when he learned that two of his wives had been involved in the trade makes it abundantly clear that their married status made a very big difference indeed. One early morning in March 1828, when Henry Williams was trying hard to conciliate rival parties and avoid further hostility, Tohitapu approached him in a very foul mood:

> I soon learnt that two of Tohitapu's wives had been on board one of the ships during his absence, and that he was much distressed, that he was determined to hang himself, and had sent for his friends to witness his death. In the afternoon, hearing that he had been inflicting punishment on some of his neighbours, I went to his place, and found him apparently in great sorrow. He said that he had not eaten food since his return, neither could he unless he were to kill someone, then his heart would be at ease; but that he had been restrained by us, and he must die. I could not but feel considerably for him. . . .[16]

Sexual hospitality

Prior to Christianity making inroads into their moral code, Māori ideas of hospitality, or manaakitanga, were such that male visitors of rank would typically be offered the comfort of a temporary wife. If the young women commanded by their elders to perform such duties conceived a child from the liaison, the ties of kinship formed as a consequence would be deemed a bonus by way of alliance building and defence.[17] Sexual hospitality was a custom that appears to have been extended to European visitors deemed worthy of similar respect. Richard Cruise, apparent author of *Journal of a Ten Months' Residence in New Zealand*, recorded many details of the interaction between the ship's company of the *Dromedary* and Māori during their 1820 'residence'. Having landed a shipment of convicts at New South Wales, the *Dromedary* was directed to New Zealand in search of spars for the British Navy, but what was intended to be a short visit turned into a much-extended one. Fortunately for history, the length of their stay has resulted in some detailed accounts of the experiences and impressions of at least four of the ship's officers whose shipmates might have otherwise been destined to very long periods of celibacy.[18]

For example, on an expedition to Motukorea, or Browns Island, in the Hauraki Gulf to shoot birds, Cruise and his companions received hospitality in several forms from their Māori hosts. As well as the present of a cat, apparently intended as their dinner, a large canoe full of women came alongside their ship during the evening. They were not a bad-looking group, he thought, intended as 'wives for the white men'. Once on board, the women lined up on deck and their rangatira, Tetatta (?), approached the officers, asking them 'very politely and individually ... to select what number of wives they wanted'. Their host 'seemed much disappointed that this mark of attention and hospitality was declined by those to whom he wished most to show it'. Their visit did not go to waste, however, as a number of the women found 'husbands' among other members of the crew and the entire ship's complement was entertained with dancing and singing well into the night. Cruise pronounced that 'the harmony of their voices, the gracefulness of their movements, as well as in personal appearance' put them a notch above those from tribes they had previously encountered.[19]

Reverend John Butler, who arrived in New Zealand in 1819, wrote home to his boss Josiah Pratt, Secretary of the CMS, the same year as the *Dromedary*'s visit. Having explained that the principal sins to which Māori were 'addicted' were 'pride, lust, and cruelty', he went on to say that 'the first thing a chief will offer you as a compliment, is a fine woman'. So although Butler clearly recognised that it was a compliment, he nonetheless declined an offer from Hīnaki to supply him with a temporary wife during a visit to that rangatira's home at Mokoia (Panmure). He dealt with the situation by saying that he was 'tabood' and that his God would destroy him if he 'committed such wickedness' — a response that must have bemused his host.[20] In the case of Butler and the officers of the *Dromedary*, there is no suggestion that any immediate 'payment' was requested — although long-term benefit was surely expected by way of securing preferential treatment in future dealings. Not all of their countrymen were so coy when it came to accepting offers, though, and most were perfectly willing to pay for services rendered. As the *Dromedary*'s surgeon Dr Fairfowl subsequently told Commissioner Bigge's inquiry in 1821,[21] New Zealand women went aboard the ship willingly: 'Prostitution is not reckoned a crime or a disgrace amongst the unmarried women, and the chiefs come and offer their sisters and daughters for prostitution and expect a present in return.'[22]

These instances confirm that sexual hospitality and a sex trade were both occurring in 1820. But even so, Fairfowl's use of the word prostitution betrays his understanding of what his Māori hosts may have considered to be an exchange of gifts: an act of hospitality acknowledged by a gift of thanks. For the Wesleyan William Wade, who travelled from Northland to the Bay of Plenty in 1838, the sex trade was an innovation brought by wicked Westerners. He was disgusted by the 'spectacle of every seaman on board [a vessel] appearing to lay claim to more girls than one; and in the Bay of Plenty, though less frequented by shipping, there was a lamentable extent of imported crime', he said.[23] So, at what point did sexual hospitality become a sex industry? Was it an 'imported crime', as Wade claimed, or was it merely an adaptation as Māori hosts began to recognise their visitors' quite different ideas regarding reciprocation and adjusted their approach? And when did either of these institutions turn into acknowledged marriage?

At South Island whaling stations, for example, men who came and went to and from Sydney with their cargoes of oil were regularly supplied with local wives for 'the season' by the women's senior relatives. In these cases, expectations went beyond sexual duties to include what a Western man of the period would consider other wifely roles and might even involve a free trial. According to Edward Jerningham Wakefield (known as Jerningham), son of Edward Gibbon Wakefield:

> Regular bargains were struck between the experienced headsman or boat-steerer and the relations of the girls selected and in most cases the bargains were punctually adhered to. In cases where the wife was negligent or slow to learn her duties of cooking, clothes-mending, and washing, the uncle or father would often take away the delinquent and bring another more fitted to perform his part of the bargain. The whaler's part consisted in a payment made on the completion of the bargain, and in a certain degree of indulgence to the begging visits of his new relations during the season.[24]

The mention of uncles and fathers implies that these were unlikely to have been female captives but women of some rank who would be expected to facilitate economic advantages for their kin. And 'begging visits' might mean that the husband was slow to share the profits he had been able to earn from having been given trading rights within his in-laws' tribal territory. In this milieu of different understandings and expectations, reminders of those expectations might sometimes have been necessary. Foreign seamen considered arrangements to be between themselves and the individual women concerned, but it was not prostitution and the reciprocity due was to the women's wider community.

As the 1820s and 1830s progressed, men from several overseas countries began setting up trading operations on various parts of the New Zealand coast. Most of those men were incorporated into the local community through marriages, formal or otherwise, with women from their host tribe. These arrangements were often of long or even lifelong standing. And those wives were typically of the rangatira class, daughters of leading men who enhanced the trader's level of patronage and protection while the local people gained an agent who could maximise their own opportunities for trade. So there were both personal and economic benefits for each of the parties, but the husband was expected to share his wealth with his extended family in return for the trading rights he received from them.[25]

Although many of these arrangements lasted until death did indeed part them, they were sometimes seen in terms of a 'temporary marriage' by Western visitors. Edward Markham commented on these liaisons when news of the arrival of a whaler called the *Tigress*, a fairly regular twice-annual visitor to the Bay of Islands, reached three women in the village where he was staying in 1834. These three, who had 'tane', or husbands, on board, drove three large pigs down to the Bay where they put them into canoes and paddled out to live, once again, with the men they had voyaged with previously. Markham described the pigs as 'the only thing they had in shape of property', adding, 'I call that Affection'. In other words, whether 'marriages' were temporary or permanent, gifting went both ways: hardly commercial transactions or prostitution as Westerners would normally define it.

The development of a sex trade

Nevertheless, since the mid-1810s, as foreign ship visits had become more regular, the sex trade did become a major money-spinner, especially for Northland tribes who encouraged visits by more and more whalers each year. Not surprisingly, the sailors on board, who had often spent many months or even years at sea, were an eager market for female favours. But the temptations of the situation were likely just as great from the point of view of the women who welcomed them. Sometimes the men lived ashore with the women, but other times, the women lived on board ship. When on board for any length of time, they would provide the services typical of any wife of the day, such as doing their men's washing.[26] As for the going rate, it was to be expected that it would alter according to time, place, and the duration of the arrangement.

When the *Dromedary* visited the Bay of Islands in 1820, parents are said to have handed over their daughters without stipulating how much they should receive nor who among the men on board were to be their companions. But when the ship reached Whangaroa in June, fewer women were made available to them and their relatives were far clearer as to the material value of their services and the conditions on which they might visit the ship.[27] By November, the local rangatira Te Puhi attempted to tighten his conditions even further. When one of the women from his tribe was rejected by her lover, he attempted to throw overboard the Bay of Islands women who had sailed from the previous port, arguing that he had the right to do so while the vessel was in an area under his mana.[28] His reaction was typical of those where material exchange was concerned. Rangatira were determined to monopolise lucrative trade opportunities and keep them within their patch. Market forces were at work but could be tempered by the wishes of the people. Just a few months earlier, Te Puhi's brother Ngāhuruhuru had demanded that a girl whose services he had sold for 'more than the usual stipend' be taken off the ship and relieved of her duties. All of his people supported Ngāhuruhuru and abandoned their work in protest. She later returned under her own steam, 'begging to be admitted on board', but although the *Dromedary*'s officers thought it prudent to turn her down, the to-ing and fro-ing went on over several days.[29]

Dr Maynard of the *Ville de Bordeaux* wrote of a young girl who was probably about thirteen years old in 1840 when, despite having a young Māori fiancé, she was carrying on a shipboard relationship with a crew member while it was anchored at Banks Peninsula in the South Island. The arrangement earned her 'a red woollen counterpane, an old cavalry sabre, and a pair of boots'. The young woman in this case was not a slave, but the goods she earned were shared with her family, as might have been expected. The counterpane or bedspread was cut in half to give each of her parents 'a kind of shawl', the boots had the soles stripped away so that her uncle could wear them despite their being too small for his feet, and the sabre went to her fiancé who swore to use it to kill Te Rauparaha should he attempt to enter their tribal area again.[30] That threat was in response to that particularly devious attack in 1830 when Te Rauparaha had infamously induced Captain Stewart, master of the *Elizabeth*, to transport a war party to the South Island.

Sex and muskets

It was probably from about 1820 that the sex industry as such had got under way on a regular basis with men engaging more in its promotion and the deployment of female captives. Ship visits had already increased by then. At least 25 visited the Bay of Islands that year and the number would continue to rise.[31] But this period coincided with the beginnings of the 'musket wars' when an arms race was in play. That circumstance surely encouraged greater involvement in the fledgling industry as an important currency of exchange.

Naturally, the price of muskets rose and fell according to demand, with the value usually measured in terms of pigs, baskets of potatoes, or tons of dressed flax. Precise figures are impossible to confirm, but in 1820 it was said to be 1 ton of dressed flax or ten large pigs.[32] Augustus Earle, a travelling painter who spent eight months in New Zealand during 1827 and 1828, claimed that ten large pigs or 120 baskets of potatoes was the fixed price at that time. Frederick Maning, who did not arrive in New Zealand until 1833, noted even then, when the price had dropped along with demand, that Māori still had to give a ton of flax, 'scraped by hand with a shell, bit by bit, morsel by morsel, half-quarter of an ounce at a time', for just one or two muskets.[33] Figures were less often cited with regard to the cost of sex, but a fairly standard rate for a contract between an individual sailor and a woman for the duration of his stay in the Bay of Islands is said to have been a dress or similar item for her and a musket for her tribe.[34]

Since flax dressing was a more customary occupation for women, a comparison of the labour expended on that pursuit compared to a sex contract might put their attitudes to alternative methods of bringing home the musketry bacon in perspective. Admittedly, estimates of how much flax a woman could prepare in a day are not reliable, varying from 5 to 20 pounds, and do not include the time spent gathering the flax or transporting it to the ship or the trader.[35] However, since there were 2240 pounds in a ton, we can assume that it would take anything between 112 and 448 days for one woman to produce a ton of dressed flax. Given how labour-intensive and time-consuming the work was, some women may well have considered that sexual favours, especially with one temporary 'husband', offered a much better option. James Belich calculated that a sex contract represented a tenfold improvement over the income earned from flax processing.[36] It may have been even more than that. Combined with the better meals and other comforts that women were likely to enjoy while living aboard ship with Western lovers, it was probably an attractive form of employment. But the nature of the 'ruling price' may also have encouraged the trade. When access to muskets was not only important for political dominance, but also critical for survival, the booming sex trade made significant contributions to Bay of Islands arsenals. Ensign McCrae's estimate that they had 'no less than 500 stand of arms' in 1820 is probably a better one than his shipmate Richard Cruise's suggested 100 for that year. According to missionary Thomas Kendall, the number had grown to at least 2000 by 1821, and Richard Davis said there were 'many thousand stands of arms . . . both in the Bay and at the River Thames' by 1826.[37] And, from the rangatira's point of view, flax dressing was probably a less productive use of his captive labour force. There were few shore-based traders anywhere in New Zealand during the 1820s and the missionaries were officially forbidden to deal in muskets, so visiting ships were a vital means of access.[38] Te Rauparaha employed large numbers of women at Kāpiti to produce the 'cash' in hand to purchase muskets, but flax was less abundant in the Bay of Islands and the area's ability to supply foodstuffs declined over time, so sex was a more sustainable source of income and arms.[39]

Māori attitudes

But if, over time, Māori men became more anxious to deploy their womenfolk in the business, women often found that their experience enhanced their feminine appeal as well as giving them greater control over the arrangements. By the 1830s, it was not uncommon for rangatira to marry young women who had previously been involved in the sex trade or lived with whalers aboard ship.[40] The negligible, if any, value placed on premarital chastity was evident in the marriage of the high-ranking Bay of Islands chief Tara to a young woman known as Mrs Goshore. According to John Liddiard Nicholas, her 'face was familiar to all the

English sailors that happened to touch' at the Bay of Islands and her name was assumed to have derived from the words 'go on shore', which he thought was a siren call she was remembered for using. Several weeks spent aboard ship with Captain Jones, master of a Port Jackson-based vessel, had given her a very useful facility with the English language. Besides that, Tara's senior wife was as 'old and infirm' as himself, so Mrs Goshore's youthful beauty surely played a part in his affection for her, too.[41] Nicholas wrote that Tara always preferred her 'fondling assiduities . . . to the less endearing attentions of his head spouse':

> Mrs. Goshore, notwithstanding all her irregularities, had the art of preserving the unabated affection of this old man; and studying upon all occasions the peculiarities of his humour, she was ardently beloved, and he never once imagined but the flame was mutual.[42]

She was evidently good in bed.

Aside from honing their sexual skills, living with temporary husbands on British ships for weeks at a time (or even longer in some cases) gave the women greater familiarity with Western ways as well as the English language. As the men aboard the *Dromedary* found, they also 'imitated as far as they could the English manner of dress' and 'conformed themselves to English customs'.[43] The skills acquired made them not only social assets but also economic ones as they could facilitate advantageous commercial dealings on behalf of their tribal group.[44] Edward Markham, in Northland in 1834, found it 'a curious Thing' that chiefs of recent times had often married girls who had been living aboard whaling ships. It appears that those who had been well trained in Western ways could attract higher fees or clients of higher status and then settle down with a husband of rank.

Markham remarked on the missionaries' hatred of ships coming into the Bay of Islands. Anything from 30 to 35 whalers were coming in annually by that time, each staying some three weeks. The 400 to 500 men aboard these ships had been at sea perhaps for a year, or, in one case at least, 32 months. Consequently, 'the Ladies were in great request'. Even more galling for their god-fearing employers at the Paihia mission was that relatives of their servants would call and take their kin away to take advantage of those opportunities. When Henry Williams reported that his wife Marianne had lost her 'most useful girl' to the ships, he said it was 'a common case. As soon as the girls become useful they are carried off.'⁴⁵ '[I]n spite of all their prayer lessons', as Markham put it, the women would be very satisfied with the three weeks they spent on board, coming away with a fowling piece for their male relatives as well as blankets, gowns, and other goods: worth as much as they would earn from the mission in a year. Markham not only understood why they would want to take part in the trade but also felt that the sailors had done at least as much towards 'Civilizing the Natives' as the missionaries had: possibly more.⁴⁶ Nonetheless, he acknowledged that they sometimes went too young and became infertile as a result of sexually transmitted disease.

From the Māori point of view, the rank or status of the client or temporary husband was an important factor. So, in the case of shipping, attention was first directed at the officers, with the more lowly members of crew being something of a consolation prize. The Frenchman Captain Cyrille-Pierre-Théodore Laplace, who visited the Bay of Islands in 1831 aboard *La Favorite*, referred to 'hard women who pocketed their presents and gave up nothing' — a cultural misunderstanding, perhaps, since what is referred to as 'gift exchange' in Māori society did not necessarily require an immediate return. Nevertheless, he and his companions found this all the more annoying because the women he referred to were the cleanest and prettiest among a group of rangatira women. They knew from their white chemises, their well-arranged hair, high-quality necklaces, and 'gentle and reserved little airs' that they were awaiting particular whaling captains or officers who would return the following winter. When those men of rank had departed their shores previously, their chiefs had placed them under tapu so that 'their fidelity became a matter for the atoua [atua, or gods], and judging from what [he] saw, it was strictly observed'. Laplace regretted that such a fine institution for protecting absentee husbands was not only unknown in his country but, he felt, was unlikely to 'take root there without great difficulty'.⁴⁷ Nevertheless, those remarks tend to confirm that women of some rank in Māori society were generally matched with the officer class aboard Western vessels and suggest that captives more commonly found their clients among the rank and file of ship's crew.

Enthusiastic participants?

Back in the 1770s, one member of the *Resolution*'s crew had written that women 'offer'd themselves for sale with as much ease & assurance as the best Strand walker in London would do' and that their services were available 'for much less than you could get a fish for your dinner'. As Cook had intimated, the laws of supply and demand appear to have been at work here as well as the suppliers learning what the customers might be willing to pay, because the price of sex would be much higher when Western ship visits became more frequent in the early nineteenth century.[48] But comparative values were also relevant. It was not fish that the crew made payment with. The cost of a fish may have been low in England and of approximately equivalent value to the nails, fish-hooks, second-hand clothing, and other items in great demand by Māori at this time.[49] However, nails, metal tools, and European clothing were among items not previously known or available to them. In the wake of Cook's first voyage when Māori were introduced to some of those items, recognition of their many practical advantages gave them a considerably higher value than fish.

Even at that early date, previous experience led to expectations evident in 1773 when William Hodges, the *Resolution*'s artist, sought to sketch a young woman during his stay at Tōtara-nui (fig. 46). Having been well paid to descend into the saloon, she assumed that she was required to give a certain type of service so was bemused when directed to sit on a chair. Bewildered as to how this strange man intended to have his way with her, she did her best to oblige by first sitting in a prone position across the chair.[50] What she thought of her experience as an artist's model is hard to guess.

Half a century later, the sex trade had really taken off in more popular ports of call such as the Bay of Islands. René Primevère Lesson, a naturalist and doctor aboard the French corvette *Coquille* in 1824, stressed the enthusiasm of the women of Kahuwera for a trade 'they found more lucrative' than that of provisions or curiosities:

> Canoes arrived crammed (the word is not too strong) full of women, and our bridge was overrun with swarms of girls; for the seventy-man crew, more

than a hundred and fifty samples of this unorthodox merchandise came like a flock of ewes in search of buyers.

Lesson claimed that despite the captain's vain attempts to remove 'this lascivious livestock', for every ten women who left one side of the corvette, twenty more clambered up the other. In other words, they were very keen to participate in the business. Yet he interpreted their carefree ways as symptomatic of 'the moral degradation produced by the disgrace they [had] fallen into'.[51] It is unlikely that the women felt any such disgrace. However, Lesson may also have believed that their enthusiasm was inspired by the threat of punishment if they failed to take home sufficient earnings. He wrote that one beautiful young girl, taken to the vessel with a view to her pleasing one of the officers, was struck by her mistress when she failed in her mission.[52]

Access to sought-after commodities was a very important goal and the women were not slow in coming forward when it came to displaying their charms. Laplace reported that Kororāreka Māori were persistent in their attempts to obtain ammunition and biscuits from his sailors and that the local young women attempted to distract them from their fishing by running in front of them. Nor was this eagerness limited to the Bay of Islands. Dumont d'Urville, who visited Otago in 1840, wrote that 'as night fell the ships in harbour were visited regularly by troops of women'.[53]

It might be wondered whether the enthusiasm of women to take advantage of opportunities arising from ship visits was bolstered somewhat by the exotic character of the visiting white men. Might they have had particular appeal, such as women of our own time might presume that an Italian or Frenchman would prove a better lover than one of Anglo-Saxon stock? Or as a first-rank sports hero or movie-star boyfriend might give a woman kudos within female society? At a time when Westerners were the source of exciting new and highly desirable manufactured goods and luxury items, such men would surely have been perceived as wealthy and powerful. As one woman of very high rank sang in a waiata, or song, she composed, the beautiful clothes she had enjoyed would disappear over the horizon with William Mayhew, her American whaler husband. As he sailed away, she would return to her 'rags' and to her 'nothing-at-all':

Te kaipuke
E waihape atu ra noa
na, i Te Hu
He tau a Pohiwa e rere ana ia
Te tai ki Europi homai e Toru
Tetehi ki a au ahu mehume tahi
te taku a te tipua kati au ka hoki
Ki aku pepepora
Ki aku kore noa iho

But see whose ship is that which tacks
Is it yours, O Hu [Mayhew]
you husband of Pohiwa
sailing away on the tide to Europe
O Toru pray, give some of your fine things
to me: for beautiful are the clothes of the whiteman
Enough of this, I must return to my rags, and to my nothing-at-all[54]

Western attitudes

The worldview of the visitors was quite different from that of their hosts, but their publicly expressed opinions are far more readily accessible. Whatever their true feelings towards the situation, a number of ship's captains proclaimed their repugnance towards the goings-on between Māori women and their crews. Laplace was one who was keen to avoid responsibility for the 'dissolute conduct' that occurred when 'the attractive ladies of Korora-Reka' played a 'new trick' on him:

> The sentries entrusted with announcing to the officer of the watch the approach of boats, had been on duty for two hours and the distant strains of the Sirens were the only sounds to trouble the silence that reigned on board the *La Favorite*. Suddenly, several small canoes that were not large enough to arouse suspicion, but whose numerous passengers had noisy shrill voices, causing one to recognise them immediately as friendly, came alongside the corvette at all quarters at once. The surprise was all the

more difficult to avoid because the enemy, displaying an agility that easily put the sailors of the watch off the scent, clambered up the channels, and guided by accomplices, invaded the interior of the ship in a trice. At such a critical juncture, M. Verdier leapt into action and displayed strong principles worthy of better success; but perfidy had corrupted all hearts. As for myself, whose authority was invoked, I went to sleep again so I would not have to witness such disgraceful things; when, in the morning, I desired, perhaps a little late, to protect the morals of my crew, the female cohort had decamped.[55]

But if officers often expressed abhorrence at the level of sexual interaction in New Zealand, some remarks suggest that the disgust was really aimed at their readers at home. The words of René Primevère Lesson, for example, strike the reader as those of a man under strain, much like a priest whose vow of celibacy was being sorely tried:

Among these accommodating creatures some were not, however, to be ignored; a dulcet voice, expressive glances, a well filled mouth, fresh and rounded lines, mirth, enthusiasm for pleasure, and even a dash of coquettishness, all ought to have seduced me. But I was repelled by their very teasing, as much as by the immodesty demonstrated in the mimed scenes which each evening, after being with crew members, marked the moment of separation. As soon as the daylight failed, all these young girls placed themselves in a line one behind the other and began, while singing and beating their hands, a sort of lewd dance, which, as they warmed to it, ended up in obscene contortions and gestures.[56]

Yet, on another occasion, Lesson described the entertainment provided by those girls who remained on board overnight somewhat differently. At Kahuwera, he wrote that 'having become an integral part of the crew', the girls 'were kind enough to repay their cordial reception with games and dances'. Although the erotic nature of the dances was still noted, his response had less of a scandalised tone to it. Perhaps he was becoming acculturated?[57]

Kororāreka: the hell-hole of the Pacific?

Kororāreka's various epithets of ignominy included 'Gomorrah, the scourge of the Pacific' and 'Hell hole of the Pacific', or, as one alliterati put it, '[l]icentious lasciviousness was restricted only by satiety'.[58] Writing in 1859, Arthur Thomson said that, 27 years earlier, when only 100 white settlers lived there permanently, Kororāreka was dubbed the Cyprus of the Southern Ocean where 'life was one unceasing revel' and that local chiefs 'lived in affluence by pimping for the crews of whale ships'.[59] Charles Hursthouse, an avid promoter of British immigration to New Zealand and critic of missionary support for Māori sovereignty, also compared the Bay of Islands with places of disrepute in Europe:

> . . . blasphemy and the debauchery of drunkenness, were all intensified by debauchery in women. Dark Helens, aboriginal Messelinas, swarmed in Kororareka. Every resident kept a mistress, every visitor came for one. Native women were as common an article of barter between chiefs and whalers as native pigs; and to the daily fights and quarrels which arose in such a community through rum and whiskey were to be added those which arose through the passion of jealousy and the disputed possession of the slave girl. There was neither magistrate nor policemen at Kororareka, neither law nor order nor gospel; every ruffian, and there were many, did what seemed good to him; and in 1831, this New Zealand village port was the veritable "Alsatia" of the Pacific, dashed with a "Convict Wapping."[60]

Missionary frustration and all-too-frequent disappointment when young Māori women from their Paihia station were tempted to cross the Bay to join in the sex trade at Kororāreka entered into local lore. It is said that, on one occasion, a girl who decamped from the mission and crossed over when ships arrived was 'told in disgust to go to Hell in her own way'. Having reached the other side, her sailor friends decided to reciprocate by calling Paihia 'Heaven'.[61] It was certainly perceived as the more godly side by the Bay's Pākehā residents, many of whom were Christian by custom or expectation only. Ironically, mission training may have had the unexpected and unwanted by-product of making the girls more marketable to Western clients.

Missionary attitudes

At Kaeo, the still single Wesleyan missionary John Hobbs was made to 'feel unpleasant sensations' when a chief came to ask when he was leaving for Port Jackson to get his 'wife'. The question being brushed off, the visitor made the reason for his inquiry 'more plain'. Hobbs managed to overcome his horror long enough to avoid falling into a trap a friend in Tasmania had alerted him to:

> One assaulted in New Zealand by a Chief and his Daughter with base designs cannot exclaim with indignation "You filthy strumpet get away", as in England without exposing himself to the danger of being killed and eaten by these wretched Cannibals.

Having been forewarned, Hobbs managed to keep himself in check and avoided temptation by portraying his feelings through his 'countenance'.[62] Married missionaries were open to temptation too — and sometimes succumbed.[63] However, the moral education of non-missionaries — both European and Māori — was part of the missionary project.

After a regular Sunday service in March 1828, Henry Williams boarded the ship *Ann* in the Bay of Islands, apparently intending to preach. But, finding that no preparations had been made for his visit, he went ashore to Captain Robert Duke's house, where he found a room full of willing listeners and spoke to them from Psalm XXIII. 'Their attention was good', he reported, but 'their course of life depraved'. 'The boys' (presumably those from the mission) told him that as the boat from Paihia had drawn near, 'the girls were hurried out of the ship to go on shore'.[64] Duke had attended CMS services since he first called at the Bay of Islands in 1825, had often hosted Williams's Sunday services, and had even given the missionary a subscription to the Bethel Union Society, but was consistently ill-treated by him.[65] Williams was, quite literally, a man on a mission. A few months later and feeling a 'need to speak seriously upon the abominable practice of sending their daughters on board the shipping', he 'assembled all who would come near'. But it was a thankless task. His audience 'walked away one by one' until he was left alone and had to admit that they 'did not approve of what [he] had to say'.[66]

Māori who had been baptised or aspired to baptism were being taught a very new moral code, which many accepted, but it was not a process without trauma. CMS missionary Richard Davis lost a young man called Philip who was removed from the mission by Rewa for having tried to stop one of his relatives being taken away by the rangatira assuming that she was to be used for prostitution. 'The Chief treated me with great contempt', bewailed Davis: 'They have never acted in this way before.' Davis referred to the young woman concerned as a slave, so her mother and Philip were probably captives, too. But despite their being very upset about the situation ('a prostitute she could not be', were the words Davis used), she was returned 'to her rightful owner' the next day.[67] This was in 1836, when captives were often being released, which suggests that those readily deployed to the sex trade retained their economic value.

'Slave labour' in the sex trade

According to Te Kāhui (Poukōhatu Te Kāhui Kararehe) of Taranaki, chief informant for Percy Smith's *History and Traditions of the Maoris of the West Coast*, it was enslaved women who were given to Europeans. He also felt the need to add that some were even 'given to niggers who were on board the ships at the same price as the others'.[68] Born in 1846, Te Kāhui was taught Taranaki traditional knowledge by tribal elders during his early years, but Christian ideas were surely instilled by his father, a Methodist minister, that may have influenced his understandings.[69]

Rather than being standard procedure from the start, the use of female war captives in the sex trade may have been a practice that gained favour over time. Dr Fairfowl told Commissioner Bigges's 1821 inquiry somewhat ambiguously that although the numbers of women who offered themselves for prostitution at the Bay of Islands were not particularly great when the *Dromedary* visited in 1820, 'the whole unmarried female population appeared to be at the service of the ship'. He was aware of only one instance in which a master took a female slave aboard the *Dromedary*, adding that he returned the following morning expecting that he would receive some remuneration for her hire. When he learned that she had failed in her mission (like the woman who would fail to score an officer from the *Coquille* in 1824), the 'master' conveyed his disappointment by beating her.[70] Since this was evidently witnessed by the officers and crew, we might wonder whether the beating was, in part, intended to arouse their sympathies and ensure her of more custom the next day. A more detailed account of what appears to be the same incident suggests that was the plan.

Cruise, who was also aboard the *Dromedary*, wrote that the girl was taken back out to the ship in a canoe and furiously attacked by two men as the crew looked over the side, telling them 'to desist'. The men in the canoe responded by tying her hands and feet and paddling back to shore. Having been told that she was now about to be killed and eaten, some of the officers headed straight for the beach where they found she had been untied but left on her own, crying. Having seen the men from the *Dromedary* arrive, her abuser warned that unless they bought the girl, he would kill her. The rangatira of the group, who was evidently a friend of the Englishmen, immediately put their minds at rest by assuring them it was a performance for their benefit and that nothing would happen to the girl. Disappointed by having nothing to show for sending her aboard, her master was throwing his toys out of the metaphorical cot.[71]

However, the *Dromedary* visited in 1820, during the early stages of the 'musket wars' and possibly before the northern tribes had built up a significant stock of captives. If that was the case, it may not have been until a slightly later date, when more such women were available and less often required for other duties like potato cultivation or flax dressing, that they were redeployed to the sex trade on a more regular basis.

A couple who often appear in European accounts of the trade during this period are Tuai and his wife. Lesson may have misunderstood the nature of the arrangement when he wrote that Māori marriages were 'arranged by purchase', but his remark that Tuai, then chief of Kahuwera on the Paroa peninsula, 'bought' his wife with two muskets and a male slave is not unenlightening. She was said to have been from a distinguished family of high rank, so that, in return for his gifts, Tuai received 'mats' and three family slaves to look after her.[72] However, Ensign Charles Hector Jacquinot, Lesson's crewmate aboard the

Coquille, wrote that because Tuai 'was sufficiently attached to' his first wife, he chose not to take any others, which strongly implies that they were a genuine love match.[73]

As a young man, Tuai had visited England with Titeri in 1818 at the request of Samuel Marsden. But although the missionaries had great hopes of his Christian convictions, they were probably disappointed in the longer term. He not only boasted about the favours he had received from a missionary's daughter (probably Elizabeth Marsden) during his stay in Australia but also participated very eagerly in the sex trade when back in New Zealand.[74] According to Lesson and others, Tuai and his wife 'Ehidi' (perhaps Hiri) were both benefiting from the sexual services offered to sailors by their captives. Perhaps much of what he did learn during his sojourn overseas related to commercial opportunities rather than theology.

Tuai told Ensign Lottin, another member of the *Coquille*'s crew, that he had 25 slaves: that the men went fishing with him, took him about in his canoe, harvested potatoes, and gathered other foods. The women, he said, performed much the same duties but proved even more profitable when sent aboard ship, where, he said, 'they reap a plentiful harvest'.[75] At one point in his account, Lesson wrote of 'thirty or so slave girls who had settled down on board to trade their charms [and] gave us regularly every evening an exhibition of their love dances', that number suggesting that they may not all have belonged to Tuai.[76] Nevertheless, he said that the couple 'never failed to summon and to visit their slaves each evening to take possession of their day's yield'. Powder for their owners' muskets was what the women dutifully requested from their sailor friends.[77] For Lesson, having to hand over part or all of their earnings represented exploitation, but it was not out of line with normal practice. Even in later years, when individual workers were paid wages for their labour, it was normal for them to share a significant portion of the cash or goods they received with their rangatira or wider tribal group. Men, whether captives or free, who worked as crew on Western ships were said to have presented one 'fowling piece' or shotgun to their chief on their return but to have kept the balance of their earnings.[78] Individual wealth had little place in a communal society although workers typically received some personal consideration.[79]

Théodore Julien de la Calande de Blois, another member of the *Coquille*'s crew, thought that 'as a general rule, the girls who came on board [were] slaves', but added that 'free girls who belong to the first families may also play the same role without the slightest scruple' — at least until they were married.[80] Perhaps some better insight into the differences between free and captive women, the status of their clients, and the nature of their offerings comes from his shipmates Jacquinot and Lesson. Much like other visitors to New Zealand shores during the 1820s, Jacquinot wrote that: 'A ship is barely anchored before she is filled with women who by their gestures and movements promote the purchase of their favours, which they are always ready to grant for the least trifle.' However, his subsequent comments are even more enlightening:

> The women who sink to the lowest level of prostitution are all slaves that their masters employ in this way in order to acquire a few European things. In any case, these unhappy women do not seem angered by this obligation, they are on the contrary in a state of perpetual gaiety.[81]

Lesson's impressions were much the same, though far less kind to their hosts:

> The young girls who come crowding to offer their bodies for mere trifles or even for a morsel of bread, are the slaves that these disgusting blood-covered savages take in war ...

Yet he, too, acknowledged that they were 'always full of the most exuberant gaiety'.[82]

So those comments seem to confirm that higher-ranking Māori women set their sights on liaisons with higher-ranking Western men but also suggest that this particular aspect of a young captive's duties was not the most odious from her point of view. Female captives were expected to be sexually available to their masters, so the same expectations with regard to foreigners might not have altered their lot dramatically, except that in the new situation, there were added bonuses in the form of gifts or other treats for those services.[83] Moreover, as discussed earlier, war captives came from the various ranks of Māori society. That might mean that rangatira women from other tribes were not as badly treated as those of lower rank or that they were more likely offered to officers or Westerners of rank than those of more lowly origins.

Lesson had sympathy for those 'victims of greed' whose parents 'had been killed and even eaten by their barbarous proprietors' and thought 'their bosoms as lovely as one could hope to find'. But although he insisted that he found their smell revolting, he accepted that the seamen found them appealing. 'Temporary unions were contracted, and these unhappy girls showed themselves to be faithful', he wrote.[84] Why they should need to be faithful if their lot was so miserable is unclear. They may have been obliged to uphold the deal arranged by their master or mistress, but the Frenchman's response was likely informed by his own social mores. His shipmate Jacquinot had, after all, previously described them as 'unhappy women . . . in a state of perpetual gaiety'.

Whatever the case, they do not seem to have greatly resented their situation. During the *Coquille*'s visit, an elderly woman from the shore settlement was carried out to sea in a canoe that had been tied to the side of the corvette but broke free in a storm. Hearing her cries, some of the captives employed as sex workers 'threw themselves into the ice-cold water' and brought the woman and the canoe back to safety. One of her rescuers was a cheerful girl whom the seamen called Nanette and 'whose irrepressible gaiety was the delight of the hammocks'.[85]

As we know, income from the sex trade was often measured in muskets during the 1820s arms race. Because northern tribes were generally well supplied with them by about 1820, well before those in less economically favourable locations, they became an important component in intertribal trade from that date.[86] So, with access to guns not only the key to political power but also a matter of life or death, it might be wondered whether this period of peak demand was also related to a more 'hard sell' approach. Records suggest that the industry gained considerable traction from around 1820. George Clarke, who had arrived in New Zealand aboard Duperrey's vessel *Coquille* the previous year, wrote in March 1825 that:

> For a musket a New Zealander will make great sacrifices, he will labour hard and fare hard for many months to obtain his musket, in fact it is his idol he values it above all he possesses, he will not only part with his slaves for

one, but even prostitute his children to diseased sailor [sic] for one of those instruments of destruction.[87]

The increasing use of 'slave' women in the sex trade might explain the 1826 instance when 'a number' of Māori women were exchanged for muskets and taken away permanently.[88] If they were captives, their 'owners' may have been tempted to trade them with another Māori group. But 'slave owners' and missionary 'redeemers' were often at odds over their transactions. In 1829, some time after James Kemp had paid blankets and other articles to redeem a slave girl, her rangatira arrived to reclaim her. He now wanted a musket and intended to take her to the 'Shipping where he [might] obtain one for her'. Kemp pursued the man and brought her back, but the 'crafty fellow' who had consigned her to him now returned some of the articles paid 'after they had been worn several months'. He threw them over the fence to Kemp, who promptly threw them back. A slapstick comedy followed as items from the rangatira's wardrobe went back and forth over the fence and he kept up his 'teasing' for several hours. Finally wearying of the game, he headed off inland, away from the coast and his ticket to musket ownership.[89]

Over the next five or six years, most tribes became fully armed. That is to say, they had one gun for every one to three of their warriors, so the scramble for muskets began to subside.[90] But there were still many other economic benefits to be had. Pōmare, who purpose-built a pā at Ōtūihu around 1830 to serve as a centre of rest and recreation for visiting mariners, is said to have had some 96 slave girls on hand to provide for their sexual needs. Arthur Thomson commented that the missionaries in the area 'magnified and widely circulated glowing accounts of the scenes which daily occurred; and stated that the [British] Resident, although he had the British flag flying over his house, had no power to put down the floating brothels which polluted the bay under its protection'.[91] Writing in 1927, some 70 years after Thomson, Thomas Donne, who, perhaps appropriately, had once been secretary of the government's infant Department of Tourist and Health Resorts, pointed out that the New Zealand situation had hardly been unique. Māori were 'following the procedure of the Lords of the Admiralty' of the time, who sent 'a draught of officially approved harlots on board' ships that returned to England after foreign service. There they evidently remained for several days before the unmarried sailors and marines were given shore leave.[92]

As late as 1840, another of the many ship's doctors who have bequeathed their reminiscences of activities in New Zealand ports described the salesmanship of a man from Akaroa, probably a low-ranked rangatira, whom he referred to as an 'honest procurer'. Dr Louis Thiercelin, from the whaler *Ville de Bordeaux*, saw this man as something of a 'village mayor' who was keen to facilitate good relations with visiting vessels and had acquired a collection of certificates attesting to his kind assistance. Over dinner with the captain, John, as he was known, offered to supply the ship's complement with 'female companions whose fidelity was guaranteed for the whole duration' of their visit.[93] Thiercelin was especially impressed by 'a fat, pleasant and healthy-looking girl in her thirties', offered to the captain personally, who turned out to be John's sister. She became their 'daily companion', accompanying their party on their walks and proving an invaluable source of local information.[94] So, once again, the line between commercial sex, sexual hospitality, temporary marriage, and, perhaps, a personal assistant was blurred.

But if Dr Fairfowl had been correct in his statement that only one slave woman was involved when the *Dromedary* visited in 1820, the activities of Tuai and others in 1824 suggest that attitudes had changed considerably in the interim. According to Fairfowl's evidence, Māori were aware, even in 1820, that sexually transmitted disease had been introduced by seamen. They called it 'the Europe god'. Fairfowl had noted only fourteen or fifteen cases during his stay in the Bay of Islands, explaining that it had not spread to any great degree because those infected were placed under tapu.[95] The situation may have changed by 1824, though, as Ensign Lottin, who did not shirk from apportioning blame, said that '[v]enereal disease was prevalent', and being a patriotic fellow, insisted that it was 'no use the English denying it, they are the true culprits'.[96] His shipmate, Lesson, recorded in his medical journal that:

> the native men try to prevent as much as they can all relations between
> their women and the Europeans, and send a large number of young slaves
> on board the ships, to satisfy the desires of the crews and to obtain from this

FIGURE 32. 'Slave girl, Putiki', by J. A. Gilfillan, 1847. *Sketchbook, Vol. 1:19, 1847, Hocken Library, Dunedin*

FIGURE 33. Te Waru with his left hand raised over his downcast young daughter, then under threat of being charged with murdering her brother's slave-lover. *'Te Waro', engraving by Whitby, after a sketch by Joseph Jenner Merrett, 1843, L. Haghe, lith. Day & Haghe, London: A-259-010, Alexander Turnbull Library, Wellington*

FIGURE 34. This painting by Earle shows the steepness of Rangihoua where a young girl and another 'slave' were thrown down inside potato baskets. *Augustus Earle, 'Ranghe Hue [i.e. Rangihoua], a New Zealand fortified village, the residence of Warri-Pork [i.e. Wharepoaka]', [1827]: Rex Nan Kivell Collection, NK12/141, National Library of Australia, Canberra*

FIGURE 35. 'Tohitapu, chief and tohunga of the Roroa', from a sketch by Archdeacon Henry Williams. *Reproduced from J. R. Elder, ed.,* The Letters and Journals of Samuel Marsden, 1765–1838, *Dunedin, 1932, p. 472*

FIGURE 36. Ships at Kororāreka in 1842. *Louis Le Breton, 'Anchorage of Kororareka (Bay of Islands) Mouillage de Korora-Reka (Baie des Iles)', 1842: 2002-0036-2, Museum of New Zealand Te Papa Tongarewa, Wellington*

FIGURE 37. Sketch of a slave giving a drink to a chief. *John White,* Illustrations Prepared for White's Ancient History of the Maori, *1891*

FIGURE 38. This painting shows Fox, Heaphy, Brunner, and Kehu (smoking) by a campfire. *William Fox, 'On the grass plain below Lake Arthur. 8th & 9th Feb. 1846': B-113-014, Alexander Turnbull Library, Wellington*

FIGURE 39. This scene, from the Bay of Islands during Augustus Earle's visit in the late 1820s, shows a man addressing a group of warriors. Most are armed with muskets, although one on the far right holds a taiaha (fighting staff). It is a time of transition but muskets were the key to success. *Augustus Earle, 'War speech', 1838: PUBL-0015-09, Alexander Turnbull Library, Wellington*

FIGURE 40. A group of people at Te Aro pā, including members of Ngāti Ruanui and Ngāti Awa, 1847. *George French Angas,* The New Zealanders Illustrated, *London, 1847: PUBL-0014-40 PAINTING 22701759, Alexander Turnbull Library, Wellington*

FIGURE 41. This 1827 painting of Te Rangituke of Kawakawa with his wife and son is an example of old and new weapons sitting side by side. The rangatira holds a taiaha while his son holds a long-barrelled musket. *Augustus Earle, 'Portrait of Aranghi Tooker [i.e. Rangituke] Chief of Cower Cower [i.e. Kawakawa] Bay of Islands, New Zealand, with his wife and son, painted at New Zealand', 1827: G-634, Alexander Turnbull Library, Wellington*

FIGURE 42. This lithograph appears to show a woman overseeing a group of female workers in such a way that they are likely to have been war captives. *Louis Auguste de Sainson, 'Défrichement d'un champ de patates', from Dumont d'Urville,* Voyage pittoresque autour du monde, *Paris, 1839: PUBL-0034-2-387, Alexander Turnbull Library, Wellington*

FIGURE 43. The trader Phillip Tapsell and his daughter in later years. *Unknown photographer (n.d.): DU402.2 T172, Auckland War Memorial Museum Library*

FIGURE 44. A soldier asleep in a whare (house), being watched over by a Māori woman, between 1845 and 1858. *Robert Henry Wynyard: A-113-034, Alexander Turnbull Library, Wellington*

FIGURE 45. Mission station at Paihia, by Henry Williams. *Church Missionary Quarterly Papers, No. 79, Michaelmas, 1835: PUBL-0031-1835-03, Alexander Turnbull Library, Wellington*

FIGURE 46. Sketch of William Hodges's subject at Tōtaranui, or Queen Charlotte's Sound. *William Hodges, 'Woman of New Zealand', from J. Cook,* A Voyage Towards the South Pole and Round the World, *London, 1777, pl. 58: C-051-027, Alexander Turnbull Library, Wellington*

form of speculation, various items they value. A religious principle makes a New Zealand man consider vile and foul any relations he might have with these unhappy prostitutes, torn from the bosom of their tribes and abandoned, by the ferocity of their captors and at the risk of being left with smarting souvenirs, to the brutality of the firstcomer.[97]

But despite Māori efforts to prevent the spread of disease, another ship's surgeon, John Watkins, went so far as to claim that 49 out of 50 women at Kororāreka had sexually transmitted disease by 1834. Another, John Downing Tawell, who was at pains to differentiate between the habits of Christian and non-Christian Māori, said that he was aware of only five or six cases during his 1837 visit and that 'those were among the Heathen Tribes'.[98] So, according to the Frenchman, the English were the main purveyors of the disease, and according to the Englishman, the heathens the most numerous victims. Ernst Dieffenbach, a scientist employed by the New Zealand Company whose interests were better served by condemning the missionary presence, claimed that although members of the CMS were generally very willing to offer medical assistance to Māori, they always refused if there was 'anything sexual in the disease'.[99] Māori themselves may have used kawakawa, a native pepper tree, to treat gonorrhoea. It was previously used to treat skin diseases, by older men as an aphrodisiac, and for other medical purposes, which may have suggested that the plant would treat this new disease.[100]

The problem of illegitimacy

Lesson was probably correct in thinking that the use of captive women was linked to attempts to avoid the spread of sexually transmitted disease. But there might have been other reasons for using women from outside one's own tribal group. Unmarried women were usually free to initiate sexual liaisons, but the importance of whakapapa, or genealogy, and its implications for status and land rights meant that the birth of children outside a formally acknowledged marriage was problematic.

A number of Māori words and phrases equate roughly to the English terms 'bastard' or 'illegitimate' and indicate that children born from informal relationships or who were not recognised by their fathers lacked status.[101] One well-known example occurs in the oral tradition of the Ngāti Porou ancestor Paikea's journey from Hawaiki to New Zealand. In a version told by the Reverend Mohi Tūrei of Waiapu, Uenuku had two sons: Ruatapu, born to him by a slave wife, and Kahutiaterangi, whose mother was of high rank. One day, when Ruatapu's kite came to rest on top of Uenuku's house and he climbed up onto the roof to retrieve it, his father called out: 'Who is this, trampling on my house?' To which Ruatapu replied, 'It is I, Ruatapu.' His father's harsh reply that he must get down and not walk over his tapu head sorely hurt the son's feelings. It might have been alright if it was his brother Kahutiaterangi who did this, said Uenuku, because he was 'honorably begotten', but Ruatapu was merely 'the offspring of passion' (he tama meamea noa ra koe naku).[102] In another version involving the same characters, Ruatapu was berated using other phrases:

> E hika, nāku tonu koe; he tama meamea koe nahaku; he moenga rau-kawakawa, he moenga hau!

> Son, while you are mine, you are a bastard son, you were conceived on a bed of leaves, outdoors.[103]

The status of female captives chosen to cohabit with one of their conquerors is implied by an account relating to Ngāpuhi's sacking of the island of Mokoia in Lake Rotorua. According to Te Maranui of Ngāti Manawa, one of the Ngāpuhi chiefs took two young Te Arawa women from among his share of the prisoners to be his concubines. When they were each about to give birth, their master told them that, if their babies were boys, he would make them his wives, but if they were girls, he would kill both them and their children. One of these young women, fearing an unfortunate outcome, fled into the bush where she did indeed give birth to a daughter. Daring not go back to her master, both she and her daughter soon died, probably of exposure.[104] It would seem, therefore, that the status of captive women and their children, including whether they were considered to be legitimate or not, depended entirely on the attitude of their captor 'husbands'. That supposition supports the suggestion that the 'wives' South Island men offered for prostitution were female captives whose status was more in the nature of a concubine than a formally acknowledged wife.

During the early phase of sexual interaction between Māori women and Western sailors, new terms were coined for the children born of their relationships. These included: 'utu pihikete' (paid for in biscuits), 'huipaina' (paid in hoop iron), and 'o te parara' (out of the [whaler's] barrel). They implied that the child was the inadvertent result of a commercial transaction.[105]

The boom in ship visits, naturally increasing the scale of sexual interaction, must have raised concerns about sexually transmitted disease and illegitimate children as well as the impact of both. It was a situation in which female captives from other tribes would have been considered more expendable, especially for lower-ranked seamen with little status. Such men were unlikely to bring any peripheral advantage to the local community — or provide support for their offspring. Reports of infanticide or of elderly or sickly captives being killed are often related to a lack of familial support. The same rationale was applied to the children of Westerners who might also be put to death when they were orphaned or their fathers moved on to pastures new.[106] A woman at the Waimate mission, who had previously lived as a captive nearby, told Richard Davis's wife Mary of her experiences. She had given birth to two children during her career as a ship girl, but both were killed by her master because they 'had been begotten by Europeans who would not help to bring them up'.[107]

Following Hongi Hika's attack on Mokoia the previous year, John Butler's wife gave two axes in exchange for a half-caste child, 'belonging (as the natives say) to the doctor of the "Coromandel," in order to save its life'.[108] According to Butler, the child would otherwise have been condemned to death because its mother was dead and the infant was still unable to walk.[109] So, once again, it seems that the local people did not feel they could cope with a totally dependent child whose father was not one of their own. Later that year, 1822, John King reported that a 'slave at Rangiua [Rangihoua?]' killed a baby girl she had just given birth to because 'many Females do not like the Trouble of Infants & destroy them before they are brought forth; Female Infants are often killed as they are not accustomed to war'.[110] As mentioned in Chapter 3, however, King reported in 1825 that another woman tried to hang her child before committing suicide because her husband had been killed in battle. That woman told Mrs King 'that she reasoned within herself thus, my husband is dead, I will hang myself but who will nurse & feed my child, so I intended to hang my child & then myself'. '[I]n this manner', wrote King, 'they are driven to desperation and death'.[111] Such fates were not restricted to captives or their offspring, though. As mentioned in Chapter 3, Richard Taylor thought it not uncommon for infants resulting from liaisons not sanctioned by a woman's father to be destroyed by their grandfathers.[112] Simple, old-fashioned jealousy might also incite a mother to kill her own child. According to Joel Polack, the senior wife of the Bay of Islands rangatira Manu killed her own child when a slave of her husband's presented him with a recently born infant.[113]

The involvement of very young girls

There are reports of very young girls — ten years old and under — being offered to visiting sailors. According to Augustus Earle, it was the 'great deal of interest' a child wife belonging to the rangatira Rukiruki aroused amongst the Europeans that led to her 'husband' offering to dispose of her to any of them. Rukiruki was visiting the village where Earle was staying to be tattooed by Rangi, the war captive renowned for his skill in the art. Accompanied by four of his ten wives, including the one Earle judged to be 'not more than ten years of age', Rukiruki 'importuned us incessantly on the subject', he said, 'saying she was his slave, and [offering] her in exchange for a musket'.[114] But, once again, it might be wondered if this young girl was a formally recognised wife or a captive intended as a concubine.

Reverend James Watkin was another who referred to girls of a 'tender age' being offered to foreign visitors to Otago, 'often before any sign of puberty has appeared'.[115] And at Ōtūmoetai in the Bay of Plenty, a local Christian called Hamuera, who had previously lived at the Paihia mission station, told William Wade that all the girls aged over ten or eleven years had been involved in the trade.[116] Nathaniel Turner, too, wrote in 1838 that 'there was scarcely a single girl turned eleven that had not been taken on board ship for purposes of prostitution'.[117] So the situation must have been common, but to what extent it was different from previous times is not at all clear. William Brown claimed that Māori women matured 'very early' and frequently married at the age of eleven, so just how unusually young these girls were to be sexually active is equally unclear.[118]

George Forster, aboard Cook's *Resolution* in 1773, doubted 'whether they ever debased themselves so much as to make a trade of their women, before we created new wants by shewing them iron-tools'.[119] But the sex trade was probably not an 'imported crime', as William Wade had put it, but rather something that evolved more naturally over time from a form of hospitality to a service offered in exchange for payment. It is also possible that the enormous economic benefits to be gained from a trade that required little capital or labour investment encouraged some stretching of the boundaries — regarding the age of the girls involved and possibly regarding the involvement of married women. Though, in the second case, their involvement may have required great discretion lest their husbands caught wind of their wives' extramural activities as Tohitapu did. The shift over time towards a greater usage of captive women, especially in the more casual aspects of the trade, was a means of offsetting the risks of disease and fatherless children. Rangatira women, on the other hand, were important for the relationships they might form with Western traders and retaining them and their economic benefits within their tribal areas.

The missionaries had been distressed by what they saw as the immorality of any sex outside formal marriage and railed still louder against sex for material reward. But, while all this was going on and Kororāreka gained a Pacific-wide reputation as a 'hell-hole' and den of iniquity, Britain had seized the higher moral ground over the United States and other countries involved in the slave trade by taking the path of abolition. So, within a short period of time, European responses to the involvement of war captives in the sex trade were not only based on long-standing ideas of sexual morality, but perhaps even more on other more newly acquired ideas about the immorality of slavery, as they believed war captives to be. Britain was taking its recently acquired horror of that institution to the furthest corners of the world.

CHAPTER SIX

Taking British liberty and freedom to Māori

AFRICAN SLAVERY HAD BEEN AN IMPORTANT COMPONENT IN THE rise of Britain's power during the Industrial Revolution, but despite its economic benefits, the British were proud of being the first nation to abolish the slave trade. Given key aspects of their national identity, that should probably not be surprising.

In a 1941 issue of *LIFE* magazine, a famous British military man, General Smuts (twice Prime Minister of South Africa and an early advocate of racial segregation), claimed that the British Empire was 'the widest system of organised human freedom which has ever existed in human history'.[1] Smuts was far from alone in his extravagant notions of British freedom. Almost half a century earlier, in his book *John Bull & Co.*, Max O'Rell had proclaimed that 'the Anglo-Saxons are the only people on this earth who enjoy perfect liberty' and that the new British colonies, including New Zealand, were 'nurseries of liberty'.[2] Since being annexed to the Empire in 1840, New Zealanders, too, have liked to boast that their nation was founded on neither slavery nor convicts, thus conferring special status on the country — apparently. Liberty or freedom and the idea of the 'free-born Englishman' are fundamental to English and, by extension, from the union of Scotland and England in 1707, to a subsequently British national identity. But to what extent did Britain propagate liberty in New Zealand and did Māori become more or less free on becoming British subjects?

The term 'free-born Englishman' is associated with John Lilburne, a member of a seventeenth-century radical political group, the Levellers. Before Lilburne, the phrase 'free-born subject' was the standard parliamentarian (and pre-civil war) rallying cry. But, over time, Lilburne's phrase lost the word 'subject' to be replaced with 'Englishman'.

Whether Englishmen or Britons, the connections between liberty and English/British identity are well entrenched. Take the song 'Rule, Britannia!', first performed in 1740. It was composed to commemorate the accession of George II and the third birthday of the Princess Augusta. Traditionally performed in the BBC's Last Night of the Proms, it is well known around the world, and the line 'Britons never, never, never shall be slaves' is still sung with gusto.

It was, perhaps, natural that a culture of liberty would eventually, albeit slowly, lead to an abhorrence of slavery. As far back as 1753, the famous British jurist Sir William Blackstone said that slavery was 'repugnant to reason' and consequently had no place in English law. When an attempt was made during the mid-sixteenth century to institutionalise the enslavement of 'idle vagabonds' who would be fed upon bread and water, be refused meat, wear a ring of iron round their neck or limbs, and be compelled to work as directed, he claimed that 'the spirit of the nation could not brook this condition, even in the most abandoned rogues'.[3]

The symbols of these ideals are pervasive in British classical art, too, in which the Phrygian cap of liberty, given to freed Roman slaves, is a recurring motif.[4] On a 1757 statue of Liberty as a young woman, designed by Daniel Garrett for estate owner and coal baron George Bowes, she holds a Staff of Maintenance in her right hand, to symbolise the benevolent authority of the state, and a Cap of Liberty in her left, representing freedom from slavery.[5] Representations of Britain as John Bull, Britannia, and the British Lion frequently appeared in caricatures alongside the cap of liberty or scales of justice from about 1760 to 1820.[6] The propaganda would have been very hard to miss.

A legal case that received much publicity during the early 1770s, relating to an African slave on British soil, had a profound impact on the language used by the nascent abolitionist movement and gave impetus to its cause. In 1769, a man called Charles Stewart had taken a slave, whose name was James Somerset, with him to England from Boston, then part of a British crown colony. Somerset managed to escape in 1771 but was captured and imprisoned aboard a ship bound for Jamaica where he was to be resold. But while the unfortunate man was so detained, three people who styled themselves his godparents applied to the Court of King's Bench for a writ of habeas corpus, which meant that the court would determine whether his imprisonment was legal or not.

Lord Mansfield, Chief Justice of the King's Bench, presided over the case which was not heard until February 1772. The points of issue revolved around a slave's liberty and his status as property. Having heard from various advocates who spoke on Somerset's behalf in what turned out to be a series of three hearings, Mansfield finally delivered his judgment in June of that year. He affirmed that despite the fact that slavery was permitted in the colonies, he was bound to apply the law of the land where the person was present, and since that was England, it was not lawful there 'to take a slave by force to be sold abroad because he deserted from his service'. Ultimately, Lord Mansfield declared that chattel slavery was inconsistent with the tradition of English liberty. Somerset was discharged. As scholars have pointed out, 'racial slavery', the commodification of black people by white, had originated in the American and Caribbean colonies rather than in the British Isles. Different attitudes in the metropolis meant that even those who defended slavery and the slave trade did not attempt to justify their arguments with the suggestion that black people were in any way subhuman. As Douglas Lorimer pointed out, 'unlike the colonial variety', eighteenth-century English law was colour blind.[7]

Although the decision did not end the slave trade, many people assumed that it had done so in England.[8] Perhaps more significantly, though, the decision brought arguments for and against slavery to the fore. It also saw important shifts in the focus and vocabulary of the debate, with the illegality of slavery under English law a key point. Anti-slavery activists praised the higher moral calibre of English civil law and, as a study of the rhetoric relating to the slave trade and its connection with British national identity showed, 'arguments in favour of "liberty" trumped those favoring colonial property rights' or the economic concerns cited by anti-abolitionists.[9] Because African slavery was a critical component of the imperial economy, most of those directly involved in the case had been anxious not to upset the economic applecart. And while many are likely to have shared Mansfield's opinion that slavery was 'odious', they were more concerned with keeping slavery out of England and restricting it to the colonies so that it could continue to benefit mercantile interests without affecting the civil liberties of Englishmen.

Whereas the early historiography of British abolitionism focused on the philanthropy of figures like William Wilberforce and the evangelical Clapham Sect (who will be discussed shortly), more recent scholarship has taken a less celebratory view of the process and explored other motivations for the shift towards ending slavery. The same shift has taken place with regard to abolition in other European countries such as Portugal, Spain, and France. As was the case following the Somerset decision, myths grew around various notices, orders, and decrees issued in Portugal, which were also increasingly misunderstood or seen to offer greater freedom to slaves than was actually the case. The 'free soil principle', a term commonly applied to the idea that people in bondage could become free once they crossed particular state borders, was exploited by Somerset's supporters as it was in Portugal following a 1761 royal decree which prohibited the transportation of slaves to that kingdom and declared all those who arrived after that date to be free. But it has also been demonstrated that in all four countries – Britain, Portugal, Spain, and France – the legal shifts were less about freeing slaves per se than about protecting the countries' own citizens and bolstering their images on the world stage. In Britain, marketing the expansion of empire to those who might have had misgivings was also very important.[10]

A tide was welling in Western Europe. The French first abolished slavery following the revolution of 1789, but Napoleon revived the institution during the wars which bear his name. However, the French Revolution and its flow-on effects also altered the connotations of the cap of liberty, a long-standing symbol of British libertarianism. Reformers of the day did occasionally use the symbol but, following the Napoleonic Wars, radicals sought to reappropriate and refashion old symbols. So it was that the symbolism of the cap of liberty re-entered both the vocabulary and rituals of radicalism with a newly refined patriotic tinge, emphasising national unity in a republican future. In this new political environment — very worrying for established elites who feared revolution in England — the right to display the cap of liberty was denied. And, horror of horrors, it was even removed from the coinage. As *Cobbett's Weekly Political Register*, a radical paper dedicated to the cause of parliamentary reform and the enfranchisement of the working classes, commented in October 1819:

> What would an old king of England have said, if he had been advised to take the *Cap* from the half-penny, lest his subjects should, by the sight of it, be urged on to *sedition* and *revolution*? Everything that could be done has been done to keep the emblems of our country's former liberty from our sight and to extirpate the recollection of it from our minds; but, all the efforts having this object in view have failed.[11]

So these events reveal the ever-changing understandings of liberty itself, how much of it ordinary Britons should be able to claim, as well as the use of its symbols — all of which were subject to shifting political sands.

Various periods from around 1780 to 1850 and beyond have been referred to as Britain's 'Age of Reform'. 'Reformers' sought changes to Parliament, government, the law, the church, and more besides. In response to changes in British public feeling, the slave trade was made illegal in 1807. However, existing slaves were still not free and the passing of that legislation did little to improve the conditions under which those in British colonies such as Jamaica, Barbados, and Demerara laboured, and the poor health of slave women was believed to be the major contributing factor to their failure to reproduce themselves. The consequent labour shortage, coupled with the effects of the American War of Independence, saw sugar exports from those islands fall dramatically. The war had not only interrupted trade routes leading to higher costs but also led the Americans to source their sugar from French and Dutch sugar producers. It was a crisis that led to rebellion in Jamaica and further agitation in Britain. Fears for their safety following the Jamaican slave rebellion of 1831 saw plantation owners warm to the idea that abolition might prove a lesser evil. Meanwhile, abolitionists in Britain, campaigning for parliamentary reform, made some headway with the passing of the 1832 Reform Act. That Act widened the franchise to include many members of the middle class whose votes led to a large number of pro-slavery Members of Parliament losing their seats. The resulting shift in the balance of political power allowed the Slavery Abolition Act to pass in 1833 so that slavery itself, not merely the trade in slaves, officially, became non-existent throughout the Empire.[12]

Although the reality was less clear cut,[13] many Britons still take pride in the idea that their nation was the first to completely abolish slavery and that Britain then turned to campaigning for other countries to stop using slave labour. That campaigning was new, but the rhetoric glorifying Britain and the favoured parts of Europe as centres of freedom was not. In 1772, around the same time as abolitionist sentiments had begun to appear, Arthur Young, a keen agriculturist with an interest in political economy, estimated the world's total population at 775 million inhabitants (it was, perhaps, a little higher). All but 33 million of these, who lived in western Europe and the 'northern Anglo-American colonies', were slaves in one form or another, he wrote. Adam Smith, the 'father' of economics, agreed with Young's claim, adding that the unfree were likely to remain so for ages to come, if not forever.[14] So it was that the public relations campaign, which began life in the 1770s, had, by the 1830s, seized the moral high ground and borne long-lasting fruit.

Freedom — long a strong component in the British psyche — had combined with an abhorrence of slavery to become a pivotal facet of national identity and was promoted as both a motivation and justification for colonisation. As the Empire expanded, those ideals were also embodied in the symbolisms of the British flag — the Union Jack. And, as was the case in New Zealand, it served as another plank in the campaign assuring as yet uncolonised lands that they were better off going with Britain than their allegedly less noble foreign rivals. As the original words of the poem by James Thomson extolled:

> The nations, not so blest as thee,
> Must, in their turns, to tyrants fall;
> While thou shalt flourish great and free,
> The dread and envy of them all.

"Rule, Britannia! rule the waves:
"Britons never will be slaves."

There was considerable irony in the image, of course, as subsequent chapters will show.

Motivations behind abolitionism

Historians of abolition have argued the need to consider the economic, political, and spiritual reasons behind the surge of support for abolition in the British mind from the late eighteenth century into the 1840s, but it is equally necessary to consider those reasons in connection with British attitudes towards what they saw as slavery in Māori society.

A common theme in recent studies of abolition is the idea of atonement as a response to crises inflicted on Britain and assumptions that these represented divine retribution for national sins. Political evangelicalism is said to have begun in the early 1780s, but as the 1790s rolled on, the fear that Britain was suffering from God's displeasure gained momentum. Revolution in France and fears of insurrection at home, the Napoleonic Wars and the threat of invasion, disease and scarcity, followed by national debt and the discomfort of a mad king (George III), were surely harbingers of divine punishment. And, as if these signs were not enough, Malthus's famous work *An Essay on the Principle of Population* kept reappearing. His publications, which argued that mankind's tendency to reproduce itself until resources are outstripped, led to the conclusion that poverty and starvation were necessary to maintain balance. It was a heady mix. The end of the world was surely nigh.[15]

Slavery has been described as 'the symbolic opposite of free agency under God'.[16] So the national crises and fear of divine retribution fostered the belief that emancipation would be an act of atonement for the sin of slavery. 'We are all guilty', proclaimed William Wilberforce when he launched the first anti-slavery debate in the British House of Commons in 1789. And, as Linda Colley put it: 'Was it really to be expected that a nation that sold the heathen for selfish gain instead of endeavouring to make them Christians would be allowed to flourish?'[17]

There was also a feeling that a lack of virtue was the reason for Britain losing the war with America. Perhaps God was not on their side after all. But there was hope. In 1838, Bishop J. B. Sumner charged the clergy of the diocese of Chester with changing England through the Gospel. Drawing on 1 Peter 2:9, he insisted that England could become 'a chosen generation, a royal priesthood, a holy nation, a peculiar people!'[18] 'The eschatological importance of emancipation was that of an act of redemption — redemption of the abolitionists as well as redemption of the slaves.'[19] Perhaps the nation could still be saved from the fires of hell: but there was a long way to go.

The 'saints' come marching in

A sense of impending doom is said to have led to a jump in the number of evangelical members of the British Parliament. One study conservatively identified 112 in the period 1784–1832, and of these some 30 were adherents of what became known as the Clapham Sect.[20] Members of that influential 'sect' were among the congregation of John Venn, founder of the CMS, in Clapham, South London. Several leading abolitionists, including the well-known William Wilberforce, as well as Venn's son Henry, James Stephen, and Josiah Pratt, were among the congregation. '[F]rom that little knot of men emanated all the Bible societies, and almost all the missionary societies in the world', wrote Lord Macaulay, son of leading Clapham reformer Zachary Macaulay.[21] A number of those individuals were also responsible for directing missionaries or government officials in New Zealand.

Clapham Sect member Sir James Stephen, Undersecretary for the Colonies, not only drafted the Slavery Abolition Act in 1833, but also Lord Normanby's instructions to Captain Hobson regarding the Treaty of Waitangi.[22] Stephen had entered the Colonial Office in order to help end slavery in the British Empire, but also sought to protect indigenous peoples from colonial exploitation. So the two campaigns often overlapped, regardless of some significant conflicts between their respective aims. And those joint projects explain many of the Clapham Sect's attitudes including why their interest in Māori slavery was related to and coloured by the contemporary focus on the trans-Atlantic trade in Africans.

But while all of this was going on, other minds were focused on problems at home. The United Kingdom's population had increased from just over 16 million in 1801 to almost 27 million by 1841.[23] That rapid increase and the poverty that came with it were seen to be causing considerable social ills — as well as triggering great anguish for the better off who bore the cost of poor relief. Many thought that emigration — shifting unemployed workers offshore — would be a good way of dealing with crime, disease, and other social problems associated with Britain's alleged 'surplus' population. With these issues in the public mind and an eye on self-promotion and profit, Edward Gibbon Wakefield appeared on the scene.

He was certainly an unlikely hero. Having been a holy terror at every school he was sent to and lived a rather transitory life afterward, Wakefield first eloped and married a sixteen-year-old heiress and ward of chancery, Eliza Anne Frances Pattle. Eliza died after only four years of marriage, having given birth to two children. Some six years later, Wakefield abducted an even younger schoolgirl, Ellen Turner, the daughter of a wealthy manufacturer and county sheriff. The couple had never met but he imagined that, having made the girl his wife, her father would be obliged to help him enter political life. The plan began well. He enticed her away from school with a message that her mother was dangerously ill, and then tricked her into marriage with a cock-and-bull story about her father's grave financial difficulties which, he insisted, could only be remedied by her marrying him. The marriage apparently took place at Gretna Green, Scotland's celebrated marriage venue for runaway couples, before they fled to France. This attempt at gaining a political leg up was a dismal failure. Subsequently apprehended, Edward and his brother William, a co-conspirator, were tried and imprisoned for three years. Not one to take defeat lightly, though, he read widely while serving his time in Newgate Prison and drew on that reading to put together his theories of systematic colonisation. Wakefield's ideas were at first published anonymously in newspapers in instalments and later as a book, *A Letter from Sydney*, which appeared at the end of 1829.

There were, in reality, many problems with the theory — or gaps between theory and reality — but, despite his social faux pas, Wakefield gained influential supporters and backers who allowed him to play a leading role in the setting up of the scheme's promotional body, the New Zealand Association, in early 1837. That brought other battles, though, with the Church Missionary Society and the Colonial Office, who thought colonisation was contrary to Māori wellbeing. Since the late eighteenth century, Evangelicals had often argued that Britain was guilty of two sins: the enslavement of Africans and imperial rapine, especially in the Indian subcontinent. So the British not only had an obligation to spread the Gospel that was proportional to their previous iniquities, but the work of the missionaries '[i]n the eastern parts' was needed to atone for 'the cruelty and tyranny' of avaricious fortune-seekers who merely bore 'the name of Christians'.[24]

Protecting the aborigines

Many people in Britain felt that New Zealand was ripe for colonisation and the Association gained considerable traction. But, having finally achieved what might have appeared to be total abolition of slavery throughout the then British Empire, many of its key supporters had turned their attention to other parts of the world and the threats they perceived to indigenous peoples from schemes such as Wakefield's.

Thomas Fowell Buxton, MP for Weymouth, who had succeeded Wilberforce as leader of the parliamentary anti-slavery campaign, carried through the Bill against slavery. Taking matters further, he called for a select committee to consider what measures might be put in place to protect the native inhabitants of places settled by the British, seeking not only to protect them but also 'to lead them to the peaceful and voluntary reception of the Christian religion'.[25] He and his wider family were not only passionate about their causes but were also expert lobbyists with many friends in high places, including the Colonial Office where Buxton was a regular caller. They sought to cajole the government into action by convincing individuals in power that it was their moral, religious, and national duty, while simultaneously proposing plausible reforms and rallying support from the wider public.[26] Buxton argued that the British owed reparation to indigenous peoples who had been dispossessed throughout the Empire. He suggested that 'civilisation' and conversion to Christianity, which could be combined with missionary endeavour and very restricted colonial settlement, would provide that reparation.[27] It was perhaps inevitable then that Buxton would chair the subsequent House of Commons Select Committee on Aborigines in British Settlements.

This was a propaganda war and the Buxtons were very able exponents. In August 1835, as the Committee hearings began and evidence was being heard, Thomas had written to his family from the committee rooms. One such letter is very clear as to what they had been looking for when they prepared their lists of witnesses and questions to be asked:

> Tell Anna we had Capt[ain] Stockenstrom today and that his evidence has been most delightfully frightful and most cheeringly horrid. Oh such a set of villains[,] such robbers[,] such murderers. And Stockenstrom did answer most nobly. It was worth all the trouble Anna had. I think the enquiry will do the greatest possible good. I begin to hope we shall be able to alter the whole of our policy to savage nations.[28]

Buxton's cousin Anna Gurney would write the bulk of the Committee's final report.

One example of their manipulation of witnesses and evidence to support the need for increased British intervention in order to protect allegedly hapless Māori concerned the British naval vessel HMS *Alligator*'s expedition to Taranaki in 1833. It was sent to rescue members of the Guard family and crew of the whaling ship *Harriet* that had been wrecked on the Taranaki coast, then subsequently attacked and plundered. Several of those on board, including the wife of the captain, her two children, and other members of the crew, had been held hostage. They were ultimately rescued, but only after a series of punitive actions that saw a number of Māori killed and several of their villages destroyed. The *Alligator*'s assistant surgeon William Barrett Marshall, author of *A Personal Narrative of Two Visits to New Zealand*, had previously nailed his colours to the mast as it were by dedicating the profits from the publication of his book to the Church Missionary Society.

Both he and the *Alligator*'s master, Captain Lambert, gave evidence concerning the incident before the House of Commons Select Committee on Aborigines in 1836. However, Marshall's account of the *Alligator*'s actions, which was damning, was favoured for presentation in the Committee's report. His interview also lasted more than twice as long as that with Captain Lambert, who was defended by the Admiralty, commended by other authorities, and ultimately retired a full Admiral.[29] It seems that, in this case as in others, Buxton and his collaborators distorted the circumstances surrounding the *Alligator*'s expedition and its impact to strengthen their campaign for British 'protection' of New Zealand Māori and other South Pacific islanders who were alleged to be the victims of evil Europeans. But the emphasis was always on indigenous people as being in need of paternalistic protection through Christianisation and an accompanying process of 'civilisation'.[30]

There had been increasing concern about the effects of European contact on indigenous peoples. The notion of 'fatal impact' — the belief that indigenous people were destined to die out in the face of competition from allegedly superior white people — was nagging consciences. Perhaps fearful for their own souls, the campaigners hoped that some of God's wrath had been deflected by their campaigns. As the report of the Select Committee on Aborigines explained: 'Great Britain in former times, countenanced evils of great magnitude, — slavery and the slave trade; but for these she has made some atonement.'[31] Whatever machinations went on behind the scenes, the report was significant for its impact on the humanitarians of the day and the Aborigines' Protection Society, instituted in 1836.[32] The Society, which drew in many of those previously involved in the movement to abolish slavery, was dedicated to ensuring that the necessary reforms identified by the Select Committee were followed through by government.[33] Buxton was one of its founders. Not that he had deserted the cause of slavery.

Interlinked ideas put forward by Buxton were that Christianity could not be introduced until the slave trade was suppressed and that civilisation would follow legitimate commerce. His 1839 book *The African Slave Trade* advocated commerce and diplomacy with African nations to end the slave trade. Also relevant, though somewhat late in the case of New Zealand, is that the first of six appendices to Part II of his 1840 edition called *The Remedy* (copies of which were presented to leading British parliamentarians)[34] was entitled 'On Facilities of making Treaties'.[35] Even though these publications may have appeared too late to be of immediate influence on the annexation of New Zealand and the Treaty of Waitangi, they nonetheless reflected the developing viewpoint of like-minded contemporaries.

Inquiring minds

The British Parliament had held 41 debates on slavery between the end of the Napoleonic Wars and 1830, followed by another 90 from 1830 to 1840. Parliamentary committees were a well-established method of enquiring into social and political issues by then, so the Select Committee on Aborigines was hardly a unique event.[36] Abolitionist sentiments and humanitarian attitudes were now prominent as circumstances pushed the British to seriously consider intervening in the government of New Zealand. It was a climate that saw inquiries held in 1821, 1838, and subsequent to annexation in 1844, ask many questions about slavery in Māori society.

Ensign McCrae of the 84th Regiment appeared before Commissioner Bigge's 1821 inquiry. He had visited New Zealand the previous year aboard HMS *Dromedary* while it was obtaining a cargo of spars for the British Navy after delivering convicts to New South Wales. Based on that experience, McCrae was asked whether Māori chiefs could compel their tribes to work for them. 'No, they cannot', he replied. When asked if slaves were compelled to cook and whether they formed 'a separate class from their masters', he replied in the affirmative. He no doubt confirmed the commissioner's suspicions, too, when he assured him that Māori slaves were treated very cruelly, were 'very badly clothed and seem[ed] to be in a wretched condition'. McCrae added that they were 'put to death as offerings and a sacrifice for any person of the chief's family who happens to die'.[37]

The prominence of abolitionist sympathies and more general humanitarian sentiments, widespread in the Colonial Office at the time, were surely behind the more particular concern with the issue of slavery in the much more extensive 1838 inquiry into 'the state of New Zealand' held on the eve of British annexation. However, those involved in this inquiry in particular had competing agendas. The New Zealand Association, which advocated colonisation, did not like the missionaries, and the missionaries wanted to be left to evangelise without interference. The political lobbying that ensued took on an air of jousting on a grand scale with a professed concern for indigenous people suiting their respective purposes.

Questions concerned the size of the slave population, whether British subjects were employing their labour, whether tribal leaders would agree to release their slaves, and many other matters. Much of the questioning revealed a lack of appreciation that what was referred to as slavery in Māori society was very different from the trans-Atlantic trade in Africans. However, it was also evident that some witnesses recognised that the immediate abolition of 'slavery' might involve some injustice. The problem, though, for people like New Zealand Association member Reverend Samuel Hinds, was not that it would impact upon the authority of rangatira but that applying the British criminal code would be unfair to 'barbarous people' such as the Māori. Unlike civilised men, he said, 'the savage would not be aware that he was committing so great a crime'. So, for Hinds, it would be like trying a child of eight or nine years of age for a murder and hanging him.[38] While the general tenor of the questions and answers was against slavery and about the possibility of ending it, concerns about retaining the social hierarchy and superior status of the rangatira were also apparent. That would prove to be the major fault line running through humanitarian intentions. How could the superior status of the rangatira be upheld while everyone else, including slaves, was raised to equality with them? They may have been equal before God, but not in this earthly world.

Questions and answers

Witnesses to that 1838 inquiry included missionaries, merchants, people connected with the New Zealand Association, and one Māori man. They were asked a number of questions relating to the status of slaves, their own use of slave labour, and the terms under which they were employed, including how they were treated within Māori society and by Europeans. They were also asked whether Spanish or Portuguese slave traders might be able to get their hands on some.

John Flatt, who had previously served as a catechist for the CMS in New Zealand, was asked whether it was necessary to obtain chiefly consent when hiring individuals for work and whether it was necessary to make any payments to the chiefs or parents of young men employed. 'No', he said: 'except when a Slave was purchased, then there would be a Remuneration given to the Chief, and he would become the Property of the European; he would not expect so large a Payment as those that were not purchased.'[39] This implies that a slave or war captive would be paid at a lower rate than a free member of the tribal group, which was later government practice. But it is also interesting that he should refer to slaves being purchased and becoming the property of the European. A meeting of a CMS subcommittee in New Zealand, held in May 1839 to respond to the evidence given at the London inquiry, was clearly alarmed by Flatt's comments, insisting that they 'redeemed' them.[40] As *The Times* of London somewhat cynically suggested, Flatt, 'this worthy servant of all work', happened to be 'out of place just now' and was, perhaps, hoping to gain support from the New Zealand Association and a new line of work.[41]

A number of witnesses had spent little time in New Zealand. Surgeon John Watkins was there for about six months in 1833 but John Downing Tawell for only two months in 1837. Still others had never set foot on New Zealand soil.[42] Predictably, responses to some questions varied wildly and some appear to have been severely off track, especially those of J. B. Montefiore, a merchant who spent just four months in New Zealand in 1830 without venturing far once he got there. As the CMS missionaries in New Zealand would subsequently tell London, many of Montefiore's ideas were quite wrong. For example, he stated that the children of slaves were also slaves. That was rarely so — only when both parents were slaves, which was an uncommon occurrence. He also stated that chiefs never marry slaves: 'they uphold their Aristocracy', he said, but, again, it is well known that many rangatira took captive wives in addition to wives of higher rank. Those women were typically of rangatira birth or were physically attractive — perhaps the literal equivalent of today's trophy wife? Montefiore was also 'certain that if the Settlers in South America had known it, they might have got Cargoes of Slaves [in New Zealand], they are so fond of Trade'. He felt that Māori slaves were badly treated and frequently killed, but revealed his rather jaundiced view of Māori men by saying that free men did not work at all — only fought. When asked if he thought Māori chiefs would be pleased to find out that under British sovereignty every slave would be instantly free, he thought otherwise but felt they would accept monetary compensation. The Commission suggested £20,000,000 but Montefiore thought that a few thousands would do. Twenty million pounds was the amount of compensation paid to British slave owners after the abolition of slavery in 1833, so, once again, Māori slavery was directly related to the trans-Atlantic trade and, presumably, thought to be of similar economic value.

Parliament also gave some thought to which Britons might actually go to New Zealand. A number of European colonies were populated by planters who owned or managed plantations of one sort or another, but rather than planning to stay permanently, they typically intended to return home after making their fortunes. Besides, such places were often thought unsuitable for wives and families. In the sugar colony of Jamaica, for example, the white population comprised two men for every woman.[43] So, after Montefiore had attested that the land of a European trader living in New Zealand's Poverty Bay was cultivated by slaves, he was asked whether there would be any need to send Europeans out to cultivate the land and raise produce. No, he replied, 'not if they can compel the Slaves ... to work'.[44] What this would mean in reality is that there would have to be a continuation of warfare to the same extent as it had been taking place during the 'musket wars' in order to keep up the supply of 'slaves' or captives. That scenario would, of course, run counter to other ideas justifying colonisation on the basis that it would bring an end to 'endemic warfare'. However, the inquiries did not highlight those sorts of discrepancies.

Sometime Bay of Islands trader Joel Polack, who spent around six years in New Zealand during the 1830s, was probably more realistic in his view that Brazilian, Portuguese, or Spanish vessels would unlikely be able to ship cargoes of slaves from New Zealand. They might take them by treachery or force, he said, but not as 'articles of merchandize'. Somewhat ambiguously, he continued that he had purchased slaves himself — 'Boys whom I liked for their quiet Conduct' — but added that 'that would not hold good'. 'The Natives among one another purchase Slaves', he said, 'but from Europeans the Slaves run away, and go back to their Master', who 'inveigles' and protects them. Polack went on to explain that it was very difficult to purchase a slave, but as to whether his land was cultivated by free men or slaves, he responded that he had employed principal chiefs as well as slaves and that there was very little difference between the greatest chief and the most abject fellow.[45]

But just how real was British concern for Māori slaves? Several of the witnesses described them as a different and inferior 'race' to the higher ranks, although, as Montefiore's remarks confirm, they used the word 'race' in its more contemporary sense of class:

> I think the Chiefs are a superior Race of Men; there is the same Line which may be drawn in this Country between People of Education and the lower Orders.[46]

If the unequal distribution of power was to be justified, as supporters of the New Zealand Association thought it should, belief in the equality of individuals presented a dilemma. So, race offered one marker of hierarchy while class offered another.[47] And, if class was not a category of social distinction that applied in Māori society, it could be invented.

Although widely applauded, the humanitarian ideas of the day were certainly not shared by everyone and attitudes towards Māori slaves were often less than kindly. Polack revealed his own class sensitivities when he complained that:

> The Slaves of New Zealand are very impertinent; they are given to Invention and Lies, and those are Things which cause more Wars between the Natives than any thing else.[48]

But he was not immune to scorn either. *The Times*, with unabashed anti-Semitism and language indicative of its attitude towards New Zealand Association supporters, joined the political tussle, calling him 'a worthy and wandering off-shoot of the seed of Abraham' and 'retailer of ardent spirits to sailors and fugitives in New Zealand'.[49]

When asked how colonisation would prevent intertribal wars, Polack chose to overlook the fact that they had already declined, and failed to acknowledge any contributions made by the missionaries or other factors in bringing that about. Instead he insisted that a reduction in warfare could be achieved:

> By employing their Minds and their Bodies; by Europeans settling between them; by Europeans taking up the Slaves as Farm Servants.[50]

In other words, colonisation along the lines promoted by the New Zealand Association. But, like Wakefield, he also thought that the 'Chiefs ought to have an Authority'. He claimed to have written to the various chiefs from whom he purchased land, saying that 'in the event of the Place being colonized' he would 'allow them every Year an annual Stipend; and [hoped] every other European' would do the same.[51] So their authority would be based on an annual stipend — not on inherited or acquired mana as it had been customarily.

Polack's evidence revealed little sympathy for the plight of Māori slaves. Instead, he cautioned that the abused would become abusers:

> Slaves who have experienced the bitterness of their condition, and afterwards become masters and influential men in council and battle, are among the worst of tyrants, visiting with additional severity, the punishments they may have suffered when similarly situated, on the persons of their slaves. Obscenity and lying are among the practices most persisted in by the slaves ... they may be justly regarded as the greatest drawback to the prosperity and civilization hitherto of the New Zealanders.

As a supporter of Wakefield's form of colonisation, Polack was no friend of the missionaries, nor they of him. So when he had been subjected to a taua muru five years earlier, Henry Williams reported:

> The news of the day, Mr Polack stript of the whole of his property by a small party of natives from Waiomio; the assigned reason, that he swore at them.

This person is one of those free and independent men, full of threats and great boastings as to his treatment of these people; and as he had expressed himself thus to me upon one occasion, my sympathy was not very great.[52]

The 1838 Committee also took evidence from a Māori whose name was recorded as 'Nayti' — in reality, Te Whaiti, a junior relative of the high-ranking chief Te Rauparaha. Te Whaiti, who spent two years living with Edward Gibbon Wakefield in London's Chelsea, said that he was keen to have more English people settle in his country, especially if they were 'gentlemen'. A true Wakefieldian, perhaps, he demonstrated an awareness of the British social order and likened his slaves to England's poor. He explained that when his chief died, a slave was not entitled to land in any sense of ownership but was given the right to grow food, saying:

> They can grow Potatoes and Cabbage, and so on. It is all Gentleman's Land; the Cookees [one term for slaves or captives] work upon it. In England it is different, for a poor Man is obliged to walk about the Road, and has no Place to grow Potatoes.[53]

The implication is that he felt Māori slaves were better off than Britain's poor. Some British witnesses agreed.

Four months before he appeared as a witness, Te Whaiti's appearance was used to bolster the notion that Māori, like other indigenous people, could be 'improved' by British training. In this case, though, it was the New Zealand Association that got the credit for the apparent transformation. The *Saturday Magazine*, a paper sponsored by the Society for Promoting Christian Knowledge, described 'Nayti' when first taken 'to the rooms of the [New Zealand] Association'. He was said to be 'a complete savage; unshorn, very dirty, stupefied with astonishment, unable to express himself, or to comprehend what was said to him, and altogether a pitiable object'. Within five months, however, he was miraculously reborn as a man 'far more civilized than very many Englishmen; more cleanly, obliging, and intelligent; with more respect for himself and others; and with elevated views as to the improvement of his country'. 'He once hated the Missionaries', the magazine announced, 'having been taught to do so by some English ruffians at New Zealand', but now fully appreciated 'the utility of missionary labours'.[54]

The New Zealand Association, meanwhile, was also planning to use 'Nayti', who was said to be 'perfectly aware of the value of land in England', to help explain to his countrymen that 'a tenth of the land will be far more valuable than the whole was before'.[55] That remark related to the fact that the Association, intending to buy huge tracts of land from Māori, had promised to set aside one tenth of the acreage purchased as native reserves. Their 'mode of proceeding' had been 'fully explained to Nayti' who took pride in 'being a *rangatira* or gentleman', but they were also anxious about his fate on that very account: 'He is no longer a New Zealander in manners, habits, or tastes, but has acquired those of a well-bred Englishman.' The subsequent New Zealand Land Company's Chief Agent was urged to ensure that he was treated as such in order to continue 'the relative superiority of their chief families' and encourage his countrymen to embrace the Company's aims and objectives.[56] Despite being related to Te Rauparaha, Te Whaiti was probably not of very high rank. That was immaterial in the circumstances, though, as he was being used by both sides, much as protestations of humanitarian concern were, to serve their respective agendas.

The letters and journals missionaries sent back to Britain during the 1820s and 1830s were full of the horrors of slavery and cannibalism. Were they deliberately stressing Māori ferociousness in order to bolster support for their mission or to discourage settlers from coming to New Zealand as George Butler Earp told the 1844 Select Committee? Perhaps, but Earp was not a neutral witness either. He would publish a book in 1853 promoting immigration to New Zealand, an enterprise in which he claimed long experience.[57] So he had reasons for downplaying aspects of Māori society that might have deterred potential migrants.

British government in New Zealand

The Protestant missionaries were keen for British intervention, but although the CMS subcommittee responded to the 1838 Select Committee's report, it had arrived too late for them to influence government plans. The single copy of the report sent to them, which had to be circulated among their members, had taken many months to arrive. Consequently, they were not able to consider their response until May 1839, just over eight months before the treaty, which became known as the Treaty of Waitangi, was presented to Māori, and it would take almost as long to reach London. In fact, William Hobson, who was appointed to treat with the Māori, sailed from Plymouth in August that year. The tyranny of distance did not allow for effective communication.

Meanwhile, plans for colonisation had continued, with liberty and freedom as common themes. Hobson drew on those themes when he outlined his ideas for administration to Lord Glenelg, Secretary of State for the Colonies, in 1839. He concluded his thirteen-page letter by warning that Britain would have no legal power to remedy the 'aggressions of Foreigners', 'unless Her Majestys Government at once [resolve] to extend to that highly Gifted Land the blessings of civilization and liberty, and the protection of English Law, by assuming the sovereignty of the whole Country and by transplanting to its Shores, the nucleus of a moral and industrious population'.[58] So liberty was to come through Britain's assumption of sovereignty over what had been a Māori country and the importation of more 'moral and industrious' residents.

In May 1839, some four months after Hobson submitted his proposals to Glenelg, the New Zealand Association was reconstituted as the New Zealand Company. Fearing that the Crown would annex New Zealand to protect Māori interests and shut the Company out, Wakefield organised the despatch of a ship called the *Tory* on a preliminary expedition to New Zealand. The battle lines were drawn: the businessmen versus the humanitarians.

The instructions Hobson received from Glenelg's successor Lord Normanby, just before he departed from Britain in August, included stamping out 'savage practices' such as human sacrifice and cannibalism:

> [S]uch atrocities, under whatever plea of religion they may take place, are not to be tolerated within any part of the dominions of the British Crown.[59]

But there was no mention of slavery. Nevertheless, when, as Lieutenant Hobson, he arrived in the Bay of Islands to offer a treaty under which New

Zealand would be annexed to Britain, Lieutenant Thomas McDonnell, a merchant and one-time Additional British Resident, who was never a shrinking violet, claimed to have advised him to proclaim that slaves were to have their liberty and reminded him 'that the British flag never flew over a nation of slaves'.[60]

Following the signing of the 'Treaty of Waitangi' by some 300-plus rangatira, New Zealand became a colony of New South Wales for a short period.[61] That colony's first governor, Arthur Phillip, was of a strongly abolitionist frame of mind. In September 1786, shortly after being appointed by the British Secretary for Home Affairs, he had composed a detailed memorandum outlining his plans for the proposed new colony. In one paragraph he wrote that:

> The laws of this country [England] will of course, be introduced in [New] South Wales, and there is one that I would wish to take place from the moment his Majesty's forces take possession of the country: That there can be no slavery in a free land, and consequently no slaves.[62]

The land was, of course, to be populated by transported convicts who may have had difficulty perceiving their situation as 'free'.

The idea of creating new societies without slavery was not an entirely new one. But in claiming to have reminded Hobson of what the British flag did not fly over, Thomas McDonnell was echoing contemporary, post-abolition rhetoric, especially that of the Anti-Slavery Society and other like-minded groups. John Stoughton, for example, speaking at their headquarters of Exeter Hall during the English winter of 1845–46, recalled the awakening of 'the slumbering genius of British freedom' when:

> To her unutterable horror, she found that the demon of slavery had her fast in his embrace; then she started up, shuddering, and with loathing indignation flung the hideous incubus away from her presence for ever.
>
> ... And this spirit of justice to all men has since increased in its strength, leading to an entire abolition of the accursed trade on the part of England, throughout her colonies, so that now the sun, in his daily circuit, as he girdles the British Empire, never sheds his rays upon a slave.[63]

In the same lecture series, Reverend William Arthur quoted from an American poem reflecting the poet's indignation at the sin of his own country:

> Shall every flap of England's flag
> Proclaim that all around are free . . .[64]

So British suns and English flags did not shine or flap over nations of slaves. However, the gulf between the ideological concerns of British government officials and the realities for that nation's residents in New Zealand was particularly evident when another parliamentary select committee interviewed McDonnell in 1844. It became clear to the committee members that he and others were probably employing Māori slaves and they pursued this line of questioning like dogs with a bone. When asked by Commissioner John Arthur Roebuck, a Utilitarian radical and supporter of the New Zealand Company, whether English settlers purchased slave labour, McDonnell explained that everyone worked, including chiefs. Roebuck pressed the point, rewording his question to ask whether the English 'hired' slave labour. McDonnell explained that a chief would come with a party requesting work, that he offered a contract without enquiring whether they were free men or slaves, and that they all worked together, chiefs, slaves, and free men. Still not satisfied, Roebuck asked whether this meant that slave labour was purchased. Obviously uncomfortable at this stage, McDonnell said it was a question he would 'rather decline in answering; it admit[ted] of so many constructions'.[65] Why Roebuck should have caused McDonnell to squirm so is rather curious, because he would write only five years later that it was 'requisite for [Englishmen] to pass over the original tribes' that inhabited the lands they colonised because they were going to disappear anyway. As contemporary racial theory had it:

> When the European comes in contact with any other type of man, that other type disappears. Let us not shade our eyes, and pretend not to see this result.

In Roebuck's view, 'New Zealand [had] been a favourite field for the freaks [whims] of Colonial Secretaries of State'.[66]

Māori responses to British government

Some 'freaks' of the Colonial Office initially prevailed, so that when British government was established in 1840, slavery was, theoretically, abolished — but that proved problematic. Māori chiefs expected that English law would uphold their rangatiratanga, or chiefly authority, and protect their interests, as was specifically guaranteed by te Tiriti o Waitangi, the Māori-language version of the Treaty of Waitangi, that the vast majority of signatories had signed.[67] But they were soon disillusioned. Ironically, given British ideas regarding the symbolism of the Union Jack, it was displeasure with British government that led Hone Heke, the northern chief who had been first to sign the Treaty, to chop down the British flagstaff in July 1844. In early October of that year, then Governor Robert FitzRoy responded by holding a conference with disaffected Northland chiefs in which he attempted to counter Heke's claims that the flag represented the oppression of Māori chieftainship by stressing that '[t]he British Flag is the signal of freedom, liberty, and safety'.[68] Still unconvinced, Heke was responsible for chopping the flagstaff down four times in total, instigating a war which lasted from March 1845 to January 1846.

The two sides were certainly talking past each other, for Heke wrote to FitzRoy in May 1845 asking:

> Where is the correctness of the protection offered by the treaty? Where is the correctness of the good will of England? Is it in her great guns? Is it in her Congreve rockets? Is the good will of England shown in the curses of Englishmen and in their adulteries? Is it shown in their calling us slaves? Or is it shown in their regard for our sacred places? The Europeans taunt us. They say, "Look at Port Jackson, look at China, and all the islands; they are but a precedent for this country. That flag of England which takes your country is the commencement." After this the French, and after them the Americans, told us the same. Well, I assented to these speeches ... and in the fifth year (of these speeches) we interfered with the flagstaff for the first time. We cut it down and it fell. It was re-erected; and then we said, "All this we have heard is true, because they persist in having the flagstaff up."[69]

So Heke did not feel that the British flag had supplied the gifts FitzRoy and Hobson had spoken of, although the *New Zealander* newspaper continued to repeat the message that as a consequence of British government:

> no one injures or molests [the Māori people], their lands are secured to them, and . . . they are perfectly free. The British Flag is the signal of freedom, liberty, and safety. That Flag is considered most sacred, because it defends and protects us. In sharing its advantages with you, we make you our brothers; we place you on equal terms with ourselves. Every advantage that we obtain through that Flag, is open to you, and we are instructing you how to make use of those advantages. Can we do more? No.[70]

The government that was established after the Treaty was signed claimed that slavery was illegal but recognised its importance in the Māori social order and often tolerated it or turned a blind eye. But it was a situation they could not allow to continue indefinitely. 'Slavery', or the servitude of war captives, gradually faded away but the symbolism of the British flag lived on far longer.

The British Empire was, and still is, seen by many as a moral concept, a bringer of justice and liberty to societies allegedly lacking those ideals. School journals published for New Zealand children during the first half of the twentieth century reinforced such ideas. A 1909 journal explained that: 'Wherever the Union Jack flies, those who live under its folds, dark and white races alike, enjoy liberty and justice such as cannot be found under any other flag.' Sixteen years later, children were told that 'wherever our flag flies we shall be able to sweep away everything that is wrong and evil' and that that self-same flag 'will always stand for all that is best and noblest on earth'.[71] But 90 years after that, a tradition of annual protest on the anniversary of the signing of the Treaty reveals that not everyone considers colonisation by Britain to have been an unmitigated benefit and other flags do battle with regard to the representation of Māori freedom. The flag of the United Tribes, selected by a number of northern chiefs in 1834, and the Tino Rangatiratanga flag designed in 1989 and unveiled on Waitangi Day 1990, have each symbolised the Māori desire for self-determination (figs 58 and 59).

But to return to those nineteenth-century parliamentary inquiries, they are, of course, artefacts of their time, and despite the ostensible concern with the pros and cons of colonising New Zealand, there remained a strong undercurrent of abolitionist sentiment. Within that mindset, colonisation could be justified morally and scruples about its potentially damaging effects overcome — at least in part — if the allegedly universally wretched state and cruel treatment of Māori slaves could be ameliorated by English law or the propagation of Christian teachings. But perhaps the benefit of hindsight was necessary to see that by declaring their slaves — effectively their servants — to be free, the British would usurp chiefly authority, deny their mana and rangatiratanga, and undermine their economic base in one fell swoop. The *London Quarterly Review* had an inkling of that in 1854:

> One of the inconvenient consequences which followed the universal adoption of Christianity was the relaxation of the tie between chief and vassal, master and slave. It would be a great mistake to judge of the general character of these feudal institutions merely by their abuses, monstrous as these have been.

Yet that publication's understanding of a Māori class system was also revealed when it claimed that:

> The lower classes are engaged in road-making, whale-fishing, building, tending cattle, and tilling the soil; the chiefs becoming landed proprietors, millers, ship-builders, and ship-owners.[72]

As Joel Polack had told the 1844 inquiry, he employed chiefs as well as slaves. Chiefly rank was not a ticket to a life of indolence in Māori society. Rangatira worked alongside the lower ranks on the roads and other public works as they had aboard whaling ships. And once tribal groups owned trading ships, flourmills, and other plant communally, they, too, were worked by all sections of Māori society.

Christopher Leslie Brown has suggested that '[i]f the English in the eighteenth century made a fetish of liberty, they tended to consider it a national possession peculiar to English soil and inappropriate for less civilized people and to define it in a way that reinforced social hierarchies rather than undermined them'.[73] That idea might explain the discrepancies in the New Zealand context — where, as we shall see, the rhetoric does not correspond with reality.

It might then be asked whether Max O'Rell was correct to claim that New Zealand was a nursery of liberty or whether Māori lost many of their previous freedoms in the process of colonisation. As philosopher Sir Isaiah Berlin said, liberty is a 'protean word', one that might be stretched to fit a multitude of situations and purposes. Sir Isaiah wisely chose not to discuss its 'more than two hundred senses'.[74]

CHAPTER SEVEN

Plucking brands from the burning

MUCH OF THE CONCERN FOR THE SECULAR ASPECTS OF MĀORI welfare was still in the future when the first missionaries arrived in New Zealand at the end of 1814. Although questions relating to the morality of slavery were already prominent, so, too, was the urgency of saving heathen souls. Taking the light of Christianity to the dark and benighted areas of the world would surely go a long way towards achieving atonement.

New Zealand's formal introduction to Christianity did not come about without teething problems, though. Te Pahi from Te Puna in the Bay of Islands, who visited Sydney in late 1805 and early 1806, had discussions with Samuel Marsden which encouraged the clergyman to put forward his first proposal for a New Zealand mission in 1807. But the initial plans to establish a CMS station under Te Pahi's protection were foiled by the murder of the crew of the British trading ship the *Boyd* in 1809 for which he was, unjustly, held responsible.[1] Following Te Pahi's death in 1810, however, Ruatara offered land at Rangihoua for the first mission.

Marsden had been recruited for the New South Wales penal colony by none other than William Wilberforce, the abolitionist famous for his part in persuading the English Parliament to end the slave trade.

Wilberforce was also a founding vice-president of the CMS. Marsden's appointment reflected the humanitarian sentiments then prevalent in Britain's Colonial Office but did not relate directly to the abolition of what was referred to as slavery in Māori society. The evangelical focus was firmly on personal religious transformation, although some may have expected that 'slavery' would disappear as a natural process associated with the 'civilisation' that they understood to accompany the adoption of Christian principles. For CMS and Wesleyan missionaries in New Zealand, Christianity was 'the only basis on which "true" civilization could be founded' and faith in Christ the only truly moral foundation for human life. Secular concepts of civilisation, which included the trappings of modern life found in Western towns and cities, settled agriculture, human industry, and formalised systems of education, were also expected to have moral as well as practical outcomes.[2]

Representatives of the Wesleyan-Methodist Missionary Society, who shared the evangelical beliefs of the CMS, followed the Anglicans and established a mission at Kaeo in 1823. Fortunately for history, missionaries were prolific writers. Their early letters and journals are 'time capsules' of contemporary political and ideological influences, including the evangelical theology that informed their preconceptions and often varied responses to Māori 'slavery' as well as their fundamental faith in the benefits their mother country could bestow. But as well as their concerns and what they hoped to achieve, those writings also reveal changes in their responses over time.

Marsden's thoughts certainly reflected popular British rhetoric as he beheld the scene from the deck of his ship on Christmas Day 1814, the day after his arrival at the mission site. Ruatara had gone to considerable lengths to prepare for the occasion, including setting up a flagpole:

> I saw the English flag flying, which was a pleasing sight in New Zealand. I considered it as the signal and the dawn of civilization, liberty, and religion, in that dark and benighted land. I never viewed the British Colours with more gratification; and flattered myself they would never be removed, till the Natives of that island enjoyed all the happiness of British Subjects.[3]

Early missionary attitudes toward slavery

Two months after Christmas, Marsden returned to Sydney leaving his recruits William Hall, Thomas Kendall, and John King to bring his plans to fruition. But, as his words indicate, Christianity and civilisation were virtually one and the same thing in their minds, and their teachings extended well beyond biblical injunctions. Their 'to do' list was extensive, but any efforts to abolish slavery had less energy behind them than those accorded to stamping out polygamy, utu, muru, feasting, tattooing, and other customary practices. Perhaps more significantly, there is little to indicate that those early arrivals were concerned about the position of war captives. Their condemnations were more often directed towards the ritual killing (and especially the eating) of those people and other treatment they considered to be abuse. Their use as a labour force was a taken-for-granted state of affairs that typically passed without comment. That was evident in May 1819, when John King visited Hongi Hika's settlement at Kerikeri with Samuel Leigh and a Mr Hansen.[4] Having arrived with their 'natives', they stopped for refreshment and looked over the local cultivations which they estimated to cover an area of some 20 or 30 acres (8–12 hectares). Having offhandedly noted that Hongi had left a chief there 'in charge of a few Captives to cultivate the Land', King added that it was both 'pleasing & promising' that they were clearing still more.[5] Neither he nor his companions appear to have felt any aversion to the forced labour. Even their concern for the killing of captives was not unequivocal. For example, having reported the execution of several people for stealing food supplies from their captors, King went on to remark that 'if the slaves had not stolen contrary to the law of Jehovah they would not have been killed for stealing'.[6] So it served them right apparently. They got their just deserts. It seems to have made perfect sense to him that war captives would be required to work for their captors, just as the British would have expected of their prisoners of war, but crimes such as theft were an entirely different matter. The somewhat different responses of later arrivals probably reflect a better understanding of Māori society as well as the greater unease associated with 'slavery' that had developed after the pioneer missionaries left Britain.

Some of King's brethren were more sympathetic than he, but even so, there is little in their writings to suggest that the idea of slavery posed ethical issues for them. Nor was it evident when Marsden made his third visit to New Zealand in 1820. At Coromandel, a subordinate chief named 'Amoppa', under threat of death for allegedly stealing a mat from the son of the 'Areekee' (ariki: a very senior chief), asked him to intervene on his behalf. Harmony was restored when Amoppa's party agreed to compensate the victims by handing over a canoe and a slave as utu, or compensation.[7] So hostilities were avoided but Marsden did not hint that he was troubled by the inclusion of a 'slave' as part of the payment.

Despite Henry Williams writing in 1827 that '[m]en, women and children, the gentry of the different orders and their slaves, all are on one footing with us',[8] others felt that the lowly status of slaves was in line with God's preordained social order. William Yate, who had served as a CMS missionary in New Zealand from the beginning of 1828, was of that mind. He described a group baptism he performed in 1834 when chiefs and slaves were admitted into the church together. His account of this event reveals his understanding that, despite that shared experience, God intended the individuals involved to remember their rightful place:

> One, named Atua-haere, (that is "the walking god") is the great man of Kaikohi [Kaikohe]: he, and several of his slaves from some of whom he first heard of the Gospel stood side by side, as brethren; and all their distinction of rank was merged at that moment in the name of Christian. Not that his dependants will cast off their duty to their earthly master, in acknowledging a heavenly one; nor that they now think themselves his equal. Such is not the design of the Gospel: it will place all ranks of men in their just relation: it will make servants obedient and faithful, and masters kind and tender; thus enabling every one to fulfil his relative duties in that station of life to which it has pleased God to call him.[9]

When asked subsequently by an 1836 select committee whether Māori had any 'repugnance to the introduction of Christianity', Yate replied quite similarly: 'None whatever; . . . it has made them more comfortable, their slaves more obedient, their wives more faithful.'[10] So, Christianity was a boon to Māori slave owners and dull husbands.

Missionary writings provide much of the evidence for how captives were treated in the early years of the nineteenth century. It must be remembered, though, that their journals were not personal diaries but more like ship's logbooks, required by the societies in Britain that sponsored them. Selected extracts were often published in contemporary journals such as the CMS's *Missionary Register,* which ran from 1813 to 1855. Containing monthly reports from mission stations around the world, including New Zealand, they were not necessarily matter-of-fact daily accounts but intended to impress their superiors as well as members of church congregations and the government back in Britain. If emphasising the 'savage' treatment of Māori 'slaves' heightened the perception of their work's importance and urgency, it could be expected to improve the health of the mission's funds as well. With that in mind, it might be wondered to what extent such accounts of barbarism were, at least in some part, marketing exercises. It was in the missionaries' own interests to not only show themselves in a good, even heroic, light, but also to stress the woe-begotten state of the heathens they had been sponsored to save. Journals from their earliest years in New Zealand often have a 'shock-horror' flavour to them. Recounted with especially grisly fervour were incidents involving the killing of women or children for what, in their minds, were minor crimes as well as instances of eating human flesh.

An example of both occurred in 1819, when John King recounted the killing of a little boy, aged about seven, who had been brought as a captive from the South Island. The lad had stolen kūmara that had been placed under tapu by the rangatira — a capital offence. So his death was justified under Māori law, but King described the preparation of his body for cooking and consumption in graphic detail. As it happened, the death coincided with the arrival of the Wesleyan Samuel Leigh aboard the missionary vessel *Active* 'upon a visit for the good of his Health', which may not have been improved by his coming across the body on a fire. Leigh paid an axe for the boy's body which he took to the missionary settlement and buried very publicly in full view of their Māori neighbours.[11] King's journal entries regarding these events were likely intended to impress his audience at home with the vital importance of their work, while the public burial of the boy showed Māori how 'civilised' folk dealt with the dead.

Adults who stole from tapu kūmara stores were also liable to the death penalty, but it may have been the case that small children were particularly susceptible. The taking of captives was, in large part, a practical response to a need for labour, and the very young would have had less value in that regard. It is interesting to note then, that in Nigeria, where child slavery was common, the age of six was considered the point of usefulness. In that part of Africa, infants and toddlers younger than six were considered to be of no benefit to potential buyers.[12] Māori may have assessed them similarly.

Over time, though, the missionaries became better acquainted with Māori tikanga, or laws, and the rationale for different levels of punishment. So, by the end of 1823, Marsden was able to explain what he referred to as the difference in Māori law between religious theft and ordinary theft. By religious theft he meant stealing items under tapu or from a tapu place such as the incident that King reported. He was responding to a series of questions posed by the Church Missionary Society's committee in London. When asked: 'Is it a custom among the New Zealanders to kill and eat those who are convicted of thefts?' Marsden explained:

> Thefts are of different kinds — common and sacred. Sacred thefts are often punished with death. I saw one young woman who was killed for sacred theft, such as breaking into the sweet potato houses when tabooed, or into the sepulchre of the dead to carry away the bones, or into any sacred ground, especially if the offender be a slave. If any of their own friends are guilty of theft they are liable to be punished some other way. The New Zealanders do not think that theft is a crime of that magnitude generally as to merit death.[13]

So stealing from 'sacred' places was likely to incur capital punishment but the difference in attitude towards captives versus members of the kin group that Marsden also mentioned likely explains why William Fairburn failed to redeem a condemned man, described by Henry Williams as 'a reputed thief'. The pair of blankets Fairburn offered was not enough incentive to stay the execution, which may have been necessary as a warning to other captives inclined to being light-fingered.[14]

More gently does it

Writing several years after the 1831 execution of the 'reputed thief', Polack remarked that '[t]he situation of a slave or taurekareka is less burdensome to the northward than it was within a very few years back'.[15] In his view, 'the profits accruing from their employment in rearing pigs, and planting provisions, cutting timber, and cleaning flax' had also resulted in an end to the practice of sacrificing captives to accompany deceased chiefs in the spirit world.[16] He had told the 1838 Select Committee that they could and did refuse the commands of their chiefs 'because they know they are under the Protection of the Europeans; that they cannot kill them; they know that the Europeans will not trade with them if they do'.[17] Other European observers agreed that the heightened demand for labour had resulted in a tendency to acquire greater numbers of prisoners of war and reduced the frequency of their being put to death for ritual purposes.[18] That was evident when Hongi had ordered that none of his slaves be killed for his wife's adultery and again when, on his deathbed, he asked that none be sacrificed at his passing.[19]

However, while Polack and others considered a gradual amelioration of attitudes towards slaves to be related to economic factors, missionary writings suggest it was due to their teachings. Alfred Brown, for example, reported an apparently softer response than he expected when one of Tohitapu's slaves committed adultery in 1832. The Te Roroa rangatira and tohunga had been satisfied with throwing stones at the man and breaking a 'spear' across his back.[20] In terms of custom law, this crime might well have been punishable by death, so Brown attributed the rangatira's more lenient approach to the influence of God. Tohitapu was a good friend of the mission despite never becoming a Christian. However, capital punishment was not universal in such cases. Nor had Brown indicated who the slave had committed the offence with. It would have been serious indeed if it had been a woman of high rank and it is unlikely that, in this case, the woman was a wife of Tohitapu himself. He had been extremely upset over three years earlier when two of his wives were found to have been aboard the ships and he had threatened to make a public spectacle of hanging himself.[21] But if the lover of the adulterous slave was of low rank, the need for retribution might well have been moderate — with or without Christian influence. Nor was Tohitapu a man without compassion. He had reacted angrily four years earlier when his people sacrificed an elderly female slave because a little girl had drowned.[22] Minimal information, a lack of context, and monocultural perspectives on events, often from a single observer, tend to leave questions unanswered with regard to differences in the ways that miscreants were punished.

Regardless of whatever lay behind responses to individual events, Brown clearly agreed with Polack's impression that, by the 1830s, war captives were less likely to be killed to accompany their captors to the afterlife. The day after Tītore, rangatira of Kororāreka, died, he wrote that:

> We were surprised at seeing some chiefs eating food within the sacred enclosure where Titore was laid out — the women too appeared to have laid aside their usual violent mode of shewing grief by cutting and gashing their arms and breasts — nor does it seem probable that any of Titore's slaves will be killed out of honour to him, which are so many proofs that the edifice of superstition is crumbling away beneath the irresistible power of the glorious Gospel . . .'[23]

Brown's interpretation of the reasons for change may have been coloured by his own beliefs and expectations, especially as he admitted that few of the people had been converted by that time. But something had changed. What is not clear is whether changes in attitude towards 'slaves' had been affected by missionaries, by the increased value of captive labour as Polack suggested, or whether it was simply that a period of aberration was coming to an end.

Success in terms of widespread conversion was slow in coming, but the missionaries did not falter in their attempts to instil new values and beliefs. In 1831, George Clarke reported to his superiors in London that having established a new mission station at Waimate the previous year, he and his brethren were now in close reach of many more villages and concentrated centres of population. On top of that, a wider respect for the Sabbath day had also enhanced their opportunities to provide religious instruction. Clarke was 'very thankful to see the slave beginning to claim his day of rest and his master allowing the justness of the claim'.[24]

So captives now had a designated day off but their free time was to be spent enjoying the mission's teachings.

From slaves to servants

Missionary journals record a number of instances when they 'redeemed' Māori slaves by offering axes, hoes, or other goods in exchange. But the degree to which the latter became truly 'free' following the transaction is not entirely clear. The question is perhaps a semantic one as most of them were employed as servants in the mission settlements. They may have been fed and housed to a better standard, but freedom has different meanings for different people.

As we know, the first missionary arrivals were rarely disconcerted by Māori use of captives as 'slave' labour. So, after having gained a favourable impression of the work of a few captives left to cultivate some of Hongi's land at Kerikeri in 1819, Messrs King, Leigh, and Hansen continued their journey until they reached Hongi himself, some 15 miles (24 km) away at Waimate. King reported that their host responded hospitably by ordering his servants 'to dress some food'.[25] In other words, to perform the same duties as the missionaries' servants.

If differences in custom law and spiritual beliefs are set aside (and, admittedly, they are considerable), there appear to have been few differences between the way Māori treated their captives and the way the missionaries treated those they redeemed with trade goods and subsequently employed as servants. They were expected to work long hours and were subject to strict discipline. Missionaries certainly complained about the unwillingness of their servants, whether rangatira or slaves, to work continuously, year round, regardless of season or circumstance. As Marianne Williams, wife of Henry, found:

> The moment a boat arrives, down scamper all hands, men, boys and girls to the beach. If there is anything to be seen, or anything extraordinary occurs in Newzealand [sic], the mistress must do the work, while the servants gaze abroad. She must not scold them either: for if they are rangatiras, they will run away in a pet: and if they are Kukus [slaves], they will laugh and tell her

she has "too much of the mouth". Having been forewarned of this, I wait and work away till they choose to come back.[26]

Working conditions at the mission

As Marianne's lament makes clear, those employed as servants in the missions were certainly not all 'slaves' or captives. Men and women from any rank in Māori society might see such work as an opportunity. The wife of a rangatira, hired to do laundry, did so under the tuition of her own slave, while the slave girl took care of missionary children, watching over them when out of doors.[27] And those hired as servants received wages in addition to their 'bed and board'. When Henry and Marianne arrived at Kerikeri in 1823, Mrs Butler kindly offered to have their linen washed by two Māori servants. One had been a servant to Mrs Butler herself and the other to Mrs Kemp. Curious to know how much they were paid, Marianne was told that when they had washed four times they were given a hoe. They were paid once in three months, an axe one time, and a hoe the next.[28] John King had mentioned the previous year that indoor and outdoor servants were 'all fed & paid out of the society's store'.[29] However, the *Missionary Register* reported that, if they had not been 'redeemed' from their former masters, 'the greater portion of the wages which [slaves] might earn' were given up to the master.[30] Marianne confirmed that, saying that Tom and Dicky, slaves of Te Koki, ate and slept with the other servants, 'but the payments they receive all go to their mistress, Te Koki's head wife, while the others do what they like with theirs'.[31] James Kemp indicated that the arrangement was a standard one, saying that his wife:

> keeps two females in the house one of them have been with her for two years and is very much attached to us they can do the domestic work in the house and are very useful they both belong to Shunghee [Hongi] and we pay him for their service [sic].[32]

The remark that they belonged to Hongi indicates that they were his captives. However, given the nature of these payments (an axe and a hoe), it seems likely that such goods would have gone to the community among whom they lived anyway, whether they were free girls or captives, 'slaves' or 'redeemed'.

Marianne Williams was very impressed by the servants' English-isms when she visited Mrs Kemp in 1823:

> 'Everything around was neat as wax, and three Newzealand [sic] girls tidily dressed in English bedgowns and aprons, welcomed me with a courtesy [curtsy?], and "How do you do Ma'm" in English in answer to my "Tina raka kue" [sic].[33]

But she changed her tune dramatically two days later:

> The state of the natives is most deplorable. As an instance of their savage nature, we were told that Jane, the native girl in this house, upon the return of the fight from the river Thames, killed two prisoners herself, the instant the canoes landed at Hongi's point.[34]

Given Jane's response to the new shipment of prisoners, it must be assumed that she was not a captive herself but a member of the local community by birth. Her reaction on this occasion was likely a response to the loss of one or more close relatives in the battle.

Being a servant to the Williamses may not have been every girl's dream, but dissatisfaction went both ways and was not always cross-cultural. They became so fed up with Betsy, the English-born convict girl they brought with them from Sydney, who, among other sins, teased 'the natives', they sent her back there, deciding to rely on Māori girls instead.[35]

'Redeemed' slaves seem to have been perceived much like apprentices: effectively 'bonded' for a period — even, perhaps, for life. Eliza White was 'truly grieved' when one of her servants ran away, saying that she had been with her 'four months and was getting very useful'.[36] As late as 1853, thirteen years after the establishment of English law in New Zealand, ex-missionary William Colenso wrote to a government official disputing a charge of assaulting a Māori who had employed a slave redeemed by another missionary but raised and trained by himself.[37] Colenso ranted long and hard about the 'illegality' of the charge against him on the basis that theirs was a master/child relationship, and lambasted the slave, who had promised never to leave him but had the temerity to take alternative employment.[38] His biographer Peter Wells described that 'essentially deranged letter' as the work of Colenso's agitated state of mind, and so it likely was, but the attitudes are not dissimilar to those of others — albeit more stridently expressed.[39]

Just how much freedom redeemed captives had gained is no clearer than how grateful they were. They were certainly not always as grateful as they were expected to be. Perhaps the late eighteenth-century trope of the 'grateful slave' — the idea that total freedom was not important if slaves were well treated — raised expectations of gratitude from those redeemed? It was a convenient idea that emerged at a time when racial difference was evolving as a means of justifying slavery, especially in the West Indies where British interests had suffered a severe blow from the Somerset case. The grateful slave, a literary device that was used in a number of late eighteenth-century novels, suggested that non-white people could be subdued by kindness which would arouse their passionate gratitude. Within that mindset, real freedom was not necessary — only kindly (and condescending) treatment.

As George Boulukos, author of *The Grateful Slave: The Emergence of Race in Eighteenth-Century British and American Culture*, explained:

> The trope begins with a nod to human similarity, in the sentimental attention to slave suffering, but ends with the suggestion of meaningful difference, as the slaves are so overwhelmed by passionate, irrational gratitude that they enthusiastically accept their state of slavery. This implies distinctions from the rationality, desire for independence, and rejection of slavery expected from whites.[40]

It was a form of literature that was pervasive and very persuasive.

John King, Samuel Leigh, and the Butlers were all born in the 1780s; Henry and Marianne Williams and the Kemps in the 1790s. So the grateful slave was a concept they would have grown up with. Indeed, Governor George Grey had one novel of the genre, *Robinson Crusoe*, translated into the Māori language by the Kemps' son, Henry Tacy Kemp, in 1852, and the diary of British naval officer Theodore Morton Jones, written while he was in New Zealand in 1853, records his impressions of *Uncle Tom's Cabin* first published two years earlier. Having noted that it had already gone through ten editions, he called it 'one of the most intensely thrilling stories' he had ever read.[41]

If, as seems likely, the trope of the 'grateful slave', ever-indebted to a white master or mistress for kindly treatment, was an ingrained idea, especially among 'humanitarians' such as those of the missionary societies, it may explain their indignation when 'redeemed slaves' employed as their servants were ungrateful or disobedient; and their complaints when they left after being made useful through training. Unfortunately, missionary writings do not always clarify whether a particular servant was a redeemed slave or a free person. But their attitudes to desertion — whether permanent or temporary — were generally consistent. Their shared despair was probably revealed in Eliza White's heartfelt words: 'We leave all that is dear to us on earth for their sake and they do all they can to irritate and make us angry.'[42]

The Bible and slavery

In order to understand early nineteenth-century missionary motivations and attitudes towards slavery, it should be useful to look at what the Bible has to say about the subject. The Good News version, first published in 1976, mentions the words 'slave' or 'slavery' 349 times, whereas the New Revised Standard version of the Bible, which was first published in 1989 and claims to be the most accurate translation, uses the words 153 times. However, early missionaries in New Zealand would have used the authorised King James version. And that Bible only includes the word twice: in Jeremiah and Revelation, although it does include over a hundred references to bondage, bondman, bondwoman, and so on.[43]

The root of the problem lies in the Greek word *'doulos'* which may be used to mean either a slave or a servant so that the translation into English depends on how the translator understands the word in context.[44] Modern translators are more likely to think of a person in bondage as a slave, whereas in earlier times, many people lived in a state of bondage, whether permanent or temporary, and their status may have been seen as a normal, even acceptable, situation. So while the New Revised Standard version renders Paul's words to Titus in the New Testament as:

> Tell slaves to be submissive to their masters and to give satisfaction in every respect; they are not to talk back, not to pilfer, but to show complete and perfect fidelity, so that in everything they may be an ornament to the doctrine of God our Saviour[45]

the missionaries' King James Bible has him say:

> Exhort servants to be obedient unto their own masters, and to please them well in all things; not answering again. Not purloining, but shewing all good fidelity; that they may adorn the doctrine of God our Saviour in all things.

The implication is that slaves, servants, bondsmen, and bondswomen were considered to have much the same status, so the missionaries' servants might have had the same obligations as the New Revised Standard version's slaves. Paul lived and preached in places where slaves constituted a very significant proportion of the population: places such as Ephesus and Corinth.[46] It has also been argued quite persuasively, that, in the context of his time, Jesus would have used the word equivalent to an unpaid slave rather than a servant who received some form of payment for his or her duties.[47]

Translations are representations of what the translator understood the words in the original language were intended to convey. So how early nineteenth-century missionaries understood these words should be evident in the Māori-language version of the Bible, Te Paipera Tapu, since it was members of the CMS in New Zealand who translated it. Curiously, the harsh Māori word 'taurekareka' appears there only four times: in Romans 7:23, Galatians 4:24, Hebrews 2:15, and Revelation 13:10,[48] and those instances correspond with bondage or being led into captivity in the King James Bible — none of them being translations of 'slave' or 'slavery'. Nevertheless, this does confirm that the people referred to were either war captives or in bondage and, in either case, not 'free'. Yet, in the two instances where the word 'slave' appears in the King James Bible, the Māori translation is 'pononga' which tends more towards the meaning of servant. All of this would seem to suggest that the kind of servant they had in mind was not one free to quit their employment but more like a bonded apprentice in Britain who, until 1814, was obliged to serve a fixed term, typically of seven years, as payment for the skills they had acquired.[49] Pononga may have been used to convey the sense of a subservient person who gave faithful service to a benign master or mistress, implying a relationship similar to that of parent and child or master and apprentice.

Like much of English law, that concerning apprentices appears to be derived from the Bible. For example, Deuteronomy 15:12 says:

> If your brother, a Hebrew man, or a Hebrew woman, is sold to you and *serves you six years, then in the seventh year you shall let him go free* from you. And when you send him away free from you, you shall not let him go away empty-handed; you shall supply him liberally from your flock, from your threshing floor, and from your winepress. From what the Lord your God has blessed you with, you shall give to him. You shall remember that you were a slave in the land of Egypt, and the Lord your God redeemed you; therefore I command you this thing today. [emphasis added]

In this passage, redemption equates with physical freedom or freedom from bondage rather than spiritual redemption, but it also implies that God had the right to command the Hebrew people as a quid pro quo for his securing their release from slavery.

Missionary understandings of slave redemption

As already mentioned, some nine months after the report of the 1838 Select Committee inquiry was published, the CMS missionaries in New Zealand took the opportunity to respond to various sections of the evidence. In refuting John Flatt's remark that slaves were 'purchased', they underscored the key word in their riposte: 'Slaves are <u>redeemed</u> by the Missionaries.'[50] But what precisely did they mean by redemption?

Sometimes missionaries got lucky and were given slaves as presents or were able to negotiate exchanges. After a taua muru had visited the mission at Paihia in April 1829, for example, the mission agreed to return a musket seized from the plundering party in exchange for a small slave girl who was given to the Māori convert Taiwhanga.[51] Curiously, though, when the mission vessel called at the home place of some captives from the Bay of Plenty region, who were on board in 1826, Henry Williams had not allowed them to return to their people on a permanent basis:

> Their fathers, mothers and other relations came alongside . . . and I gave them permission to return with them on shore specifying a time when I expected to see them back. I was a little surprised to see them according to promise. They told me their friends had endeavoured to persuade them to remain behind, but they would not.[52]

Perhaps the captives were not redeemed and Williams was anxious not to jeopardise the mission's relationship with their patrons. That seems to have been the case six years later when Tāreha came to the Williamses' home one dinner time enquiring after two slave girls living in the settlement. Henry feared that the rangatira 'was prepared to use violent measures' had the missionaries shown any hesitation in allowing him to take them away, so they 'told him, that as they were not [their] slaves, of course they must depart with him if he thought proper'.[53] While Williams's attitude might now seem strange, it was not inconsistent with his stronger emphasis on evangelising Māori rather than attempting to change long-standing customs. Whereas CMS policy had previously focused on 'civilising' Māori before attempting to convert them, Henry Williams altered that approach when he took over leadership of the mission. Not one Māori had been converted when he arrived in New Zealand in 1823, but after reversing their approach to make spiritual teaching and conversion the first priority, their work began to bear real fruit during the 1830s.[54]

Nevertheless, the journals of early missionaries in Northland proudly proclaimed a number of slave 'redemptions' that they facilitated, usually through the payment of goods. However, their accounts of the circumstances suggest that, rather than being unwilling to take back loved ones who had been captured, their friends and family were very often only too anxious to secure their return. When a group from the Hauraki area came seeking a peace agreement with his Ngāpuhi neighbours at Kerikeri in early 1823, John Butler was moved by a request from a chiefly member of the party. The man, who Butler referred to as Tee Toee from Mokoia (Panmure), was a relative of Hīnaki from Ngāti Pāoa, who had been killed by Hongi Hika in 1821. He was bereft over the loss of his small son named John Butler, then about seven years old, who had been taken as a slave to a Hokianga chief named 'Kawaddu' (Kawharu?). The boy had received Butler's name over two years previously, at his father's behest, when the missionary was at the River Thames. That was more than two years before the first Christian baptism, but the circumstance of the naming proved very helpful in bringing about the boy's safe return. Butler assured 'Tee Toee' he 'would do all in [his] power to redeem him', to which the '[p]oor creature', with 'tears of joy' in his eyes, replied, '"Ka pai, E Tangata pai" (Very good, good man)'.[55] Eleven days later, Butler expressed the heartfelt pleasure he felt from redeeming the boy:

> [His master] talked about having a gun, but I told him I could not give any such thing, but I must have the child nevertheless, and I urged my name, which he had received, as well as a father's feelings. I told him that I could not endure the thought of my child being a slave, who was called after my name. He then said he would take the above articles of trade [two axes and a hoe], which were readily paid, [and I] took the boy into my house and sent for his father. On presenting his child unto him, he could scarcely speak. I cannot write his feelings, but those who are parents, and have an only son torn from their bosoms by ravages of war, and reduced to slavery for life, to have such a one redeemed by a stranger, and returned to their embrace, at a time when according to their own prospects, there was not the least reason to expect any such thing could take place — if such an unexpected deliverance would overwhelm their hearts, then let them remember that something like this was doubtless the feelings of this poor heathen.[56]

Butler seems to have been aware of the significance of tapatapa to Māori whereby a person of mana might name something after themselves which would have the effect of giving them some claim over it — in this case, the boy. Such an understanding would have been very useful in obtaining the lad's release.

In other cases, however, and even when payment had been made to secure an individual's 'redemption', missionaries, like merchants, found that those who had accepted their payments were all too often inclined to take the people back whenever extra labour was required. Demands for their return, even if on a temporary basis, were particularly common when crops required planting or harvesting or at other times when labour was most needed.

Arguments over what sort of rights the 'redeemers' of slaves actually had were surely behind Alfred Brown and William Fairburn's arranging for Tohitapu to sign a document (fig. 61), acknowledging receipt of six blankets, two iron pots, and two axes, in exchange for the redemption of his slaves Rahi, Painga, Kotuku, and Rawa. Tohitapu signed with his moko (tattoo design) but, since he was unlikely to have understood the paperwork, we can only speculate as to how he understood the arrangement.

Just a month later, another CMS missionary, Charles Baker, formally recorded his payment of two blankets in exchange for a slave who was about to be killed. In this case, the document was witnessed by Thomas Chapman of the CMS and John Hobbs from the Wesleyan mission.[57]

In 1842, by which time he had obviously learned that the purchase of slaves was not necessarily considered a permanent arrangement, Reverend John Warren did a deal with an elderly woman of chiefly rank from Waimā in the Hokianga. The woman had heard that Warren wanted a servant and offered someone Warren described as 'one of the lowest and most wretched kind of a slave'. 'I am dying with love for my slave', the woman told him. 'He is cold and naked: I want him to work for you, that he may get a blanket, to keep him warm during the winter.' But Warren replied that he was tired of hiring slaves, 'because as soon as they are clothed you come and strip them'. So he offered a written agreement which would bind her to allowing the man to stay with him for a year on the basis that he would receive monthly wages, half of which would go to her. The document was apparently signed and witnessed, but when the planting season came around two months later, the woman ordered the man to plant her potatoes. Thoroughly displeased with Warren's response, she threatened to kill the slave if he did not commence the work within two days.

When she subsequently caught and beat the man, Warren grabbed her, causing her to fall, which inflamed the situation even further. Now absolutely livid, the woman returned at sunset with 30 men in tow, all demanding to take the slave away. Having anticipated such a visit, the overly loved man had fled into Warren's bedroom, hiding under the bed while Mrs Warren, with babe in arms and backed by some mission girls, barred the door. After a few hours and much commotion, one of the men threatened to smash the door with a hatchet but thought better of it and instead accused the woman of embroiling them all in a 'trespass' on the missionary's home. Warren seized that opportunity to offer to redeem the man in return for 'a considerable amount of property'. Some of her companions were keen to accept the offer, but the irony was not lost on the woman who responded very righteously:

> So you want me to sell him! Is that your gospel? Who ever heard of an English lady selling the man that she loved?

Her idea of love surely differed from the missionaries', though. It related to the fact that she had reared him from childhood after her people had 'killed and ate' his parents in the Waikato and that she had subsequently thrown him the occasional potato.

Fortunately for Warren and the man at the centre of the dispute, an elderly chief broke the impasse by singing a love song in which:

> he satirically complimented the old lady on her surpassing beauty, and recited the many conquests she had made, only they were many years ago; and then, addressing her, said: "Madam, you are a great lady, and you have been badly used in this affair: you never made a written agreement with the white man: you were not the aggressor in this matter: you did not come and shed blood in the missionary's garden: you were very much hurt by falling into the river; and if you had been only a common woman, you would have been killed. But you are a priestess, and full of the Atua Maori (native god) [Māori spirituality], so there is no killing you. All that you have said of your great love to the slave is perfectly true. We know that when you fed your pig you threw the slave a potato, but it was after the pig would eat no more; and we know that when you had got the pig nice and fat, you did not object to sell

him for a blanket. My advice is, that you do the same with this slave. Shall I take care of these goods for you? What say you?"

Having concluded his performance, he stooped, as if to listen for the answer, 'Ae? ae. Ae? ae.' (Yes, yes, yes, yes.) She could hardly contradict him now, so, having gathered her party together, they all left and the protesting woman gained only a small portion of the goods Warren had offered. But, as he proudly declared, 'the poor slave was free'.[58]

It may be gleaned from all of this that the Māori owners understood the redeemers to have acquired only limited use rights. As Māori frequently objected to claims that land had been 'purchased' in the sense of permanent alienation rather than a right of occupation, cross-cultural misunderstandings were equally evident in these human transactions. Māori clearly did not consider that missionary redemption altered the status of those people nor their mana over them.

Henry Williams had vented his frustration with this practice of commandeering redeemed slaves in his journal for December 1831. Tohitapu had become 'very troublesome', he wrote, because he had insisted on taking a slave 'who had been redeemed' from the service of fellow missionary Alfred Brown. Williams felt that the 'old man' was being 'very insolent' in not returning him. Tohitapu, however, was in the 'same humour' the next day when he arrived at the mission house carrying a small staff, intent on driving out the slave's wife who had 'taken shelter' with the missionaries. Since Brown was absent at the time, Williams 'was obliged to turn him out'.[59] Was the slave one of those named in the document Brown and Fairburn had drawn up the previous month? Unfortunately, Williams did not say.

However, the constancy of status of redeemed slaves had been made clear one Sunday in 1833 when a number of Māori had gathered to witness the marriage of Ropata Oru, previously redeemed and baptised, to his fiancée Turanga, who had been living at the CMS mission for several years by then. As proceedings were about to begin, 'a distant relative' of the bride arrived on the scene, rather like the wicked witch of European fairy tales. The new arrival claimed that, as the groom was a slave, he would not allow the union to go ahead and intended to kill the would-be husband. John King was bemused. Having 'redeemed' Ropata well before that time, he assumed the transaction had changed his status in Māori eyes as well as his own. On this occasion, happily, a present given to the objector 'had the desired effect' and the betrothed couple were able to be married in the presence of the bride's parents and other relations. King noted, though, that 'the chiefs who attended looked on with surprise'.[60]

Although missionaries consistently spoke of 'redeeming' slaves, other Westerners used different vocabulary, and not all such transactions worked out well. Joel Polack, for example, was less coy in his language when he reported purchasing a slave boy 'for a blanket, a musket, a bag of duck shot, and some well thumbed leaves of the "Penny Magazine"'. As he explained, the *Penny Magazine* 'was appropriated as wadding for the "diffusion" of shot . . . it being the season for pigeon shooting'. Polack was as disappointed and annoyed as his Christian neighbours, when, despite that 'purchase', Te Tawa, the boy's master, enticed the lad from his service. He was even more annoyed when he visited Te Tawa to demand the boy back and was told that the great man had better things to do than run after slave boys, and that if Polack had chosen to buy one, the only solution he could suggest for preventing them returning was 'to kill and roast them'. Polack responded that if he did not get the boy by the next day, the chief would 'not have him'. We might wonder what he meant by that riposte, but having heard the threat repeated 'with exaggerations', the lad understood it to mean that he was bewitched so 'took to his bed, refused all sustenance, and within a fortnight died'.[61] Polack was not the most sympathetic of souls and the boy's reaction to the situation suggests that he did not feel that the transaction was in his favour. Those who chose to run back to their previous 'owners' — from missionary redeemers or trader-purchasers like Polack — may have been hinting that they enjoyed more personal freedom under Māori masters than Western ones.

Spiritual redemption

Many of the attitudes expressed by the missionaries may have stemmed from their belief that Māori 'slavery' was more benign than the trans-Atlantic trade in Africans. But regardless of the extent to which that was the case, a fundamental shared conviction remained that liberty and freedom from slavery were blessings that British colonisation would bestow. And like most of their countrymen, they took it for granted that those blessings were symbolised by the British flag. Indeed, Henry Williams opted to fly the white ensign, based on the cross of St George with the union flag in the top left corner, on the CMS vessels. For him the flag would have symbolised all the noble ideals that Britain, or, perhaps more precisely, England, stood for — ideals that had been reflected in Marsden's words as he prepared for his first service in New Zealand.

There was another, probably more important, aspect to missionary 'redemptions', though. Their writings frequently reveal that when they redeemed or assumed that they had redeemed Māori slaves, it was spiritual redemption, rather than physical freedom in this earthly world, that was foremost in their minds. That was their primary objective when entering missionary service and may explain why the word 'manumission' does not seem to have been used when payment was made in exchange for slaves.

It is widely accepted that many of Christianity's earliest converts came from within the Roman Empire's slave populations. That circumstance, and the fact that redemption has been offered as one of the three key words of the Apostle Paul's theology, may help to explain the extraordinary role of slave metaphors in the symbolic structure of Christianity. In theological terms, redemption means release from enslavement. Sin condemns a person to slavery but believers are emancipated from sin through Christ.[62] Christ is consequently referred to as the 'Redeemer', and the missionaries surely felt that they were doing his work in a very literal sense. So metaphors may hold the key to understanding not only missionary attitudes but also, perhaps, those of contemporary Britons more generally towards slavery.

Both Wesleyan and CMS missionaries emphasised the doctrine of Christ's atonement over his incarnation in early nineteenth-century New Zealand. Nathaniel Turner wrote that his soul delighted to dwell on 'the Doctrine of General Redemption'.[63] John King embodied the same sentiment in his address to Māori at Rangihoua in 1823 about the 'slavery of sin and the freedom of the service of Christ', and again the following year when he offered his listeners a choice between being 'children of Jehovah or slaves of Satan', a concept referred to as the 'hinge of Christian truth'.[64] Some ten years later, Richard Davis wrote of his fears that Māori were 'dying fast' from their exposure to 'haunts of vice', adding: 'O that the Lord would but subdue the power of Satan and save those wretched, though willing captives from eternal death!' Freedom lies at the core of Christianity's promise of salvation.[65] Thus, Davis used the word 'captives' metaphorically to mean those Māori who had not converted to Christianity and were thus captives of Satan rather than prisoners of war.[66]

Plucking brands from the burning

Davis referred to a relative of Rāwiri Taiwhanga's wife as a slave whom he had redeemed 'when she was about to be sacrificed by being sent on board the ships', in other words, to cater for the sex trade. Following her subsequent baptism in 1830, he trusted that the Lord had 'plucked her as a brand from the burning, and made her a partaker of saving grace'.[67] William Williams used the same phrase when reporting his deathbed baptism of another ex-ship girl some three or four years later.[68]

'Plucked as a brand from the burning' appears quite frequently in missionary journals during the 1820s and 1830s. When one of the mission servants, a young man from 'Te Puki' (Te Puke?) and very likely a war captive from the Bay of Plenty area,[69] became seriously ill, Davis urged his congregation to strive to 'pluck him as a brand from the burning'. Davis's exhortation had the desired effect. Previously disinclined to accept Christian teachings, but near death, the man confirmed that he 'desired to die and to go to Christ'. He was baptised the next day, just three days before he expired. Davis believed that he had been 'received into everlasting glory as a gem to the Redeemer's crown'.[70] Not all made such last-minute conversions, however. One who did not was Naonao, a physically frail young man, said to be a good worker who could read and write well and knew the basics of arithmetic. But for William Yate, being a good and steady man was all that could be said in his favour: 'to the day of his death' they 'never saw any thing in him, but hardness of heart, unbelief, and contempt of God's Word and Commandments'. So, despite Naonao's claims 'that he had never done any harm' but simply would not believe and 'did not want a saviour', in Yate's eyes, he was never 'free': 'He died as he had lived — apparently without God, and without hope.'[71] As Boyd Hilton explained: 'it is not sinful activity but lack of faith for which men are condemned to Hell, an apparently innocent life is often more dangerous spiritually than a career of heinous crime'.[72]

Davis's pride in his successful redemptions is apparent in a November 1828 diary entry which announced that he had redeemed another slave that day: 'I have now redeemed five, and they all turn out well.' He was also gratified that another breakthrough had been made: 'slaves living with us are permitted to marry free girls'. There had been two such instances among his servants by that time: 'Oh that they may speedily be united in the bonds of redeeming love!'[73] 'Free' girls they may have been, but Davis was keen to discourage too much freedom. Some nine months earlier, he had asked one of the mission boys, Poutu by name, to select a partner from among the mission girls:

> His note intimated his desire to take one, but that he could not understand the lady's mind on the subject, especially as we kept so strict a look-out. I desired him to enquire in person; but he considered that it would be better that I should propose the question.[74]

Having nudged things along and performed a Christian marriage service, Davis felt: 'exceedingly thankful that this girl, for whom we have felt much anxiety, was now likely to be respectably settled in life'. She had dodged one of Satan's musket balls.[75]

The tenets of Christian faith that missionaries sought to introduce to Māori could not be divorced from their evangelical worldviews with regard to ideas of moral propriety and social functionality.[76] So, as Angela Wanhalla noted: 'Marriage, and the process of baptism which preceded the ceremony, was the main work of missionaries in early New Zealand.'[77] They 'maintained the traditional Christian stress on the importance of marriage' as the only appropriate context for sexual activity.[78] But, as

John King discovered in the case of Turanga and Ropata, slaves were still not always considered eligible to marry a free spouse.

'Plucked as a brand' — from the burning or the fire — was said of various individuals and by Wesleyans as well as Anglicans, but perhaps most often of women who had been involved in the sex trade. So that phrase is the key to what missionaries had in mind when they 'redeemed' slaves: salvation of the soul — redemption in Christ. And that was tied up with moral redemption, including being plucked from the sex trade and immoral relationships. Having said that, William Yate offered a somewhat different rationale for redeeming female slaves (he specified 'female'). 'When any of them have been redeemed', he said, 'it is for the purpose of being married; that, after their marriage, their masters may not have any claim upon them, nor take them away by force from their husbands.' While this implies a specific purpose, he had claimed immediately before this statement that mission families frequently 'redeemed their domestics' so that they might have their liberty and 'an opportunity of being married to the person of their choice, or that they may secure to themselves the wages which they receive for their labour'.[79] Although he did not stipulate the gender of the 'domestics' in this sentence, marriage may have given women protection from being reclaimed by previous owners. If that were the case, widowhood may have exposed a woman to vulnerability yet again.

William Barrett Marshall's *A Personal Narrative of Two Visits to New Zealand* is a passionate plea in favour of the missionary cause, timed to coincide with British deliberations regarding the possible colonisation of New Zealand. In it, Marshall related a story of romance and redemption that centred on a couple who lived at the Paihia mission with their small baby. Although neither had been baptised, he was touched by 'the simplicity of their manners and the modesty of their behaviour'. Wera, the woman, 'had been one of the wretched race of native prostitutes, who earn for themselves disease, misery, and an untimely death, while letting out their bodies for hire, at the bidding of their covetous masters'. Happily, though, Marshall was able to report that Wera was 'emancipated at a very tender age' from 'so degraded a condition' by marriage. But when her husband left for distant parts with a war party soon after, she could only pine for his return in a wretched state of suspense and anxiety. Wretchedness appears to have dogged her whilst she remained a heathen. But Marshall tells us that, during this time of great stress, another man, named Keno, fell in love with her. Coincidentally, it was also during this period that Wera conceived 'a deep concern for the salvation of her soul'. The story has little sympathy for the husband who fell in battle as Wera had feared, but implies considerable admiration for Keno who, after awaiting 'the gradual subsidence of her grief, declared his hitherto secret passion'. A subsequent wedding, conducted by the missionaries, allowed the couple to live happily ever after and 'spend the remainder of their lives with their offspring, in the free service of the Most High, and at the same time in full enjoyment of the glorious liberty of the sons of God'.[80] So, two more lost souls gained redemption and liberty via the twofold process of religious conversion and Christian marriage.

The idea of being 'plucked as a brand from the burning' originates with the prophets of the Old Testament. It is used there in the sense of the nation of Israel being saved from destruction in order to fulfil God's purpose. In other words, the sense is of their having been given a second chance — specifically, from destruction like that suffered by Sodom and Gomorrah or by allowing their return from exile in Babylon.[81] John Wesley used this phrase of himself, in recalling that he was saved from a house fire as a child. But Anglicans were also aware of the usage to refer to individuals being rescued from certain death, which experience was expected to cause them to reflect soberly on the miracle which that represented and consider God's call on them.[82] No doubt with that in mind and recalling how he was saved when his own family home burned to the ground in 1838, the son of Wesleyan missionary Nathaniel Turner referred to himself as 'a brand plucked from the burning' in more senses than one.[83]

In 1894, long after most would consider that 'slavery' in the sense of bonded war captives was past, an article entitled 'God's Year of Release' appeared in *Te Hoa Maori*, a newspaper published by the Plymouth Brethren. While stressing the vital importance of redemption, it also emphasised metaphors of enslavement. Redemption equalled freedom or liberty, it explained, but although lust or desire was enough to enslave a person, slaves to passion did not feel their bondage because they loved such excitement. 'God proclaims liberty' and '[o]nly God can redeem'. Drawing heavily on Leviticus 25 pertaining to the redemption of slaves, the article clearly distinguished between physical and spiritual enslavement. But, by reading between the lines, it becomes apparent that freedom from physical and social bondage was expected to lead to religious conversion and spiritual salvation. However, one section from this lengthy article would have had particular resonance for Māori who were still fighting for the return of their land. That was the one which assured readers that not only would enslaved persons become free through Christ but also that 'forfeited inheritances return to their owners, and so the land shall return to the Jew'.[84]

CHAPTER EIGHT

Breaking the spiritual bonds

THE INTRODUCTION OF CHRISTIANITY OFFERED NEW WAYS OF dealing with a new environment even though many of the practices Māori chose to adopt sat side by side with older ones. Sometimes new procedures replaced customary ones but with similar purpose. Wheaten bread, for example, unknown to Māori before European contact, was adopted as a staple food. But as bread has applications in Christian ritual, some Māori communities used it as a replacement for the more customary cooked kūmara in ceremonies to whakanoa, or lift the tapu or restrictions from a person or place.[1] In other words, while practices might alter in their detail, fundamental concepts were not necessarily overridden by new religious ideas. What changed was the social, political, and spiritual context.

Tapu was an important cohesive force in Māori society because it not only linked individuals to the ancestors but also to their wider tribal network. The system placed each person in an interdependent relationship with their extended family and tribal group with responsibilities and obligations to uphold the tapu and the mana of the group.[2] But that interdependent relationship began to loosen as new ideas about the nature of tapu and individual responsibility began to take hold. Christian principles of human equality, which held that salvation was a matter of individual responsibility, as well as the privileging of individual rights by British institutions more generally, cut across collective systems. However, missionary teachings were not the only instigators of change in the social, political, and spiritual worlds of Māori. The modification of tikanga, or customary ways of doing things, in order to secure the benefits of new trading opportunities, was closely connected with those changes.[3] That economic pragmatism played an important part in eroding the strength of tapu's restrictive power and straining social cohesion.

The Māori aptitude for business was evident as soon as they and late eighteenth-century European explorers made their first fumbling attempts at cross-cultural trade. But while infringements of tapu were quickly punished initially, rangatira soon appreciated that longer-term trading prospects were better served by making allowance for their visitors' ignorance of Māori laws and protocols.[4] So, once regular trading relationships had been established, breaches of tapu by traders and other outsiders were often overlooked or handled with particular diplomacy to avoid losing those all-important economic opportunities. One of many such examples occurred when the baby daughter of a merchant negotiating with the rangatira Patuone seized his topknot. The head being the most tapu part of the body, such a travesty against a man of great mana might have incurred the death penalty. In this case, however, Patuone acquitted baby Julia on the grounds of insanity. He declared her to be pōrangi (mad).[5] It was hardly a good business move to kill the geese which laid the golden eggs (or their offspring); but such allowances had long-term implications.[6]

Māori spiritual beliefs, underpinned by the principles of tapu and mana, were all-pervasive, and the position of war captives was just one aspect of the changes that were about to occur. But because the juxtaposition of 'slave' and rangatira was such a significant and symbolic component of Māori society's hierarchical structure, those changes would have domino effects on other aspects of power relations.

Why were captives released?

Unprecedented numbers of captives had been acquired during the 1820s especially, when the demand for labour was great. Unfortunately for historiography, however, this period followed closely on the heels of the first missionary arrivals and increasing visits from European mariners. Consequently, it is their writings that have formed the basis of most publications on the subject of Māori warfare and captive taking.[7] But it was an atypical era, during which the balance of power altered dramatically to favour leaders at locations preferred by Western shipping. And muskets enabled the victors not only to take huge numbers of captives, but also to walk or paddle them back to their home areas far more readily. The capacity for mass capture was now well beyond what could be achieved with hand-to-hand weapons. So a situation that has been assumed to be normal was, in fact, extremely abnormal in many ways. Within a relatively short period of time, however, the trend reversed. During the 1830s that unseemly scramble to acquire captive labour was followed by an equally dramatic reversal with many captives being set free — even if their lands were not always available to reoccupy.

In 1851 the Reverend Thomas Buddle told members of the Auckland Mechanics' Institute that: 'Christianity has produced its usual results in reference to slavery. When the tribes embraced the Gospel, they gave their slaves leave to return and occupy their own lands.'[8] He was not alone in claiming that it was missionary teachings, even before the introduction of English law, which ended Māori slavery. It has remained a common refrain from the mid-nineteenth century to the present.[9] But what part did Christianity play in the process or in alleviating the lot of that section of society?

The missionaries active in the 1830s made considerable efforts to restore peace to a disturbed land but made no loud claims to have ended slavery. Religious conversion was far from general by that time, especially not among the chiefly classes, which raises the suspicion that shifts in the perspectives of writers over time, noted in accounts of the *Endeavour* incident, were responsible for this retrospective claim.[10] Only 2000 Māori had been baptised by 1840 although Henry Williams recorded that 30,000 were then under instruction.[11] Christians were still a minority five years later, yet even chiefs who remained non-Christian might refuse to fight on Sundays for fear of offending missionaries.[12] With the advantage of hindsight, Christianity appears less a religious conviction for some leaders than an excuse for putting the brakes on warfare that had reached unprecedented levels in extent and killing power.[13] Besides, the freeing of captives was very convenient at this time.

The availability of huge numbers of captives as a compliant labour force would have had great appeal when they could be utilised to increase production for foreign trade. But they came with ongoing costs. They had to be fed, housed, and clothed — even if in the most begrudgingly thrifty manner. So keeping them had to make economic sense, and there is much evidence to suggest that the economic justifications weakened over time. Market forces varied according to geographic location, but in Northland, by the early 1830s, changes in demand for Māori trade goods meant that enormous labour forces were no longer great assets and idle labourers had become a burden. The trade in flax, which required vast armies of female workers to prepare it for sale, was giving way to timber and, while slave labour was useful for cutting and dragging logs from inland to the water's edge, it required far fewer workers. And although there is no evidence that food production in the Bay of Islands diminished in the wake of departing slaves, the initial rush to expand agricultural land for growing potatoes and other crops petered out.[14] Enough had been cleared to meet demand. Not only did the decline in warfare leave their own men free to spend more time in the gardens rather than on the battlefield, but the acquisition of more metal tools also made agricultural work more efficient, requiring less manual labour.

During his lifetime, Hongi Hika's military and political dominance had allowed him to restrict missionary activities to Northland. He had jealously guarded 'his' missions to the point that other tribal groups did not dare show interest.[15] But after his death in 1828, the missionary societies were able to extend their evangelisation programmes further afield. The release of captives was evident soon after that, too. Thousands are believed to have been released during the 1830s: first by Ngāpuhi, then by the Waikato tribes, Ngāi Tahu, and others.[16] So the two circumstances coincided to a large degree but were not necessarily directly connected.

By that time, there was not only a reduced demand for labour but also a lessening enthusiasm for further warfare. The loss of lives had been significant, albeit often exaggerated, but so, too, was the social disruption that accompanied it.[17] Even though the lands of the vanquished had not been occupied by the northern tribes, there was a high level of migration and resettlement. Some groups were pushed out of their homelands and onto the lands of others. Those wars were not about the acquisition of territory but about settling old scores and acquiring labour forces. Nevertheless, the flow-on effects were very significant.

Tribal groups from the Bay of Islands and, subsequently, other areas of Northland had initially held the whip hand in terms of armoury but, over time, others throughout the country had caught up. By around 1835, they were mostly as well-armed as their erstwhile tormentors and would surely seek to turn the tables on those who had beaten them so easily.[18] Rather than sitting back and waiting for retribution, releasing and returning their captured kinfolk was not only economically expedient but also an excellent peacemaking initiative.[19] In that light, their emancipation might be viewed as less the result of Christian teaching than an instinctive response to changed circumstances.

Like the other great war leader Hongi Hika, Te Rauparaha did not become a Christian. As late as 1839, he killed one of his 'slaves' to feed guests at a feast. Yet, around 1840, a number of Ngāi Tahu people, including the leading rangatira Iwikau, Memo, and Paora Tau, were returned to Banks Peninsula from Kāpiti Island after some nine or ten years in captivity. Two sources claim that Te Rauparaha, their captor, was moved to free them as a consequence of near-defeats at the hands of Ngāi Tahu and fear of further retaliation. However, as Hilary and John Mitchell point out, it served Ngāi Tahu's interests to associate such motives with their great enemy.[20] Besides, customary protocols had always allowed for the freeing of captives. Ema Turumeke told how she successfully escaped from her Ngāti Toa captors around 1829 after her mother had been formally released. Her mother was formally freed when their captor's wife climbed onto the roof of a house to issue a decree to that effect.[21] That incident is reminiscent of the more famous occasion when Te Ao-kapurangi of Ngāti Rangiwewehi was able to save her kinfolk from a Ngāpuhi raid on Te Arawa at Mokoia Island in 1823. Te Ao-kapurangi, who had been captured earlier, became the wife of the Ngāpuhi rangatira Hauraki. So when his people prepared to assault Mokoia, she asked to accompany them, knowing that members of Ngāti Rangiwewehi, against whom Ngāpuhi had no grudge, would be present. Hongi Hika, the Ngāpuhi leader, agreed to a concession: those of her people who

FIGURE 47. Kororāreka Beach, 1831, by the artist aboard Laplace's vessel, *La Favorite*. This was where the women tried to distract the men from their fishing. *Barthélemy Lauvergne, from C. P. J. Laplace,* Voyage autour du monde, Paris, *1835: B-098-005, Alexander Turnbull Library, Wellington*

FIGURE 48. This scene, recorded in Tolaga Bay, shows Māori men and women on board the *Astrolabe* performing a less salacious dance than Lesson described. A French officer is on the right. *Louis Auguste de Sainson, 'Baie Houa-Houa; Naturels executant une danse a bord de l'Astrolabe (Nouvelle-Zelande)', 1833: B-052-021, Alexander Turnbull Library, Wellington*

FIGURE 49. French sailors from Dumont d'Urville's ship the *Astrolabe* washing their clothes and relaxing by a stream flowing out into Astrolabe Roadstead, Tasman Bay (now Watering Bay). *Date: 1827 By: Sainson, Louis Auguste d, 'Aiguade a l'Anse de l'Astrolabe [January 1827]', B-052-003, Alexander Turnbull Library, Wellington.*

FIGURE 50. The man in European clothes standing near the prow of the canoe has been identified as Tuai (Bell, *The Maori in European Art*, p. 22–24). *Jules Louis Lejeune, 'N[ouvel]le Zelande. Habitans et pirogue', [copied 1825 or 1826 by Antoine Chazal from an 1824 drawing by Jules Louis Lejeune]: C-082-098, Alexander Turnbull Library, Wellington*

FIGURE 51. Portrait of Wesleyan missionary John Hobbs. *1/2-022079-F, Alexander Turnbull Library, Wellington*

FIGURE 52. 'An officer and sailor with natives on board a ship'. *From 'Drawings and Sketches in New Zealand', c. 1853 (colour litho): BL254429, British Library, London, UK; © British Library Board*

FIGURE 53. Pōmare's centre for rest and recreation at Ōtūihu in the Bay of Islands being destroyed by detachments of the British Army's 58th and 96th Regiments. Pomare was taken prisoner aboard HMS *North Star*. *John Williams, 'HMS North Star, destroying Pomare's pa, Otiuhu, Bay of Islands', 1845: A-079-032, Alexander Turnbull Library, Wellington*

FIGURE 54. This painting of half-castes of Pōmare's pā at the Bay of Islands shows a woman with a baby, said to be the daughter of the Chevalier Peter Dillon, a sea captain who had been trading in the Pacific since 1809. To the left of her is Jane, who was 'famous for her personal attractions'. *Richard Aldworth Oliver, 'Half-castes of Pomare's pah (Bay of Islands)', 1851: PUBL-0032-6, Alexander Turnbull Library, Wellington*

FIGURE 55. This 1792 cartoon contrasts the thin and hungry Frenchman's jubilation at becoming a 'Free Citizen', with no more slavery and no more tax to pay, with that of the obviously well-fed and prosperous Briton who complains of being enslaved and starved by taxation. The image reinforces the idea that slavery is a matter of perception. *By James Gillray, published by H. Humphrey, London, 1792*

FIGURE 56. This monumental painting depicts the 1840 convention of the British and Foreign Anti-Slavery Society. It shows Thomas Clarkson, the society's founder, addressing more than 500 delegates, including Henry Beckford, a liberated slave. *Benjamin Robert Haydon, 'The Anti-Slavery Society Convention', 1840*

FIGURE 57. Hone Heke with his wife Hariata around the time of the Northern War. *Joseph Jenner Merrett, 'Johny Heke & wife', c. 1845: E-309-q-2-033, Alexander Turnbull Library, Wellington*

FIGURE 58. Coloured reproduction of a version of the United Tribes Ensign of 1834 which has been copied from a plate in the Admiralty Library's 'Book of flags', 1845. *MS-Papers-0009-09-01, Alexander Turnbull Library, Wellington*

FIGURE 59. Tino rangatiratanga flag

FIGURE 60. Studio portrait of Marianne Williams, taken c. 1860s by an unidentified photographer. *1/2-052460-F, Alexander Turnbull Library, Wellington*

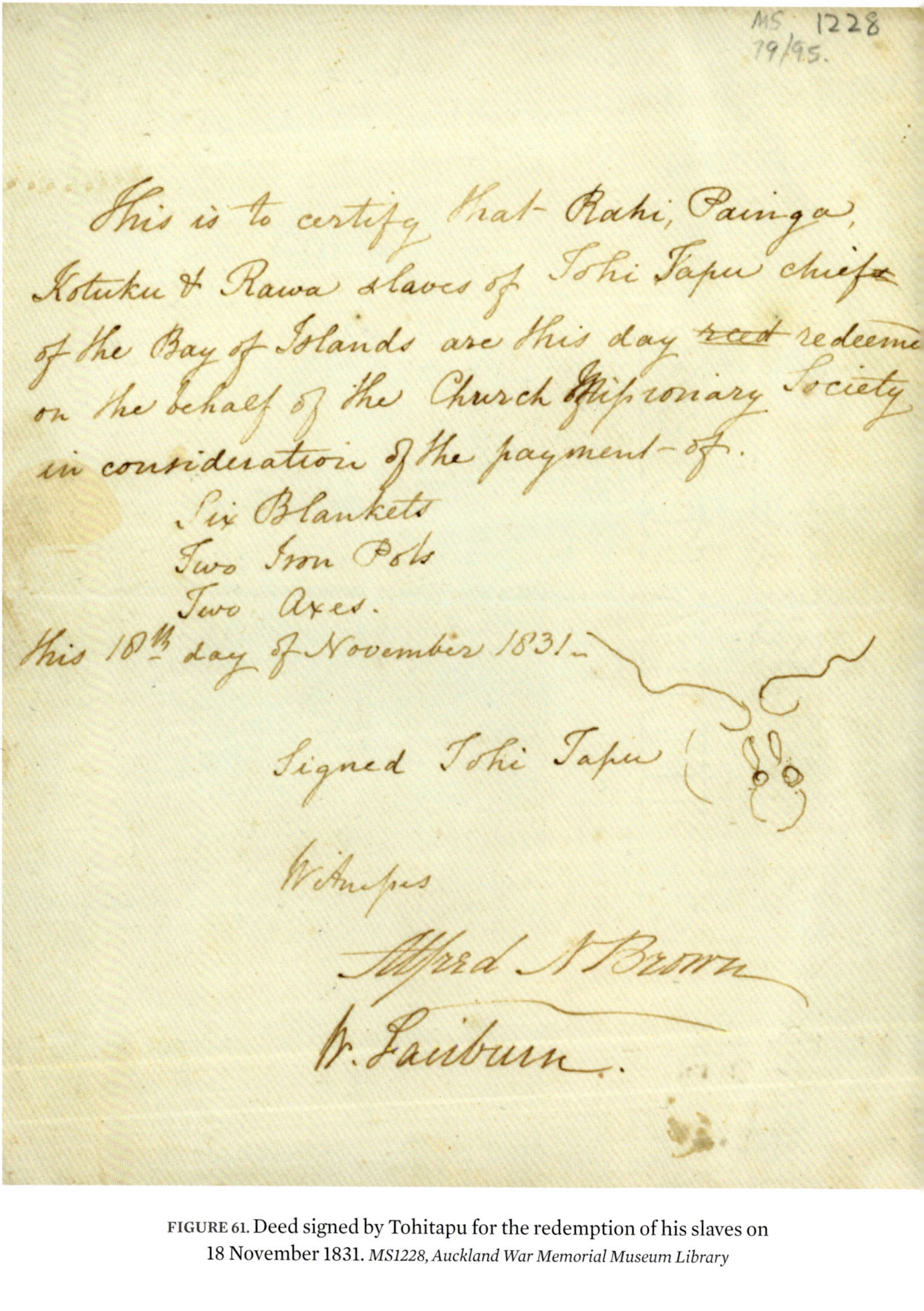

MS 1228
79/95.

This is to certify that Rahi, Painga, Kotuku & Rawa slaves of Tohi Tapu chief of the Bay of Islands are this day ~~recd~~ redeemed on the behalf of the Church Missionary Society in consideration of the payment of.
 Six Blankets
 Two Iron Pots
 Two Axes.
This 18th day of November 1831 —

  Signed Tohi Tapu

 Witness

  Alfred N Brown
  W. Fairburn.

FIGURE 61. Deed signed by Tohitapu for the redemption of his slaves on 18 November 1831. *MS1228, Auckland War Memorial Museum Library*

passed between her thighs would be spared. Determined to take full advantage of the opportunity, Te Ao-kapurangi climbed onto the roof of their wharenui, or meeting house, Tama-te-kapua, and stood astride of the ridgepole, so they might pass through 'between her thighs' into the house and be saved.

John White recounted another occasion when Hongi appeared to show compassion for his captives. He explained that the great warrior suffered severe pain in his knee while aboard a ship near Kororāreka. Believed to be the effect of mākutu (sorcery) by a Thames chief, this spiritual assault required a military response. Because that could not be served up immediately, his people proposed to appease the gods in the meantime by sacrificing some of his 'slaves'. But Hongi tipped them off and told them to flee to 'his relatives' (presumably some other relatives) for safety.[22] Whether that was an act of pure compassion or a way of retaining still valuable workers may never be known, but it was just one of several occasions when he sought to avoid the death of his captives.

Released captives as converts, teachers, and catechists

Whereas in other societies, including North America and the Caribbean where African slaves were debarred from attending school or learning to read or write, Māori war captives were often allowed to attend mission schools and are believed to have been more likely to do so than rangatira. Unfortunately, there are no reliable statistics that can be drawn on to establish levels of Māori literacy by 1840 nor any clear evidence as to whether those of high or low rank were more likely to be literate.[23] But anecdotal evidence suggests that Māori literacy was greater than that of Europeans. We also know that many tribal leaders used scribes in order to communicate in writing, that those people were likely drawn from among the teachers and catechists who had been taught in mission schools, and that a high proportion of these were freed captives. So it was typically released or redeemed captives who took their Christian teachings back to their home communities. When the CMS missionaries were in the process of establishing a new mission at the East Cape in 1838, Davis wrote of three couples who had lived with him in Northland but were now returning to their homes to become teachers to their respective tribes: 'They were all brought to this Country as Slaves but through the blessed influence of Christianity they are not only freed from slavery but are, I trust, become free men in Christ Jesus.'[24]

It was through the work of such people that the mission field was able to extend further south. In a number of instances, missionaries arriving at unfamiliar places found that the ground had already been prepared for them. William Yate was astonished to arrive at pastures new intending to impart the 'first principles or truths of our holy religion' only to be told 'we know all that'. The advance guard had beaten him to it. Interestingly, too, Yate mentioned that as well as those who had 'by some means obtained their freedom', others of those teachers were captives who had 'received permission, from the chief to whom they belonged, to depart for a season', using the opportunity to take 'their little stock of knowledge' and begin 'the work of instruction'.[25] So perhaps those temporary releases were granted in the same spirit as captives 'redeemed' by Pākehā were expected to be still available to their previous masters during busy periods? Presumably, the 'season' in which they took this break from normal duties was one of downtime in the Māori horticultural year.

When he made his first journey south to Wairoa, a month after he and his family had opened their new mission station at Tūranga (Poverty Bay), William Williams found that a keen former slave named Putoko had paved the way for them. Having settled there some eighteen months earlier, Putoko had already built a chapel and established a regular congregation. Although a believer, he had never been baptised.[26] So Māori who had adopted the Christian religion were spreading the faith and its practices, regardless of whether or not they had been personally selected to do so. Commenting in 1840 on the great pleasure that Māori took from hymn singing 'every morning and evening', William Brown noted the debt owed to the 'missionary natives'. Whether at their own home villages or during their travels, they held regular Sunday services, with hymn singing and Bible reading, and frequently delivered an exhortation, 'conducting themselves with the utmost solemnity and propriety'. They were also very strict observers of the Sabbath.[27]

Jerningham Wakefield claimed that their fervour showed itself in other ways, too. He accused Māori missionaries of being jealous of the authority that hereditary chiefs continued to wield, saying that they hoped to become leaders themselves in matters temporal as well as spiritual.[28] However, Wakefield was being harassed by one-time captives who converted to Christianity during their time in the Bay of Islands. Reihana Te Kamo, who was mentioned earlier (see Chapter 4), was based at Pipitea, and Minarapa Te Rangihatuake of Ngā Māhanga was at Te Aro, serving the CMS and Wesleyan missions respectively. They had both been taken back to work among their own people as teachers but also fought to secure the return of their land, allegedly bought by William Wakefield for the New Zealand Company but in questionable circumstances.[29] It was almost certainly those activities that got under his skin. Nevertheless, many of those released captives who became Christian teachers did wield far more power than hereditary chiefs — at least in their own fields of endeavour. They might punish 'backsliders' by banishing them from their communities, fining them, or excluding them from classes, and could summon whole communities to prayer several times a day – things that rangatira were very unlikely to have achieved.[30]

Rangatira conversions

Quite apart from the many documented examples of non-Christian rangatira releasing their captives, the missionaries themselves acknowledged that, in reality, those who did convert did not necessarily release theirs. Although John Downing Tawell had told the 1838 Select Committee that 'as soon as a man is baptised it is understood that he has no slaves', the missionaries on the ground in New Zealand responded the following year that, while they hoped that situation would eventuate, it was still 'not currently the case'.[31]

It was a slow process. Thirteen years later, John King could say only that '*most* of the slaves are liberated who had been taken in war' (emphasis added).[32] Another ten years after that, in 1862, Richard Davis told the CMS in London that it was only during the previous year that Waikato, the rangatira at Te Puna, had allowed all his slaves to return home. In other words, not until almost half a century after the missionaries arrived in the region and 30 years after the mission was established on his doorstep.[33] However, physical 'release' and movement away from the captors' community may not have been the key factor for many people. Dr Karl Scherzer, a member of the Austrian expedition that visited New Zealand during its circumnavigation of the world in 1857, 1858, and 1859, wrote long after the era of intertribal captive taking that:

> Slavery, to the extent that existed among the aborigines in former times, is no longer to be found, though many prisoners taken in war are still held as slaves by their captors. In many cases the slaves prefer to stay with their present masters, if they have been well treated, rather than return among their own race, from whom they feel themselves estranged, and by whom it is probable they have long been forgotten.[34]

As with ancient Rome, it is widely believed (although there is some dispute on this point) that war captives were typically the first and most eager Māori converts to Christianity. A religion that denied the existence of tapu and mana was likely to have greater appeal to those who suffered a loss of those attributes than to those of greatest mana. Chiefs, on the other hand, especially ruling chiefs whose mana came from their personal achievements rather than those whose rank was hereditary, recognised the threat to their authority. As Hongi Hika is famously quoted as saying, 'Christianity might be suited to a nation of slaves but was irrelevant for one of warriors'.[35] Having visited England in 1820, he was well aware of Britain's military power. According to Frederick Maning, as he lay dying in 1828 with his people gathered round him, Hongi urged them to be kind to missionaries and other Europeans but to fear the arrival of British soldiers: 'When you see them, make war against them. . . . Be brave that you may not be enslaved, and that your country may not become the possession of strangers.'[36]

Tāreha was another who had said that Christianity was for slaves and Europeans, not for a free and noble people like Ngāpuhi.[37] The idea that Christianity was more attractive to captives than rangatira was also implied by William Williams's remark that Te Ripi Paratene, baptised in 1831, was 'the first person of high rank who had ventured to stand forth on the side of Christianity'.[38] But even if those of chiefly rank were slower to accept Christian teachings, they certainly felt the impact. In 1837, over twenty years after establishing the New Zealand mission, Samuel Marsden wrote to the Secretary of the CMS in London concerning a visit he had made to New Zealand that year. In it, he mentioned that he had been given a written appeal by a chief who had succeeded Hongi, the mission's earlier patron. It was a response to the introduction of Christianity and the confusion that had resulted as to correct ways of behaving in the new environment. In order to comply with Christian requirements, the letter writer asked that Māori be given new laws for six enumerated circumstances before concluding with:

> Another thing, which we are afraid of, and which also degrades us, is this — slaves exalting themselves above their masters. Will you give us a law in this also?[39]

So this chief did not expect any change in the social order as a consequence of new religious ideas.

Whether their conversions took place early or late in the process of evangelisation, many rangatira were eventually, albeit gradually, converted. Their captives may not have been freed as a consequence but they were now even more likely to be exposed to Christian ideas. Richard Davis recounted the story of Tupapa, a Taranaki rangatira who, having been captured by a Waikato tribe, was being taken north with his family to be exchanged for muskets with the Hokianga leader Moetara. However, as fate would have it, they passed through the territory of Te Ripi Paratene, the early rangatira convert, where they were recognised by other captives taken there previously. Those folk talked Tupapa and his family into hiding themselves in the woods until after the Waikato people had left the area. They took that advice, coming out of the forest when the coast was clear, and put themselves under the protection of Te Ripi's people where they, too, came under the influence of the mission.[40] Given the circumstances, they are likely to have been willing students of the new faith.

The assessment of when individuals had been truly converted may have altered from around 1830 when the CMS missions were under threat of closure for their apparent ineffectiveness in achieving converts.

Prospects for the missions' survival would have been improved if a more generous view of the candidate's conversion served to lift their annual baptism statistics. It is, of course, impossible to measure the extent or depth of faith of historical converts. But as real 'conversion' (whatever that may mean) is necessarily gradual, so too was the process of changing attitudes through Christian teachings.[41] In 1823, before any Māori had been baptised, John Hobbs and his brethren spoke to a man about to cook a slave he had killed because of his age and infirmity. The offender asked 'if the Atua-nui [great or almighty God] were angry with him' to which they replied that he was. Hobbs was uncertain how effective their words would be but felt that they were making inroads. 'We think they understand some of the instructions given', he wrote, adding, more curiously, 'and what we can say we endeavour to say as if we believed it ourselves'.[42] Perhaps Hobbs was not entirely confident about the extent of God's anger towards Māori?

Some sixteen years later, however, Richard Davis confirmed that leaders of great mana were open to new ideas presented to them — even by far more lowly personages. He reported that some slaves from his home at Waimate had returned from a visit to Tāreha, who was very ill. Although Davis did not say that these men were converts, it was implied by the fact that they had been sent to implore the elderly rangatira to turn to Christ before his demise. Having arrived at this place, they were reluctant to approach the sick chief without his direct invitation. As Davis put it: 'the place being sacred all around him'. However, they sought and received permission to approach and found a willing listener in the elderly man who asked that they spend the night with him so he could learn more about Christ and the possibility of saving his soul.[43] That was the same Tāreha who had previously said Christianity was for slaves and Europeans; not for a free and noble people like Ngāpuhi.

The times were a-changing, but although captives were being released somewhat contemporaneously with increased numbers of baptisms, the two were not necessarily interdependent. Acceptance of Christian tenets or British moral codes may have allowed chiefs to relieve themselves of some of the obligations of 'slave owning' while gaining other benefits simultaneously. Freeing their captives may have put them in the missionaries' good books but would also have impressed the relatives of those liberated with their merciful magnanimity and deterred them from seeking utu.⁴⁴ Those taken during the wars of the 1820s and 1830s had been absent for less than a generation so their 'ahi kaa', or home land rights, had not been extinguished, and they generally seem to have been able to reintegrate with their original kin groups.

Missionaries as peacemakers

The release of captives was one trend that missionaries encouraged and sometimes facilitated, but their intervention proved useful in peacemaking as well. An 1828 invitation to Henry Williams to mediate in a dispute between the Hokianga and Bay of Islands tribes may have been the first time Māori asked a missionary to help bring about a peaceful resolution but many more would follow.⁴⁵ Although peace may have been desired, it needed to be obtained without loss of mana, so declaring peace through missionary agency could be an effective face-saving/mana-preserving approach. Something of that sort may have influenced the Northland rangatira Moka when one of his wives ran off with another man. Thoroughly fed up, he told the missionaries that he would commit murder if they did not restrain him. Moka had been led to believe that she and her paramour had debunked to live in Te Morenga's settlement at Taiāmai — and Moka considered Te Morenga his enemy. Perhaps that was one reason for his asking missionary Richard Davis to accompany him on his journey. Moka told Davis that he had repudiated the woman so they were effectively divorced. He added that she had 'not been as a wife to me for some time', which is an interesting remark for the implication that he could not force his attentions on her. Nevertheless, while he was not willing to lose her as a slave, Davis understood him to agree that if the man she had gone with were to return with her and become his slave, too, they could live together as man and wife.

Despite Moka's alleged fears, Te Morenga received the two men warmly when they reached Taiāmai. However, his people assured the visitors that the runaway couple was not with them but most likely 'in the woods'. Should they see the woman, they would be sure to return her to him, they promised. Moka told the Taiāmai people that had he come alone and found his errant wife, he would have killed her, but the missionary had come with him to soothe his 'angry heart'.[46] So while this incident is an example of successful missionary intervention in a potentially lethal situation, it was nonetheless engineered by Moka. It occurred in 1833 when northern Māori were, perhaps, tiring of war and beginning to release their captives. Yet, while it took place in that context, it is also an example of how missionaries were used in potentially fraught situations. Moka clearly wanted to preserve his mana but without further hostilities. Taking the missionary with him secured both aims.

William Yate, who had left New Zealand for Britain in 1834, told the 1836 House of Commons Select Committee on Aborigines that his brethren could not attack slavery as a general principle until there was 'a more thorough recognition of Christianity'. For him, outlawing slavery could only be taught in terms of it being a Christian duty, so it would be essential for Māori to grasp the benefits of his religion before they could perceive that duty and release their slaves.[47] Evangelical faith in the power of Christianity to change and transform cultures would have lain behind that view.[48] Consequently, Yate's understanding could explain missionary claims that the widespread release of slaves from the 1830s was due to Christian teachings when twenty-first-century hindsight suggests other possibilities. He had identified this decade as the one when Christian evangelisation began to bear real fruit and the numbers of converts increased noticeably.[49] So while his mind likely tied the two events together, to the exclusion of other factors, the reality may not have been so simple.

Slaves who did not want to go free

Faith in the power of their teachings and an expectation of gratitude for their intervention were such that missionaries tended to take for granted that conversion would logically follow the release of captives – even if the situation had to be carefully managed. But some captives chose not to leave their captors. As we know, it was not uncommon for captives to marry into their conquerors' tribe. Others had different reasons for opting to stay where they were. Bishop George Augustus Selwyn discovered that in 1848 when, during a visitation tour through his diocese, he called at a small village called Onetea in Croisilles Harbour in the Marlborough Sounds. He was accompanied by Henry Mauhara, a Māori friend and Christian teacher who hoped to free his mother from slavery. Having come ashore, Mauhara sat down to await his mother's approach. Their meeting was an emotional one, as the Bishop recalled:

> No words were spoken, but tears such as no civilized man can shed rolled down the cheeks of both. They had not met for many years; and now the son was returning with stores of tempting presents earned in my employment, to redeem her from slavery.

Once the tangi (lamentation) was over, Selwyn began a speech, in which he described Mauhara's faithful services and explained that he hoped to return his kindness by arranging his mother's release. Her 'master', who had been baptised a Christian, was offered 'the choice proposed by St. Paul to Philemon, of giving them up freely in a spirit of Christian love, or of receiving payment as the price of [her] redemption'. Despite his Christianity, the old chief was not disposed to give the woman up, but his response was such that Selwyn felt it 'strongly illustrated the mild character of slavery in New Zealand'. He was an old man, he said, and because he could no longer work for himself, he needed her help. Besides, he added, it would not be long before he was in his grave so the Bishop's request would soon come to pass. The old woman responded in much the same vein, describing the domestic work she did for him and explaining that if she were no longer there for him, the old man would have no one to fetch him water, light his fire, or boil his pot. She concluded by saying that 'she loved her master' and, consequently, was not prepared to 'go out free'.[50] The old man at Onetea may have been a kindly master but that did not necessarily mean that he accepted the whole Christian 'package' offered by the missionaries. The absorption of Christian tenets was an ongoing process and converts were inclined to cherry-pick the rules they chose to live by.

The demands of conversion

Twenty years earlier, when the Māori world was in the early stages of transition, Christian teachings had been causing much confusion. In February 1828, for example, when it was discovered that the recent robbery of men associated with the Paihia mission had been committed by slaves from Haumi and Taiāmai, two men from the mission, Te Kaue and Pūmuka, set out to apprehend them. They managed to catch one, a slave of Te Kaue, and recover some of the stolen goods. The other, one of Tohitapu's slaves, had escaped into the forest. Everyone from the mission was annoyed with them so the missionaries gathered the Māori inhabitants together and explained the British system of trial by jury. Having done so, they asked them to consider the matter and decide on an appropriate punishment for the thief who had been caught. The majority felt that he should be shot but, thinking that rather over the top, their teachers persuaded them to give him a flogging instead. A 'thieves' cat' was duly prepared and the members of the 'jury' gave him one lash each.[51] But some changes were not so easily made.

For Māori to take on Christian beliefs and mores led to much soul-searching, by both missionaries and their converts. That was especially so when converts endeavoured to comply with the Christian ban on polygamy. A chief at Māwe in Northland had asked Davis to redeem one of his wives, who was a slave, 'because he heard it was not right to have two wives, and therefore wished to put her away'. Apparently happy to oblige, the missionary noted that she was now free to marry again. Te Ripi Paratene had 'put away' two of his wives, but the requirement was creating practical difficulties for Māori communities. 'Slave' wives were more likely to lose the coin toss in such instances as the summary dismissal of a rangatira wife would cause such offence as to be unthinkable. Clearly troubled by these difficulties, the CMS missionaries wrote to the London committee about the issue and prayed that God would direct their 'steps aright'.[52] But it was a requirement that also chipped away at chiefly mana. Although a practising Christian when he died, the leading Taupō chief Iwikau refused to put away his 'excess' wives in order to be baptised. Hospitality was highly valued and an important responsibility for one of great mana. An inability to produce and maintain a substantial food supply with which to feed visitors would damage his status to a point he could not accept: 'You have taken away all my slaves', he said, 'if I send away my wives I shall have no one to plant food for my visitor. Now I am a slave.'[53]

That was something that Jacky Marmon, an Australian-born sailor who became one of the first to live in New Zealand as a 'Pākehā-Māori',[54] well understood:

> A chief, by uniting himself to a goodly number of wives, if they were of rank, by this means greatly extended his hospitality, for each lady dwelt on her own land, which was cultivated by her slaves, and thus she was able to receive her husband and his friends with fitting honour when they came to see her, and to entertain them as became her station.

Marmon quoted a proverb: 'A man with many wives never wanted food, but with only one can never receive his friends according to their rank', to explain why he set out to secure a goodly number for himself. He boasted that his mana as a 'tohunga' became so great that 'little wooing was required' on his part.[55]

Equally damaging to chiefly status was the condition sometimes insisted on in order to be baptised: the release of their captives. As constitutional lawyer Jock Brookfield noted, once lost or diminished as the new legal order superseded customary systems, rangatiratanga could not be restored.[56] The point is an important one but it must also be remembered that the resultant loss of chiefly authority was not only immediate over released captives but more long term over their tribal group. A lack of compliant workers eroded their mana by reducing their labour force, productivity, and ability to offer hospitality to guests.

Christianity's war on mana and tapu

Providing lavish hospitality was an important means of asserting and building mana, but missionaries worked hard to bring an end to the customary practice of treating other tribal groups to hākari, or feasting, which they considered unnecessarily extravagant. Māori did not always accept such attacks on important and well-established traditions lying down, however, even when they had reached proportions well beyond those of pre-European contact times.[57] So it was in 1835, when the Anglicans attempted to put an end to such events by tying flags to the poles of the tiered platforms of a hākari stage at the Hokianga. Notices attached to the flags advising that the current feast was to be the last were not at all well received. During the great hubbub that followed, one rangatira responded by attempting to place his tapu over a pile of kūmara. Richard Davis considered it 'Satan's last effort' because, at that moment, Nene leapt to his feet, calling on his people to divide the food immediately — in other words, before the tapu could be applied. General anger seems to have followed in the wake of the missionaries' departure, leaving the two parties, hosts and visitors, to sort things out between themselves. Both sides blamed Christian spoilsports for ruining the occasion.[58]

Material matters aside (and Pākehā tended to see hākari as material rather than spiritual events), Protestant missionaries in particular felt it necessary to wipe out 'heathen' spiritual beliefs in order to impose Christian ones. Consequently, those who elected to become Christian were required to disavow tapu — a process that might involve more than verbal professions of faith. Converts were frequently subjected to what might be analogous to baptisms of fire — such as being asked to undergo the torment of washing their hair in cooking vessels. The head being the most tapu part of the body, such an act would be so fearful an ordeal that many rangatira refused to accept it. But not all. Some were so committed to the new faith they were prepared to put their lives on the line. The Waikato rangatira 'William Tawaiti', or Wiremu Naylor, determinedly made his conversion finite by cutting his hair and throwing it into a fire that was cooking food for his slaves. Another, who became a Wesleyan catechist, is believed to have been the one who derived a process for baptism that involved washing the head in a cooking pot while the convert confessed their sins. The term adopted for this practice was 'kokiro', meaning to release from tapu.[59] The great Ngāpuhi rangatira Mohi Tāwhai is said to have done much the same: washing his head in a pot that his slave had cooked food in and eaten from. If he was still alive when the sun set, that would be the appointed sign telling him that the Christian god was the true god and he would be a disciple. Tāwhai told John White that he 'perspired with deadly fear' as he underwent the ordeal.[60] Fear was a regular accompaniment to missionary teachings. Hobbs told the man about to eat the elderly slave he had killed, 'that both he and the body about to be consumed would rise again from the dust, to stand before the judgment seat of Christ'.[61] Becoming Christian was not for the squeamish or insecure.

The Catholics, who arrived in New Zealand in 1838, took a somewhat different approach. Rather than denying the power of tapu or of the Māori gods, they identified them with Satan and sought to replace them with their church's more powerful sanctions. Father Baty used prayer and the sign of the cross to efface the power of tapu. Others used their voices, getting into a 'holy rage' to denounce the evil one in a manner they thought simulated the way in which Māori called upon their gods.[62]

The concept of tapu was being assailed from many quarters and in many ways. That did not mean that it ceased to exist, but apart from new applications in the Christian sense of holy or sacred, the tapu of individuals suffered from a lack of acknowledgement. As Hirini Moko Mead explained: 'The idea of tapu works best when this personal attribute is recognised, known and accepted by the community at large.'[63] And therein lies the rub. Thanks to missionary teachings and the attitudes of secular authorities who privileged individual rights, the power of tapu was being eroded by a lack of recognition. And that lack of recognition was being fostered by the spread of Christian ideas, with or without the efforts of European missionaries.

Whatever the approach and whoever the messenger, the old spiritual bonds came to be broken, not only by outsiders but also by those Māori who accepted and spread new beliefs and values. In some cases, overturning chiefly authority may have been deliberate, but in others, the effect was inadvertent. Either way, the impact on social cohesion was real and already irreversible, but the British legal systems that followed, and which stressed the rights of the individual over the collective, would embed those impacts still further.

When Te Ngahue was baptised in the presence of Governor Grey on 29 December 1849, G. S. Cooper wrote that: 'It was a truly imposing and touching sight, to see the old savage — one of the Maori chiefs of the old school, who had often led his tribes to deeds of blood and savage warfare, and had feasted, time after time upon the flesh of his enemies — now meekly offering himself as a candidate for admission into the Church of Christ.'[64] Grey sent the original drawing on which a subsequent painting was based (see fig. 66) to the CMS who published it. As Leonard Bell noted: 'It advertised missionary and governmental success among Māori.'[65]

CHAPTER NINE

'Offensive to the English in the next degree to man eating'?

BACK IN BRITAIN, AS WE KNOW, AN AWAKENING TO THE INJUSTICE of chattel slavery had roused a heightened humanitarian consciousness which was particularly strong in the Colonial Office when the annexation of New Zealand was being considered. One early response to Māori concerns about the lawlessness and disorder resulting from the increased interaction between themselves and unruly Westerners such as whalers was to appoint an official British Resident. Having already spent time in Australia and reported to the Office on matters relating to New Zealand, James Busby got the job and arrived at Waitangi in the Bay of Islands in May 1833.

However, government policy and practice from the beginning of that official British presence did not necessarily respond to the attitudes and concerns of the lobbyists, which were coloured by perceptions of the trans-Atlantic slave trade. And when they did, it was not always to the advantage of Māori.

The Busby era

Joel Polack claimed that slaves — that is, war captives — were treated more kindly from the 1830s due to their greater economic value as well as being 'under the Protection of the Europeans'.¹ But, as mentioned in Chapter 3, Dumont d'Urville had found them to be 'treated fairly kindly' in 1824 when the scramble for more captives and muskets was in full swing and they were more valuable. So the fact that prisoners were being allowed to return home from the 1830s, having largely served their captors' economic needs, may not mean that attitudes had undergone significant fundamental change so much as the circumstances. The 1820s may have been the more abnormal period, the 1830s one of a return to more customary practice. Rewa's comments to Marsden that little boys taken captive were expected to grow up without enmity towards their captors suggest that long-term relationships were fostered, even if, as outsiders, they stayed at the bottom of the pecking order and closer to the front of the line when human sacrifice was required.

Children would have had fewer options, but missionaries and others mentioned adult slaves attempting to run away from the 1820s if not earlier.² Most were sympathetic towards those who took a chance — but not everyone was. Captain Sadler, of HMS *Buffalo*, which was in New Zealand waters in 1834 in search of spars for the British Navy, was incensed when a female slave had the temerity to try to escape by stowing away in his ship's hold at Whangaroa. When she was discovered the next morning, he sent her ashore and asked Busby how his office 'had better dispose of her' because 'New Zealanders are a great annoyance. I wish I was clear of them all', he said, underlining the phrase that emphasised his aggravation. However, a tinge of compassion was slipped into a postscript to his letter to Busby:

> This unhappy slave girl gives me much pain as I learn from a brother of her owner who I am giving a passage to the Thames — that (Effeue? her owner) [sic] will certainly kill her the moment she returns.³

What is unclear from Sadler's letter is whether running away was her only transgression or whether she was trying to escape capital punishment for other wrongdoing. As we know, a crime in Māori society was not necessarily one in English law and vice versa. But disputes between individuals and groups are a universal fact of life even if the triggers are not. In this case, however, the journal of Thomas Laslett, a timber surveyor aboard the *Buffalo*, probably refers to this same unfortunate young woman and suggests that her escape was depriving her master of her earnings. Laslett recorded that a young slave girl had been concealed aboard the ship when it left Whangaroa, probably by one of the sailors, because she had not been detected when the usual search for strangers was made before sailing. His account agrees with Sadler's that the captain had put her ashore at Kororāreka with the expectation that she could get back to Whangaroa from there: 'The journey was long, but it was thought a native woman would get over it without difficulty, and the chance whether prudent or not was given her to do so.' When the *Buffalo* returned to Whangaroa a few months later, however:

> The girl was seen by some of our people safe among her tribe, and it was thought she was all right, but young Shoungie her master having failed to find the man who employed the girl on board, and consequently to obtain the Hutu [utu] or payment which he considered due to him, killed her.[4]

Presumably, Busby had suggested or agreed to the idea of letting her find her own way 'home'.

Anglican and Wesleyan missionaries had been promoting British methods of justice well before Busby arrived on the scene, so many of those systems, including the concept of juries, were not new to Māori. What was new from 1833 was an official British presence. Busby's handling of a murder that took place five years later, in which a 'slave' was one of the accused, was, therefore, a demonstration of British forms of justice played out in what was then still a non-British location. Precisely what happened between the victim and the accused in this instance has never been clearly determined, but based on a combination of various available sources, some basic facts are evident. Henry Biddle, a Pākehā sawyer who had been living at Whirinaki in the Hokianga Harbour, had been shopping in the small township of Rāwene (then known as Herd's Point) and needed a lift home. However, after hitching a canoe ride with two Māori men, he turned up dead on a river bank. A quarrel had erupted along the way when one of the men, a middle-aged slave named Kite, demanded that Biddle hand over some of his property as payment. Kite and his master, a young rangatira about twelve years old, who was also in the canoe, admitted that Kite had held Biddle's head under water, but claimed that he had walked away from the confrontation and died later as he tried to cross the creek where his body was found.

Busby's appointment was intended to offer protection to British traders and settlers and to Māori from crimes committed by Britons as well as to apprehend any convicts who turned up from Australia. But he had no jurisdiction in a Māori country. Although he had previously mediated in other disputes that pitted Māori against European, the office of official British Resident came with only limited powers and no means of enforcing his authority. Consequently, he had little choice but to work with Māori rangatira and apply what Sir George Gipps, then Governor of New South Wales, suggested was justice independent of law. To deal with Biddle's death, he set up a court in the Wesleyan chapel at nearby Mangungu. Presiding effectively as a judge, Busby employed the 60 or so Europeans who came along to witness proceedings as a jury. Having heard the evidence, the vast majority decided that Kite was guilty of murder and the senior rangatira in the area agreed that he should be executed. Eric Ramsden called it 'the first legal execution in New Zealand's history'.[5] It was certainly not the first under Māori law but was it legal under British? Gipps, Busby's boss, was not sure.

In retrospect, and in terms of English law, the sentence would seem to have been unjust on several counts. Nathaniel Turner thought it was manslaughter at worst, a view that may have been shared by the one or two other 'jurors' who did not agree with the guilty verdict.[6] But, significantly, no responsibility was laid at the feet of Kite's master who, despite his age, should, perhaps, have had some responsibility for his actions, especially since he was present while whatever happened took place. Called as a witness during the trial, the young rangatira was not treated as a suspect in the way that Kite was. Moreover, since Biddle was living at Whirinaki, he might have expected the protection of his patrons, the young man's wider kin group. As we know, Tohitapu had been distraught three years earlier when one of his slaves was identified as a thief, refusing to eat and insisting that he be tied up as the thief had been. In both examples, though, appearances may not have reflected long-standing custom law. Māori did not wish to drive away the economic advantages brought to their areas by a Pākehā presence and Busby would have sought to protect British interests by placating both sides of the cultural divide. Consequently, the proceedings comprised a patchwork of British and Māori law. The former was drawn on for the concept of a court with judge and jury while the latter lay behind the decision of the local rangatira to hand over the older man and carry out his execution. Busby was well aware that the co-operation of the leading rangatira was essential to satisfying all the parties.

Once the matter had been dealt with, news of what had taken place reached the Colonial Secretary in a despatch from Busby explaining that the 'satisfactory' outcome could be attributed entirely to the fact that the guilty man was a slave.[7] Turner and others recorded that Kite died a Christian, and John White, who had lived in the Hokianga with his Wesleyan family from boyhood and wrote an account of these events some 33 years later, noted rather poignantly that when Kite's body was taken away, part of the New Testament was found in his armpit.[8] So neither his Christian faith nor the intervention of English law could save him from what appears to have been a fate heavily influenced by his social status — or lack of it.

Busby's unsympathetic attitude to 'slaves' had been evident earlier when he sought the execution of a man called Reti and his two slaves for an attack on his home in 1834. Windows were broken, shots fired (one of which had caused Busby to be injured by splinters of wood from a doorframe), and goods may have been stolen. But, as Henry Williams suggested, the offence was hardly 'worthy of death', and since the slaves were likely acting under Reti's authority, to demand that they also be killed was an especially callous response.[9] However, the office of British Resident became redundant following the signing of the Treaty of Waitangi so Busby's views would subsequently count for little.

Following the Treaty

For one writer, the signing of the Treaty marked a major turning point. His description of it as 'a great event for many Māori, none more so than the slaves who became free men and women' conjures up images of suddenly freed people singing and dancing into the night.[10] But we know that while many captives had already been released through the 1830s, others were not freed for another twenty years or more. February 1840 was not significant for Māori war captives. John Hobbs tried in vain the following year 'to tell a chief that slaves are all liberated now'.[11] Nor could they be, given that the wording of the treaty signed by the vast majority of Māori signatories guaranteed to uphold 'the unqualified exercise of their chieftainship' over their lands, villages, and all dimensions of their tribal group's estate.[12] As mentioned in Chapter 3, some rights appear to have been granted to 'slaves' after this time but they were limited.

In June 1842, very soon after his arrival in New Zealand, Bishop Selwyn, together with his chaplain William Cotton and George Clarke, was sent to investigate the looming renewal of hostilities between Ngāti Tamaterā leader Tāraia Ngākuti Te Tumuhuia in the Thames Coromandel area and Ngāi Te Rangi from the Bay of Plenty. Clarke initially recommended that Tāraia be forcibly arrested but prudently changed his mind. It was another deputation, sent the following month, which managed to arrange a settlement between the parties.[13] But Selwyn told his mother that his group had succeeded in convincing that rangatira to release his slaves during their meeting with him (fig. 67).[14] That promise clearly did not hold, however, because Tāraia, who neither signed the Treaty, nor accepted Christianity, was seen to punish a slave for infringing his personal tapu as late as 1866.[15]

With the formal establishment of British government in 1840, Māori chiefs clearly expected it to uphold their rangatiratanga and protect their interests as the Treaty promised. So, in January 1842, Wharepapa of Te Ihutai in the Hokianga wrote to the government seeking action over the desertion of one of his slaves. Because the correspondence is no longer extant, the response he received remains unknown, but registers at Archives New Zealand record that he wrote again about the matter four months later. Perhaps he was not satisfied by the reply he received because, shortly after Hone Heke had arranged for the flagstaff to be cut down for the fourth and last time — in April 1845 — Wharepapa wrote again to the government complaining about the conduct of its ally Tāmati Wāka Nene who would fight against Heke.[16] For his part, Wharepapa not only joined Heke against the British but is also said to have superintended the building of the 'rebel' pā at Ōhaeawai.¹⁷ The design of that pā proved very successful in protecting its defenders from bombardment by British cannons. So Wharepapa's disillusionment with British government seems to have gone well beyond any disappointment with its response to his runaway slave.

According to reports in nineteenth-century newspapers, runaways who made it to Auckland could face either a gallant rescue or the complicity of the authorities in returning them to cruel owners who threatened to murder them. For example, in July 1880, the *New Zealand Herald* recounted the efforts of the late Captain McIntosh in rescuing a male slave he had previously employed as a chainman some 37 years earlier on various surveying expeditions. As he walked in town McIntosh found the man being held down by Pōmare. Having been unsuccessful in reclaiming his slave that day, Pōmare returned two or three weeks later with backup support only to come face to face with another hero, Colonial Surgeon Dr Johnson, who gave him 30 minutes to reboard his vessel and leave town. After much kōrero, or discussion, the rangatira and his men apparently did so, 'quietly but sulkily'. Like Johnson, McIntosh was hailed as a hero: 'The Auckland citizens were loud in their praise of McIntosh's gallantry and humanity in saving one of an alien race from a frightful death at the risk of his own life.'¹⁸ Yet back in December 1844, the *Nelson Examiner*, in what was admittedly a highly opinionated piece, blasted the authorities for helping another rangatira to retrieve his runaway slave. In this case, the slave was a woman who had taken refuge with relatives in Auckland. The fact that those involved in returning her to her owner, Tāraia Ngākuti (who had promised to release all his slaves two years earlier), included the Police Magistrate and Protector of Aborigines Edward Shortland did not go down well with some. 'Weak concession after concession', screeched the *Examiner*.¹⁹

Neither of these stories made the papers at the time they are alleged to have occurred so their credibility must be suspect, especially as they were each reported to make a point: in the first, to praise the 'gallant deed' of a recently deceased 'old colonist', and, in the second, to criticise the 'imbecile' government's alleged pandering to the natives. The *Nelson Examiner*, mouthpiece of the New Zealand Company, objected to the idea of a Protector of Aborigines (an office inspired by the now fading humanitarian climate) and, indeed, any other obstacles to establishing their settlement unhindered. But the timing of their article is also telling. Having failed to obtain the vast areas of land needed to carry out its plans, the settlement had been struggling. The Company had expected to purchase 200,000 acres (over 800 sq. km) — an aspiration that proved to be sorely over-optimistic (and especially awkward when the first shipload of immigrants, who arrived in early 1842, were quickly followed by a rush of others). Within eighteen months there were over 3000 eager settlers in the area — most with little or no capital but anxious to fulfil their Wakefieldian dreams. The Company's plans had to be suspended in 1843, but the building tensions over access to land had had dramatic results in June of that year when Arthur Wakefield and Henry Thompson attempted to seize land from Māori owners who denied having sold it. Wakefield and 21 other settlers as well as four Māori lost their lives in what has become known as the Wairau affray. Although the newly arrived Governor Robert FitzRoy considered that the Māori defenders had been provoked by the Company's actions, many settlers blamed them and referred to the deaths of the Europeans as a 'massacre'. The *Nelson Examiner*'s sympathies shone through clearly in its editorial as did the view that rangatira had no rights over their 'slaves'.

Five years later and further north, Tāmati Ngāpora expressed his disquiet about the ways in which the new political environment had affected the rights of slave owners and the related impact on chiefly mana. He wrote to Governor Grey pointing out that his slaves were prisoners of war held as compensation for their own people who had fallen. Now, they refused to obey his orders and social disorder had resulted:

> The slaves of my village will not obey me; when I ask them to work, they will not regard me; the result of this conduct is theft and adultery. . . . I learn from Europeans that servants who rebel or disobey their master are taken before the magistrates and judged. . . . Is it right for a servant to be indolent, and disobey his master? . . . If our slaves had been recently taken captive, no law would be required; but they were taken captive a long time ago, long before you Europeans came hither. Our slaves were taken in battle; we kept them as a payment for our relatives who fell in battle. . .[20]

Like Te Whaiti in his evidence to the 1838 inquiry, Ngāpora equated Māori slaves with British domestic servants, but with the additional implication that their service was the recompense for sparing their lives and, perhaps, to replenish their own labour force after losses in battle.[21] His letter was forwarded to Earl Grey, Secretary of State for the Colonies, in London. George Grey's accompanying despatch supported the rangatira's concerns and pointed out 'the evils' resulting from the weakening of chiefly authority 'without any equivalent efficient power for the punishment of crime':

> The chiefs feel as I do, that the Maori laws, which compelled subordination, and restrained the violence of the evil-disposed multitude, are being rapidly swept away, whilst the local Government find it difficult, if not impossible, to spread their administration of the European law into the interior of the country so rapidly as the influence of Maori law disappears.[22]

Ngāpora's feelings of lost authority were evident again in the lead-up to the government's invasion of the Waikato in 1863 when he spoke to the Reverend Arthur Guyon Purchas, Vicar of Onehunga. Having assured Purchas that he would be sure to 'let the Europeans know before any acts of violence were committed', he admitted that he was less confident of his ability to influence his people:

> He said that formerly, regard to his safety would have ensured their giving notice of their intentions, but now he was no better than a *kuri* (dog), and it was quite possible that they might disregard him and leave him to his fate ...[23]

New legal systems were severely eroding the authority of hereditary leaders throughout the country.

Not that Māori leaders were necessarily aware of any new rules regarding prisoners of war. In January 1846, after the final battle in the Northern War, Sir Everard Home was obliged to write to Governor Grey from the British naval ship *North Star* explaining that he was carrying two wounded men. They were Wiremu Wāka Turau, who supported the British, and a 'Kawiti native' — in other words, a 'rebel'. Both had been wounded and Sir Everard sought advice as to what to do with them:

Kawiti's man believes . . . he is to be made a slave of and I believe Waka has an eye towards him for that purpose. I hope he will be taught that as he fights in support of our constitution here, that slavery forms no part of it and is offensive to the English in the next degree to man eating.

I hope when he is recovered he will be set free.[24]

It was somewhat ironic that Wiremu Wāka Turau, brother of Tāmati Wāka Nene, perhaps the only major military leader, Māori or Pākehā, to manage a real victory over Heke and Kawiti (at Te Ahuahu in June 1845), would be denied what he would have considered his rightful 'spoils of war'.[25]

Protecting New Zealand's aborigines

Following a recommendation in the report of the Select Committee of the House of Commons on Aborigines, the office of the Protector of Aborigines had been established very shortly after British annexation of New Zealand had been declared. George Clarke, the CMS missionary who would accompany Selwyn and Cotton on their visit to Tāraia in 1842, was appointed the first Protector. His mission was officially to protect Māori from injustice and cruelty, establish and maintain friendly relations with them, encourage the 'development of their capacities', preserve their health and general wellbeing, educate their youth, and teach them about Christianity (the last being a particularly appropriate role for Clarke).[26]

Neither Hobson's instructions to Clarke nor Lord Russell's subsequent instructions to Hobson mentioned slavery.[27] Hobson did, however, advise Clarke that the British government would hold Māori rights of property inviolate and that their 'native customs' would not be infringed, adding more ambiguously, 'except in cases that are opposed to the principles of humanity and morals'. It was, perhaps, the latter that led both Hobson and Russell to refer specifically to human sacrifice, cannibalism, and infanticide and the need to wean Māori away from those practices.[28] London was clearly looking for a gently-does-it approach to transforming Māori society into a more British model.

No record has been found of any Act or ordinance being passed outlawing the Māori practice of slavery.[29]

Just how deliberate the omissions were is hard to say. But more than eight years after the signing of the Treaty, Earl Grey wrote to George Grey expressing concern that changes brought about through 'the progress of civilization' and the introduction of English law would see rangatira 'speedily sink to the general level of their Countrymen', 'unless some special means [were] adopted to guard against it'. '[T]he consideration they enjoyed depended in no small degree upon the superiority in wealth . . . which was derived from their absolute command of the services of their slaves', he wrote. Earl Grey feared that simply removing the obligation of slaves towards their former masters would not be in the best interests of either and suggested that they be given the right to cultivate enough land for their own subsistence and give some modest payment or tithe in return.[30] George Grey chose to ignore Earl Grey's despatch entirely. Preferring not to reinforce chiefly authority, he neither minuted it nor replied to it.[31] So, there appears to have been a realistic recognition in London that abolishing 'slavery' would have a negative impact on the authority of rangatira and, consequently, on Māori society more generally. Although there were some in New Zealand who agreed with that prognosis, many did not.

One who did not was A. Hamilton Russell, Captain of the 58th Regiment and Superintendent of Military Roads, who submitted a report concerning progress in road making in the Wellington area where parties of Māori workers were employed. Having noted that they included 'minor chiefs, freemen and slaves', he added that:

> the influence of the former appears to have declined, — it was never exercised for good, but frequently to produce dissatisfaction, and cause a strike, in which they formerly succeded [sic], but latterly have always been unsuccessful. They are now treated in all respects like the other workmen, and are equally under control.[32]

As to those strikes, someone was still succeeding in that regard because, in April 1848, soon after Hamilton Russell's report was compiled, a dispute over how the men were to be paid brought work to a standstill in Auckland.[33] All but one of the overseers of the work parties had been deducting money from their wages to pay for flour and potatoes supplied for their meals. Not only had truck systems like this been made illegal by law, but government also considered that the prices charged were exorbitant. Still more unjustly, deductions had been made even when the workers' relatives had sent provisions from their home places. The workmen 'declared that they were not slaves; that they were the Queen's subjects equally with the white men, and that they would be treated and paid like white men'. Citing the Māori's 'well known improvidence', the *New Zealander* claimed that because they were surviving on nothing but flour and potatoes while doing heavy labour, the workers' refusal to buy meat meant that they were exhausted before they had completed their expected ten hours of daily work. While the newspaper did not explicitly say so, it is evident that the men, who had mostly, if not all, travelled to Auckland to undertake the work, hoped to receive as much cash in hand as possible to take home. It was an aim that was being thwarted. As one man said, 'if it takes five shillings a week to feed me, how am I to support the rest of my family on the remaining four'?[34] There seems little doubt that they were being cheated or paid insufficiently, even to support their own immediate families. Yet the rewards of their labour were almost certainly intended to benefit a much wider kin group. Engagement on public works was often undertaken in order to raise funds for communal projects such as flourmill construction, the purchase of sailing ships, or agricultural equipment. Much like the humanitarians of the previous decade, however, the *New Zealander*'s focus was not on protecting their right to manage their own affairs but on how the men themselves might be best managed for government purposes and settler convenience.

The communal nature of Māori society was an important feature government determined to alter, even if those concerned with achieving such a change disagreed as to how to go about it. For some, rangatira authority amounted to feudal authority, which was to be abhorred, whereas others argued in favour of introducing a European-style feudal system on the basis that, although 'slavery' was losing favour, its value to the Māori and, by extension, the New Zealand economy had value. But however Pākehā understood Māori systems, respect for them was rare. The necessity of change was a given, and particularly heavy emphasis was placed on individualising land ownership. Consequently, the rhetoric portrayed both communal work and communal land ownership as slavery. Not surprisingly then, the *Daily Southern Cross* agreed with the New Zealand Company's view that Māori were better off with a small area of land than with the whole of it as had been the case before Europeans arrived on their shores: 'As a possessor of land in common with other members of his tribe, the Maori is nobody — he is but the abject thrall of his chief.' Individual land ownership, on the other hand, would 'emancipate the Maori from his present degrading condition of unwilling vassalage'. Rescuing Māori from this 'vassalage' was a matter, the *Cross* argued, that the Aborigines' Protection Society 'would do well to consider'.[35]

Slaves or prisoners of war?

As communal land ownership might be called vassalage, Māori war captives were called slaves, implying that their treatment was not civilised. But Māori treatment of their prisoners of war was not very different from British treatment of theirs. During the Napoleonic Wars, which raged from 1793 to 1815, over 100,000 French prisoners were taken to Britain. As seems to have been the case with rangatira in Māori society, officers received much better treatment than enlisted soldiers and seamen, many of whom were confined in horrific conditions on moored hulks or derelict ships. The luckier ones were housed in a specially built prison on Dartmoor in the south of England, as were American prisoners from the war of 1812. They were employed reclaiming the desolate moorland for farming.[36] Over 1100 French nationals died at Dartmoor, as did 218 Americans.[37] Officers, however, (assumed to be gentlemen?) were offered the opportunity to give their parole, or word of honour, in writing, not to escape. Those who did so could live relatively normal lives in lodgings in certain, specified British towns.[38]

The period between the French Revolution and the Napoleonic Wars was a turning point in the history of prisoners of war, however. That was when the nationalisation of war led to the demise of long-established practices such as their release on parole, the exchange of prisoners for money, and impressment into the captor's armed forces. Those practices, remarkably similar to Māori ones, were no longer politically feasible in Europe. The breakdown of traditional rules and customs lay behind the creation of a legally codified prisoner regime that began in the nineteenth century and became generally accepted between European polities. But, as Sibylle Scheipers suggested, 'colonial warfare seems to stand out as the starkest illustration that European standards only applied in Europe . . . not in Europe's encounters with the "uncivilised" world'. Scheipers qualified that point by saying that the lines between the two settings 'become blurred' because exposure to warfare within Europe and the colonies led European armies to develop 'surprisingly persistent patterns of operational thinking and behaviour'.[39] In New Zealand, however, colonial government made the rules. Māori 'slaves' were, if not all, almost all war captives. Yet Māori captured by the British during the New Zealand Wars of the nineteenth century were treated in ways not entirely dissimilar to how they might have been treated by other tribal groups. They were typically removed from their home areas — even overseas — and expected to work for their keep.

In his journal entry for 17 December 1827, Richard Davis had referred to two Māori having been 'transported' to Australia for setting adrift a vessel belonging to a European (possibly Captain Duke), causing it to be driven on shore and lost. Davis did not know the names of these two men but he knew one to be the son of the Kororāreka rangatira Kira. No other record has been found concerning this apparent transportation or of any Māori being transported to Van Diemen's Land (Tasmania) before 1846.[40] However, it is possible that they were taken to New South Wales, as convict transports and trading vessels could acquire prisoners at their ports of call.[41]

Records are available, though, for five Māori political prisoners who arrived in Tasmania aboard the *Castor* in 1846. These five men had been captured as supporters of Te Rangihaeata, having been tracked down following an attack on a government redoubt on the Hutt Valley farm of a settler named Almon Boulcott. That attack, during which several British soldiers were killed, was one outcome of a long period of tension following the arrival of settlers into the Wellington area. Disputes over the New

Zealand Company's alleged land purchases created considerable friction between Māori and settlers. So much so, that an altercation between British troops and Ngāti Tama and Ngāti Rangatahi in the Hutt Valley two months earlier, in March 1846, had led Governor Grey to declare martial law in Wellington. However, as one newspaper correspondent pointed out, martial law was rarely reverted to except in extreme circumstances, such as when Elizabethan England was threatened by a Spanish invasion. That writer, who called himself 'An Englishman', wondered whether the step was warranted given the threat it posed to English liberties. The imposition of martial law effectively suspended the right to be tried before the civil courts. 'An Englishman' was also concerned that the prisoners were 'not notorious criminals' but 'taken in a foraging expedition' after the attack on the farm. 'To try them now by court martial, and then hang them, now that there is no necessity for such a proceeding, would be a gross act of wanton barbarity.' And what sort of message would it give to Māori, he wondered?

> It has been the object of Government for some time past to convince the natives that its proceedings are guided by fixed principles and fixed laws. They have been informed that criminals are tried according to regular forms, before an impartial jury, so that in order to exclude any enemy or supposed enemy, or prejudiced person from influencing the decisions of the jury they have the right of challenge. What, I ask, is the effect likely to be produced on the natives generally, if, on the first disturbance that has occurred in this district, they find that all these much-vaunted laws and privileges are suspended by a proclamation to suit the occasion?[42]

Although the letter writer used a pseudonym, it has been noted that the letter bears the hallmarks of Bishop Selwyn's work. Whether the writer was the Bishop remains uncertain, but as his biographer notes, Selwyn's 'advocacy of Maori rights brought bitter reproaches, including charges of disloyalty to the Crown'. That remark may explain why the letter also stresses his admiration for the Governor.[43]

Since martial law had been declared, those captured should have been treated as prisoners of war, but Grey ordered a court martial on the grounds that they had rebelled against the Queen's authority. They had no legal counsel and only an interpreter to plead their cause. None had sufficient English to conduct their own defence. Having pleaded guilty, they were convicted of rebellion, among other crimes, and sentenced to be 'transported as Felons for the Term of their Natural lives' (see figs 68 and 69). According to Grey, under Māori law, their 'several murders and many robberies' would have brought a death sentence, so transportation was a 'merciful alternative'. Others saw it very differently — especially in Tasmania. The Hobart newspaper, the *Courier,* reported their arrival in November 1846, noting that 'the Local Government has not been indifferent to the peculiar case' of this group and that bringing it to the notice of the 'Home Government' was being contemplated.[44] Fortunately for the prisoners, C. J. La Trobe, acting Lieutenant-Governor of Van Diemen's Land, elected to send them to the Darlington probation station on Maria Island off the coast as a more humane alternative to Norfolk Island, the more usual destination for convicts.[45] The *Courier* felt that 'their greatest offence seems to have been the defence of their country against what, with erring views, they conceived to be foreign aggression, or doubtful implication in a murder committed under the excitement of hostilities and in the reckless violence of warfare'. A more humanitarian attitude still prevailed in Tasmania — at least towards 'superior natives' like the Māori prisoners. Sadly, different attitudes applied to the local Aboriginal people who were dangerously close to extinction by that time as a result of their particularly brutal frontier experiences.[46]

Nevertheless, the wellbeing of the Māori exiles continued to be a matter of concern in Tasmania, and Grey was castigated by the Home Office in London on the basis that their court martial was probably illegal. Eventually, in February 1848, official notice was received that they had been pardoned and the four survivors could return to New Zealand. One of their number, Te Umuroa, had died of tuberculosis the previous year, when Governor William Denison, recognising the spiritual impact of their captivity, told London that the despondency felt by his compatriots would soon have seen them succumb, too.[47]

A month before the trial leading to their transportation, another of Te Rangihaeata's warriors, Matene Ruta (Martin Luther) Te Whareaitu, had been captured and court-martialled by officers of the various British regiments then serving in the Wellington area. One officer was appointed as an interpreter, but there, too, no legal counsel was provided. The sentence handed down, that Te Whareaitu was to be hanged, was also considered extreme — even by the local settlers — and it proved difficult to find a willing executioner. The time-honoured inducement of a generous financial reward eventually saw that one was found, but the deed may have hung heavily on the soldier who carried it out. When he drowned just over a year later in shallow water, friends blamed his premature death on his role as executioner. They said that his involvement 'in the killing . . . had clung to him like a curse'.[48]

Māori were often keen scholars of the Bible, and, given missionary teachings that connected Christianity closely with civilisation and civilisation with English law, some confusion between civil and canon law was probably inevitable. For example, in July 1860, some four months after the North Taranaki war had begun and two and a half weeks after he had guided British troops into position for their attack on Puketākauere pā, Īhāia Kirikūmara and his brother Tāmati Tiraurau sent a letter to the settlers at New Plymouth from Waitara. Tensions had been rising in Taranaki over the proposed sale of land at Waitara which Īhāia supported against the wishes of Wiremu Kīngi Te Rangitāke who vehemently opposed it. Their enmity went back many years and Īhāia's attitude was more likely about undermining Te Rangitāke than that of a disinterested party. Īhāia, who belonged to Te Āti Awa, is thought to have been baptised a Christian while living as a captive in Waikato following an 1833 assault on Pukerangiora pā, on the Waitara River.[49] That might explain why their letter began with a reference to Māori having done 'wrong' in the past, mentioning warfare, cannibalism, and slavery. It went on to give their history of the land in question, saying that, as a result of conquest in battle, the land had been vacated prior to the arrival of British settlers. Those living there at the time were merely 'a remnant, a handful returned from slavery', who were happy for the settlers to buy the land because they expected their enemies to return and evict them again anyway. As well as the references to the historical sins of the Māori, their letter employed biblical expressions, saying that those 'living in the house of bondage' and others who had fled, learned of the sale and returned. On that basis, they claimed that European purchases of the land had allowed them to resettle and live together with the settlers in harmony.[50] Īhāia and Tāmati appear to have played the slavery card in order to increase the level of sympathy for their cause — a cause that suited the settler government.

It was also in July 1860, following the outbreak of war in Taranaki and the alleged threat posed by the establishment of a Māori King, that then Governor Thomas Gore Browne convened a conference at Kohimarama, Auckland. Leaders of tribal groups considered loyal to the government were invited in hopes of shoring up support for British sovereignty and ratification of the Treaty of Waitangi. Many of those who attended were now Christian, and the mental connection between biblical and Westminster law was evident when Hōhepa Tāmaihengia of Ngāti Toa referred to a government blue book as 'that Bible'.[51]

Similar cross-fertilisation of Christian ideas and English law seems to have occurred in 1865 following the ritual execution of missionary Reverend Carl Sylvius Völkner, who had provided intelligence to the government and was considered by his executioners to be a spy.[52] Representatives of the people involved in his execution wrote to the government explaining that he had been crucified:

> according to the laws of the New Canaan [as they referred to their settlement in Ōpōtiki], in the same manner as it has been ordained by the Parliament of England, that the guilty man be crucified.

In reality, Völkner was hung from a tree, so the reference to crucifixion was a metaphor — perhaps their perception of a biblical form of capital punishment. Their letter also gave conditions for the release of another missionary, Thomas Grace. A Jewish man named Morris Levy, a local storekeeper who had captained the ship that had taken the two missionaries home to Ōpōtiki, was asked to act as a messenger and was not harmed.[53] Pātara, the leader of the warriors, but who had not been present at the execution, explained to Levy that he was very fond of Jews because they had once been 'a grand people, but were now reduced to a very small one through the persecutions they had gone through' — persecutions they felt to be much the same as those that Māori now suffered.[54]

Disputes over land raised tensions in southern Taranaki, too. Tītokowaru, a Ngā Ruahine leader, had engineered a number of acts of peaceful resistance against the colonial forces during the 1850s and

1860s.⁵⁵ But when George Grey proclaimed the whole of the South Taranaki coast to be confiscated in 1865, a series of bloody campaigns ensued between the local Ngāti Ruanui and Ngā Rauru tribes and colonial forces. Ngāwaka Taurua was one leader caught between his attempts to keep the peace, despite broken promises from government, and Tītokowaru's military campaigns.⁵⁶ Precisely what part Taurua played in the resistance is not clear, but ironically, given that chiefly authority was being denied in other respects, he was held responsible for his Pakakohe people who were alleged to have taken a prominent part in Tītokowaru's resistance. Ninety-six men were tried for treason, and 74, including Taurua, were initially sentenced to death, a sentence subsequently commuted to penal servitude. They were sent to Dunedin gaol for periods varying from three to seven years.⁵⁷ During his time in Dunedin, Taurua acted as overseer of road-building gangs around Otago Harbour. But captivity and exile had a profound impact on his spirit. He referred to their day of departure for Dunedin as 'the darkest day in his life'.⁵⁸

Te Āti Haunui-a-Pāpārangi leaders had interceded on Taurua's behalf after the trial, but Premier William Fox told them that his 'offence was great.... He had gone to the government at Wellington and swore to be faithful but then joined Titokowaru in his evil work.'⁵⁹ Keen to keep the land between Kai Iwi and Waingongoro 'clear of Natives', Fox informed Thomas McDonnell that: 'Our mutual friend Tauroa and his numerous family — at least the male part of it, are safely lodged in Dun Eden [sic] gaol.'⁶⁰ When Fox visited the gaol in April 1870, the pain of being held captive was very clear yet again. He had a long interview with Taurua who sang 'a mournful song' bewailing 'his expatriation from his native wilds'.⁶¹ Eventually sent back to Whanganui by Native Minister Donald McLean in 1872, Taurua was promised reserves at Ōtauto, Wai-o-Turi, and Matangirei, but unsatisfactory surveys meant that the struggle lingered on.⁶²

In our own time, the phrase 'sent to Siberia' has become a metaphor for isolation, demotion, disgrace, or loss of status. But its origins lie in the cold, harsh conditions and isolation of the geographic Siberia as a place of banishment and forced labour camps. Dunedin's climate may be mild compared to North Asia, but Māori political prisoners were nonetheless sent to distant places colder than their home areas. It is frequently asserted that the men sent to Dunedin were sometimes kept in cold, damp caves around Dunedin's causeway. Local folklore says that while trusted prisoners were returned to their cells at night, troublesome ones were locked in the caves overnight. Although official records do not mention that practice, they do confirm that eighteen of the prisoners died between November 1869 and February 1872. Thirteen of those are recorded as dying from forms of tuberculosis.[63] A generation later, when Hokianga Māori were protesting a tax on dog ownership, rumours were rife that they were to be sent to an 'icy country' where they would be 'frozen to death' as punishment for their resistance. It was a fear they had taken 'very much to heart'.[64]

Te Kooti Arikirangi Te Tūruki, another political prisoner and one who had fought with the government at Waerenga-a-hika near Gisborne in 1865, was arrested as a spy for the second time in 1866 and sent to Wharekauri, or Chatham Island — also a cooler place, far from his home. Educated by members of the Church Missionary Society and mentored as a businessman by Thomas Grace, he is remembered as a warrior and a prophetic leader who lives on today as founder of the Ringatū Church. Te Kooti always fought for his people's rights, but warned them of dangers to come through predictions and a large body of waiata, or songs, that he composed. Before the missionaries began reducing Māori to a written language, the culture was an oral one in which people expressed not only their history but also their emotions in oral form. Like Taurua's 'mournful song', Te Kooti's more than one hundred compositions were such expressions. Most were adaptations of older songs, altered to suit new circumstances. For example, his most famous song, 'Pinepine te kura' ('Little tiny treasure'), arose from his arrest and asked why the law was abused and why 'hatred' (te mau-a-hara) prevailed.[65] Spiritual pain inspired many a Māori composer.

But their pain also had more material manifestations. Grey's nominal confiscation of land north of the Waingongoro River in South Taranaki was one example, and one that would bring more trouble to that district. Seventy thousand acres of the confiscated land had been formally returned and no objections had been raised to the people's returning home. Nor had the Crown made any attempt to occupy the land or exercise any right of ownership. As the Waitangi Tribunal found:

After the war had ended, the Government had, to all intents and purposes, abandoned the confiscation in central Taranaki for the whole of the district that had Parihaka at its heart, from the Hangatahua River to the Waingongoro River. No European had settled one acre in that entire area.⁶⁶

Under those circumstances, a community had been established by Te Whiti-o-Rongomai and Tohu Kākahi, at a place called Repanga, which they renamed Parihaka to commemorate the warfare that had occurred there. Pari was Māori for a steep cliff from where people would haka, or perform a posture dance, in defiance of war parties intent on assaulting their pā. Although pacifist in their outlook, this community was determined in its resistance, with biblical imperatives underpinning their peaceful approach.

Feeling secure, they had been cultivating the land and re-establishing their community at Parihaka. However, in 1878, when the government sent surveyors to prepare it for Pākehā settlement, the people responded with peaceful obstruction. They systematically removed the survey pegs, erected fences across road lines, and ploughed settler farms. Ploughing the land was a way of disrupting the survey but also a biblical symbol of peace.⁶⁷ The resisters were arrested and held without trial. Then, in 1879, 170 of the prisoners, known as the 'Ploughmen of Taranaki', were transferred from New Plymouth Prison to the Mount Cook Prison in Wellington. Like Taurua, they were mournful and spoke of the effect on their spirit in a haka they composed while held there. The words of the haka, recorded by Rāniera Erihana, or Ellison, who supported the prisoners, express their feelings of oppression. They lament being tossed about by the waves of fortune and having to survive on insufficient food but urge each other to be united and stand firm. The haka also refers to the injuries they suffered: 'te kuru i ngā ture' — pummelling by laws manipulated to settler advantage. One line of the haka refers to the ploughmen as 'hipi hiroki', or lean sheep, the symbolism of which appears to go beyond the deficiency of their food supply to invoke the Bible. In Ezekiel 30:20, God says 'Nana, maku, maku tonu nei e whakarite te whakawa a te hipi momona raua ko te hipi hiroki', or 'Behold, I, even I, will judge between the fat cattle and between the lean cattle'.⁶⁸ The implication seems to be that it was the prisoners, the 'mauherehere' (literally: someone restrained or tied up), who were the righteous ones.[69]

As for comparisons between the treatment of Māori captives and that of British prisoners, early Western observers of Māori society often stressed the poor quality of food given to slaves and, as mentioned above, the *New Zealander* criticised Māori road workers for limiting their diet to flour and potatoes which it considered inadequate sustenance for men performing heavy labour. Yet the ploughmen's diet is said to have consisted of just water and potatoes while they undertook similar work. So poor were their rations that Erihana felt compelled to provide them with extra food from his own resources.[70]

The numbers of Parihaka men imprisoned continued to climb, but determined to end the obstruction of surveyors, government decided on more decisive action. So it was that, in November 1881, a combined force of over 1500 descended on Parihaka. In another symbolic expression of peace, women and children met the troops, offering them fresh loaves of bread, but failed to prevent the destruction of their homes and the eviction of some 1600 residents. Now homeless, they spread through other areas of Taranaki without shelter or livelihood while the soldiers looted and then destroyed most of their remaining buildings. Te Whiti-o-Rongomai and Tohu Kākahi were both arrested and spent six months awaiting trial before special legislation was passed allowing them to be held indefinitely. After sixteen months' imprisonment in the South Island, they returned home to reconstruct Parihaka as a model village with many modern facilities. Te Whiti was arrested again in 1886 when the ploughing campaign restarted, returned in 1887, but was declared bankrupt four years later. Despite this and many other trials, Parihaka maintained its non-violent resistance to settler laws until both prophets passed away in 1907.

British promises to take liberty to colonised nations made for good rhetoric, but Māori went further than Britain in their application of Christian principles and their application of pacifist approaches to political struggles.[71] What this suggests is that the horror invoked by the word 'slavery', when applied to Māori war captives, had more to do with British self-belief than true humanitarianism.

CHAPTER TEN

Enslaved by the British?

AS WE KNOW, MĀORI LEADERS WERE COMPLAINING TO MISSIONaries that slaves were 'exalting themselves above their masters' even before British annexation. Indeed, from the early 1820s, many went further, claiming that the British intended — or had already succeeded in — enslaving them. Some of these claims might be dismissed as merely rhetorical devices, but certainly not all. Filipinos, keen to gain independence from the United States in later times, would maintain that colonialism was a form of slavery, but the spiritual aspects of captivity were critical for Māori.[1] Bearing the associations of tapu and mana in mind, the sentiments expressed in New Zealand might make better sense. As British missionaries and government authorities increasingly denied the existence of either quality, they were effectively confirming the Māori's worst fears.

Fears of enslavement were already evident at Whangaroa in 1823 when John Hobbs recorded that he and his fellow Wesleyans had been troubled by 'the conduct of George' (Te Ara), the local rangatira who had threatened to shoot the Reverend Turner. Although Hobbs did not believe that the threat would be carried out, Te Ara was nonetheless 'in a dreadful rage'. He had no interest in hearing about Jesus Christ and was unhappy that the members of the mission had given them nothing of substance, saying that they had instead come 'to make slaves of them'. Hobbs attempted to defend himself by insisting that he worked 'every day as much as the Natives from morning till Night'. But the two men were clearly talking past each other because Māori leaders did work alongside their people. 'Slavery' had quite different meanings in this conversation. For the missionary it meant hard labour, for the rangatira it was a matter of status and recognition of his mana and tapu. Moreover, he would have felt that his patronage and protection warranted some quid pro quo beyond the religious teaching he had not sought.[2] At this stage in the Māori–missionary relationship, the latter were valued for providing access to material rather than spiritual blessings. That was made even clearer four years later when the Wesleyan mission at Kaeo on the Whangaroa Harbour was destroyed by the local Ngāti Uru people and Hobbs and his fellow missionary James Stack were forced to flee. Despite accumulating a good supply of trade goods, they had failed to let the locals purchase them. It was a lesson learned the hard way.

Missionary motives continued to arouse suspicion, however. In 1833, ten years after Te Ara's outburst and six from the sacking of the Kaeo mission, the Anglican Richard Davis was also upset by Māori accusations. They believed that he and his fellow missionaries had written to England saying that the reason they wanted them to accept the new religion was so they could sell them as slaves after having 'got them into our power'. Davis blamed other Europeans for giving them that idea and for telling them that the missionaries were only pārau — 'the most abject ... appellation that they can make use of'.[3] Pārau is one of many Māori words that have been translated into English as slave. Davis had been reporting similar mischief-making for at least six months by that time and it seems likely that when Māori asked visiting seamen whether the rumours were true, many were only too happy to irritate the moral guardians of their watering holes and fan the flames a little higher.

That was confirmed after a service at Kororāreka the following month, when one of the local rangatira asked Henry Williams to explain some very worrying information he had received from someone called 'Tami' (Tommy?) and Captain 'Boulger'. They had assured him that the missionaries were receiving a bounty for every 'tangata wakapono' or Christian believer they achieved. Williams lamented that:

> Satan, through the means of these, his agents, has been very industriously circulating the idea of our intention to seize the chiefs in a short time, and have them conveyed to England, and that for those who received our instruction, we are to receive dollars, according to the rank of the individual.[4]

William Bolger, master of the whaling ship *Governor Halket*, which visited the Bay of Islands between 25 March and 21 April 1833 as well as on a number of other occasions, was surely responsible for this fanciful example of anti-missionary muckraking.[5] Sailors looked to ports like Kororāreka for a bit of fun after months of sea and tended to see missionaries as the ultimate killjoys. Nevertheless, Māori questioning was further evidence that they feared their position was being compromised.

Pākehā as slaves of the Māori

Prior to 1840 and the arrival of British government, there were instances of Māori enslaving non-Māori. According to William Yate, one Māori community 'nearly five hundred miles from the Bay of Islands' was so keen for Christian instruction in 1834 that they planned to hold him against his will for just that purpose. He said that he heard some of them talking while he lay in his tent one night:

> "We must hold a Committee," they said, "about keeping him here. We must not let him go. He says he is going to England, and the ship is here to take him; but he shall not go. He shall be our slave: not our slave to fetch us wood or to draw water for us; no, but our Talking Slave. Yes, he shall be our slave to talk to us and to teach us."[6]

It would be interesting to know which Māori word Yate translated as slave. Perhaps it embodied the sense of a captive or hostage?

More often, the non-Māori taken and treated like captives or slaves were those whom Māori recognised as people of little status in the

Western world. From the 1820s, New Zealand port towns, especially the Bay of Islands, drew a few escaped convicts from Australia — people transported there after being convicted of crimes in England. Māori were aware of their status and seem to have been more inclined to turn them in (albeit often for a fee) than to give them refuge. If they did gain 'refuge' they would be treated much as ordinary Māori captives were. Clearly aware of the status of these people in terms of English law, they were known to refer to them as 'George's slaves', that is, slaves of King George IV. They were not 'free' men (or women, as was less often the case) but captives, and so, in Māori terms, they had little, if any, mana.

An example of those prevailing attitudes occurred in 1827 when a ship called the *Wellington* was assigned to carry 74 British convicts to Norfolk Island. Far outnumbering their guards, the prisoners managed to overpower them. Taking control of the vessel only a few days before they should have reached Norfolk Island, they changed course for New Zealand's Bay of Islands where several British whalers in the harbour were initially taken in by the new command. However, the true situation was eventually revealed and, together with local Māori, the British mariners soon recaptured the convicts. The prisoners asked to be landed at Kororāreka, which the Māori allowed, but, aware that they were 'slaves' of King George 'who had broken loose', they subsequently seized and bound all but six of them, stripping them of their clothes and escorting them aboard the whaling ships.[7]

Twenty years later, in February 1847, a Hokianga trader reported that the captain of a vessel called the *Janet* had accused a Māori slave and a Malay who had lived locally for a number of years of harbouring a group of runaway sailors. John Webster, the trader, abhorred the cruel barbarity meted out to the two men who were tied together by their hands and thrown overboard. The Malay barely survived while the Māori drowned. Webster remarked that 'there would have been a fine rumpus' if either of the men had been rangatira. But he also added that local Māori had refused to give up the runaways, intending to make slaves of them themselves. They presumably saw them as 'stray slaves', available for claiming as Māori ones might have been.[8] Later still, in 1865, after the American-born British army soldier Kimble Bent deserted, he fell into the hands of Tito Hanataua. Although protected by the Ngāti Ruanui leader, he was also obliged to fill the role of his servant.[9] Given the likely fate of a deserter, Hanataua's protection probably offered a reasonable alternative.

'Enslavement' through land loss

The old ordered ways of 'chief' and 'slave' within Māori society had been changing as disorderly elements were coming in from outside, and the two factors reinforced one another. Runaway convicts, sailors, and adventurers with little reverence for Māori law or Christian morality were creating havoc. It was those changes, as portrayed by the missions and merchants, each for their own reasons, which helped to draw the attention of the British Parliament to the situation.

Their lobbying, supported by the Aborigines' Protection Society, had nudged the Colonial Office to rather reluctantly consider the annexation of New Zealand. The 'humanitarian' climate in the Office at that time had been particularly conscious of the ill effects suffered by indigenous peoples previously subject to European colonisation and sought to protect Māori from those potentially harmful consequences. Colonisation by the commercially oriented New Zealand Association was an especially worrying prospect, although, somewhat ironically, the Association had proclaimed its intention to strengthen, rather than weaken, chiefly authority. Their literature implied that they proposed to transform the ownership of New Zealand land in much the same way as had occurred in the Scottish Highlands, where clan lands were converted into personal property. Māori rangatira were to become landed gentry.[10] That would have created a very different situation from the long-established system in New Zealand whereby rangatira had mana over the land but no 'ownership', and their status was very different from that of a landed gentry. The dramatic changes envisaged by Wakefield were outlined in his published plans for the colonisation of New Zealand. Using the metaphor of fully grown trees, he explained what he deemed the necessity of transplanting 'not people merely' but a whole society into the new colony.[11]

For Māori, disorder among the rowdy Europeans visiting their shores and the crimes they were committing were a big problem. Their irregular comings and goings hindered Māori ability to deal with their activities according to custom law. But fraudulent claims and serious misunderstandings relating to what Westerners considered their purchases of Māori lands aroused even greater anxiety. Having no concept of land ownership, Māori had no concept of its sale, and in most, if not all, cases, had understood the rights granted to foreigners to be merely those of usufruct, or rights of use, not permanent alienation.[12] The loss of their land and, therefore, of mana whenua, or control over their territories, was another pathway to slavery in the Māori worldview. Conquest in battle, when accompanied by the occupation of the land of the defeated, removed their mana whenua. A tribe without territory, without resources — for its own sustenance and for the provision of hospitality — was at best in a state of vassalage to its conquerors.

Missionaries were worried about this, too. Two years before the signing of the Treaty of Waitangi and fearful of the New Zealand Association's plans, Henry Williams warned the CMS in London that 'unless some protection [was] given by the British Government, the country [would] be bought up, and the people pass into a kind of slavery, or be utterly extirpated'.[13] So he, too, was linking land sales with the potential subjection of Māori. Land was what Europeans wanted more than anything, and fear for its loss a matter of increasing alarm. Nor were Māori unaware of the impact of colonisation in other parts of the world.

The speeches made by chiefs during the treaty negotiations focused strongly on their desire to protect their land from unscrupulous 'buyers'. Some idea of their concerns can be gleaned from the words of Te Kēmara — one of several who expressed fears that the Queen's consul William Hobson could offer him few benefits: 'I am not pleased towards thee', he said, before pointing out that English law could work against him:

> I will not consent to you remaining here in this country. If you stay as Governor, then, perhaps, Te Kemara will be judged and condemned. Yes, indeed, and more than that — even hung by the neck.[14]

The advantages of British justice were not as apparent to Māori as the Queen's representatives felt they should be. And, once again, the blame for their fears was placed firmly on the heads of less than pious foreign advisors. Henry Williams complained that Hobson had barely been in the country twelve hours before other Europeans had 'commenced using most infamous and exciting language to the natives — that the country was gone to the Queen, and that the Maori were *taurekareka* (slaves)'.[15]

How much influence such suggestions had on Māori attitudes is difficult to judge, but the loss of land up to that point and fears for further loss were a common refrain during those discussions — as was criticism of Williams, his fellow missionaries, and British Resident James Busby. To quote Te Kēmara again:

> "... my land is gone, gone, all gone. The inheritances of my ancestors, fathers, relatives, all gone, stolen, gone with the missionaries. Yes, they have it all, all, all. That man there, the Busby, and that man there, the Williams, they have my land. The land on which we are now standing this day is mine. This land, even this under my feet, return it to me.... Say to Williams, 'Return to Te Kemara his land.' You (pointing and running up to Henry Williams), you, you, you bald-headed man — you have got my lands. O Governor! I do not wish you to stay."[16]

Rewa, one of the first chiefs to speak, had also told Hobson to go home, complaining about land lost to the missionaries and insisting that Māori were in charge of their country. Māori had been travelling overseas for at least two decades by then and were familiar with the experience of indigenous Australians, as his words reveal:

> No, no, no; return. What! This land to become like Port Jackson [Sydney] and all other lands seen [or located] by the English.[17]

Other leaders expressed their concerns about the potential subordination of their status vis-à-vis the British in terms of slavery. Tāmati Wāka Nene from the Hokianga told Hobson: 'You must not allow us to become slaves! You must preserve our customs, and never permit our lands to be wrested from us!'[18] Rewa went further, warning others to:

> Send the man away; do not sign the paper; if you do, you will be reduced to the condition of slaves, and be obliged to break stones for the roads. Your land will be taken from you, and your dignity as chiefs will be destroyed.[19]

They were certainly very conscious of the implications of land loss for their chiefly mana.

But despite their doubts, the decision by Hone Heke to sign the Treaty turned the tide and encouraged others to do the same. Heke had a close relationship with the CMS missionaries and their influence may have enhanced his fear that if Māori did not align with Britain, France might present a worse alternative.[20]

Having gathered as many signatures as possible from various (but by no means all) parts of the country, Hobson proclaimed British sovereignty over New Zealand in May 1840. What Māori understood they had agreed to was an entirely different matter but, on the basis of Hobson's understanding, colonial government was established.[21]

During the preceding years, as the Colonial Office debated the ins and outs of colonising New Zealand, it had considered entering into an agreement with the New Zealand Association, the New Zealand Company, or its other incarnations. However, when the Company learned that the new Colonial Secretary Lord Normanby was not inclined to go ahead with that, its officers had taken matters into its own hands. As already mentioned, they had quickly despatched the *Tory* to head off the government and buy up whatever tracts of land they could before the Colonial Office could intervene. That affront was countered by Normanby's amendment to James Stephen's first draft of Hobson's instructions. The focus would now be on state-controlled colonisation, supported by the Crown's right of pre-emption (the exclusive right of purchase under which land could only be transferred to the government), which, Normanby believed, would strengthen the protective aspects of British colonisation and offer greater benefits to Māori. True to his task, Hobson had announced pre-emption by proclamation as soon as he arrived.

Yet, less than two years later, in December 1841, over a hundred European residents in Kororāreka petitioned Governor Hobson for the removal of that Crown right, arguing that Māori would attempt to regain their independence if this 'badge of slavery' were not removed from them.²² That emotive wording appears to have been a genuine reflection of Māori concerns pertaining to lost revenue but would also have helped the petitioners to gain sympathetic ears in London. Their objective was to reduce 'red tape', enabling them to buy land directly and more cheaply from the owners. However, that phrase, 'badge of slavery', may also have inspired Governor FitzRoy's comments just over two years later when he announced his unilateral decision to waive the Crown's right of pre-emption. His proclamation included the remark that Māori saw that provision as a 'mark of oppression — even of slavery', though he sought to justify the original proclamation by adding that it was 'in reality an effect of parental care'.²³ His despatch to Lord Stanley the Colonial Secretary in London a few months later accused settlers of alerting Māori to the provisions of the Treaty of Waitangi:

> The attention of the natives has also been repeatedly, I may say frequently and purposely, drawn to the last article of the treaty of Waitangi, by which Her Majesty "imparts to them all the rights and privileges of British subjects;" and they have been told that while unable to sell their own land, that article is not executed, and they are no better than slaves (taurekareka) taken in war, who have not the disposal of their own lands, while occupied by the conquerors.²⁴

So the settlers may have been stirring the pot to make it easier for them to buy land, and FitzRoy, having taken a very dangerous and controversial step without authority, would have chosen his words carefully to appease humanitarian sympathies in London. But they struck a very loud chord with Māori nonetheless.

'Humanitarian language' like that used by the Colonial Office and Aborigines' Protection Society during the 1830s had been employed across the political spectrum — by opponents and supporters of aboriginal rights — and was eventually applied to support policies that violated indigenous rights. The upshot was a shift away from Māori management of their own affairs and land rights to one of subjection under English law. In the process, their ability to enjoy and enforce their rights in land came to be discussed in terms of a paternalistic rhetoric of 'protecting' their beneficial interests. In other words, they were being treated as children under the law, incapable of rational action on their own account and in need of protection by benevolent guardians. But the protectors were hardly neutral.[25]

Perhaps not surprisingly, the first major challenge to the colonial government's authority had come when representatives of the New Zealand Company and Māori came to blows over the disputed land purchase in the Wairau Valley in 1843. But regardless of the *Nelson Examiner*'s view (cited in the previous chapter), one newspaper put the blame firmly on the settlers' shoulders. Having previously been 'accused of a suicidal advocacy of the rights of the natives', the *Daily Southern Cross* could now boast its foresight and suggested that had the Nelson settlers paid proper respect and attention to the rights of the Māori, the 'melancholy event' would not have occurred. 'Reason, justice, and good Government demand a different treatment on behalf of the New Zealanders', it said. 'Their own superior intelligence and sense of right will never allow of their tamely degenerating into slavery.'[26]

As we know, while these events and their aftermath were going on in the south, Hone Heke in the north had also become pretty disillusioned by the first years of British rule. He chose to demonstrate that disillusionment by having the British flagstaff chopped down because he saw it as a symbol of dispossession — an unauthorised claiming of sovereignty rather than the protection promised. It is highly probable that he would have seen it as equating with a very similar symbol of authority in Māori society. Pou rāhui, frequently painted red, the colour of tapu and mana, were posts used traditionally to indicate that a resource was under chiefly authority. Moreover, as Heke pointed out at the time, it was he who had supplied the pole to fly the 1834 flag of Māori sovereignty that had hung there previously and the British had never paid for it. In another act of defiance and as an assertion of Māori rangatiratanga, mana, and tapu, he hoisted a red shirt to replace the British flag.

After the fourth chopping down, the Bay of Islands port town of Kororāreka was sacked and most of the buildings (except for those belonging to the church) were burned. European residents were evacuated to Auckland and hostilities began in earnest. Heke had made his perception very clear during the ensuing Northern War when he asked Governor FitzRoy the whereabouts of Britain's goodwill and protection, adding: 'That flag of England which takes your country is the commencement.'[27] When the CMS missionary Richard Taylor heard about Heke's comments, he was unable to comprehend such a reaction to the 'protection' of the British flag and specifically blamed Americans and French priests for putting such ideas in his head.[28] But Heke was far from alone in his response to the experience of British protection.

The support Heke received during the Northern War attested to the strength of feeling in that part of the country. Northern Māori had been the primary promoters of the Treaty but suffered a dramatic economic downturn seven months after signing when the capital was moved from Kororāreka to Auckland. But feelings of betrayal, closely linked to the alienation of Māori land, were felt throughout the country. Numerous letters and reports of meetings with rangatira reveal that they understood the sale of their land to settlers would have the effect of enslaving them. It was often Westerners who sowed the seeds of that idea. In Māori custom law, land was held in common with the mana whenua, or authority over its use, residing with the rangatira. So it may have been their fear that Māori did not comprehend the idea of a permanent alienation that prompted those Westerners to try and get the message across in ways they might better grasp.

For a man named Poharama,[29] the realisation of the implications of land sale had been a gradual process. As he explained to Captain King, a magistrate investigating disputed land claims in the Whanganui area in 1844:

> The land from Ngamotu to Waiwakaiho (Witoki in the centre) belongs to me. I will not part with it. Some time ago I was foolish, and would have sold it; but now that I know the value of it, I will not. I don't want to part with my land, and to be made a slave of by the Europeans.[30]

In other words, he now recognised that by selling one's land, the mana over the land was forfeited; and that, to him, was akin to being enslaved.

From the settlers' point of view, people who gave such advice were traitors. Reporting on his visit to Mōkau in 1852, George Sisson Cooper, a government Native Land Purchase Officer, was very forthright in his condemnation of a locally based trader called Josiah Hopkins. Hopkins had told local Māori that they were wrong to sell their lands, 'using the usual argument that they would become slaves to the Europeans, &c'. When that did not put them off, 'he told them only to let the land go in small blocks, as they would thereby obtain a much larger payment for it'. Cooper was frustrated by the influence the trader had over the local people. He complained that the protection Hopkins enjoyed from their rangatira allowed him to be a nuisance to the resident missionary. Although he felt that 'the mischief he [was] doing [was] very great', Cooper could not see 'how at present any proceedings could be taken against this man'.[31] So, some settlers, embarrassed by the methods being used to divest Māori of their lands, were trying to warn them.

One Waikato leader, Niutone Te Pakaru, wrote to Governor Grey in 1852 to ask his advice concerning the potential for land sale to enslave his people. In a letter written on his behalf by his son, Te Pakaru explained that when he had visited the Governor's office in Auckland, a Pākehā had told him that: 'ka riro te whenua i ngā Pākehā, ka taurekareka tatou nga Māori' ('the Pākehā will take the land and make slaves of the Māori'). The consequence, it had been suggested to him, was that his people would have no land left to live on; the Pākehā would take it all. Te Pakaru remained uncertain but trusted Grey to make the decision for him.[32]

The denial of chiefly mana

From the mid-1850s, however, Māori leaders were once again talking of being 'enslaved' by what was now, following the Constitution Act of 1852, a settler government, no longer directed from London. By then, it was not only the loss of land that was undermining their mana but also denials that they had any mana to undermine. That denial of chiefly mana was a particular cause of resentment and one that already had a long history.

A failure to recognise or acknowledge differences in rank had begun as soon as Māori men began signing on as crew aboard whaling ships. Frenchman Dumont d'Urville blamed the sailors rather than the masters of visiting ships for not acknowledging differences in rank, and recommended that interaction between sailors and the local indigenous people be limited to the minimum possible.[33] But wherever the fault lay, war captives and others of low status serving on the same ships as rangatira all too often witnessed the tapu and mana of men of rank violated by their being subjected to physical punishment.[34] Perhaps the most famous, or infamous, example of that is believed to have triggered what has gone down in history as the '*Boyd* Massacre', 'the burning of the *Boyd*', or the '*Boyd* incident', an event that delayed the establishment of the first Christian mission and kept whalers and other shipping away from New Zealand for several years. The sailing ship *Boyd*, which was on its way to Whangaroa from Sydney in 1809 for a cargo of kauri spars, had 70 people on board including the then young chief from Whangaroa named Te Ara.[35] It is suspected that the captain, John Thompson, fresh from England, may not have met any Māori prior to this voyage and was not used to treating rangatira with the respect generally paid by others when they visited Sydney.[36] But for whatever reason, Thompson treated Te Ara like a common member of the crew and subjected him to a flogging from a cat-o'-nine-tails.[37] Moehanga, who had visited England earlier and later hoped to acquire a red jacket from India, told Peter Dillon that Te Ara had been framed by the ship's cook who had accidentally thrown some pewter spoons overboard with a bucket of water. The spoons had come from the captain's mess, so, fearing that he would be hanged from the yardarm, the cook told him that they had been stolen by Te Ara and his attendant.[38] Whether he was punished for his alleged thievery or because he was seriously ill and unable to work, as he told John Nicholas, we do know that he suffered the flogging and was denied food. Thompson is also said to have called him a cookie, or slave, despite the protestations of other Māori on board who assured him of Te Ara's high status. To make matters even worse, when the ship arrived at Whangaroa, his home port, he had been stripped of all the goods he had acquired during his travels, right down to the clothes he was wearing. Not only was his near-nakedness a great indignity, but so too was his inability to present any gifts to his people. When they learned how severely he had been mistreated, such humiliation to the entire tribal group was beyond any diplomatic turning of the cheek.[39] The dramatic response was unexpected by the crew but necessary in terms of utu, or restoring their lost mana.

Oblivious to the severity of the offence they had caused, the *Boyd*'s captain and several crew members, who went ashore in search of a cargo, were attacked, killed, and eaten. Then, as night fell, the ship was assaulted and most of those left on board were also killed. The following day, the ship was pillaged, gunpowder stored on board exploded, and the vessel burned to the waterline. However, a few of the ship's passengers and crew did survive. One was a fifteen-year-old apprentice named Thom Davis who was spared because he had looked after Te Ara when he was flogged.[40] Another survivor, the second mate, fared differently, however. Treated as a war captive, he was put to work making fish-hooks from hoop iron, items of Western technology that Māori were keen to acquire. But when his skills or his output disappointed, he succumbed to the fate of his fellow crew members.[41] Enslaving problematic Europeans like the *Boyd*'s second mate was one way of keeping order.

The *Boyd* incident was a particularly dramatic one, but the shipboard circumstances were not uncommon. Another young rangatira, whose name may have been Kawiti, Kawhiti, or Kowiti,[42] who visited Marsden in Parramatta in 1811, had been sent to Port Jackson by his elders to discover more about the wider world and acquire useful goods for his people. Instead, the ship's master put him ashore with a sealing gang at bitterly cold Macquarie Island and left him there for ten months with few provisions. Even worse than that, both aboard ship and on shore, he had been ordered to make fires and cook, which was, of course, slaves' work. His father was going to be very angry, he told Marsden.[43] But it was not only mariners who paid little heed to rank in Māori society. Over much the same period, missionaries had been preaching the gospel of egalitarianism: the idea that slaves were as good as their masters, or, in this case, rangatira.

As when Sir Everard Home asked for confirmation that Wiremu Wāka Turau would not be allowed to take Kawiti's man prisoner, the British Government did not allow 'new' slaves to be created but quite happily used existing ones as and when it suited. That had been evident in the composition of the gang employed to build military roads in Wellington in 1846. The superintendent, a nephew of the warrior chief Te Rauparaha, was paid 3s a day for his services and was assisted by other relatives of the great rangatira who received 2s 6d a day to oversee four men each. The rest of the gang, who included six of Te Rauparaha's slaves, received 2s a day. So the British administration was preserving the social order here. It was no doubt working in their favour by way of maintaining worker obedience. Yet eighteen months later, Hamilton Russell reported that he had imposed a system of ignoring the different ranks of men employed on government road-building projects. He acknowledged that there was rarely any difference in the clothing, food, or manner of living of the slaves and their masters, but did not like the fact that 'however slightly the authority of the master may be exercised' it appeared to be indisputable. That authority had meant that 'masters' were able to deprive slaves of the 'fruits of their industry' that government considered to be their individual reward rather than earnings for the communal pool — often intended for specific tribal projects. Consequently, it had become a matter of policy to 'gradually do away with' the 'classes' among the Māori they employed.[44]

Pākehā had their ranks but all Māori were held to be equal in social and political status. As the great Ngāti Tūwharetoa leader Iwikau Te Heuheu told Governor Browne in 1862, 'when an English serf visited the Maories, he was treated like a Chief; but if a Māori Chief of the highest rank visited Auckland he was treated like a slave by all except the Governor and a few officials'. Browne added that it was impossible to prevent that from being the case. 'The middle class of Englishmen will not recognise as an equal — still less as a superior — a Maori Chief, who may without loss of caste sell fish or fruit, or perhaps even beg for a shilling, as Potatau has done more than once', he said.[45] However, Te Heuheu's reference to the Governor and a few officials was probably made as a matter of diplomacy. Governors and their officials did not make a habit of upholding chiefly mana unless it suited their purposes to do so.[46]

Even Reverend Buddle's Wesleyan newspaper joined the chorus in assuring Māori that it was Queen Victoria who now held mana over the land and that theirs was a lost cause:

> E pai kia matau wawe te tangata Maori ekore e taea e ia te roromi te mana o te Kuini, e whawhai noa nei ia.

> It is well that the Māori people quickly understand that they will never be able to crush the *mana* of the Queen, they fight in vain.[47]

Because maintaining and improving the material wellbeing of the tribal group was a fundamental role of hereditary chiefs, the Crown's denial of their mana reduced their influence significantly. Christian teachings as well as English law lessened their ability to manage the tribal labour force and build its communal wealth. During the 1830s and 1840s that was in part due to a reduction in the available labour pool. Missionary insistence on monogamy meant that as well as losing the labour of released slaves, chiefs lost the support of more than one wife, and children's labour was diverted to the mission stations where they could get the advantages of literacy and a British education. Counterbalancing that, however, given that missionary influence did play a part in reducing the extent of inter-tribal warfare, it could be argued that by reducing the loss of life in battle and freeing up warriors for more productive work, some depletion of the labour pool was avoided.

Arresting rangatira

But things were to get worse as the 1840s wore on and tensions ratcheted up, especially in connection with alleged land purchases by the New Zealand Company and following the affair at Wairau. As well as dealing with the Northern War, newly arrived Governor Grey had plans for securing the Wellington region for the settlers. In addition to the military roads, those plans included building forts, stockades, and blockhouses as well as stationing 25 police and 220 soldiers at Porirua to supplement others at the Hutt. As Patricia Burns and other have pointed out, his intentions were clear. In April 1846, five months after his arrival, he wrote that 'it is not sufficient that the Government should merely conquer, and remain in possession of certain portions of [New Zealand]'. In a long, secret memorandum he had set out a policy of long-term, total conquest.[48] Grey went on to take other steps to reduce the power of rangatira and their protections. During 1846 he abolished the Protectorate of Aborigines and repealed the Native Exemption Ordinance, established by his predecessor Robert FitzRoy. That ordinance had provided for Māori to be arrested only by their own chiefs so that a degree of authority over their own people would have been retained.[49] That was not deemed to be in settler interests, however, and it was settler lobbying that lay at the root of such changes. According to William Fox, the New Zealand Company agent at Nelson who went on to become Premier on four occasions, the Native Exemption Ordinance was 'a sort of cloak to cover the design of the government to render the natives independent of British law'.[50] Chiefly mana was up against an invading army of spin doctors.

The settlers looked to Grey to secure the imperial muscle that would back their interests. As Timothy Keegan said of his subsequent policies as Governor of the Cape Colony, South Africa:

> The assimilationist ideals which he espoused in the 1850s, based on dismantling the rule of chiefs and expanding mission schooling, have been regarded as a high point of liberal administration at the Cape. And yet to the Xhosa these were years of despair, when their independence was lost, their culture was subverted, and they were reduced in the main to a state of dependence on colonial labour markets.[51]

Grey had practised that dismantling of chiefly rule during his first New Zealand governorship. As mentioned in the previous chapter, violence related to dubious land claims in the lower North Island had flared in May 1846 when Te Mamaku of Whanganui led the attack on troops stationed at Almon Boulcott's farm in the Hutt Valley. Rumours then surfaced that Wellington would be next. Grey claimed to suspect treachery on the part of Te Rauparaha, although whether he had real reason for such fears is far from certain. Te Rauparaha had established a reputation for treachery among the settlers well before they had arrived in New Zealand and it proved hard to shift even after he signed the Treaty of Waitangi. Despite his protestations and a lack of any real evidence, Grey claimed that Te Rauparaha was supporting his nephew Te Rangihaeata, said to have ordered the attack on Boulcott's farm. As it was, Te Rauparaha had agreed to vacate some of the disputed land and a previously close relationship between him and Te Rangihaeata had become strained.

Having sought a peaceful resolution to the disputes, Te Rauparaha was living quietly at his Taupō pā near Porirua when Grey visited him on the naval vessel *Driver* in July. But then, soon after the Governor's departure, the vessel returned and, two hours before dawn, seized him ignominiously from his bed, where he lay naked between his two wives, and took him aboard as a captive. He was subsequently transferred to another naval vessel, the *Calliope*, where he was held without charge for ten months, as the vessel sailed 'aimlessly up and down the coast of the North Island', before he was allowed to live in Auckland.[52] Illegally detained for eighteen months, he was not returned to his people at Ōtaki until January 1848 after petitioning for his own release. George Grey, his wife Eliza, and various Māori leaders, including Pōtatau Te Wherowhero, accompanied him on the journey home but the damage to his mana had been done.[53]

Grey had not been in the country long when Te Rauparaha was arrested and it is difficult to assess the extent to which his action was a conscious assault on the mana of a highly respected rangatira, designed to destroy him as a leader in the Māori world. Grey was certainly flexing his muscles, and it has long been suggested that he was building up a dossier of supposed evidence, to the point of reaching 'new heights of absurdity' in order to incriminate Te Rauparaha.[54] Whatever the level of intent, the impact of holding the Ngāti Toa leader in captivity was devastating. As we know, unless there was real reason to do otherwise, Māori were careful to respect the mana and tapu of their rangatira captives, as the British respected the rank of American and European prisoners of war. It was, therefore, a key point of difference. Māori respected the rank of other Māori much as the British respected the rank of other white-skinned men. But the rank of Māori rangatira was another matter — one more example of European standards applying only to warfare in Europe and not in its encounters with the 'uncivilised' world.[55]

As Iwikau Te Heuheu told Grey in September 1846, the detention of Te Rauparaha had taken things another step beyond the Māori comfort zone:

> This is a grievous thing, to me the way in which you have beaten Te Rauparaha, and for this reason you are getting a bad name, but now the natives have seen your evil disposition, and they will now be suspicious of your mode of adjusting matters. You are showing your mode of proceeding in taking land and enslaving Te Rauparaha as he is now.[56]

The ripples from Te Rauparaha's capture spread far and wide, impacting the influence of even the government's staunchest allies. Tāmati Wāka Nene, who had supported the government in the recent Northern War, was now:

> rather alarmed about his own position, as it is impossible to persuade the natives in his district, and at Hokianga, that we have not killed Rauparaha!!! And they lay the blame to Waka; therefore, he asked me to request your Excellency to send him down to the south to visit the chiefs there, and to see Rauparaha.[57]

Even in the 1860s, Captain John Campbell Johnstone was conscious that: 'The old Maori feeling which numbered prisoners amongst the dead is not yet extinct.' Johnstone recalled telling a rangatira he came across that he had met Tireni Te Oriori who was taken prisoner at Rangiriri but allowed to live in Auckland on parole because he had saved several European lives during the hostilities. The rangatira corrected him, saying that he was 'very wrong to say that [he] had seen Te Ori-ori; he is dead'.[58] Te Oriori himself, while still held aboard a hulk in January 1864, had written to his people with a brief greeting which was translated as: 'This is sufficient greeting from such a thing as a slave.'[59] Andrew Vayda accounted for these attitudes by suggesting that the effective functioning of kin groups was dependent on unity and residence in the same locality. In reality, related groups living elsewhere might be called on and respond to calls for assistance, whether in military or other projects. But Vayda's point is that 'non-residence tended to cut people off from their kinship affiliations', so, by regarding captured kinsmen as dead, the solidarity of the group could be maintained without obligation to undertake costly expeditions to either rescue them or avenge their deaths.[60] Te Rauparaha is likely to have suffered similar emotions to Te Oriori. Imprisonment is a very powerful weapon and there are those who suspect that George Grey knew exactly what the impact on his mana would be when he had him arrested in 1846. As Belich remarked wryly: 'Grey had removed Te Rauparaha and slotted into his place, the sorcerer dethroned by his apprentice.'[61]

The economy of chiefly mana

However, other changes were also impacting on chiefly authority. The bust that followed a boom in the Māori economy in the mid-1850s saw chiefly authority suffer by way of collateral damage. Northland tribes, who had the advantage of most of the overseas ship visits and trading opportunities, had been doing very well economically during the 1830s. However, six months before the Treaty of Waitangi was signed, the CMS subcommittee told London that although the tribes once had immense numbers of slaves, they now did not have enough available to cultivate their lands. They claimed that the situation had come about because large numbers had been killed in battle and male slaves were generally not allowed to marry. The second point was said to have reduced the supply of 'home born' slaves, meaning that the stock was not replenished.[62] They did not mention here that they had been redeeming captives themselves and that many others had been released by that time. But it was correct that the loss of captive labour was having a negative impact on the mana of rangatira and on tribal cohesion.

John Jolliffe reported from the Hokianga in 1851 that a local leader named Rangatira had:

> hitherto been much against the missionaries declining to become a Christian himself and preventing any of his slaves from becoming Christians, the reason he assigns is that if he becomes a Christian, and his slaves also become Christians, he can [in the?] spirit of the new religion have no more power over them, and consequently they will not work for him & he would lose their services altogether, and rather than do this, he to use his own words, "was always a devil and prefers remaining a devil."[63]

Tribes in a number of other North Island areas made great economic strides during the 1840s and into the 1850s. By the early 1850s, they were growing vast quantities of wheat, had purchased a number of water-powered flourmills to produce the settlers' staple food, and dominated the coastal shipping industry. Their agricultural production and other commercial activities kept the colony afloat and their purchases contributed more to the revenue than those of the European settlers did.

But in the mid-1850s a number of virtually simultaneous events affected both the agricultural and shipping industries. The damage to the viability of those enterprises was dramatic, sending many tribal economies into something of a tailspin from which they would not recover. It was during this time of great financial stress that the shift in the social order came to be particularly evident and worsened their economic difficulties. Whereas in pre-colonial times individuals needed to maintain ties with a tribal group for support in times of illness or old age as well as for military defence, the advent of Christianity and English law meant that those connections were no longer essential. Security could now be sought elsewhere. As Resident Magistrate Fenton wrote in 1858: 'Rawiri, Katatore and Ihaia were all slaves in Waikato, but it is very doubtful whether the returned slaves would recognise the influence of their former rangatiras.'[64] During the boom time, many of those from the lower social orders, especially freed captives, had taken the opportunity to cut ties with their previous masters. While rangatira were still obliged to distribute their wealth — by custom and to preserve their mana — more humble individuals could keep theirs in the hope of growing rich.

Chiefly mana was built and maintained by the distribution of wealth rather than its accumulation, so it could only suffer as the economic position of hereditary chiefs diminished along with their resources, their ability to support their people, or to offer hospitality to visitors. One government official remarked that many chiefs had received considerable sums from the sale of tribal land but that that wealth was dissipated in presents. Given that it was tribal land, it would, of course, have been necessary and correct for them to distribute the proceeds.

During his first governorship, from 1846 to 1853, George Grey had behaved in the manner of a supreme chief, or rangatira, in order to be comprehended as such by Māori. Octavius Hadfield, a CMS missionary, reported that Māori leaders had already been expressing their concern about these trends for some three or four years by 1856 and had been discussing ways of reasserting their authority. But despite that awareness, Hadfield recommended that government should endeavour to lessen chiefly influence 'by every legitimate means, especially by raising the position of inferior men through the equal action of the law'.[65] That viewpoint apparently differed from his previous attitude, as Jerningham

Wakefield had earlier applauded Hadfield for 'wisely' introducing new ideas 'without destroying the native aristocracy'.[66]

Twenty years later, in 1876, two of the government's land purchase officers explained the approach they had been taking to weaken chiefly authority:

> It has been our practice . . . to ignore the *mana*, because it professes to be perfectly distinct from the ownership of the soil . . . . It does seem strange indeed that in these times, when Maori rule is almost annihilated by European usages, that any chiefs . . . should be found to assert their *mana* and to base their pretensions on it, and this seems doubly strange when we take into consideration the fact that all the leading chiefs of the Arawa are receiving Government salaries, by which act they have to all intents and purposes virtually abandoned the Maori notions of authority.

For their part, those chiefs had understood the government salaries they received to be an acknowledgement of their authority in their tribal areas. But the officers' report went on to repeat the fiction that 'slaves were emancipated' with the introduction of Christianity and to sum up the process of giving them equal status with the chiefs:

> [W]hen Christianity was introduced into New Zealand all Maori slaves were emancipated, and every individual Maori was looked upon as the owner of his land, the chiefs having been disrobed of their *mana* power.[67]

One of those officers was Charles O. B. Davis who had been clerk and interpreter to the Auckland office of the Protectorate of Aborigines in 1842. As was the case with others charged with protecting the 'aborigines' through that department, he was obliged to become a land purchase agent during the 1870s. The two roles were, of course, in direct contradiction to each other. Charged with acquiring large areas of Māori territory, however, Davis was pleased to be able to report having achieved a reduction in the size of a reserve from 100 acres to just 5 in 1875 on the basis that it would prevent the Māori owners from privately letting an important mineral springs area.[68]

The trend to deny chiefly mana, increasingly evident from 1860 when interracial tensions reached new heights, was a key component in the attacks on Māori authority. As Patu Hohepa explained, 'mana cannot be self-imposed', the measurement of one's mana is done by others.[69] So mana denied is mana non-existent. Without mana, one could only be a slave, and denying chiefly mana was government policy.

The Wesleyan missionary John Whiteley, sent to Taranaki in 1856, was one who denied that 'the mana of a Chief over land' had existed 'before Europeans began to buy land'. To make the point even more conclusively, he added that if it had existed earlier, it was ceded through the Treaty of Waitangi.[70] As his biographer pointed out, in 1847 Whiteley had joined protests against Earl Grey's instructions to George Grey that he should treat unoccupied land as Crown land, and as available for sale to settlers. At that time, Whiteley argued that all land in the country had customary claimants, and that the Crown would contravene both the letter and spirit of the Treaty if it were to take it. Yet his stance had shifted dramatically by 1860 when he wrote to Thomas Buddle denying chiefly mana. Whiteley was a prolific letter writer whose arguments now supported the settler community. He claimed that armed opposition to the sale of land was rebellion against the Crown. His attitude was certainly hardening to the point that, by 1868, he would write:

> It has been said, "The natives are fighting for their lands." But "the earth is the Lord's" & for 600 years he has been waiting for them to "occupy", 600 years more would find them with millions upon millions of still unoccupied acres; and Providence indicates that now shall this portion of his earth be occupied by those who are able and willing to bring forth the fruits thereof.

This was a view that conveniently overlooked the fact that, prior to British troops invading the Waikato, home to vast tracts of wheat, fruit, and vegetable gardens, in 1863, Māori were producing the vast bulk of the country's food supplies. Whiteley was killed over five and a half years later, in February 1869, on his way to minister to the garrison at a redoubt at Pukearuhe (White Cliffs). Three military settlers and the family of one were killed that same day in the course of an attack on the redoubt, which had blocked the path from Mōkau to Taranaki where fighting was then in progress. Whiteley had been warned not to proceed.[71]

Fishing up the island: hardening attitudes and the Kīngitanga

War and the propaganda that both encourages and accompanies it went a long way towards hardening attitudes between the parties. But the relationship between settler and Māori had already been strained by the 1850s, and humanitarian sympathies in Britain had long waned. Fiscal considerations as well as rebellions in other parts of the Empire had dampened British ardour for colonisation and for protecting indigenous peoples.[72] A new era of free trade had dawned in the wake of the abolition of the East India Company's monopoly, and the corn laws that had protected British farmers from imports. Colonial powers like Britain would receive far less return for their investment in colonies that were now expected to be self-sufficient and internally administered.[73] Although representative government had been officially established in New Zealand in 1852, Māori were effectively disenfranchised until 1867 when four electorates were set up specifically for Māori men. That was because the vote was dependent on individual property qualifications and their remaining land was still communally owned. The effects of that disenfranchisement were compounded by the fact that immigration saw Pākehā outnumber Māori in their own country by about 1858.

Their declining political authority and the rapid alienation of their land had become matters of great concern to Māori well before the wars of the 1860s, so the idea of having their own sovereign under whose mana the land could be placed and protected from sale was a concept that appealed to some North Island tribes. After much consultation and debate as to who might have the mana and resources to hold such a position, Pōtatau Te Wherowhero, a Waikato rangatira of high rank and wealth with genealogical connections to many tribes, had been established as the first Māori King in 1858.

Donald McLean, the Native Secretary, wrote to Governor Gore Browne in May of 1860 to report on a meeting at Ngāruawāhia that month. McLean reported that the principal purpose of the meeting was to confirm Pōtatau Te Wherowhero as King and to erect his flag. But as British troops had assaulted Wiremu Kīngi Te Rangitāke's pā at Te Kohia just two and a half months earlier, igniting the first Taranaki War, it was inevitable that the possibility of giving military support for Kīngi would be high on the agenda. Under severe criticism for their inability 'to secure a rapid and cheap assertion of sovereignty', Governor Browne and his military commander Colonel Gold were in the hot seat and very conscious of the threat posed by the possibility of military intervention from supporters of the King Movement, or Kīngitanga.[74] McLean was there to observe and assess the degree of support for the movement, but he, too, was conscious of how colonisation had affected the position of hereditary leaders:

> It is evident that Potatau has for years past felt, whatever he may say to the contrary, that his connexion with the Europeans, and his residence at Mangere, near Auckland, has divested him of much of the extensive influence and power which he had previously swayed over the Waikato tribes, and deprived him of the homage of his people, and the full recognition by them of his high position.

McLean also claimed that Te Wherowhero's followers had taunted him for being a 'plate licker', a term of derision for 'those who partially throw off their nationality, and become so far incorporated with Europeans as to assume English customs'. Remarking on the lack of acknowledgement of his mana by Europeans when he visited settler towns, McLean pointed out that it was very different from the deference he was used to in Māori communities. Some supporters of the movement were said to feel that they had invited Pākehā to their country 'in their days of childish ignorance; but now they have become wiser they seem resolved, to use their own expression, "to fish up the island," and to preserve what remained as a lasting inheritance'.[75]

Although he recognised the problems being faced by rangatira of high rank, McLean felt they would not be readily overcome 'unless the chiefs are invited to take a more prominent part, *subject to Government control*, in the management of the various tribes owing allegiance to them' (emphasis added). He appreciated that the Kīngitanga was not supported 'with a view to the regaining of national independence' so much as 'a means of exacting such a recognition of their rights as may ensure the preservation of the declining influence and power of their chieftainship'.⁷⁶ Being 'subject to Government control' was, of course, the very thing that would continue to adversely affect their mana.

Nevertheless, true to his mission, McLean attempted to convince the people at that meeting that the government's disputed purchase of land at the Waitara in Taranaki was appropriate and proper and sought to discourage them from giving military support to Kīngi's resistance. He 'reminded them of the release of the Ngatiawa [Taranaki] slaves by Waikato chiefs, and the consequent transfer of *mana* to those so released over the several districts occupied by them as well as the transfer of the right of the Waikato, acquired by conquest, to the Government'. His use of the word 'mana' is significant because, as mentioned below, it was during this year that other supporters of the government's position were denying that the word had any meaning or that Māori had any right to claim it.⁷⁷

While some claimed that those who did not support the Kīngitanga had become slaves to the government, Te Rangi Topeora, mother of Hēnare Mātene Te Whiwhi, a key instigator of the Kīngitanga (but who had subsequently rejected it), saw things differently. She wrote to McLean in 1861 condemning those 'taurekareka' (scoundrel) tribes who had wantonly or foolishly installed a king ('kei te pokea au enei iwi taurekareka poka noa ki te hanga kingi').⁷⁸ Regardless of the true motives behind the Kīngitanga, the government and settlers either perceived it or sought to portray it as a challenge to the Queen's sovereignty over New Zealand.

The 1860 Kohimarama Conference, prompted by these concerns, became a forum for establishing whether the leaders invited to attend accepted the mana (or sovereignty) of the Queen. Their speeches, quoted in the government's bilingual newspaper, reveal the rangatira's concerns regarding the mana of the land. In other words, who had authority over it. It is noteworthy, therefore, that the published report denied that British settlers were claiming mana over the land to the exclusion of Māori (as had evidently been suggested at the meeting), saying that the mana claimed for the Queen was nothing more than 'the right to protect'. More tellingly, the newspaper asked: 'Where was the "mana" of New Zealand before the Queen took these Islands under the protection of her flag and made all its people her subjects?' implying that it did not exist.

The article continued with what Māori would surely have considered a very confused discussion including asking what the consequences would be if the Queen removed her flag and gave up the mana of the country. 'Would the Māori Chiefs possess more "mana" than they now do?' it asked before answering: 'It is foolish therefore to object to the "mana" of the Queen. Those who do so cannot understand what they are talking about.'[79]

This event appears to have instigated a raft of correspondence to various English-language newspapers around the country on the question of 'mana' and whether Māori were entitled to claim it. An 1860 newspaper editorial probably summed up the crux of contemporary feeling among settlers. In connection with Wiremu Kīngi's objections to the forced sale of land at Waitara, the cause of war breaking out in Taranaki, it proclaimed that: 'His claim is to the "mana," — the chieftain's veto — the sovereignty. To allow his pretension is to sanction the authority of [the Māori King].'[80] Later that year, James Mackay Jnr, Assistant Native Secretary and Acting Land Purchase Commissioner, responded to criticism of the government's actions in Taranaki by suggesting that Māori mana was useless and damaging: 'Wherefore do you cry about this mana which never did any good, has it not always been a source of evil.'[81]

John Morgan, a CMS missionary based in the Waikato area, told Governor Gore Browne the following year that the Kīngitanga was fostering the belief that the movement was essential to Māori independence, 'that if they submit to be ruled by British law, they will be only slaves to the Europeans, and finally lose their lands. This is now what binds them together and they consider as their enemies all persons who reason with them on their folly.'[82] The idea had spread around the country. As a Christian teacher told a government agent who visited the Urewera tribes in 1862:

> You urge these things on us that we may come under the Queen! Then away goes our land, and we become slaves to the Queen! The Queen comes coaxing [whakapatipati] us with money that she may get the "mana" of the land.[83]

However, as Lyndsay Head has pointed out, Wiremu Tāmihana Tarapīpipi, one of the early initiators of the Kīngitanga, an early convert to Christianity, and admirer of British systems (settlers referred to him as the 'King Maker'), saw the situation very differently. Tāmihana had come under the influence of Christian teachings in 1835 when Alfred Brown established a mission near Matamata pā and was a firmly committed convert.[84] His religious convictions, coupled with the new environment in which many hereditary leaders now found themselves, may have led him, as it did many others, to seek a different form of leadership. The weakening of traditional spiritual beliefs meant that the mana of Māori leaders was no longer supported by tapu — at least not in the way it had previously been. Now sidelined in many of their customary roles and denied a role in colonial government, they needed to grasp opportunities for leadership outside either context. For Tāmihana, the concept of a king appeared to unite two streams of foreign power — that of the Old Testament's righteous king and that demonstrated by Britain's king at the Battle of Waterloo.[85]

As for the Pākehā community, while few supported the proposal for a Māori king, some expressed their own concerns about the undermining of chiefly authority. As James West Stack, a New Zealand-born clergyman and son of a missionary, described the situation in 1876:

> The whole social system of the Maoris is disorganized; they are loosed from the old restraints, and are not bound by the new; the slave sits on the same mat with his master . . .[86]

He had warned three years earlier that:

> The Maoris would probably have sooner become reconciled to their altered condition if some method could have been devised to prevent the chiefs from being reduced to the level of their slaves.

Stack assured the Native Minister that the chiefs' complaints were echoed by their inferiors, adding that '[i]f the largest share of the reserved land had been assigned to the chiefs, they would have been spared much humiliation'.[87] But that was not how it was.

FIGURE 62. 'Native Catechist at Waitotara', 1839, by Charles Heaphy. *PD56(19), Auckland War Memorial Museum Library*

FIGURE 63. Because 'E Wai' (the woman on the left) was recovering from an illness when Angas visited, she had 'been placed under a tapu so strict, that every spot of ground whereon she sat was rendered sacred for a certain number of days; one of these tapued places is represented ... fenced around with twigs that its sanctity may not be infringed upon'. *'E Wai, his wife. Na Horua or Tom Street, (elder brother of Rauparaha). Tuarau or Kopai (his son), at Kahotea near Porirua', from George French Angas,* The New Zealanders Illustrated, *London, 1847: PUBL-0014-19, Alexander Turnbull Library, Wellington*

FIGURE 64. A group of war canoes on an expedition to Tauranga in 1833. The missionary schooner *Active*, flying a White Ensign, is in the centre of the image. *Church Missionary Quarterly Papers, No. 77, Lady Day, 1835: PUBL-0031-1835-1, Alexander Turnbull Library, Wellington*

FIGURE 65. 'Henry and William Williams calming hostile Maori by speaking extracts of the Bible in Maori'. *'The power of God's Word', from* Illustrations of Missionary Scenes, *vol. 2, 1856: PUBL-0151-2-013, Alexander Turnbull Library, Wellington*

FIGURE 66. The baptism of Te Ngahue in 1849. *W. W. McCarty, 'Baptism of Te Ngahue, an aged New Zealander chief at Te Ariki on the lake of Tarawera, 1849', 1875, nla.pic-an2253447, National Library of Australia, Canberra*

FIGURE 67. Sketch of the scene when Selwyn, Clarke, and Cotton met with Tāraia in 1842. *From an original letter sent by Bishop Augustus Selwyn to his mother, courtesy of the Master and Fellows of Selwyn College, University of Cambridge*

FIGURES 68 AND 69. Two of the prisoners transported to Tasmania. Te Rāhui (left) and Hōhepa Te Umuroa (right). *John Skinner Prout, 'Ko Pi Ta Ma, Te Ra Ni [Te Rahui], New Zealand' and 'Hohepa Teumuroa [Hohepa Te Umuroa], New Zealand', 1846: Reg. No. Oc2006,Drg.27 and 29 © The Trustees of the British Museum*

FIGURE 70. These prisoners, captured at Weraroa pā, Waitotara, South Taranaki in 1865, were photographed aboard a hulk in 1866. Māori prisoners were often photographed, much like trophies, a circumstance that must have added to their feelings of humiliation and loss of mana. *'Maori prisoners, members of the Hauhau church, under guard on board a prison hulk in Wellington harbour': 1/2-103605-F, Alexander Turnbull Library, Wellington*

FIGURE 71. A reconstruction of the burning of the *Boyd* in 1809. *Louis Auguste de Sainson, 'Enlevement du Boyd par les Nouveaux Zealandais', from Dumont d'Urville,* Voyage pittoresque autour du monde, *Paris, 1839: PUBL-0034-2-390, Alexander Turnbull Library, Wellington*

FIGURE 72. Portrait of Te Rauparaha in the 1840s. *R. Hall, 'Te Raparaha [Te Rauparaha], chief of the Kawias [Kāwhia]', [after 1843]: A-114-047, Alexander Turnbull Library, Wellington*

FIGURE 73. Photograph of Wiremu Tāmihana Tarapīpipi Te Waharoa, c. 1865. *New Zealand Parliamentary Library: 1/2-053942-F, Alexander Turnbull Library, Wellington*

FIGURE 74. The top flag is that of Te Ua Haumēne. The middle one is Tītokowaru's and the bottom one is that of Te Peehi Tūroa: both followers of Te Ua. *Māori rebel flag: Flag of Te Ua (Hau Hau originator): 1992-0035-1631/8A, Museum of New Zealand Te Papa Tongarewa, Wellington*

FIGURE 75. Hīona (Zion). Rua Kēnana, Te Kooti's successor, is the third figure from the left on the platform leading to the upper level. *Rua Kenana Hepetipa's wooden circular courthouse and meeting house at Maungapohatu, c. 1908: 1/2-002915-F, Alexander Turnbull Library, Wellington*

FIGURE 76. 'A slave woman, preparing potatoes by scraping them with a mussel shell', by Angas. *George French Angas,* The New Zealanders Illustrated, *London, 1847: PUBL-0014-59, Alexander Turnbull Library, Wellington*

FIGURE 77. This drawing is an example of how images can also distort historical details even if they appear relatively minor. Based on Angas's 1844 painting, it was made some 50 years later as an illustration for John White's *Ancient History of the Maori*, most of which was published in 1897. The woman's hair is no longer cut short and hanging loose but held back in a topknot, a style usually associated with men. *John White,* Illustrations Prepared for White's Ancient History of the Maori, *1891*

FIGURE 78. A slave woman cooking kānga pirau, or fermented corn. *George French Angas, Sketchbook, 1844: A-020-034-2-3, Alexander Turnbull Library, Wellington*

FIGURE 79. Distinctions of status certainly mattered to rangatira. The Mōkau chief Taonui was so annoyed that George French Angas had chosen to paint his 'ugly' slave rather than someone of greater mana that the travelling artist was obliged to appease him before painting the rangatira and his family in front of their home. This painting may be the work that so offended Taonui. *George French Angas, 'E Kupa, son of Taonui, Jacky a slave, and Koturi Weti, son of Tariki', 1844: Accession No: 1992/25, Auckland Art Gallery Toi o Tāmaki*

FIGURE 80. 'Spoils to the Victor', by Louis John Steele, 1908. *Accession No: 1912/7/1, Auckland Art Gallery Toi o Tāmaki*

According to some nineteenth-century sources, Wiremu Tāmihana also encountered the objection that British systems were leading Māori into slavery.[88] As Edwin Hodder explained:

> The King Movement had its origin in rather a singular manner. "William Thompson Tarapipipi, principal chief of Ngatihana [sic: Ngāti Hauā], a man of high rank in Maori society, and son of Te Waharoa, a renowned warrior of the last generation, was its chief promoter. Thompson, in conversation with a friend, expressed his great admiration of some of our usages, and especially of the manner in which justice is administered in our Courts. His friend replied, 'E tomo koe i raro i aku huha.' (Your path is through underneath my thighs.) He inquired the meaning of this strong figure, and received for reply, 'Me rapu koe.' (Search it out.) He thought, he pondered, and at length arrived at the conclusion that it must point to oppression and slavery. 'That path,' he reasoned, 'is the path of dogs only; then are we to be treated like dogs? Does the Pakeha intend to put us beneath his feet? But he shall not be permitted.' And he resolved on devising some means to preserve himself and countrymen from the degradation thus figuratively described."[89]

For Lyndsay Head, Tāmihana's Christianity meant that he put God above the Queen, so his rejection of the Treaty of Waitangi and attempt to establish a modernised model of Māori political independence were in line with those most deeply held beliefs. Despite Hodder's account, Head argues that Tāmihana did not believe that the Treaty was intended to make slaves of Māori.[90]

A number of tribal groups and individuals did remain loyal to the government and clung steadfastly to their Christian faith, but disillusionment was casting wider shadows over the land. Some embraced the Kīngitanga, but another initiative, also designed to reassert Māori control over their own affairs, was a series of gatherings or parliaments organised by Ngāti Whātua's Paora Tūhaere. The first of these was held at Ōrākei in 1879 in commemoration of the Kohimarama Conference nineteen years earlier. Te Hēmara Tauhia from Mahurangi was one of the disillusioned who attended that meeting. He advocated adherence to the Treaty and the Gospel but 'complained that the missionaries had directed the eyes of the Maoris to Heaven, while taking their lands'. Although Te Hēmara laid some of the blame on Māori themselves, he complained that Pākehā Land Court judges were awarding land to people who possessed no real claim to it. 'The fault of the pakeha', he said, 'was in depriving the chiefs of their *mana*'. Patoromu felt that Māori should ask the government to restore their mana along with their lands and fisheries. Like Paora Tūhaere, a number of other speakers placed a portion of the blame on Māori themselves and expressed a willingness to abide by the Treaty, but several condemned the Native Land Court system as the fundamental base of their problems.[91]

The Native Land Court, established in 1865 to convert customary land-holdings into individual titles and facilitate sale, has been described as an 'engine of destruction' and a 'Kooti Tango Whenua', or land-taking court.[92] It was one aspect of government policy intent on overriding rangatira authority over the land and their ability to allocate resources. The West Waiuku land block, a little south of Auckland, provides one example of the confusion and discord that resulted from those processes. That land had been confiscated in 1865 under the New Zealand Settlements Act of 1863 designed to punish tribal groups alleged to have been in rebellion against the Crown. So-called 'loyal' Māori living there were promised that their villages, cultivations, and burial places would be returned to them, surveyed and under Crown grant. Of just over 47,000 acres taken, some 6600 were returned — in 36 Crown grants made out to six or seven rangatira to be held in trust for their people. However, Māori land rights are more complex than Western ones with often overlapping rights of use to the same geographic area. That was a reality government officials had great difficulty comprehending and led to very many travesties of justice. In this case, it was not long before people who felt they should have benefited from those grants complained that the trusts specified were either inappropriate or they did not agree that those appointed as trustees were 'fitting persons to have control over their lands'. Another complaint was that land was being leased, timber being sold, or income generated from the land under trust but that the assigned rangatira were not accounting for the proceeds. On the surface, such complaints suggest that the people had been strongly influenced by the individualist teachings of the church and government, but the reality seems to have been less simple. The Commissioner of Native Reserves explained that 'the young men would not, with any heart, clear or cultivate land that was not secured at least to the head of the family, nor defined from that of the tribe by an intelligible boundary'. So, on one hand, they were anxious that their labours contributed to the family economy which was controlled by its 'head', but, on the other, they did not want their rights to land subsumed under that of the 'tribe'. However, since the government had chosen those who were to decide what land belonged to which tribal group and felt it necessary to establish so-called 'intelligible' boundaries, that aspect of their concern may have related to the possibility of their contributions going to a group they did not affiliate to.[93]

Government ideas as to what was in the best interests of Māori and who were the appropriate people to manage their affairs differed greatly from those of the people who were supposed to benefit from its official 'protection'. But differing perceptions as to who was qualified or equipped to carry out tribal or public functions were evident on many levels. Because mana was the basis of authority and, therefore, necessary for the overseeing of important decisions, the British practice of trial by a jury 'of one's peers' was another that did not sit well with rangatira. Disappointed by his expectation that a Pākehā who had murdered a Māori would be executed for the crime, Te Ao-o-te-Rangi complained that the jurors were not of the class that he expected — not appropriate people for the task. He had learned that that they were the likes of cart drivers and labourers (people employed breaking stones on the roads was how he put it):

He kai rohi i hohorotia e tenei hunga; kati ano i reira to ratou mohio.

They can eat a loaf of bread greedily enough; and this is the amount of their ability.[94]

For him, the system was unthinkable. It should have been people of mana who determined such matters and, in his opinion, ordinary workers, who he equated with slaves, did not have the authority and, perhaps, not the wisdom either, to decide a fitting punishment.

Abolished by George Grey in 1846, the position of Protector of Aborigines turned out to be a short-lived institution. But whether it would have supported the retention of rangatira authority over their own people is doubtful. Equally difficult to know is how conscious Māori were of the Aborigines' Protection Society in its early days, although they were certainly aware of it by the 1860s. In September 1864, after its members had urged Grey to protect Māori lands, Te Kou Rehua and five others from Hauraki wrote to the Society praising them for 'fulfilling the words of Christ'. Their address concluded by saying:

> All the Maoris are agreed on these two points, for the blood of the Europeans is shed in his money, but as to the blood of the Maori it is shed on his own land.[95]

Te Oha Taotao, Katikati, and Te Kou wrote again from Horotiu the following month asking that representatives of the Society visit New Zealand to investigate the causes of the war then raging and bring an end to it. Adding that war was the work of Satan and peace that of God, they asked the Society to raise them back up to stand on their own feet once more and return to Christianity. War, they said, had driven Christianity far from them.[96]

The Committee of the Aborigines' Protection Society forwarded the letters to the Secretary of State for the Colonies, Edward Cardwell, endorsing the rangatira's request for an impartial investigation into the causes of the war. They were convinced 'that a great wrong would be permitted, if the absolute conduct of native affairs were transferred to the colonists before the Maoris are placed in the enjoyment of all the rights solemnly guaranteed to them by the Treaty'. They added that such a commission would provide 'crowning proof of the determination of the Imperial Government to grant them . . . justice'. It was critical that 'the natives draw a broad line between the Colonial Government as such, and the authority of the Queen to which the large majority of them instinctively bow'. However, Cardwell replied that he did not think a commission, 'independent of the Governor and constituted authorities of New Zealand, would be likely to produce any beneficial result'.[97] Settler government was now fully in control.

Lady Mary Martin, the daughter of a clergyman and wife of New Zealand's first Chief Justice, looked back nostalgically in her 1884 book

Our Maoris. In it she applauded the sincerity of the 'old warrior[s]' and 'fierce barbarians' who freed their slaves:

> One by one the chiefs, who depended on those over whom they had exercised despotic sway for the cultivation of their lands, freed them and let them return to their own homes.

But she also recognised that:

> This noble act of manumission told, in time, very unfavourably on the position of the New Zealand chiefs. They lost much of their prestige by having to work with their own hands, and they lost the power of exercising the large hospitality which had made their names great in the land.[98]

Her ideas were intended kindly but were naive. Māori rangatira had always worked 'with their own hands' alongside their people, but there were limitations on the types of work they could do to preserve their mana. However, she was correct in her appreciation of the impact on their ability to offer hospitality.

Distrust of the Pākehā's long-term goals was inevitable and rumours were rife. Extravagant stories of Māori victories over British troops were particularly evident in the early months of war but were overtaken by fearful tales of the sweeping subjugation some neutral tribes claimed the colonists intended for Māori. As Alan Ward put it, 'there was too much substance in the latter rumours' for officers of the Native Department to be entirely convincing in their denials of such plans. But cultural factors probably exacerbated matters, too. In Māori, as in other Polynesian societies, extravagant rumour, which implied special personal knowledge on the part of the teller, was a traditional strategy used by those seeking to gain influence.[99] That would seem to be the ploy adopted by one such rumour-monger following hostilities at Waitōtara in 1864. A man snatched a newspaper from an old woman who had been using it to wrap clothing in. Claiming that he could read English, the man announced to his Māori audience that it reported the loss of 3800 British troops and that Queen Victoria 'wished it to be perfectly understood that when the present war was over, all the surviving friendly natives [those who had fought in support of the government] should be used as beasts of burden, or to sweep the streets and cleanse the most filthy localities in European towns'.[100] So, if Māori did not already feel that they had become the slaves of the British, such home-grown propaganda might yet convince them.

It was a process that crept on, but Ward was quite specific when he identified 1893 as the year in which '[t]he *mana* of the land and the *mana* of the people had clearly passed into Pakeha hands'. Māori had by then been largely subordinated to settler legal and political systems. They were required to assume the obligations of the former, but the four seats in Parliament set aside for Māori under the 1867 Maori Representation Act proved quite inadequate. The Native Department was treating Māori representation in Parliament as a public relations exercise rather than a genuine attempt at democratic process. Although the legislation overcame the previous property qualification which denied most Māori the vote, the limit of four Māori members was hardly equivalent to the then 72 Pākehā members. It also imposed an unrealistic workload on those four: three for the more heavily populated North Island and one for the entire South Island.[101] And despite the anxiety for land loss expressed at the 1840 Treaty negotiations, post-war confiscations under the 1863 Settlements Act, followed by both Crown and private purchases under the Native Land Acts from 1865, had resulted in a dramatic loss of Māori land ownership. The period from 1865 to 1890 was, according to Ward, the main period of Crown and private purchases.[102]

And it was also around 1893 that government wound up the special machinery of administration tailored to Māori requirements. The rūnanga system had been closed down in 1865 and other systems of self-government once envisaged were abandoned.[103] The Native Department, which had employed Māori as assessors, police, and members of school committees, was never intended to be a lasting institution and was dismantled in 1892.[104] The Resident Magistrates' Courts were closed and numbers of Māori assessors (leading rangatira appointed to work with resident magistrates in Māori districts and with judges in the Native Land Courts) were substantially reduced. The government was abandoning all ideas of comprehensive self-government.[105] But the writing had been on the wall for some time and two further Māori initiatives aimed at self-government had been set in motion the previous year. The Kīngitanga's Kauhanganui and the Kotahitanga parliament had both met for the first time in 1892. The Kauhanganui parliament was founded by the second Māori King, Tāwhiao, after his proposal to establish a pan-Māori institution as a counterpart to the colonial Legislative Council was denied. Supported by the Kīngitanga tribes, it had a council of twelve tribal representatives (called the Tekau-mā-rua). Under its 1894 constitution, the Kauhanganui parliament established its own courts and police force independent of the government institutions. The Kotahitanga (unity) parliaments were another initiative aimed at setting up a pan-tribal system of self-government. These were political responses to the loss of Māori autonomy, but there were also religious ones.

Bound for Canaan

Changes in religious adherence and practice — in the past as in the present — inevitably connect with human experience — with physical suffering, but perhaps more so with spiritual and emotional pain. Religion offers a way of handling those experiences. So, as John Seed has pointed out, to understand the role of religion in any given society or age requires an investigation of what he called the 'affective life' of the people — in other words, their emotional and spiritual realities, and 'how their "religious experience" connected to the ways in which they confronted and transformed reality in their everyday lives'. The Māori world had been confronted with many new ideas and realities; technical, economic, political, and spiritual. As the circumstances of life change, the ways in which human beings respond to those changes alter too, and so it was with Māori.[106]

Since the introduction of Christianity to New Zealand, there has been a long-standing tradition of Māori spiritual leaders identifying their people with the Jews of the Old Testament. That has been particularly evident in movements aimed at the recovery of Māori authority and freedom from oppression. Canaan, the promised land of the Bible, was a recurring theme, as was the idea that the Māori situation was similar to that of the

Israelites in Egypt. For many, Canaan, usually rendered as Kēnana in the Māori language, became the sought-after promised land within New Zealand. Excerpts from Genesis as well as Exodus 20, which refers to God's role in saving the Israelites from slavery in Egypt, were among the first selections from the Bible to be published in Māori. Old Testament stories in particular, with their prophets and lengthy genealogies, were about people not entirely dissimilar to themselves. Stories about Moses leading Jacob's descendants out of slavery in Egypt to the 'Promised Land' of Canaan strengthened their feelings of kinship.

Taumata-ā-Kura, who had been taken to the Bay of Islands as a captive when Ngāpuhi attacked Waiapu in 1823, is credited with taking knowledge of Christianity to Ngāti Porou in the 1830s. During his time in the north, he had learned to read and write, and his return to his own people at Whakawhititerā near the Waiapu River was negotiated by the missionary William Williams. Mohi Tūrei told that shortly after his return home, Taumata-ā-Kura (baptised Piripi, or Phillip) hoisted what Tūrei referred to as 'te haki a te kuini', or the Queen's flag, to announce that it was the Sabbath day.[107] One of his first sermons focused on how God took the children of Israel out of Egypt, the ten miracles he performed through Aaron and Moses, and the Passover that commemorates their liberation.[108] However, many of the prophets who formulated new syncretic religions, incorporating Christian teachings into Māori spiritual beliefs and practices, went further in associating Māori with the people of Exodus.

One of the earliest Māori prophets, whose teachings came to light in the early 1830s, was Papahurihia, also known as Te Atua Wera. He may have been the first to identify Māori as Jews, referring to them as Hūrai, a people lost in their own lands. Māori interest in Judaism grew from that time as the Old Testament became more available to them. Papahurihia's teaching and symbols drew on those books as well as Jewish traditions of authority and lost land regained. As Jews, Papahurihia's followers were not Christians but understood themselves to be the chosen people of God. Saturday, the Jewish Sabbath day, became their day of worship.[109]

Identification with the Jews and concepts of Canaan as a promised or recovered land featured in other prophetic movements that followed. Missionary teachings may have nourished the concept but, as an aspiration, Canaan was not necessarily visualised in the same way. Wesleyan missionary Nathaniel Turner composed a hymn in Māori which began with the words:

Me haere tatou nei	Let us all go
Kit era wahi pai,	To that good place
Ki runga ra ki Kenana	Above in Canaan,
Ko reira noho ai.	And there stay.

Turner had clearly intended Canaan as a metaphor for Heaven in this composition, which was 'sung with great feeling' during a service at Mangungu.[110] But so did an unknown Māori who composed another hymn, apparently on the death of a relative. He or she also placed Kēnana above (in Heaven?):

Naku koe i tuku atu,
Ki te motu o Ihowa;
I ahu to wairua,
Ki runga ki Kenana.[111]

Like Taumata-ā-Kura, Mahika of Waitaha, a tribe belonging to the Te Arawa confederation, was also taken north after a Ngāpuhi attack in 1823. During his time in the Bay of Islands, he, too, was brought under Christian influence and baptised Hākaraia (Zachariah). A student of Reverend Thomas Chapman, Hākaraia followed Chapman and his wife to Rotorua around 1836 and lived on the shores of the lake where many of his kinsmen had settled after the 1823 raid. In 1840, he moved with the Chapmans to Te Ngae on the lake's eastern shores and extended his activities as a native teacher, or kaiwhakaako. A few years later, however, he settled on the site of an old pā called Muriwharau in his own tribal area where he established a Christian village named Kēnana, now a suburb of Te Puke in the Bay of Plenty. Canaan had connotations of political autonomy and land regained for many people, but for Hākaraia they were more literal. His people's territory having been occupied by an invading tribe for more than twenty years, they must have been overjoyed to be able to return to it after so long.[112]

Still later, during the wars of the 1860s, a time of great disillusionment for Māori, Te Ua Haumēne came to prominence as a prophet. Having been taken to the Hokianga area as a captive while still a child, he had studied Scripture there and continued that study when he eventually returned to his Taranaki homeland. Following a number of visions, including appearances by the angels Gabriel and Michael, he led a new movement based around instructions to be 'good and peaceful' (Pai Mārire). Te Ua saw himself as a new Abraham or Moses while his followers considered themselves God's chosen people: the Tiu, or Jews. For them, New Zealand was the New Canaan. In 1864 he would write that he was 'the Hau Marire [gentle wind] standing on the half of Canaan which has ascended up out of the darkness and peace', and signed himself 'The Ua a peaceable Jew'. At his Christian baptism, Te Ua was given the name Horopāpera (Zerubbabel), the name of the leader of the first group of Jews who returned from captivity in Babylon. A man who spent a day and a night with his followers at Kāwhia reported that they delighted each other with stories of the escape of the Israelites into the wilderness — as well as how the Scots had gallantly maintained their independence from the English.[113] Te Ua, who had classified the Pākehā as 'Samaritans', prophesied that God would ultimately banish them from the 'New Canaan' of his 'chosen people', the Māori.[114]

Like Te Ua and others, Te Kooti was mission educated. Having founded the Ringatū Church following a series of visions while imprisoned at Wharekauri, he established Saturday as their Sabbath day and included other Jewish practices such as declaring the first of January the celebration of Kapenga, or the Jewish Passover. He also insisted that Abraham, Isaac, Jacob, and David were the ancestors of Māori.[115] The followers of his successor, Rua Kēnana, were called Iharaira (Israelites), and lived much as a Hebraic community would. Until 1915, they kept themselves apart from others and the men did not cut their hair. The building called Hīona, or Zion, in which his council of Rīwaiti, or Levites, met, was painted in blue, gold, and white, colours among those used by the priestly class of Israelites (fig. 75).[116]

The people of Parihaka in Taranaki felt similar connections with the Jews. Like a number of other Māori prophets, Te Whiti developed a strong belief in the affinity of Jew and Māori but went even further, telling James Cowan: 'We came from the land of Canaan . . . Kenana was our first Hawaiki; our last Hawaiki was Rangiatea.'[117] Hawaiki is a reference to the previous Polynesian homeland of the Māori people and Rangiātea is the Māori name for Ra'iatea, in the Society Islands, the likely birthplace of some of their ancestors. The report by Native Affairs Minister John Bryce, who directed the assault on Parihaka, makes it quite clear that he understood the significance of mana and tapu to Māori. In that report he remarked that Te Whiti's wharenui, or meeting house, was smashed and its timbers scattered over the marae (the courtyard or gathering place in front of the building) 'to deprive it of its sacred character, and break the magic spell'.[118] These events ensured that the people's feelings of oppression and identification with Jewish slavery continued in their aftermath.

The Parihaka settlers who were removed following the assault in November 1881 understood themselves to be prisoners but, according to the *Hawera and Normanby Star*, they had actually been 'deported'.[119] Many of these people had come from Pātea, Whanganui, and Waikato in support of the cause and to replace the ploughmen who had been imprisoned earlier. However, because so many were now taken back to their supposed home areas and the crops at Parihaka had been destroyed by the invading constabulary, feeding the 'deportees' had become a problem. Those taken to Whanganui were initially given customary hospitality by their hosts, but the large numbers of people and the length of their stay meant that supplies were soon exhausted.[120] Bryce announced his intention not to provide any food to people displaced without it having been worked for. The *Auckland Star* responded to this news by saying:

> It is thought an attempt will be made to make the natives turn to road work, after the manner lately pursued in the case of the unemployed, giving them a minimum of pay, just sufficient to find them in rations. Even taking the estimate of acres destroyed as published in the telegrams from Parihaka, it is abundantly shown that the late and present inhabitants of Parihaka are anything but a lazy people; in fact, the extent of the cultivations in that neighbourhood was the admiration of all — even of the colonial army. It appears to me an entirely new phase in the policy of the British colonists, this uncharitable and wanton destruction of the food in the first place, and

the taking advantage of the destitution so produced to obtain cheap labour for the construction of roads in the Taranaki district.[121]

Historian Dick Scott described the policy as: 'a refinement in cruelty — they could be employed on the works which were dividing their land'.[122] However, a 'travelling correspondent' from the more locally based *Hawera and Normanby Star* was far less sympathetic, suggesting that 'the pride of independent savages' would cause them to 'scorn to gain their living by the sweat of their brow'. More tellingly, he reported that, for their part, the 'deportees' had likened that proposal 'to the slavery of Israel in Egypt, the colonists of New Zealand being the Egyptians, who will appoint taskmasters for the oppression of the chosen people'.[123]

The shadow of oppression and loss continued into the twentieth century with many of the same symbols. As a response to landlessness, homelessness, disease, and poverty among her people, Piupiu Te Wherowhero, a granddaughter of the first Māori King, established a new community called Kēnana on the south-eastern slopes of Maungatautari in the Waikato during the 1920s. The first houses were made from sacking. Benzene boxes served for chairs. Without any assistance from government or elsewhere, the community struggled to establish farms and gardens before eventually having to move as the swampy land on which they had settled was liable to flooding.[124]

In that same decade, Elsdon Best claimed to have had confidential talks with 'old native friends' who felt that the Māori had 'become a common, graceless being, like unto the slaves of old' who would 'never regain his old-time physical, intellectual, and spiritual vigour'. 'The noa [free from tapu] condition of the mauri ora [life force] is the cause of the decadence of the race — so says the Maori.'[125] This was a particularly pessimistic viewpoint and one that was commonly expressed by Pākehā during this period when their own society was experiencing a period of considerable gloom.[126] Native Minister Sir Āpirana Ngata put it somewhat differently in a 1934 speech in support of the Maori Purposes Fund, but referred to the same underlying premise when he quoted a saying: 'Divorce the Maori from the land, and you will make him a slave.'[127] Another half-century after that, in Witi Ihimaera's 1986 novel *The Matriarch*, the old lady of the title is said to declare that Māori lost everything if they lost their land.

'We also become nothing', she said. Putting the point into even sharper perspective, Ihimaera had her continue that Māori 'had to endure confiscation and to become no more than a black slave in the new antipodean white South'. The Pākehā settlers were 'like a plague of locusts in the land of Egypt'.[128] These words sum up an enduring conviction.

Given the close connection between the mana, or political power, of tribal groups and their mana over their territories, attacks on communal land ownership had the effect of breaking down the authority of hereditary leaders over tribal members — and even over war captives. That led, ultimately, to a breakdown of the wider political, social, and economic order. But since the key aspect of 'slavery', in Māori terms, was a loss of mana and tapu, their responses and their claims of enslavement by government are more understandable. That reality also increases the relevance of the questions: What is slavery? And who were the slaves?

CHAPTER ELEVEN

The language of slavery

Any attempt to discover what life was like for war captives in Māori society and whether slavery is an appropriate term to apply to it is bound to be confounded by the barriers and hazards common to any investigation of the past. A lack of sources can be a barrier, but even when they exist in abundance, they are almost always subject to hazards of bias. Whether written, oral, or pictorial, and whether they were produced for bureaucratic purposes, to glorify or condemn historical figures, or for any other purpose, the truth may be bent — deliberately or inadvertently. In the course of researching this particular aspect of New Zealand history, however, inconsistencies in vocabulary or the way in which words were applied emerged as having a major part to play in confounding the evidence. The study had begun with the expectation that analysis of the language used in Māori texts, especially early ones, would reveal the more specific meanings of the various terms applied to people of low status. That hope was soon dashed. Whether in the original Māori language or English translation, those texts revealed less about the true meaning of particular words than how language use, which relates to perception, changed as attitudes towards past customs changed. Not only were words used loosely as forms of derision but their meaning has been confused by what appears to be the early adoption of 'political correctness' in Māori language — but in its positive sense. In other words, attempts seem to have been made to avoid not only the stigmatisation of individuals but also past customs through the use of softer, kindlier terms. Unfortunately, this phenomenon, almost certainly the product of Western contact and the assumption of Christian values, has also had the effect of obscuring original meanings and, therefore, the status of the people being discussed.[1] The lack of consistency in terms used to refer to captives, servants, and people of low status proved so confusing that some of many big questions came to be: 'Who or what was a slave?' and 'Whether or at what point did captives became slaves?' As previous chapters have shown, not all of those captured can be said to have been treated as slaves. Were those of rangatira rank who were allowed to maintain their dignity and mana considered to be hostages rather than permanent prisoners? And were all hostages rangatira?

Prisoners of war have been described as slaves or as doing slave labour throughout the ages. In sixth century BC Babylon, prisoners of war were given to the temples as slaves.[2] The men obliged to labour on the Burma–Siam railway during the Second World War, the subject of the 1957 film *The Bridge on the River Kwai*, offer another, more recent, example.

The politically astute have always known the value of manipulating language. So, as far back as April 1789, when abolitionists were pitted against the pro-slavery West Indies lobby, a mischievous correspondent using the nom de plume 'No Planter' wrote to the English *Gentleman's Magazine* cynically suggesting that because '[t]he vulgar are influenced by names and titles':

> Instead of SLAVES, let the Negroes be called ASSISTANT-PLANTERS; and we shall not then hear such violent outcries against the slave trade by pious divines, tender-hearted poetesses, and short-sighted politicians.[3]

But while 'sanitary engineer' and 'assistant planter' may have more positive connotations than rubbish collector or slave, the reverse is equally powerful. Whether deliberately or unconsciously, words may conjure up more negative connotations.

Words carry a lot of baggage. The well-known but harsh word 'taurekareka' has been applied not only to captives or people 'enslaved' but also as a more general term of derision. However, like the somewhat gentler words 'pononga' and 'mōkai', another more specific and less damning word for captives than taurekareka is herehere. Mauherehere (or mau herehere), to be held captive, was sometimes applied to hostages, implying that their captivity was temporary with the likelihood of ransom or some form of negotiated release. And that raised the question of whether war captives (herehere) and slaves (taurekareka) were one and the same or whether it depended on how they were perceived and treated in their captors' community. In evidence to the Waitangi Tribunal on behalf of Ngāti Toa, Te Waari Carkeek referred consistently to prisoners as 'herehere' and, speaking of the time before missionary influence, said that serving and maintaining the honour of the rangatira as a slave was an obligation captives acquired for the sparing of their life.[4] Nor were all captives considered 'lesser mortals just because they were captured in battle', he added, but were often given considerable responsibility.[5] The respect afforded to rangatira captives as compared with commoners and ways in which captives with useful skills or ability could rise in status within their conquerors' communities are evidence of that.

If captives became 'slaves', it was not mere captivity that brought it about. As mere conquest was not enough for the victors to gain mana whenua, or land rights, over the vanquished — it had to be followed by ahi kaa (continuous occupation) and ringa kaha (strong defence) — the case appears to have been similar with captives. Factors such as their previous rank or perceived usefulness certainly affected how they were perceived and treated, so they may not have suffered significant loss of tapu or mana until other things had taken place. Being obliged to undertake tapu-destroying work such as lighting fires, cooking, and so on may have been the effective means of subjugation, as might absence from one's own people for a substantial length of time.

As the Appendix illustrates, many different words have been applied to war captives, prisoners, and people of low status. Some derive from ancient usage in other parts of Polynesia, some are likely dialectal — being more common or even confined to particular tribal areas — and others may be metaphorical. So there are many difficulties in deciding just who was a debased war captive and who was a free-born servant or personal attendant to someone else.

The word used in any given context reflected the speaker or storyteller's attitude towards the person being discussed or the situation they found themselves in. That was and is still the case when English speakers use the term slavery in a myriad of circumstances, but especially when they feel that workers are being exploited. For example, at a time when all slaves were assumed to be 'black', campaigners for workers' rights often spoke of 'white slavery'. The term, in use from the first decade of the nineteenth century, gained more widespread use following publication of an 1888 article by Annie Besant. 'White Slavery in London' drew attention to the appalling conditions and low wages suffered by girls employed at the Bryant & May match factory in the East End of London.[6] But the word has many more metaphorical applications in English, too. 'He is a slave to drink' comes to mind.

As with Māori language use more generally, many of the metaphorical terms for people of low status fell into disuse. But to confuse matters even further, a variety of words has often been applied to the same person in the same context and in the same text, which is a strong indication that their use was more literary than precisely lexical.

The changing vocabulary of 'slavery'

For example, in the famous love story of 'Hine-moa' published in Sir George Grey's 1853 collection of oral traditions, *Nga Mahi a Nga Tupuna*, the man who acts as an intermediary between Hinemoa and her beloved Tūtānekai following her legendary swim from the mainland to be with him, is referred to firstly as a 'taurekareka', then as a 'pononga', before he becomes a 'mokai'. This may simply be a reflection of the man's status as a captive who served as a servant to Tūtānekai before becoming a more favoured, albeit still subservient, attendant. However, the translation, published as 'The Story of Hinemoa (The Maiden of Rotorua)' in *Polynesian Mythology*, refers to him as a servant six times and as a slave four times. The narrative alternates the terms, even in the same sentence. It is especially curious that the word taurekareka in *Nga Mahi a Nga Tupuna* is translated as servant in the English, while pononga and mōkai are, with one exception, rendered as slave: the opposite of what might have been expected.[7] The earlier, Māori version of the story moves progressively from using taurekareka to pononga to mōkai, increasingly kindly words, whereas the English translation appears to be more random. What was the status of Tūtānekai's attendant? Based on this rendition, that is difficult to say.

As with the story of Hinemoa, words that may have had neutral or even quite different meaning in other Māori texts were very often translated into English as slave. For example, the government newspaper the *Maori Messenger* referred to a waiata beginning:

Kua riro herehere na to matua . . . [Your father has been taken captive]

translating it as:

Your father has been taken slave[8]

The translator has assumed that to be captured necessarily means enslavement.

Because Western writers and translators referred to Māori war captives as slaves, regardless of how they were treated, this highly emotive word could be used as 'evidence' of a barbaric institution to be eradicated by 'civilisation' and Christianity. Even when not necessarily indicated in the original Māori text, use of the slavery word has strengthened the impression that either the missionaries or colonisation by the British 'abolished' an allegedly uncivilised institution. But as allowance must be made for the cultural, political, and religious baggage inherent in the observations of Europeans as well as the context of their time, it must also be acknowledged that, as they accepted Christianity, Māori were affected by the same influences and ideals. No society is static in its culture or its way of thinking. Beliefs and attitudes are ever evolving as are sensitivities to the beliefs and attitudes of other cultures. It would seem, then, that Christian teachings, English law, and the hostile attitudes of outsiders towards using war captives as a labour force may have influenced what Māori have said at different points in time, as well as how they have said it, and even how they understood past practices themselves.

A broad overview of Māori texts from the 1850s into the twentieth century certainly suggests that Māori language use was being influenced by European or Christian sensitivities. There was an apparent shift away from use of the word 'taurekareka' towards more charitable words, especially 'pononga'. Māori who became Christian may have felt some discomfort about earlier practices and altered their language to obscure what they came to see as an uncivilised or unchristian system. A Native Land Court witness's reference to the pre-Christian period as being 'in Satan's time' certainly gives that impression.[9] According to Lesley Kelly, sensitivities aroused by the adoption of Christian values even led to a change in some recitations of whakapapa pertaining to a man named Kaitangata. Kaitangata translates into English as man-eater, and such was the missionary condemnation of cannibalism that someone chose to alter this man's name to Noa. The reasoning behind the change is said to have been that Kaitangata's son was Hema, which is also the missionary translation of Shem, and the father of the biblical Shem was Noah.[10]

The case of the Moriori signals how not only Māori language but also attitudes towards war captives changed as a consequence of contact with Westerners. Sealers and whalers from New South Wales appear to have been particularly influential by way of introducing Māori to foreign ideas of racial hierarchy and hardened the way conquered people were treated in that instance. But the effect of one culture on another is not one-directional. The arrival of Christian missionaries, first in Northland and gradually through the rest of the country, had a different impact. A reduction in the use of the word 'taurekareka' and its replacement with softer words such as 'pononga' and 'mōkai' may, perhaps, have been prompted by the equivalent shift in the translated Bible, Te Paipera Tapu.

As previously mentioned, one of the first extracts from the Bible to be translated and published was Exodus 20:2–3, which, in the King James version, reads: 'I am the Lord thy God, which have brought thee out of the land of Egypt, out of the house of bondage.' More modern translations of the Bible tend to use 'slavery' rather than bondage, but whatever English word is used, it generally refers to involuntary confinement and removal from one's native home. However, that passage from Exodus was translated into Māori as: 'Ko Ihowa ahau, ko tou Atua, naku koe i whakaputa mai i te whenua o Ihipa, i te *whare pononga*' (emphasis added). The 'whare pononga' might more literally mean the servants' house or quarters and indicates that the language used here, as elsewhere in the Bible, has been softened. Missionary translators may have wanted to avoid using the much more derisory word 'taurekareka' for 'God's chosen people'. Perhaps they were afraid that potential converts would not be interested, let alone inspired, by stories of taurekareka: people who were at best of no account, or, at worst, despised wretches.

As Peter Lineham noted: 'Scholars are increasingly appreciating the way in which Bible translations have affected cultures.'[11] There are concepts in the Bible that the missionary translators found difficult to convey in Māori, and concepts in the Māori world that are difficult to translate into English. So, if English-speaking immigrants who found themselves living in a Māori-speaking world during the nineteenth century used translations of the Bible as learning aids, as the Beetham family on the Brancepeth Station in the Wairarapa did, the miscommunication would have been intensified. *Ko te tahi wahi Te Kawenata Tawhito* (the Old Testament) and *Ko te Kawenata Hou* (the New Testament), published in 1848 and 1852 respectively, were the texts the Beethams and their staff used beside Williams's 1844 *Dictionary of the New Zealand Language* to learn how to communicate with their neighbours.[12] The understandings that those settler learners of the Māori language gained from the Old and New Testaments were framed by a British Christian worldview rather than a Māori one and are likely to have entrenched the use of Bible language still further — by both peoples.

In the beginning was the word

As those who translated the Bible into Māori used the word 'taurekareka' only four times, compared with 'pononga', which appears 777 times, much the same phenomenon began to occur in subsequent Māori writing.[13] In correspondence, letters to newspapers, minutes of meetings, and other writings, taurekareka was used less frequently as time went on. The sheer vastness of Māori literature from the 1830s to the present inhibits a thorough and complete analysis of how often any particular word has been used, but taurekareka appears to have lost favour from around 1860 and into the twentieth century. Pononga seems to have replaced it. As people in today's English-speaking world tend to shy away from insensitive or derogatory terms commonly used by previous generations (such as those applied to people of colour or with mental or physical disabilities), Māori appear to have opted for less emotionally charged terms for war captives. Taurekareka became a dirty word not to be used in polite company.

What may be one of the earliest examples of 'pononga' being used by a Māori writer to refer to captives appears in a will written by Wiremu Tāmihana in 1843. In that, he outlined who was to inherit his settlements, eel-weirs, and other possessions such as pigs and potatoes as well as his 'pononga tane' and 'pononga wahine', or male and female attendants.[14] Since he was bequeathing these things, he surely had mana over them and saw them as personal assets. In other words, those 'pononga' were almost certainly war captives rather than free servants. The fact of his even preparing a written will speaks volumes with regard to the extent he had taken on Western ways of doing things. Given his strong commitment to the new faith and its values, it is somewhat curious that he did not feel they debarred him from bequeathing those human beings he referred to as his 'pononga' but retained a more customary perspective. As the CMS missionaries explained in their response to the 1838 parliamentary inquiry concerning New Zealand, when a person died, their 'slaves' would be claimed by surviving family members.[15]

Many years later, however, in April 1863, when tensions between Māori and settler were high and the government had ordered Waikato Māori to leave Auckland, then the capital, Tāmihana was concerned about the tit-for-tat expulsion of Pākehā men from the Waikato. Hoping to avoid unnecessary unpleasantness, he assured the half-caste James Fulloon, a government interpreter, that neither his 'mōkai' (pet Pākehā) nor the 'Ministers' would be violently ejected. 'They must depart in peace', he said.[16] So, Tāmihana not only avoided using the word taurekareka, by referring to his captives or slaves as pononga, but distinguished between them and the Western traders and missionaries living under his mana, whom he referred to as mōkai. Yet, while Māori were uttering

THE LANGUAGE OF SLAVERY

the word taurekareka less often themselves, Christian evangelists were less coy about applying it to other people when it suited their purposes. For example, in an 1860 edition, the Wesleyan newspaper *Te Haeata* told its Māori readers that there were many believers among the former slaves of the West Indies who were eagerly raising money for the Gospel through which they had been elevated from 'taurekareka' to 'rangatira'.[17]

For Māori though, taurekareka retained its usefulness as a term of heartfelt abuse. The word allowed an angry person to vent considerable steam, but could not be overlooked by the recipient or their wider kin group — as resident magistrates charged with overseeing George Grey's rūnanga system discovered (see Chapter 3).

The power of words may explain the extent to which the word 'pononga' came to be the new taurekareka, because the apparently new understanding of the term was sometimes spelled out quite clearly. In an 1898 Northland Land Court hearing, for example, Ngāpuhi claimed that the status of people taken prisoner had been reduced to that of pononga.[18] In more recent times, it was explained that these pononga were the survivors of battles who had been taken captive and thereby suffered a loss of mana. As such, they were reduced to being tonotono, or servants, obliged to follow orders from whoever had captured them.[19] Even more interesting is an example from John White's *The Ancient History of the Maori*, published in 1887, where in a story concerning a man named Timuaki, who is turned into a mountain by Poutiri, he is referred to as his 'ropa'. But when the word 'ropa' is first used in the Māori text, 'pononga' follows it in brackets. White appears to be inserting a gloss to explain rōpā (slave or servant) in terms of more contemporary usage.[20]

Under section 16 of the Maori Lands Administration Act 1900, papatupu block committees were established in some areas, especially in Northland. Their purpose was to allow elected committees to assist the Land Court by determining which individuals or families had an interest in their lands according to customary law and usages, and who should, therefore, have title when those lands were transferred into the British system of title. The existence of the committees turned out to be short-lived but many of the Māori-language minute books they produced are still extant.[21] Witnesses who gave evidence at these gatherings appear to use the word 'pononga' rather than taurekareka or any other term, perhaps exclusively. That was certainly the case in *Karanga Hokianga*, published in 1987, being a history of a local area as presented by thirteen rangatira at a papatupu block committee meeting at Te Karaka, Northern Hokianga, in 1903. That text, taken from the original minutes, does not contain a single example of the word 'taurekareka'. 'Mokai' appears once and 'pononga' 19 times.[22] This is in marked contrast to Sir George Grey's 1853 *Nga Mahi a Nga Tupuna*, which included 16 instances of 'taurekareka' versus 13 of 'pononga' and 23 of mōkai.[23]

More curiously, in 'The Tale of Rokiroki — A Memory of the Mokau', by Sir Māui Pōmare, which was published in English after his death in 1930, a man is referred to as a 'runaway *mokai*':

> For cannibal he was — he was hungry for man! The dead stranger was an escaped *mokai*, a slave. He was a man of the Atiawa tribe, of Taranaki, and had been taken as prisoner of war at the sacking of Pukerangiora. His captors took him to the Waikato, and after a while he escaped, and, taking to the bush, was making his way through the wilderness towards his old home in the south. He was famished for food when he reached the Mokau banks, and when he saw Rokiroki in the plantation he designed to slay him and drag his body into the secret parts of the bush and feast upon it.[24]

Of course, this thoroughly unpleasant fellow got his comeuppance. But since the word 'mōkai' more often refers to someone regarded favourably even if of junior or inferior status, this word usage is curious. Pōmare left no room for doubt as to the man's status but chose not to use an apparently more accurate, if harsh, term for a war captive. Yet he also calls him a cannibal which implies that his motive was not related to any embarrassment relating to older, pre-Christian practices. Perhaps it was the storyteller's way of stressing how evil this man was.

On the other hand, this might be an early example of another shift — to the use of mōkai instead of pononga. In other words, a further softening of the terms used for 'slave'. While still far from being examples based on scientific analysis of all instances published, some more recent publications indicate such a shift. For example, *Te Ao Hou* magazine's 1963 bilingual account of the story of Ponga and Puhihuia refers to Ponga's subordinate variously as a rōpā or a mōkai, the words being translated as attendant or slave, apparently indiscriminately.[25] Then, later still, in 1990, *He Kōrero Pūrākau mo Ngā Taunahanahatanga a Ngā Tūpuna*, which includes two stories referring to slaves, does much the same. In 'Te Haerenga o Tōhē rāua ko tana Mōkai', or 'Tōhē: A Last Journey', the elderly rangatira's companion is referred to as a mōkai in the Māori text but variously as a 'servant', 'devoted slave', and 'slave' in the English.[26] The same occurs in 'Ngātoro i Rangi rāua ko Tia', or 'Ngātoro i Rangi and Tia: Mountains of Fire'. Ngāuruhoe, a mōkai in the Māori version, is a slave or 'faithful slave' in the English.[27]

Quite apart from the influence of new value systems and moral codes, some more prosaic uses of English conventions are also evident in nineteenth- and twentieth-century Māori writing. In 1900, for example, Waata Hīpango, editor of the Māori-language newspaper *Te Tiupiri*, signed a letter published within his paper 'Na te [sic] koutou mokai' (your assistant/servant?).[28] The phrases 'pononga iti' or 'hoa pononga iti rawa', closer equivalents to the English term 'your humble servant', appear quite regularly in Māori letters to government officials and newspaper editors during the nineteenth and early twentieth centuries.[29] Perhaps Hīpango was ahead of the trend — or even set it? Yet this adoption of contemporary British letter-writing etiquette was not dissimilar to earlier practices. When Pōtatau Te Wherowhero referred to himself as 'a person of small influence', Donald McLean explained to Governor Gore Browne that: 'These expressions of humility are often used by chiefs of high rank, out of compliment to the person they are addressing, some of whom ... are frequently of inferior rank.'[30]

Political correctness

Although the phrase tends to be used pejoratively, the purpose of so-called political correctness in our own world is to eliminate prejudice. It is believed that by replacing negative, hurtful, or demeaning terms for people of different race, religion, gender, or physical or mental capacity with more neutral or inclusive ones, society will better value all people. It is about changing minds and attitudes. Although a shift to British or Western ways of thinking was apparent beyond mere language, the two

— mindset and word use — are likely to have been mutually supporting in a similar way. As changes in attitude encourage changes in vocabulary, so does vocabulary affect attitude. As was discussed in Chapter 1, a particularly poignant example of changing language use had occurred much earlier — after the 1835 invasion of Rēkohu. It is widely accepted that Moriori were treated more harshly than was customary and the circumstances behind their being referred to as 'paraiwhara' (black fella) not only reflect new attitudes towards conquered people but also hint at some of the broader ideological changes that were occurring. Moreover, the coining of the word 'paraiwhara' reminds us that languages, too, are living and ever-changing things. It is not simply a matter of adding new words to the Māori vocabulary but of changes in usage, and on a long-term basis. If pononga and mōkai meant something different from taurekareka, and slave meant something different from war captive, then the meaning derived from the texts would also be distorted and, as guides to past practice or experience, offer false evidence as well as implanting false memories.

However, it may not be coincidental that shifts in word usage became evident at a particular point in time. As previous chapters explained, Pākehā attitudes towards Māori had undergone significant change by the 1850s and tensions were high. Altering aspects of their vocabulary may have been one response to the new political climate, even if it was only one thread in the great fabric of change taking place within Māori society and between Māori and Pākehā.

New attitudes towards women, many of which were supported by Christian teachings and, often, formalised by legislation, were very evident. For example, among other 'lessons' addressed to Māori, the government's Māori-language newspaper *Ko Te Karere o Nui Tireni* published correct behaviours for readers (evidently presumed to be men) travelling to Pākehā towns to trade.[31] One of their rules was not to take women with them. The reason for this advice was not explained and was probably ignored as large numbers of women continued to accompany their menfolk on those journeys.[32] However, the limited legal capacity of women under English law was apparent from the moment Māori were offered a treaty with Britain and most rangatira women, despite their protests, were prevented from signing on the basis of their gender. Like their Pākehā counterparts, they would also be denied the right to vote for many years after self-government was introduced in 1852.

Well beyond this period of history, in 1908, the female war captive as sex object or victim of male lust was represented in terms of erotic beauty. Louis J. Steele, who painted the well-known 'Spoils to the Victor' (fig. 80), specialised in subjects from Māori history. But, as the Auckland Art Gallery's guide explained:

> he often deviated from fact for the sake of the aesthetic concept and the tastes of his European audience. The *Spoils to the Victor* has a clear affinity with the nineteenth-century European penchant for exotic subjects. The captive, half-naked Māori woman replaces the African slave or Turkish odalisque . . .[33]

So, as language is a reflection of the speaker's time and place, so is art the artist's.

Summing up

The lives of war captives, too, were a reflection of time and place. The vastness of time and the variations in geographic location, coupled with the very wide variety of impressions recorded since European contact began, do not allow for any neat conclusions. Nor can we answer the question: 'Were Māori war captives slaves?' because 'slave' is a Humpty Dumpty word. As that famous character in Lewis Carroll's book *Through the Looking-Glass* said: 'When I use a word . . . it means just what I choose it to mean, neither more nor less.' What is clear, though, is that being captured in Māori warfare was not necessarily the route to a predetermined new life but a kaleidoscope of potential conditions: not all black and white nor black and red. And while it is usually assumed that the people referred to as 'slaves' were war captives, it appears that some were not. People banished from their own communities for serious wrongdoing and, perhaps, unfortunates, like 'Reko's slave girl' (see Chapter 3), deemed to have limited economic or practical value to the community, were obliged to fill similar roles.

It seems probable that only small numbers of captives were seized prior to European contact and that most of them were women and children — the everyday needs of food preparation, cooking, and similar work being their primary function. Whether more were taken during the era of pā building or for other major engineering projects is a matter of conjecture. Male 'slaves' are mentioned in oral traditions, but changes in the use of vocabulary have made it more difficult to know whether they might have been captured as adults, raised from childhood, or were simply men of lower rank serving as companions to their masters. It is tempting to suggest, as many have, that captives received better treatment over time — either as a consequence of Western, especially Christian, influence, or because they became more valuable as economic assets. But all too often, other evidence confounds those ideas. Contrary to frequent assertions, it was clearly not okay to kill a captive without lawful reason, captives were often treated kindly, and many were welcome home, even before 1820.

In contrast to many other systems, however, the roles of those people supported distinctions of rank more than they did social distance. Captives provided a labour force but the rangatira laboured, too. The division of labour was a key difference. Captives or slaves maintained and built the authority and prestige of strong leaders through the preservation and enhancement of mana and tapu. By lighting and tending fires, cooking food, carrying loads on their backs, and performing other menial chores, they freed the rangatira for more strategic activities; from further warfare to managing the tribal economy. But as the numbers of captives taken increased over time, as they surely did during the 1820s, the demise of slavery was an equally logical phenomenon.

A very new era had begun around 1818, when the 'musket wars', which represented a big change in themselves, ushered in many other changes. The fact that the Bay of Islands and surrounding areas drew most of the overseas shipping to their shores altered the balance of power very quickly. As those communities sought more labourers to expand production and make the most of their new trading opportunities, the muskets they were able to access gave them the ability to take larger numbers of captives to answer that need. Muskets also allowed those well-positioned tribal groups to cherry-pick individuals with specialist skills from the ranks of the enemy, gaining the practical advantages of their expertise as well as enhancing their mana still further. And while experiences varied greatly by time, place, and individual inclination, the heightened concern for security — of food and arms — especially where captives were plentiful, may have encouraged harsher treatment during the 1820s. They probably went hungrier then as food stores were the cashboxes essential for purchasing more arms, and empty stomachs may have increased the temptation to steal. Other changes were apparent during the 1830s, though, as society began to rebalance. As the focus of trade shifted towards timber, and exports of potatoes and flax dropped, there was less need for workers to clear and prepare land for cultivation or to scrape flax.[34]

War captives had both spiritual and economic value but the two worked in tandem. As political tension fostered warfare, warfare provided compliant workers. More captives meant greater mana, but greater demands for the labour that would maintain and build that mana encouraged the taking of greater numbers. In the Christian era, however, as the communal society was increasingly replaced by an individualistic one, the once vital importance of tapu to the functioning of Māori society lessened. And whereas people may still be credited with mana today, the term tends to be applied in the sense of deep respect. In Lyndsay Head's words: 'the personal sacredness that policed chiefly authority evaporated with the collapse of native religion'.[35] 'Native religion' may be less prominent now but is far from extinct. Key elements have blended with Christian beliefs and practices, so tapu, like mana, may also mean different things in the twenty-first century. While many traditional practices pertaining to tapu are still observed, the word is also used as a synonym for sacred in its more Christian sense. Māori society has changed but many fundamental underpinnings have survived.

Given that CMS missionaries arrived in 1814, captives were being released from around 1830, and British government did not begin until 1840, Christianity might well seem the leading contender for bringing an end to Māori forms of bondage. Yet the second wave of missionaries, those who arrived in the 1820s and 1830s, had evinced greater concern for these captives' plight than their predecessors. Thomas Buddle, speaking in 1851, may have been the first missionary to claim that his predecessors had been responsible for ending customary practices (see Chapter 8). No earlier claims have been located, only remarks that 'slaves' were gradually being released. Christianity had begun to make its first serious inroads during the 1830s when reports of their release became more common, but there was no clear correlation between the adoption of the new faith and decisions to release captives. Some converts opted to retain theirs while non-Christians sometimes chose to set theirs free. The idea that British missionaries brought an end to 'slavery' may be a perception formed through the rose-coloured glasses of hindsight. But they did, if sometimes indirectly, facilitate the ending of intertribal warfare which, in itself, ensured an end to enslavement. As that warfare came to an end, so did captive taking. The source of new 'recruits' dried up. Missionaries, particularly the Protestant ones, were eager to redeem Māori captives when they could, but through Christ rather than through payments made to their captors. Spiritual redemption was far more important to them than the physical or social freedom of captives in the here and now — or there and then as the case may be. Balance was ultimately restored but the impetus for change had come from within Māori society.

Nor can British government be readily credited with making a dramatic change to the captives' situation. Widespread releases had been reported before this governance commenced and the process would continue for at least two more decades. There were no sudden celebrations among those who remained captives when the Treaty was signed. English law served only to ensure that the process of reduction continued. But while that process was probably a good thing for most of those individuals, it did have a very damaging impact on the authority of hereditary leaders and the cohesiveness of Māori society.

There seems to be little doubt that the extent to which enemies were captured and used as a labour force had fluctuated historically as circumstances, including economic and political conditions, altered. And conditions certainly changed from the time of the first European arrival on New Zealand shores. Trade with the early explorers, whalers, sealers, and shore-based traders; interaction with missionaries; the availability of muskets; unprecedented warfare; new methods of dispute resolution; and English law all played their part in influencing the increase or decline of Māori captive taking. But Māori had made conscious choices, including the adoption of Christianity and new mechanisms for maintaining social order, as they engaged with the world beyond their shores. There was not one catalyst for any aspect of change. Nevertheless, given the essentially spiritual nature of captivity in Māori society, with its intrinsic loss of tapu and mana, the denial of those forces by the settler government, together with the political subjugation of their leaders, was bound to convince many Māori that they had indeed been enslaved by the colonisers.

Moreover, despite the many voluntary adaptations made by Māori, the newly introduced moral codes that became entrenched as intertribal warfare and the taking of captives waned also had real impact on the way that Māori themselves perceived earlier practices. In many ways, changes in language use are part of a wider phenomenon of redefining words for political or other purposes. As the English word 'slavery' has been applied to a multitude of circumstances in Māori society historically, it has corrupted not only the original meanings of the various Māori words but also our understanding of social practices. There is a symbiotic relationship between concepts and vocabulary. Words conjure up perceptions in our minds. Beth Heke from *Once were Warriors* was deceived by a word. Māori 'slavery' was *not* 'just like them poor Negroes had to endure in America'.

This study is the personal perspective of an outsider, as we all must be to some extent. So many generations have passed since the cast of players were alive. There will be many other interpretations of how it really was. But so, too, will there always be limitations on our understanding of the past and our ability to see into the minds of those long dead. As one old man said to historian Thomas William Downes over a hundred years ago when he enquired about a Ngāti Apa ancestor who had arrived in the *Kurahaupō* waka centuries earlier:

> "Look yonder," . . . "behold those distant hills" (pointing to the Ruahine
> Range). "On those mountains are growing the totara and rimu, the maire and
> miro tree; but who can tell from this distance what they are? Our forefathers
> could have told you of these things; we cannot: the haze and mist of time and

distance obscure all detail, and our vision cannot pierce the fog. Say, friend, can you tell me of your great navigator Cook, all who were with him, and what they did?"[36]

To misquote L. P. Hartley in *The Go-Between*: 'The past is a foreign country: they [spoke] differently there.' The haze and mist of time have combined with the foreign language of nineteenth-century abolitionism to change the meanings of words and the responses they evoke. But those, like Jake the Muss, who are still troubled by captives in their whakapapa or family tree, might reflect on the words of Te Waari Carkeek who said: 'We can be proud of our heritage no matter what the circumstances of the past were for our tupuna [ancestors].'[37] There is still much to know and understand about the lives of Māori war captives, but if a new conversation can begin, a clearer image might emerge from the gloom and bring the 'outcasts' of history into the light of day.

APPENDIX: TERMS IN TE REO MĀORI

General te reo terms

ahi kaa roa	long-burning fires or continuous occupation
ariki	paramount chief
atua	god
haka	fierce rhythmical dance; posture dance
hākari	feast
hapū	tribal group
hei tiki	item of personal adornment; usually made from pounamu and worn around the neck
ika	fish
iwi	tribe
kāinga	village or settlement
karakia	incantation
kāuta	cookhouse
Kīngitanga	Māori King Movement
kōrero	talk, discussion, story
kūmara	sweet potato
mākutu	to bewitch
mana	influence, prestige, power; a psychic force
mana whenua	control, authority over land
Māori	indigenous New Zealander
mauri ora	life force
muru	retributive plundering raid
noa	free from tapu
pā	fortified settlement
Pākehā	person of European descent
pare	lintel
pātaka	storehouse
pou rāhui	post signifying that the area is under tapu
pounamu	greenstone or nephrite jade
puhi	ritually set aside virgin
rangatira	chief or person of high rank
rangatiratanga	chiefly authority
Rēkohu	the Chatham Islands
take	cause, grounds for dispute
taniwha	supernatural creature
tangata whenua	local people; those with mana over the area
tangi	wailing, lamentation or funeral
tapatapa	to call an article by someone's name to confer sanctity on it
tapu	spiritual restriction
taua	war party
taua muru	retributive plundering party
tika	correct or just
tikanga	correct way of behaving; customary law
tohunga tā moko	master tattooist
tohunga whakairo	master carver

tuku whenua	gifting of land rights
utu	revenge, retaliation, restoration of balance
whānau	family
whakapapa	genealogy
wharenui	meeting house

Terms relating to captivity, servitude and low status

The following list of words relating to captivity, servitude and low status gives definitions and explanations for the terms, further notes, and relevant examples of usage.

apa   a group of workers and slaves, or a slave, work gang. (The root 'apa' does not in itself indicate subjugation, as a related term, aparangi, refers to a company of important persons.)
- *Ka whakaorangia ētahi hei apa, hei mahi*. Some were left alive to be slaves, to do the work.
- *He apa mātou nō Hongi*. We're Hongi's slaves.
- Related phrases seem to appear frequently in the Bible: e.g. Genesis 27:37 'kua hoatu hoki ona tuakana katoa ki a ia hei apa' / 'and all his brethren I have given to him as servants'.
- Deuteronomy 20:11 'katahi ka waiho nga tangata katoa e kitea e koe ki reira hei kaihomai takoha ki a koe, hei apa ano ratou mau' / 'that all the people that is found therein shall be tributaries unto them, and they shall serve thee'.

awhenga   vassal people, as a weak tribe saved from destruction out of pitying contempt (as opposed to 'awhina', assisting kin). See Elsdon Best, 'Notes on the Art of War', p. 212.

hunga   people, a group or crowd of people, the masses; can also be used in the sense of 'a slave'. Related to the term kahunga.

kahunga   seems to have 'slave' as its primary meaning. Possibly relates to *kaunaga* in Tonga, East Fortuna, West Uvea and East Uvea (www.pollex.org.nz).
- *He kahunga koe noku.*

kaihaumi   applied to a person who wanders over lands of others where he has no rights and takes resources (Williams, 2004). Possibly Ngāi Tahu usage.

kaitonotono (or tonotono)   literally one who takes orders (and therefore including slaves)

kakanga   derived from kanga, 'to curse'. Possibly a Te Rarawa term.

karokaro   slave. The reduplicated form of karo ('pick out of a hole'); from Proto Fijiic *kalo ('pick something out of a hole, excavate'), denoting a marauding party as well as a slave.

kikiki   drunken or mad slave, idiot or fool; also a name for Europeans

konene   stranger or wanderer; a person belonging to a tribe that has been broken up or scattered

kuki   slave. Loan word or transliteration from the English word 'cook'.

mahimahi   term for low-born or plebeian (primary meaning 'copulate')

mau herehere   hostage, someone held captive

mōkai   slave, captive, subject, servant, pet. Also young child, especially the youngest in the family. 'Kaura mōkai' is a term of derision occurring in a Ngāti Porou haka (cited in Orbell, 1968).
- *Ko tāna mōkai i hōmai e tōna tuakana hei whāngai māna*. Her older sister gave her a child to foster.
- *Mōkai pai mā māuiui whakatere*. Illness can humble even a strong person.

- *Ko tōku pononga mōkai tēnā.* That one is my servant.
- *He kurī tāna mōkai.* She had a pet dog.

mōri   person of no account. From Proto Central Eastern Polynesian *mōrï, 'a person of low rank'.

ngongo   low-born or plebeian. Core meaning to waste away or languish physically or psychologically, thus 'to become thin; to pine, to be sad and withdrawing'; also to be an invalid – from Proto Fijiic [cf. 'mori', a bone] *ngongo* (weak, wasted away).

ngoringori   a small black eel; slave. As 'slave', possibly restricted to Taranaki; for an example of usage, see 'Raumahora and Takarangi. A Legend of the Taranaki Tribes', *Journal of the Polynesian Society*, 36, 143, 1927, pp. 239–59. Ngoringori are not mentioned in R. M. McDowall's *Ikawai* which does include ngorengore, a smelt (fish not eel).

- *[Tūmatauenga] ing, āhua. He tangata kore mana ka mauheretia hei kaimahi mā tētahi atu. Whakamaua ai he mekameka rino ki ngā waewae o ngā ngoringori kia kore ai rātou e oma.*

ora   slave. The word 'ora' (normally referring to being alive, healthy and well) was also sometimes used to denote a slave, as someone who had been saved from a worse fate (this meaning of ora may come not from Proto Polynesian *ora, 'alive' etc., but from *sola, 'flee'); such survival may have been somewhat tenuous, judging by expressions such as toenga kai 'left-over food', a contemptuous expression for an enslaved survivor whose comrades or relatives had been eaten, and taitai waka, referring to a ceremony of dedicating a canoe, which included the sacrifice of a slave to complete the proceedings.

- Margaret Orbell, *Traditional Māori Stories*, p. 126 by unknown author from Te Akau, north of Raglan, re 'He puhi makutu (The terrible Head)'.
- George Grey, *Nga Mahi a Nga Tupuna*, p. 156: 'Ka haere tonu atu māua ko taku ora.' 'My slave and I journeyed on.'

pahī   serf, slave, person of low birth. Pahī, a term indicating a large ocean-going vessel in most Eastern Polynesian languages (including Māori), extends its scope to refer to expeditions, groups of travellers, places where such people camp temporarily, sections of a tribe, and also to slaves and people regarded as being of little worth; may be connected with pahī, as someone seized by an expedition. See also 'pori' and Jim Williams's remarks concerning that word.

- Minutes of CMS Sub-Committee, May 1839, CN/M M11, Micro-MS-Coll-4 33, ATL, Wellington, p. 424: 'There are those who being broken up as a people fly to some other tribe. These are called pahis, and may be considered as holding a middle station between freeman and slaves.'

paihi   slave; 'uneasy in mind'. See ngongo above.

paraiwhara   Moriori people conquered by Māori. A transliteration of 'black fellow', applied by Māori to Moriori.

parakau   slave; young flounder

pararau   slave, dependant. Term of opprobrium, with connotations of lack of merit, indolence or personal worthlessness.

pararau ware   person of no consequence

pārau   slave or war captive. 'Rau' can mean catch, as in a net. Also possibly relevant is that *parau* refers to a black pearl oyster shell in Cook Islands Māori and *matau parau* to a trolling lure, while *ahu parau* refers to a mourner's chest apron in Society Islands.

- Richard Davis, Journal, 20 March 1833: 'Parau … the most abject name or appellation that they can make use of.'
- *Ka riro taku tamaiti i te parau.* My child has been taken captive (as a slave).

paruauru   labourer

- *Te Wananga*, 24 August 1878, p. 418: *E kore te Maori e pai kia riro ana whenua ki te iwi ke, i te mea kei kiia ai he Hunga, he Pori, he Paruauru, i te mea hoki he ingoa*

	kino aua kupu ana kiia ki a ia e te iwi ke. The Māori would never like his lands to be taken by another people lest he is called a slave, a dependant, a labourer because those words are bad names when he is called that by another race.
piriawaawa	leech or metaphorical term for a homeless wanderer, skulk, or loafer. See William Colenso, *The Authentic and Genuine History of the Signing of the Treaty of Waitangi*, p. 22.
piringa	persons who have claims to land from their family connections, but of secondary importance to the claims of those who reside on and cultivate them; from 'piri,' sticking; possibly Ngāi Tahu usage. See Edward Shortland, *The Southern Districts of New Zealand*, p. 312.
piritoka	limpet or metaphorical term for a homeless wanderer, skulk, or loafer. See William Colenso, *The Authentic and Genuine History of the Signing of the Treaty of Waitangi*, p. 22.
poketara	low class of people without rights to resources, a landless class; suggests one who has been ejected from society due to an anti-social action; possibly Ngāi Tahu usage
pononga	slave, captive, subject, pet, disciple; servant, stalwart, one who takes responsibility for being of service to others. Examples from *Taitokerau Māori Dictionary*: • *Tino pononga tēnā tangata nā taua whānau rā*. He was a real slave to that family. • *Ko toku pononga mokai tēnā*. That one is my servant. • *I roto i ngā whānau katoa ko ngā pononga anōē kei muri e mahi ana i ngā mahi*. In all families one will always find the same people carrying the responsibilities for the rest of the family. • *Ina, te pononga a te Ariki*. Behold the handmaid of the Lord. (Possibly derived from pono [2] 'come upon; taunt', but the second sense echoes pono [1] 'fidelity'.) In modern Māori at least, pononga can refer to a servant or assistant who is performing that role on a voluntary basis; it has also been noted that the word pononga is now (in the twenty-first century) used to refer to people who support or believe in a chief or leader (of a religious or political group).
pori	subservient tribe or hapū, people, dependants. NB: hapori = section of a tribe or family. • *E kiia ana e Tinirau kia mahia e ana pori he whare pera me to Kae.* • *Ko nga wahine me nga tamariki o aua iwi, i waiho e Turi hei pori mana.* • Jim Williams, 'E Pākihi Hakinga a Kai', p. 122: 'Pahi are similar, the difference being that pori implies vassalage whereas pahi are fully independent, e.g. a subhapu.' • John White, *The Ancient History of the Maori*, vol. III, p. 280: reference to the personal name Taupori as meaning 'slave-attendant' (Ngāi Tahu usage?).
poroteke	slave, person in a menial position, scamp, loafer
rahi	seems to have 'slave' as its primary meaning. Ngāti Maru term (?). See Edward Shortland, *Maori Religion and Mythology*, p. 95 re rahi as vassal tribe; and Bruce Biggs, *Complete English Maori Dictionary*.
rōērā	powerless indifferent, subdued, subject, cowardly, shamed, exposed to ridicule or contempt
rōpā	slave or servant; from rōēpā, 'subordinate person or group' • *Katahi a Marutuahu raua ko tana rōēpā ka haere mai.*
tākatahara	similar to poketara; suggests one who has been ejected from society due to an anti-social action. See Jim Williams, 'E Pākihi Hakinga a Kai', p. 122. Possibly Ngāi Tahu usage.
tangata	person. Can refer also to an agricultural labourer, and analogous to English 'my man'.

taureka   slave? Used in 'He Patere', George Grey, *Ko nga Moteatea, me nga Hakirara o nga Maori*, p. 247. See 'taurekareka' below. Possibly a literary usage.

taurekareka   slave taken in war, a nobody, family worker, one spurned, larrikin, scoundrel, waster. Examples from *Te Papakupu o te Taitokerau*:
- *Kaua e whakarongo ki a ia, he mahi taurekareka kē āna nei mahi*. Don't listen to him, he is a scoundrel.
- *He taurekareka ia*. He is a nobody.
- *Koia ano te tikanga a te taurekareka*. Such is the dastardly action of a larriken [sic].

The entry in Te Papakupu o te Taitokerau goes on to read: '[Note from *Te Mātāpunenga*] **Taurekareka**. A common term applied to a prisoner of war, and a slave, and by extension a rogue or scoundrel. Taurekareka is the reflex of a Proto-Polynesian word *taulekaleka, meaning "youth, young man; handsome".' Similarly, Edward Tregear, in 'Curious Polynesian Words', pp. 540–1, says: 'Taurekareka, a slave; a rascal, a scoundrel. There is no such meaning to be found in the other island dialects. In Samoan taule'ale'a is a young man: in Tahiti taurearea means the young, healthy, and vigorous of the people. In Tongan toulekaleka is a beauty, a handsome man; goodly; well-proportioned. Ext. Poly.: In Sikayana taurekareka is handsome. There is evidently a remarkable reversal of meaning in the New Zealand word, exactly akin to the European degradation of the word slav, glorious (a member of the Slavonic race), into our English slave. If the process by which taurekareka was thus degraded could be traced, it would doubtless have historical value.'

tia   may denote slave or servant.
- Margaret Orbell, *Traditional Māori Stories*, p. 33: the phrase 'he tia ma ratou' appears in the story 'Ruru-teina'. The youngest son in this story was treated very badly by brothers. Treated like slave (original source MS: Wohlers, Ruapuke Island, 1876 MS, original date c. 1850).

tipai   untattooed face; a sign the man would be made a slave of (Taylor, 1855); mollusc or scallop. See Richard Taylor, *A leaf from the natural history of New Zealand, or, A vocabulary of its different productions, &c., &c*, p. 79.

toenga, kai toenga, kaitia toenga kainga   left-over food. See 'ora' above; and see Bruce Biggs, *Complete English Maori Dictionary*: kept as a slave = toenga kaitia.

tonotono   see kaitonono: 1. (stative) be bossy; 2. (noun) dogsbody, gofer, lackey. Probably a modern term.

tūmou / tūmau   refers simultaneously to both 'slave' and 'cook'. Tūmou: 1. slave, servant; 2. cook (because cooking was destructive of tapu).

tūtūā   mean; low-born.
- *E kore te rangatira o te Mahuremahure e pai kia moe tuutuua tana tama a Hoone*. The chief of Mahurehure did not want his son Hone to marry a low-born.

ware / wareware   a term for someone of low social status, but who is not a slave. Wareware: 'of no account, mean, low-born'. From Proto-Polynesian *wale, 'mad, ignorant, unskilled'. Ihaaka Takanini & others in the *Maori Messenger: Ko Te Karere Maori*, 15 December 1860, p. 14 used the word 'ware' as a synonym for tūtūa.

whakarau   prisoner. For examples of usage, see Judith Binney, '"In-between" Lives: Studies from within a Colonial Society', in *Disputed Histories: Imagining New Zealand's Pasts*, p. 112; Ernst Dieffenbach, *Travels in New Zealand*. Wakarau = making a hundred, collecting a number of slaves together (translated by a Pākehā) in *Maori Messenger: Ko Te Karere Maori*, 18 July 1863 re invasions of early England.

Sources

A number of sources were used in compiling this list of terms and many, especially dictionaries, gave identical definitions. For ease of use and in order to avoid extensive referencing, most sources have not been individually identified. However, the principal references are as follows.

Bennion, Tom, *Māori Law Review*, May 2001, at: http://maorilawreview.co.nz/2001/05/
Benton, Richard A., ed., *Te Papakupu o te Taitokerau* (*Taitokerau* Māori Dictionary), 2001, revised 2006
Benton, Richard, Alex Frame & Paul Meredith, *Te Mātāpunenga: A Compendium of References to the Concepts and Institutions of Māori Customary Law*, Hamilton, 2013
Best, Elsdon, 'Notes on the Art of War, as Conducted by the Maori of New Zealand, with Accounts of Various Customs, Rites, Superstitions, &C., Pertaining to War, as Practised and Believed in by the Ancient Maori', New Plymouth, 1902
Biggs, Bruce, *The Complete English Maori Dictionary*, Auckland, 1992 (first published 1981)
Colenso, William, *The Authentic and Genuine History of the Signing of the Treaty of Waitangi*, Wellington, 1890
Dieffenbach, Ernst, *Travels in New Zealand: With Contributions to the Geography, Botany, and Natural History of That Country*, London, 1843
Grey, George, *Ko nga Moteatea, me nga Hakirara o nga Maori*, Wellington, 1853
——, *Nga Mahi a Nga Tupuna: Ha Mea Kohikohi Mai*, London, 1854
McDowall, R. M., *Ikawai: Freshwater Fishes in Māori Culture and Economy*, Christchurch, 2011
Niupepa Māori: Māori Newspapers, at: http://www.nzdl.org/cgi-bin/library.cgi?a=p&p=about&c=niupepa
Orbell, Margaret, *Maori Folktales in Maori and English*, Auckland, 1968
——, *Traditional Māori Stories*, introduced and translated by Margaret Orbell, Auckland, 1997
Pollex (Polynesian Lexicon Project Online), at: http://pollex.org.nz/
Shortland, Edward, *The Southern Districts of New Zealand; A Journal, with Passing Notices of the Customs of the Aborigines*, London, 1851
——, *Maori Religion and Mythology*, London, 1882
Taylor, Richard, *Te Ika a Maui: New Zealand and Its Inhabitants*, London, 1855
Te Aka Māori-English, English-Māori Dictionary and Index, at: http://www.maoridictionary.co.nz/
Tregear, Edward, 'Curious Polynesian Words', *Transactions and Proceedings of the New Zealand Institute* (*TPNZI*), 23, 1890, pp. 540–1
Wakareo ā-ipurangi, at: http://www.reotupu.co.nz/WSLiveWakareo/Default.aspx
White, John, *The Ancient History of the Maori, His Mythology and Traditions*, 13 vols, Hamilton, 2001
Williams, H. W., *A Dictionary of the Maori Language*, 7th edn, Wellington, 2000
Williams, Jim, 'E Pākihi Hakinga a Kai', PhD thesis, 2004, University of Otago, Dunedin

NOTES

Introduction

1. Alan Duff, *Once Were Warriors*, Auckland, 1994, pp. 102–3.
2. For example, John Robinson, 'Why the Treaty?', in *Twisting the Treaty: A Tribal Grab for Wealth and Power*, Wellington, 2013, p. 26. More grass-roots examples appear in internet blogs and letters to the editors of newspapers at: http://www.kiwiblog.co.nz/, www.kilts.co.nz/mhorruairidh.htm, www.siliconinvestor.com/, & www.whitenewsnow.com/new-zealand-news-white-new-zealand/14578-celtic-viking-traces-ancient-new-zealand-3-print.html (all accessed 18 May 2014) & *New Zealand Herald*, 11 February 2014.
3. For example, Robinson, *Twisting the Treaty*, pp. 18–19 & 22; John Robinson, *The Corruption of New Zealand Democracy: A Treaty Overview*, Wellington, 2011. Internet blogs and letters to editors are also readily accessible promoters of these ideas, too, as at: v8-coupe, at www.fishing.net.nz/asp_forums/200m-with-taranaki-iwi_topic86177_p3.html, accessed 18 May 2014. A *New Zealand Herald* correspondent claimed similarly that 'had it not been for the interfering Europeans their campaign of extermination and domination of other tribes would likely have been completed' (11 February 2014).
4. Robinson, *Twisting the Treaty*, p. 20.
5. Among those who thought it benign were: William Colenso, 'On the Maori Races of New Zealand', *Transactions and Proceedings of the New Zealand Institute*, 1, 1868, p. 22; Edward Tregear, *The Maori Race*, Wanganui, 1904, p. 155; & James Busby cited in Angela Ballara, 'Warfare and Government in Ngapuhi Tribal Society: 1814–1833', MA thesis, University of Auckland, 1973. Other examples are cited in Chapter 3. Examples of more negative representations also appear in the text but include Robert McNab, *Historical Records of New Zealand*, 2 vols, vol. 1, Wellington, 1908, pp. 538 & 543.
6. Examples of this perspective include: *A Historical Guide to World Slavery*, New York, 1998, p. 307; Angela Ballara, *Taua: 'Musket Wars', 'Land Wars' or Tikanga? Warfare in Māori Society in the Early Nineteenth Century*, Auckland, 2003, pp. 100–1; Harry C. Evison, *Te Wai Pounamu — The Greenstone Island: A History of the Southern Maori During the European Colonization of New Zealand*, Wellington, 1993, pp. 10 & 51; Noelene Hall, "*I Have Planted . . .*" *A Biography of Alfred Nesbit Brown*, Palmerston North, 1981, p. 44; Karl Scherzer, *Narrative of the Circumnavigation of the Globe by the Austrian Frigate Novara*, 3 vols, vol. 3, London, 1863, p. 117; Charles Darwin, *Journal of Researches into the Geology and Natural History of the Various Countries Visited by H.M.S. Beagle*, London, 1839, p. 505.
7. Ballara, *Taua*, pp. 100 & 101.
8. See, for example, David Brion Davis, *Inhuman Bondage: The Rise and Fall of Slavery in the New World*, Oxford, 2005, p. 89; E. S. D. Fomin, *A Comparative Study of Societal Influences on Indigenous Slavery in Two Types of Societies in Africa*, Ceredigion, pp. 198–201.
9. Suzanne Miers, 'Slavery: A Question of Definition', *Slavery & Abolition*, 24, 2, 2003, p. 1.
10. Stanley L. Engerman, *Slavery, Emancipation, and Freedom: Comparative Perspectives*, Baton Rouge, 2007, p. 91.
11. David Brion Davis, *Slavery and Human Progress*, New York, 1984, p. 12.
12. Edvard Hviding explained that interisland raiding in New Georgia was 'founded above all on the regular ritual cycles that required *mana* for the propitiation of ancestral and other spirits': Edvard Hviding, *Guardians of Marovo Lagoon: Practice, Place, and Politics in Maritime Melanesia*, Honolulu, 1996, p. 89.
13. Tregear, *The Maori Race*, pp. 156–7; Raymond Firth, *Economics of the New Zealand Maori*, 2nd edn, Wellington, 1959, p. 214.
14. Atholl Anderson, *The Welcome of Strangers: An Ethnohistory of Southern Maori A.D. 1650–1850*, Dunedin, 1998, p. 225, fn. 2.
15. The idea that New Zealand represented a possibly unique example of idealist or humanitarian colonial development, suggested in work such as Keith Sinclair, 'Why Are Race Relations in New Zealand Better Than in South Africa, South Australia or South Dakota?', *New Zealand Journal of History*, 5, 2, 1971, had been challenged by Ian Wards, *The Shadow of the Land: A Study of British Policy and Racial Conflict in New Zealand 1832–1852*, Wellington, 1968 and later by Alan Ward, *A Show of Justice: Racial 'Amalgamation' in Nineteenth Century New Zealand*, Auckland,

1995. Research related to claims put forward to the Waitangi Tribunal since 1995 has also added much to the critique of Crown policies towards Māori. Recent work suggesting that missionaries may have received greater credit than their due includes Allan Davidson, 'Early Protestant Missionary Beginnings in New Zealand through Different Lenses', in *Te Rongopai 1814 — 'Takoto te pai!': Bicentenary Reflections on Christian Beginnings and Developments in Aotearoa New Zealand*, Allan Davidson, Stuart Lange, Peter Lineham & Adrienne Puckey, eds, Auckland, 2014, p. 45 & Geoffrey Troughton, 'Missionaries, Historians & the Peace Tradition', in *Te Rongopai 1814 — 'Takoto te pai!': Bicentenary Reflections on Christian Beginnings and Developments in Aotearoa New Zealand*, Allan Davidson, Stuart Lange, Peter Lineham & Adrienne Puckey, eds, Auckland, 2014, p. 234.

16 'Swamping' is a term used by James Belich for this process in his book *Making Peoples: A History of the New Zealanders From Polynesian Settlement to the End of the Nineteenth Century*, Auckland, 1996, p. 249.

17 The various versions were published between 1824 and 1878: Alexander Maxwell & Evan Roberts, 'The Whangaroa Incident, 16 July 1824: A European–Maori Encounter and Its Many Incarnations', *The Journal of Pacific History*, 49, 1, 2014, p. 75 & passim.

18 Ibid., p. 66.

19 See Hazel Petrie, *Chiefs of Industry: Maori Tribal Enterprise in Early Colonial New Zealand*, Auckland, 2006, pp. 182–6.

20 Andrew P. Vayda, *Maori Warfare*, Wellington, 1960.

21 Andrew P. Vayda, 'Maori Prisoners and Slaves in the Nineteenth Century', *Ethnohistory*, 8, 2, 1961.

22 Andrew P. Vayda, 'Maoris and Muskets in New Zealand: Disruption of a War System', *Political Science Quarterly*, 85, 4, 1970.

23 Ballara, *Taua*, 2003.

24 Ibid., pp. 17–28.

25 Boyd Hilton has examined the ways in which new religious ideas about the nature of God and the Atonement affected contemporary thinking more widely in Boyd Hilton, *The Age of Atonement: The Influence of Evangelicalism on Social and Economic Thought 1785–1865*, Oxford & New York, 1991.

26 As early as the seventeenth century, promoters of colonisation insisted that the 'humanity of the English' would effect 'much gaine upon' the indigenous peoples of the Americas: *New Englands First Fruits*, London, 1643, cited in Michael Guasco, 'To "Doe Some Good Upon Their Countrymen": The Paradox of Indian Slavery in Early Anglo-America', *Journal of Social History*, 41, 2, 2007, p. 391.

27 It has been argued that the Apprenticeship scheme in Jamaica and various other examples of freed slaves being less than completely free defy the idea that slavery was abolished in toto. There is much literature on this subject including Catherine Hall, *Civilising Subjects: Metropole and Colony in the English Imagination, 1830–1867*, Oxford, 2002 & Anita Rupprecht, '"When He Gets among His Countrymen, They Tell Him That He Is Free": Slave Trade Abolition, Indentured Africans and a Royal Commission', *Slavery & Abolition*, 33, 3, 2012. Marika Sherwood's provocative study pays particular attention to the ways in which Britain continued to benefit from the slave trade after official abolition: Marika Sherwood, *After Abolition: Britain and the Slave Trade since 1807*, London, 2007.

28 *New Zealand Spectator and Cook's Strait Guardian*, 7 June 1845, p. 2.

29 Some historians have touched on the reasons for the release of many slaves from the 1830s, especially as a peacemaking process. See, for example, Belich, *Making Peoples*, p. 168 & Vincent O'Malley, *The Meeting Place: Māori and Pākehā Encounters, 1642–1840*, Auckland, 2012, p. 202.

30 An 1874 survey found that *Self Help* was one of the most commonly held books in Auckland provincial libraries — which might be further evidence that independence and self-reliance were values held even more strongly by settlers in New Zealand than back in their original homeland: Glenda Northey, 'Accessible to all? Libraries in the Auckland Provincial Area, 1842–1919', MA thesis, University of Auckland, 1998, Appendix XI, p. 178.

31 R. W. Emerson, *Self Reliance*, 1841 (serialised in *Blackwood's Edinburgh Magazine*, vol. 62 (386), December 1847, p. 646).

32 Davis, *Slavery and Human Progress*, pp. 8–9.

33 Thomas Lambert, *The Story of Old Wairoa and the East Coast District, New Zealand, or, Past, Present and Future: A Record of over Fifty Years' Progress*, Dunedin, 1925, p. 117.

34 Paul Moon, *This Horrid Practice: The Myth and Reality of Traditional Maori Cannibalism*, Auckland, 2008, p. 191. 'Viewpoint', a 2005 paper by Mr I. Parker of Taranaki making the same point about captives being a source of protein food, once available on the New Zealand Human Rights Commission's website (in June 2009) is still available

at time of writing via the Google search engine in 2014 at: http://www.hrc.co.nz/hrc/worddocs/3%20-%20Mr%20I%20Parker%2019%20May%202005.doc.
35 Robinson, *Twisting the Treaty*, p. 20.
36 Lea argued that he had been misquoted and misrepresented by 'media hype' in a subsequent article: Rod Lea & Geoffrey Chambers, 'Monoamine Oxidase, Addiction, and the "Warrior" Gene Hypothesis', *New Zealand Medical Journal*, 120, 1250, 2007.
37 Christina A. Thompson, 'A Dangerous People Whose Only Occupation Is War: Maori and Pakeha in 19th-century New Zealand', *The Journal of Pacific History*, 32, 1, 1997, p. 113; Franchesca Walker, '"Descendants of a Warrior Race": The Maori Contingent, New Zealand Pioneer Battalion, and Martial Race Myth, 1914–1919', *War & Society*, 31, 1, 2011, p. 10.
38 For example, Junius P. Rodriguez, *Chronology of World Slavery*, Santa Barbara, 1999. The *Cambridge World History of Slavery* currently covers only the Ancient Mediterranean world, Africa, Asia, Eastern Europe, and the Americas. *A Historical Guide to World Slavery* devotes one page to indigenous slavery in Oceania generally; *The Historical Encyclopedia of World Slavery* discusses only external slavery in Oceania from the second half of the nineteenth century.
39 Seymore Drescher & Stanley L. Engerman, eds, *A Historical Guide to World Slavery*, New York, 1998, p. 364.
40 The *Journal of the Polynesian Society* devoted a special issue to 'Essays on Head-Hunting in the Western Solomon Islands' in 2000 but these essays make frequent reference to captives and slaves.
41 Debra McDougall, 'Paths of *Pinauzu*: Captivity and Social Reproduction in Ranongga', *Journal of the Polynesian Society*, 109, 1, 2000, pp. 99 & 101.
42 Guasco, 'To "Doe Some Good Upon Their Countrymen"', p. 399.
43 For a discussion regarding the existence of these principles across the regions covered by the orthodox categories of Polynesia, Melanesia, and Micronesia, see, for example: Paul Rainbird, 'Taking the Tapu: Defining Micronesia by Absence', *The Journal of Pacific History*, 38, 2, 2003.
44 Raymond T. Smith, 'Race, Class and Gender', in *The Meaning of Freedom: Economics, Politics, and Culture after Slavery*, Frank McGlynn & Seymour Drescher, eds, Pittsburgh & London, 1992; Cleve Barlow, *Tikanga Whakaaro: Key Concepts in Maori Culture*, Auckland, 1992, p. 61.

45 Barlow, *Tikanga Whakaaro*, p. 128.
46 Davis, *Inhuman Bondage*, p. 78.
47 Some of the many varieties are discussed in works such as *Native American Adoption, Captivity, and Slavery in Changing Contexts*, New York, 2012; James F. Brooks, 'Epilogue: Captive, Concubine, Servant, Kin: A Historian Divines Experience in Archaeological Slaveries', in *Invisible Citizens: Captives and Their Consequences*, Catherine M. Cameron, ed., Salt Lake City, 2008.
48 For example, concerning the Amazonian countries of South America, see Brenda J. Bowser, 'Captives in Amazonia: Becoming Kin in a Predatory Landscape', in *Invisible Citizens: Captives and Their Consequences*, Catherine M. Cameron, ed., Salt Lake City, 2008.
49 Theda Perdue, *Slavery and the Evolution of Cherokee Society 1540–1866*, Knoxville, 1979, cited in Steve Russell, 'Apples Are the Color of Blood', *Critical Sociology*, 28, 1, 2002, p. 70.
50 Judith A. Bennett, *Wealth of the Solomons: A History of a Pacific Archipelago, 1800–1978*, Honolulu, c. 1987, p. 13; Fomin, *A Comparative Study of Societal Influences on Indigenous Slavery*, p. 13.

Chapter 1: By black and red together, the work is done

1 Richard Taylor, *Te Ika a Maui: New Zealand and Its Inhabitants*, London, 1855, p. 127.
2 William Colenso, 'Art. VII.—Contributions Towards a Better Knowledge of the Maori Race', *Transactions and Proceedings of the New Zealand Institute*, 12, 1879, p. 116.
3 Bronwen Douglas, 'Slippery Word, Ambiguous Praxis: "Race" and Late-18th-Century Voyagers in Oceania', *The Journal of Pacific History*, 41, 1, 2006, p. 3.
4 Morgan Godwyn, *The Negro's and Indians Advocate*, London, 1680, cited in Guasco, 'To "Doe Some Good Upon Their Countrymen"', p. 399.
5 Mukti Barton, 'I Am Black and Beautiful', *Black Theology: An International Journal*, 2, 2, 2004.
6 Davis, *Inhuman Bondage*, p. 57.
7 Archdeacon Walsh, 'Art. II.—On the Maori Method of Preparing and Using Kokowai', *Transactions and Proceedings of the New Zealand Institute*, 36, 1903, p. 8.
8 George French Angas, *Savage Life and Scenes in Australia and New Zealand: Being an Artist's Impressions of Countries and People at the Antipodes*, 2 vols, vol. 2, London, 1847, p. 101.

9. Andrew Sharp, *Duperrey's Visit to New Zealand in 1824*, Andrew Sharp, ed., Wellington, 1971, p. 87.
10. George Grey, *Ko Nga Whakapepeha Me Nga Whakaahuareka a Nga Tipuna o Aotea-Roa*, Cape Town, 1857, p. 54.
11. Elsdon Best, *The Maori as He Was: A Brief Account of Maori Life as It Was in Pre-European Days*, Wellington, 1934, p. 233.
12. Anne Salmond, 'Te Ao Tawhito: A Semantic Approach to the Traditional Maori Cosmos', *Journal of the Polynesian Society*, 87, 1978, p. 12.
13. Hirini Moko Mead & Neil Grove, *Ngā Pēpeha a Ngā Tīpuna: The Sayings of the Ancestors*, Wellington, 2004, p. 426.
14. Ibid.
15. James Morrison, 'The Journal of James Morrison, Boatswain's Mate of the Bounty, Describing the Mutiny and Subsequent Misfortunes of the Mutineers Together with an Account of the Island of Tahiti', in *Exploration & Exchange: A South Seas Anthology: 1680–1900*, Vanessa Smith, Jonathan Lamb & Nicholas Thomas, eds, London, 2000, p. 52.
16. George Grey, *Polynesian Mythology and Ancient Traditional History of the New Zealand Race*, Auckland, 1885, pp. 88–89.
17. Walter L. Buller, 'On the Addition of the Red-Tailed Tropic Bird (Photon Rubricauda) to the Avifauna of New Zealand', *Transactions and Proceedings of the Royal Society of New Zealand*, 10, 1877, p. 219.
18. W. B. Monkhouse, *The Journals of Captain James Cook on His Voyages of Discovery* (Journal, Appendix IV), J. C. Beaglehole, ed., Kraus Reprint edn, vol. 1, pt 2, Millwood, NY, 1988, pp. 572 & 573.
19. Personal communication, Maureen Lander, 2006. James Barry was a lay member of the Church Missionary Society.
20. T. T. R. Mokena, 'The Structural Framework of the Māori Quest Story', PhD thesis, University of Auckland, 2005, p. 300.
21. David A. Chappell, *Double Ghosts: Oceanian Voyagers on Euroamerican Ships*, Armonk, NY, c. 1997, p. 49.
22. Edward Markham, *New Zealand or Recollections of It*, Wellington, 1963, pp. 46–47.
23. *Te Ao Hou*, 51, June 1965, p. 15.
24. Anne Salmond, *Two Worlds: First Meetings of Maori and Europeans 1642–1772*, Auckland, 1993, p. 62.
25. Grove & Mead, *Ngā Pēpeha a Ngā Tīpuna*, p. 179.
26. Martin Wikaira, 'Patupaiarehe — Encounters with patupaiarehe', in *Te Ara — the Encyclopedia of New Zealand*, updated 22 September 2012, at: http://www.TeAra.govt.nz/en/patupaiarehe/page-2. It is possible that the offence caused by cooked food and restrictions on various resources could imply that the term patupaiarehe may have related to earlier inhabitants of the land who had greater mana than the newer Māori arrivals.
27. Chris D. Paulin, 'Perspectives of Māori Fishing History and Techniques. Ngā Āhua me Ngā Pūrākau me Ngā Hangarau Ika o te Māori', *Tuhinga*, 18, 2007, p. 18.
28. *Te Puke ki Hikurangi*, 1 September 1905, p. 6.
29. *Te Toa Takatini*, 1 June 1926, p. 413.
30. Translation by Hohipere Tarau.
31. George Grey, *Polynesian Mythology & Ancient Traditional History of the New Zealanders as Furnished by Their Priests and Chiefs*, London, 1855, p. 106.
32. J. F. H. Wohlers, 'The Mythology and Traditions of the Maori in New Zealand', *Transactions and Proceedings of the Royal Society of New Zealand*, 7, 1874, p. 51.
33. Christine Tremewan, *Traditional Stories from Southern New Zealand: He Kōrero Nō Te Wai Pounamu*, Christchurch, 2002, p. 271.
34. Taylor, *Te Ika a Maui*, p. 111; Mokena, 'The Structural Framework of the Māori Quest Story', p. 124.
35. 'The Story of Reiapanga', Alexander Shand, 'The Moriori People of the Chatham Islands: Their Traditions and History: Chapter X.—Moriori Stories', *Journal of the Polynesian Society*, 5, 4, 1896, p. 196.
36. Taipari Munro, in *Waka Huia*, TV ONE, New Zealand, October 2005, transcribed and translated by Hohipere Tarau. Although the word pononga implies a person more like a servant, the information that he was in the habit of sleeping in the embers of the fire suggests he was a very lowly person, most probably a slave.
37. John Turnbull Thomson, *Rambles with a Philosopher, or, Views at the Antipodes*, Dunedin, 1867, p. 65.
38. William Yate, Journal & Diary, 1 November 1833, MS-2544, ATL, Wellington. Nankeen was a pale brownish-yellow cloth.
39. Personal communication, Maureen Lander, 4 November 2008.
40. John Alexander Wilson, *Missionary Life and Work in New Zealand — Part III: Tauranga, 1836–39. Being the Private Journal of the Late Rev. John Alexander Wilson*, C. J. Wilson, ed., Auckland, 1889, p. 51.
41. *Auckland Star*, 4 February 1882, Supplement, p. 1.

42 George Robertson, *The Discovery of Tahiti: A Journal of the Second Voyage of H.M.S. Dolphin Round the World, under the Command of Captain Wallis, R.N. In the Years 1766, 1767 and 1768*, Hugh Carrington, ed., London, 1948, p. 179.
43 Ibid., p. 227.
44 Victor Charles Lottin, 'Journal of Victor Charles Lottin', in *Extracts from New Zealand Journals Written on Ships under the Command of d'Entrecasteaux and Duperrey: 1793 and 1824, Early Eyewitness Accounts of Maori Life: 3 and 4*, Wellington, 1986, p. 121.
45 William Colenso, 'On the Maori Races of New Zealand', *Transactions and Proceedings of the New Zealand Institute*, 1, 1868, p. 5.
46 Taylor, *Te Ika a Maui*, p. 203.
47 Tuta Tamati, 'A Reply to Mr. A. S. Atkinson's Paper, "What Is a Tangata Māori?"', *Journal of the Polynesian Society*, 2, 1893, p. 62.
48 Davis, *Inhuman Bondage*, p. 51.
49 Edward Tregear, *The Maori-Polynesian Comparative Dictionary*, Wellington, 1891.
50 Jeffrey Paparoa Holman, *Best of Both Worlds: The Story of Elsdon Best and Tutakangahau*, Auckland, 2010, pp. 87–89.
51 Kerry Howe, *The Quest for Origins: Who First Discovered and Settled New Zealand and the Pacific Islands?*, Auckland, 2003, p. 143.
52 Ferdinand von Hochstetter, *New Zealand: Its Physical Geography, Geology and Natural History with Special Reference to the Results of Government Expeditions in the Provinces of Auckland and Nelson*, Stuttgart, 1867, pp. 199–200.
53 Ibid., p. 201.
54 Robert Carey, *Narrative of the Late War in New Zealand*, London, 1863, p. 36.
55 The Bishop of Wellington, 'Notes on the Maoris of New Zealand and Some Melanesians of the South-West Pacific', *Journal of the Ethnological Society of London*, 1, 4, 1869, p. 395.
56 *Maori Messsenger: Ko Te Karere Maori*, 19 January 1849, p. 1.
57 McNab, *Historical Records of New Zealand*, vol. 1, p. 267. Philip Gidley King had been Governor of Norfolk Island when Tuki Tahua was taken there in 1793 (see Judith Binney, 'Tuki's Universe', *New Zealand Journal of History*, 38, 2, October 2004) and became Governor of New South Wales in 1800.
58 Anne Salmond, *Between Worlds: Early Exchanges between Maori and Europeans 1773–1815*, Auckland, 1997, pp. 351–5.
59 Transliteration is the process of converting a word from one language into the alphabet of another.
60 Nigel Prickett, 'Trans-Tasman Stories: Australian Aborigines in New Zealand Sealing and Shore Whaling', in *Islands of Inquiry: Colonisation, Seafaring and the Archaeology of Maritime Landscapes*, Geoffrey Clark, Foss Leach & Sue O'Connor, eds, Canberra, 2008.
61 Lynette Russell, '"A New Holland Half-Caste": Sealer and Whaler Tommy Chaseland', *History Australia*, 5, 1, 2008, p. 11.
62 Waitangi Tribunal, *Rekohu: A Report on Moriori and Ngati Mutunga Claims in the Chatham Islands*, Wai 64, Wellington, 2001, 3.12 & 7.1.
63 Elsdon Best, *Polynesian Voyagers: The Maori as a Deep-Sea Navigator, Explorer, and Colonizer*, Wellington, 1923, p. 38.
64 See, for example: Peter Clayworth, '"An Indolent and Chilly Folk": The Development of the Idea of the "Moriori Myth"', PhD thesis, University of Otago, 2001.
65 H. Beattie, 'Traditions and Legends Collected from the Natives of Murihiku. (Southland, New Zealand.) Part XIV', *Journal of the Polynesian Society*, 31, 124, 1922, p. 194.
66 Clayworth, '"An Indolent and Chilly Folk"', p. 175.
67 Angas, *Savage Life and Scenes in Australia and New Zealand*, vol. 2, p. 280.
68 Willoughby Shortland Esq. to Lord Stanley, 18 January 1845, No. 2, *GBPP*, Vol. 33, No. 2, p. 10.
69 Ranginui Walker, 'The Relevance of Maori Myth and Tradition', in *Te Ao Hurihuri: Aspects of Maoritanga*, Michael King, ed., Auckland, 1992, p. 182.
70 Ibid.

Chapter 2: Tapu and mana: losing and regaining

1 Maori Marsden, 'God, Man and Universe: A Maori View', in *Te Aohurihuri*, Michael King, ed., 1975, pp. 194–5.
2 Ibid., pp. 193–4.
3 Much the same was the case in the Western Solomon Islands and probably elsewhere in the Pacific: Debra McDougall, 'Paths of Pinauzu: Captivity and Social Reproduction in Ranongga', *Journal of the Polynesian Society*, 109, 1, 2000, p. 100.
4 Richard Benton, Alex Frame & Paul Meredith, *Te Mātāpunenga: A Compendium of References to the Concepts and Institutions of Māori Customary Law*, Hamilton, 2013, p. 426.
5 Rev. W. Wyatt Gill, 'Concerning the Name Unga for "Slave" at Rarotonga, South Pacific', *Journal of the Polynesian Society*, 20, 1911,

pp. 128–9. Gill supported his explanation by adding: 'The correctness of this interpretation is evidenced by the Raro-tongan phrase for "dust" — *ungaungā* = one, literally "grains of earth." Again, in the Rarotongan Bible (Matt. XV., 29, and Mark VII., 28) for "crumbs" we have *ungaungā* kai, literally "grains of food." In these phrases the plural is made by repeating the noun *unga* = grain. The underlying idea is that the slave (*unga*) is but an insignificant grain or unit, that in the nature of things can never rise to anything great.'

6 The New Zealand Māori 'hunga' is a genuine cognate of the Rarotongan 'unga, from the Proto-Polynesian (PPN) *funga, which seems to have the core sense of 'small piece or fragment'. I am grateful to Ross Clark of Auckland University for his very helpful comments on this and other matters relating to Polynesian linguistics.

7 Benton, Frame & Meredith, *Te Matapunenga*, p. 426.

8 My thanks go to Vavao Fetui for alerting me to this possibility.

9 Tai Tokerau Dictionary, previously at: http://search.atomz.com/whakaheke, accessed 12 September 2010.

10 The Samoan word *pologa* also means slave and may be connected to *polo* meaning to cut fish into pieces or serve kava to a chief (both the work of slaves), although *polo* may not be the word's immediate origin. Similarly, the Māori pononga is often thought to derive from 'pono' meaning loyal, faithful, or true but that is also uncertain. It has been suggested that it might be an irregular development from poronga, hence a cognate with the Samoan *polonga*: personal communication, Ross Clark, 23 June 2014.

11 Taylor, *Te Ika a Maui*, p. 203. See Chapter 1.

12 Although McLean's words would have been a translation of what the King actually said in the Māori language, they nonetheless indicate the point he was making: McLean to Browne, 31 May 1860, Enc. 1 in No. 26, Brown to the Duke of Newcastle, *GBPP*, Vol. 12, p. 69.

13 Davis, the son of Irish migrants to Australia, who edited the paper for several years, had good Māori language skills and published a book of hymns and other British songs translated into Māori.

14 The sentence read 'Tokorua aua tama a Kanute i āhua ngoringori, kaore i kitea he tohungatanga i a rāua': *Te Korimako*, 15 July 1884, p. 7.

15 *Te Aka Māori–English, English–Māori Dictionary and Index* at: http://www.maoridictionary.co.nz/.

16 H. W. Williams, *A Dictionary of the Maori Language*, 7th edn, Wellington, 2000.

17 Elsdon Best, 'Raumahora and Takarangi: A Legend of the Taranaki Tribes', *Journal of the Polynesian Society*, 36, 143, 1927, pp. 243 & 252.

18 Te Ariki-tara-are, 'History and Traditions of Rarotonga, Part VII, Translated by S. Percy Smith', *Journal of the Polynesian Society*, 28, 112, 1919, p. 187 & Paul Wallin & Helene Martinsson-Wallin, 'The "Fish" for the Gods', *Rapa Nui Journal*, 15, 1, 2001, p. 6.

19 Tim Thomas, 'Communities of Practice in the Archaeological Record of New Georgia, Rendova and Tetepare', in *Lapita: Ancestors and Descendants*, P. Sheppard, T. Thomas & G. R. Summerhayes, eds, Auckland, 2009, p. 128.

20 T. A. McDonnell, *A Maori History of the War: Being a Native Account of the Pakeha-Maori Wars in New Zealand*, Auckland, 1887, p. 532.

21 Richard Taylor, *Leaf from the Natural History of New Zealand*, Auckland, 1870, p. 79.

22 Marsden, 'God, Man and Universe', p. 206.

23 Williams, *A Dictionary of the Maori Language*.

24 Jim Williams, 'E Pākihi Hakinga a Kai', PhD thesis, University of Otago, 2004, p. 24. Morganatic means 'Designating or relating to a marriage in which a man of high rank marries a wife of lower rank.... Also (occas.): designating a similar arrangement between a woman of high rank and a man of lower rank': *Oxford English Dictionary*.

25 Raymond Firth, *Primitive Economics of the New Zealand Maori*, London, 1929, p. 204 & Firth, *Economics of the New Zealand Maori*, 2nd edn, Wellington, 1959, p. 215. The first edition of his book was based on his earlier doctoral thesis.

26 Robinson, *Twisting the Treaty*, p. 20.

27 M. P. Shirres, 'Tapu', *Journal of the Polynesian Society*, 91, 1, 1982, p. 32.

28 Tregear, *The Maori Race*, pp. 156–7.

29 Firth, *Economics of the New Zealand Maori*, p. 214.

30 Christine Dureau, 'Oceania', in Seymore Drescher & Stanley L. Engerman, eds, *A Historical Guide to World Slavery*, New York, 1998, p. 307.

31 Elsdon Best, *The Maori*, vol. 1, Wellington, 1924, pp. 251–2.

32 Barry Brailsford, *Greenstone Trails: The Maori Search for Pounamu*, Wellington, 1984, p. 8.

33 Robert Joseph, 'Māori Customary Laws and Institutions — Crimes Against the Person, Marriage, Interment, Theft (Draft)', Te Mātāhauariki Research Institute, University of Waikato, Hamilton, 1999, at: lianz.waikato.ac.nz/PAPERS/Rob/

Custom%20Law.pdf, p. 15, accessed 5 September 2014.
34 Male captives were employed to paddle canoes, for example.
35 Shirres, 'Tapu', p. 33.
36 Ibid., p. 35.
37 Ibid., pp. 32, 39 & 40.
38 J. S. Polack, *New Zealand: Being a Narrative of Travels and Adventures During a Residence in That Country between the Years 1831 and 1837*, London, 1838, reprint edn, Christchurch, 1974, vol. 2, p. 253.
39 Ibid., p. 260.
40 *Missionary Register*, December 1835, p. 555.
41 William Brown, *New Zealand and Its Aborigines*, 2nd edn, London, 1851, p. 13.
42 Tregear, *The Maori Race*, pp. 156–7.
43 Church Missionary Society, Minutes of Sub-Committee appointed to examine the Report from the Select Committee of the House of Lords, on the present state of New Zealand, Letters Received, CN/M M11, Micro-MS-Coll-04-33, ATL, Wellington (hereafter CMS, Minutes of Sub-Committee, May 1839).
44 Shirres, 'Tapu', p. 35.
45 Raymond Firth's remark that 'being a class of people who were free from any attributes of sacredness [slaves] could attend to the degrading tasks connected with cooking and the bearing of burdens' and that 'cooked food and all its adjuncts had no destructive effect upon him' was interpreted by Orlando Patterson to mean that because the slave lived 'outside the mana of the gods' he could 'cross the boundaries with social and supernatural impunity': Orlando Patterson, 'Authority, Alienation and Social Death', in *African-American Religious Thought: An Anthology*, Cornel West & Eddie S. Glaude Jr, eds, Louisville, Kentucky, 2003, p. 117. For an in-depth study of slavery and social death, see also Orlando Patterson, *Slavery and Social Death: A Comparative Study*, Cambridge, Mass., 1982.
46 For example: Ballara, *Taua*, 2003, pp. 78 & 81; Arthur S. Thomson, *The Story of New Zealand: Past and Present — Savage and Civilized*, vol. 1, London, 1859, p. 149; Augustus Earle, *A Narrative of a Nine Months' Residence in New Zealand in 1827: Together with a Journal of a Residence in Tristan d'Acunha, an Island Situated between South America and the Cape of Good Hope*, London, 1832, p. 124; Lieut.-Col. Gudgeon, 'Maori Wars', *Journal of the Polynesian Society*, 16, 1, 1907, p. 31; Scherzer, *Narrative of the Circumnavigation of the Globe by the Austrian Frigate Novara*, vol. 3, p. 116.
47 K. R. Howe, 'Tregear, Edward Robert', *Dictionary of New Zealand Biography: Te Ara — the Encyclopedia of New Zealand*, updated 30 October 2012, at: http://www.TeAra.govt.nz/en/biographies/2t48/tregear-edward-robert.
48 Tregear, *The Maori Race*, p. 157.
49 Earle, *Narrative of a Nine Months' Residence*, pp. 124–5.
50 J. S. Polack, *Manners and Customs of the New Zealanders*, London, 1840, reprint edn, Christchurch, 1976, vol. 2, p. 103.
51 Ann R. Parsonson, 'He Whenua Te Utu (The Payment Will Be Land)', PhD thesis, University of Canterbury, 1978, p. 146.
52 Ann R. Parsonson, 'The Expansion of a Competitive Society: A Study in Nineteenth-Century Maori Society', *New Zealand Journal of History*, 14, 1, 1980, p. 55.
53 James Kemp was one who confirmed that slaves who failed in their attempt to escape could expect to be punished with death. However, he recorded an 1827 incident when several of Rewa's slaves were caught on their way to join a larger group who were absconding in a canoe. Because they were caught within the bounds of the mission, Rewa agreed not to harm them as long as they returned to his settlement quietly: Journal, 17 February 1827, PC-0075, Hocken Library, Dunedin.
54 William Yate dated the first Christian breakthrough as coming in 1828 but there were few converts before the 1830s: Judith Binney, 'Christianity and the Maoris to 1840: A Comment', *New Zealand Journal of History*, 3, 2, October 1969, pp. 148–51.
55 John White, *The Ancient History of the Maori: Tainui*, vol. 5, Hamilton, 2001, pp. 92–93.
56 http://www.patuone.com/files_main/whaka-papa.html and personal communications from Dr Benjamin Pittman, Kaua'i, Hawai'i, November 2011.
57 J. Holbech, ed., *Captain Thomas Sødring's Diary, Kept During the First Danish Expedition to the South Seas*, translation from Danish, 1841, pp. 45–46.
58 For example, Ballara, *Taua*, p. 426; Parsonson, 'A Study in Nineteenth-Century Maori Society', p. 55; Andrew P. Vayda, 'Maori Prisoners and Slaves in the Nineteenth Century', *Ethnohistory*, 8, 2, 1961, p. 146.
59 There is an extensive literature on this subject, for example: Olatunji Ojo, 'Child Slaves in Pre-Colonial Nigeria, c.1725–1860', *Slavery & Abolition*, 33, 3, 2012; Gwyn Campbell, 'Slavery and Other Forms of Unfree Labour in the Indian Ocean World', *Slavery & Abolition*, 24, 2, 2003; Brenda J.

Bowser, 'Captives in Amazonia: Becoming Kin in a Predatory Landscape', in Catherine M. Cameron, ed., *Invisible Citizens: Captives and Their Consequences*, Salt Lake City, 2008; Pauline Turner Strong, 'Transforming Outsiders: Captivity, Adoption, and Slavery Reconsidered', in *A Companion to American Indian History*, Philip J. Deloria & Neal Salisbury, eds, Malden & Oxford, 2002; James F. Brooks, *Captives & Cousins: Slavery, Kinship, and Community in the Southwest Borderlands*, Williamsburg, Virginia, c. 2002; Christina Snyder, *Slavery in Indian Country: The Changing Face of Captivity in Early America*, Cambridge, Mass., 2010; Catherine M. Cameron, 'Introduction: Captives in Prehistory as Agents of Social Change', in *Invisible Citizens: Captives and Their Consequences*, Catherine M. Cameron, ed., Salt Lake City, 2008. The word *pinausu*, used in Marovo for slave, is also the term for 'pet animal', much like the Māori word 'mōkai'. But the verb from which the word derives, *pausu*, is the Marovo term most closely approximating 'adoption', that is, '*koburu ta pausu*' (adopted child): Hviding, *Guardians of Marovo Lagoon*, p. 394; Thomas, 'Communities of Practice'; McDougall, 'Paths of *Pinauzu*'.
60 John White, *The Ancient History of the Maori: Notes for Ancient History of the Maori (Maori/English)*, vol. 12, Hamilton, 2001.
61 Belich, *Making Peoples*, pp. 163 & 173–8.
62 Ian Pool, 'Population change — Māori population change', *Te Ara — the Encyclopedia of New Zealand*, updated 13 July 2012, at: www.TeAra.govt.nz/en/population-change/page-6.
63 J. R. Elder, ed., *The Letters and Journals of Samuel Marsden, 1765–1838*, Dunedin, 1932, p. 173.
64 Barnet Burns, *A Brief Narrative of a New Zealand Chief: Being the Remarkable History of Barnet Burns, an English Sailor, with a Faithful Account of the Way in Which He Became a Chief of One of the Tribes of New Zealand*, Gisborne, 1871, p. 39.
65 Ballara, *Taua*, p. 118.
66 Ian Pool estimated the decrease at between 10% and 30% by 1840: Ian Pool, *Te Iwi Maori: A New Zealand Population, Past, Present & Projected*, Auckland, 1991, p. 234.
67 Elder, ed., *The Letters and Journals of Samuel Marsden, 1765–1838*, p. 175.
68 Shortland Manuscripts, MS2b, UAL, pp. 57–59. This karakia has been used for other purposes in more recent times — for example, in connection with suicide.
69 J. W. Stack, 'Art. V.—Sketch of the Traditional History of the South Island Maoris', *Transactions and Proceedings of the New Zealand Institute*, 10, 1877, p. 73; Arthur Hugh Carrington, *Ngāi Tahu: A Migration History — The Carrington Text*, Te Maire Tau & Atholl Anderson, eds, Wellington, 2008, pp. 84–85. Stack refers to the tohunga as Tauhiku.
70 Stack, 'Traditional History of the South Island Maoris', p. 73.
71 Firth, *Economics of the New Zealand Maori*, p. 214.
72 White, *The Ancient History of the Maori*, vol. 12, unpaginated.
73 Ballara, *Taua*, p. 89.
74 Burns was a trader who lived among Māori at the Uawa River during the 1830s but returned to England, heavily tattooed, where he gave lectures on his adventures dressed in Māori costume. He also wrote a book called *A Brief Narrative of a New Zealand Chief: Being the Remarkable History of Barnet Burns*.
75 William Williams, *Christianity among the New Zealanders*, London, 1867, pp. 162–3; William Yate, Journal & Diary, 19 December 1833, MS-Copy-Micro-0453, ATL, Wellington; Joseph Angus Mackay, *Historic Poverty Bay and the East Coast, N.I., N.Z.*, Gisborne, 1949, p. 156; Theodore Morton Jones, Journal, qMS-1075, ATL, Wellington, pp. 349–51. Mackay cites William L. Williams, who was not present at the time; Morton Jones cites his father Archdeacon William Williams for similar details.
76 William Yate, Journal & Diary, 19 December 1833, MS-Copy-Micro-0453, ATL, Wellington.
77 William Yate, 25 December 1833, Journal & Diary, 1833–45, MS-2544, ATL, Wellington. Another CMS missionary, John Butler, visited the Hauraki region very briefly aboard HMS *Dromedary* in 1820 but Yate states that it was the returned captive who taught them hymn singing.
78 Ibid., 8 January 1834.
79 Wilson, *Missionary Life and Work in New Zealand*, pp. 40–41.
80 Tregear, *The Maori Race*, p. 155.
81 Wilson, *Missionary Life and Work in New Zealand*, p. 51.
82 Cooked kūmara were used in various ceremonies to whakanoa, or remove tapu, but uncooked ones were also used for other ritual purposes which are less clear.
83 Peter Henry Buck, *The Coming of the Maori*, Wellington, 1949, p. 401.
84 Marsden, 'God, Man and Universe', p. 206.
85 Pat Hohepa, 'My Musket, My Missionary and My Mana', in *Voyages and Beaches: Pacific*

Encounters, 1769–1840, Jonathan Lamb, Alex Calder & Bridget Orr, eds, Honolulu, 1999, p. 197.
86 Elsdon Best, *Notes on the Art of War*, Jeff Evans, ed., Auckland, 2001, p. 215.
87 Henry Williams, Journal, 24 March 1828, cited in Angela Ballara, 'The Role of Warfare in Maori Society in the Early Contact Period', *Journal of the Polynesian Society*, 85, 4, 1976, p. 500. Ngāti Manu was a section of the Ngāpuhi group of tribes. Te Wharerahi belonged to Ngāi Tawake, another branch of Ngāpuhi.
88 Steven Oliver, 'Te Pehi Kupe — Biography', *Dictionary of New Zealand Biography: Te Ara — the Encyclopedia of New Zealand*, updated 30 October 2012, at: http://www.teara.govt.nz/en/biographies/1t55/te-pehi-kupe. Te Maire Tau says that Te Rauparaha's warriors disinterred the body of a Ngāi Tahu woman named Te Ruaki at Tuahiwi and ate her corpse, which act was one of the reasons for making Te Pēhi's bones into fish-hooks: Te Maire Tau, *I Whanau Au Ki Kaiapoi: The Story of Netanahira Waruwarutu as Recorded by Thomas Green*, Dunedin, 2011, p. 35.
89 Best, *Notes on the Art of War*, p. 209.
90 T. A. Pybus, *The Maoris of the South Island*, Wellington, 1954, p. 48.
91 Stack and the Mitchells say that her father pushed her body through a porthole: James West Stack, *The Sacking of Kaiapohia*, Christchurch, 1906, p. 138 & Hilary & John Mitchell, *Te Tau Ihu o Te Waka: A History of Maori of Nelson and Marlborough*, 2 vols, vol. 1, Wellington, 2005, p. 118. Another version of the story recorded by John White has it that it was Captain Stewart who had her body thrown overboard to avoid it being eaten by Te Rauparaha's people: White, *The Ancient History of the Maori*, vol. 6, pp. 116 & 131. T. A. Pybus simply alluded to a 'worse' fate than slavery: Pybus, *The Maoris of the South Island*, p. 48.
92 Taylor, *Te Ika a Maui*, pp. 327–8.
93 Carrington, *Ngāi Tahu: A Migration History*, p. 183.
94 Different versions of the events say that he was flogged either because of his defiant demeanour or because he had strangled his daughter.
95 John Butler, *Earliest New Zealand: The Journals and Correspondence of the Rev. John Butler*, R. J. Barton, comp. & ed., Masterton, 1927, p. 216.
96 Earle, *Narrative of a Nine Months' Residence*, p. 123.
97 Polack, *New Zealand: Being a Narrative of Travels and Adventures*, vol. 2, p. 62.
98 Sharp, *Duperrey's Visit to New Zealand in 1824*, p. 38.
99 Richard Davis, Journal, 3 November 1834, Letters & Journals, typescript, MS-1211-3, Hocken Library, Dunedin.
100 Raine, Ramsay, and Browne of Sydney had established a dockyard at Hōreke by the 1820s.
101 http://www.patuone.com/files_life/commerce.html, accessed 14 November 2011 & James Brown, Chief Executive Officer of Ngai Tai Te Waka Totara Trust, cited at: http://www.movetonz.org/forum/general-nz-chat/4831-maori-2.html, accessed 21 April 2013.
102 Henry Williams, Journal, 21 March 1835, cited in Hugh Carleton, *The Life of Henry Williams: Archdeacon of Waimate*, revised edn, Wellington, 1948, p. 179.
103 Alexander McCrae, *Journal Kept in New Zealand in 1820 by Ensign Alexander McCrae, of the 84th Regiment, Together with Relevant Documents*, The Hon. Sir Frederick Revans Chapman, ed., *Alexander Turnbull Library, Bulletin No. 3*, Wellington, 1928, p. 25.
104 Ballara, 'The Role of Warfare in Maori Society in the Early Contact Period', p. 496.
105 Polack, *New Zealand: Being a Narrative of Travels and Adventures*, vol. 2, p. 62.
106 G. A. Phillipson, *Rangahaua Whanui District 13: The Northern South Island*, Part 1, June 1995 (report commissioned by the Waitangi Tribunal), p. 21.
107 Jenifer Curnow, 'Te Rangikaheke, Wiremu Maihi — Biography', *Dictionary of New Zealand Biography: Te Ara — the Encyclopedia of New Zealand*, updated 1 September 2010 & Wiremu Maihi Te Rangikaheke, 'He Waiata Haka Oriori', *Te Ao Hou*, 3, Summer 1853.
108 http://collections.tepapa.govt.nz/objectdetails.aspx?oid=58631, accessed 14 December 2009 & Pania Waaka, 'Hei tiki and issues of representation within contemporary Māori arts', *MAI Review*, 2007, 1, Intern Research Report 7, http://www.review.mai.ac.nz/index.php/MR/article/view/38, accessed 14 December 2009.
109 http://collections.tepapa.govt.nz/ObjectDetails.aspx?oid=71840, accessed 21 May 2013.
110 Monty Soutar, 'Ngāti Porou Leadership — Rāpata Wahawaha and the Politics of Conflict', PhD thesis, Massey University, 2000, pp. 86 & 88. Rāpata and Rōpata are alternative Māori versions of the English name Robert.

111 Ballara, 'The Role of Warfare in Maori Society in the Early Contact Period', p. 495.
112 Ballara, *Taua*, p. 100 & Angela Ballara, 'Kawepo, Renata Tama-ki-Hikurangi', *Dictionary of New Zealand Biography: Te Ara — the Encyclopedia of New Zealand*, updated 30 October 2012, at: http://www.TeAra.govt.nz/en/biographies/1k3/kawepo-renata-tama-ki-hikurangi.
113 Ballara, *Taua*, pp. 427 & 447.
114 For example, in the course of a long-running dispute over title to the Ōmāhu Block in Hawke's Bay after Kawepō's death, Airini Donnelly claimed that as a consequence of his having been captured, he 'bore lasting opprobrium as having been a slave': *Ashburton Guardian*, 23 January 1889, p. 2. But, for a very different perspective, see the reference to Tāmati Hone Ōraukawa, a candidate for the first Māori kingship, below.
115 Lyndsay Head, 'Te Ua Haumene', *Dictionary of New Zealand Biography: Te Ara — the Encyclopedia of New Zealand*, updated 30 October 2012, at: http://www.TeAra.govt.nz/en/biographies/1t79/te-ua-haumene.
116 http://www.lindaueronline.co.nz/maori-portraits/hakopa-te-ata-o-tu, accessed 16 July 2014. Te Rauparaha, who died in 1849, did not embrace Christianity but Te Ata-o-Tū did. The relevance of Christian conversion concerning his release may be based on an assumption, however. In an 1883 obituary, for example, the *Press* newspaper reported that 'through the introduction of Christianity he was at liberty to return to his own tribe': 10 September 1883, p. 3. As will be seen in subsequent chapters, the adoption of Christianity and the release of captives were not necessarily concurrent. Some were released prior to or without their masters' conversion, and others were obliged to continue in subservient roles within their captors' communities even after their masters' or mistresses' baptism.
117 James Cowan, *Evening Post*, 3 August 1912, p. 10. These would have been the Ngāti Raukawa people who had left their previous home at Maungatautari and moved south to join forces with Ngāti Tūwharetoa in the west Taupō district.
118 Hākopa Te Ata-o-Tū died at Kaiapoi in 1883: per 'Lindauer online' at: http://www.lindaueronline.co.nz/maori-portraits/hakopa-te-ata-o-tu, accessed 16 July 2014.
119 Report by I. E. Featherston, Superintendent of Wellington, enclosed with memorandum by Willliam Fox, *GBPP*, Vol. 14, Enc. 2 in No. 22, pp. 79–81.
120 Ballara, *Taua*, p. 155.
121 For example, Elsdon Best, 'Notes on the Art of War, as Conducted by the Maori of New Zealand, with Accounts of Various Customs, Rites, Superstitions, &C., Pertaining to War, as Practised and Believed in by the Ancient Maori', *Journal of the Polynesian Society*, 12, 3, 1903, p. 161.
122 Ibid., p. 162.
123 T. Lindsay Buick, *An Old New Zealander: Or, Te Rauparaha, the Napoleon of the South*, London, 1911, pp. 46–47; S. Percy Smith, *History and Traditions of the Maoris of the West Coast, North Island of New Zealand Prior to 1840*, New Plymouth, 1910, pp. 288–9; & Teremoana Sparks, 'Topeora, Rangi Te Kuini', *Dictionary of New Zealand Biography: Te Ara — the Encyclopedia of New Zealand*, updated 30 October 2012, at: http://www.TeAra.govt.nz/mi/biographies/1t103/topeora-rangi-te-kuini. Vayda cited S. Percy Smith's report that a European whaler named Billy Bundy was saved in a similar manner by a chief's daughter who cast her mat over him but there is little supporting evidence for this: Vayda, *Maori Warfare*, p. 103.
124 Tregear, *The Maori Race*, p. 155.
125 T. W. Downes, 'History of Ngati-Kahu-Ngunu', *Journal of the Polynesian Society*, 25, 97, 1916, p. 7.
126 Lieut. Col. Gudgeon, 'Maori Wars', *Journal of the Polynesian Society*, 16, 1, 1907, p. 32.
127 White, *The Ancient History of the Maori*, vol. 9, (B No.1 White), p. 142.
128 James Cowan, *The New Zealand Wars: A History of the Maori Campaigns and the Pioneering Period*, vol. 1, Wellington, 1955, p. 334.
129 White, *The Ancient History of the Maori*, vol. 5, p. 102.
130 Ian Church, 'Oraukawa, Tamati Hone', *Dictionary of New Zealand Biography: Te Ara — the Encyclopedia of New Zealand*, updated 30 October 2012, at: http://www.TeAra.govt.nz/en/biographies/1o4/oraukawa-tamati-hone.
131 Elsdon Best, 'The Land of Tara and They Who Settled It. Part III', *Journal of the Polynesian Society*, 27, 106, 1918, p. 68.
132 Brief of Evidence of Te Waari Carkeek, 9 June 2003, relating to Wai 207 & Wai 785, pp. 13–14, at: http://www.ngatitoa.iwi.nz/wp-content/uploads/PhotoGallery/2011/10/Te-Waari-Carkeek.pdf, accessed 9 September 2010.
133 Roger Neich, *Painted Histories: Early Maori Figurative Painting*, Auckland, 1994, p. 68.
134 Roger Neich, *Carved Histories: Rotorua Ngati Tarawhai Woodcarving*, Auckland, 2001, p. 10.

135 For example, D. M. Stafford, *Te Arawa: A History of the Arawa People*, Auckland, 2002, p. 179.
136 Earle, *Narrative of a Nine Months' Residence*, pp. 133–6.
137 William Williams noted that Te Ripi Paratene, baptised in 1831, was 'one of the first chiefs in authority to incline to religion': Ballara, *Taua*, p. 425.
138 Nicky Conrad interviewed by Whai Ngata, *Waka Huia*, TV ONE, New Zealand, 27 June 1987, transcribed and translated by Hohipere Tarau.
139 Cowan, *The New Zealand Wars*, vol. 1, p. 57. John White, 'Lectures on Maori Customs', *AJHR*, 1861, E No. 7, p. 48. Cowan calls him Pirihonga, White Pirihongo.
140 William Colenso, 'On the Maori Races of New Zealand', *Transactions and Proceedings of the New Zealand Institute*, 1, 1868, p. 22.
141 *A Dictionary of New Zealand Biography*, vol. II, Wellington, 1940, p. 76.
142 Ballara, 'Warfare and Government in Ngapuhi Tribal Society: 1814–1833', p. 284.
143 Dan Munn, 'Ngati Manu: An Ethnohistorical Account', MA thesis, University of Auckland, 1981, p. 218. Vayda suggested that the motive for captives joining their conquerors in subsequent warfare was to take revenge on their own tribal groups for being captured, but that would only make sense when they fought against their own relations and would not account for other instances: Vayda, *Maori Warfare*, p. 109.
144 Clipping from the *Sun*, 17 July 1929, p. 11, courtesy of Auckland War Memorial Museum.
145 Probably Maramatautini.
146 Withdrawn file card courtesy of the Auckland War Memorial Museum. The carving has since been returned to Ngāti Hine. 'Kapetoru', which could mean 'threepence', may be a nickname.
147 Ballara, *Taua*, pp. 11–12.

Chapter 3: The roles, status, and rights of Māori war captives

1 Ballara, *Taua*, p. 134.
2 Busby, Letters, 6 April 1835, cited in Ballara, 'Warfare and Government in Ngapuhi Tribal Society: 1814–1833', p. 56.
3 William Colenso, 'On the Maori Races of New Zealand', *Transactions and Proceedings of the New Zealand Institute*, 1, 1868, p. 22.
4 Thomas Buddle, *The Aborigines of New Zealand: Two Lectures Delivered by Thos. Buddle at the Auckland Mechanics' Institute on the Evenings of the 25th March and 12th May, 1851*, Auckland, 1851, p. 46.
5 *Report from the Select Committee on New Zealand with the Minutes of Proceedings*, in *GBPP*, London, 1844, p. 22.
6 Evidence of Rev. Wilkinson, in Parliament of Great Britain, *Report from the Select Committee of the House of Lords, Appointed to Inquire into the Present State of the Islands of New Zealand*, Vol. 1, *GBPP*, reprinted as *Colonies: New Zealand, I*, Shannon, 1968 (orig. pub. 1838), p. 96. Wilkinson had previously been Chaplain of New South Wales.
7 Ibid., pp. 97, 133 & 169.
8 The cohesiveness of the iwi or 'tribe' is a relatively recent phenomenon. For a detailed discussion of the history and dynamics of Māori tribal organisation see Angela Ballara, *Iwi: The Dynamics of Maori Tribal Organisation from c. 1769 to c. 1945*, Wellington, 1998.
9 John Liddiard Nicholas, *Narrative of a Voyage to New Zealand, Performed in the Years 1814 and 1815, in Company with the Rev. Samuel Marsden*, 2 vols, vol. II, London, 1817, p. 143.
10 Elder, ed., *The Letters and Journals of Samuel Marsden, 1765–1838*, p. 118.
11 Arthur S. Thomson, *The Story of New Zealand: Past and Present — Savage and Civilized*, vol. 1, London, 1859, p. 149.
12 Gudgeon, 'Maori Wars', pp. 34–35.
13 Anonymous storyteller, possibly from Ngāti Pāoa. Translation by Orbell in Margaret Orbell, *Traditional Māori Stories*, introduced and translated by Margaret Orbell, Auckland, 1997, pp. 161–4. Personal communication, Hone Sadler, 23 May 2012.
14 Steven Oliver, 'Te Kani-a-Takirau — Te Kani-a-Takirau', *Dictionary of New Zealand Biography: Te Ara — the Encyclopedia of New Zealand*, updated 30 October 2012, at: http://www.TeAra.govt.nz/en/biographies/1t41/te-kani-a-takirau.
15 Earle, *Narrative of a Nine Months' Residence*, p. 124; Ballara, *Taua*, p. 100.
16 His phrase 'to the southward' is vague but may suggest places less visited by shipping with less incentive to increase production for foreign trade.
17 Polack, *New Zealand: Being a Narrative of Travels and Adventures*, vol. 1, pp. 95–96.
18 For example, the diary of J. G. Butler, 31 May 1820, cited in Butler, *Earliest New Zealand*, p. 80 & Marsden to Pratt, 21 March 1821, cited in Robert McNab, *Historical Records of New Zealand*, 2 vols, vol. 2, Wellington, 1914, p. 520.
19 John King, Journal, 2 June 1825, Letters

& Journals, MS Vol. 73, PC-0152, Hocken Library, Dunedin.
20 Extracts from the journal of Mr. Francis Hall, 22 December 1821, *Missionary Register*, 1823, p. 506.
21 John Hobbs, Diary, 27 November 1823, Diaries & letter books, MET 10, Kinder Library, Auckland.
22 Journal of William Williams, 16 July 1826, typescript, Vol. 1, qMS-2248, ATL, Wellington.
23 V. S. Jackson letter to Miss Wilton: [c. 1919?], MS Papers-1052, ATL, Wellington.
24 The battle of Tūtūrau in 1836–37.
25 John Hall-Jones, *John Turnbull Thomson: First Surveyor-General of New Zealand*, Dunedin, 1992, pp. 32–33.
26 *Nelson Examiner and New Zealand Chronicle*, 12 September 1846, p. 111.
27 Brailsford, *Greenstone Trails*, p. 43.
28 Atholl Anderson, *The Welcome of Strangers: An Ethnohistory of Southern Maori A.D. 1650–1850*, p. 225, fn. 2.
29 Wohlers, 'The Mythology and Traditions of the Maori in New Zealand', p. 23 & Tremewan, *Traditional Stories from Southern New Zealand*, p. 17.
30 William Yate, *An Account of New Zealand*, 2nd edn, London, 1835, p. 94.
31 White, *The Ancient History of the Maori*, vol. 3, pp. 192–4.
32 Angela Ballara, 'Tamairangi', *Dictionary of New Zealand Biography: Te Ara — the Encyclopedia of New Zealand*, updated 30 October 2012, at: http://www.TeAra.govt.nz/en/biographies/1t8/tamairangi. The Carrington Text indicates that Te Kēkerengū did seduce Te Rangihaeata's wife: Carrington, *Ngāi Tahu: A Migration History*, p. 172.
33 Patricia Burns, *Te Rauparaha: A New Perspective*, Wellington, Sydney, Auckland & Christchurch, 1980, pp. 145–6 & related by Ema Turumeke and translated by her daughter Mrs C. J. Harden, 'Narrative of the Battle of Omihi', *Journal of the Polynesian Society*, 3, 2, 1894, pp. 107–8.
34 Rev. J. Beecham, Dandeson Coates & Rev. W. Ellis, *Christianity the Means of Civilization: Shown in the Evidence Given before a Committee of the House of Commons, on Aborigines*, London, 1837, p. 247.
35 CMS, Minutes of Sub-Committee, May 1839, ATL, Wellington, p. 431.
36 Ibid., pp. 427–8.
37 G. S. Cooper, *Journal of an Expedition Overland from Auckland to Taranaki: By Way of Rotorua, Taupo, and the West Coast*, Auckland, 1851, p. 276.

38 Lottin, 'Journal of Victor Charles Lottin', p. 120.
39 Sharp, *Duperrey's Visit to New Zealand in 1824*, p. 74.
40 Ibid., p. 87.
41 Lottin, , 'Journal of Victor Charles Lottin', p. 120.
42 John Johnson, 'Notes from a journal', in *Early Travellers in New Zealand*, Nancy Taylor, ed., Oxford, 1959, p. 182.
43 Cooper, *Journal of an Expedition Overland from Auckland to Taranaki*, p. 280.
44 Firth, *Economics of the New Zealand Maori*, p. 216.
45 Burns, *Te Rauparaha*, p. 131.
46 Edward Shortland, *Traditions and Superstitions of the New Zealanders: With Illustrations of Their Manners and Customs*, 2nd edn, London, 1856, p. 88.
47 R. A. Cruise, *Journal of a Ten Months' Residence in New Zealand*, London, 1824, pp. 106–7.
48 Caroline Fitzgerald, *Letters from the Bay of Islands: The Story of Marianne Williams*, Auckland, 2004, p. 81.
49 Elsdon Best, *Tuhoe: The Children of the Mist*, 2nd edn, 2 vols, vol. 1, Wellington, 1971 (first published 1925), p. 343.
50 Buck, *The Coming of the Maori*, p. 393.
51 *Te Ao Hou*, 50, March 1965, p. 13.
52 Elsdon Best, *The Maori*, vol. 1, 1924, p. 257. The frequency of words or phrases being spoken or actions carried out three times suggests that the number had a particular significance in custom law which was likely to have a spiritual origin.
53 Sharp, *Duperrey's Visit to New Zealand in 1824*, pp. 38–39.
54 Darwin, *Journal of Researches*, p. 505.
55 Tregear, *The Maori Race*, p. 157 & Grey, *Polynesian Mythology*, 1885, p. 196.
56 Sharp, *Duperrey's Visit to New Zealand in 1824*, p. 38.
57 Butler, *Earliest New Zealand*, p. 106.
58 Cited in Hall, *"I Have Planted . . ."*, p. 44.
59 Davis, *Inhuman Bondage*, p. 81.
60 See, for example, Tāmati Ngāpora in Chapter 9.
61 Sarah Dingle, 'Gospel Power for Civilization: The CMS Missionary Perspective on Maori Culture 1830–1860', PhD thesis, University of Adelaide, 2009, p. 12; John Stenhouse, Tony Ballantyne, and Lyndsay Head also discuss the theological understandings of the Evangelicals in John Stenhouse, ed., assisted by G. A. Wood, *Christianity, Modernity and Culture: New Perspectives on New Zealand History*, Adelaide, 2005.

62 The *Atlas*, London, 23 August 1845, p. 538.
63 Brown, *New Zealand and Its Aborigines*, pp. 63 & 68.
64 Yate, *An Account of New Zealand*, p. 120.
65 For example, Vayda, 'Maori Prisoners and Slaves in the Nineteenth Century', p. 146.
66 Davis from Waimate, 25 April 1831, cited in J. N. Coleman, *A Memoir of the Rev. Richard Davis*, London, 1865, p. 134.
67 Ibid., 3 September 1831, p. 137.
68 Johnson, *Early Travellers in New Zealand*, p. 168.
69 Angas, *Savage Life and Scenes*, p. 101.
70 Johnson, *Early Travellers in New Zealand*, p. 124.
71 Berys N. Heuer, 'Maori Women in Traditional Family and Tribal Life', *Journal of the Polynesian Society*, 78, 4, 1969, p. 457.
72 Tregear, *The Maori Race*, pp. 158–9.
73 Heuer, 'Maori Women in Traditional Family and Tribal Life', p. 457.
74 Dr Tuutere Wiirepa, 'Ko Te Whetuu-Matarau: The Many-Pointed Star', in *He Whiriwhiringa: Selected Readings in Maori*, Bruce Biggs, ed., Auckland, 1997, pp. 173–4.
75 CMS, Minutes of Sub-Committee, May 1839, ATL, Wellington, p. 430.
76 Ibid., p. 426.
77 Taylor, *Te Ika a Maui*, p. 59, fn. 2.
78 John King, Journal, 2 June 1825, Letters & Journals, MS Vol. 73, PC-0152, Hocken Library, Dunedin; Extracts from the journal of Mr. Francis Hall, 22 December 1821, *Missionary Register*, 1823, p. 506; John Hobbs, Diary, 27 November 1823, Diaries & letter books, MET 10, Kinder Library, Auckland; Journal of William Williams, 16 July 1826, transcript, Vol. 1, qMS-2248, ATL, Wellington; John King, Journal, 8 August 1824, Letters & Journals, MS Vol. 73, PC-0152, Hocken Library, Dunedin.
79 Possibly Thomas McLean.
80 Markham, *New Zealand or Recollections of It*, p. 82.
81 Ward, *A Show of Justice*, pp. 51–52.
82 James Rutherford, *Sir George Grey, K.C.B., 1812–1898: A Study in Colonial Government*, London, 1961, pp. 214–15.
83 Teremoana Sparks, 'Topeora, Rangi Te Kuini', *Dictionary of New Zealand Biography: Te Ara — the Encyclopedia of New Zealand*, updated 30 October 2012, at: http://www.TeAra.govt.nz/en/biographies/1t103/topeora-rangi-te-kuini.
84 John King, Journal, 10 September 1824, Letters & Journals, MS Vol. 73, PC-0152, Hocken Library, Dunedin.
85 There may have been exceptions to this, however, as the Kaihuanga feud suggests (see text at note 115).
86 Ballara, *Taua*, p. 101.
87 John Hobbs, Diary, March 1841, Papers, Vol. 4, typescript, MS 144, AWMML, Auckland.
88 *Maori Messenger: Ko Te Karere Maori*, 31 May 1860, p. 7.
89 C. O. Davis, *The Life and Times of Patuone, the Celebrated Ngapuhi Chief*, Auckland, 1876, pp. 63–64.
90 John Webster, *Reminiscences of an Old Settler in Australia and New Zealand*, Christchurch, Wellington & Dunedin, 1908, p. 263.
91 It is now in the collection of the Auckland Art Gallery Toi o Tāmaki, at: http://www.nzmuseums.co.nz/.
92 Elder, ed., *The Letters and Journals of Samuel Marsden, 1765–1838*, p. 478.
93 John White, *The Ancient History of the Maori*, vol. 10 (English), Wellington, 1887, p. 135 (Book 4A).
94 Earle, *Narrative of a Nine Months' Residence*, p. 117.
95 James Kemp, Journal, 23 April 1824, Letters & Journals, MS Vol. 70, PC-075, Hocken Library, Dunedin.
96 Tregear, *The Maori Race*, p. 158.
97 Polack, *New Zealand: Being a Narrative of Travels and Adventures*, vol. 2, p. 107.
98 *New Zealand Gazette and Wellington Spectator*, 10 February 1844, p. 3.
99 They were tapu while growing in the field and during the harvest but became noa, or free from tapu, while being carried to the storehouse. However, once there, they were tapu again until they were removed for cooking: David V. Williams, *Matauranga Maori and Taonga: The Nature and Extent of Treaty Rights Held by Iwi and Hapu in Indigenous Flora and Fauna*, Wellington, 2001, p. 114.
100 John King, Journal, 2 June 1819, Letters & Journals, MS Vol. 73, PC-0152, Hocken Library, Dunedin.
101 Ibid., 29 May & 23 August 1822.
102 Ibid., 25 November 1823.
103 John Hobbs, Diary, 13 February & 3 March 1824, Diaries & letter books, MET 10, Kinder Library, Auckland.
104 Ibid., 31 October 1827.
105 Cruise, *Journal of a Ten Months' Residence in New Zealand*, p. 94.
106 B. H. Fletcher, 'Phillip, Arthur (1738–1814)', *Australian Dictionary of Biography*, at: http://adb.anu.edu.au/biography/phillip-arthur-2549, accessed 11 April 2013.
107 Cruise, *Journal of a Ten Months' Residence in New Zealand*, p. 42.

108 James Kemp, Journal, 17 February 1827, Letters & Journals, MS Vol. 70, PC-0075, Hocken Library, Dunedin.
109 Ibid., 14 February 1824.
110 G. W. Rusden, *History of New Zealand*, 2 vols, vol. 1, Melbourne, 1883, p. 117; John Rutherford, *The White Chief: A Story of Adventure in New Zealand*, Christchurch, Wellington, Dunedin, Melbourne, London, 1908, p. 195. The ultimate fate of Hongi's armour has been the subject of much scholarly debate.
111 Henry Williams, Journal, 11 February 1824, cited in Henry Williams, *Te Wiremu — Henry Williams: Early Years in the North*, Caroline Fitzgerald, ed., Wellington, 2011, p. 41.
112 Anderson, *The Welcome of Strangers*, p. 78.
113 Evidence of Ta Tipene Gerard O'Regan on behalf of the Rūnanga o Ngāi Tahu and the Department of Conservation, concerning an application to amend the National Water Conservation (Lake Ellesmere) Order 1990, at: http://ecan.govt.nz/publications/Plans/lake-ellesmere-wco-applicant-evidence-ta-tipene-oregan-310511.pdf, pp. 9–10, accessed 27 May 2014. Atholl Anderson stated that the first man killed was a slave belonging to one of Murihaka's relatives but Ta Tipene O'Regan's statement that it was one of her relatives who had become a slave may be the more likely scenario (ibid.).
114 James Kemp, Journal, 13 February 1825, cited in Ballara, *Taua*, p. 100.
115 Henry Williams, Journal, typescript, 25 & 26 February 1828, qMS-2224, ATL, Wellington.
116 James Kemp, Journal, 19 October 1826, Letters & Journals, MS Vol. 70, PC-0074, Hocken Library, Dunedin.
117 *Maori Messenger: Ko Te Karere Maori*, 4 March 1855, pp. 54–55.
118 Cruise, *Journal of a Ten Months' Residence in New Zealand*, p. 96.
119 Carleton, *The Life of Henry Williams*, p. 81.
120 James Cowan cited in Tony Sole, *Ngāti Ruanui: A History*, Wellington, 2005, p. 170.
121 Ibid., pp. 170–1.
122 Henry Williams, Journal, typescript, 17 January 1835, qMS-2224, ATL, Wellington.
123 Fitzgerald, *Letters from the Bay of Islands*, pp. 228–9.
124 Winthrop D. Jordan, *The White Man's Burden: Historical Origins of Racism in the United States*, New York, 1974, pp. 70 & 78–79. See also Vincent O'Malley, *Agents of Autonomy: Maori Committees in the Nineteenth Century*, Wellington, 1998 & Fomin, *A Comparative Study of Societal Influences on Indigenous Slavery*.
125 Report by Mr. Hanson Turton Respecting the Runanga Maori, *AJHR*, 1862, E No. 5A, No. 1, p. 4.
126 Report from C. Hunter Brown, Esq, of an official visit to the Urewera tribes, June 1862, *AJHR*, 1862, E No. 9, Sec. IV, p. 31.
127 Vincent O'Malley, *Beyond the Imperial Frontier: The Contest for Colonial New Zealand*, Wellington, 2014, p. 104.
128 *AJHR*, 1862, E No. 9, Sec. IV, p. 28.
129 O'Malley, *Beyond the Imperial Frontier*, p. 105.
130 *Daily Southern Cross*, 9 January 1869, p. 3.
131 Robinson, *Twisting the Treaty*, p. 19. Similar examples include: Dureau, 'Oceania', p. 307; Evison, *Te Wai Pounamu*, pp. 10 & 51; Hall, "I Have Planted . . .", p. 44; Scherzer, *Narrative of the Circumnavigation of the Globe by the Austrian Frigate Novara*, vol. 3, p. 117; Earle, *Narrative of a Nine Months' Residence*, p. 124; Darwin, *Journal of Researches*, p. 505; Butler, *Earliest New Zealand*, pp. 386–7; Buck, *The Coming of the Maori*, p. 402; Vayda, *Maori Warfare*, p. 105; & Ballara, *Taua*, pp. 100–1.
132 Thomson, *The Story of New Zealand*, vol. 1, p. 149; T. E. Donne, *The Maori: Past and Present*, London, 1927, p. 138.
133 'He kohuru na te tamariki' ('Murder by children') in John White, *The Ancient History of the Maori*, vol. 10, chapter III, (39).
134 'He kohuru, he aroha, me te Whakamomori' ('Murder, love, and suicide') in ibid.
135 Tregear, *The Maori Race*, p. 157; Ross Bowden, 'Tapu and Mana: Ritual Authority and Political Power in Traditional Maori Society', *The Journal of Pacific History*, 14, 1, 1979, p. 58.
136 Sharp, *Duperrey's Visit to New Zealand in 1824*, p. 38.
137 Thomas Wayth Gudgeon, *The History and Doings of the Maoris: From the Year 1820 to the Signing of the Treaty of Waitangi in 1840*, Auckland, 1885, p. 220.
138 Michael P. J. Reilly, 'Tuakana-Teina Relationship and Leadership in Ancient Mangaia and Aotearoa', *The Journal of Pacific History*, 45, 2, 2010, p. 225.
139 Rongowhakaata Halbert, *Horouta: The History of the Horouta Canoe, Gisborne and East Coast*, new edn, Auckland, 2012, pp. 103 & 267.
140 Elsdon Best, *The Stone Implements of the Maori*, Wellington, 1974, pp. 207 & 211.
141 Ballara, *Taua*, pp. 101–2.
142 Mackay, *Historic Poverty Bay and the East Coast*, p. 466.
143 John White, *AJHR*, 1861, p. 18.
144 See Chapter 1 regarding Manaia realising that his wife had slept with a slave when he saw the ashes transferred from his body to hers.

145 Parliament of Great Britain, *Report from the Select Committee of the House of Lords, Appointed to Inquire into the Present State of the Islands of New Zealand*, p. 30. Watkins was the surgeon aboard HMS *Buffalo* which was in New Zealand from December 1833 to June 1834 collecting spars for the British Navy, so, like many of the witnesses, his evidence was limited by his experience. Nevertheless, his opinion on these matters is supported by longer-standing residents such as Joel Polack and was not disputed by the CMS missionaries.
146 *Australasian Chronicle*, 9 July 1840, p. 2.
147 Richard Davis, Journal, 15 April 1936, Letters & Journals, typescript, MS-1211-3, Hocken Library, Dunedin.
148 Yate, *An Account of New Zealand*, p. 120.
149 White, *AJHR*, 1861, p. 17.
150 Firth, *Economics of the New Zealand Maori*, p. 110 & Brown, *New Zealand and Its Aborigines*, p. 29.
151 *Wanganui Herald*, 14 January 1885, p. 2.
152 S. M. D. Martin, *New Zealand in a Series of Letters*, London, 1845, p. 284.
153 John White, *Maori Customs and Superstitions: Being the Subject of Two Lectures Delivered at the Mechanics' Institute in Auckland During the Year 1861*, facsimile edn, Christchurch, c. 1999, pp. 192–4.
154 *Hawera and Normanby Star*, 4 October 1905, p. 5.
155 Waitangi Tribunal, *Ngai Tahu Land Report*, Appendix 04 Maori Appellate Court Decision, 4.1 4 South Island Appellate Court Minute Book 672, Appendix 4, Wai 27, Wellington, 1991.
156 White to McLean, 24 August 1871, Object # 1022811, Inward letters — John White, MS-Papers-0032-0632, ATL, Wellington.
157 Evidence of Heremaia Kauere, concerning the Waimamaku Block, 14 June 1875, Northern MB 2, p. 201.
158 Evidence of Ruatara Taurapoko, concerning the Hariru Block, 27 October 1887, Northern MB 8, p. 390.
159 See various witnesses, Native Land Court, Hauraki MB 48, pp. 140–50 & Hauraki MB 51, pp. 3–33.
160 *Star*, 9 August 1907, p. 2.
161 Nin Tomas, 'Key Concepts of Tikanga Maori (Maori Custom Law) and Their Use as Regulators of Human Relationships to Natural Resources in Tai Tokerau, Past and Present', PhD thesis, University of Auckland, 2006, pp. 122–3.
162 Firth, *Economics of the New Zealand Maori*, pp. 213–15.
163 Tregear, *The Maori Race*, pp. 154–5.
164 Best, 'Notes on the Art of War', p. 165.
165 Williams's *Dictionary* offers 'Ko nga wahine me nga tamariki o aua iwi, i waiho e Turi hei pori mana' ('Turi left the women and children of those tribes as his "pori"') as an example of that usage.
166 Edward Shortland, *Maori Religion and Mythology*, London, 1882, p. 95.
167 The kiore, a native rat, was an important food source as New Zealand had few sources of animal protein other than fish.
168 Best, 'Notes on the Art of War', p. 165.
169 Shortland, *Maori Religion and Mythology*, pp. 95–96.
170 Mitchell, *Te Tau Ihu o Te Waka*, vol. 1, p. 131 & Waitangi Tribunal, *Te Tau Ihu o te Waka a Maui: Report on Northern South Island Claims*, 3 vols, vol. 1, Wai 785, Wellington, 2008.
171 Edward Jerningham Wakefield, *Adventure in New Zealand, from 1839 to 1844*, 2 vols, vol. 1, London, 1845, p. 89.
172 Ibid., p. 94.
173 Best, *The Maori as He Was*, p. 107.
174 Polack, *New Zealand: Being a Narrative of Travels and Adventures*, vol. 2, p. 110.
175 Taylor, *Te Ika a Maui*, p. 97.
176 John Owens, 'Religious Disputation at Whangaroa 1823–7', *Journal of the Polynesian Society*, 79, 3, 1970, p. 290.
177 Martin, *New Zealand in a Series of Letters*, p. 284.

Chapter 4: The value of captives and the impact of muskets

1 Mark. W. Allen, 'Transformations in Maori Warfare', in *The Archaeology of Warfare: Prehistories of Raiding and Conquest*, Elizabeth N. Arkush & Mark W. Allen, eds, Gainesville, Florida, 2006, p. 193.
2 Ibid., pp. 194–5.
3 See, for example, W. H. Skinner, 'Ancient Maori Canals. Marlborough, N.Z.', *Journal of the Polynesian Society*, 21, 3, 1912 & D. M. Wilson, 'Ancient Drains Kaitaia Swamp', *Journal of the Polynesian Society*, 30, 119, 1921.
4 Ian Barber, 'Diffusion or Innovation? Explaining Lithic Agronomy on the Southern Polynesian Margins', *World Archaeology*, 42, 1, 2010, p. 85 & *Karanga Hokianga*, Henare Tate, ed., compiled and researched by Teresa Paparoa, Kohukohu, 1987, pp. 107–8.
5 Mark Allen suggested that although all Polynesian societies have similar concepts for maintaining mana against attack, the Māori

ideology of utu evolved under conditions of endemic warfare as a strong deterrent against all transgressions. 'Fierce and assured counterstrikes' were the best means of maintaining land and protecting a polity: Allen, 'Transformations in Maori Warfare', p. 208.
6 Ballara, *Taua*, p. 426.
7 Elsdon Best, *Tuhoe: The Children of the Mist*, 2nd edn, 2 vols, vol. 1, Wellington, 1971 (first published 1925), pp. 112–13.
8 Paora Tokoahu, letter to the editor in *Te Waka Maori o Niu Tirani*, 4 April 1875, p. 89.
9 Evidence of Te Piri re Pāraeroa Block, Waipiro Wp7B/272 of 19 March 1885, cited in Soutar, 'Ngāti Porou Leadership', p. 78.
10 Joseph Banks, *The Endeavour Journal of Joseph Banks 1768–1777*, J. C. Beaglehole, ed., vol. 2, Sydney, 1962, p. 12.
11 Le Dez, 'Summary of a new voyage to Australasia in 1772', in *Extracts from the Journals of the ships Mascarin and Marquis de Castries 1772*, transcribed and translated by Isabel Ollivier, Wellington, 1985, p. 329.
12 Lottin, 'Journal of Victor Charles Lottin', p. 117.
13 Butler, *Earliest New Zealand*, p. 173.
14 See, for example, Shortland, *Traditions and Superstitions of the New Zealanders*, p. 19.
15 Firth, *Economics of the New Zealand Maori*, p. 214.
16 Harry Morton, *The Whale's Wake*, Dunedin, 1982, p. 183; R. P. Hargreaves, 'Changing Maori Agriculture in Pre-Waitangi New Zealand', *Journal of the Polynesian Society*, 72, 2, 1963, p. 103.
17 Angela Ballara, 'Ruatara', *Dictionary of New Zealand Biography: Te Ara — the Encyclopedia of New Zealand*, updated 30 October 2012, at: http://www.TeAra.govt.nz/en/biographies/1r19/ruatara.
18 Rangihoua was quite unsuitable for horticulture which was essential for the mission to be sustainable.
19 Elder, ed., *The Letters and Journals of Samuel Marsden, 1765–1838*, p. 176.
20 Williams, *Christianity among the New Zealanders*, pp. 176–7 & Ballara, 'Warfare and Government in Ngapuhi Tribal Society: 1814–1833', pp. 12 & 258.
21 Cited in Burns, *Te Rauparaha*, p. 139.
22 S. Percy Smith, 'History and Traditions of the Taranaki Coast', *Journal of the Polynesian Society*, 18, 4, 1909, p. 179.
23 John King, Journal, 11 February 1823, Letters & Journals, MS Vol. 73, PC-0152, Hocken Library, Dunedin.
24 Ballara, 'Warfare and Government in Ngapuhi Tribal Society: 1814–1833', p. 80.
25 Roger Philip Wigglesworth, 'The New Zealand Timber and Flax Trade, 1769–1840', PhD thesis, Massey University, 1981, p. 78.
26 Waitangi Tribunal, *Te Tau Ihu o Te Waka a Maui: Report on Northern South Island Claims*, 3 vols, vol. 1, Wai 785, Wellington, 2008, p. 116.
27 White, *The Ancient History of the Maori*, vol. 6, p. 30.
28 C. O. Davis, *The Renowned Chief Kawiti and Other New Zealand Warriors*, Auckland, 1855, p. 11.
29 Best, 'Notes on the Art of War', p. 163.
30 White, *The Ancient History of the Maori*, vol. 9, n.p.
31 Elsdon Best, *Maori Religion and Mythology: Being an Account of the Cosmogony, Anthropogeny, Religious Beliefs and Rites, Magic and Folk Lore of the Maori Folk of New Zealand*, Wellington, 1976–1982, p. 497.
32 A New South Wales trading vessel purchased seven to eight tons of 'very fine' potatoes that year: Hargreaves, 'Changing Maori Agriculture in Pre-Waitangi New Zealand', p. 103 & Rhys Richards & Jocelyn Chisholm, *Bay of Islands Shipping Arrivals and Departures, 1803–1840*, Wellington, 1992, n.p.
33 Belich, *Making Peoples*, p. 159. As Vincent O'Malley pointed out, 'the most intensive period of intertribal warfare in the 1820s coincided with a phase of dramatic growth in cultivated land at the Bay [of Islands]': O'Malley, *The Meeting Place*, p. 125.
34 Archdeacon Walsh, 'Art. II.—The Cultivation and Treatment of the Kumara by the Primitive Maoris', *Transactions and Proceedings of the New Zealand Institute*, 35, 1902, p. 18; William C. Schaniel, 'European Technology and the New Zealand Maori Economy: 1769–1840', *The Social Science Journal*, 38, 1, 2001, p. 139.
35 Elder, ed., *The Letters and Journals of Samuel Marsden, 1765–1838*, p. 113.
36 Ibid., p. 176.
37 Richards & Chisholm, *Bay of Islands Shipping Arrivals and Departures, 1803–1840*, n.p.
38 Savage, who visited in 1805, remarked on Māori eagerness to obtain metal tools, especially axes, adzes, and hatchets, at that time: John Savage, *Some Account of New Zealand; Particularly the Bay of Islands, and Surrounding Country*, originally published, London, 1807, facsimile reprint, Christchurch, 1973, p. 56.
39 Wigglesworth, 'The New Zealand Timber and Flax Trade, 1769–1840', p. 106.
40 Shortland, *Traditions and Superstitions of the New Zealanders*, p. 19; Alister Matheson & Steven Oliver, 'Tupaea, Hori Kingi',

Dictionary of New Zealand Biography: Te Ara — the Encyclopedia of New Zealand, updated 1 September 2010, at: www.TeAra.govt.nz/en/biographies/1t112/1.
41. Mokena, 'The Structural Framework of the Māori Quest Story', p. 353.
42. Yate, *An Account of New Zealand*, p. 121.
43. 'Utu for a slave', White, *The Ancient History of the Maori*, vol. 12, n.p.
44. Lottin, 'Journal of Victor Charles Lottin', p. 120.
45. For example, 'Biography: Obituary and Notices of Tupapa, an aged New-Zealand Chief', *Missionary Register*, December 1835, p. 530. Minarapa Te Rangihatuake, who went on to be a Wesleyan teacher at Mangungu, had been captured by Waikato and on-sold to Ngāpuhi before coming under missionary influence: Gary Clover, 'More Heroes of the Faith: Minarapa Te Rangi-Hatu-Ake and Te Aro Pa, 1839–1841', *Wesley Historical Society Journal*, Proceeding 95, 2012, p. 36.
46. Polack, *New Zealand: Being a Narrative of Travels and Adventures*, vol. 2, pp. 109–10. As Polack had not arrived in the country until 1831 and, as far as is known, the only Westerners resident in New Zealand in 1814 were the first missionaries who arrived in December, it must be assumed that the three or four slaves being purchased for a small hatchet that year were either redeemed immediately as mission servants or sold to visiting ships, perhaps as crew?
47. Ballara, *Taua*, p. 397.
48. As Pat Hohepa explained, 'Weapons, tools, artifacts, and heirlooms with *mana* are usually given names, and once they have a name and a connected narrative [as in this case], they become *taonga* (things inanimate or animate that have exceptional value). Naming a musket would give it potential attributes of *mana*': Hohepa, 'My Musket, My Missionary and My Mana', p. 197.
49. Best, *Tuhoe: The Children of the Mist*, vol. 1, p. 520.
50. 'Sketches of New Zealand', *Sydney Herald*, 12 June 1837, p. 3.
51. Ballara, 'The Role of Warfare in Maori Society in the Early Contact Period', pp. 491–2 & Ballara, *Taua*, p. 103.
52. Richard Davis, Journal, 26, 27 & 30 June 1836, Letters & Journals, typescript, MS-1211-3, Hocken Library, Dunedin.
53. Ibid., 19 October 1824.
54. See Chapter 6 regarding Joel Polack's evidence to the 1838 Select Committee of the House of Lords.
55. He may be said to have married three Māori women but the first, Maria Ringa from the Bay of Islands, fled the scene the very day that the marriage service took place in 1823. His subsequent wife had died before he married again.
56. James Cowan, *Tales of the Maori*, Wellington, 1982, pp. 89–90.
57. H. C. Jacobson, *Tales of Banks Peninsula*, 3rd edn, Christchurch, 1976, p. 214.
58. Williams, *A Dictionary of the Maori Language*, p. 122.
59. R. S. Oppenheim, *Maori Death Customs*, Wellington, Sydney & London, 1973, pp. 52–53.
60. Cruise, *Journal of a Ten Months' Residence in New Zealand*, p. 42.
61. Brown, *New Zealand and Its Aborigines*, p. 79.
62. Best, *Tuhoe: The Children of the Mist*, vol. 1, p. 1060.
63. Elsdon Best, 'Art. XXV.—Maori Eschatology: The Whare Potae (House of Mourning) and Its Lore; Being a Description of Many Customs, Beliefs, Superstitions, Rites, &C., Pertaining to Death and Burial among the Maori People, as Also Some Account of Native Belief in a Spiritual World', *Transactions and Proceedings of the New Zealand Institute*, 38, 1905, p. 166.
64. Tregear, *The Maori Race*, pp. 154–5.
65. Tau, Rāniera Tei Ringa (Sonny), 'History of Ngāpuhi', 14 December 2007, at: http://www.ngapuhi.iwi.nz/ngapuhi-history.aspx, accessed 6 May 2013.
66. Polack, *New Zealand: Being a Narrative of Travels and Adventures*, vol. 2, p. 81.
67. John Hobbs, Diary, 19 January 1824, Papers, typescript, Vol. 4, MS 144, AWMML.
68. Ballara, *Taua*, p. 101.
69. Tregear, *The Maori Race*, p. 156.
70. Richard Davis, Journal, 19 September 1836, Letters & Journals, typescript, Vol. 3, MS-1211-3, Hocken Library, Dunedin.
71. Paul Monin, *Matiatia: Gateway to Waiheke*, Wellington, 2012, pp. 22, 24 & 52.
72. *Wanganui Herald*, 27 November 1886, p. 2 & *Auckland Star*, 1 July 1884, p. 3.
73. Mary K. Watson & Brad R. Patterson, 'The Growth and Subordination of the Maori Economy in the Wellington Region of New Zealand, 1840–52', *Pacific Viewpoint*, 26, 3, 1985, p. 528 & Jenny Murray, 'Moving South with the CMS', in Robert Glen, ed., *Mission and Moko: Aspects of the Work of the Church Missionary Society in New Zealand 1814–1882*, Christchurch, 1992, p. 120.
74. Carleton, *The Life of Henry Williams*, pp. 239–40.
75. Ibid., pp. 107–8; R. A. A. Sherrin & J. H. Wallace, *Early history of New Zealand: from*

earliest times to 1840 by R. A. A. Sherrin; from 1840 to 1845 by J. H. Wallace, Thomson W. Leys, ed., Auckland, 1890, p. 592.
76 Evidence of G. B. Earp, 13 June 1844, Minutes of evidence taken before the Select Committee on New Zealand, *GBPP*, Vol. 2, pp. 108 & 153.
77 John Johnson, 'Notes from a Journal', in Nancy M. Taylor, ed., *Early Travellers in New Zealand*, Oxford, 1959, p. 18.
78 CMS, Minutes of Sub-Committee, May 1839, ATL, Wellington, p. 425.
79 Ballara, *Taua*, p. 426.
80 Evidence of T. McDonnell, 23 May 1844, Minutes of evidence taken before the Select Committee on New Zealand, *GBPP*, Vol. 2, p. 21.
81 Charles Baker, 15 January 1829, Journal, Charles Baker Papers, Series 2, Vol. 1, MS 22, AWMML.
82 Tregear, *The Maori Race*, p. 157.
83 Polack, *New Zealand: Being a Narrative of Travels and Adventures*, vol. 2, p. 110.
84 *Nelson Examiner and New Zealand Chronicle*, 14 March 1846, p. 5.
85 *Nelson Examiner and New Zealand Chronicle*, 7 March 1846, p. 3.
86 Hilary & John Mitchell, *Te Tau Ihu o Te Waka: A History of Maori of Nelson and Marlborough*, vol. 2, Wellington, 2007, p. 287.
87 Kahutoi Te Kanawa & John Turi-Tiakitai, 'Te Mana o Te Kākahu: The Prestige of Cloaks', in *Whatu Kākahu: Māori Cloaks*, Awhina Tamarapa, ed., Wellington, 2011, p. 23.
88 Judith Binney, *The Legacy of Guilt: A Life of Thomas Kendall*, Wellington, 2005, p. 136.
89 Neich, *Painted Histories*, pp. 67–68.
90 McCrae, *Journal Kept in New Zealand in 1820*, pp. 14–15.
91 Cruise, *Journal of a Ten Months' Residence in New Zealand*, pp. 24–26. Richard Cruise is the reputed writer of the journal but it has been suggested that McCrae, a young subaltern, may have been the real author.
92 Petrie, *Chiefs of Industry*, p. 21. Archaeologist Nigel Prickett agrees that although houses in the north were mostly small and undecorated in the 1820s, a number of elaborately carved storehouses had been built by experts imported from further south: Neich, *Painted Histories*, p. 57.
93 Evidence of Piri Teira, 24 November 1885, Whirinaki Block, Native Land Court, Northern MB 7, p. 277.
94 Roger Neich, 'Waitere, Tene — Biography', *Dictionary of New Zealand Biography: Te Ara — the Encyclopedia of New Zealand*, updated 1 September 2010, at: http://www.TeAra.govt. nz/en/biographies/3w1/1.
95 McCrae, *Journal Kept in New Zealand in 1820*, p. 17.
96 Facial moko contained information about a person's ancestry, tribal connections, occupation, rank, and deeds.
97 Christian Palmer & Mervyn L. Tano, *Mokomokai: Commercialization and Desacralization*, International Institute for Indigenous Resource Management, Part of: The Moko Texts Collection, Denver, August 2004, n.p.
98 With regard to head-hunting in the Solomon Islands, Shankar Aswani pointed out that, in Roviana, New Georgia, there was a clear distinction between the ritual functions of the heads of deceased kin and those of slain enemies. In general terms, to keep the head of a chief or relative was 'an act of ritual consecration, a means to subsequently secure the power of the ancestors as vectored through the skull's physical presence' whereas the skulls of enemies were mere 'vessels containing nothing that could be supernaturally taken (i.e., mana) but, rather, something that could be supernaturally denied'. By severing and taking those heads, Roviana warriors could preclude any possibility of the enemy securing the power of their own ancestors: Shankar Aswani, 'Changing Identities: The Ethnohistory of Roviana Predatory Head-Hunting', *Journal of the Polynesian Society*, 109, 1, 2000, p. 55.
99 Palmer & Tano, *Mokomokai: Commercialization and Desacralization*, n.p.; Elder, ed., *The Letters and Journals of Samuel Marsden, 1765–1838*, p. 168.
100 Elder, ed., *The Letters and Journals of Samuel Marsden, 1765–1838*, p. 196.
101 Banks, *The Endeavour Journal of Joseph Banks 1768–1777*, p. 31.
102 Salmond, *Between Worlds*, p. 474.
103 *Sydney Monitor*, 20 September 1828, p. 2. The article refers to the presentation having been made in October, which implies that it occurred almost a year previously. As Winthrop Jordan pointed out, the English discovered chimpanzees, which were then called 'orang-outang', at approximately the same time as they first encountered sub-Saharan West Africans in much the same area. An early seventeenth-century publication, *Historie of Foure-Footed Beastes*, which described apes generally as venerous and lustful, may have begun much of the stereotypical associations between Africans and apes that persisted for generations after: Jordan, *The White Man's Burden*, pp. 15–18.

Historie of Foure-Footed Beastes was written by Edward Topsell in 1607. It should be noted, though, that simian or apelike qualities could also be applied to white people, including the Irish in the nineteenth century.
104 *Sydney Gazette and New South Wales Advertiser*, 8 January 1820, p. 3.
105 For example, in the *Morning Chronicle*, 10 November 1820.
106 *Morning Chronicle*, 26 September 1828.
107 *Morning Chronicle*, 23 September 1822.
108 *Morning Post*, 6 January 1827, p. 1.
109 Māori were widely referred to as New Zealanders at this time.
110 *The Times*, 15 April 1835, p. 6.
111 See, for example, Angas, *Savage Life and Scenes*, pp. 48–49.
112 Major-General Robley, *Moko; or Maori Tattooing*, London, 1896, pp. 146–7.
113 Salmond, *Between Worlds*, p. 474.
114 Lottin, 'Journal of Victor Charles Lottin', p. 119.
115 René Primevère Lesson, 'Journal of René Primevère Lesson', in *Extracts from New Zealand Journals Written on Ships under the Command of d'Entrecasteaux and Duperrey: 1793 and 1824*, transcribed and translated by Isabel Ollivier, ed., Wellington, 1986, p. 142.
116 Ibid.
117 *Sydney Herald*, 23 April 1835, p. 2.
118 Butler, *Earliest New Zealand*, pp. 36, 166–7 & 194.
119 Alison Twells, *Civilising Mission and the English Middle Class 1793–1850: The 'Heathen' at Home and Overseas*, Basingstoke & New York, 2009, p. 206.
120 *York Herald and General Advertiser*, 6 December 1828 & *York Herald*, 13 January 1844, p. 6.
121 *York Herald*, 13 January 1844, p. 6.
122 Robert McNab, *The Old Whaling Days: A History of Southern New Zealand from 1830 to 1840*, Wellington, 1913, pp. 160–1.
123 J. Pitts Johnson, *Plain Truths, Told by a Traveller, Regarding Our Various Settlements in Australia and New Zealand*, London, 1840, pp. 62–63. Despite suggestions that captives were sometimes tattooed in order to sell their subsequently preserved heads, there is no reliable primary evidence for the practice: Ballara, *Taua*, p. 133.
124 C. Wilkes, *Narrative of the United States Exploring Expedition: During the Years 1838, 1839, 1840, 1841, 1842*, vol. II, Philadelphia, 1845, pp. 399–400.
125 There appears to be no record of the enforcement of this proclamation or any accounts of the financial penalty for transgressions being levied: Ngahuia Te Awekotuku with Linda Waimarie Nikora, Mohi Rua & Rolinda Karapu, *Mau Moko: The World of Māori Tattoo*, Auckland, 2007, p. 49.
126 Diana Beaglehole, 'Whanganui region — European settlement, 1840–1860', *Te Ara — the Encyclopedia of New Zealand*, updated 28 January 2010, at: http://www.TeAra.govt.nz/en/whanganui-region/5 & David Young, *Woven by Water: Histories from the Whanganui River*, Wellington, 1998, p. 15.

Chapter 5: Dark Helens and aboriginal Messelinas

1 Salmond, *Between Worlds*, pp. 119–20.
2 Archdeacon Walsh, 'Art. II.—On the Maori Method of Preparing and Using Kokowai', p. 6.
3 Sharp, *Duperrey's Visit to New Zealand in 1824*, p. 87.
4 Salmond, *Between Worlds*, p. 121.
5 June 1773, cited in J. C. Beaglehole, ed., *The Journals of Captain James Cook on His Voyages of Discovery: II. The Voyage of the Resolution and Adventure 1772–1775*, Cambridge, 1961, pp. 174–5.
6 Le Dez, 'Summary of a new voyage to Australasia in 1772', p. 327.
7 Brown, *New Zealand and Its Aborigines*, p. 71. The first edition of this book was written in 1840.
8 Salmond, *Between Worlds*, pp. 75–76.
9 With regard to the crime of adultery, see, for example, Hazel Petrie, 'Satisfaction in a Horse: The Perception and Assimilation of an Exotic Animal into Maori Custom Law', in *Invasive and Introduced Plants and Animals: Human Perceptions, Attitudes and Approaches to Management*, Ian D. Rotherham & Robert A. Lambert, eds, Washington, DC, 2011.
10 From Anderson, *The Welcome of Strangers*, p. 129 & Olive Wright, *Voyage of the Astrolabe, 1840: An English Rendering of the Journals of Dumont d'Urville and His Officers of Their Visit to New Zealand in 1840 Together with Some Account of Bishop Pompallier and Charles, Baron De Thierry*, Wellington, 1955, p. 22.
11 Lesson, 'Journal of René Primevère Lesson', p. 138.
12 Salmond, *Between Worlds*, p. 76.
13 Salmond, *Two Worlds*, p. 376.
14 Nicholas, *Narrative of a Voyage to New Zealand*, vol. I, pp. 201–2.
15 Bruce Biggs, *Maori Marriage: An Essay in Reconstruction*, vol. 1, Polynesian Society

Maori Monographs, Wellington, Auckland, Sydney & Melbourne, 1960, reprinted 1970, p. 15.
16 Henry Williams, Journal, typescript, 27 March 1828, qMS-2224, ATL, Wellington.
17 Ballara, *Taua*, p. 399.
18 Few of those who recorded their impressions of the sex trade admit to personal experience of it.
19 Cruise, *Journal of a Ten Months' Residence in New Zealand*, pp. 202–3.
20 Butler, *Earliest New Zealand*, pp. 105–6.
21 Thomas Bigge was appointed a special commissioner to examine the government of the Colony of New South Wales.
22 Evidence of Dr Fairfowl, May 1821, McNab, *Historical Records of New Zealand*, vol. 1, p. 554.
23 William Wade, *A Journey in the Northern Island of New Zealand: Interspersed with Various Information Relative to the Country and People*, Hobart, 1842, pp. 71–72.
24 Wakefield, *Adventure in New Zealand*, vol. 1, p. 323.
25 Petrie, *Chiefs of Industry*, p. 48.
26 Johnson, *Plain Truths, Told by a Traveller*, p. 64.
27 Cruise, *Journal of a Ten Months' Residence in New Zealand*, p. 166.
28 Ibid., pp. 251–2.
29 Ibid., pp. 166–71. Ballara suggested that she was possibly of high rank and was already promised as a bride: Ballara, 'Warfare and Government in Ngapuhi Tribal Society: 1814–1833', p. 58.
30 Felix Maynard & Alexandre Dumas, *The Whalers*, London, 1937, p. 221.
31 Twenty-eight were recorded in 1821, 1822, and 1824 with 33 known to have called in 1823. The number reached 60 in 1831 and 127 in 1834: Richards & Chisholm, *Bay of Islands Shipping Arrivals and Departures, 1803-1840*, n.p.
32 R. D. Crosby, *The Musket Wars: A History of Inter-Iwi Conflict, 1806–45*, Auckland, 1999, p. 372. In 1818, 60 tons of New Zealand flax, re-exported from Sydney, were valued at £2,600 ($5,200) or just over £43 per ton: Muriel Lloyd Prichard, *An Economic History of New Zealand to 1939*, Auckland & London, 1970, p. 15. Although this would have been a much higher amount than that received by Māori producers, it offers an indication of its value.
33 F. E. Maning, *Old New Zealand: A Tale of the Good Old Times and a History of the War in the North Told by an Old Chief of the Ngapuhi Tribe*, New Zealand Classics, Auckland & Christchurch, 1973 (first published 1887), pp. 211–12.
34 Belich, *Making Peoples*, p. 153.
35 Wigglesworth, 'The New Zealand Timber and Flax Trade, 1769–1840', p. 212. Robert McNab suggested that a woman working quickly could prepare 9 lbs a day but that the average was 5 lbs: Robert McNab, *Murihiku and the Southern Islands: A History of the West Coast Sounds, Foveaux Strait, Stewart Island, the Snares, Bounty, Antipodes, Auckland, Campbell and Macquarie Islands, from 1770 to 1829*, Invercargill, 1907, p. 203.
36 Belich, *Making Peoples*, p. 153.
37 Kathleen Anne Shawcross, 'Maoris of the Bay of Islands, 1769–1840: A Study in Changing Maori Attitudes Towards Europeans', MA thesis, University of Auckland, 1966, p. 257 & Harrison M. Wright, *New Zealand, 1769–1840: Early Years of Western Contact*, Harvard Historical Monographs, Cambridge, Mass., 1959, p. 91.
38 In reality, missionaries sometimes had little option but to deal in muskets in order to survive in a world still ruled by Māori.
39 D. U. Urlich, 'The Introduction and Diffusion of Firearms in New Zealand 1800–1840', *Journal of the Polynesian Society*, 79, 4, 1970, p. 406.
40 Markham, *New Zealand or Recollections of It*, p. 65.
41 Nicholas, *Narrative of a Voyage to New Zealand*, vol. I, pp. 210 & 229. Captain Jones was probably L. Jones, master of a Sydney whaler called the *King George* which visited the Bay of Islands in 1812: Richards & Chisholm, *Bay of Islands Shipping Arrivals and Departures, 1803–1840*, n.p.
42 Nicholas, *Narrative of a Voyage to New Zealand*, vol. I, p. 229.
43 Cruise, *Journal of a Ten Months' Residence in New Zealand*, p. 259.
44 Markham, *New Zealand or Recollections of It*, p. 67.
45 Henry Williams, Journal, 14 December 1826, cited in Fitzgerald, *Letters from the Bay of Islands*, p. 120.
46 Markham, *New Zealand or Recollections of It*, p. 65.
47 Keith V. Sinclair, *Laplace in New Zealand, 1831*, Waikanae, 1998, p. 100.
48 Salmond, *Between Worlds*, p. 121.
49 Ibid., pp. 110, 111, 127, 141 & 142.
50 Ibid., p. 78.
51 Sharp, *Duperrey's Visit to New Zealand in 1824*, pp. 55–56.
52 Lesson, 'Journal of René Primevère Lesson', p. 138.

53 Anderson, *The Welcome of Strangers*, p. 129.
54 Transcript and translation per Edward Shortland Papers, MS 22, UAL.
55 Sinclair, *Laplace in New Zealand, 1831*, pp. 101–2.
56 Ibid., p. 101.
57 Sharp, *Duperrey's Visit to New Zealand in 1824*, p. 55.
58 Donne, *The Maori: Past and Present*, p. 223.
59 Thomson, *The Story of New Zealand*, vol. 1, pp. 284–5.
60 Charles Hursthouse, *New Zealand, or, Zealandia, the Britain of the South*, vol. 1, London, 1857, p. 32.
61 Jack Lee, *I Have Named It the Bay of Islands . . .*, Auckland, 1983, p. 154.
62 John Hobbs, Diary, 19 January 1824, Papers, typescript, Vol. 1, MS 144, AWMML.
63 Thomas Kendall, William Colenso, and William White were among those known to have succumbed.
64 Henry Williams, Journal, typescript, 30 March 1828, qMS-2224, ATL, Wellington.
65 He had been denied the opportunity of staying at the mission when he arrived at the Bay in poor health in 1827, as was his wife when in an advanced state of pregnancy and in need of midwifery assistance and support: Henry Williams, *The Early Journals of Henry Williams*, Lawrence M. Rogers, ed., Christchurch, 1961, pp. 76, 273 & 276. The Bethel Union Society was a religious organisation for seafarers founded in 1819.
66 Henry Williams, Journal, typescript, 20 June 1828, qMS-2224, ATL, Wellington.
67 Richard Davis, Journal, 6 May 1836, Letters & Journals, typescript, Vol. 3, MS-1211-3, Hocken Library, Dunedin.
68 S. Percy Smith, *History and Traditions of the Maoris of the West Coast*, New Plymouth, 1910, p. 418.
69 Ailsa Smith, 'Te Kahui Kararehe, Wiremu', *Dictionary of New Zealand Biography: Te Ara — the Encyclopedia of New Zealand*, updated 1 September 2010, at: http://www.TeAra.govt.nz/en/biographies/3t14/te-kahui-kararehe-wiremu.
70 McNab, *Historical Records of New Zealand*, vol. 1, p. 554.
71 Cruise, *Journal of a Ten Months' Residence in New Zealand*, pp. 138–9. Threatening to kill slaves may have been a regular ploy adopted to either extort payment or gain support from Pākehā. When Te Ara claimed to have speared a slave who had stolen some tools from John Hobbs in 1823 and insisted on his determination to punish all thieves with death, Marsden believed it to be 'mere pretence': Elder, ed., *The Letters and Journals of Samuel Marsden, 1765–1838*, p. 349.
72 Sharp, *Duperrey's Visit to New Zealand in 1824*, p. 99.
73 Charles Hector Jacquinot, 'Journal of Charles Hector Jacquinot', in *Extracts from New Zealand Journals Written on Ships under the Command of d'Entrecasteaux and Duperrey: 1793 and 1824*, transcribed and translated by Isabel Ollivier, Wellington, 1986, p. 99.
74 Sharp, *Duperrey's Visit to New Zealand in 1824*, p. 56.
75 Lottin, 'Journal of Victor Charles Lottin', p. 119.
76 Sharp, *Duperrey's Visit to New Zealand in 1824*, p. 48.
77 Ibid., p. 44.
78 Evidence of Charles Enderby, in Parliament of Great Britain, *Report from the Select Committee of the House of Lords, Appointed to Inquire into the Present State of the Islands of New Zealand*, GBPP, Vol. 1, reprinted as *Colonies: New Zealand, I*, Shannon, 1968 (orig. pub. 1838), pp. 74–75.
79 For a more detailed discussion of personal ownership rights, see, for example, Petrie, *Chiefs of Industry*, pp. 179–82.
80 Theodore Julien de Blois de la Calande, 'Journal of Theodore Julien De Blois De La Calande', in *Extracts from New Zealand Journals Written on Ships under the Command of d'Entrecasteaux and Duperrey: 1793 and 1824*, transcribed and translated by Isabel Ollivier, Wellington, 1986, p. 131.
81 Jacquinot, 'Journal of Charles Hector Jacquinot', p. 99.
82 Lesson, 'Journal of René Primevère Lesson', p. 138.
83 Jean Marie Kehoe, 'Medicine, Sexuality, and Imperialism: British Medical Discourses Surrounding Venereal Disease in New Zealand and Japan: A Socio-Historical and Comparative Study', PhD thesis, Victoria University, 1992, p. 122.
84 Sharp, *Duperrey's Visit to New Zealand in 1824*, p. 55.
85 Ibid., p. 75.
86 Urlich, 'The Introduction and Diffusion of Firearms in New Zealand 1800–1840', p. 403.
87 Clarke, George, [Senior], Letters & Journals, 26 March 1825, Vol. 1, MS 0060, PC-0054, Hocken Library, Dunedin.
88 William Williams, Journal, 19 October 1826, cited in Ballara, *Taua*, p. 399.
89 Baker, Charles, Journal, 16 May 1829, Charles Baker Papers, Series 2, Vol. 1, MS 22, AWMML.
90 Urlich, 'The Introduction and Diffusion

of Firearms in New Zealand 1800–1840', pp. 408–9 & Ballara, *Taua*, pp. 399–400.
91 Thomson, *The Story of New Zealand*, p. 285.
92 Donne, *The Maori: Past and Present*, p. 224.
93 Dr Louis Thiercelin, *Travels in Oceania: Memoirs of a Whaling Ship's Doctor*, 1866, trans. Christiane Mortelier, Dunedin, 1995, p. 138.
94 Ibid.
95 McNab, *Historical Records of New Zealand*, vol. 1, p. 555.
96 Lottin, 'Journal of Victor Charles Lottin', p. 119.
97 Lesson, 'Journal of René Primevère Lesson', p. 161.
98 Parliament of Great Britain, *Report from the Select Committee of the House of Lords, Appointed to Inquire into the Present State of the Islands of New Zealand*, p. 121.
99 Ernst Dieffenbach, *Travels in New Zealand: With Contributions to the Geography, Botany, and Natural History of That Country*, vol. II, London, 1843, Capper Reprint, 1974, p. 161.
100 P. M. E. Williams, *Te Rongoā Māori: Māori Medicine*, Auckland, 1996, p. 23 & L. K. Gluckman, *Medical History of New Zealand Prior to 1860*, Auckland, 1976, p. 162.
101 They include: kōkuhu, meamea, moenga, pōnahanaha, pōriro, raparere, and tīraumoko.
102 *Te Waka Maori o Niu Tirani*, 22 May 1877, p. 134.
103 Basil Keane, 'Tūranga i te hapori — status in Māori society — Tribal traditions of status and rank', *Te Ara — the Encyclopedia of New Zealand*, updated 13 July 2012, at: http://www.TeAra.govt.nz/en/turanga-i-te-hapori-status-in-maori-society/page-2.
104 Stephenson Percy Smith, *Maori Wars of the Nineteenth Century*, Christchurch, 1910, p. 258.
105 Suzanne Boyes, 'Mai i ngā Ao e Rua — From Two Worlds: An investigation into the attitudes towards half castes in New Zealand', BA (Hons) thesis, University of Otago, 2006, p. 5.
106 Brown, *New Zealand and Its Aborigines*, p. 41.
107 Richard Davis to Dandeson Coates, 25 January 1834, Letters & Journals, typescript, MS-1211-1, Hocken Library, Dunedin.
108 This may have been the Mr Hume mentioned by Samuel Marsden in his third New Zealand journal: Elder, ed., *The Letters and Journals of Samuel Marsden, 1765–1838*, p. 255.
109 Butler, *Earliest New Zealand*, p. 216.
110 John King, Journal, 22 September 1822, Letters & Journals, MS Vol. 73, PC-0152, Hocken Library, Dunedin.
111 Ibid., 2 June 1825.
112 Taylor, *Te Ika a Maui*, p. 59.
113 Polack, *New Zealand: Being a Narrative of Travels and Adventures*, vol. 1, p. 377.
114 Earle, *Narrative of a Nine Months' Residence*, p. 139.
115 Anderson, *The Welcome of Strangers*, p. 129.
116 Wade, *A Journey in the Northern Island of New Zealand*, pp. 71–72.
117 Cited in J. M. R. Owens, 'Missionary Medicine and Maori Health: The Record of the Wesleyan Mission to New Zealand before 1840', *Journal of the Polynesian Society*, 81, 4, 1972, p. 427.
118 Brown, *New Zealand and Its Aborigines*, p. 38.
119 Salmond, *Between Worlds*, p. 76.

Chapter 6: Taking British liberty and freedom to Māori

1 *Life*, 28 December 1941.
2 Max O'Rell, *John Bull & Co. — The Great Colonial Branches of the Firm: Canada, Australia, New Zealand and South Africa*, London, 1894, p. 318.
3 Sir William Blackstone, *Commentaries on the Laws of England in Four Books*, 1893 edn, vol. 1, chapter XIV: 'Of Master and Servant', Philadelphia, 1753, p. 424.
4 http://www.askaboutireland.ie/reading-room/arts-literature/irish-traditional-music/turlough-ocarolan/the-harp-a-symbol-of-irel/.
5 The National Heritage List for England, at: http://list.english-heritage.org.uk/resultsingle.aspx?uid=1025166, accessed 11 December 2013.
6 Tamara L. Hunt, *Defining John Bull*, Aldershot & Burlington, 2003, pp. 121–69.
7 Douglas A. Lorimer, 'Black Slaves and English Liberty: A Re-examination of Racial Slavery in England', *Immigrants and Minorities: Historical Studies in Ethnicity, Migration and Diaspora*, 3, 2, 1984, pp. 122 & 123. See also Linda Colley, *Britons: Forging the Nation, 1707–1837*, rev. edn, New Haven [Conn.] & London, 2009.
8 Lorimer, 'Black Slaves and English Liberty'.
9 Srividhya Swaminathan, *Debating the Slave Trade, 1753–1815: Rhetoric of British National Identity*, Farnham, Surrey, 2009, pp. 86–87.
10 See, for example, Cristina Nogueira da Silva & Keila Grinberg, 'Soil Free from Slaves: Slave Law in Late Eighteenth- and Early Nineteenth-Century Portugal', *Slavery & Abolition*, 32, 3, 2011; Sue Peabody & Keila Grinberg, 'Free Soil: The Generation and

Circulation of an Atlantic Legal Principle', *Slavery & Abolition*, 32, 3, 2011.
11 James Epstein, 'Understanding the Cap of Liberty: Symbolic Practice and Social Conflict in Early Nineteenth-Century England', *Past and Present*, 122, 1989, pp. 90–94.
12 Hall, *Civilising Subjects*, p. 72. There had been earlier slave revolts in Haiti, Barbados, and Demerara.
13 For example, fixed-term contracts were imposed on 'free' slaves in Jamaica, a system that was not abolished until 1838.
14 Seymour Drescher, 'Abolitionist Expectations: Britain', *Slavery & Abolition*, 21, 2000, p. 41.
15 Hilton, *The Age of Atonement*, pp. 204–5. Malthus's essay was published in six editions between 1798 and 1826.
16 Ibid., p. 209.
17 Colley, *Britons: Forging the Nation, 1707–1837*, p. 360.
18 Cited in Robert Glen, 'Those Odious Evangelicals', in *Mission and Moko: Aspects of the Work of the Church Missionary Society in New Zealand 1814–1882*, Robert Glen, ed., Christchurch, 1992, p. 23.
19 C. Duncan Rice, *The Scots Abolitionists, 1833–1861*, Baton Rouge, Louisiana, 1981, cited in Hilton, *The Age of Atonement*, p. 209.
20 Ibid., p. 205.
21 Quoted in Peter Thorold, *The London Rich: The Creation of a Great City, from 1666 to the Present*, London, 1999, p. 232.
22 Normanby was Secretary of State for the Colonies.
23 These figures cover England, Wales, Scotland, and Ireland.
24 The Reverend John Newton cited in Matthew Wyman-McCarthy, 'Rethinking Empire in India and the Atlantic: William Cowper, John Newton, and the Imperial Origins of Evangelical Abolitionism', *Slavery & Abolition*, 35, 2, 2014, p. 314.
25 James Heartfield, *The Aborigines' Protection Society: Humanitarian Imperialism in Australia, New Zealand, Fiji, Canada, South Africa, and the Congo, 1837–1909*, London & New York, 2011, pp. 9–10.
26 Zoë Laidlaw, '"Aunt Anna's Report": The Buxton Women and the Aborigines Select Committee, 1835–37', *The Journal of Imperial and Commonwealth History*, 32, 2, 2004, p. 2.
27 Ibid., pp. 3–4.
28 Cited in ibid., p. 14.
29 Jane Samson, 'The 1834 Cruise of HMS Alligator: The Bible and the Flag', *Northern Mariner*, 3, 4, October 1993, p. 43.
30 Ibid.
31 Aborigines' Protection Society, *Report of the Parliamentary Select Committee on Aboriginal Tribes (British Settlements)*, reprinted, with comments, by the Aborigines' Protection Society, London, 1837 edn, p. 104.
32 Laidlaw, '"Aunt Anna's Report"', p. 21.
33 Heartfield, *The Aborigines' Protection Society*, pp. 8–9.
34 Howard Temperley, *British Antislavery, 1833–1870*, London, 1972, pp. 50 & 53.
35 Sir Thomas Fowell Buxton, *The African Slave Trade: Part II: The Remedy*, London, 1840, p. 339.
36 A. G. L. Shaw, 'British Attitudes to the Colonies, ca. 1820–1850', *The Journal of British Studies*, 9, 1, 1969, p. 78.
37 McNab, *Historical Records of New Zealand*, vol. 1, pp. 538 & 543.
38 Parliament of Great Britain, *Report from the Select Committee of the House of Lords, Appointed to Inquire into the Present State of the Islands of New Zealand*, Vol. 1, pp. 133–4.
39 Ibid., p. 49.
40 CMS, Minutes of Sub-Committee, May 1839, ATL, Wellington, p. 426.
41 *The Times*, 6 November 1838, p. 4.
42 Members of the CMS in New Zealand would note that of the 'nineteen witnesses, above one half had never been within many thousands of miles of the country and people they professed to be perfectly well acquainted with; their evidence consequently referred, not to what they had personally seen, experienced, and mentally digested, but in most cases to what they had casually read or accidentally heard', and that others had made only brief visits, often to one place only while they remained aboard ship: Elder, ed., *The Letters and Journals of Samuel Marsden, 1765–1838*, p. 238.
43 Hall, *Civilising Subjects*, p. 72.
44 Parliament of Great Britain, *Report from the Select Committee of the House of Lords, Appointed to Inquire into the Present State of the Islands of New Zealand*, pp. 68–69.
45 Ibid., p. 90.
46 Ibid., p. 70. In his monumental study of the mid-nineteenth-century London poor, first published in 1861, Henry Mayhew distinguished so-called civilised people from their uncivilised counterparts amongst whom he placed the poor of London. Whilst acknowledging some intermediate groups, the two extremes, which Mayhew referred to as 'races', were dichotomised as wanderers versus settlers, vagabonds versus citizens, and nomadic versus civilised: Henry Mayhew, *London Labour and the London Poor*, vol. 1, New York, 1968, pp. 2–3.

47 Smith, *The Meaning of Freedom*, pp. 258–9.
48 Parliament of Great Britain, *Report from the Select Committee of the House of Lords, Appointed to Inquire into the Present State of the Islands of New Zealand*, p. 81.
49 *The Times*, 6 November 1838, p. 4.
50 Parliament of Great Britain, *Report from the Select Committee of the House of Lords, Appointed to Inquire into the Present State of the Islands of New Zealand*, p. 81.
51 Ibid.
52 Henry Williams, Journal, typescript, 3 July 1833, qMS2224, ATL, Wellington.
53 Parliament of Great Britain, *Report from the Select Committee of the House of Lords, Appointed to Inquire into the Present State of the Islands of New Zealand*, p. 115.
54 *Saturday Magazine*, vol. 11, December 1837, p. 262.
55 Extracts from the instructions of the Chief Agent of the New Zealand Land Company, cited in *Extracts from the Papers and Proceedings of the Aborigines' Protection Society, No. 1*, London, May 1839, p. 23.
56 Ibid., pp. 25–27.
57 George Butler Earp, *New Zealand: Its Emigration and Gold Fields*, London, 1853.
58 Hobson to Glenelg, 21 January 1839, Original correspondence, New Zealand, 1838–1846, CO209/4 (1), p. 93.
59 Normanby to Hobson, 14 August 1839, *GBPP*, vol. 23, pp. 37–40. Normanby had succeeded Glenelg on 20 February that year.
60 *Report from the Select Committee on New Zealand with the Minutes of Proceedings*, in *GBPP*, London, 1844, p. 21. McDonnell had arrived in New Zealand around 1830 and established various business interests in the Hokianga. Hobson died in 1842 so could not confirm or contradict McDonnell's statement.
61 The name 'Treaty of Waitangi' is more properly applied to an English-language version of the Treaty, which is not a true translation of the Māori-language document (known as Te Tiriti o Waitangi) signed by almost all the Māori signatories.
62 Cited in Keith Windschuttle, 'Abolition of the Slave Trade: The Australian Connection', *Quadrant*, April 2007, at http://www.sydney-line.com/Abolition%20of%20slave%20trade.htm, accessed 30 December 2011.
63 John Stoughton, 'Ancient Rome and Modern London: Intended to Illustrate the Past and Present State of Civilisation', in *Lectures Delivered Before the Young Men's Christian Association 1845–46*, vol. 1, London, 1869, p. 94.
64 William Arthur, 'The Extent and the Moral Statistics of the British Empire', in *Lectures Delivered Before the Young Men's Christian Association 1845–46*, vol. 1, London, 1869, p. 54.
65 *Report from the Select Committee on New Zealand with the Minutes of Proceedings*, p. 21.
66 John Arthur Roebuck, *The Colonies of England: A Plan for the Government of Some Portion of Our Colonial Possessions*, London, 1849, pp. 117 (fn.) & 138.
67 It was not commonly recognised until an article was published by Ruth Ross in 1972 (Ruth Ross, 'Te Tiriti o Waitangi: Texts and Translations', *New Zealand Journal of History*, 6, 2, 1972) that the English-language version of the Treaty, considered to be the official one, was not an accurate translation of the Māori-language text agreed to by the vast majority of signatories. This subsequently spawned a considerable body of literature debating issues relating to translation, cross-cultural understandings, and other matters. See, for example, Bruce Biggs, 'Humpty-Dumpty and the Treaty of Waitangi', in *Waitangi: Maori and Pakeha Perspectives of the Treaty of Waitangi*, I. H. Kawharu, ed., Auckland, 1989 & Appendix, including Kawharu's translation of the Māori text, pp. 319–21.
68 *Nelson Examiner and New Zealand Chronicle*, 12 October 1844, p. 3.
69 John William Pokai (Heke) to Governor FitzRoy, 21 May 1845, *The Treaty of Waitangi*, New Zealand Room (1990), Canterbury Public Library, Christchurch.
70 *New Zealander*, 19 November 1845, p. 1.
71 E. P. Malone, 'The School Journal and Imperial Ideology', *New Zealand Journal of History*, 7, 1, 1973, pp. 14–15.
72 *London Quarterly Review*, American edition, New York, July 1854, pp. 103–4.
73 Christopher Leslie Brown, *Moral Capital: Foundations of British Abolitionism*, Williamsburg, Virginia, c. 2006, p. 52.
74 Frank Evelyn McDermott, ed., *Self-determination in Social Work: A Collection of Essays on Self-determination and Related Concepts by Philosophers and Social Work Theorists*, London, 1975, p. 141.

Chapter 7: Plucking brands from the burning

1 This incident is discussed in further detail in Chapter 10.
2 Dingle, 'Gospel Power for Civilization', pp. 11–12 & 230.
3 *Missionary Register*, November 1816, p. 471.
4 His journal says 'W' Hansen but it seems

likely to have been a reference to Captain Thomas Hansen who commanded the vessel *Active*, which brought the first missionaries to New Zealand in 1814.

5. John King Journal, 25 May 1819, Letters & Journals, MS Vol. 73, PC-0152, Hocken Library, Dunedin.
6. Ibid., 26 November 1823.
7. Elder, ed., *The Letters and Journals of Samuel Marsden, 1765–1838*, p. 276.
8. *Missionary Register*, 1829, p. 127.
9. Yate, *An Account of New Zealand*, p. 235.
10. Rev. William Yate, evidence, *Report from the Select Committee on Aborigines (British Settlements)*, 13 February 1836, GBPP, Vol. 7, p. 199.
11. John King, Journal, 4 June 1819, Letters & Journals, MS-007, PC-0152, Hocken Library, Dunedin.
12. Ojo, 'Child Slaves in Pre-Colonial Nigeria, c.1725–1860', p. 429.
13. Elder, ed., *The Letters and Journals of Samuel Marsden, 1765–1838*, p. 409.
14. Henry Williams, Journal, 29 December 1831, typescript, qMS-2224, ATL, Wellington.
15. Polack, *New Zealand: Being a Narrative of Travels and Adventures*, vol. 2, p. 105.
16. J. S. Polack, *Manners and Customs of the New Zealanders*, vol. 2, London, 1840, reprint edn, Christchurch, 1976, pp. 78–79.
17. Parliament of Great Britain, *Report from the Select Committee of the House of Lords, Appointed to Inquire into the Present State of the Islands of New Zealand*, Vol. 1, p. 84.
18. O'Malley, *The Meeting Place*, p. 176.
19. Carleton, *The Life of Henry Williams*, p. 62.
20. Letter from Brown, 1 August 1831, *Missionary Register*, 1832, p. 191.
21. Henry Williams, Journal, 27 March 1828, typescript, qMS-2224, ATL, Wellington.
22. Ibid., 16 & 17 February 1828.
23. Alfred Nesbitt Brown, Journal, 2 June 1837, MSS & Archives A-179, UAL. Ballara pointed out that although he remained unconverted when he died, Titore had not killed any of his slaves when his son or other relatives had died: Ballara, *Taua*, p. 424.
24. George Clarke to the CMS, 6 September 1831, Letters & Journals, folios 137–139, PC-0054, Hocken Library, Dunedin.
25. John King, Journal, 25 May 1819, Letters & Journals, MS Vol. 73, PC-0152, Hocken Library, Dunedin.
26. Fitzgerald, *Letters from the Bay of Islands*, p. 56.
27. Ibid., p. 67.
28. Ibid., pp. 59–60.
29. John King, Journal, 10 May 1822, Letters & Journals, MS Vol. 73, PC-0152, Hocken Library, Dunedin.
30. *Missionary Register*, 1835, p. 436.
31. Fitzgerald, *Letters from the Bay of Islands*, p. 93.
32. Kemp to Pratt, 11 February 1824, Letters & Journals, MS Vol. 70, PC-0074, Hocken Library, Dunedin.
33. Fitzgerald, *Letters from the Bay of Islands*, p. 58.
34. Journal of Marianne Williams, 10 August 1823, Letters & Journals written by the Rev. Henry & Mrs Marianne Williams & the Rev. William and Mrs Jane Williams, 1822–1864, typescript, Vols 1 & 2, qMS-2225–2227, ATL, Wellington.
35. Williams, *Te Wiremu — Henry Williams*, Fitzgerald, ed., pp. 64 & 251.
36. 20 February 1832, cited in Frances Porter, Charlotte Macdonald & Tui MacDonald, eds, *My Hand Will Write What My Heart Dictates: The Unsettled Lives of Women in Nineteenth-Century New Zealand as Revealed to Sisters, Family and Friends*, Auckland, 1996, pp. 77–78.
37. As a fourteen-year-old, Colenso had been bonded to a printer for six years in order to learn the trade that would eventually bring him to New Zealand in 1834 in the service of the CMS. He was subsequently dismissed in 1852.
38. Colenso to McLean, 18 January 1853, Object #1005971, MS-Papers-0032-0221, ATL, Wellington.
39. Peter Wells, *The Hungry Heart: Journeys with William Colenso*, Auckland, 2011, pp. 242–4.
40. George Boulukos, *The Grateful Slave: The Emergence of Race in Eighteenth-Century British and American Culture*, Cambridge, 2008, p. 4.
41. Theodore Morton Jones, Journal, March 1853, Vol. 2, qMS-1075, ATL, Wellington.
42. Porter, McDonald & McDonald, eds, *My Hand Will Write What My Heart Dictates*, pp. 77–78.
43. http://www.biblegateway.com/.
44. The word 'ebed', also sometimes translated into English as servant, was used to refer to slavery in the Hebrew version.
45. Titus 2:9–10.
46. Aside from those in the process of being traded, it has been conservatively estimated that one third of the population of Corinth were slaves and another third were 'freedmen' or ex-slaves: Patterson, *Freedom in the Making of Western Culture*, p. 320.
47. Ibid., p. 451, fnn. 32 & 33 & Elias J. Bickerman, 'The Maxim of Antigonus of Socho', *Harvard Theological Review*, 44, 4, 1951, p. 154 & passim.

48 Cleve Barlow, *He Pukapuka Whakataki Kupu o Te Paipera Tapu: A Concordance of the Holy Bible*, Rotorua, 1990.
49 See, for example, John Tidd Pratt, *The Laws Relating to the Poor: Being a Supplement to the Sixth Edition of Bott's Poor Laws, as Well as to the Fourth Edition of Nolan's Treatise on the Same Subject: Including All the Cases and Statutes to the Day of Publication*, London, 1833, pp. 104 & 106.
50 CMS, Minutes of Sub-Committee, May 1839, ATL, Wellington, p. 426.
51 Coleman, *A Memoir of the Rev. Richard Davis*, p. 124.
52 Fitzgerald, *Letters from the Bay of Islands*, p. 109.
53 Henry Williams, Journal, typescript, 16 August 1832, qMS-2224, ATL, Wellington.
54 Robin Fisher, 'Williams, Henry', *Dictionary of New Zealand Biography: Te Ara — the Encyclopedia of New Zealand*, updated 30 October 2012, at: http://www.TeAra.govt.nz/en/biographies/1w22/williams-henry.
55 Butler, *Earliest New Zealand*, pp. 98 & 252. During the missionary's visit to the Thames area in November 1820, the boy's father, who considered the naming 'a great favour', presented Butler with a mat which was reciprocated with a return gift of fish-hooks.
56 Ibid., pp. 254–5.
57 *Taranaki Herald*, 12 January 1889, p. 2.
58 James Buller, *Forty Years in New Zealand: Including a Personal Narrative, an Account of Maoridom, and of the Christianization and Colonization of the Country*, London, 1878, pp. 211–14.
59 Henry Williams, Journal, typescript, 28 & 29 December 1831, qMS-2224, ATL, Wellington.
60 John King, Journal, 18 & 19 November 1833, Letters & Journals, MS Vol. 73, PC-0152, Hocken Library, Dunedin.
61 Polack, *New Zealand: Being a Narrative of Travels and Adventures*, vol. 2, p. 264.
62 Patterson, 'Authority, Alienation and Social Death', pp. 138–9.
63 Nathaniel Turner, Journal, 19 February 1826, Turner-WMS, 22 March 1826, MMS, Trinity College, Auckland, cited in Owens, 'Religious Disputation at Whangaroa 1823–7', p. 295.
64 John King, Journal, 19 November 1823 & 9 September 1824, Letters & Journals, MS Vol. 73, PC-0152, Hocken Library, Dunedin; Patterson, 'Authority, Alienation and Social Death', p. 33.
65 Patterson, *Freedom in the Making of Western Culture*, p. 294.
66 Richard Davis, Journal, 4 August 1833, Letters & Journals, typescript, MS-1211-3, Hocken Library, Dunedin. Michael Guasco has shown that in the American colonies of the seventeenth century, English colonists understood that slavery might actually be an agent of conversion and consequently redeem the Pequot Indians: Guasco, 'To "Doe Some Good Upon Their Countrymen"', p. 399.
67 Coleman, *A Memoir of the Rev. Richard Davis*, p. 132.
68 Williams, *Christianity among the New Zealanders*, p. 169.
69 Elder, ed., *The Letters and Journals of Samuel Marsden, 1765–1838*, pp. 260–1.
70 Letter from Paihia, 24 August 1830, in Coleman, *A Memoir of the Rev. Richard Davis*, pp. 130–1.
71 Yate, *An Account of New Zealand*, pp. 289–91.
72 Hilton, *The Age of Atonement*, p. 13.
73 Coleman, *A Memoir of the Rev. Richard Davis*, p. 111.
74 Carleton, *The Life of Henry Williams*, pp. 59–60.
75 Ibid., p. 61.
76 Dingle, 'Gospel Power for Civilization', p. 11.
77 Angela Wanhalla, '"The Natives Uncivilize Me": Missionaries and Interracial Intimacy in Early New Zealand', in *Missionaries, Indigenous Peoples and Cultural Exchange*, Patricia Grimshaw & Andrew May, eds, Brighton, Portland & Toronto, 2010, p. 25.
78 Tony Ballantyne, 'The Reform of the Heathen Body', in *When the Waves Rolled in Upon Us: Essays in Nineteenth-Century Maori History*, Dunedin, 1999, p. 32.
79 Yate, *An Account of New Zealand*, p. 121.
80 W. B. Marshall, *A Personal Narrative of Two Visits to New Zealand in His Majesty's Ship, Alligator, A.D. 1834*, London, 1836, pp. 34–35.
81 '[Y]ou were like a firebrand plucked from the burning' (Amos 4:11) and 'Is this not a brand plucked from the fire?' (Zechariah 3:2).
82 Personal communication, Dr Martin Sutherland, 19 August 2010.
83 Josiah G. Turner, *The Pioneer Missionary: Life of the Rev. Nathaniel Turner, Missionary in New Zealand, Tonga, and Australia*, Melbourne, 1872, p. 199.
84 *Te Hoa Maori*, 1 April 1894, pp. 6–8.

Chapter 8: Breaking the spiritual bonds

1 For example, touching bread or water might be used to remove the tapu from individuals leaving a cemetery, or from a building following a death: Hazel Petrie, 'The Sanctity of Bread: Missionaries and the Promotion

of Wheat-Growing among the New Zealand Maori', in *Food and Faith in Christian Culture*, Ken Albala & Trudy Eden, eds, New York, 2011, p. 143; Anne Salmond, *Hui: A Study of Maori Ceremonial Gatherings*, Auckland, 2004, p. 43; Tai Tokerau Dictionary, previously at: http://search.atomz.com/whakaheke, accessed 12 September 2010.
2   New Zealand Ministry of Justice, *He Hinatore Ki Te Ao Maori: A Glimpse into the Maori World: Part 1 — Traditional Maori Concepts*, Wellington, 2001.
3   Ballara, *Taua*, pp. 412 & 415.
4   Wigglesworth, 'The New Zealand Timber and Flax Trade, 1769–1840', p. 231.
5   Frank Rogers, 'Ranulph Dacre and Patuone's Topknot', *Stout Centre Review*, 5, 1, 1995, p. 17.
6   See Petrie, *Chiefs of Industry*, pp. 62–64. Harrison Wright suggested that customary notions of mana were disturbed by innovations such as the tattooing of captive heads before or after death to increase the sale value of their preserved heads, although there appears to be little contemporary evidence for this assertion: Wright, *New Zealand, 1769–1840: Early Years of Western Contact*, p. 146.
7   Angela Ballara's *Taua: 'Musket Wars', 'Land Wars' or Tikanga? Warfare in Māori Society in the Early Nineteenth Century* is a notable exception.
8   *New Zealander*, 17 May 1851, p. 2. He repeated much the same statement in 1873: Supplement to the *Nelson Evening Mail*, 30 August 1873, p. 11.
9   For example, Williams, *Christianity among the New Zealanders*, pp. 39–40; Buller, *Forty Years in New Zealand*, p. 214; *AJHR*, 1876, G-5, p. 33; C. W. Vennell, *The Brown Frontier*, Auckland, Wellington & Sydney, 1967, p. 113; John Blacket, *Missionary Triumphs among the Settlers in Australia and the Savages of the South Seas*, London, 1914, p. 283; & Te Waaka Melbourne, 'Te Wairua Kōmingomino o Te Māori: The Spiritual Whirlwind of the Māori', PhD thesis, Massey University, 2011, p. 148.
10 Maxwell and Roberts's analysis of accounts of that incident was noted in the Introduction.
11 Ballara, *Taua*, p. 425.
12 Ibid., pp. 412, 420, 423 & 424.
13 Belich, *Making Peoples*, pp. 164–5; O'Malley, *The Meeting Place*, p. 173.
14 Shawcross, 'Maoris of the Bay of Islands, 1769–1840', p. 347.
15 Belich, *Making Peoples*, p. 167.
16 Ibid., p. 168. Ngāti Toa were releasing their Ngāi Tahu slaves in 1839: Carrington, *Ngāi Tahu: A Migration History*, p. 191.
17 Belich, *Making Peoples*, p. 163.
18 Urlich, 'The Introduction and Diffusion of Firearms in New Zealand 1800–1840', p. 409.
19 Belich, *Making Peoples*, p. 167.
20 Mitchell, *Te Tau Ihu o Te Waka*, vol. 2, p. 463.
21 Harden, 'Narrative of the Battle of Omihi', p. 108.
22 White, *The Ancient History of the Maori*, vol. X (English), p. 198.
23 Anecdotal and circumstantial evidence suggests that Māori literacy was high and that mission-educated Māori were teaching others in areas without access to schools. William Williams's report from the East Coast in January 1840 that lack of access to paper and pen had led Māori to create their own writing materials certainly suggests that there was eager engagement with the new form of communication. He received a written request for books 'written upon a wooden slate . . . which is first rubbed with oil and then plunged into wood ashes, which give it a slight coat on which the writing is made with a pointed stick. Many of these are in use among the natives for want of better. I obtained from another a copy of hymns written with gunpowder': William Williams, *The Turanga Journals, 1840–1850: Letters and Journals of William and Jane Williams*, Wellington, 1974, p. 81.
24 Richard Davis to Dandeson Coates, 6 December 1838, Letters & Journals, typescript, Vol. 1, MS-1211, Hocken Library, Dunedin.
25 Yate, *An Account of New Zealand*, p. 240.
26 Bronwyn Elsmore, *Mana from Heaven: A Century of Maori Prophets in New Zealand*, Auckland, 1999, p. 48.
27 Brown, *New Zealand and Its Aborigines*, pp. 82–83.
28 Mitchell, *Te Tau Ihu o Te Waka*, vol. 1, p. 267.
29 Clover, 'More Heroes of the Faith', passim.
30 Ballara, *Taua*, p. 427.
31 CMS, Minutes of Sub-Committee, May 1839, ATL, Wellington, p. 430.
32 King to the CMS, 10 May 1852, Letters & Journals, MS Vol. 73, PC-0152, Hocken Library, Dunedin.
33 Richard Davis, Annual letter, 1 January 1862, Letters & Journals, typescript, Vol. 3, MS-1211-3, Hocken Library, Dunedin.
34 Scherzer, *Narrative of the Circumnavigation of the Globe by the Austrian Frigate Novara*, vol. 3, pp. 116–17.
35 Binney, 'Christianity and the Maoris to 1840: A Comment', p. 146.
36 Maning, *Old New Zealand*, p. 240.
37 Carleton, *The Life of Henry Williams*, p. 135.

38. Williams, *Christianity among the New Zealanders*, p. 109.
39. *Church Missionary Register*, 1838, p. 219, cited in Elder, ed., *The Letters and Journals of Samuel Marsden, 1765–1838*, p. 533, fn. The letter writer was Wiremu Hau of Ngāi Tāwake: Ballara, *Taua*, p. 428.
40. 'Biography: Obituary and Notices of Tupapa, an aged New-Zealand Chief', *Missionary Register*, December 1835, p. 530.
41. Belich, *Making Peoples*, p. 167; Dingle, 'Gospel Power for Civilization', p. 22.
42. John Hobbs, Diary, 27 November 1823, Papers, typescript, Vol. 1, MS 144, AWMML.
43. Richard Davis, Journal, 23 July 1839, Letters & Journals, typescript, MS-1211-3, Hocken Library, Dunedin.
44. James Belich and Vincent O'Malley have noted the value of releasing captives as a peacemaking strategy: Belich, *Making Peoples*, p. 168; O'Malley, *The Meeting Place*, p. 202.
45. Binney, 'Christianity and the Maoris to 1840: A Comment', p. 148.
46. Richard Davis, Journal, 18 June 1833, Letters & Journals, typescript, MS-1211-3, Hocken Library, Dunedin.
47. Coates, Beecham & Ellis, *Christianity the Means of Civilization*, p. 248.
48. Dingle, 'Gospel Power for Civilization', p. 12.
49. Binney, 'Christianity and the Maoris to 1840: A Comment', p. 151.
50. Bishop Selwyn to Mr Hawkins, 23 June 1848, from *Undine* schooner, off Banks's Peninsula, at: http://anglicanhistory.org/nz/spg20.html, accessed 19 August 2011.
51. Henry Williams, Journal, typescript, 25 & 26 February 1828, qMS-2224, ATL, Wellington.
52. Coleman, *A Memoir of the Rev. Richard Davis*, p. 154.
53. Guy H. Scholefield, *Taupo Haurau: Incidents of a Tribe*, Wellington, 1944, p. 8.
54. The term 'Pākehā-Māori' was applied to Western men, usually traders, whalers, or sealers, who chose to live among Māori communities as part of the tribal group.
55. *Otago Witness*, 11 February 1882, p. 26.
56. F. M. (Jock) Brookfield, *Waitangi and Indigenous Rights: Revolution, Law and Legitimation*, Auckland, 2006, p. 142.
57. Petrie, *Chiefs of Industry*, pp. 53–55.
58. Richard Davis, Journal, 27 May 1835, Letters & Journals, typescript, Vol. 3, MS-1211-3, Hocken Library, Dunedin.
59. Carleton, *The Life of Henry Williams*, pp. 222–3.
60. White, *Maori Customs and Superstitions*, p. 164.
61. Owens, 'Religious Disputation at Whangaroa 1823–7', p. 298.
62. Philip Turner, 'The Politics of Neutrality: The Catholic Mission and the Maori 1838–1870', MA thesis, University of Auckland, 1986, p. 206.
63. Hirini Moko Mead, *Tikanga Maori: Living by Maori Values*, Wellington, 2003, p. 46.
64. Cooper, *Journal of an Expedition Overland from Auckland to Taranaki*, pp. 223–4.
65. Leonard Bell, *Colonial Constructs: European Images of Maori, 1840–1914*, Auckland, 1992, p. 43.

Chapter 9: 'Offensive to the English in the next degree to man eating'?

1. Polack, *New Zealand: Being a Narrative of Travels and Adventures*, vol. 2, p. 105; Parliament of Great Britain, *Report from the Select Committee of the House of Lords, Appointed to Inquire into the Present State of the Islands of New Zealand*, Vol. 1, p. 84.
2. Few of their journals are available prior to 1820.
3. Sadler to Busby, 7 January 1834, AABS 8156, BR1/1, Microfilm 6908, ANZ, Wellington.
4. Thomas Laslett, Journal, MS-Papers-8349-1, ATL, Wellington, pp. 36–37.
5. Eric Ramsden, *Busby of Waitangi: H.M.'s Resident at New Zealand, 1833–40*, Wellington & Dunedin, 1942, p. 188.
6. This is somewhat curious as Turner reported that two doctors had agreed that Biddle's death was the result of injuries sustained before he was thrown into the water whereas Busby accepted the view that he had drowned. 'Rev. Nathaniel Turner — journal, 1836-Aug. 1846', A 1873, Mitchell Library, State Library of NSW, at: http://acms.sl.nsw.gov.au/_transcript/2010/D04581/a2223.pdf, accessed 1 April 2013 & Jennifer Ashton, '"So Strange a Proceeding": Murder, Justice and Empire in 1830s Hokianga', *New Zealand Journal of History*, 46, 2, 2012, p. 151.
7. Ramsden, *Busby of Waitangi*, p. 186.
8. John White Papers, MS Papers-0075-109, Microfilm 0765-12, ATL, Wellington.
9. Williams, *The Early Journals of Henry Williams*, Rogers, ed., p. 398.
10. Robinson, *Twisting the Treaty*, p. 26. Much like the singing and cheering black slaves who would greet the army of liberation that entered Richmond, Virginia, in 1865 as the American Civil War came to an end: Davis, *Inhuman Bondage*, p. 297.
11. John Hobbs, Diary, 31 January 1841,

typescript, Papers, Vol. 4, MS 144, AWMML.
12. I. H. Kawharu, 'Translation of Maori Text', Appendix, in Kawharu, ed., *Waitangi: Māori & Pākehā Perspectives of the Treaty of Waitangi*, pp. 319–20.
13. Angela Ballara, 'Taraia Ngakuti Te Tumuhuia', *Dictionary of New Zealand Biography: Te Ara – the Encyclopedia of New Zealand*, updated 30 October 2012, at:www.TeAra.govt.nz/en/biographies/1t13/taraia-ngakuti-te-tumuhuia.
14. 'George Clarke and Maori at Teraia's pa, 1842', part of Letters from Bishop Selwyn and others, qMS-1775-42, ATL, Wellington.
15. His response to a written insult from a Ngāi Te Rangi Christian community was to attack, kill, and eat some of the members of that hapū. He then taunted Christians within his own hapū area by rolling the heads of the deceased into the midst of a prayer service: Ballara, 'Taraia Ngakuti Te Tumuhuia'.
16. MA 1, Registry of Native Letters, 1845/198, ANZ, Wellington.
17. Webster, *Reminiscences of an Old Settler*, p. 275.
18. *New Zealand Herald*, 10 July 1880, p. 6.
19. *Nelson Examiner and New Zealand Chronicle*, 21 December 1844, p. 166.
20. Official translation of Ngapora to Grey, 19 February 1848, Enclosure No. 7 in Governor Grey to Earl Grey, 3 April 1848, *GBPP*, Vol. 6, p. 19.
21. His letter was passed on to Earl Grey, the Secretary of State for the Colonies, whose solution to the problem was to suggest that chiefly authority be upheld by granting chiefs land titles and local jurisdiction. This suggestion was not taken up by the Governor, however.
22. Ngapora to Grey, 19 February 1848, *GBPP*, Vol. 6, p. 19.
23. Statement by the Rev. A. G. Purchas, 7 July 1863, Enc. 6, No. 30, *AJHR*, 1863, E-3, Sec. I, p. 61.
24. Home to the Governor, 20 January 1846, GLNZ H32.6, ACL, Auckland.
25. Angela Ballara, 'Nene, Tamati Waka', *Dictionary of New Zealand Biography: Te Ara – the Encyclopedia of New Zealand*, updated 30 October 2012, at: http://www.TeAra.govt.nz/en/biographies/1n2/nene-tamati-waka.
26. 'Clarke, George', from *An Encyclopaedia of New Zealand*, A. H. McLintock, ed., originally published 1966, *Te Ara – the Encyclopedia of New Zealand*, updated 23 April 2009, at: http://www.TeAra.govt.nz/en/1966/clarke-george.
27. Te Iwi Moriori Claim Rekohu/Wharekauri (Chatham Islands) / Evidence of Dr Ashley Gould, 1994, part of King, Michael (Dr), 1945–2004: Papers, 97-042-04/07, ATL, Wellington, p. 26.
28. Normanby to Hobson, 14 & 15 August 1839, *GBPP*, Vol. 3, p. 40.
29. Te Iwi Moriori Claim Rekohu/Wharekauri (Chatham Islands)/Evidence of Dr Ashley Gould, p. 30.
30. Earl Grey to Grey, 27 December 1848, G 1/22 no. 97, cited in Ward, *A Show of Justice*, p. 84.
31. Ibid., p. 85.
32. A. Hamilton Russell to the Lieutenant Governor of New Zealand, 1 January 1848, Enc. in No. 26, Governor Grey to Earl Grey, 4 March 1848, *GBPP*, Vol. 6, p. 78.
33. *New Zealand Spectator and Cook's Strait Guardian*, 7 June 1848, p. 3.
34. *New Zealander*, 15 April 1848, p. 2.
35. *Daily Southern Cross*, 21 February 1854, p. 3.
36. Richard Cavendish, 'Dartmoor Prison Is Founded: March 20th, 1806', *History Today*, 56, 3, 2006, p. 61.
37. http://www.napoleon.org/en/reading_room/articles/files/474017.asp.
38. http://www.devon.gov.uk/index/councildemocracy/record_office/, accessed 22 August 2013.
39. Sibylle Scheipers, 'Prisoners and Detainees in War', in *European History Online*, 15 November 2011, at: http://ieg-ego.eu/en/threads/alliances-and-wars/war-as-an-agent-of-transfer/sibylle-scheipers-prisoners-and-detainees-in-war.
40. Information courtesy of Jacqui Hughes, State Library of Tasmania & Tasmanian Archive and Heritage Office, 11 October 2010.
41. Marie Jones, *From Places Now Forgotten*, Cardiff, NSW, 1996, reference courtesy of Emily Hanna, Senior Archivist Access and Information, The State Records Authority of New South Wales, 23 October 2010.
42. Kristyn Harman, *Aboriginal Convicts: Australian, Khoisan and Maori Exiles*, Sydney, 2012, p. 221; *Wellington Independent*, 7 October 1846, p. 2.
43. Warren E. Limbrick, 'Selwyn, George Augustus', *Dictionary of New Zealand Biography: Te Ara – the Encyclopedia of New Zealand*, updated 30 October 2012, at: http://www.TeAra.govt.nz/en/biographies/1s5/selwyn-george-augustus.
44. *Courier*, 28 November 1846, p. 2.
45. Ruth Wilkie, 'Te Umuroa, Hōhepa', *Dictionary of New Zealand Biography: Te Ara – the Encyclopedia of New Zealand*, updated 30 October 2012, at: http://www.TeAra.govt.nz/mi/biographies/1t80/te-umuroa-hohepa.
46. Harman, *Aboriginal Convicts*, pp. 225–6.

47 Ibid., pp. 237–8.
48 Ibid., p. 220.
49 Steven Oliver, 'Te Kirikumara, Ihaia', *Dictionary of New Zealand Biography: Te Ara — the Encyclopedia of New Zealand*, updated 30 October 2012, at: http://www.TeAra.govt.nz/en/biographies/1t44/te-kirikumara-ihaia.
50 Extracts from letter from Ihaia & Tamati to New Plymouth Settlers, from Waitara, 15 July 1860, *AJHR*, 1861, E-1, No. 4, pp. 46–47.
51 *Maori Messenger: Ko Te Karere Maori*, 3 August 1860, p. 27.
52 Evelyn Stokes noted in Völkner's biography that '[t]he evidence that Völkner acted as a spy is well documented in letters he sent to Governor George Grey in January and February 1864': Evelyn Stokes, 'Völkner, Carl Sylvius', *Dictionary of New Zealand Biography: Te Ara — the Encyclopedia of New Zealand*, updated 30 October 2012, at: http://www.TeAra.govt.nz/en/biographies/1v5/volkner-carl-sylvius.
53 The committee of Ngatiawa, Whakatohea, Urewera & Taranaki to the Office of the Government, 6 March 1865, *AJHR*, 1865, E-5, No. 5, Enc. 2, p. 9.
54 Bronwyn Elsmore, *Like Them That Dream*, Auckland, 2011, p. 101.
55 Ngā Ruahine are a section of Ngāti Ruanui.
56 Native Minister J. C. Richmond had promised his people the land between the Patea and Whenuakura rivers as compensation for other land lost through confiscation, but surveyors cut a baseline through that land to link the Patea and Waitara surveys.
57 Jane Reeves, 'Maori Prisoners in Dunedin, 1869–1872 and 1879–1881: Exiled for a Cause', BA (Hons) thesis, University of Otago, 1989, p. 8. See also Margaret Wilson, 'Deed of Settlement between the Crown and Ngati Ruanui 2/5', 4 September 2000, at: http://www.beehive.govt.nz/feature/deed-settlement-between-crown-and-ngati-ruanui-25.
58 Sole, *Ngāti Ruanui: A History*, pp. 352–3.
59 Ian Church, 'Taurua, Ngawaka', *Dictionary of New Zealand Biography: Te Ara — the Encyclopedia of New Zealand*, updated 30 October 2012, at: http://www.TeAra.govt.nz/en/biographies/1t20/taurua-ngawaka.
60 Cited in Sole, *Ngāti Ruanui: A History*, p. 353.
61 *Otago Witness*, 30 April 1870, p. 15.
62 Church, 'Taurua, Ngawaka'.
63 Sole, *Ngāti Ruanui: A History*, pp. 353–4.
64 *New Zealand Herald*, 5 July 1898, p. 3 and 9 July 1898, p. 3.
65 Judith Binney, 'Te Kooti Arikirangai Te Turuki, c.1832–17 April 1893', *Kōtare*, 7, 2, 2008, p. 44.
66 Waitangi Tribunal, *The Taranaki Report: Kaupapa Tuatahi*, Wai 143, Wellington, 1996, 8.5.
67 For example, Isaiah 2:4, Joel 3:10 & Micah 4:3: 'They shall beat their swords into ploughshares, and their spears into pruning hooks.' For specific reference to the connection between ploughing and peace in New Zealand, see also Petrie, *Chiefs of Industry*, pp. 104–6 & Petrie, 'The Sanctity of Bread'.
68 It is unclear why the cattle of the King James Bible were translated as hipi, or sheep, in Te Paipera Tapu.
69 Megan Pōtiki, 'Te haka nā ngā herehere', unpublished paper presented to the New Zealand Historical Association Conference, Dunedin, 2013.
70 Ibid.
71 Lyndsay Head has discussed the ways in which Wiremu Tāmihana's deep Christian convictions and reading of the Bible led him to place the authority of God above that of the Queen: Head, 'Wiremu Tamihana and the Mana of Christianity', in John Stenhouse, ed., assisted by G. A. Wood, *Christianity, Modernity and Culture: New Perspectives on New Zealand History*, Adelaide, 2005. A number of other Māori leaders took a similar approach to their relationships with government.

Chapter 10: Enslaved by the British?

1 They allegedly went so far as to distort historical records to show that chattel slavery had never existed in their islands: Miers, 'Slavery: A Question of Definition', p. 9.
2 John Hobbs, Diary, 26 November 1823, Diaries & letter books, MET 10, Kinder Library, Auckland. The missionaries referred to Te Ara as George. He was the same Te Ara whose ill-treatment had led to the burning of the *Boyd*.
3 Richard Davis, Journal, 20 March 1833, Letters & Journals, typescript, Vol. 3, MS-1211-3, Hocken Library, Dunedin.
4 Henry Williams, Journal, 21 April 1833, typescript, qMS-2224, ATL, Wellington.
5 Richards & Chisholm, *Bay of Islands Shipping Arrivals and Departures, 1803–1840*, n.p.
6 *Missionary Register*, 1835, p. 308.
7 Earle, *Narrative of a Nine Months' Residence*, pp. 127–30.
8 4 February 1847, John Webster, Maori Journal, 1 January–8 July 1847, ACL, NZMS 116–117.
9 W. H. Oliver, 'Bent, Kimble', *Dictionary*

of *New Zealand Biography: Te Ara — the Encyclopedia of New Zealand*, updated 5 June 2013, at: http://www.TeAra.govt.nz/mi/biographies/1b19/bent-kimble.
10 Morton, *The Whale's Wake*, p. 223.
11 E. G. Wakefield, *The British Colonization of New Zealand: Being an Account of the Principles, Objects and Plans of the New Zealand Association, together with particulars concerning the position, extent, soil and climate, natural production and native inhabitants of New Zealand*, London, 1837, pp. xii–xiii.
12 The extent to which Māori understood Western concepts of land ownership and sale became a matter of intense academic and public debate in the wake of the 1985 amendment to the Treaty of Waitangi Act 1975, which allowed Māori groups to make claims against the Crown for breaches of the Treaty. That debate in turn spawned a vast body of literature from the early 1990s, arguing for and against Māori claims that they had not understood land transactions to be permanent alienations. Although that debate, especially the point at which Māori came to understand the concept of sale, remains open, there can be little doubt that, as well as cases of outright fraud, there would have been considerable misunderstanding in the early days of settlement by Westerners.
13 Williams to the CMS, 11 January 1838, cited in Carleton, *The Life of Henry Williams*, pp. 231–2.
14 William Colenso, *The Authentic and Genuine History of the Signing of the Treaty of Waitangi*, Wellington, 1890, reprint, Christchurch, 1971, p. 17.
15 Fitzgerald, *Letters from the Bay of Islands*, p. 247.
16 Colenso, *The Authentic and Genuine History of the Signing of the Treaty of Waitangi*, p. 18.
17 Ibid., p. 19.
18 Waitangi Tribunal, *He Whakaputanga me te Tiriti The Declaration and the Treaty: The Report on Stage 1 of the Te Paparahi o Te Raki Inquiry*, Wai 1040, Wellington, 2014, 7.6.2.
19 Ibid.
20 Colenso, *The Authentic and Genuine History of the Signing of the Treaty of Waitangi*, p. 26.
21 There is a considerable body of literature concerning the different understandings and discussions of the differences between the two versions of the agreement. The vast majority of signatories agreed to the Māori-language version. Only a few Māori, who could not read English, signed the English-language version which is not a translation of the Māori. See, for example, Claudia Orange, *The Treaty of Waitangi*, Wellington, 1987, passim.
22 Peter Adams, *Fatal Necessity: British Intervention in New Zealand 1830–1847*, Auckland, 1977, p. 201.
23 *Daily Southern Cross*, 19 October 1844, p. 3.
24 Despatch 23, FitzRoy to Stanley, 14 October 1844, *GBPP*, 1845, Vol. 33, No. 369, p. 20, cited in Ross, 'Te Tiriti o Waitangi: Texts and Translations', p. 130.
25 Hannah Robert, '"Satisfying the Saints" — Colonial Entrepreneurs in the 1830s and 1840s and the Elasticity of Language', in *Writing Colonial Histories: Comparative Perspectives*, Tracey Banivanua Mar & Julie Evans, eds, Melbourne, 2002, pp. 10–11.
26 *Daily Southern Cross*, 28 October 1843.
27 John William Pokai (Hone Heke) to Governor FitzRoy, 21 May 1845, *The Treaty of Waitangi*, New Zealand Room (1990), Canterbury Public Library, Christchurch.
28 R. Taylor to D. Coates, 18 August 1845, in ATL-Micro-MS-Coll-04-35 (CMS Archives CN/M v. 15 p. 549), at: http://www.treatyofwaitangi.govt.nz/quotes/.
29 Probably Poharama Te Whiti.
30 Donald McLean, Extract from Journal, 9 September 1844, Object #1023874, MS-Papers-0032-0127, ATL, Wellington.
31 G. S. Cooper to the Civil Secretary, 24 October 1852, in H. Hanson Turton, *An Epitome of Official Documents Relative to Native Affairs and Land Purchases in the North Island of New Zealand*, Wellington, 1883, p. 361.
32 Nuitone Te Pakaru to Governor Grey, 6 September 1852, Object #1032265, MS-Papers-0032-0676D-12, ATL, Wellington.
33 Sharp, *Duperrey's Visit to New Zealand in 1824*, p. 39.
34 Morton, *The Whale's Wake*, p. 221.
35 Wade Doak, *The Burning of the 'Boyd': A Saga of Culture Clash*, Auckland, 1984, p. 93. Te Ara was the same man who would later be called George by the missionaries.
36 Whereas Doak, writing in 1984, pointed out that Māori chiefs were due and usually received deferential treatment in Sydney, Dillon, writing in 1829, had a different view: 'Captain Thomson's behaviour in this affair cannot be too much censured. Savages are characterized by a peculiar susceptibility of indignity, while they are equally susceptible of gratitude. In fact, the extreme to which these opposite passions predominate in their breasts, forms one of the principal traits in the uncivilized mind. There cannot be the

least doubt that from the moment George's appeals were disregarded, the *Boyd* and those on board were marked for destruction, as the only means of appeasing his thirst for revenge': Peter Dillon, *Narrative and Successful Result of a Voyage in the South Seas*, London, 1829, p. 219.
37 Doak, *The Burning of the 'Boyd'*, pp. 93–94.
38 Dillon, *Narrative and Successful Result of a Voyage in the South Seas*, p. 218.
39 O'Malley, *The Meeting Place*, pp. 62–63.
40 It has been suggested that Davis's having a club foot was also a factor in his survival on the basis that Māori 'regarded the deformity with awe and sometimes made such people tohungas or priests': Doak, *The Burning of the 'Boyd'*, p. 101. Bentley makes the same suggestion: Trevor Bentley, *Pakeha Maori: The Extraordinary Story of the Europeans Who Lived as Maori in Early New Zealand*, Auckland, 1999, p. 120.
41 Doak, *The Burning of the 'Boyd'*, p. 101.
42 Marsden referred to him as 'Coweetee Teetooa' in one place and 'Toweetee Teetooa' in another. He was described as a son of Tara (probably the one from Kororāreka).
43 Marsden to Pratt, 20 November 1811, in *Marsden and the New Zealand Mission: Sixteen Letters*, P. Havard-Williams, ed., Dunedin, 1961, pp. 40–41.
44 A. Hamilton Russell to the Governor, 8 June 1846, Enc. in No. 20, *GBPP*, Vol. 5, pp. 29–30 & A. Hamilton Russell to the Lieutenant Governor of New Zealand, 1 January 1848, Enc. in No. 26, *GBPP*, Vol. 6, p. 78.
45 Browne to Duke of Newcastle, 13 July 1861, *AJHR*, 1862, E-1, p. 24.
46 For example, Donald McLean, who visited Hawke's Bay in late 1850 to investigate the availability of land for purchase by the government, met Te Hāpuku of Ngāti Te Whatuiapiti there. Although he was told that Tāreha, Kurupō, Te Moananui, and Pūhara were of equal mana to Te Hāpuku, 'he seems to have made a conscious decision that his best chance of acquiring extensive territory was through the latter': Angela Ballara, 'Te Hapuku', *Dictionary of New Zealand Biography: Te Ara — the Encyclopedia of New Zealand*, updated 30 October 2012, at: www.TeAra.govt.nz/en/biographies/1t28/te-hapuku.
47 *Te Haeata*, 1 February 1861, p. 1. Translation from Yvonne Louisa Sutherland, 'Te Reo o Te Perehi: Messages to Maori in the Wesleyan Newspaper *Te Haeata* 1859–1862', MA thesis, University of Auckland, 1999, p. 167.
48 Burns, *Te Rauparaha*, p. 271.
49 Ibid.
50 Fox to [the New Zealand Company?], typescript, 22 April 1845, Aborigines' Protection Society Papers, Micro-MS-Coll-20-2432, ATL, Wellington, cited in Vincent O'Malley, 'Runanga and Komiti: Maori Institutions of Self-Government in the Nineteenth Century', PhD thesis, Victoria University, Wellington, 2004, p. 17.
51 Timothy Keegan, *Colonial South Africa and the Origins of the Racial Order*, Charlottesville, 1996, p. 284.
52 Wards, *The Shadow of the Land*, p. 279; Belich, *Making Peoples*, p. 206; Harman, *Aboriginal Convicts*, p. 218.
53 Pōtatau Te Wherowhero would become the first Māori King.
54 Burns, *Te Rauparaha*, p. 274 & Wards, *The Shadow of the Land*, p. 280.
55 Scheipers, 'Prisoners and Detainees in War'.
56 W. W. Carkeek, *The Kapiti Coast: Maori History and Place Names of the Paekakariki-Otaki District*, Auckland, 2004, pp. 114–15.
57 Graham to Grey, 12 March 1847, Enc. 1 in No. 14, Grey to Earl Grey, 10 April 1847, *GBPP*, Vol. 6, p. 21.
58 J. C. Johnstone, *Maoria: A Sketch of the Manners and Customs of the Aboriginal Inhabitants of New Zealand*, London, 1874, p. 72. In the Western Solomon Islands, too, captives may have been understood to be dead in the eyes of their kin: McDougall, 'Paths of Pinauzu', p. 100.
59 Tioriori [Te Oriori] to Patara, and to the Tribe at the Au o Waikato, 6 January 1864, *AJHR*, 1864, E-1, Appendix I, p. 61. Unfortunately, his actual words in Māori are not quoted.
60 Vayda, *Maori Warfare*, p. 108.
61 Belich, *Making Peoples*, p. 206.
62 CMS, Minutes of Sub-Committee, May 1839, ATL, Wellington, p. 428.
63 John Jolliffe, New Zealand Journals, 1851–1856, Microfilm 10154:1–2, Hocken Library, Dunedin, p. 166.
64 Reports from Mr. Fenton, R. M., As to Native Affairs in the Waikato District, *AJHR*, 1860, E No. 1c, p. 31.
65 Octavius Hadfield, *The New Zealand War: The Second Year of One of England's Little Wars*, London & Edinburgh, 1861, p. 53.
66 Edward Jerningham Wakefield, *Adventure in New Zealand, from 1839 to 1844*, 2 vols, vol. 2, London, 1845, p. 3.
67 *AJHR*, 1876, G-5, p. 3.
68 Alan Ward, 'Davis, Charles Oliver Bond', *Dictionary of New Zealand Biography: Te Ara — the Encyclopedia of New Zealand*, updated 30 October 2012, at: http://www.

TeAra.govt.nz/en/biographies/1d3/davis-charles-oliver-bond.
69 Patu Hohepa, *Mana Tiriti: Mana Tangata*, Auckland/Tamaki Makaurau, 2013, p. 7.
70 Whiteley to Buddle, 9 May 1860, aMS-2178; IRN 1573360, transcript courtesy of Eileen Barrett-Whitehead, 26 March 2013.
71 Graham Brazendale, 'Whiteley, John', *Dictionary of New Zealand Biography: Te Ara — the Encyclopedia of New Zealand*, updated 30 October 2012, at: http://www.TeAra.govt.nz/en/biographies/1w20/whiteley-john.
72 Rebellions included the 1848 Matale rebellion in Ceylon (Sri Lanka), the 1856–7 Xhosa cattle-killings in South Africa, the Santhal insurrection of 1855–6, and the Indian Rebellion of 1857–8.
73 Keegan, *Colonial South Africa and the Origins of the Racial Order*, pp. 44–45.
74 James Belich, *The New Zealand Wars and the Victorian Interpretation of Racial Conflict*, Auckland, 1986, pp. 82–83.
75 Report of Mr. McLean of Native Meeting on the Waikato, 31 May 1860, Enc. 1 in No. 26, *GBPP*, Vol. 12, pp. 72–73.
76 Ibid., p. 71.
77 Ibid.
78 Te Kuini Topeora to Sir Donald McLean, MS-Papers-0032-0685D-10, ATL, Wellington, at: http://natlib.govt.nz/records/22706682.
79 *Maori Messenger: Ko Te Karere Maori*, 15 March 1860, pp. 6–9. For a fuller discussion of how their speeches at this meeting were translated in bilingual newspapers, see Hazel Petrie & Hohipere Tarau, 'Maori Texts and Official Ventriloquism', *New Zealand Journal of History*, 46, 2, 2012.
80 *Taranaki Herald*, 19 May 1860.
81 James Mackay Jnr to the Native Secretary, Report of Pelorus Hui, 12 October 1860, Outwards letterbook, MA-Collingwood, 2/1:173–178, ANZ, Wellington, cited in Mitchell, *Te Tau Ihu o Te Waka*, vol. 2, p. 461.
82 J. Morgan to Sir Thomas Robert Gore Browne, 13 March 1861, Object #1032947, MS-Papers-0032-0459, ATL, Wellington.
83 Report from C. Hunter Brown, Esq, of an official visit to the Urewera tribes, June 1862, *AJHR*, 1862, E No. 9, Sec. IV, pp. 28–29.
84 When Brown and the British missionaries were absent from the CMS mission at Tauranga, Tāmihana took 'the lead in all school matters'. In 1838 he began construction on a Christian village at Te Tāpiri, not far from Matamata pā, where his rules dictated that the precepts of the Ten Commandments were to be followed. By March 1839, the village, complete with chapel and school, had some 300 residents: Evelyn Stokes, 'Te Waharoa, Wiremu Tamihana Tarapipipi', *Dictionary of New Zealand Biography: Te Ara — the Encyclopedia of New Zealand*, updated 30 October 2012, at: http://www.TeAra.govt.nz/en/biographies/1t82/te-waharoa-wiremu-tamihana-tarapipipi.
85 Head, 'Wiremu Tamihana and the Mana of Christianity', pp. 63–66.
86 J. W. Stack to Under-Secretary of the Native Department, 12 June 1877, *AJHR*, 1877, G-4, p. 22.
87 Report to Hon. The Native Minister, 30 April 1873, 'Reports from Officers in Native Districts', *AJHR*, 1873, G-1, p. 20.
88 J. Alexander, *Incidents in the Maori War*, London, 1863, p. 227; Rev. Buddle cited in the *Otago Witness*, 12 January 1861, p. 6, *New Zealand Herald*, 29 June 1887, p. 6, and elsewhere.
89 Edwin Hodder, *Memories of New Zealand Life*, 2nd edn, London, 1863, pp. 205–6.
90 Head, 'Wiremu Tamihana and the Mana of Christianity', pp. 67 & 69.
91 *AJHR*, 1879, Session II, G-8, pp. 2–3.
92 I. H. Kawharu, *Maori Land Tenure: Studies of a Changing Institution*, Oxford & New York, 1977, p. 18 & David V. Williams, *'Te Kooti Tango Whenua': The Native Land Court 1864–1909*, Wellington, 1999.
93 Report of Commissioner of Native Reserves, 30 June 1875, *AJHR*, 1875, G-05, p. 1.
94 *Maori Messenger: Ko Te Karere Maori*, 4 March 1855, p. 54.
95 Te Kouorehua, Tauhuritapoki, Te Tiki Te Whatarau, Te Potahi, Te Riuti, Te Rongotoa and all the tribe to the Aborigines' Protection Society, in Secretary of State to Governor Grey, 27 September 1865 [sic], A6, No. 25, Sub-enclosure in Encl. 1, AJHR, 1865, Session I, A-06, p. 22 (as their letter was enclosed with a response from the Society, dated 15 March 1864, it is assumed that the date of the first Māori letter is a typographical error).
96 Te Oha Taotao, Katikati, Te Kou and all their tribes to the Aborigines' Protection Society, 29 October 1864, A6, No. 25, Sub-enclosure 2 in Encl. 1, AJHR, 1865, Session I, A-06, pp. 22–23.
97 C. Fortescue to the President of the Committee of the Aborigines' Protection Society, 31 March 1865, Enc. 2 in No. 25, *AJHR*, 1865.
98 Lady Mary Martin, *Our Maoris*, Auckland, 1970, reprinted 1970 (first published 1884), p. 210.
99 Ward, *A Show of Justice*, p. 171.
100 John White, R. M. to The Hon. the Colonial

Secretary, 29 April 1864, *AJHR*, 1864, E No. 8, p. 10.
101 Ward, *A Show of Justice*, p. 209.
102 Alan Ward, *An Unsettled History: Treaty Claims in New Zealand Today*, Wellington, 1999, p. 163.
103 Ward, *A Show of Justice*, p. 204.
104 Ibid., p. 302.
105 Ibid., pp. 305–6.
106 John Seed, '"Secular" and "Religious": Historical Perspectives', *Social History*, 39, 1, 2014, pp. 6 & 7.
107 Mohi Turei, 'Te Haki a Te Kuini', in *Mohi Turei: Ana Tuhinga i Roto i Te Reo Maori*, Wiremu & Te Ohorere Kaa, eds, Wellington, 1996, p. 95. The flag may have been the red ensign which was often used by CMS missionaries to indicate the Sabbath day. However, Turei's description is likely to have been a reference to the fact that the Treaty of Waitangi was between Māori on one side and the Queen and her heirs and successors on the other, not with Britain as a nation. That personal relationship lay behind the attempts of several delegations that travelled to England seeking an audience with her to discuss breaches of the Treaty.
108 Ibid., p. 96.
109 Judith Binney, 'Papahurihia, Penetana', *Dictionary of New Zealand Biography: Te Ara — the Encyclopedia of New Zealand*, updated 30 October 2012, at: http://www.TeAra.govt.nz/en/biographies/1p4/papahurihia-penetana.
110 Alfred Barrett, *The Life of the Rev. John Hewgill Bumby*, London, 1852, p. 255 & William Morley, *The History of Methodism in New Zealand*, Wellington, 1900, p. 85.
111 Charles Davis, who recorded this hymn, supplied a very free rather than a literal translation. However, it does suggest that the composer's hope was for his relative's spirit to ascend to heaven: C. O. Davis, *Maori Mementos*, Auckland, 1855, p. 224.
112 Mark Derby, 'Hakaraia Mahika — prophet of peace or son of Satan?', unpublished paper presented to the New Zealand Historical Association conference, Dunedin, 22 November 2013, and personal communication.
113 Paul Clark, *'Hauhau': The Pai Marire Search for Maori Identity*, Auckland & Oxford, 1975, p. 79.
114 Ngatiawa, Whakatohea, Urewera & Taranaki to the Office of the Government, 6 March 1865, Enc. 2 in No. 5, *AJHR*, 1865, E-5, p. 9.
115 Tony Ballantyne, 'Christianity, Colonialism and Cross-Cultural Communication', in *Christianity, Modernity and Culture: New Perspectives on New Zealand History*, John Stenhouse, ed., assisted by G. A. Wood, Adelaide, 2005, p. 56.
116 Elsmore, *Mana from Heaven*, p. 313.
117 James Cowan, 'Famous New Zealanders — No. 19 — Te Whiti, of Taranaki. — The Story of a Patriot and Peacemaker', *New Zealand Railways Magazine*, 9, 7, 1934, p. 18.
118 Hazel Riseborough, *Days of Darkness: The Government and Parihaka, Taranaki 1878–1884*, revised edn, Auckland, 2004, pp. 177–8.
119 *Hawera and Normanby Star*, 9 January 1882, p. 2.
120 Dick Scott, *Ask That Mountain: The Story of Parihaka*, Auckland, 1975, pp. 129–30.
121 *Auckland Star*, 9 January 1882, p. 2.
122 Scott, *Ask That Mountain*, p. 131.
123 *Hawera and Normanby Star*, 9 January 1882, p. 2.
124 Angela Ballara, 'Te Wherowhero, Piupiu', *Dictionary of New Zealand Biography. Te Ara — the Encyclopedia of New Zealand*, updated 30 October 2012, at: http://www.TeAra.govt.nz/en/biographies/3t26/te-wherowhero-piupiu.
125 Elsdon Best, *Spiritual and Mental Concepts of the Maori*, Wellington, 1922, p. 24.
126 The Pākehā's previously implacable faith in ruralism, hard work, and capital accumulation had been severely shaken by economic depression by this time, and historians are agreed that it was a period of psychological trauma as the settler population was embittered, disillusioned, and, eventually, radicalised. When Keith Sinclair wrote *A History of New Zealand*, he designated the period from 1914 to the early 1930s 'Insecurity'. The economy, which had slumped from about 1920, rallied only briefly between 1923 and 1925 and continued to fluctuate until the Wall Street Crash plunged New Zealand into a far deeper depression. P. J. Gibbons referred to 'cheer up days' held to boost morale, and Sinclair spoke of 'loud talk and little faith': P. J. Gibbons, 'The Climate of Opinion', in *The Oxford History of New Zealand*, W. H. Oliver with B. R. Williams, eds, Auckland, 1987, p. 321 & Keith Sinclair, *A History of New Zealand*, revised edn, Auckland, 1988, p. 245. For a fuller discussion, see Petrie, 'The "Lazy Maori"', pp. 109–10.
127 *Evening Post*, 8 November 1934, p. 13.
128 Witi Ihimaera, *The Matriarch*, Auckland, 1986, pp. 238–9.

Chapter 11: The language of slavery

1. A similar phenomenon has been noted in Samoa and is likely to have occurred elsewhere: Vavao Fetui, personal communication, 13 May 2014.
2. *The Cambridge Ancient History: Assyrian and Babylonian Empires and Other States of the near East from the Eighth to the Sixth Centuries B.C.*, 2nd edn, vol. 3, pt 2, Cambridge, 1992, p. 269.
3. *The Gentleman's Magazine*, vol. 59, January–June, April 1789, at: http://www.bl.uk/learning/histcitizen/campaignforabolition/sources/proslavery/planterletter/plantersletter.html.
4. The term 'here-here' was also used by the *Star* newspaper almost 100 years earlier when reporting a claim brought before the Native Land Court at Paeroa in 1907: *Star*, 9 August 1907, p. 2.
5. Brief of Evidence of Te Waari Carkeek, 9 June 2003, relating to Wai 207 & Wai 785, pp. 13–14, at: http://www.ngatitoa.iwi.nz/wp-content/uploads/PhotoGallery/2011/10/Te-Waari-Carkeek.pdf, accessed 26 May 2014.
6. The *Oxford English Dictionary* cites examples of similar use dating from 1807.
7. George Grey, *Nga Mahi a Nga Tupuna*, Wellington, 1953, pp. 106–13; *Polynesian Mythology & Ancient Traditional History of the New Zealanders as Furnished by Their Priests and Chiefs*, London, 1855, pp. 235–45.
8. *Maori Messenger: Ko Te Karere Maori*, 3 August 1860, p. 64.
9. Ballara, *Iwi*, p. 48.
10. Lesley G. Kelly, 'Some Problems in the Study of Maori Genealogies', *Journal of the Polynesian Society*, 49, 194, 1940, p. 241.
11. Peter Lineham, 'To Make a People of the Book', in *Mission and Moko: Aspects of the Work of the Church Missionary Society in New Zealand 1814–1882*, Robert Glen, ed., Christchurch, 1992, p. 166.
12. Lydia Wevers, *Reading on the Farm: Victorian Fiction and the Colonial World*, Wellington, 2010, p. 53.
13. http://www.biblegateway.com/.
14. Shortland, *Traditions and Superstitions of the New Zealanders*, p. 271 & *Maori Religion and Mythology*, pp. 95–96.
15. CMS, Minutes of Sub-Committee, May 1839, ATL, Wellington, p. 430.
16. Judith Binney, '"In-between" Lives: Studies from within a Colonial Society', in *Disputed Histories: Imagining New Zealand's Pasts*, Tony Ballantyne & Brian Moloughney, eds, Dunedin, 2006, p. 96. Tāmihana's letter was dated 27 April but the expulsions did not take place until July.
17. *Te Haeata*, 1 January 1860, p. 4.
18. Tomas, 'Key Concepts of Tikanga Maori', p. 122.
19. Interview with Hinerangi Rapihana at Kaitaia on 6 February 2005, cited in ibid., p. 186.
20. John White, *The Ancient History of the Maori, His Mythology and Traditions: Horo-Uta or Taki-Tumu Migration*, vol. 2, Wellington, 1887, p. 36.
21. Davis, *Inhuman Bondage*, pp. 70–76. The committees were abolished in 1909.
22. Tate, *Karanga Hokianga*.
23. It also included one instance of 'taurereka', four of pārau, and one of rōpā: Ray Harlow, *A Name and Word Index to Ngā Mahi a Ngā Tūpuna*, Dunedin, 1990.
24. Sir Maui Pomare, *Legends of the Maori*, vol. 2, Auckland, 1987, p. 116.
25. *Te Ao Hou*, 44, 1963, pp. 17–24 & 37–45.
26. New Zealand Geographic Board, *He Kōrero Pūrākau Mo Ngā Taunahanahatanga a Ngā Tūpuna: Place Names of the Ancestors, a Maori Oral History Atlas*, Wellington, 1990, pp. 19–23.
27. Ibid., pp. 31–36.
28. *Te Tiupiri*, 18 January 1900, p. 8.
29. See 'Niupepa: Māori Newspapers', at: www.nzdl.org.nz.
30. McLean to Browne, 31 May 1860, Enc. 1 in No. 26, *GBPP*, Vol. 12, p. 72.
31. *Ko Te Karere o Nui Tireni*, 1 February 1845, p. 5.
32. The numbers are confirmed by police returns of canoe traffic into Auckland between 1852 and 1858 published in the *AJHR* and elsewhere.
33. http://www.nzmuseums.co.nz/account/3236/object/1375/Spoils_to_the_victor. Odalisque: 'A female slave or concubine in a harem, esp. in the seraglio of the Sultan of Turkey (now *hist.*). In extended use: an exotic, sexually attractive woman; a representation of a sexually attractive figure in art': *Oxford English Dictionary*.
34. Although prices were volatile, flax exports through Sydney dropped from a peak of £830.75 in 1831 to £96.35 in 1836, and potatoes from £1,040 in 1836 to £328 in 1838: Wigglesworth, 'The New Zealand Timber and Flax Trade, 1769–1840', Appendices 12 & 13.
35. Head, 'Wiremu Tamihana and the Mana of Christianity', p. 63.
36. T. W. Downes, 'Art. XI.—Early History of Rangitikei, and Notes on the Ngati Apa Tribe', *Transactions and Proceedings of the New Zealand Institute*, 42, 1909, p. 76.
37. Brief of Evidence Te Waari Carkeek, 9 June 2003, relating to Wai 207 & Wai 785, p. 14.

BIBLIOGRAPHY

PRIMARY SOURCES

Unpublished archives and manuscripts

Archives New Zealand (ANZ), Wellington
Sadler to Busby, 7 January 1834, AABS 8156, BR1/1, Microfilm 6908

Alexander Turnbull Library (ATL)
Church Missionary Society, Minutes of Sub-Committee appointed to examine the Report from the Select Committee of the House of Lords, on the present state of New Zealand, Letters Received, CN/M M11, Micro-MS-Coll-04-33
Laslett, Thomas, 1811–1887: Journals, MS-Papers-8349-1
McLean, Donald, Papers, 1832–1927, MS-Papers-0032
Morton Jones, Theodore, 1828–1895: Private journals, qMS-1075
White, John, Papers, MS-Copy-Micro-0765
Williams, Henry, Journal, 1827–1840, typescript, qMS-2224
Williams, Marianne, Journal, Letters & Journals written by the Rev. Henry & Mrs Marianne Williams & the Rev. William and Mrs Jane Williams, 1822–1864, typescript, Vols 1 & 2, qMS-2225–2227
Williams, William, Journal, 16 July 1826, typescript, Vol. 1, qMS-2248
Yate, William, Journal and diary, 1833–1845, MS-Copy-Micro-0453

Auckland City Library (ACL)
Grey, George, Grey New Zealand letters, GLNZ H32.5.
Webster, John, Maori Journal, 1 January–8 July 1847, Auckland City Library, NZMS 116–117

Auckland War Memorial Museum Library (AWMML)
John Hobbs, Papers, 1800 1883, typescript, Vol. 1, MS 144
Baker, Charles, Journal, Charles Baker Papers, Series 2, Vol. 1, MS 22

Hocken Library, University of Otago
Clarke, George, [Senior], Letters & Journals, 1822–1849, Vol. 1, MS 0060, PC-0054
Davis, Richard, Journal, Letters & Journals, 1824–1863, typescript, 3 vols, MS-1211
Jolliffe, John, New Zealand Journals, 1851–1856, Microfilm 10154:1–2
Kemp, James, Letters & Journals, 1819–1857, MS Vol. 70, PC-0074
Kemp, James, Letters & Journals, 1819–1857, MS Vol. 70, PC-0075
King, John, Letters & Journals, 1819–1853, MS Vol. 73, PC-0152

John Kinder Theological Library, Auckland
Hobbs, John, Diaries & letter books, 1823–1860, MET 10

Māori Land Court Minute Books
Hauraki MB 48
Hauraki MB 51
Northern MB 2
Northern MB 7
Northern MB 8

University of Auckland Library (UAL)
Brown, Alfred Nesbitt, Journal, typescript, MSS & Archives A-179
Edward Shortland Papers, Maori MSS 95/1

Published primary sources

Official publications
Appendices to the Journals of the House of Representatives (AJHR)
Great Britain Parliamentary Papers (GBPP)
McNab, Robert, *Historical Records of New Zealand*, vol. 1, Wellington, 1908
McNab, Robert, *Historical Records of New Zealand*, vol. 2, Wellington, 1914
Turton, H. Hanson, *An Epitome of Official Documents Relative to Native Affairs and Land Purchases in the North Island of New Zealand*, Wellington, 1883

Newspapers and periodicals
Auckland Star
Australasian Chronicle
Blackwood's Edinburgh Magazine
Courier
Daily Southern Cross
Evening Post
Gentleman's Magazine
Hawera and Normanby Star
Ko Te Karere o Nui Tireni
LIFE
Maori Messenger: Ko Te Karere Maori
Missionary Register
Morning Chronicle
Nelson Evening Mail
Nelson Examiner and New Zealand Chronicle
New Zealand Gazette and Wellington Spectator
New Zealand Herald
New Zealand Spectator and Cook's Strait Guardian
New Zealander
Otago Witness
Saturday Magazine
Sun
Sydney Gazette and New South Wales Advertiser
Sydney Herald
Sydney Monitor
Taranaki Herald
Te Ao Hou
Te Haeata
Te Hoa Maori
Te Puke ki Hikurangi
Te Tiupiri
Te Toa Takatini
Te Waka Maori o Niu Tirani
The Times
Wanganui Herald
York Herald
York Herald and General Advertiser

Books
A Dictionary of New Zealand Biography, vol. II, ed., G. H. Scholefield, Wellington, 1940
Alexander, J., *Incidents in the Maori War*, London, 1863
Angas, George French, *Savage Life and Scenes in Australia and New Zealand: Being an Artist's Impressions of Countries and People at the Antipodes*, 2 vols, vol. 2, London, 1847
——, *The New Zealanders Illustrated*, London, 1847
Banks, Joseph, *The Endeavour Journal of Joseph Banks 1768–1777*, ed., J. C. Beaglehole, vol. 2, Sydney, 1962

Beaglehole, J. C., ed., *The Journals of Captain James Cook on His Voyages of Discovery: II. The Voyage of the Resolution and Adventure 1772–1775*, Cambridge, 1961

Blackstone, Sir William, *Commentaries on the Laws of England in Four Books*, 1893 edn, vol. 1, chapter XIV: 'Of Master and Servant', Philadelphia, 1753

Brown, William, *New Zealand and Its Aborigines*, 2nd edn, London, 1851

Buddle, Thomas, *The Aborigines of New Zealand: Two Lectures Delivered by Thos. Buddle at the Auckland Mechanics' Institute on the Evenings of the 25th March and 12th May, 1851*, Auckland, 1851

Buller, James, *Forty Years in New Zealand: Including a Personal Narrative, an Account of Maoridom, and of the Christianization and Colonization of the Country*, London, 1878

Butler, John, *Earliest New Zealand: The Journals and Correspondence of the Rev. John Butler*, compiled & ed., R. J. Barton, Masterton, 1927

Calande, Theodore Julien de Blois de la, 'Journal of Theodore Julien De Blois De La Calande', in *Extracts from New Zealand Journals Written on Ships under the Command of d'Entrecasteaux and Duperrey: 1793 and 1824*, transcribed and translated by Isabel Ollivier, Wellington, 1986

Carey, Robert, *Narrative of the Late War in New Zealand*, London, 1863

Carrington, Arthur Hugh, *Ngāi Tahu: A Migration History – The Carrington Text*, ed., Te Maire Tau & Atholl Anderson, Wellington, 2008

Coates, Dandeson, Rev. J. Beecham & Rev. W. Ellis, *Christianity the Means of Civilization: Shown in the Evidence Given before a Committee of the House of Commons, on Aborigines*, London, 1837

Coleman, J. N., *A Memoir of the Rev. Richard Davis*, London, 1865

Cooper, G. S., *Journal of an Expedition Overland from Auckland to Taranaki: By Way of Rotorua, Taupo, and the West Coast*, Auckland, 1851

Colenso, William, *The Authentic and Genuine History of the Signing of the Treaty of Waitangi*, Wellington, 1890, reprint, Christchurch, 1971

Cruise, R. A., *Journal of a Ten Months' Residence in New Zealand*, London, 1824

Darwin, Charles, *Journal of Researches into the Geology and Natural History of the Various Countries Visited by H.M.S. Beagle*, London, 1839

Davis, C. O., *Maori Mementos*, Auckland, 1855

—, *The Renowned Chief Kawiti and Other New Zealand Warriors*, Auckland, 1855

—, *The Life and Times of Patuone, the Celebrated Ngapuhi Chief*, Auckland, 1876

Dieffenbach, Ernst, *Travels in New Zealand: With Contributions to the Geography, Botany, and Natural History of That Country*, vol. II, London, 1843, Capper Reprint, 1974

Dillon, Peter, *Narrative and Successful Result of a Voyage in the South Seas*, London, 1829

Dumont d'Urville, Jules-Sébastien-César, *Voyage pittoresque autour du monde*, Paris, 1839

Earle, Augustus, *A Narrative of a Nine Months' Residence in New Zealand in 1827: Together with a Journal of a Residence in Tristan d'Acunha, an Island Situated between South America and the Cape of Good Hope*, London, 1832

—, *Sketches Illustrative of the Native Inhabitants and Islands of New Zealand*, London, 1838

Earp, George Butler, *New Zealand: Its Emigration and Gold Fields*, London, 1853

Elder, J. R., ed., *The Letters and Journals of Samuel Marsden, 1765–1838*, Dunedin, 1932

Fitzgerald, Caroline, *Letters from the Bay of Islands: The Story of Marianne Williams*, Auckland, 2004

Grey, George, *Polynesian Mythology & Ancient Traditional History of the New Zealanders as Furnished by Their Priests and Chiefs*, London, 1855

—, *Ko Nga Whakapepeha Me Nga Whakaahuareka a Nga Tipuna o Aotea-Roa*, Cape Town, 1857

—, *Polynesian Mythology and Ancient Traditional History of the New Zealand Race*, Auckland, 1885

—, *Nga Mahi a Nga Tupuna*, Wellington, 1953

Hadfield, Octavius, *The New Zealand War: The Second Year of One of England's Little Wars*, London & Edinburgh, 1861

Hochstetter, Ferdinand von, *New Zealand: Its Physical Geography, Geology and Natural History with Special Reference to the Results of Government Expeditions in the Provinces of Auckland and Nelson*, Stuttgart, 1867

Hodder, Edwin, *Memories of New Zealand Life*, 2nd edn, London, 1863

Holbech, J., ed., *Captain Thomas Sødring's Diary, Kept During the First Danish Expedition to the South Seas*, translation from Danish, 1841

Hursthouse, Charles, *New Zealand, or, Zealandia, the Britain of the South*, vol. 1, London, 1857

Jacquinot, Charles Hector, 'Journal of Charles Hector Jacquinot', in *Extracts from New Zealand Journals Written on Ships under the Command of d'Entrecasteaux and Duperrey: 1793 and 1824*, transcribed and translated by Isabel Ollivier, Wellington, 1986

Johnson, J. Pitts, *Plain Truths, Told by a Traveller, Regarding Our Various Settlements in Australia and New Zealand*, London, 1840

Johnson, John, 'Notes from a journal', in Nancy Taylor, ed., *Early Travellers in New Zealand*, Oxford, 1959

Johnstone, J. C., *Maoria: A Sketch of the Manners and Customs of the Aboriginal Inhabitants of New Zealand*, London, 1874

Le Dez, 'Summary of a new voyage to Australasia in 1772', in *Extracts from the Journals of the ships Mascarin and Marquis de Castries 1772*, transcribed and translated by Isabel Ollivier, Wellington, 1985

Lesson, René Primevère, 'Journal of René Primevère Lesson', in *Extracts from New Zealand Journals Written on Ships under the Command of d'Entrecasteaux and Duperrey: 1793 and 1824*, transcribed and translated by Isabel Ollivier, Wellington, 1986

Lottin, Victor Charles, 'Journal of Victor Charles Lottin', in *Extracts from New Zealand Journals Written on Ships under the Command of d'Entrecasteaux and Duperrey: 1793 and 1824*, transcribed and translated by Isabel Ollivier, Wellington, 1986

McCrae, Alexander, *Journal Kept in New Zealand in 1820 by Ensign Alexander McCrae, of the 84th Regiment, Together with Relevant Documents*, ed., The Hon. Sir Frederick Revans Chapman, Alexander Turnbull Library, Bulletin No. 3, Wellington, 1928

Maning, F. E., *Old New Zealand: A Tale of the Good Old Times and a History of the War in the North Told by an Old Chief of the Ngapuhi Tribe*, New Zealand Classics, Auckland & Christchurch, 1973 (first published 1887)

Markham, Edward, *New Zealand or Recollections of It*, Wellington, 1963

Marsden, Samuel, *Marsden and the New Zealand Mission: Sixteen Letters*, ed., P. Havard-Williams, Dunedin, 1961

Marshall, W. B., *A Personal Narrative of Two Visits to New Zealand in His Majesty's Ship, Alligator, A.D. 1834*, London, 1836

Martin, Lady Mary, *Our Maoris*, Auckland, 1970, reprinted 1970 (first published 1884)

Martin, S. M. D., *New Zealand in a Series of Letters*, London, 1845

Mayhew, Henry, *London Labour and the London Poor*, vol. 1, New York, 1968 (first published 1861)

Monkhouse, W. B., *The Journals of Captain James Cook on His Voyages of Discovery* (Journal, Appendix IV), ed., J. C. Beaglehole, Kraus Reprint edn, vol. 1, pt 2, Millwood, NY, 1988

Morrison, James, 'The Journal of James Morrison, Boatswain's Mate of the Bounty, Describing the Mutiny and Subsequent Misfortunes of the Mutineers Together with an Account of the Island of Tahiti', in Vanessa Smith, Jonathan Lamb & Nicholas Thomas, eds, *Exploration & Exchange: A South Seas Anthology: 1680–1900*, London, 2000

Nicholas, John Liddiard, *Narrative of a Voyage to New Zealand, Performed in the Years 1814 and 1815, in Company with the Rev. Samuel Marsden*, vols I & II, London, 1817

O'Rell, Max, *John Bull & Co. — The Great Colonial Branches of the Firm: Canada, Australia, New Zealand and South Africa*, London, 1894

Polack, J. S., *New Zealand: Being a Narrative of Travels and Adventures During a Residence in That Country between the Years 1831 and 1837*, London, 1838, reprint edn, Christchurch, 1974, vols 1 & 2

——, *Manners and Customs of the New Zealanders*, London, 1840, reprint edn, Christchurch, 1976, vols 1 & 2

Porter, Frances, Charlotte Macdonald & Tui MacDonald, eds, *My Hand Will Write What My Heart Dictates: The Unsettled Lives of Women in Nineteenth-Century New Zealand as Revealed to Sisters, Family and Friends*, Auckland, 1996

Pratt, John Tidd, *The Laws Relating to the Poor: Being a Supplement to the Sixth Edition of Bott's Poor Laws, as Well as to the Fourth Edition of Nolan's Treatise on the Same Subject: Including All the Cases and Statutes to the Day of Publication*, London, 1833

Robertson, George, *The Discovery of Tahiti: A Journal of the Second Voyage of H.M.S. Dolphin Round the World, under the Command of Captain Wallis, R.N. In the Years 1766, 1767 and 1768*, ed., Hugh Carrington, London, 1948

Roebuck, John Arthur, *The Colonies of England: A Plan for the Government of Some Portion of Our Colonial Possessions*, London, 1849

Rutherford, John, *The White Chief: A Story of Adventure in New Zealand*, Christchurch, Wellington, Dunedin, Melbourne, London, 1908

Savage, John, *Some Account of New Zealand; Particularly the Bay of Islands, and Surrounding Country*, originally published, London, 1807, facsimile reprint, Christchurch, 1973

Scherzer, Karl, *Narrative of the Circumnavigation of the Globe by the Austrian Frigate Novara*, 3 vols, vol. 3, London, 1863
Strachan, A., *The Life of the Rev. Samuel Leigh: Missionary to the Settlers and Savages of Australia and New Zealand*, London, 1870
Tate, Henare, *Karanga Hokianga*, ed., compiled and researched by Teresa Paparoa, Kohukohu, 1987
Tau, Te Maire, *I Whanau Au ki Kaiapoi: The Story of Netanahira Waruwarutu as Recorded by Thomas Green*, Dunedin, 2011
Taylor, Richard, *Te Ika a Maui: New Zealand and Its Inhabitants*, London, 1855
——, *Leaf from the Natural History of New Zealand*, Auckland, 1870
The Bishop of Wellington, 'Notes on the Maoris of New Zealand and Some Melanesians of the South-West Pacific', *Journal of the Ethnological Society of London*, 1, 4, 1869
Thiercelin, Dr Louis, *Travels in Oceania: Memoirs of a Whaling Ship's Doctor*, 1866, translated by Christiane Mortelier, Dunedin, 1995
Thomson, John Turnbull, *Rambles with a Philosopher, or, Views at the Antipodes*, Dunedin, 1867
Tregear, Edward, *The Maori-Polynesian Comparative Dictionary*, Wellington, 1891
Turei, Mohi, 'Te Haki a Te Kuini', in Wiremu & Te Ohorere Kaa, eds, *Mohi Turei: Ana Tuhinga i Roto i Te Reo Maori*, Wellington, 1996
Wade, William, *A Journey in the Northern Island of New Zealand: Interspersed with Various Information Relative to the Country and People*, Hobart, 1842
Wakefield, Edward Jerningham, *Adventure in New Zealand, from 1839 to 1844*, 2 vols, London, 1845
Webster, John, *Reminiscences of an Old Settler in Australia and New Zealand*, Christchurch, 1908
Williams, H. W., *A Dictionary of the Maori Language*, 7th edn, Wellington, 2000
Williams, Henry, *The Early Journals of Henry Williams*, ed., Lawrence M. Rogers, Christchurch, 1961
——, *Te Wiremu — Henry Williams: Early Years in the North*, ed., Caroline Fitzgerald, Wellington, 2011
Williams, William, *Christianity among the New Zealanders*, London, 1867
——, *The Turanga Journals, 1840–1850: Letters and Journals of William and Jane Williams*, Wellington, 1974
Wilson, John Alexander, *Missionary Life and Work in New Zealand — Part III: Tauranga, 1836–39. Being the Private Journal of the Late Rev. John Alexander Wilson*, ed., C. J. Wilson, Auckland, 1889
Wright, Olive, *Voyage of the Astrolabe, 1840: An English Rendering of the Journals of Dumont d'Urville and His Officers of Their Visit to New Zealand in 1840 Together with Some Account of Bishop Pompallier and Charles, Baron De Thierry*, Wellington, 1955
Yate, William, *An Account of New Zealand*, 2nd edn, London, 1835

Electronic sources
Ancient Celtic / Scottish Viking sites in New Zealand!(?), www.kilts.co.nz/mhorruairidh.htm
Ask about Ireland, http://www.askaboutireland.ie/reading-room/arts-literature/irish-traditional-music/turlough-ocarolan/the-harp-a-symbol-of-irel/
Bible Gateway, http://www.biblegateway.com/
Carkeek, Te Waari, 'Brief of Evidence Regarding the Northern South Island Inquiry (Wai 785)', 9 June 2003, www.ngatitoa.iwi.nz/wp-content/uploads/PhotoGallery/2011/10/Te-Waari-Carkeek.pdf
Devon County Council, http://www.devon.gov.uk/index/councildemocracy/record_office/
Human Rights Commission, http://www.hrc.co.nz/hrc/worddocs/3%20-%20I%20Parker%2019%20May%2005.doc
Kiwiblog, http://www.kiwiblog.co.nz/
Lindauer online, http://www.lindaueronline.co.nz/maori-portraits/
Mai Review, http://www.review.mai.ac.nz
Move to New Zealand, http://www.movetonz.org/forum/general-nz-chat/4831-maori-2.html
Museum of New Zealand Te Papa Tongarewa, http://collections.tepapa.govt.nz/
New Zealand History: Nga kōrero a ipurangi o Aotearoa, www.treatyofwaitangi.govt.nz/quotes/
Ngapuhi: Te Runanga a iwi o Ngapuhi, http://www.ngapuhi.iwi.nz/
Nuipepa Māori, http://www.nzdl.org/cgi-bin/library.cgi?a=p&p=about&c=niupepa
NZ Museums, http://www.nzmuseums.co.nz/
Robinson, Chris, 'Dartmoor Prison: the French connection', http://www.napoleon.org/en/reading_room/articles/files/474017.asp
Scheipers, Sibylle, 'Prisoners and Detainees in War', *European History Online*, 15 November 2011, http://ieg-ego.eu/en/threads/alliances-and-wars/war-as-an-agent-of-transfer/sibylle-scheipers-prisoners-and-detainees-in-war

Silicon Investor (SI), www.siliconinvestor.com/
Tano, Mervyn L. & Christian Palmer, *Mokomokai: Commercialization and Desacralization*, International Institute for Indigenous Resource Management, Part of: The Moko Texts Collection, Denver, August 2004, online at New Zealand Electronic Text Collection, 2007
Te Aka Māori-English, English-Māori Dictionary and Index, http://www.maoridictionary.co.nz/
Te Ara — the Encyclopedia of New Zealand, http://www.TeAra.govt.nz/
The Gentleman's Magazine, vol. 59, January–June, April 1789, http://www.bl.uk/learning/histcitizen/campaignforabolition/sources/proslavery/planterletter/plantersletter.html
The National Heritage List for England, http://list.english-heritage.org.uk/resultsingle.aspx?uid=1025166
The Patuone website, http://www.patuone.com/files_main/whakapapa.htm
Turner, Nathaniel, Journal, 1836–Aug. 1846, Mitchell Library, State Library of NSW, http://acms.sl.nsw.gov.au/_transcript/2010/D04581/a2223.pdf
Wikaira, Martin, 'Patupaiarehe — Encounters with patupaiarehe', *Te Ara — the Encyclopedia of New Zealand*, updated 22 September 2012, http://www.TeAra.govt.nz/en/patupaiarehe/page-2
White News Now.com, www.whitenewsnow.com/new-zealand-news-white-new-zealand/14578-celtic-viking-traces-ancient-new-zealand-3-print.html
Windschuttle, Keith: 'Abolition of the Slave Trade: The Australian Connection', *Quadrant*, April 2007, http://www.sydneyline.com/Abolition%20of%20slave%20trade.htm

Video recordings
Conrad, Nicky, interviewed by Whai Ngata, *Waka Huia*, TV ONE, New Zealand, 27 June 1987, transcribed and translated by Hohipere Tarau
Munro, Taipari, 'Parihaka pā', *Waka Huia*, TV ONE, New Zealand, October 2005, transcribed and translated by Hohipere Tarau

SECONDARY SOURCES

Books and articles
A Historical Guide to World Slavery, New York, 1998
Adams, Peter, *Fatal Necessity: British Intervention in New Zealand 1830–1847*, Auckland, 1977
Allen, Mark W., 'Transformations in Maori Warfare', in Elizabeth N. Arkush & Mark W. Allen, eds, *The Archaeology of Warfare: Prehistories of Raiding and Conquest*, Gainesville, Florida, 2006, pp. 184–213
Anderson, Atholl, *The Welcome of Strangers: An Ethnohistory of Southern Maori A.D. 1650–1850*, Dunedin, 1998
Ariki-tara-are, Te, 'History and Traditions of Rarotonga, Part VII, Translated by S. Percy Smith', *Journal of the Polynesian Society*, 28, 112, 1919, pp. 183–208
Ashton, Jennifer, '"So Strange a Proceeding": Murder, Justice and Empire in 1830s Hokianga', *New Zealand Journal of History*, 46, 2, 2012, pp. 142–56
Aswani, Shankar, 'Changing Identities: The Ethnohistory of Roviana Predatory Head-Hunting', *Journal of the Polynesian Society*, 109, 1, 2000, pp. 39–70
Ballantyne, Tony, 'The Reform of the Heathen Body', *When the Waves Rolled in Upon Us: Essays in Nineteenth-Century Maori History*, Dunedin, 1999, pp. 31–41
—, 'Christianity, Colonialism and Cross-Cultural Communication', in John Stenhouse, ed., assisted by G. A. Wood, *Christianity, Modernity and Culture: New Perspectives on New Zealand History*, Adelaide, 2005
Ballara, Angela, 'The Role of Warfare in Maori Society in the Early Contact Period', *Journal of the Polynesian Society*, 85, 4, 1976, pp. 487–506
—, *Iwi: The Dynamics of Maori Tribal Organisation from c. 1769 to c. 1945*, Wellington, 1998
—, *Taua: 'Musket Wars', 'Land Wars' or Tikanga? Warfare in Māori Society in the Early Nineteenth Century*, Auckland, 2003
Barber, Ian, 'Diffusion or Innovation? Explaining Lithic Agronomy on the Southern Polynesian Margins', *World Archaeology*, 42, 1, 2010, pp. 74–89
Barlow, Cleve, *He Pukapuka Whakataki Kupu o Te Paipera Tapu: A Concordance of the Holy Bible*, Rotorua, 1990
—, *Tikanga Whakaaro: Key Concepts in Maori Culture*, Auckland, 1992

Barrett, Alfred, *The Life of the Rev. John Hewgill Bumby*, London, 1852
Barton, Mukti, 'I Am Black and Beautiful', *Black Theology: An International Journal*, 2, 2, 2004
Beattie, H., 'Traditions and Legends Collected from the Natives of Murihiku. (Southland, New Zealand.) Part XIV', *Journal of the Polynesian Society*, 31, 124, 1922, pp. 193–7
Belich, James, *The New Zealand Wars and the Victorian Interpretation of Racial Conflict*, Auckland, 1986
—, *Making Peoples: A History of the New Zealanders From Polynesian Settlement to the End of the Nineteenth Century*, Auckland, 1996
Bell, Leonard, *The Maori in European Art*, Wellington, 1980
—, *Colonial Constructs: European Images of Maori, 1840–1914*, Auckland, 1992
Bennett, Judith A., *Wealth of the Solomons: A History of a Pacific Archipelago, 1800–1978*, Honolulu, c. 1987
Bentley, Trevor, *Pakeha Maori: The Extraordinary Story of the Europeans Who Lived as Maori in Early New Zealand*, Auckland, 1999
Benton, Richard, Alex Frame & Paul Meredith, *Te Mātāpunenga: A Compendium of References to the Concepts and Institutions of Māori Customary Law*, Hamilton, 2013
Best, Elsdon, 'Art. LXV.—The Art of the Whare Pora: Notes on the Clothing of the Ancient Maori, Their Knowledge of Preparing, Dyeing, and Weaving Various Fibres, Together with Some Account of Dress and Ornaments, and the Ancient Ceremonies and Superstitions of the Whare Pora', *Transactions and Proceedings of the New Zealand Institute*, 31, 1898, pp. 625–58
—, 'Notes on the Art of War, as Conducted by the Maori of New Zealand, with Accounts of Various Customs, Rites, Superstitions, &C., Pertaining to War, as Practised and Believed in by the Ancient Maori: Part VII', *Journal of the Polynesian Society*, 12, 3, 1903, pp. 145–65
—, 'Art. XXV.—Maori Eschatology: The Whare Potae (House of Mourning) and Its Lore; Being a Description of Many Customs, Beliefs, Superstitions, Rites, &C., Pertaining to Death and Burial among the Maori People, as Also Some Account of Native Belief in a Spiritual World', *Transactions and Proceedings of the New Zealand Institute*, 38, 1905, pp. 143–239
—, 'The Land of Tara and They Who Settled It. Part III', *Journal of the Polynesian Society*, 27, 106, 1918, pp. 49–71
—, *Spiritual and Mental Concepts of the Maori*, Wellington, 1922
—, *Polynesian Voyagers: The Maori as a Deep-Sea Navigator, Explorer, and Colonizer*, Wellington, 1923
—, *The Maori*, vol. 1, Wellington, 1924
—, 'Raumahora and Takarangi: A Legend of the Taranaki Tribes', *Journal of the Polynesian Society*, 36, 143, 1927, pp. 239–59
—, *The Maori as He Was: A Brief Account of Maori Life as It Was in Pre-European Days*, Wellington, 1934
—, *Tuhoe: The Children of the Mist*, 2nd edn, 2 vols, vol. 1, Wellington, 1971 (first published 1925)
—, *The Stone Implements of the Maori*, Wellington, 1974
—, *Maori Religion and Mythology: Being an Account of the Cosmogony, Anthropogeny, Religious Beliefs and Rites, Magic and Folk Lore of the Maori Folk of New Zealand*, Wellington, 1976–1982
—, *Notes on the Art of War*, ed., Jeff Evans, Auckland, 2001
Bickerman, Elias J., 'The Maxim of Antigonus of Socho', *Harvard Theological Review*, 44, 4, 1951, pp. 153–65
Biggs, Bruce, *Maori Marriage: An Essay in Reconstruction*, vol. 1, Polynesian Society Maori Monographs, Wellington, Auckland, Sydney & Melbourne, 1960, reprinted 1970
—, 'Humpty-Dumpty and the Treaty of Waitangi', in I. H. Kawharu, ed., *Waitangi: Maori and Pakeha Perspectives of the Treaty of Waitangi*, Auckland, 1989, pp. 300–12
Binney, Judith, 'Christianity and the Maoris to 1840: A Comment', *New Zealand Journal of History*, 3, 2, October 1969, pp. 143–65
—, 'Tuki's Universe', *New Zealand Journal of History*, 38, 2, October 2004, pp. 215–32
—, *The Legacy of Guilt: A Life of Thomas Kendall*, Wellington, 2005
—, '"In-between" Lives: Studies from within a Colonial Society', in Tony Ballantyne & Brian Moloughney, eds, *Disputed Histories: Imagining New Zealand's Pasts*, Dunedin, 2006
—, 'Te Kooti Arikirangai Te Turuki, c.1832–17 April 1893', *Kōtare*, 7, 2, 2008, pp. 39–47
Blacket, John, *Missionary Triumphs among the Settlers in Australia and the Savages of the South Seas*, London, 1914
Boulukos, George, *The Grateful Slave: The Emergence of Race in Eighteenth-Century British and American Culture*, Cambridge, 2008

Bowden, Ross, 'Tapu and Mana: Ritual Authority and Political Power in Traditional Maori Society', *The Journal of Pacific History*, 14, 1, 1979, pp. 50–61

Bowser, Brenda J., 'Captives in Amazonia: Becoming Kin in a Predatory Landscape', in Catherine M. Cameron, ed., *Invisible Citizens: Captives and Their Consequences*, Salt Lake City, 2008, pp. 262–82

Brailsford, Barry, *Greenstone Trails: The Maori Search for Pounamu*, Wellington, 1984

Brookfield, F. M. (Jock), *Waitangi and Indigenous Rights: Revolution, Law and Legitimation*, Auckland, 2006

Brooks, James F., *Captives & Cousins: Slavery, Kinship, and Community in the Southwest Borderlands*, Williamsburg, Virginia, c. 2002

——, 'Epilogue: Captive, Concubine, Servant, Kin: A Historian Divines Experience in Archaeological Slaveries', in Catherine M. Cameron, ed., *Invisible Citizens: Captives and Their Consequences*, Salt Lake City, 2008

Brown, Christopher Leslie, *Moral Capital: Foundations of British Abolitionism*, Williamsburg, Virginia, c. 2006

Buck, Sir Peter, *The Coming of the Maori*, Wellington, 1949

Buick, T. Lindsay, *An Old New Zealander: Or, Te Rauparaha, the Napoleon of the South*, London, 1911

Buller, Walter L., 'On the Addition of the Red-Tailed Tropic Bird (Photon Rubricauda) to the Avifauna of New Zealand', *Transactions and Proceedings of the Royal Society of New Zealand*, 10, 1877, pp. 219–20

Burns, Barnet, *A Brief Narrative of a New Zealand Chief: Being the Remarkable History of Barnet Burns, an English Sailor, with a Faithful Account of the Way in Which He Became a Chief of One of the Tribes of New Zealand*, Gisborne, 1871

Burns, Patricia, *Te Rauparaha: A New Perspective*, Wellington, Sydney, Auckland & Christchurch, 1980

Cameron, Catherine M., 'Introduction: Captives in Prehistory as Agents of Social Change', in Catherine M. Cameron, ed., *Invisible Citizens: Captives and Their Consequences*, Salt Lake City, 2008

Campbell, Gwyn, 'Slavery and Other Forms of Unfree Labour in the Indian Ocean World', *Slavery & Abolition*, 24, 2, 2003, pp. ix–xxxii

Carkeek, W. W., *The Kapiti Coast: Maori History and Place Names of the Paekakariki-Otaki District*, Auckland, 2004

Carleton, Hugh, *The Life of Henry Williams: Archdeacon of Waimate*, revised edn, Wellington, 1948

Carocci, Max & Stephanie Pratt, eds, *Native American Adoption, Captivity, and Slavery in Changing Contexts*, New York, 2012

Cavendish, Richard, 'Dartmoor Prison Is Founded: March 20th, 1806', *History Today*, 56, 3, 2006, pp. 60–61

Chappell, David A., *Double Ghosts: Oceanian Voyagers on Euroamerican Ships*, Armonk, NY, c. 1997

Clark, Paul, *'Hauhau': The Pai Marire Search for Maori Identity*, Auckland & Oxford, 1975

Clover, Gary, 'More Heroes of the Faith: Minarapa Te Rangi-Hatu-Ake and Te Aro Pa, 1839–1841', *Wesley Historical Society Journal*, Proceeding 95, 2012, pp. 30–52

Colenso, William, 'On the Maori Races of New Zealand', *Transactions and Proceedings of the New Zealand Institute*, 1, 1868, pp. 5–76

——, 'Art. VII.—Contributions Towards a Better Knowledge of the Maori Race', *Transactions and Proceedings of the New Zealand Institute*, 12, 1879, pp. 108–47

Colley, Linda, *Britons: Forging the Nation, 1707–1837*, rev. edn, New Haven & London, 2009

Cowan, James, 'Famous New Zealanders — No. 19 — Te Whiti, of Taranaki. — The Story of a Patriot and Peacemaker', *New Zealand Railways Magazine*, 9, 7, 1934, pp. 17–21

——, *The New Zealand Wars: A History of the Maori Campaigns and the Pioneering Period*, vol. 1, Wellington, 1955

——, *Tales of the Maori*, Wellington, 1982

Crosby, R. D., *The Musket Wars: A History of Inter-Iwi Conflict, 1806–45*, Auckland, 1999

Davidson, Allan, 'Early Protestant Missionary Beginnings in New Zealand through Different Lenses', in Allan Davidson, Stuart Lange, Peter Lineham & Adrienne Puckey, eds, *Te Rongopai 1814 — 'Takoto te pai!': Bicentenary Reflections on Christian Beginnings and Developments in Aotearoa New Zealand*, Auckland, 2014

Davis, David Brion, *Slavery and Human Progress*, New York, 1984

——, *Inhuman Bondage: The Rise and Fall of Slavery in the New World*, Oxford, 2005

Doak, Wade, *The Burning of the 'Boyd': A Saga of Culture Clash*, Auckland, 1984

Donne, T. E., *The Maori: Past and Present*, London, 1927
Douglas, Bronwen, 'Slippery Word, Ambiguous Praxis: "Race" and Late-18th-Century Voyagers in Oceania', *The Journal of Pacific History*, 41, 1, 2006, pp. 1–29
Downes, T. W., 'Art. XI.—Early History of Rangitikei, and Notes on the Ngati Apa Tribe', *Transactions and Proceedings of the New Zealand Institute*, 42, 1909
—, 'History of Ngati-Kahu-Ngunu', *Journal of the Polynesian Society*, 25, 97, 1916
Drescher, Seymour, 'Abolitionist Expectations: Britain', *Slavery & Abolition*, 21, 2000, pp. 41–66
Duff, Alan, *Once Were Warriors*, Auckland, 1994
Dureau, Christine, 'Oceania', in Seymore Drescher & Stanley L. Engerman, eds, *A Historical Guide to World Slavery*, New York, 1998, pp. 306–8
Elsmore, Bronwyn, *Mana from Heaven: A Century of Maori Prophets in New Zealand*, Auckland, 1999
—, *Like Them That Dream*, Auckland, 2011
Engerman, Stanley L., *Slavery, Emancipation, and Freedom: Comparative Perspectives*, Baton Rouge, 2007
Epstein, James, 'Understanding the Cap of Liberty: Symbolic Practice and Social Conflict in Early Nineteenth-Century England', *Past and Present*, 122, 1989
Evison, Harry C., *Te Wai Pounamu — The Greenstone Island: A History of the Southern Maori During the European Colonization of New Zealand*, Wellington, 1993
Firth, Raymond, *Primitive Economics of the New Zealand Maori*, London, 1929.
—, *Economics of the New Zealand Maori*, 2nd edn, Wellington, 1959
Fischer, David Hackett, *Fairness and Freedom: A History of Two Open Societies: New Zealand and the United States*, Oxford & New York, c. 2012
Fomin, E. S. D., *A Comparative Study of Societal Influences on Indigenous Slavery in Two Types of Societies in Africa*, Ceredigion, 2002
Gibbons, P. J., 'The Climate of Opinion', in W. H. Oliver with B. R. Williams, eds, *The Oxford History of New Zealand*, Auckland, 1987, pp. 302–30
Gill, Rev. W. Wyatt, 'Concerning the Name Unga for "Slave" at Rarotonga, South Pacific', *Journal of the Polynesian Society*, 20, 1911, pp. 128–9
Glen, Robert, 'Those Odious Evangelicals', in Robert Glen, ed., *Mission and Moko: Aspects of the Work of the Church Missionary Society in New Zealand 1814–1882*, Christchurch, 1992
Gluckman, L. K., *Medical History of New Zealand Prior to 1860*, Auckland, 1976
Grove, Neil & Hirini Moko Mead, *Ngā Pēpeha a Ngā Tīpuna: The Sayings of the Ancestors*, Wellington, 2004
Guasco, Michael, 'To "Doe Some Good Upon Their Countrymen": The Paradox of Indian Slavery in Early Anglo-America', *Journal of Social History*, 41, 2, 2007, pp. 389–411
Gudgeon, Lieut. Col., 'Maori Wars', *Journal of the Polynesian Society*, 16, 1, 1907, pp. 13–42
Gudgeon, Thomas Wayth, *The History and Doings of the Maoris: From the Year 1820 to the Signing of the Treaty of Waitangi in 1840*, Auckland, 1885
Halbert, Rongowhakaata, *Horouta: The History of the Horouta Canoe, Gisborne and East Coast*, new edn, Auckland, 2012
Hall-Jones, John, *John Turnbull Thomson: First Surveyor-General of New Zealand*, Dunedin, 1992
Hall, Catherine, *Civilising Subjects: Metropole and Colony in the English Imagination, 1830–1867*, Oxford, 2002
Hall, Noelene, *"I Have Planted . . ." A Biography of Alfred Nesbit Brown*, Palmerston North, 1981
Harden, Mrs C. J., related by Ema Turumeke and translated by her daughter, 'Narrative of the Battle of Omihi', *Journal of the Polynesian Society*, 3, 2, 1894, pp. 107–9
Hargreaves, R. P., 'Changing Maori Agriculture in Pre-Waitangi New Zealand', *Journal of the Polynesian Society*, 72, 2, 1963, p. 17
Harlow, Ray, *A Name and Word Index to Ngā Mahi a Ngā Tūpuna*, Dunedin, 1990
Harman, Kristyn, *Aboriginal Convicts: Australian, Khoisan and Maori Exiles*, Sydney, 2012
Head, Lyndsay, 'Wiremu Tamihana and the Mana of Christianity', in John Stenhouse, ed., assisted by G. A. Wood, *Christianity, Modernity and Culture: New Perspectives on New Zealand History*, Adelaide, 2005
Heartfield, James, *The Aborigines' Protection Society: Humanitarian Imperialism in Australia, New Zealand, Fiji, Canada, South Africa, and the Congo, 1837–1909*, London & New York, 2011
Heuer, Berys N., 'Maori Women in Traditional Family and Tribal Life', *Journal of the Polynesian Society*, 78, 4, 1969, pp. 448–94
Hilton, Boyd, *The Age of Atonement: The Influence of Evangelicalism on Social and Economic Thought 1785–1865*, Oxford & New York, 1991

Hohepa, Pat, 'My Musket, My Missionary and My Mana', in Jonathan Lamb, Alex Calder & Bridget Orr, eds, *Voyages and Beaches: Pacific Encounters, 1769–1840*, Honolulu, 1999

Hohepa, Patu, *Mana Tiriti: Mana Tangata*, Auckland/Tamaki Makaurau, 2013

Holman, Jeffrey Paparoa, *Best of Both Worlds: The Story of Elsdon Best and Tutakangahau*, Auckland, 2010

Howe, Kerry, *The Quest for Origins: Who First Discovered and Settled New Zealand and the Pacific Islands?*, Auckland, 2003

Hunt, Tamara L., *Defining John Bull*, Aldershot & Burlington, 2003

Hviding, Edvard, *Guardians of Marovo Lagoon: Practice, Place, and Politics in Maritime Melanesia*, Honolulu, 1996

Ihimaera, Witi, *The Matriarch*, Auckland, 1986

Jacobson, H. C., *Tales of Banks Peninsula*, 3rd edn, Christchurch, 1976

Jordan, Winthrop D., *The White Man's Burden: Historical Origins of Racism in the United States*, New York, 1974

New Zealand Ministry of Justice, *He Hinatore Ki Te Ao Maori: A Glimpse into the Maori World: Part 1 – Traditional Maori Concepts*, Wellington, 2001

Kawharu, I. H., *Maori Land Tenure: Studies of a Changing Institution*, Oxford & New York, 1977

Keegan, Timothy, *Colonial South Africa and the Origins of the Racial Order*, Charlottesville, 1996

Kelly, Lesley G., 'Some Problems in the Study of Maori Genealogies', *Journal of the Polynesian Society*, 49, 194, 1940, pp. 235–42

Laidlaw, Zoë, '"Aunt Anna's Report": The Buxton Women and the Aborigines Select Committee, 1835–37', *The Journal of Imperial and Commonwealth History*, 32, 2, 2004, pp. 1–28

Lambert, Thomas, *The Story of Old Wairoa and the East Coast District, New Zealand, or, Past, Present and Future: A Record of over Fifty Years' Progress*, Dunedin, 1925

Lea, Rod & Geoffrey Chambers, 'Monoamine Oxidase, Addiction, and the "Warrior" Gene Hypothesis', *New Zealand Medical Journal*, 120, 1250, 2007, pp. 5–10

Lee, Jack, *I Have Named It the Bay of Islands . . .*, Auckland, 1983

Lineham, Peter, 'To Make a People of the Book', in Robert Glen, ed., *Mission and Moko: Aspects of the Work of the Church Missionary Society in New Zealand 1814–1882*, Christchurch, 1992

Lorimer, Douglas A., 'Black Slaves and English Liberty: A Re-examination of Racial Slavery in England', *Immigrants and Minorities: Historical Studies in Ethnicity, Migration and Diaspora*, 3, 2, 1984, pp. 121–50

McDermott, Frank Evelyn, ed., *Self-determination in Social Work: A Collection of Essays on Self-determination and Related Concepts by Philosophers and Social Work Theorists*, London, 1975

McDonnell, T. A., *A Maori History of the War: Being a Native Account of the Pakeha-Maori Wars in New Zealand*, Auckland, 1887

McDougall, Debra, 'Paths of *Pinauzu*: Captivity and Social Reproduction in Ranongga', *Journal of the Polynesian Society*, 109, 1, 2000, pp. 99–113

Mackay, Joseph Angus, *Historic Poverty Bay and the East Coast, N.I., N.Z.*, Gisborne, 1949

McNab, Robert, *Murihiku and the Southern Islands: A History of the West Coast Sounds, Foveaux Strait, Stewart Island, the Snares, Bounty, Antipodes, Auckland, Campbell and Macquarie Islands, from 1770 to 1829*, Invercargill, 1907

——, *The Old Whaling Days: A History of Southern New Zealand from 1830 to 1840*, Wellington, 1913

Malone, E. P., 'The School Journal and Imperial Ideology', *New Zealand Journal of History*, 7, 1, 1973

Marsden, Maori, 'God, Man and Universe: A Maori View', in Michael King, ed., *Te Ao Hurihuri: Aspects of Maoritanga*, Wellington, 1975, pp. 191–219

Maxwell, Alexander & Evan Roberts, 'The Whangaroa Incident, 16 July 1824: A European–Maori Encounter and Its Many Incarnations', *The Journal of Pacific History*, 49, 1, 2014, pp. 50–75

Maynard, Felix & Alexandre Dumas, *The Whalers*, London, 1937

Mead, Hirini Moko, *Tikanga Māori: Living by Māori Values*, Wellington, 2003

Miers, Suzanne, 'Slavery: A Question of Definition', *Slavery & Abolition*, 24, 2, 2003, pp. 1–16

Mitchell, Hilary and John, *Te Tau Ihu o Te Waka: A History of Maori of Nelson and Marlborough*, 2 vols, vol. 1, Wellington, 2005

Mitchell, Hilary and John, *Te Tau Ihu o Te Waka: A History of Maori of Nelson and Marlborough*, 2 vols, vol. 2, Wellington, 2007

Monin, Paul, *Matiatia: Gateway to Waiheke*, Wellington, 2012

Moon, Paul, *This Horrid Practice: The Myth and Reality of Traditional Maori Cannibalism*, Auckland, 2008

Morley, William, *The History of Methodism in New Zealand*, Wellington, 1900
Morton, Harry, *The Whale's Wake*, Dunedin, 1982
Murray, Jenny, 'Moving South with the CMS', in Robert Glen, ed., *Mission and Moko: Aspects of the Work of the Church Missionary Society in New Zealand 1814–1882*, Christchurch, 1992
Neich, Roger, *Painted Histories: Early Maori Figurative Painting*, Auckland, 1994
——, *Carved Histories: Rotorua Ngati Tarawhai Woodcarving*, Auckland, 2001
New Zealand Geographic Board, *He Kōrero Pūrākau Mo Ngā Taunahanahatanga a Ngā Tūpuna: Place Names of the Ancestors, a Maori Oral History Atlas*, Wellington, 1990
Nogueira da Silva, Cristina & Keila Grinberg, 'Soil Free from Slaves: Slave Law in Late Eighteenth- and Early Nineteenth-Century Portugal', *Slavery & Abolition*, 32, 3, 2011, pp. 431–46
O'Malley, Vincent, *Agents of Autonomy: Maori Committees in the Nineteenth Century*, Wellington, 1998
——, *The Meeting Place: Māori and Pākehā Encounters, 1642–1840*, Auckland, 2012
——, *Beyond the Imperial Frontier: The Contest for Colonial New Zealand*, Wellington, 2014
Ojo, Olatunji, 'Child Slaves in Pre-Colonial Nigeria, c.1725–1860', *Slavery & Abolition*, 33, 3, 2012, pp. 417–34
Oppenheim, R. S., *Maori Death Customs*, Wellington, Sydney & London, 1973
Orbell, Margaret, *Maori Folktales in Maori and English*, Auckland, 1968
——, *Traditional Māori Stories*, introduced and translated by Margaret Orbell, Auckland, 1997
Owens, J. M. R., 'Missionary Medicine and Maori Health: The Record of the Wesleyan Mission to New Zealand before 1840', *Journal of the Polynesian Society*, 81, 4, 1972, pp. 418–36
Owens, John, 'Religious Disputation at Whangaroa 1823–7', *Journal of the Polynesian Society*, 79, 3, 1970, pp. 288–304
Parsonson, Ann R., 'The Expansion of a Competitive Society: A Study in Nineteenth-Century Maori Society', *New Zealand Journal of History*, 14, 1, 1980, pp. 45–60
Patterson, Orlando, *Slavery and Social Death: A Comparative Study*, Cambridge, Mass., 1982
——, *Freedom in the Making of Western Culture*, vol. 1, New York, c. 1991
——, 'Authority, Alienation and Social Death', in Cornel West & Eddie S. Glaude Jr, eds, *African-American Religious Thought: An Anthology*, Louisville, Kentucky, 2003
Paulin, Chris D., 'Perspectives of Māori fishing history and techniques. Ngā āhua me ngā pūrākau me ngā hangarau ika o te Māori', *Tuhinga*, 18, 2007, pp. 11–47
Peabody, Sue & Keila Grinberg, 'Free Soil: The Generation and Circulation of an Atlantic Legal Principle', *Slavery & Abolition*, 32, 3, 2011, pp. 331–9
Perbi, Akosua Adoma, *A History of Indigenous Slavery in Ghana: From the 15th to the 19th Century*, Legon, Accra, 2004
Petrie, Hazel, *Chiefs of Industry: Maori Tribal Enterprise in Early Colonial New Zealand*, Auckland, 2006
——, 'The Sanctity of Bread: Missionaries and the Promotion of Wheat-Growing among the New Zealand Maori', in Ken Albala & Trudy Eden, eds, *Food and Faith in Christian Culture*, New York, 2011
——, 'Satisfaction in a Horse: The Perception and Assimilation of an Exotic Animal into Maori Custom Law', in Ian D. Rotherham & Robert A. Lambert, eds, *Invasive and Introduced Plants and Animals: Human Perceptions, Attitudes and Approaches to Management*, Washington, DC, 2011
Petrie, Hazel & Hohipere Tarau, 'Maori Texts and Official Ventriloquism', *New Zealand Journal of History*, 46, 2, 2012, pp. 129–40
Pomare, Sir Maui, *Legends of the Maori*, vol. 2, Auckland, 1987
Pool, Ian, *Te Iwi Maori: A New Zealand Population, Past, Present & Projected*, Auckland, 1991
Prichard, Muriel Lloyd, *An Economic History of New Zealand to 1939*, Auckland & London, 1970
Prickett, Nigel, 'Trans-Tasman Stories: Australian Aborigines in New Zealand Sealing and Shore Whaling', in Geoffrey Clark, Foss Leach & Sue O'Connor, eds, *Islands of Inquiry: Colonisation, Seafaring and the Archaeology of Maritime Landscapes*, Canberra, 2008
Pybus, T. A., *The Maoris of the South Island*, Wellington, 1954
Rainbird, Paul, 'Taking the Tapu: Defining Micronesia by Absence', *The Journal of Pacific History*, 38, 2, 2003, pp. 237–50
Ramsden, Eric, *Busby of Waitangi: H.M.'s Resident at New Zealand, 1833–40*, Wellington & Dunedin, 1942
Rangikaheke, Wiremu Maihi Te, 'He Waiata Haka Oriori', *Te Ao Hou*, 3, Summer 1853
Reilly, Michael P. J., '*Tuakana-Teina* Relationship and Leadership in Ancient Mangaia and Aotearoa', *The Journal of Pacific History*, 45, 2, 2010, pp. 211–27

Richards, Rhys & Jocelyn Chisholm, *Bay of Islands Shipping Arrivals and Departures, 1803–1840*, Wellington, 1992

Riseborough, Hazel, *Days of Darkness: The Government and Parihaka, Taranaki 1878–1884*, revised edn, Auckland, 2004

Robert, Hannah, '"Satisfying the Saints" — Colonial Entrepreneurs in the 1830s and 1840s and the Elasticity of Language', in Tracey Banivanua Mar & Julie Evans, eds, *Writing Colonial Histories: Comparative Perspectives*, Melbourne, 2002, pp. 7–22

Robinson, John, *The Corruption of New Zealand Democracy: A Treaty Overview*, Wellington, 2011

—, 'Why the Treaty?', in *Twisting the Treaty: A Tribal Grab for Wealth and Power*, Wellington, 2013, pp. 17–26

Robley, Major-General, *Moko; or Maori Tattooing*, London, 1896

Rodriguez, Junius P., *Chronology of World Slavery*, Santa Barbara, 1999

Rogers, Frank, 'Ranulph Dacre and Patuone's Topknot', *Stout Centre Review*, 5, 1, 1995, pp. 13–18

Ross, Ruth, 'Te Tiriti o Waitangi: Texts and Translations', *New Zealand Journal of History*, 6, 2, 1972, pp. 129–57

Rupprecht, Anita, '"When He Gets among His Countrymen, They Tell Him That He Is Free": Slave Trade Abolition, Indentured Africans and a Royal Commission', *Slavery & Abolition*, 33, 3, 2012, pp. 435–55

Rusden, G. W., *History of New Zealand*, 2 vols, vol. 1, Melbourne, 1883

Russell, Lynette, '"A New Holland Half-Caste": Sealer and Whaler Tommy Chaseland', *History Australia*, 5, 1, 2008, pp. 08.1–08.15

Russell, Steve, 'Apples Are the Color of Blood', *Critical Sociology*, 28, 1, 2002, pp. 65–76

Rutherford, James, *Sir George Grey, K.C.B., 1812–1898: A Study in Colonial Government*, London, 1961

Salmond, Anne, 'Te Ao Tawhito: A Semantic Approach to the Traditional Maori Cosmos', *Journal of the Polynesian Society*, 87, 1978, pp. 5–28

—, *Two Worlds: First Meetings of Maori and Europeans 1642–1772*, Auckland, 1993

—, *Between Worlds: Early Exchanges between Maori and Europeans 1773–1815*, Auckland, 1997

—, *Hui: A Study of Maori Ceremonial Gatherings*, Auckland, 2004

Samson, Jane, 'The 1834 Cruise of HMS Alligator: The Bible and the Flag', *Northern Mariner*, 3, 4, October 1993, pp. 37–47

Schaniel, William C., 'European Technology and the New Zealand Maori Economy: 1769–1840', *The Social Science Journal*, 38, 1, 2001, pp. 137–46

Scholefield, Guy H., *Taupo Haurau: Incidents of a Tribe*, Wellington, 1944

Scott, Dick, *Ask That Mountain: The Story of Parihaka*, Auckland, 1975

Seed, John, '"Secular" and "Religious": Historical Perspectives', *Social History*, 39, 1, 2014, pp. 3–13

Shand, Alexander, 'The Moriori People of the Chatham Islands: Their Traditions and History: Chapter X.—Moriori Stories', *Journal of the Polynesian Society*, 5, 4, 1896, pp. 105–211

Sherrin, R. A. A. & J. H. Wallace, *Early History of New Zealand: From Earliest Times to 1840 by R. A. A. Sherrin; from 1840 to 1845 by J. H. Wallace*, Thomson W. Leys, ed., Auckland, 1890

Sherwood, Marika, *After Abolition: Britain and the Slave Trade since 1807*, London, 2007

Shirres, M. P., 'Tapu', *Journal of the Polynesian Society*, 91, 1, 1982

Shortland, Edward, *The Southern Districts of New Zealand; A Journal, with Passing Notices of the Customs of the Aborigines*, London, 1851

—, *Traditions and Superstitions of the New Zealanders: With Illustrations of Their Manners and Customs*, 2nd edn, London, 1856

—, *Maori Religion and Mythology*, London, 1882

Sinclair, Keith, 'Why Are Race Relations in New Zealand Better Than in South Africa, South Australia or South Dakota?', *New Zealand Journal of History*, 5, 2, 1971, pp. 121–7

—, *A History of New Zealand*, revised edn, Auckland, 1988

Sinclair, Keith V., *Laplace in New Zealand, 1831*, Waikanae, 1998

Skinner, H. D., *Comparatively Speaking: Studies in Pacific Material Culture 1921–1972*, Peter Gathercole, Foss Leach & Helen Leach, eds, Dunedin, 1974

Skinner, W. H., 'Ancient Maori Canals. Marlborough, N.Z.', *Journal of the Polynesian Society*, 21, 3, 1912, pp. 105–8

Smith, Raymond T., 'Race, Class and Gender', in Frank McGlynn & Seymour Drescher, eds, *The Meaning of Freedom: Economics, Politics, and Culture after Slavery*, Pittsburgh & London, 1992, pp. 257–90

Smith, S. Percy, 'History and Traditions of the Taranaki Coast', *Journal of the Polynesian Society*, 18, 4, 1909, pp. 157–82
——, *History and Traditions of the Maoris of the West Coast, North Island of New Zealand Prior to 1840*, New Plymouth, 1910
Smith, Stephenson Percy, *Maori Wars of the Nineteenth Century*, Christchurch, 1910
Snyder, Christina, *Slavery in Indian Country: The Changing Face of Captivity in Early America*, Cambridge, Mass., 2010
Sharp, Andrew, *Duperrey's Visit to New Zealand in 1824*, ed., Andrew Sharp, Wellington, 1971
Sole, Tony, *Ngāti Ruanui: A History*, Wellington, 2005
Stack, J. W., 'Art. V.—Sketch of the Traditional History of the South Island Maoris', *Transactions and Proceedings of the New Zealand Institute*, 10, 1877, pp. 57–91
Stack, James West, *The Sacking of Kaiapohia*, Christchurch, 1906
Stafford, D. M., *Te Arawa: A History of the Arawa People*, Auckland, 2002
Stenhouse, John, ed., assisted by G. A. Wood, *Christianity, Modernity and Culture: New Perspectives on New Zealand History*, Adelaide, 2005
Strong, Pauline Turner, 'Transforming Outsiders: Captivity, Adoption, and Slavery Reconsidered', in Philip J. Deloria & Neal Salisbury, eds, *A Companion to American Indian History*, Malden & Oxford, 2002, pp. 339–56
Stoughton, John, 'Ancient Rome and Modern London: Intended to Illustrate the Past and Present State of Civilisation', in *Lectures Delivered Before the Young Men's Christian Association 1845–46*, vol. 1, London, 1869
Swaminathan, Srividhya, *Debating the Slave Trade, 1753–1815: Rhetoric of British National Identity*, Farnham, Surrey, 2009
Tamati, Tuta, 'A Reply to Mr. A. S. Atkinson's Paper, "What Is a Tangata Māori?"', *Journal of the Polynesian Society*, 2, 1893
Te Awekotuku, Ngahuia with Linda Waimarie Nikora, Mohi Rua & Rolinda Karapu, *Mau Moko: The World of Māori Tattoo*, Auckland, 2007
Te Kanawa, Kahutoi & John Turi-Tiakitai, 'Te Mana o Te Kākahu: The Prestige of Cloaks', in Awhina Tamarapa, ed., *Whatu Kākahu: Māori Cloaks*, Wellington, 2011
The Cambridge Ancient History: Assyrian and Babylonian Empires and Other States of the near East from the Eighth to the Sixth Centuries B.C., 2nd edn, vol. 3, pt 2, Cambridge, 1992
Thomas, Tim, 'Communities of Practice in the Archaeological Record of New Georgia, Rendova and Tetepare', in P. Sheppard, T. Thomas & G. R. Summerhayes, eds, *Lapita: Ancestors and Descendants*, Auckland, 2009
Thompson, Christina A., 'A Dangerous People Whose Only Occupation Is War: Maori and Pakeha in 19th-century New Zealand', *The Journal of Pacific History*, 32, 1, June 1997, pp. 109–19
Thomson, Arthur S., *The Story of New Zealand: Past and Present — Savage and Civilized*, vol. 1, London, 1859
Tregear, Edward, *The Maori Race*, Wanganui, 1904
Tremewan, Christine, *Traditional Stories from Southern New Zealand: He Kōrero Nō Te Wai Pounamu*, Christchurch, 2002
Troughton, Geoffrey, 'Missionaries, Historians & the Peace Tradition', in Allan Davidson, Stuart Lange, Peter Lineham & Adrienne Puckey, eds, *Te Rongopai 1814 — 'Takoto te pai!': Bicentenary Reflections on Christian Beginnings and Developments in Aotearoa New Zealand*, Auckland, 2014, pp. 228–45
Turner, Josiah G., *The Pioneer Missionary: Life of the Rev. Nathaniel Turner, Missionary in New Zealand, Tonga, and Australia*, Melbourne, 1872
Twells, Alison, *Civilising Mission and the English Middle Class 1793–1850: The 'Heathen' at Home and Overseas*, Basingstoke & New York, 2009
Urlich, D. U., 'The Introduction and Diffusion of Firearms in New Zealand 1800–1840', *Journal of the Polynesian Society*, 79, 4, 1970, pp. 399–410
Vayda, Andrew P., *Maori Warfare*, Wellington, 1960
——, 'Maori Prisoners and Slaves in the Nineteenth Century', *Ethnohistory*, 8, 2, 1961, pp. 144–55
——, 'Maoris and Muskets in New Zealand: Disruption of a War System', *Political Science Quarterly*, 85, 4, 1970, pp. 560–84
Vennell, C. W., *The Brown Frontier*, Auckland, Wellington & Sydney, 1967
Walker, Franchesca, '"Descendants of a Warrior Race": The Maori Contingent, New Zealand Pioneer Battalion, and Martial Race Myth, 1914–1919', *War & Society*, 31, 1, 2011, pp. 1–21

Walker, Ranginui, 'The Relevance of Maori Myth and Tradition', in Michael King, ed., *Te Ao Hurihuri: Aspects of Maoritanga*, Auckland, 1992, pp. 170–82

Wallin, Paul & Helene Martinsson-Wallin, 'The "Fish" for the Gods', *Rapa Nui Journal*, 15, 1, 2001, pp. 7–10

Walsh, Archdeacon, 'Art. II.—The Cultivation and Treatment of the Kumara by the Primitive Maoris', *Transactions and Proceedings of the New Zealand Institute*, 35, 1902, pp. 12–24

—, 'Art. II.—On the Maori Method of Preparing and Using Kokowai', *Transactions and Proceedings of the New Zealand Institute*, 36, 1903, pp. 4–10

Wanhalla, Angela, '"The Natives Uncivilize Me": Missionaries and Interracial Intimacy in Early New Zealand', in Patricia Grimshaw & Andrew May, eds, *Missionaries, Indigenous Peoples and Cultural Exchange*, Brighton, Portland & Toronto, 2010, pp. 24–36

Ward, Alan, *A Show of Justice: Racial 'Amalgamation' in Nineteenth Century New Zealand*, Auckland, 1995

—, *An Unsettled History: Treaty Claims in New Zealand Today*, Wellington, 1999

Wards, Ian, *The Shadow of the Land: A Study of British Policy and Racial Conflict in New Zealand 1832–1852*, Wellington, 1968

Watson, Mary K. & Brad R. Patterson, 'The Growth and Subordination of the Maori Economy in the Wellington Region of New Zealand, 1840–52', *Pacific Viewpoint*, 26, 3, 1985, pp. 521–45

Wells, Peter, *The Hungry Heart: Journeys with William Colenso*, Auckland, 2011

Wevers, Lydia, *Reading on the Farm: Victorian Fiction and the Colonial World*, Wellington, 2010

White, John, 'Lectures on Maori Customs', *AJHR*, E No. 7, 1861

—, *Maori Customs and Superstitions: Being the Subject of Two Lectures Delivered at the Mechanics' Institute in Auckland During the Year 1861*, facsimile edn, Christchurch, c. 1999

—, *The Ancient History of the Maori, His Mythology and Traditions*, 13 vols, Hamilton, 2001

Wiirepa, Dr Tuutere, 'Ko Te Whetuu-Matarau: The Many-Pointed Star', in Bruce Biggs, ed., *He Whiriwhiringa: Selected Readings in Maori*, Auckland, 1997, pp. 150–77

Wilkes, C., *Narrative of the United States Exploring Expedition: During the Years 1838, 1839, 1840, 1841, 1842*, vol. II, Philadelphia, 1845

Williams, David V., *'Te Kooti Tango Whenua': The Native Land Court 1864–1909*, Wellington, 1999

Williams, P. M. E., *Te Rongoā Māori: Māori Medicine*, Auckland, 1996

Wilson, D. M., 'Ancient Drains Kaitaia Swamp', *Journal of the Polynesian Society*, 30, 119, 1921, pp. 185–8

Wohlers, J. F. H., 'The Mythology and Traditions of the Maori in New Zealand', *Transactions and Proceedings of the Royal Society of New Zealand*, 7, 1874, pp. 3–53

Wright, Harrison M., *New Zealand, 1769–1840: Early Years of Western Contact*, Harvard Historical Monographs, Cambridge, Mass., 1959

Wyman-McCarthy, Matthew, 'Rethinking Empire in India and the Atlantic: William Cowper, John Newton, and the Imperial Origins of Evangelical Abolitionism', *Slavery & Abolition*, 35, 2, 2014, pp. 306–27

Young, David, *Woven by Water: Histories from the Whanganui River*, Wellington, 1998

Theses

Ballara, Angela, 'Warfare and Government in Ngapuhi Tribal Society: 1814–1833', MA thesis, University of Auckland, 1973

Boyes, Suzanne, 'Mai i ngā Ao e Rua – From Two Worlds: An Investigation into the Attitudes Towards Half Castes in New Zealand', BA (Hons) thesis, University of Otago, 2006

Clayworth, Peter, '"An Indolent and Chilly Folk": The Development of the Idea of the "Moriori Myth"', PhD thesis, University of Otago, 2001

Dingle, Sarah, 'Gospel Power for Civilization: The CMS Missionary Perspective on Maori Culture 1830–1860', PhD thesis, University of Adelaide, 2009

Kehoe, Jean Marie, 'Medicine, Sexuality, and Imperialism: British Medical Discourses Surrounding Venereal Disease in New Zealand and Japan: A Socio-Historical and Comparative Study', PhD thesis, Victoria University, 1992

Melbourne, Te Waaka, 'Te Wairua Kōmingomino o Te Māori: The Spiritual Whirlwind of the Māori', PhD thesis, Massey University, 2011

Mokena, T. T. R., 'The Structural Framework of the Māori Quest Story', PhD thesis, University of Auckland, 2005

Munn, Dan, 'Ngati Manu: An Ethnohistorical Account', MA thesis, University of Auckland, 1981

Northey, Glenda, 'Accessible to all? Libraries in the Auckland Provincial Area, 1842–1919', MA thesis, University of Auckland, 1998
Parsonson, Ann R., 'He Whenua Te Utu (The Payment Will Be Land)', PhD thesis, University of Canterbury, 1978
Petrie, Hazel, 'The "Lazy Maori": Pakeha Representations of a Maori Work Ethic: 1890–1940', MA thesis, University of Auckland, 1998
Reeves, Jane, 'Maori Prisoners in Dunedin, 1869–1872 and 1879–1881: Exiled for a Cause', BA (Hons) thesis, University of Otago, 1989
Shawcross, Kathleen Anne, 'Maoris of the Bay of Islands, 1769–1840: A Study in Changing Maori Attitudes Towards Europeans', MA thesis, University of Auckland, 1966
Soutar, Monty, 'Ngāti Porou Leadership — Rāpata Wahawaha and the Politics of Conflict', PhD thesis, Massey University, 2000
Sutherland, Yvonne Louisa, 'Te Reo o Te Perehi: Messages to Maori in the Wesleyan Newspaper *Te Haeata* 1859–1862', MA thesis, University of Auckland, 1999
Tomas, Nin, 'Key Concepts of Tikanga Maori (Maori Custom Law) and Their Use as Regulators of Human Relationships to Natural Resources in Tai Tokerau, Past and Present', PhD thesis, University of Auckland, 2006
Turner, Philip, 'The Politics of Neutrality: The Catholic Mission and the Maori 1838–1870', MA thesis, University of Auckland, 1986
Wigglesworth, Roger Philip, 'The New Zealand Timber and Flax Trade, 1769–1840', PhD thesis, Massey University, 1981
Williams, Jim, 'E Pākihi Hakinga a Kai', PhD thesis, University of Otago, 2004

Research reports and unpublished papers

Aborigines' Protection Society, *Report of the Parliamentary Select Committee on Aboriginal Tribes (British Settlements)*, reprinted, with comments, by the Aborigines' Protection Society, London, 1837 edn
Extracts from the Papers and Proceedings of the Aborigines' Protection Society, No. 1, William Ball, Arnold, & Co., London, May 1839
Parliament of Great Britain, *Report from the Select Committee of the House of Lords, Appointed to Inquire into the Present State of the Islands of New Zealand*, Great Britain Parliamentary Papers, Vol. 1, reprinted as *Colonies: New Zealand, I*, Shannon, 1968 (orig. pub. 1838)
Phillipson, G. A., *Rangahaua Whanui District 13: The Northern South Island*, Part 1, June 1995 (report commissioned by the Waitangi Tribunal)
Report from the Select Committee on New Zealand with the Minutes of Proceedings, Great Britain Parliamentary Papers, London, 1844
Waitangi Tribunal, *Ngai Tahu Land Report*, Wai 27, Wellington, 1991
——, *The Taranaki Report: Kaupapa Tuatahi*, Wai 143, Wellington, 1996
——, *Muriwhenua Land Report*, Wai 45, Wellington, 1997
——, *Rekohu: A Report on Moriori and Ngati Mutunga Claims in the Chatham Islands*, Wai 64, Wellington, 2001
——, *Te Tau Ihu o te Waka a Maui: Report on Northern South Island Claims*, 3 vols, vol. 1, Wai 785, Wellington, 2008
——, *He Whakaputanga me te Tiriti The Declaration and the Treaty: The Report on Stage 1 of the Te Paparahi o Te Raki Inquiry*, Wai 1040, Wellington, 2014
Williams, David V., *Matauranga Maori and Taonga: The Nature and Extent of Treaty Rights Held by Iwi and Hapu in Indigenous Flora and Fauna*, Wellington, 2001 (report commissioned by the Waitangi Tribunal for the indigenous flora and fauna claim (Wai 262))

INDEX

Aboriginal Australians, 34–7, 276
Aborigines' Protection Society, 199, 273, 287, 291, 314
abortion, 97
Abraham, Bishop Charles John, 33
Active, 54, 128, 160, 219, Fig. 64
adultery, 27, 95–8, 104, 105, 112, 140, 158–9, 211, 221, 268
Africa, Africans, 1–2, 10, 14, 20, 31, 37, 90, 149–50, 188, 189–91, 196–201, 220, 236, 247, 299, 336
ahi kaa roa, 115, 116, 253, 326
Akaroa, 61, 182
American War of Independence, 192
amokura, 23, Fig. 7
Anderson, Atholl, 6, 82
Angas, George French, 5, 20, 37, 92, Fig. 79
Ann (convict ship), 128
Anti-Slavery Society, 209
Aotea, 25
Aranghie *see* Rangi
Arawa canoe, 22, 25
Ariki aka Arikinui, 73
Arthur, Reverend William, 210
aruhe (root of the bracken fern), 45, 47, 59, 86, 110
Aterea, Harehare, 69
Atereta, 108
Atua-haere, 218
Auckland Star, 321
Awatope, 69

Baartman, Saartjie, 149–50
Baker, Charles, 144, 232
Ballara, Angela, 8–9, 74, 76, 97
Banks Peninsula, 103, 165, 246; *see also* Akaroa
Banks, Sir Joseph, 126, 149
Barbados, 192
Barry, James, 24
Barton, Mukti, 19–20
Baty, Father Claude, 259
Bay of Islands, 9, 51, 56–7, 62–3, 66, 72, 74, 80, 85, 89, 96–7, 104, 106, 109, 116, 126–9, 132, 134–7, 142, 145, 147, 150, 151, 153, 157, 160, 164–77, 182, 186, 208, 215, 245, 246, 249, 253, 261, 285–6, 292–3, 318, 319, 337; *see also* names of individual places
Beetham family of Wairarapa, 330
Belich, James, 132, 167, 301
Bell, Leonard, 260
Bent, Kimble, 286–7
Berlin, Sir Isaiah, 214
Besant, Annie, 327
Best, Elsdon, 31, 36–7, 43, 46, 60–1, 69, 72, 88–9, 118, 121–2, 131, 135, 138–9, 322
Betsy, English convict girl, 225
Biddle, Henry, 263–4
Black Charley, 37
Blackbirding, 14
Blackstone, Sir William, 189
Bolger, William, 285
Boulcott, Almon, 274, 299

Boulukos, George, 226
Bowes, George, 189
Boyd, 215, 295–6, Fig. 71
British Colonial Office, 10, 12, 195, 197, 200–1, 206, 211, 216, 261, 287, 290, 291
Brookfield, Jock, 257
Brown, Charles Hunter, 107–8
Brown, Christopher Leslie, 213–4
Brown, Mr (sea captain), 97
Brown, Reverend Alfred, 90–1, 221–2, 232, 234, 310
Brown, William, 48–9, 91, 114, 157–8, 187, 248
Browne, Sir Thomas Robert Gore, 278–9, 306–7, 309, 334
Brunner, Thomas, 82, 144–5
Bryce, John, 321
Buck, Sir Peter (Te Rangi Hīroa), 59–60
Buddle, Reverend Thomas, 77, 244, 297, 305, 338
Buller, Walter, 23
burial, funerary practices, mourning, 121–2, 138–9, 142, 219
Burns, Barnett, 54, 57
Burns, Patricia, 298
Busby, James, 76–7, 261–5, 289
Butler, Hannah, 185, 224, 226
Butler, Reverend John, 62, 90–1, 127, 162, 185, 226, 231
Buxton, Sir Thomas Fowell and family, 10, 197–200

Calliope, 300
Cameroon, 15
Campbell, John Logan, 96
Canaan (Kēnana), 278, 317–22
'cannibalism', head-hunting, 2, 11–14, 37, 90–1, 127, 175, 207–8, 270, 277, 329, 333
Canute, 42
Cardwell, Edward, 314
Carey, Robert, 32–3
Carkeek, Te Waari, 72, 326, 341
Carleton, Hugh, 105
Carroll, Lewis, 336
carvers, carving, 3, 23, 68, 74–5, 122, 146–7
Chapman, Reverend Thomas, 232, 319
Chatham Islands *see* Rēkohu
Cherokee, 15
Cherry, Samuel, 153
Church Missionary Society (CMS), 28, 90, 128, 130, 162, 195, 197, 198, 202, 215–6, 219, 220, 228, 230, 236, 249, 251, 260, 280 288, 302; *see also* names of individual missionaries
Clapham Sect, 191, 195–6
Clarke, George, 180–1, 222, 266, 270, Fig. 67
cloaks, 23–4, 68–70, 87, 103, 135
Cobbett's Weekly Political Register, 192
Colenso, William, 17, 29, 30, 74, 77, 225–6
Colley, Linda, 194
Commissioner Bigge's Inquiry, 162, 176, 200
confiscation (land), 31, 279–81, 312, 316, 323
Conrad, Nicky, 73

convicts, 28, 102–3, 161, 188, 200, 209, 225, 264, 274, 276, 286–7
Cook Islands Māori (language), 41
Cook, Captain James, 23, 126, 149, 156–8, 170, 187, 340
cooks, cooking, 21, 25, 27, 37, 40, 44–9, 55–6, 59–61, 65, 67, 85–6, 91, 93, 99, 155, 163, 200, 258, 295, 296, 326, 337
Cooper, George Sisson, 85, 259–60, 293–4
Coquille, 20, 89, 134, 151, 170–1, 177–80
Coromandel (ship), 185
Coromandel (place), 218, 266
Cotton, William, 266, 270, Fig. 67
Courier (Hobart newspaper), 276
Cowan, James, 67–8, 73, 138, 321
Crozet, Julien, 159
Cruise, Major Richard, 87, 102, 138, 146, 161, 167, 177

Daily Southern Cross, 108, 273, 292
Darling, Sir Ralph, 152–3
Darlington probation station, 276
Darwin, Charles, 89
Davis, Charles Oliver Bond, 42, 304
Davis, David Brion, 15, 31
Davis, Mary, 185
Davis, Richard (missionary), 63, 91, 112–3, 136–7, 141–2, 167, 176, 185, 237–8, 247–53, 256, 258, 274, 284
Davis, Richard (Māori teacher and entrepreneur) *see* Reihana Te Kamo
Davis, Thom, 296
de Blois, Théodore Julien de la Calande, 179
Demerara, 192
Denison, Governor William, 276
Dieffenbach, Ernst, 183
Dillon, Captain Peter, 24, 295, Fig. 54
disease, 54, 81–2, 122, 169, 181–7, 194, 196, 239, 322
Donne, Thomas, 181
Doubtless Bay, 134
Downes, Thomas William, 70, 340–1
Driver, 299
du Fresne, Marion, 126, 159
Dubouzet, Joseph, 158
Duke, Captain Robert, 175, 274
Dumont d'Urville, Jules Sébastien César, 62–3, 76, 89–90, 109, 134, 171, 262, 294

Earle, Augustus, 5, 50, 62, 63, 73, 79, 99, 102, 166, 186
eels, 23, 25, 119, 124, 144–5, 331
Elizabeth (Captain Stewart's ship), 61, 165
Elizabeth (whaling ship), 56–7
Emerson, Ralph Waldo, 11–12
Endeavour (1824), 7, 244
Endeavour (1769–70) *see* HMS *Endeavour*
Erihana or Ellison, Rāniera, 281–2
Exeter Hall, 209–10
exiles, outlaws, 15, 51, 82–3, 240, 276, 279

Fairburn, William, 220, 232, 234
Fairfowl, Dr George, 162, 176, 182
feathers, 22–4, 98, 122
Firth, Raymond, 45–6, 55, 86, 114, 118, 127
fish, fishing, fish oil, 20–1, 36, 42–4, 59, 83, 86, 111, 123–4, 138, 144, 152, 157, 170, 171, 178, 213, 297, 312
FitzRoy, Robert, 77, 211–2, 268, 291–2, 298
flags, flagstaff, 10, 11, 181, 193, 209–12, 216, 236, 266, 292–3, 306, 308–9, 318, Figs 58, 59, 74
Flatt, John, 202, 229
flax, flax dressing, 20, 23, 25, 86–7, 128, 130–6, 146, 155, 166–7, 177, 221, 245, 338
Fontenelle, M. J., 150
Forster, George, 158–9, 187
Fox, William, 144, 279, 299
France, 150, 191, 194, 196, 290
French Revolution, 191, 273

Garrett, Daniel, 189
Gentleman's Magazine, 325
George III, King, 127, 194
George IV, King, 103, 129, 286
Geyser Hotel, 147
Gipps, Sir George, 264
Glenelg, Charles Grant, 1st Baron, 208
Godwyn, Morgan, 19
Gold, Colonel Charles Emilius, 307
Goshore, Mrs, 167–8
Governor Halket, 285
Grace, Thomas Samuel, 278, 280
Graham, David, 74, Fig. 16
Graham, Reverend John, 152–3
Grey, Alexander, 105
Grey, Eliza, 300
Grey, Sir George, 22, 64, 86, 96, 98, 106, 108, 226, 259, 260, 268–9, 271, 275–6, 279, 280, 294, 298–301, 303, 305, 313–4, 327, 332
Grey, Henry George, 3rd Earl Grey, 269, 271, 305
Guard family, 198
Gudgeon, Lieutenant-Colonel Thomas, 78–9, 119
Gurney, Anna, 198

Hadfield, Octavius, 303–4
Hākaraia (Mahika of Waitaha), 319
hākari (feasts), 87, 257–8
Hall, Francis, 80
Hall, William, 128, 152, 217
Hamlin, John, 100
Hamuera, 186
Hansen, Mr, 217, 223
Harriet, 198
Hauhau religion (Pai Mārire), 66, 68–9, 320
Haumia (god of fern root and wild plants), 59
Haupapa-o-te-rangi, 70
Hauturu (husband of Te Rangi Topeora), 96
Hauturu pā, 135
Hawai'i, 31, 46
Hāwea, 37
Hawera and Normanby Star, 321, 322
He Kōrero Pūrākau mo Ngā Taunahanahatanga a Ngā Tūpuna, 334
Head, Lyndsay, 310–11, 338
head-hunting *see* 'cannibalism'
Heaphy, Charles, 82, 100, 120, 144–5
Heke Pokai, Hone Wiremu, 74, 105, 211–12, 266, 270, 290, 292–3, Fig. 57
Heke, Beth, 1, 340
Heke, Jake 'The Muss', 1, 78, 341

Hema, 329
Henry VIII, King, 106
Hinds, Samuel, 77, 84, 201
Hiona, 320, Fig. 75
Hinemoa, 327–8
Hīpango, Waata, 334
HMS *Alligator*, 24, 198–9
HMS *Bounty*, 22
HMS *Buffalo*, 262–3
HMS *Dolphin*, 29
HMS *Dromedary*, 64, 138, 161–5, 168, 176–7, 182, 200
HMS *Endeavour*, 23, 149, 156–7
HMS *Resolution*, 158, 170, 187
Hobbs, John, 80, 97, 101, 175, 232, 252, 259, 266, 283–4, Fig. 51
Hobson, William, 11, 195, 208–9, 212, 270, 288–90
Hochstetter, Christian Gottlieb Ferdinand von, 32
Hodder, Edwin, 311
Hodges, William, 170, Fig. 46
Hoete, Wiremu, 47, 141
Hohepa, Patu, 60, 305
Hokianga, 28, 37, 43, 51, 53, 63, 95, 96, 98, 104, 116, 148, 231, 232, 251, 253, 258, 263, 265, 266, 280, 286, 289, 301, 302, 320, 333
Home, Sir Everard, 269–70, 296
Hongi Hika, 24, 51, 54, 64, 72, 84, 87, 103–4, 106, 128–33
137, 185, 217, 221, 223–5, 231, 245–7, 250–1, Fig. 5
Hopkins, Josiah, 293–4
Hōri Kīngi *see* Te Ānaua, Hōri Kīngi
Horouta, 37
Howe, Kerry, 32
Hughes, John, 138
human sacrifice, 43–4, 125, 138–9, 148, 200, 208, 221–2, 237, 262, 270
Hume, Alexander, 150
Hunaara, 111
Huntly, Mr, 104
Hursthouse, Charles, 174

Ihaia (war captive), 303
Ihimaera, Witi, 322–3
infanticide, 13, 80, 94–5, 98, 185–6, 270
Iwikau (of Ngāi Tahu), 246

Jacquinot, Ensign Charles Hector, 177–80
Jamaica, 190, 192, 203
Janet, 286
John Bull, 189
John Bull & Co., 188
Johnson, John, 92–3, 143, 267
Johnson, J. Pitts, 153
Johnstone, Captain John Campbell, 301
Jolliffe, John, 302
Jones, Captain, 168
Jones, Theodore Morton, 226–7

Kaeo, 175, 216, 284
Kahea, 45
Kahutiaterangi, 184
Kahuwera, 109, 170, 173, 177
Kāi Tahu *see* Ngāi Tahu
Kaiapoi, 61, 67–8, 103

Kaihuanga feud, 103
Kaikohe, 218
Kaikōura, 84
Kaitangata, 329
Kaitara, 112–3
kākā, 23, 24, 45, 86
Kapetoru, 75
Kāpiti Island, 64, 67, 84, 87, 96, 130–1, 153–4, 167, 246
karakia (incantation), 6, 54–6
Karanga Hokianga, 333
Kareroariki, 139
Katatore (war captive), 303
Kāti Māmoe *see* Ngāti Māmoe
Katikati, 314
Kauere, Heremaia, 116
Kauhanganui, 317
kawakawa (plant), 183, 184
Kawakawa (place), 132
Kawakawa River, 101
Kawepō, Rēnata Tama-ki-Hikurangi, 65–6, 71
Kāwhia, 42, 66, 70, 81, 93, 97, 120, 320
Kawiti, Kawhiti, or Kowiti, 296
Kawiti, Reverend Riri, 74
Kawiti, Te Ruki, 74–5, 270, 296
Keegan, Timothy, 299
Kehu (aka Hone Mokehakeha or Hone Mokekehu), 120, 144–5, Figs 23, 38
Kelly, Lesley, 329
Kemp, Henry Tacy, 226
Kemp, James, 99, 102–4, 144, 181, 224, 226
Kemp, Charlotte, 224–6
Kēnana *see* Canaan
Kendall, Thomas, 24, 128, 167, 217
Keno, 240
Kepa Ehau, 72
Kerikeri, 128, 136, 144, 217, 223–4, 231
Kikikoi, 97
King George *see* Te Whareumu
King, Captain Henry, 293
King, Governor Gidley, 35
King, John, 80, 94–7, 100–1, 128, 130, 136, 185–6, 217–20, 223, 224, 226, 234–6, 239, 249
King, Mrs Hannah, 186
Kīngi, Mete *see* Te Rangi Paetahi, Mete Kīngi
Kīngitanga (King Movement), 306–11, 317
Kirikūmara, Īhāia, 277
Kite, 263–5
Kiwikiwi, 73
Ko Te Karere o Nui Tireni, 335
Kōhere, Reweti T., 26
Kohimarama Conference 1860, 278, 308–9, 311
Kōkai, 111
Kokiro, 258
kōkōwai (red ochre), 20–4, 122, 156–7
Korokoro, 128
Kororāreka, 73, 105, 146, 156, 171, 174, 183, 187, 222, 247, 263, 274, 284–6, 290, 292–3, Figs 25, 36, 47
Kotahitanga parliaments, 317
Kōtiro Hinerangi, 105–6
Kotuku (war captive), 232
kūmara, 29, 59, 80, 86, 90, 100–1, 132, 219–20, 242, 258
Kurahaupō, 25, 340

La Favorite, 169, 172
La Trobe, Charles J., 276
Labé, Guillaume, 134
Lambert, Captain Robert, 199
Lambert, Thomas, 12
Laplace, Captain Cyrille-Pierre-Théodore, 169, 171–2
Laslett, Thomas, 263
Le Dez, First Lieutenant, 126, 157
Lea, Rod, 13
Leigh, Samuel, 64, 97, 217, 219, 223, 226, Fig. 1
Lesson, René Primevère, 20, 151–2, 158–9, 170–3, 177–83
Levy, Morris, 278
LIFE magazine, 188
Lilburne, John, 189
Lineham, Peter, 330
literacy, 10, 237, 247, 298, 318
London Quarterly Review, 213
Lord, William, 105
Lottin, Victor Charles, 29, 85–6, 127, 134, 151, 178, 182

Mackay, James Jnr, 309
Mahika of Waitaha *see* Hākaraia
Mahue, 110–1
Mai (of Tahiti), 156
Maketū, 59, 133
Mākutu, 56, 108, 247
Malthus, Reverend Thomas Robert, 194
Manaia, 27, 111
Māngere, 307
Mangumangu, 96
Mangungu, 264, 319
Maning, Frederick, 166, 250
Mansfield, Lord Chief Justice, 190–1
Maori Messenger: Ko Te Karere Māori, 34, 328
Markham, Edward, 5, 24, 95, 164, 168–9
Marmon, John (Jacky), 28, 257
Marquis de Castries, 126, 157
Marsden, Elizabeth, 178
Marsden, Māori, 39–40, 60
Marsden, Reverend Samuel, 54, 77–8, 99, 128–9, 132, 148–52, 160, 178, 215–8, 220, 236, 251, 262, 296
Marshall, William Barrett, 198–9, 239–40
Martin, Lady Mary, 314
Martin, Samuel, 114, 122
Matakerepō, 134
Matamata, 49, 87, 310
Mātiatia, 141–2
Mauhara, Henry, 255
Maungakiekie, 111
Maungaraki pā, taking of, 70
Maungatapu, 58
Maungatautari, 322
Māwe, 256
Maxwell, Alexander, 7
Maxwell, Thomas, 63
Mayhew, William, 171–2
Maynard, Dr Felix, 165
McCrae, Ensign Alexander, 64, 146–7, 166, 200
McDonnell, Lieutenant Thomas, 43, 77, 143–4, 209–10, 279
McIntosh, Captain, 267
McLean, Donald, 116, 279, 306–8, 334

Mead, Hirini Moko, 259
Melanesians, 31, 32, 34, 37
Missionary Register, 219, 224
Mitchell, Hilary and John, 246
moa, 123
Moehanga, 24, 295
Moetara, 251
Moka, 28, 104, 253–4
Mōkau, 293, 305, 333
moko (tattoo, tattooing) *see* tā moko
Moko (personal name), 83
Mokomōkai, 147–54
Mokoia (Panmure), 62, 162, 185, 231
Mokoia Island (Lake Rotorua), 65, 72, 184, 246
Monkhouse, William Brougham, 23
Montefiore, John Israel, 136
Montefiore, Joseph Barrow, 77, 202–4
Moremonui, battle of, 129
Morgan, John, 48–9, 140, 309
Moriori, 27, 31, 33, 35–7, 329, 335, Fig. 11
Motoki, 103
Motueka, 100, 120, 144
Motukorea (Browns Island), 161
mourning *see* burial, funerary practices
Moutoa, 68
Munn, Dan, 74
Munro, Taipari, 27
Murihaka, 103
Muriwharau pā, 319
Muru, 105, 107, 110, 125, 129, 136, 205, 217, 229–30
Museum of the Royal College of Surgeons, 150
'Musket wars', 8–9, 53–4, 101, 132, 134–5, 154, 166, 177, 203, 337
muskets, 8–9, 57, 63, 64, 67, 72, 80, 87, 101, 103, 110, 121, 123, 127–37, 146–7, 149, 166–7, 177–81, 186, 230, 235, 244, 251, 262, 337, 339

Nanette, 180
Naonao, 237–8
Napoleon, 191
Napoleonic Wars, 191, 194, 200, 273
Native Appellate Court, 115
Native Department, 315–6
Native Exemption Ordinance, 298–9
Native Land Acts, 316
Native Land Court, 6, 116–7, 141, 146, 312, 316, 329
Naylor, Wiremu (aka William Tawaiti), 258
Nayti *see* Te Whaiti
Nekepapa, 70
Nelson Examiner, 267–8, 292
Nelson, 65, 120, 292, 299
Nelson, Charles E., 147
Nene, Tāmati Wāka, 96, 98, 258, 266, 270, 289, 301
New Canaan, 278, 320
New South Wales, Sydney, Port Jackson, 35, 37, 78, 97, 102, 128, 150, 152, 161, 163, 168, 175, 200, 209, 211, 215, 217, 225, 264, 274, 289, 295, 296, 329
New Zealand Aborigines' Protection Association, 114
New Zealand Association, 197, 201–2, 204–8, 287–8, 290
New Zealand Company, 120–1, 142, 183, 208, 210, 249, 267, 273, 290, 292, 298–9
New Zealand Herald, 267

New Zealand Settlements Act 1863, 312
New Zealander, 212, 272, 282
Ngā Māhanga, 69–70, 249
Nga Mahi a Nga Tupuna, 327, 333
Ngā Rauru, 279
Ngā Ruahine, 278
Ngāhuruhuru, 165
Ngāi Tahu, 45, 55, 61, 63, 65, 67–8, 82, 103, 115, 120, 245, 246
Ngāi Tai, 63
Ngāi Tāwake, 146
Ngāi Te Rangi, 133, 266
Ngāi Te Ūpokoiri, 65–6
Ngāi Tūhoe, 69, 135–6, 138
Ngāpora, Tāmati, 268–9
Ngāpuhi, 23, 24, 28, 56–7, 63–4, 66, 72–4, 94, 99, 105, 114–5, 117, 127, 129, 131, 135–7, 139, 146–7, 184, 231, 245–6, 250–2, 258–9, 318, 319, 332
Ngare Raumati, 117
Ngata, Sir Āpirana, 322
Ngāti Apa, 120, 340
Ngāti Awa, 68–9, 120
Ngāti Hauā, 28, 59, 71, 118, 311
Ngāti Hine, 74–5
Ngāti Hotu, 25
Ngāti Ira, 25, 83, 120
Ngāti Kahungunu, 65–6, 74, 98, 114, 135
Ngāti Koata, 64, 67
Ngāti Kōpirimau, 51
Ngāti Koreha, 103
Ngāti Kōtore, 135
Ngāti Kuia, 64, 120
Ngāti Māmoe, 45, 55
Ngāti Manawa, 69, 184
Ngāti Maniapoto, 98
Ngāti Manu, 60
Ngāti Maru, 57, 107, 135–6, 140
Ngāti Mutunga, 35, 83–4
Ngāti Pāoa, 28, 47, 90, 98, 231
Ngāti Porou, 25, 30, 56, 58, 65, 79, 94, 184, 318
Ngāti Pou, 7
Ngāti Raka, 88
Ngāti Rangatahi, 275
Ngāti Rangiwewehi, 64, 246–7
Ngāti Rārua, 65, 120, 144
Ngāti Raukawa, 51, 68
Ngāti Ruanui, 32, 72, 279, 287
Ngāti Ruanuku, 119
Ngāti Tama, 35, 275
Ngāti Tamaterā, 56, 266
Ngāti Tarāwhai, 72, 147
Ngāti Toa, 61, 64–5, 67–8, 70, 72, 84, 87, 115, 120, 130–1, 143, 246, 278, 300, 326
Ngāti Toki, 51
Ngāti Tū, 105, 116
Ngāti Tūmatakōkiri, 120, 144–5
Ngāti Tūwharetoa, 94, 154, 297
Ngāti Umutahi, 105
Ngāti Uru, 7, 284
Ngāti Wai, 27, 51
Ngāti Wairangi, 120
Ngāti Whakaue, 72
Ngāti Whanaunga, 107

Ngāti Whatua, 129, 311
Ngātokorua, 59–60
Ngātoroirangi, 25
Ngeungeu, 63
Ngoi, 140
Nicholas, John Liddiard, 5, 77, 114, 167–8, 295
Nieboer, H. J., 45
Niho (personal name), 82
Norfolk Island, 35, 276, 286
Normanby, Lord (Constantine Henry Phipps, 1st Marquess), 195, 208, 290
North Star, 269
Northern War, 74, 98, 105, 269–70, 292–3, 298, 301
Nugent, Captain Charles Lavallin, 96
Nukutaurua, 66
Nukutere, 25

O'Malley, Vincent, 108
O'Rell, Max, 188, 214
Ōhaeawai, 267
Okataina, 72
Old Mihaka, 81, Fig. 21
Ōmihi, 84
Once Were Warriors, 1, 340
Onetea, 255
Ōpōtiki, 107, 278
Oppenheim, Roger S., 138
oral traditions, 3, 6, 15, 18, 21–2, 24, 26–7, 38, 43, 46, 73, 82, 88–90, 92, 93, 95, 99, 109–10, 110–11, 113, 126, 131, 133–4, 146, 184, 327–8, 332, 333–4, 337
Ōraukawa, Tāmati Hone, 71–2
Oru, Ropata, 234
Ōtaki, 300
Ōtūihu, 74, 181, Figs 53, 54
Ōtūmoetai, 186
outlaws *see* exiles, outlaws

pā building, 123–4, 126, 337
Pacific islands, 78
Paeko, 111
Paeroa, 117
Pai Mārire *see* Hauhau religion
Paihia, 88, 128, 168–9, 174, 175, 186, 230, 239–40, 256
Paikea, 184
Painga, 232
Pakakohe, 279
Pākawau pā, 82
Pakepakeha, 24
Pakoko, Eruera Te Wata (aka Eruera Puhiohio), 120
Palmer, Judge Jackson, 115
Pangopango (personal name), 73
Pāoa, 90
Paopao, 109
Paowa, 26
Papahurihia (Te Atua Wera), 318
Papatūānuku, 21, 59
Papatupu block committees, 332–3
Paratene, Te Ripi, 91–2, 250–1, 256
Pare and Hutu (story of), 88–9
Parihaka, 281–2, 320–2
Pātara, 278
Pātea, 321
Patoromu, 312

Pattle, Eliza Anne Frances, 196
Patuone, 25, 63, 98, 243
Patupaiarehe, 24–5
peacemaking, 57, 60, 64–5, 67, 69, 94, 125, 140, 148, 231, 244, 246, 253–4, 278
Penny Magazine, 235
Pera, 108
Phillip, Governor Arthur, 102, 209
Phrygian cap, cap of liberty, 189, 191–2
Pikia, 97–8
Pikiwati, 145
Pipitea pā, 142, 249, Fig. 26
Poharama, 293
Pōhatu (of Ngāi Tahu), 55
Pōhatu Pāremoremo, 45
pōhutukawa, 22–3, Fig. 8
Polack, Joel, 48, 50–1, 62–4, 79–80, 88, 122, 135–7, 139–40, 144, 186, 203–6, 213, 221–2, 235, 261–2
polygamy, 69, 96–7, 106, 132, 186, 202, 217, 256–7
Polynesia, Polynesian, 22, 29, 31–7, 40–1, 78, 315, 321, 326
Polynesian Mythology, 327
Pōmare II (Whētoi), 74, 116, 150, 151, 181, 267
Pōmare, Sir Māui, 333
Ponga and Puhihuia (story of), 333–4
Poporokewa, 27
Pōrangahau, 114
Porirua, 298–9
Port Jackson *see* New South Wales
Port Nicholson *see* Wellington
Portugal, Portuguese, 32, 191, 202–3
Pōtahi, 103
potatoes (white), 80, 86–7, 97, 101, 127, 129–30, 133, 140, 142, 155, 166, 177, 178, 206, 232, 233, 245, 272, 282, 331, 338
pounamu (greenstone, nephrite jade), 23, 46, 61, 64, 65, 68, 84, 122, 140, 152
Poutu, 238
Poverty Bay, 78, 110, 135, 203, 248
preserved heads *see* mokomōkai
prisoners of war (non-New Zealand), 14, 16, 217, 273–4, 300, 325
Protector, Protectorate of Aborigines, 267, 270, 292, 298, 304, 313
proverbs, sayings, 6, 17, 20–2, 25–6, 28, 30–1, 38, 78, 257
Pu Taewa, 118
puhi (ritually set aside virgin), 88–9, 94, 160
Puhihuia, 333
Pūkawa, 85–6
Pukearuhe (White Cliffs), 305
Pukenui, 144
Pukerangiora pā, 277, 333
Pukeroa, 96
Puketākauere pā, 277
Pūmuka, 106, 256
Punga, 30
Purchas, Reverend Arthur Guyon, 269
Putoko, 248
Putu (Paora?), 140

Queen Caroline (trial of), 106

Ra'iatea, 321
Rahi (war captive), 232
Rāhui, 97, 292
Raimona, 69
Ramsden, Eric, 264
Rangatira (of Hokianga), 95, 302
Rangi (tohunga tā moko), 72–3, 76, 142, 145, 186, Fig. 15
Rangiātea, 321
Rangihoua, 80, 101, 128, 130, 136, 148, 185, 215, 236–7
Ranginui, 21, 59
Rangiriri, battle of, 71, 301
Rangitāne, 120, 131
Rangituke, 73, Fig. 41
Rangi-whakatatae, 94
ransom, 64–7, 133, 137–8, 148, 326
Rauru, 147
Rawa (war captive), 232
Rāwene, 263
Rāwhiti, 117
Rawiri (war captive), 303
Reform Act 1832, 193
Reihana Te Kamo (aka Richard Davis), 142–3, 249
Reko, 81–2
'Reko's slave', 81, 336, Fig. 22
Rēkohu, 27, 31, 35, 36, 280, 335
representation, Māori parliamentary, 316
Rerewaka, 84
Reti, 265
Rewa, 102, 104, 127, 176, 262, 289–90
Ringatū Church, 280, 320
Rīwai (personal name), 107
Roberts, Evan, 7
Robertson, George, 29, 31
Robinson Crusoe, 226
Roebuck, John Arthur, 210
Rongomātāne (god of agriculture), 59
Rōpiha, Hami Hone (aka John Hobbs), 98
Rōpiha, Hōri, 114
Rotoaira, 94–5
Rotorua, 72, 133, 147, 184, 319, 327
Rowe, Joe, 154
Royal Institute of France, 150
Ruapuke, 82
Ruatapu, 184
Ruatara, 127–8, 215–16
Ruatara Taurapoko, 116
Ruka, 108
Rukiruki, 73, 186
Rule, Britannia!, 189, 194
rūnanga, 106–8, 316, 332
Rusden, Geoge William, 103
Russell, Captain Andrew Hamilton, 271, 297
Russell, Lord John (Colonial Secretary), 270
Ruta, Matene (Martin Luther), 276
Rutherford, John, 103

Sadler, Captain Frederick W. R., 262–3
Samwell, David, 156
Saturday Magazine, 206
Scheipers, Sibylle, 274
Scherzer, Dr Karl, 250
Scott, Dick, 322

Select Committee on Aborigines (1835–37), 84, 198–200, 218, 254, 270
Select Committee on the state of New Zealand (1838), 77, 84, 94, 111, 206–7, 221, 229, 249
Select Committee on New Zealand (1844), 77, 143, 200, 207, 210, 213
Selwyn, Bishop George Augustus, 255, 266, 270, 275, Fig. 67
Seth-Smith, Chief Judge Hugh Garden, 115
sex trade, 155–87, 237, 239
Sheffield Literary and Philosophical Society 152
Shepherd, James, 99
Shirres, Father Michael, 46–9
Shortland, Edward, 54, 87, 119, 267
slander, 106–7
slave trade, African, 2, 10, 19, 187–8, 190, 192, 196, 199, 201–3, 215, 236, 261, 325
Slavery Abolition Act 1833, 10, 193, 195
slavery, definition of, 3–4, 84
Smiles, Samuel, 11
Smith, Adam, 193
Smith, S. Percy, 176
Smuts, General Jan, 188
social death *see* spiritual death
Society for Promoting Christian Knowledge, 206
Sødring, Captain Thomas, 52
Solomon Islands, 14–5, 43, 53
Somerset, James, 190–1, 226
South Africa, 37, 149, 188, 299
Southwark, 151
Spain, Spanish people, 32, 191, 202–3, 275
spiritual death, 40, 46, 301
'Spoils to the Victor', 336, Fig. 80
St Jean Baptiste, 134
Stack, James Snr, 284
Stack, James West, 310
Steele, Louis J., 336, Fig. 80
Stephen, Sir James, 195, 290
Stewart, Captain William, 61–2, 165
Stewart, Charles, 190
Stockenström, Captain Andries, 198
Stoughton, John, 209
sugar trade, 192, 203
Sumner, Bishop J. B., 195
Sydney *see* New South Wales
Symonds, Lieutenant William Cornwallis, 95–6

tā moko, 27, 48, 72–3, 88, 145, 148–9, 232
Tahiti, Tahitian, 22, 29, 31, 43, 156
Taiāmai, 103, 113, 253–4, 256, Fig. 24
Taiaroa, Te Mātenga, 65
Tainui (canoe), 25
Tainui (people or tribe), 55
Tai Tapu, 103
Taiwhanga, Rāwiri, 230, 237
Takitimu, 25
Tama (name from oral tradition), 26–7
Tamaāhua, 46, 110
Tama-i-haranui (Te Maiharanui), 61–2, 103
Tāmaihengia, Hōhepa, 120, 278
Tamainupō, 24
Tamairangi, 83–4
Tama-i-whakanehua-i-te-rangi, 65

Tāmaki, 63
Tama-te-kapua (wharenui/meeting house), 247
Tāmati, Tuta, 30
Tāne (god of the forest), 59
Tangaroa (god of the sea), 30, 43–4, 59
Taniwha, 131
Taonui, 37
Taotao-riri, 94
Tapihana, 42
Tapsell, Phillip, 137–8, Fig. 43
Tara, 167–8
Tāraia Ngākuti Te Tumuhuia, 56, 266–7, 270, Fig. 67
Taranaki, 25, 32–3, 43, 63, 66, 69, 82, 97, 100, 117, 120–1, 130, 141, 146, 176, 198, 251, 277–82, 305, 306, 308–9, 320, 322, 333
Tarapīpipi, Wiremu Tāmihana, 118–9, 310–11, Fig. 73
Tarawheti, 146
Tasmania, 175, 274–6
tattooing *see* ta moko
Tau (war captive), 82
Tau, Rāniera (Sonny), 139
taua muru *see* muru
Tauhia, Te Hēmara, 311–2
Taumata-ā-Kura, Piripi, 58, 318, 319
Taupō, 25, 26, 66, 68, 85, 92–3, 147, 256
Taupō pā, 299
Taurua, Ngāwaka, 279–81
Tawell, John Downing, 183, 202, 249
Tāwhai, Mohi, 258–9
Tāwhaki, 26, 134
Tawhi, 64
Tāwhiao, Tūkāroto Matutaera Pōtatau Te Wherowhero, 114, 317
Tāwhirimātea (god of wind and weather), 59
Tawhitinui (Poor Knights Islands), 51
Taylor, Richard, 17, 28–31, 42, 44, 94–5, 122, 186, 293
Te Ahuahu, battle of, 270
Te Aitanga-a Māhaki, 54, 110
Te Ānaua, Hōri Kīngi, 68
Te Ao Hou, 333
Te Ao Paki, 67–8
Te Ao-kapurangi, 246–7
Te Ao-o-te-Rangi, 104, 313
Te Ara, 7, 283–4, 295–6
Te Arawa (tribal group), 26, 58, 71, 73, 75, 133, 184, 246, 304, 319
Te Aro pā, 121, 249, Fig. 40
Te Aroha, 51
Te Ata-o-Tū, Hākopa, 67–8, 74, Figs 13, 14
Te Āti Haunui-a-Pāpārangi, 279
Te Āti Awa, 70, 142, 277
Te Haeata, 332
Te Haupokia, 74
Te Heuheu, Tūkino II, Mananui, 94
Te Heuheu, Tūkino III, Iwikau, 85–6, 256, 297, 300
Te Hiko, 61, 68, 143, 153
Te Hiku-poto, 94
Te Hikutū, 51–2
Te Hoa Māori, 240
Te Ihutai, 266
Te Irirangi, Ōtara, 63
Te Kāhui (Poukōhatu Te Kāhui Kararehe), 176
Te Kani-ā-Takirau, 26, 79

Te Karaka (northern Hokianga), 333
Te Kaue, 256
Te Kēkerengū, 83–4
Te Kēmara, 117, 288–9
Te Kohia pā, 306
Te Koki, 88, 224
Te Kooti Arikirangi Te Tūruki, 280, 320
Te Korimako, 42
Te Kou Rehua, 314
Te Mamaku, 299
Te Maranui, 184
Te Maungarongo, 65
Te Mau-Paraoa, 74
Te Morenga, 72, 253
Te Mutu, 58
Te Ngae, 319
Te Ngahue, 259–60, Fig. 66
Te Oha Taotao, 314
Te Oriori, Tireni, 301
Te Pahi, 35, 215
Te Pakaru, Niutone, 93, 294
Te Pakiaka, 56
Te Papa, 88
Te Parihi, Wi (Pirihongo or Pirihonga), 73–4
Te Pēhi Kupe, 61–2, 68
Te Pehi Tahau, 67
Te Pou-o-Urutake, battle of, 88
Te Puhi, 110–11, 165
Te Pukekōhatu, 65
Te Puna, 78, 101, 105, 215, 249
Te Puni-kōkopu, 121
Te Rangi Hīroa (Sir Peter Buck), 59–60
Te Rangi Paetahi, Mete Kīngi, 69
Te Rangi Topeora, 70, 96, 308
Te Rangihaeata, 70, 84, 274, 276, 299, Fig. 10
Te Rangihatuake, Minarapa, 249
Te Rangikāheke, Wiremu Maihi, 64, 71
Te Rangitāke, Wiremu Kīngi, 32, 277, 306, 309
Te Ratu, 111
Te Rātūtonu, 69–70
Te Rauparaha, 52, 61, 64–8, 70, 72, 81, 82, 84, 87, 130–3, 165, 167, 206, 246, 296, 299–301, Fig. 72
Te Rauparaha, Tāmihana, 130
Te Riaki, 136
Te Ripi *see* Paratene
Te Roroa, 221
Te Rou, Rāpata, 117, 141–3
Te Ruaoneone, 131
Te Tātua, 51
Te Tawa, 235
Te Tiupiri, 334
Te Toa Takatini, 26
Te Tuhiwai, 65, Fig. 10
Te Tūmū pā, 58
Te Ua Haumēne, 66, 71, 320
Te Umuroa, 276, Fig. 69
Te Urikapana, 74
Te Waharoa, 28, 71
Te Waharoa, Wiremu Tāmihana Tarapīpīpī *see* Tarapīpīpī
Te Waru, 95–6, Fig. 33
Te Weherua, 156–7
Te Whaitere, 42

Te Whaiti (aka Nayti), 114, 118, 206–7, 269
Te Whanapipi, Tumakoha, 72
Te Whānau-ā-Apanui, 125
Te Whareaitu, 276–7
Te Wharepōuri, 121
Te Wharerahi (aka Te Wharenui), 60, 117
Te Whareumu (King George), 73–4, 146
Te Whata, 116
Te Wherowhero, Piupiu, 322
Te Wherowhero, Pōtatau, 42, 71–2, 297, 300, 306–7, 334
Te Whetū-Matarau, battle of, 94
Te Whi-o-te-Rangi, 111
Te Whiti-o-Rongomai III, Erueti, 281–2, 320–1
Te Whiti-o-Tū, battle of, 66
Te Whiwhi, Hēnare Mātene, 308
Te Ao-o-te-rangi, 104, 313
Terehunga, 110
The Ancient History of the Māori, 53, 109, 332
The Times, 151, 202, 204
theft, thieves, 79, 83, 100–5, 139, 140, 217–21, 256, 264–5, 268, 289, 295, 338
Thiercelin, Dr Louis, 182
Thompson, Captain John, 295
Thompson, Christina, 13
Thompson, Henry, 268
Thomson, Arthur, 78, 109, 174, 181
Thomson, James, 193
Thomson, John Turnbull, 27, 81
Through the Looking-Glass, 336
Tia, 25
Tiakiruahine, 146
Tiakitai, 66
Tigress, 164
Tikanga, 47, 109–14, 220, 243
Tinirau, 26–7
Tipako, 97
Tiraurau, Tāmati, 277
Titeri, 178
Tito Hanataua, 287
Tītokowaru, 278–9
Tītore Tākiri, 74, 136–7, 222
Tōhē, 73, 334
Tohitapu, 104, 160, 187, 221–2, 232, 234, 256, 264, Figs 35, 61
Tohu Kākahi, 281–2
tohunga (various), 55, 65, 72, 88, 104, 108, 114, 145, 146, 221
Tokomaru, 25
Toko-rākau, 120
'Toodieka', 100–1
Tory, 120, 208, 290
Treaty of Waitangi, 11, 37, 92, 95, 105, 115–6, 195, 200, 208–9, 211, 265, 278, 288, 291, 299, 302, 305, 311
Tregear, Edward, 31, 46, 49, 50, 70, 90, 99, 109, 118, 140, 144
Tuai, 85–6, 89, 109, 159, 177–8, 182, Figs 29, 50
Tūhaere, Paora, 311–2
Tūhiku, 55
Tūhua (attendant of Tamaāhua), 110
Tūhua (place name), 92
Tuki Tahua, 35
Tūmatauenga (god of war), 59

Tumu-aki, 46
Tupapa, 251
Tūranga *see* Poverty Bay
Turanga (personal name), 234, 239
Turau, Wiremu Wāka, 269–70, 296
Tūrehu, 24–5
Tūrei, Mohi, 25, 184, 318
Turner, Ellen, 196
Turner, Nathaniel, 122, 186, 236, 240, 264–5, 283, 319
Turton, Henry Hanson, 106–7
Turumeke, Ema, 246
Tūtānekai, 327–8
Tūtepourangi, 64
Tūtewaimate, 83
Tūtūrau, 81
Tūwhakairiora, 119–20

Uenuku, 184
Uncle Tom's Cabin, 227
Urewera, 108, 309
Urukēhu, 24–6
utu, 14, 51, 55, 60–2, 65, 71, 76, 83, 97–8, 106, 111–2, 124–6, 129, 136, 140, 148, 217, 218, 253, 263, 295

vassal tribes, 70, 118–21, 131, 213, 273, 288
Vayda, Andrew P., 8, 9, 301
Venn, John, 195
Ville de Bordeaux, 165, 182
Völkner, Reverend Carl Sylvius, 278
Wade, William, 58, 162, 186–7
Wahawaha, Rāpata, 65, 71
Wāhineiti, 119–20
Waiapu, 56–7, 184, 318
Waiheke Island, 63, 117, 139, 141
Waikahua, 65
Waikākahi, 103
Waikanae, 68
Waikaremoana, 12
Waikato (of Te Hikutū), 24, 51, 249, Fig. 5
Waikato (place name), 62, 63, 74, 95, 100, 233, 269, 277, 303, 305–9, 321–2, 331, 333
Waikato (tribal group), 33, 66, 117, 245, 251, 258, 294, 306–8, 331
Waimā, 60, 232
Waimamaku, 116
Waimarama, 66
Waimate North, 66, 80, 102, 185, 222–3, 252
Waingongoro, 279–81
Waiōmio, 74, 106, 205
Waiorua, battle of, 64
Waipara, 83
Wairarapa, 70, 72, 131, 330
Wairau affray, 268, 298
Wairau Valley, 65, 292
Waitaha, 37, 45, 319
Waitahora pā, 56
Waitangi, 24, 261
Waitangi Tribunal, 115, 280–1, 326
Waitara, 32, 277, 308–9
Waitere, Tene, 147
Waitōtara, 315
Wakefield, Arthur, 268
Wakefield, Colonel William, 142, 249

Wakefield, Edward Gibbon, 163, 196–7, 205–6, 208, 287
Wakefield, Edward Jerningham, 121, 163, 248–9, 303–4
Walker, Ranginui, 38
Walsh, Archdeacon Philip, 20
Wanhalla, Angela, 238
Ward, Alan, 315–6
Warren, Reverend John, 232–4
'warrior gene', 13
Watkin, Rev. James, 61, 186
Watkins, Dr John, 111, 143, 183, 202
weaving, 24, 86–7, 146
Webster, John, 286
Wellington, 53, 67, 72, 120–1, 142, 271, 274–6, 279, 281, 296, 298–9
Wellington, 286
Wells, Peter, 226
Wera, 239–40
Wero Tāroi, 147
Wesley, John, 240
Wesleyan missionaries, 101, 145, 216, 236, 239, 249, 258, 263–4, 283–4, 297, 332; *see also* names of individual missionaries
Wesleyan-Methodist Missionary Society, 216
Wētere, 146
whakairo *see* carving
Whakarewarewa, 147
Whakatāne, 125
Whakatau, 26–7, 82
whakataukī *see* proverbs, sayings
Whakatōhea, 54, 125
Whakawhititerā, 318
whalers, whaling, 24, 34, 36, 56–7, 68, 138, 145, 153, 154, 163–4, 167–9, 171–2, 174, 182, 198, 213, 261, 285–6, 294–5, 329, 339
Whangaroa, 7, 110, 165, 262–3, 283–4, 295
Wharepapa, 53, 266–7
Whau, 96
Whirinaki, 146, 263–4
White, Eliza, 225, 227
White, John, 51, 53, 56, 71, 74, 83, 109, 113–6, 131, 134, 247, 259, 265, 332
Whiteley, Reverend John, 66, 305
Wilberforce, William, 152, 191, 194–5, 197, 215–6
Wilkes, Lieutenant Charles, 153
Wilkinson, Reverend Frederick, 77
Williams, Henry, 64, 106, 142, 160, 169, 175, 205, 218, 220, 225–6, 230, 234, 236, 244, 253, 265, 284–5, 288–9, Fig. 65
Williams, Herbert William, 42, 44
Williams, Jim, 45
Williams, Marianne, 88, 223, 225–6, 230, Fig. 60
Williams, William, 56–7, 80, 237, 248, 250, 318, Fig. 65
Wilson, John, 28, 58–9
Wohlers, Johann Friedrich Heinrich, 27

Xhosa, 299

Yate, William, 28, 57–8, 82–4, 91, 113, 134, 218, 237–9, 248, 254, 285, Fig. 9
Yorkshire Philosophical Society, 152–3
Young, Arthur, 193